CONCISE EDITION

# American HORIZONS

## U.S. HISTORY IN A GLOBAL CONTEXT

### Volume I | To 1877

Michael Schaller
*University of Arizona*

Robert D. Schulzinger
*University of Colorado, Boulder*

John Bezís-Selfa
*Wheaton College*

Janette Thomas Greenwood
*Clark University*

Andrew Kirk
*University of Nevada, Las Vegas*

Sarah J. Purcell
*Grinnell College*

Aaron Sheehan-Dean
*West Virginia University*

New York Oxford
OXFORD UNIVERSITY PRESS

*To all of our students.*

*The individual authors would also like to dedicate this book to the following people.*

***Michael Schaller:*** *to GS, N, G & D*

***Robert D. Schulzinger:*** *to MES & EAS*

***John Bezís-Selfa:*** *to PCZ & JBS*

***Janette Thomas Greenwood:*** *to M, E & S*

***Andrew Kirk:*** *to L, H & Q*

***Sarah J. Purcell:*** *to H, E & M*

***Aaron Sheehan-Dean:*** *to M, L & A*

Oxford University Press, Inc., publishes works that further Oxford University's objective of excellence in research, scholarship, and education.

Oxford New York
Auckland Cape Town Dar es Salaam Hong Kong Karachi
Kuala Lumpur Madrid Melbourne Mexico City Nairobi
New Delhi Shanghai Taipei Toronto

With offices in
Argentina Austria Brazil Chile Czech Republic France Greece
Guatemala Hungary Italy Japan Poland Portugal Singapore
South Korea Switzerland Thailand Turkey Ukraine Vietnam



For titles covered by Section 112 of the US Higher Education Opportunity Act, please visit www.oup.com/us/he for the latest information about pricing and alternate formats.

Published by Oxford University Press, Inc.
198 Madison Avenue, New York, New York 10016
http://www.oup.com



Library of Congress Cataloging-in-Publication Data

American horizons : U.S. history in a global context / Michael Schaller . . . [et al.].
p. cm.
Includes index.
ISBN 978-0-19-974015-4 (volume 1: alk. paper) 1. United States—History. I. Schaller, Michael, 1947-
E178.A5527 2013
973—dc23

2011049693

Printing number: 9 8 7 6 5 4 3 2 1

Printed in the United States of America
on acid-free paper

# Brief Contents

# Contents

# Maps

# Preface

*American Horizons* is a new text for the course in American history.

For more than 400 years, North America has been part of a global network centered upon the exchange of peoples, goods, and ideas. Human migrations—sometimes freely, sometimes forced—have continued over the centuries, along with the evolution of commerce in commodities as varied as tobacco, sugar, and computer chips. Europeans and Africans came or were brought to the continent, where they met, traded with, fought among, and intermarried with native peoples. Some of these migrants stayed, while others returned to their home countries. Still others came and went periodically. This initial circulation of people across the oceans foreshadowed the continuous movement of people, goods, and ideas that made the United States. These are the forces that have shaped American history, both dividing and unifying the nation. American "horizons" truly stretch beyond our nation's borders, embracing the trading networks established during and after the colonial era to the digital social networks connecting people globally today.

*American Horizons* tells the story of the United States by exploring this exchange on a global scale and placing it at the center of that story. By doing so, we provide a different perspective on the history of the United States, one that we hope broadens the horizons of those who read our work and are ever mindful of the global forces that increasingly and profoundly shape our lives. At the same time, *American Horizons* considers those ways in which U.S. influence reshaped the lives and experiences of people of other nations.

U.S. history is increasingly perceived, interpreted, and taught as part of a global historical experience. The mutual influence of change—of global forces entering the U.S. and of American ideas, goods, and people moving out through the world—has been a consistent feature since the 16th century. While most Americans today are aware that their influence is felt abroad and are increasingly aware of the influence of events abroad on their own lives, they tend to think of these as recent developments. In fact, those earliest exchanges of beliefs and products some 500 years ago established a pattern of interaction that continues today.

We have written a narrative that encourages readers to consider the variety of pressures that spurred historical change. Some of these pressures arose within America and some came from outside its borders. In the 1820s, the global market for whale oil shaped labor conditions throughout New England. At the same time, the American political system was transformed by the unique inheritance of the American Revolution and the relative abundance of land in North America. In the 1940s and 1950s, the federal government designed a unique set of policies to help World War II veterans readjust to civilian life, while the Civil Rights Movement unfolded within a global context of decolonization in Africa and Asia. Topics such as these help us ask the reader to consider the relationship between local and global forces that shaped American history.

This book was conceived as an opportunity to present the nation's history as more than a mere sequence of events for the student to memorize. The approach of *American Horizons* reflects this. Although adhering to the familiar chronological organization of this course, our narrative style and structure provide the flexibility of shifting emphasis from time to time to the global aspects of American history. While the story of the United States is always at the center of the story, that story is told through the movement of people, goods, and ideas into, within, or out of the United States.

What qualities make the United States unique? What accounts for the diversity of dialect and lifestyle across this country? How did the United States become a major player on the world stage of nations? History includes many storylines that contribute to this narrative. *American Horizons* is the story of where this nation came from and how it has been shaped by its own set of shared values as well as its interaction with the rest of the world. It recognizes that many of the significant events in American history had causes and consequences connected to developments elsewhere and presents those events accordingly. *American Horizons* depicts this intersection of storylines from many nations that influenced, and were influenced by, the United States of America.

As readers engage the text, we encourage them to think explicitly about what makes history. What matters? What forces or events shaped how people lived their lives?

## About the Concise Edition

In addition to the comprehensive edition of *American Horizons,* we are delighted to offer this concise edition for those instructors who need to teach the course in a short term, assign readings in addition to the textbook, or prefer a more economical option for their students without sacrificing the primary advantages of the full edition. To meet this goal, the concise edition was designed with 10 percent fewer words and photographs. This was achieved without sacrificing any tables, maps, or figures, all of which are critical to the realization of *American Horizons*.

# A GUIDED TOUR OF *AMERICAN HORIZONS*

*American Horizons* is distinguished by three elements: a global theme, innovative scholarship, and features that encourage active learning.

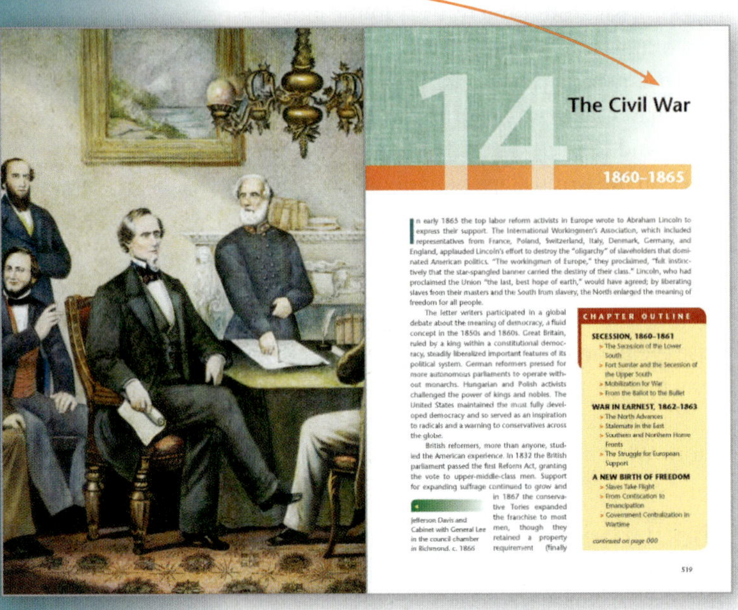

14 The Civil War

1860–1865

In early 1865 the top labor reform activists in Europe wrote to Abraham Lincoln to express their support. The International Workingmen's Association, which included representatives from France, Poland, Switzerland, Italy, Denmark, Germany, and England, applauded Lincoln's effort to destroy the "oligarchy" of slaveholders that dominated American politics. "The workingmen of Europe," they proclaimed, "felt instinctively that the star-spangled banner carried the destiny of their class." Lincoln, who had proclaimed the Union "the last, best hope of earth," would have agreed; by liberating slaves from their masters and the South from slavery, the North enlarged the meaning of freedom for all people.

The letter writers participated in a global debate about the meaning of democracy, a fluid concept in the 1850s and 1860s. Great Britain, ruled by a king within a constitutional democracy, steadily liberalized important features of its political system. German reformers pressed for more autonomous parliaments to operate without monarchs. Hungarian and Polish activists challenged the power of kings and nobles. The United States maintained the most fully developed democracy and so served as an inspiration to radicals and a warning to conservatives across the globe.

British reformers, more than anyone, studied the American experience. In 1832 the British parliament passed the first Reform Act, granting the vote to upper-middle-class men. Support for expanding suffrage continued to grow and in 1867 the conservative Tories expanded the franchise to most men, though they retained a property requirement (finally

Jefferson Davis and Cabinet with General Lee in the council chamber in Richmond. c. 1866

CHAPTER OUTLINE

**SECESSION, 1860–1861**
- The Secession of the Lower South
- Fort Sumter and the Secession of the Upper South
- Mobilization for War
- From the Ballot to the Bullet

**WAR IN EARNEST, 1862–1863**
- The North Advances
- Stalemate in the East
- Southern and Northern Home Fronts
- The Struggle for European Support

**A NEW BIRTH OF FREEDOM**
- Slaves Take Flight
- From Confiscation to Emancipation
- Government Centralization in Wartime

continued on page 000

519

## CHAPTER INTRODUCTIONS

Each chapter of *American Horizons* begins with a compelling story at the core of each chapter theme.

## GLOBAL THEME

*American Horizons* seamlessly incorporates connections to global history throughout the text, including discussion rarely found in other books.

## GLOBAL PASSAGES

"Global Passages" boxes feature a unique story connecting America to the world.

## INNOVATIVE SCHOLARSHIP

*American Horizons* is informed by the most current scholarship available. The text offers multiple perspectives and viewpoints on America's past that broaden the student's understand of America's unique place in history.

**The Story of American Indians**

**The Colonial European Empires**

**The Impact and Contributions of Hispanics and Mexican Americans**

## The Story of Immigration and Migration

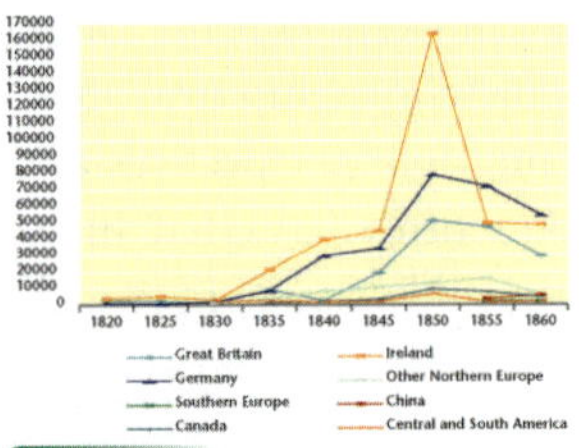


Figure 11.1

**Immigrants, by country or region, 1820–1860** Northwestern Europe sent the most immigrants to the United States in the 19th century, especially during the Famine Years in Ireland. By midcentury, however, an increasingly diverse array of immigrants found their way to the United States.

## Women in American History

MEN AND WOMEN IN ANTEBELLUM AMERICA

Women and Children in the Workplace

## LEARNING FEATURES

*American Horizons* offers vivid features to help students read, comprehend, and analyze key information, often using innovative visual aids.

### America in the World

Found in each chapter, this is a visual guide to key interactions between America and the world.

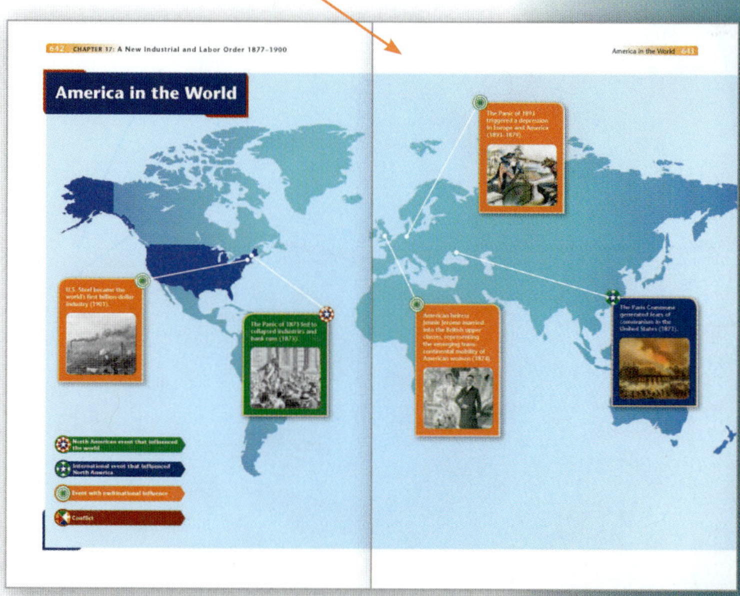

## Maps and Infographics

A rich graphics program explores essential themes in new ways.

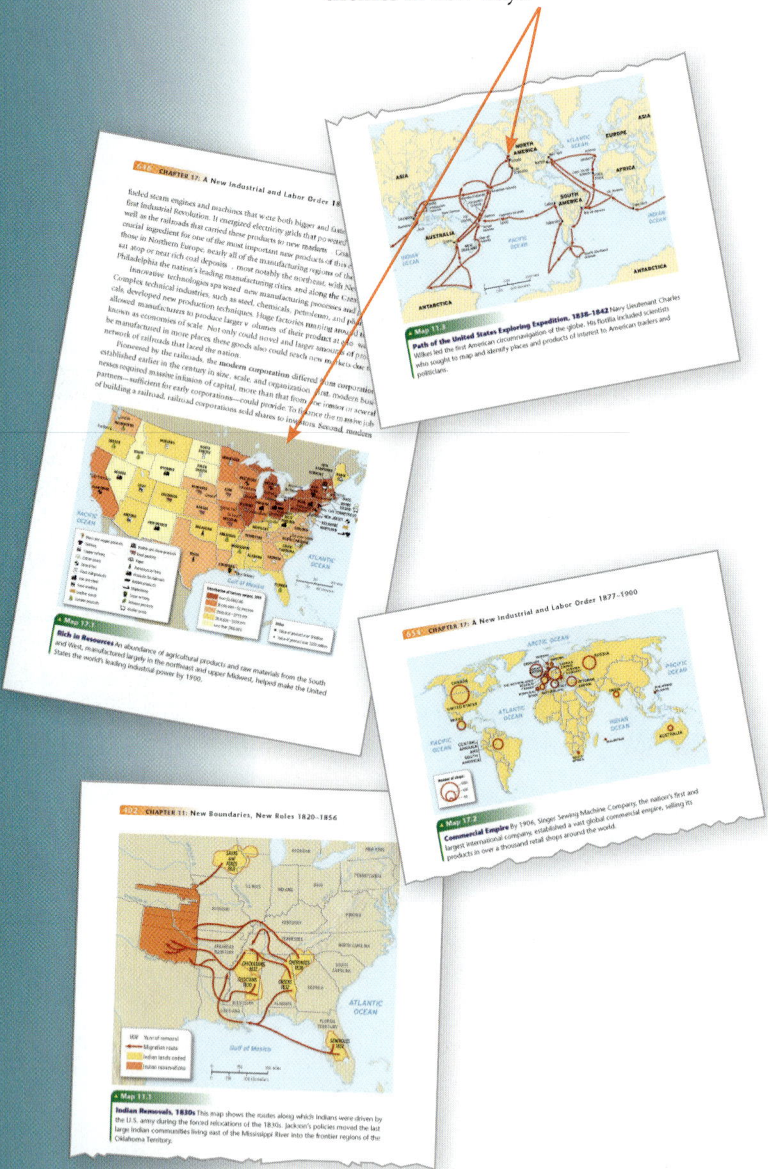

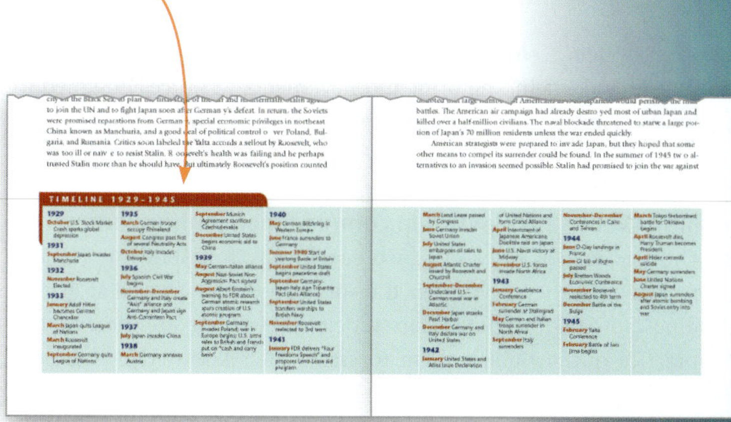


## Visual Review

At the conclusion of each chapter, this feature provides a post-reading summary to help students make links to key themes or events within a chapter.

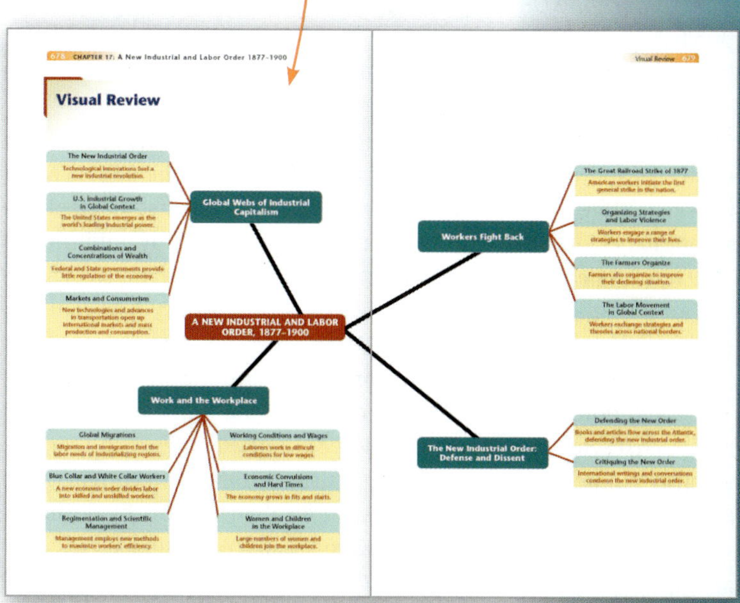

# SUPPLEMENTS

## FOR STUDENTS

Oxford University Press offers a complete and authoritative package of supplementary materials for the student, including print and new media resources designed for chapter review, primary source reading, essay writing, test-preparation, and further research.

### Student Companion Website at www.oup.com/us/americanhorizons

The open-access Online Study Center designed specifically for *American Horizons* helps students to review what they have learned from the textbook as well as explore other resources online. Note-taking guides help students focus their attention in class, while interactive practice quizzes allow them to assess their knowledge of a topic before a test.

- **Online Study Guide**, including
    - Note-taking outlines
    - Multiple-choice and identification quizzes, (two quizzes per chapter, thirty question quizzes—*different* from those found in the Instructor's Manual/Testbank)
- **Primary Source Companion & Research Guide**, a brief online Research Primer, with a library of annotated links to primary & secondary sources in U.S. history.
- **Interactive Flashcards**, using key terms and people listed at the end of each chapter, these multimedia cards help students remember who's who and what's what.

### *American National Biography Online* www.anb.org

Students who purchase a **new** copy of *American Horizons* will find an access code for a six-month (Volumes 1 or 2) or a one-year **free subscription** to this powerful online resource published by Oxford University Press.

*American National Biography* online offers **portraits of more than 17,400 women and men**—from all eras and walks of life—whose lives have shaped the nation. More than a decade in preparation, the *American National Biography* is the first biographical resource of this scope to be published in more than sixty years. Originally published in 24 volumes in 1999, the *American National Biography* won instant acclaim as the new authority in American biographies. **Winner of the American Library Association's Dartmouth Medal** as the best reference work of the year, the *ANB* now serves readers in thousands of school, public, and academic libraries around the world. The publication of the online edition makes the *ANB* even more useful as a dynamic source of information—updated semiannually, with hundreds of new entries each year and revisions of previously published entries to enhance their accuracy and currency. The *ANB Online* features **thousands of illustrations**, more than **80,000 hyperlinked cross-references**, links to select web sites, and powerful search capabilities.

**ANB Online is also a great teaching resource, since it can be actively incorporated into classroom lessons.** To assist teachers in fully utilizing ANB Online, we have prepared a Teacher's Guide to Using ANB Online. Developed with the participation of librarians and teachers, the Teacher's Guide offers six lessons that highlight the importance and value of studying biography as an end in itself and as a starting point for doing further research into the lives of those who shaped the American experience.

***Writing History: A Guide for Students*** Third edition, by William Kelleher Storey, Associate Professor at Millsaps College.

Bringing together practical methods from both history and composition, *Writing History* provides a wealth of tips and advice to help students research and write essays for history classes. The book covers all aspects of writing about history, including **finding topics** and **researching** them, **interpreting source materials, drawing inferences from sources**, and **constructing arguments**. It concludes with three chapters that discuss writing effective sentences, using precise wording, and revising. Using numerous examples from the works of cultural, political, and social historians, *Writing History* serves as an ideal supplement to history courses that require students to conduct research. The third edition includes expanded sections on **peer editing** and **topic selection**, as well as new sections on searching and using the Internet. *Writing History* can be packaged for free with *American Horizons*. Contact your Oxford University Press Sales Representative for more information.

***The Information-Literate Historian: A Guide to Research for History Students*** by Jenny Presnell, Information Services Library and History, American Studies, and Women's Studies Bibliographer, Miami University of Ohio.

This is the only book specifically designed to teach today's history student how to most successfully select and use sources—primary, secondary, and electronic—to carry out and present their research. Written by a college librarian, *The Information-Literate Historian* is an indispensable reference for historians, students, and other readers doing history research. *The Information-Literate Historian* can be packaged for free with *American Horizons*. Contact your Oxford University Press Sales Representative for more information.

## Primary Source Documents

***Our Documents: 100 Milestone Documents from the National Archives*** brings documents to life, including facsimiles side-by-side with transcripts for students to explore; explanations and a forward provided by Michael Beschloss. This primary source book can be **packaged for free** with *American Horizons*. Among the documents it contains are: Declaration of Independence; U.S. Constitution; Bill of Rights; Louisiana Purchase Treaty; Missouri Compromise; The Dred Scott decision; Emancipation Proclamation; Gettysburg Address; Fourteenth Amendment to the U.S. Constitution; Thomas Edison's light bulb patent; Sherman Anti-Trust Act; Executive order for the Japanese relocation during wartime; Manhattan Project notebook;

Press release announcing U.S. recognition of Israel; President John F. Kennedy's inaugural address, as well as many more.

Other primary source books that can be packaged with *American Horizons* include Chafe's ***History of Our Time*** and Bloom's ***Takin' It to the Streets***, as well as ***The Boisterous Sea of Liberty: A Documentary History of America from Discovery through the Civil War***; and ***Documenting American Violence: A Sourcebook***.

## FOR INSTRUCTORS

For decades, American history professors have turned to Oxford University Press as the leading source for high quality readings and reference materials. Now, when you adopt *American Horizons*, the Press will partner with you and make available its best supplemental materials and resources for your classroom. Listed here are several series of high interest, but you will want to talk with your Sales Representative to learn more about what can be made available, and about what would suit your course best.

**Instructor's Manual & Testbank.** This useful guide contains useful teaching tools for experienced and first-time teachers alike. It can be made available to adopters upon request, and is also available electronically on the Instructor's Recourse CD. This extensive manual and testbank contains:

- **Sample Syllabi**
- **Chapter Outlines**
- **In-Class Discussion Questions**
- **Lecture Ideas**
- **Oxford's Further Reading List**
- **Quizzes** (two per chapter, one per half of the chapter, content divided somewhat evenly down the middle of the chapter: twenty-five multiple choice questions each)
- **Tests** (two per chapter, each covering the entire chapter contents: each offering ten identification/matching; ten multiple-choice; five short-answer, two essay)

**Instructor's Resource CD.** This handy CD-ROM contains everything you need in an electronic format—the Instructor's Manual (PDF), PowerPoint Slides (fully customizable), Image Library with PDF versions of *all* 120 maps from the textbook, and a Computerized Testbank.

A complete **Course Management cartridge** is also available to qualified adopters. Instructor's resources are also available for download directly to your computer through a secure connection via the instructor's side of the companion website. Contact your Oxford University Press Sales Representative for more information.

## OTHER OXFORD TITLES OF INTEREST FOR THE U.S. HISTORY CLASSROOM

Oxford University Press publishes a vast array of titles in American history. Listed below is just a small selection of books that pair particularly well with *American*

*Horizons*. Any of the books in these series can be packaged with *American Horizons* at a significant discount to students. Please contact your Oxford University Press Sales Representative for specific pricing information, or for additional packaging suggestions. Please visit www.oup.com/us for a full listing of Oxford titles.

## NEW NARRATIVES IN AMERICAN HISTORY

At Oxford University Press, we believe that good history begins with a good story. Each volume in this series features a compelling tale that draws on a sustained narrative to illuminate a greater historical theme or controversy. Then, in a thoughtful Afterword, the authors place their narratives within larger historical contexts, discuss their sources and narrative strategies, and describe their personal involvement with the work. Intensely personal and highly relevant, these succinct texts are innovative teaching tools that provide a springboard for incisive class discussion as they immerse students in a particular historical moment.

*Escaping Salem: The Other Witch Hunt of 1692*, by Richard Godbeer
*Sleuthing the Alamo: Davy Crockett's Last Stand and Other Mysteries of the Texas Revolution*, by James E. Crisp
*In Search of the Promised Land: A Slave Family in the Old South*, by John Hope Franklin and Loren Schweninger
*The Making of a Confederate: Walter Lenoir's Civil War*, by William L. Barney
*"They Say": Ida B. Wells and the Reconstruction of Race*, by James West Davidson
*Wild Men: Ishi and Kroeber in the Wilderness of Modern America*, by Douglas Cazaux Sackman
*The Gentle Subversive: Rachel Carson, Silent Spring, and the Rise of the Environmental Movement*, by Mark Hamilton Lytle
*"To Everything There is a Season": Pete Seeger and the Power of Song*, by Allan Winkler

## PAGES FROM HISTORY

Textbooks may interpret and recall history, but these books **are** history. Each title, compiled and edited by a prominent historian, is a collection of primary sources relating to a particular topic of historical significance. Documentary evidence includes news articles, government documents, memoirs, letters, diaries, fiction, photographs, advertisements, posters, and political cartoons. Headnotes, extended captions, sidebars, and introductory essays provide the essential context that frames the documents. All the books are amply illustrated and each includes a documentary picture essay, chronology, further reading, source notes, and index.

*Encounters in the New World* (Jill Lepore)
*Colonial America* (Edward G. Gray)
*The American Revolution* (Stephen C. Bullock)
*The Bill of Rights* (John J. Patrick)
*The Struggle Against Slavery* (David Waldstreicher)
*The Civil War* (Rachel Filene Seidman)
*The Gilded Age* (Janette Thomas Greenwood)

*The Industrial Revolution* (Laura Levine Frader)
*Imperialism* (Bonnie G. Smith)
*World War I* (Frans Coetzee and Marilyn Shevin-Coetzee)
*The Depression and the New Deal* (Robert McElvaine)
*World War II* (James H. Madison)
*The Cold War* (Allan M. Winkler)
*The Vietnam War* (Marilyn B. Young)

### PIVOTAL MOMENTS IN AMERICAN HISTORY

Oxford's Pivotal Moments in American History Series explores the turning points that forever changed the course of American history. Each book is written by an expert on the subject and provides a fascinating narrative on a significant instance that stands out in our nation's past. For anyone interested in discovering which important junctures in U.S. history shaped our thoughts, actions, and ideals, these books are the definitive resources.

*The Scratch of a Pen: 1763 and the Transformation of North America* (Colin Calloway)
*As if an Enemy's Country: The British Occupation of Boston and the Origins of the Revolution* (Richard Archer)
*Washington's Crossing* (David Hackett Fischer)
*James Madison and the Struggle for the Bill of Rights* (Richard Labunski)
*Adams vs. Jefferson: The Tumultuous Election of 1800* (John Ferling)
*The Birth of Modern Politics: Andrew Jackson, John Quincy Adams, and the Election of 1828* (Lynn Parsons)
*Storm over Texas: The Annexation Controversy and the Road to Civil War* (Joel H. Silbey)
*Crossroads of Freedom: Antietam* (James M. McPherson)
*The Last Indian War: The Nez Perce Story* (Elliot West)
*Seneca Falls and the Origins of the Women's Rights Movement* (Sally McMillen)
*Rainbow's End: The Crash of 1929* (Maury Klein)
Brown v. Board of Education *and the Civil Rights Movement* (Michael J. Klarman)
*The Bay of Pigs* (Howard Jones)
*Freedom Riders: 1961 and the Struggle for Racial Justice* (Raymond Arsenault)

### VIEWPOINTS ON AMERICAN CULTURE

Oxford's Viewpoints on American Culture Series offers timely reflections for twenty-first century readers. The series targets topics where debates have flourished and brings together the voices of established and emerging writers to share their own points of view in compact and compelling format.

*Votes for Women: The Struggle for Suffrage Revisited* (Jean H. Baker)
*Long Time Gone: Sixties America Then and Now* (Alexander Bloom)
*Living in the Eighties* (Edited by Gil Troy and Vincent J. Cannato)
*Race on Trial: Law and Justice in American History* (Annette Gordon-Reed)
*Sifters: Native American Women's Lives* (Theda Perdue)
*Latina Legacies: Identity, Biography, and Community* (Vicki L. Ruiz)

### OXFORD WORLD'S CLASSICS

For over 100 years, Oxford World's Classics has made available a broad spectrum of literature from around the globe. With well over 600 titles available and a continuously growing list, this is the finest and most comprehensive classics series in print. Any volume in the series can be **packaged for free** with *American Horizons*. Relevant titles include Benjamin Franklin's *Autobiography and Other Writings*, J. Hector St. John de Crèvecœur's *Letters from an American Farmer*, Booker T. Washington's *Up from Slavery*, and many others. **For a complete listing of Oxford World's Classics, please visit www.oup.com/us/owc.**

## ACKNOWLEDGMENTS

A book as detailed as this draws upon the talents and support of many individuals. Our first thanks must certainly go to our families for their support and patience during the development of this textbook. We would also like to acknowledge the team at Oxford University Press for their support in making this book a reality. Thanks go first to our editor, Brian Wheel, who encouraged and challenged us at every step of the process. Oxford publisher John Challice supported the project at an early stage and spurred us to think broadly about how we envisioned it. We appreciate the able assistance of development editors Thom Holmes and Danielle Christensen. Editorial assistant Sarah Ellerton was especially helpful in wrangling the photo, map, and figure program for the book. Taylor Pilkington picked up late in the process and helped shepherd the project through to completion. Editorial assistants Laura Lancaster and Danniel Schoonebeek helped us organize and manage the project in the early stages. We thank the Oxford production team, led by managing editor Lisa Grzan, for their encouragement and help in generating this book and shaping its final form. Senior production editor David Bradley deserves special recognition for his work in coordinating the work of all the authors and for assembling the many maps, images, and graphics in the volumes. The production team also included copyeditor Deanna Hegle and proofreader Heather Dubnick. The interior and cover design were created by art director Michele Laseau and designers Binbin Li and Pam Poll, based on a plan originally conceived by Paula Schlosser. The compelling photographs were researched by Mary Rose Maclachlan and Derek Capitaine. The innovative map program was created by International Mapping through the efforts of Alex Tait, Dan Przywara, Vickie Taylor, and Kim Clark, with the consultative help of Erik Steiner, director of the Spatial History Lab at Stanford University. We also benefited enormously from the advice of all the outside readers on the manuscript. We thank them all.

### THE DEVELOPMENT STORY

The seven co-authors of this book specialize in a variety of time periods and methodologies. Based on our research and teaching, we all share the idea that the nation's history can best be understood by examining how, from the colonial era forward, the American experience reflected the interaction of many nations, peoples, and events. We present this idea in a format that integrates traditional narrative history with the enhanced perspective of five centuries of global interaction.

## MANUSCRIPT REVIEWERS

We have greatly benefited from the perceptive comments and suggestion of the many talented scholars and instructors who reviewed the manuscript of *American Horizons*. Their insight and suggestions contributed immensely to the published work.

Stanley Arnold
*Northern Illinois University*

Shelby M. Balik
*Metropolitan State College of Denver*
*University of Colorado*

Eirlys M. Barker
*Thomas Nelson Community College*

Toby Bates
*University of Mississippi*

Carol Bender
*Saddleback College*

Wendy Benningfield
*Campbellsville University*

Katherine Benton-Cohen
*Georgetown University*

Angela Boswell
*Henderson State University*

Robert Bouwman
*North Georgia College & State University*

Jessica Brannon-Wranosky
*Texas A&M University–Commerce*

Blanche Brick
*Blinn College*

Howard Brick
*University of Michigan*

Margaret M. Caffrey
*University of Memphis*

Jacqueline B. Carr
*University of Vermont*

Dominic Carrillo
*Grossmont College*

Brian Casserly
*Bellevue College*

Cheryll Ann Cody
*Houston Community College–Southwest College*

Elizabeth Collins
*Triton College*

Edward M. Cook, Jr.
*University of Chicago*

Cynthia Gardner Counsil
*Florida State College–Jacksonville*

C. David Dalton
*College of the Ozarks*

David Dzurec
*University of Scranton*

Brian J. Els
*University of Portland*

Kevin Eoff
*Palo Verde College*

Richard M. Filipink
*Western Illinois University*

Joshua Fulton
*Moraine Valley Community College*

David Garvin
*Highland Community College*

Glen Gendzel
*San José State University*

Tiffany Gill
*University of Texas–Austin*

Aram Goudsouzian
*University of Memphis*

Larry Gragg
*Missouri University of Science and Technology*

Jean W. Griffith
*Fort Scott Community College*
*Labette Community College*

Mark Grimsley
*Ohio State University*

Elisa M. Guernsey
*Monroe Community College*

Aaron Gulyas
*Mott Community College*

Michael R. Hall
*Armstrong Atlantic State University*

David E. Hamilton
*University of Kentucky*

Peggy J. Hardman
*Eastern New Mexico University*

Kristin Hargrove
*Grossmont College*

Claudrena N. Harold
*University of Virginia*

Edward Hashima
*American River College*

Robin Henry
*Wichita State University*

John Herron
*University of Missouri–Kansas City*

L. Edward Hicks
*Faulkner University*

Matt Hinckley
*Richland College*

D. Sandy Hoover
*East Texas Baptist University*

Jerry Hopkins
*East Texas Baptist University*

Kelly Hopkins
*University of Houston*

Kenneth W. Howell
*Prairie View A&M University*

Raymond Pierre Hylton
*Virginia Union University*

Bryan M. Jack
*Winston-Salem State University*

Brenda Jackson-Abernathy
*Belmont University*

Volker Janssen
*California State University–Fullerton*

Lawrence W. Kennedy
*University of Scranton*

William Kerrigan
*Muskingum University*

Andrew E. Kersten
*University of Wisconsin*

Todd Kerstetter
*TCU*

Patricia Knol
*Triton College*

Jeffrey Kosiorek
*Hendrix College*

Peter Kuryla
*Belmont University*

Peggy Lambert
*Lone Star College–Kingwood*

Alan Lehmann
*Blinn College*

Carolyn Herbst Lewis
*Louisiana State University*

Christopher J. Mauceri
*Farmingdale State College of New York*

Derrick McKisick
*Fairfield University*

Marian Mollin
*Virginia Tech*

Linda Mollno
*Cal Poly Pomona*

Michelle Morgan
*Missouri State University*

Susan Rhoades Neel
*Utah State University*

Caryn E. Neumann
*Miami University*

Jeffrey Nichols
*Westminster College*

Christopher H. Owen
*Northeastern State University*

Jeffrey Pilz
*North Iowa Area Community College*

Amy M. Porter
*Georgia Southwestern State University*

William E. Price
*Kennesaw State University*

Emily Rader
*El Camino College*

Matthew Redinger
*Montana State University–Billings*

Yolanda Romero
*North Lake College*

Jessica Roney
*Ohio University*

Walter L. Sargent
*University of Maine–Farmington*

Robert Francis Saxe
*Rhodes College*

Jerry G. Sheppard
*Mount Olive College*

Robert Sherwood
*Georgia Military College*

Terry L. Shoptaugh
*Minnesota State University–Moorhead*

Jason H. Silverman
*Winthrop University*

Nico Slate
*Carnegie Mellon University*

Jodie Steeley
*Merced Community College*

Jennifer A. Stollman
*Fort Lewis College*

James S. Taw
*Valdosta State University*

Connie Brown Thomason
*Louisiana Delta Community College*

Kurt Troutman
*Muskegon Community College*

Stanley J. Underdal
*San José State University*

David Voelker
*University of Wisconsin–Green Bay*

Charles Waite
*University of Texas–Pan American*

R. Stuart Wallace
*NHTI—Concord's Community College*
*University of New Hampshire–Manchester*

Pamela West
*Jefferson State Community College*

William Benton Whisenhunt
*College of DuPage*

Louis Williams
*St. Louis Community College–Forest Park*

Scott M. Williams
*Weatherford College*

Mary Montgomery Wolf
*University of Georgia*

Bill Wood
*University of Arkansas Community College–Batesville*

Melyssa Wrisley
*Broome Community College*

Charles Young
*Umpqua Community College*

Nancy L. Zens
*Central Oregon Community College*

# About the Authors

**Michael Schaller** (Ph.D., University of Michigan, 1974) is Regents Professor of History at the University of Arizona where he has taught since 1974. His areas of specialization include U.S. international and East Asian relations and the resurgence of conservatism in late-20th-century America. Among his publications are *Altered States: The United States and Japan Since the Occupation* (Oxford University Press, 1997), *The U.S. and China into the 21st Century* (Oxford University Press, 2002), *Right Turn: American Life in the Reagan-Bush Era* (Oxford University Press,, 2007), and *Ronald Reagan* (Oxford University Press, 2011).

**Robert D. Schulzinger** is College of Arts and Sciences Professor of Distinction of History and International Affairs at the University of Colorado–Boulder. He specializes in 20th-century U.S. history and U.S. diplomatic history. Books include *A Time for War: The United States and Vietnam, 1941–1975* (Oxford University Press, 1997), *U.S. Diplomacy Since 1900* (Oxford University Press, 2002), and *Present Tense* (Houghton Mifflin, 2004).

**John Bezís-Selfa** is Associate Professor of History at Wheaton College (Ph.D. at the University of Pennsylvania). He specializes in the history of the early Americas and teaches U.S., Latin American, and Latino/a history. Books include *Forging America: Ironworkers, Adventurers, and the Industrious Revolution* (Cornell University Press, 2004).

**Janette Thomas Greenwood** is Professor of History at Clark University (Ph.D. at the University of Virginia), and specializes in African-American history and history of the U.S. South. Books include *The Gilded Age: A History in Documents* (Oxford University Press, 2000), *Bittersweet Legacy: The Black and White "Better Classes" in Charlotte, 1850–1910* (University of North Carolina Press, 1994), and *First Fruits of Freedom: The Migration of Former Slaves and Their Search for Equality in Worcester, Massachusetts, 1862–1900* (University of North Carolina Press, 2010).

**Andrew Kirk** is Professor of History at University of Nevada, Las Vegas (Ph.D. at the University of New Mexico), and specializes in the history of the U.S. West and environmental history. Books include *Collecting Nature: The American Environmental Movement and the Conservation Library* (University of Kansas Press, 2001), and *Counterculture Green: The Whole Earth Catalog and American Environmentalism* (University Press of Kansas, 2007).

**Sarah J. Purcell** is Associate Professor of History at Grinnell College (Ph.D. at Brown University), and specializes in the Early National period, Antebellum U.S., popular culture, politics, gender, and military history. She also directs the Rosenfield Program in Public Affairs, International Relations, and Human Rights. Books include *Sealed with Blood: War, Sacrifice, and Memory in Revolutionary America* (University of Pennsylvania Press, 2002), *The Early National Period* (Facts on File, 2004), and *The Encyclopedia of Battles in North America, 1517–1916* (Facts on File, 2000).

**Aaron Sheehan-Dean** is the Eberly Professor of Civil War Studies at West Virginia University (Ph.D. at the University of Virginia), and specializes in Antebellum U.S. and the U.S. Civil War. Books include *Why Confederates Fought: Family and Nation in Civil War Virginia* (The University of North Carolina Press, 2007), *The View from the Ground: Experiences of Civil War Soldiers* (The University Press of Kentucky, 2006), and *Concise Historical Atlas of the U.S. Civil War* (Oxford University Press, 2008).

American
HORIZONS

Os montes claros em affrica:
Tropicus cācer:
Serra lioa:
Castello damina
Mare prasodu

# 1 North America Encounters the Atlantic World

## Prehistory–1565

On June 4, 1539, a tattooed man carrying a bow and arrow boldly approached a group of Spanish soldiers who had just landed near Tampa Bay, Florida. In broken Spanish he pleaded to a shocked audience: "Sirs, for the love of God and of St. Mary, do not kill me; I am Christian, like you, and I am a native of Seville, and my name is Juan Ortiz."

It took Ortiz nearly a week to summon enough Spanish to explain how he came to Florida and survived. About 12 years earlier, he and at least 20 other soldiers had arrived to join an army led by **Pánfilo de Narváez**. Ortiz and a companion volunteered to swim ashore to retrieve a sheet of paper affixed to a stick—what they hoped was a letter that would tell them where Narváez's expedition had gone. But Indians from the nearby town of Ozita had planted the letter as bait. They killed Ortiz's companion and took Ortiz hostage. The chief of Ozita had good reason to want Ortiz. Soldiers from the Narváez expedition had thrown his wife to their dogs and lopped off the tip of his nose. Ozita planned to exact revenge by burning Ortiz alive, but one of the chief's wives and his daughters intervened and saved his life. Ortiz endured three years of enslavement in Ozita before finding refuge with Mocozo, who led a nearby rival chiefdom. Mocozo saw Ortiz as the means to an alliance with the Spanish. When **Hernando de Soto** landed in Tampa Bay, Mocozo sent Ortiz to meet de Soto's fleet.

To de Soto, Ortiz was a sign that God had "taken this enterprise in His especial keeping." He needed a guide and translator—most of the Indians he had captured for that work had escaped. "This interpreter," de Soto wrote, "puts new life into us, for without him I know not what

*Monumenta Cartographia* by Alberto Cantino, c. 1502

**CHAPTER OUTLINE**



*continued on page 7*

# America in the World

Corn was cultivated in Mexico and millennia later became a food staple of North America (7000 BCE–1000 CE).

Asian Nomadic hunters began to migrate south through Alaska, populating the Americas (c. 13,000 BCE).

 North American event that influenced the world

 International event that influenced North America

 Event with multinational influence

 Conflict

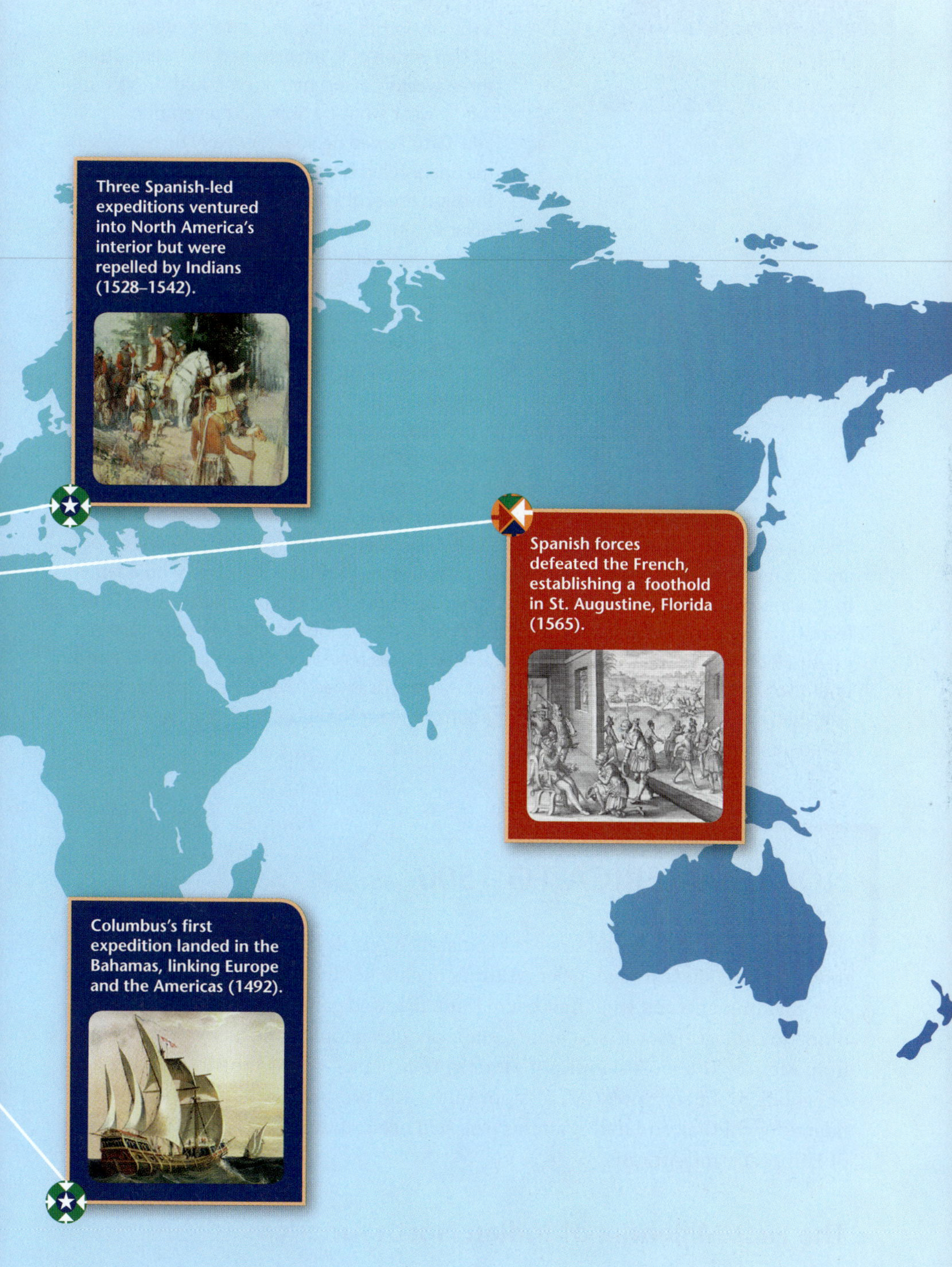
Three Spanish-led expeditions ventured into North America's interior but were repelled by Indians (1528–1542).
Spanish forces defeated the French, establishing a foothold in St. Augustine, Florida (1565).
Columbus's first expedition landed in the Bahamas, linking Europe and the Americas (1492).

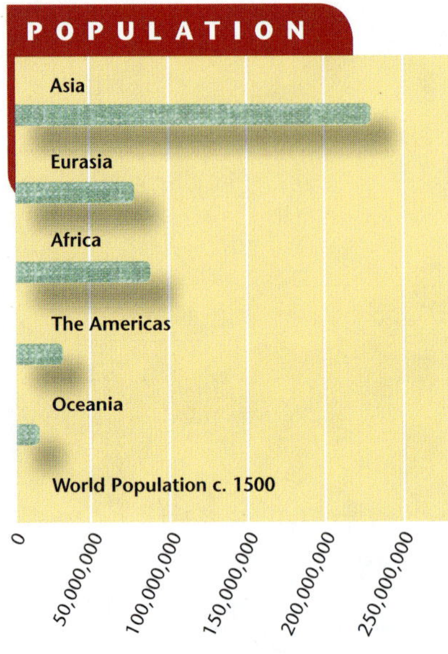


would become of us." He presented Ortiz with a suit of clothes, arms, and a horse. Because Ortiz had become so accustomed to Indian attire, three weeks passed before he could bring himself to wear what de Soto had given him.

Ortiz served de Soto for nearly three years as the Spanish-led force slashed and pillaged its way through the southeast. Ortiz died in present-day Arkansas in March 1542, leaving de Soto and his men with another captive Indian guide who barely spoke Spanish. De Soto died a few weeks later. His men sunk his body in the Mississippi River and later rafted down to the Gulf of Mexico. Then they built boats and sailed for Mexico, staggering ashore in the summer of 1543.

The fate of Juan Ortiz and of the de Soto invasion that he guided reflects centuries of Indian history as well as the first generations of contact between North America and the **Atlantic world**. The outsiders entered an ecologically and culturally diverse continent that millions of Indians had reshaped over the course of thousands of years. Outsiders like Ortiz who adapted to Indian ways and served Indian needs survived. Those who did not, particularly Ortiz's fellow Spanish conquistadors who stormed in from the Caribbean and Mexico, often perished. All of what is today the mainland United States remained entirely in Indian hands until 1565, decades after much of the rest of the Americas had fallen to the Spanish sword. Still, men like Ortiz and de Soto laid the groundwork for the subsequent European colonization of North America.

# NORTH AMERICA TO 1500

The human history of North America begins when peoples from northeast Asia arrived more than 10,000 years ago. Over centuries of climate change, they learned about the new environments and what they could hunt, fish, and gather from wild plants. In addition to cultivating local wild plants, many peoples adopted and adapted transplants from Mexico. The most significant Mexican transplant—corn—transformed the lives of peoples in the southwest, Mississippi Valley, and northeast. These long-established migratory, cultural, and trade patterns persisted in North America long after the arrival of Europeans and Africans.

## The First Millennia of Indian North America

The findings of archeologists, linguists, and geneticists indicate that Indians' ancestors left northeast Asia for North America in three distinct waves. The largest most likely walked from Siberia to Alaska during the last Ice Age at least 15,000 years ago. Most

Indians descend from those migrants, who dispersed across the Americas. The next wave crossed by water, arriving 8,000 to 10,000 years ago. Most of these migrants spoke a Na-Dene language and settled first in Alaska and northwestern Canada. The last wave of Indians traveled by boat, about 5,000 years ago. These were the ancestors of the peoples we know as the Inuit and Aleuts. Those who became the Inuit claimed the Arctic shoreline from Alaska east to Labrador and Greenland. Meanwhile, ancestors of the Aleuts settled the Aleutian Islands.

**CHAPTER OUTLINE**

*continued from page 3*



Many Indian peoples consider migration a formative part of their past. Diné (Navajo) history begins with the story of their ancestors moving among four worlds. Ojibwa say that they, along with Ottawa and Potawatomi, descend from one people who lived near the "Great Salt Sea" in northeastern North America before moving to the Great Lakes, where they parted ways to become three distinct nations. Choctaw recall an exodus east across the Mississippi to their homeland in what is today Mississippi. The west, they remembered, was the direction of death, a place that barred spirits from entering the afterworld.

The first Americans grappled with environmental changes that would profoundly alter their cultures. It took thousands of years for global warming to end the Ice Age; most of the glacial ice that had covered much of the continent had melted by 8,000 BCE. Two-thirds of the continent's animal species that weighed 100 pounds or more went extinct, including the ancestors of the modern horse and camel. Indian hunters may have accelerated such extinctions, though to what extent is controversial among scholars and Indians.

Environmental changes compelled Indians to alter their relationships to the land and to one another over the next 7,000 years. Hunters in most of North America set their sights on smaller game, such as deer, rabbits, and squirrels, while on the Plains and in the interior Northwest they teamed up to hunt bison. Peoples who lived near rivers and estuaries came to rely more heavily on fish and shellfish as sources of animal protein. The appearance of stone artifacts—slabs with hollowed-out depressions and mortars—used to grind seeds or nuts, suggests that locally available wild plants, most likely harvested and processed by women, played a more significant role in Indian diets. As Indian bands learned to make better use of a more diverse range of local resources, their populations became denser, and they confined their annual movements to smaller areas. This encouraged greater cultural differentiation, which included the rise of many of the language families that existed in North America when Europeans arrived.

About 5,000 years ago Indian women in North America began to tend patches of edible wild plants to which they returned yearly. Around 3,500 years ago southwestern peoples began to cultivate corn, a plant that originated in central Mexico. Over the next thousand years they would develop strains that fared well in the colder and more arid conditions in which they lived.

Miwok acorn granaries, California, 1870s. Miwoks interlaced branches and grass to build structures like these to store acorns. They and many other California peoples harvested acorns, a staple of their diets, from oak groves that they maintained. Indians' skillful use of California's varied ecologies enabled them to create some of North America's densest populations.

## Farmers, Hunters, and Gatherers

By 1200 CE, most people who inhabited what is today the mainland United States cultivated plants wherever the climate permitted. California and the Pacific Northwest were exceptions. California's staggering variety of microclimates and ecological zones in close proximity to one another enabled Indians to subsist on what they could hunt, fish, and gather. Salmon fishing, hunting marine mammals, and gathering wild plants enabled Indians in the Pacific Northwest to avoid agriculture and devote more time and energy to other activities, such as intricate wood carving.

By 1000 CE most North Americans grew corn, beans, and squash. Beans came from Mexico. Indians in most of the southwest grew them by 200 CE. By then women in the east had domesticated four indigenous seed plants: lamb's quarter, marsh elder, squash, and sunflower. Corn entered eastern North America around 200 CE, but centuries passed before it became the region's dominant crop. By 900 CE Indian women had created a frost-resistant variety of corn called Northern Flint. It permitted them to harvest corn in parts of the northeast and Great Lakes where growing seasons were at least 120 days long.

Cultivating corn offered Indians clear advantages over the crops and practices that Europeans introduced to the Americas. Corn provided higher yields than the grains Europeans ate. Indian agriculture was less labor and soil intensive than Europe's.

Europeans usually planted rows, plots, or fields of the same species, a technique that depletes soil more quickly and encourages weeds. Indians planted corn, beans, and squash together in small hills. Corn stalks supported climbing bean tendrils, and nodules in the beans' roots fixed nitrogen, restoring some fertility to the soil. Squash and beans created groundcover that crowded out weeds, discouraged erosion, and saved labor. The three crops were a good dietary combination as well. When eaten together, corn and beans supply a full range of essential amino acids, and squash is rich in vitamins. In short, Indian North American agriculture offered a good diet for less labor with a smaller environmental footprint than did traditional European practices.

Indian diets also differed markedly from Europeans' in their sources of animal protein. Aside from turkeys, North American Indians did not domesticate animals for food. Unlike Europe, Asia, and Africa, the Americas had few animals small and tame enough to domesticate with relative ease. Indians had little reason to raise animals because game usually provided all the animal protein that they needed. European observers noted that Indians set fires to maintain prairies or to burn away underbrush in mature forests to simplify hunting game and maintain sunny clearings that attracted deer and other favored species. Even Indians who grew corn devoted most of their territory to hunting and fishing, activities that occupied several months a year. In time, new technology made hunting a bit easier. Inuit were the first to use the bow and arrow. Archeological evidence indicates that nearly everyone north of Mexico had them as of 700 CE.

Because Indians relied on wild sources of animal protein, they did not suffer from many of the illnesses that plagued Europeans, Africans, and Asians. Many virulent diseases have resulted from millennia of microbial exchange between humans and domesticated animals. Cowpox is a close relative of smallpox, and pigs and ducks act as reservoirs for influenza viruses that mutate within humans. Indians raised few animals, so without exposure to the pathogens domesticated animals carry, they did not develop immunity to these virulent germs. That left them highly vulnerable to disease when Europeans and Africans brought their pathogens to the Americas.

## The Rise and Decline of Urban Indian North America

The rise of agriculture encouraged the creation of urban centers in North America that thrived on long-distance trade in rare commodities. The largest were in the southwest and the Mississippi Valley. Two urban societies arose in the southwest by 1000 CE—the Hohokam and the Anasazi. Leaders of both owed their influence to irrigation systems. The Hohokam began to build canals to divert river water to their fields around 800 CE. Over the next four centuries they created thousands of miles of canals that supported a population of tens of thousands. Trade helps to explain the appearance of ball courts like those found in central Mexico in Snaketown, a principal Hohokam settlement. The Hohokam probably overtaxed their environment. They stopped building ball courts after 1150. A flood destroyed most of the canal network two centuries later. Meanwhile, irrigated soils became saltier and increasingly poisonous to crops. By 1400, the Hohokam had dispersed and combined with nearby peoples to become the O'Odham. The Spanish called them Pima and Papago, as do most outsiders.

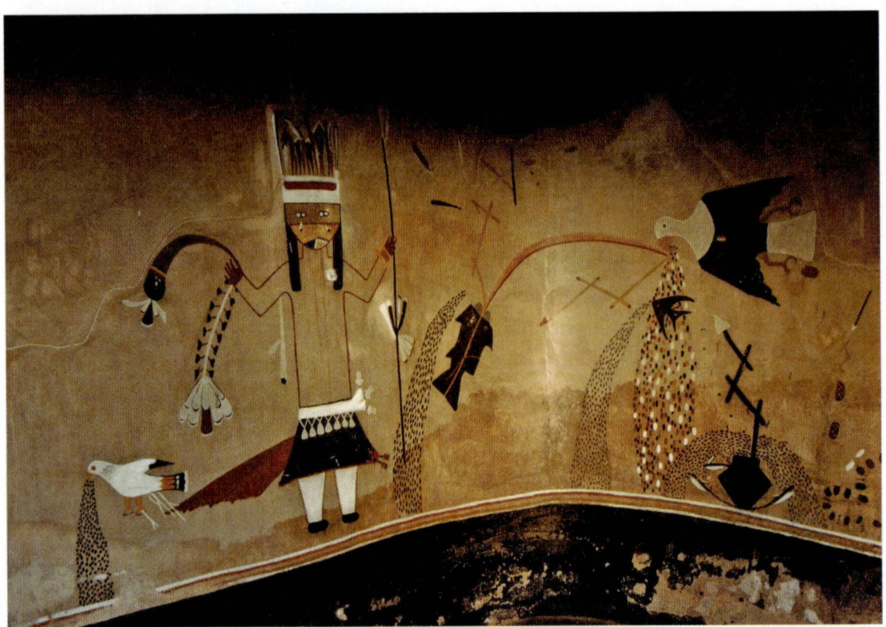

Kachina, kiva wall painting, Kuaua Pueblo, c. 1450. Kachinas are ancestral spiritual beings that Pueblo peoples believe bring rain, fertility, communal harmony, and well-being. Note the seeds, bolt of lightning, and rainbow emanating from the eagle's mouth. All symbolize fertility. Anasazi peoples constructed and settled in Kuaua Pueblo in central New Mexico during the 1300s.

As the Hohokam made more of Arizona bloom, the Anasazi developed a commercial hub in New Mexico. In 1100 Chaco Canyon contained as many as a dozen towns that together housed up to 11,000 people. Chaco residents specialized in making turquoise, which they exchanged for shells from the Gulf of California and copper bells, macaws, and feathers from Mexico. Global cooling caused severe droughts that compelled people to abandon Chaco. By 1300, many Anasazi descendants had migrated to the Rio Grande Valley and settled into small towns built of adobe, located in defensible places near reliable sources of water. These became the Hopi, Zuni, and other diverse peoples whom the Spanish collectively named Pueblos in the 1540s. A shared belief in **kachinas**, ancestral beings believed to bring rain and communal harmony, connected Pueblos, who spoke six distinct languages.

Cultivation of corn also transformed the Mississippi Valley, where what scholars call "Mississippian" societies began to form around 700 CE. **Mississippian societies** peaked between 1100 and 1300, stretching from Georgia west to Oklahoma and north to Wisconsin. Mississippians built on fertile floodplains, constructing cities with temples, earthen burial mounds, and large plazas for ceremonies and ball games like those in the southwest and Mexico. All had paramount (supreme) hereditary chiefs who collected tribute and demanded labor from commoners who erected and maintained temples and burial mounds. Chiefs mediated between their people and the sun, the source of life and their principal deity, and lived in wooden temples built atop earthen pyramids. When a chief died, his wives and servants were killed and entombed, along with rare goods, to accompany him into the afterlife.

The most famous Mississippian society peaked around 1100 at Cahokia, near today's East St. Louis, Illinois. As many as 10,000 lived in Cahokia proper and up to 30,000 in the villages that housed those whose labor sustained it. Located just south of where the Missouri met the Mississippi, Cahokians obtained copper from the Great Lakes, shells from the Atlantic coast, and obsidian (volcanic glass) from the Rockies, all items that filled the graves of chiefs and nobles.

Two centuries later, Cahokia was a ghost town. The city probably demanded more than the region and its people could provide, especially as the climate cooled

**Map 1.1**

**Trade and Selected Urbanized Indian Societies in North America, c. 700 to c. 1450** This map shows major trade routes and the goods transported along them c. 1450. Overlaid are the areas in the southwest where the Anasazi and Hohokam settled and areas in the Mississippi River Valley in which Mississippian societies flourished between roughly 700 and 1450 CE. Modern political boundaries are included to provide orientation.

and crop yields plummeted. Meanwhile, other Mississippian chiefdoms arose at Spiro in Oklahoma, Moundville in Alabama, and Etowah in Georgia. Spiro declined after 1350, when its residents and tributaries stopped erecting temples or burial mounds, and was abandoned by 1450.

The spread of corn cultivation to the northeast sparked profound changes among the Owasco, the most likely immediate ancestors of the Iroquois of upstate New York and Canada. As corn became the main source of food, Owasco women—responsible for cultivating the crop—gained importance. The rise of the longhouse during the 1100s enhanced women's status as well. Several families, all related by blood to a matriarch, occupied a longhouse where they coordinated farming, cooking, and child rearing. Meanwhile, Owasco relocated to villages situated on hilltops and surrounded by ditches and palisades for protection from worsening warfare between Owasco peoples. Villages that shared an enemy and, increasingly, a common language, banded together. Five such alliances gradually took shape. They became the Seneca, Cayuga, Onondaga, Oneida, and Mohawk, probably before the 1400s.

## Indian North America in the Century Before Contact

In 1492, scholars estimate that between 43 and 65 million people, about one-fifth of humanity, inhabited the Americas. Somewhere between 7 million and 10 million lived north of Mexico. They spoke at least 375 distinct languages, representing 21 language families. California was the most densely populated and culturally diverse

Huron woman pounding corn into meal, 1657. This image of a Huron woman at work in front of a longhouse comes from a map drawn by an Italian Jesuit who lived among the Huron in the 1640s. It illustrates the centrality of women, their labor, and their roles in the Huron and Iroquois societies.

place within what is today the United States. There were as many as 400,000 Californians, who spoke 50 different languages belonging to at least six language families. By contrast, five language families—Algonquian, Iroquoian, Muskogean, Caddoan, and Siouan—contained nearly all the tongues spoken from the Mississippi River Valley east to the Atlantic (Map 1.2). North America was one of the world's most diverse places at the moment of permanent contact with Europeans and Africans.

Migration enhanced North American diversity. Bands of Na-Dene may have introduced the bow and arrow, as well as shields, to the northwestern Plains by 700 CE. Seven centuries later, Na-Dene were settling in the southwest, where they became the Apaches and the Navajo. Their arrival affected trade and diplomacy. Na-Dene replaced Caddo and Wichita as the Pueblos' main providers of bison meat and hides, receiving

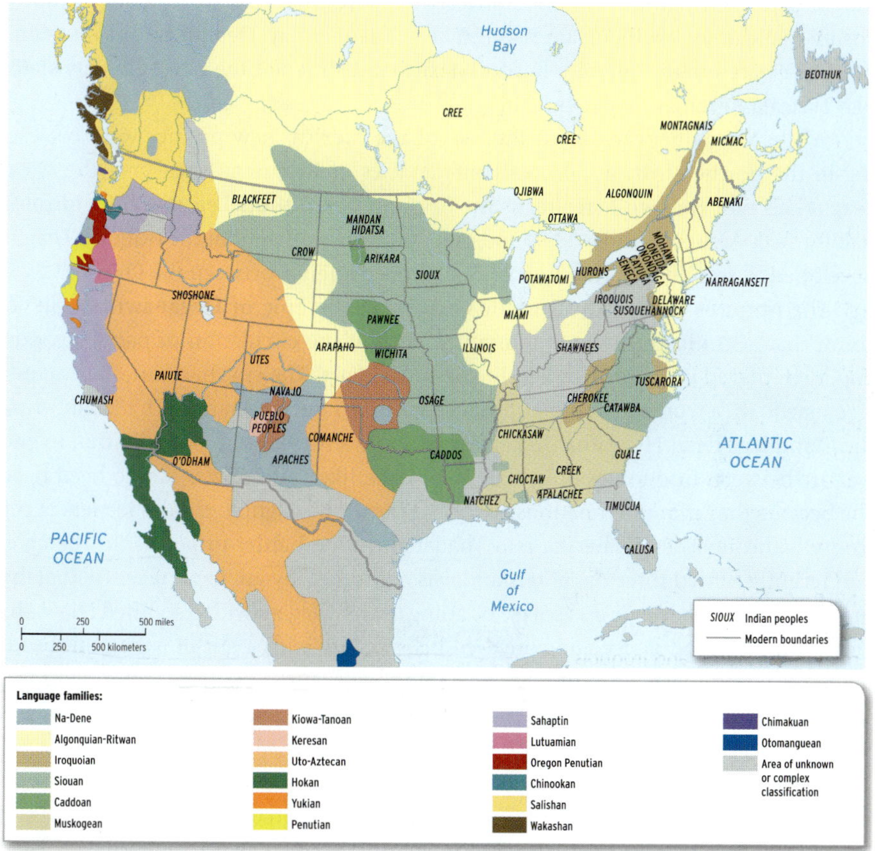


▲ **Map 1.2**

**Linguistic Map of Indian North America, with Selected Indian Peoples Included**
North America's Indians spoke nearly 400 different languages when Europeans first arrived. Above are the continent's linguistic boundaries, along with locations for a number of Indian peoples, both of which reflect the time when Europeans first made sustained contact with peoples in that region.

corn and cotton blankets in return and helping to create the southwest that Europeans and Africans encountered in the 1540s.

Meanwhile, relatively recent arrivals were also transforming central Mexico. They called themselves the Mexica. Their legends held that they had fled south from their ancestral homeland Aztlán (hence the name "Aztecs" by which the Mexica are often known), finding refuge on an island in Lake Texcoco. There, around 1325, the Mexica founded their capital Tenochtitlán. Under *tlatoani* (literally "the one who speaks," Europeans called tlatoani "emperors") Itzcoatl and Moctezuma I, the Mexica became Mesoamerica's dominant power as of the 1460s. They collected tribute from millions, many of whom, like the Mexica, spoke Nahuatl. Tenochtitlán soon had over 100,000 residents and a skyline dominated by two massive pyramids, one devoted to the Mesoamerican rain god Tlaloc, the other to the Mexica patron deity Huitzilopochtli. Mexica fought ritualized battles to seize captives who were sacrificed to Huitzilopochtli to ensure that the sun would again rise and keep death at bay. Demands for tribute and captives created many enemies for the Mexica and stiffened the resolve of city-states like Tlaxcala to remain independent.

While Mesoamericans faced the rise of the Mexica, new polities were coalescing in the northeast. By 1500, two confederacies of Iroquoian speakers—the Great League of Peace (known hereafter as the Iroquois or **Iroquois League**) and **Huron**—had formed. Archeological studies and oral traditions concur that the Iroquois League developed in response to centuries of destructive violence between the Owasco.

The Iroquois explain their league's origins in the **epic of Deganawidah**, an account that also illustrates the important roles that the circulation of people, goods, and ideas played in shaping Indian life before contact. The epic has four main actors: Deganawidah, a woman named Jikonsahseh, the Onondaga shaman Thadadaho, and the Onondaga chief Hiawatha. Deganawidah bore a message of reconciliation to end warfare between Iroquoians of upstate New York. Jikonsahseh was first to heed it, so she became the "mother of nations." Women earned the right to choose leaders of the Iroquois through her. Hiawatha and Thadadaho were harder to persuade. The chief had recently buried three daughters and was consumed by grief and rage. Thadadaho urged him to seek revenge and solace by going to war. Deganawidah soothed Hiawatha with words of condolence and conveyed his sincerity with a gift of wampum, beads made of drilled seashells strung together. He then focused on Thadadaho, who was later designated as the Firekeeper, the first chief among equals within Deganawidah's league of peace.

The structure and function of the Iroquois League honored and honors the epic of Deganawidah. The condolence ceremony and recitation of the epic began and still begin each meeting. Both rituals, accompanied by exchange of wampum, initiated diplomatic meetings with outsiders. A total of fifty chiefs, each chosen by women, represented each nation at council meetings. The Iroquois highlighted women's power and the importance of cooperation by conceiving of their confederation as a longhouse. Senecas and Mohawks guarded the western and eastern doors, respectively. The Onondaga, located at the geographic center and central figures in Deganawidah's epic, kept the fire that warmed all underneath its roof, so they hosted council meetings.

League councils could not make decisions until delegates had reached consensus and operated mainly to preserve harmony among the five peoples of the Iroquois, each of which was composed of autonomous villages. A council could not compel obedience from them, even when at war with outsiders.

Deganawidah's epic reveals longstanding practices and attitudes concerning migration between different Indian peoples. Depending on who is telling the story, Deganawidah is an adopted Mohawk, a Huron, or an otherworldly being. All agree that he was an outsider, who brought the idea of the league to their ancestors. Conscious adoption and adaptation of ideas from others shaped how Indians lived and how they understood who they were. Outsiders could be friend or foe, but could never be trusted unless they became kin. Women like Jikonsahseh were key to converting potential enemies into kin. The Iroquois League had transformed warring peoples into one another's kin, all housed under one political roof. For the Iroquois, as for most Indians, war was mainly a matter of exacting revenge on outsiders defined as enemies. The main objective was to seize captives and adopt them, not to kill or wound as many as possible. For adult male captives, that often meant ritual torture and execution. For women and children, it usually meant adoption to replace loved ones who had died. Adoption often meant enslavement. Indians practiced slavery widely and often considered slaves kin, though that did not prevent a lively slave trade between peoples that persisted well into the 1800s in North America, particularly in the southwest. The formation of the Iroquois League prompted Mohawk, Oneida, Onondaga, Cayuga, and Seneca to stop fighting **"mourning wars"** against each other and target other peoples instead.

Finally, Deganawidah's epic reveals meanings that Indians attached to exchange of goods. Deganawidah offered Hiawatha wampum because doing so told Hiawatha that he had something with spiritual power that he was willing to share. Wampum meant serious purpose, friendship, and generosity. The gift bound Hiawatha to reciprocate. Strings of shells, like other shiny portable items such as copper or turquoise—which also often came from faraway places—were considered otherworldly objects that conferred prestige and spiritual power on those who received them and on whoever gave them away. Most chiefs were expected not to amass such goods, but to redistribute them. Indians considered trade a form of diplomacy. Friends traded with friends, and did so by following customary protocols (rather than, say, a market price). Exchange of goods and people symbolized, reenacted, and maintained friendship between trading parties. That was the American way before Europeans and Africans brought Indians into an emerging global network.

## STUDY QUESTIONS FOR NORTH AMERICA TO 1500

1. **In what ways did agriculture change Indian life and politics? What changed little after Indians began to cultivate plants?**
2. **How did Indians regard the movement of people, goods, and ideas across boundaries? In what ways did such an understanding shape Indians' relations to one another and their sense of who they were?**

# MAKING AN ATLANTIC WORLD, 1400–1513

During the 1400s, western Europeans developed and refined technologies and knowledge that by the 1490s enabled them to cross the Atlantic and return home. The Spanish and Portuguese sought new sources of wealth and new allies by trading directly with sub-Saharan Africans and Asians. That led them to launch an oceanic trade in enslaved Africans that encouraged the spread of plantation agriculture to new Iberian (Spanish and Portuguese) colonies off Africa's coast, processes that accelerated the creation of a new world linked by the Atlantic Ocean. Spanish mariners brought and extended that new Atlantic world to the Americas in 1492, an act that had the most immediate impact on people of the Caribbean island of Española.

## Western Europe in the 15th Century

As the 1400s dawned, western Europe was a relatively poor region on the fringe of a prosperous Mediterranean world. Ottomans and Venetians controlled access to luxury goods—gold and ivory from sub-Saharan Africa and silks, gems, and spices from east, southeast, and south Asia—and made hefty profits as the middlemen. Merchants of the port city of Genoa, Italy, specialized in transporting bulk goods such as grains and wine. Many Christian Europeans considered the growing power of Ottoman Turks to their west and south, and the Islamic emirates in parts of southern Spain and feared that Muslims were encircling them.

Western Europeans had many interconnected reasons to venture beyond the world that they knew. Some sought to spread Christianity and make new allies for what they believed was a spiritual and ideological struggle against Islam. Monarchs in England, France, Portugal, and Spain sought revenue to fund armies and consolidate power over nobles. Ambitious men of ordinary birth saw acquisition of wealth as a path to social mobility. They concluded that the best way to become richer quickly was to circumvent the Mediterranean networks that brought them luxury goods and deal directly with Africans and East and South Asians.

By 1450 Europeans had the technology to sustain long-distance maritime commerce. The Christian conquest of Gibraltar in the late 1200s facilitated direct trade between the North Sea, the Baltic, and the Mediterranean. In time, it also gave rise to a new kind of ship in Iberian and Genoese shipyards—the caravel. Caravels combined the strength and durability required of vessels that plied stormy waters off northern Europe with the speed and maneuverability of those that operated in the relatively calm Mediterranean. They could sail in protected coastal waters or the open ocean.

Europeans also had most of what they needed to orient themselves at sea. Compasses indicated which way was north. Hourglasses permitted rough calculations of velocity. **Astrolabes** and quadrants helped to determine latitude. Long before 1400, Mediterranean mariners used portolan charts, maps with detailed images of coastlines, to decide on the best route between two ports. They also employed classical

**▲ Map 1.3**

**Global Trade, Africa, and the Making of the Eastern Atlantic World, 15th century**
The Mediterranean Basin linked Europe to Africa and Asia for thousands of years through a combination of oceanic and overland routes. Portuguese seafaring along Africa's Atlantic coast during the 15th century brought West Africa into maritime global trade networks and launched the Atlantic slave trade.

knowledge. A Latin translation of Ptolemy's *Geography* appeared in 1406. It summarized the Greek world's understanding of geography circa 100 CE and offered guidance on how to represent Earth's spherical shape on a flat map.

Meanwhile, ideas coursed more rapidly thanks to Europeans' adaptation of two Chinese inventions. One was a technique for making paper. The other was block printing, inspired by a Chinese technique whereby characters carved into wood were dipped in ink and pressed onto paper. By the 1450s, German artisans brought together movable metal typecasts of each letter of the alphabet, ink, and a machine to press inked type against paper. The printing press revolutionized access to information. Books became cheaper and more widely available. As of 1500, Europe's printers had turned out some six million books, probably more than had appeared in the previous 1,000 years.

By the 1450s Europeans had also developed techniques of warfare to support expansion. They obtained gunpowder from China by 1250, and about 70 years later

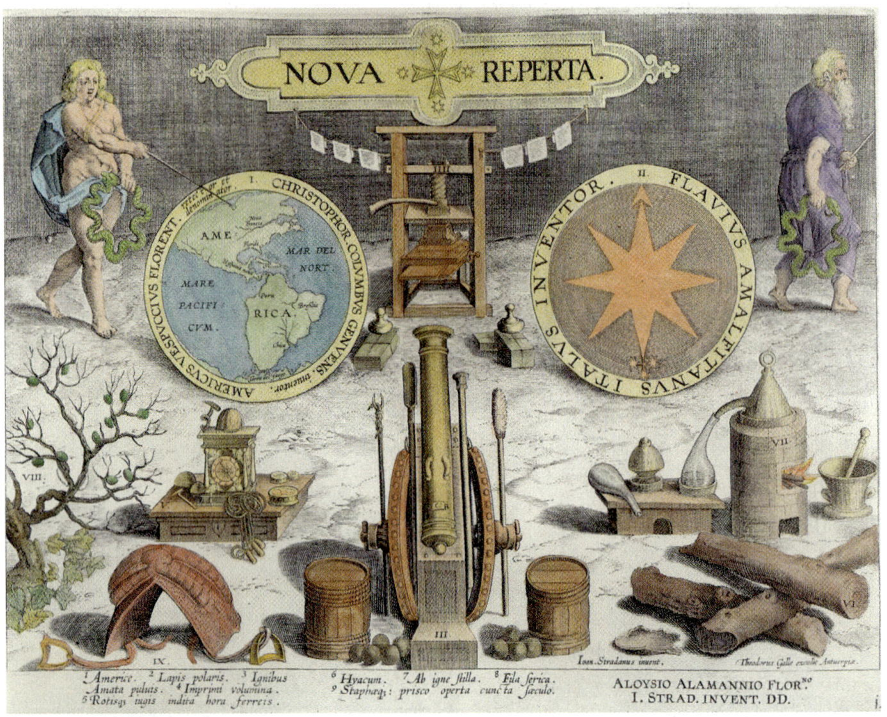


This image, from *Nova Reperta*, a book published in Antwerp in 1600, illustrates how Europeans identified their "discovery" of the Americas with technologies that they had modified and mastered. At the center a cannon, flanked by shot and barrels of gunpowder, takes aim at a printing press.

used it to propel missiles. By 1400, Europeans were producing firearms, especially artillery, which was used for sieges. By 1500, soldiers carried arquebuses, the ancestor of the musket, into battle, although their primitive design made them inaccurate. Surging metal production met demand for more weaponry. Much of it was forged into steel and beaten into pikes and swords, which remained indispensable in combat.

Christian kingdoms of the Iberian Peninsula spearheaded western European expansion during the 1400s. Those that formed modern Spain had entered the final stage of a centuries-long process of evicting Islamic emirates from Iberia. Their ***reconquista*** (reconquest) combined religious, economic, and political goals. Christians saw themselves as crusaders who were reclaiming Iberia for their faith. Monarchs could not afford to mount military campaigns themselves, so they licensed private entrepreneurs who promised to share the spoils of conquest. Those who succeeded received ***encomiendas***—grants of land that they had conquered. **Isabel of Castile's** marriage to **Ferdinand of Aragon** in 1469 united two principal Christian kingdoms. Thirteen years later, Christian forces launched the conquest of Granada, Iberia's last emirate. In January 1492, the last Muslim settlement capitulated.

Meanwhile, the Portuguese gazed south and west. Unlike Spain, England, or France, Portugal was a united kingdom at peace with its neighbors for most of the 1400s. It was also a relatively poor one with a long coastline that drew thousands of Portuguese to the sea. Located near northwest Africa and thrust far out into the Atlantic, Portugal was poised to use the ocean to link the two continents.

## Iberians, Africans, and the Creation of an Eastern Atlantic World

Europeans and Africans created an eastern Atlantic world over the course of the 15th century, largely by connecting western Africa directly to the outside world. That laid a foundation for the conquest and colonization of the Americas and for the enslavement of millions of Africans who were shipped to them.

Portugal's expansion into Africa began in 1415 with the conquest of Ceuta, a Muslim city in Morocco. Portuguese mariners soon began to map Africa's northwest coast by inching south, trading with or raiding whomever they encountered, and returning home to report and split the profits. Their efforts, sponsored by Prince Henry, had three linked objectives. One was to challenge Muslim powers in North Africa. Another was to make direct contact and ally with a Christian kingdom headed by "Prester John." By the early 1400s, Europeans associated his realm with Ethiopia, home to a large and ancient Christian community, which had begun to send emissaries to Europe. The third objective, gold, mattered most to the Portuguese. North African Muslims controlled the flow of West African gold across the Sahara and into the Mediterranean. The Portuguese wanted to divert that stream into their pockets by trading directly with West Africans. They established their first ***feitoria*** (fortified trading post) at Arguim in 1445. In 1482, the Portuguese built a feitoria at Elmina, on what Europeans called Africa's Gold Coast because of its proximity to mines (Map 1.3). Feitorias required African participation and consent. Portuguese employed locals to operate them and paid rent to their rulers.

Portuguese mariners launched the **Atlantic slave trade**. The first cargo of enslaved people shipped directly from Africa arrived in Portugal in 1441. At first the Portuguese raided for slaves, but soon found it easier and more profitable to buy them from African captors. The Portuguese lacked the military might or the antibodies to impose their will on African rulers. Like other Europeans, they had little immunity to diseases endemic to West Africa.

Slavery was common in West and West Central Africa, where slaves were the only form of private, revenue-producing property that legal systems widely recognized. Those condemned to slavery in Africa were usually criminals, war captives, or debtors. They did not inherit their status, nor did they pass it on to their children.

Africans were also familiar with long-distance slave trading. Thousands were driven across the Sahara or transported up the Red Sea to North Africa and the Middle East annually between 800 and 1600. At first relatively few entered the Atlantic slave trade—about 800 a year during the 1450s and 1460s and over 2,000 by the 1490s, about one-third of whom were sold to other Africans for gold.

Even so, Africans already figured prominently in Mediterranean slave markets. The Ottoman conquest of Constantinople, today's Istanbul, in 1453 made it harder for Europeans to purchase Slavs (hence the word "slave") from the Black Sea, a key source of enslaved labor to northern and western Europe for centuries. Most Africans enslaved in Europe served as domestics. Africans comprised about 10 percent of Lisbon's population by 1550, a reflection of Portuguese dominance of the Atlantic slave trade until the late 1500s.

The Atlantic slave trade affected how Europeans viewed Africans. By the late 1400s, Christian Europeans seldom enslaved one another, mainly for religious reasons. Muslims who ruled Iberia had distinguished between slaves on the basis of skin color: they considered darker-skinned people from sub-Saharan Africa inferior and most suitable for enslavement. Christian Iberians came to hold similar views of sub-Saharan Africans, partly because they also associated dark-skinned Africans with Muslims, whom they condemned as infidels. Demographic changes in the slave trade during the 1400s reinforced such beliefs. Ottoman control of the eastern Mediterranean and the Atlantic slave trade meant that dark-skinned Africans soon became the majority of Christian Europe's slaves, leading more Europeans to associate black skin with servility.

As the Atlantic slave trade began, Iberians were already colonizing islands off Africa's northwest coast. The most significant of these were the Canary Islands and Madeira. The conquest of the Canaries began in 1402. The islands' indigenous people, the Guanche, probably descended from Berbers of North Africa. Guanche became targets of slaving raids and fell victim to diseases to which they had no immunity. There were virtually no Guanche left by the 1490s.

Meanwhile, Portuguese colonists established sugar plantations off northwest Africa's coast on the Madeira islands. Europeans first encountered cultivation of sugar cane in the Middle East during the Crusades. For the next few centuries, Cyprus and Sicily supplied European markets with sugar, from plantations staffed by enslaved Slavs, Tatars, and Mediterranean captives. Genoese merchants brought sugar-making technology from Sicily to Iberia, and by the 1450s Sicilians ran sugar mills on Madeira. Genoese merchants financed many of them and had the sugar hauled back to Europe. By 1500 about 2,000 slaves, mostly Africans, toiled on Madeira's plantations. Spanish colonists on the Canaries also exploited enslaved Africans as they competed with Madeira to satisfy Europe's growing sweet tooth.

The imperative to spread Christianity helped to propel and justify Portuguese expansion into Africa. Papal decrees issued between 1442 and 1456 granted Portugal the right to colonize islands off Africa's coast and monopolize trade between West Africa and Europe. In exchange, Portugal agreed to establish Catholic missions in Africa. One decree permitted Portuguese to buy African captives if doing so meant that they might become converts.

The Portuguese saw missionaries as a way to forge diplomatic and commercial ties in Africa, a view that African rulers sometimes shared. To them, conversion offered a way to gain a powerful ally and bolster their own authority. In 1484, the explorer Diogo Cão left four missionaries in Kongo and returned to Portugal with four

Kongolese hostages, all nobles. They returned home three years later, having learned Portuguese. In 1491, Portuguese soldiers helped the Kongolese king Nzinga a Nkuwu put down a rebellion, and on Christmas Day he and his family were baptized. For the next 15 years Kongolese fought over who should rule them. In 1506, the victor, Afonso, committed Kongo to an alliance with the Portuguese. His son Henrique studied in Portugal, became a priest in 1518, and was appointed the first sub-Saharan African bishop two years later. Thousands of Kongolese accepted baptism and gradually infused Christianity with their traditions.

By the time Kongolese had begun to Africanize western Christianity, the Portuguese were about to open a direct water route to the Indian Ocean. In 1487, Bartolomeu Dias rounded what he named the Cape of Good Hope and entered the Indian Ocean. Eleven years later, an Arab pilot guided Vasco da Gama across the Indian Ocean to India. Da Gama returned to Lisbon with spices. King Manoel fired off a letter to Ferdinand and Isabel trumpeting da Gama's achievement.

The Portuguese dominated the eastern water route to Asia for over a century. A chain of feitorias down Africa's Atlantic coast, their cannon facing the ocean, backed Portugal's claim. But the Portuguese could not monopolize knowledge of winds and currents gleaned from thousands of voyages to Africa, Madeira, and the Canaries, which suggested that one might reach Asia by crossing the Atlantic.

This brass casting, probably made by an African artist at the royal court of Benin in the late 1500s or early 1600s, illustrates Portuguese influence in West Africa. It depicts a Portuguese mercenary fighting for the oba (king) of Benin. He carries a firearm, which the Portuguese introduced to the region.

## Columbus and the First Encounter

The man most responsible for extending the Atlantic world to the Americas emerged from the intersection of Mediterranean, Iberian, and eastern Atlantic networks. **Christopher Columbus** was born in Genoa around 1450. He likely began his maritime career in the early 1470s. Columbus soon moved to Lisbon, drawn by opportunities offered by the city's Genoese merchants. He married Felipa Muniz, daughter of Bartolomeu Perestrello. He had ties to Portugal's royal court and supervised the colonization of one of the Madeira islands. By the early 1480s, Columbus had visited Ireland, Iceland, Madeira, the Canaries, and Elmina. He knew the eastern Atlantic well.

Columbus also studied geography, sold books, and made maps. He pored over Ptolemy's *Geography*, which postulated that one could sail across the Atlantic to Asia. Ptolemy thought the distance between the continents was so great that no ship or crew could reach Asia and return. Access to the royal court alerted Columbus to a more optimistic alternative. In 1474, the Florentine cosmographer Paolo del Pazzo Toscanelli had written the king of Portugal to claim that 5,000 miles separated the Canaries and China—still a great distance but one that sounded more feasible.

Columbus needed financial and legal backing to get to Asia. He tried and failed to interest John II of Portugal, so Columbus moved to Spain in 1485. He spent the next seven years lobbying Ferdinand and Isabel for support. They approved Columbus's proposal shortly after the conquest of Granada and put up more than half the money for the voyage. The monarchs also granted him noble status and the offices of admiral, viceroy, and governor-general. Columbus had to provide one-quarter of the financing, most of which he borrowed from Italian merchants.

With three ships and 90 men under his command, Columbus departed Spain in early August 1492. In mid-October, the crew made landfall on an island in the Bahamas. The Lucayan Taínos who lived there called it "Guanahaní." Columbus, thinking he had landed near the Indian Ocean's eastern edge, called them "Indians." His account of their first encounter stressed how little clothing the Taínos wore. Europeans of Columbus's time used clothing as a benchmark to judge individuals' social status and the level of civilization that a society had attained. Columbus also interpreted Taínos' lack of clothing as a sign of their innocence. Their willingness to trade whatever they had for glass beads, coins, and copper bells was another. Both suggested to Columbus that Taínos might make suitable converts and good workers. He took seven people from Guanahaní to serve as guides and interpreters, following a practice that the Portuguese had established in West Africa. The three ships then sailed south in search of Asian ports as well as gold and other commodities that would sell in Europe.

After exploring Cuba, Columbus reached an island that Taínos called Quisqueya. He renamed it "La Isla Española"—the Spanish island, now Haiti and the Dominican Republic. On Quisqueya the visitors met Taínos who seemed more like themselves. Their ancestors had migrated from South America over a thousand years earlier. These Taínos wore gold jewelry and lived in villages of up to 2,000 people governed by chiefs called caciques. They subsisted mainly on what they grew in conucos—plots that they had slashed and burned from the forest—above all on cassava, from which they made bread. Taíno gods took physical form as zemis—carved idols that occupied places of honor in villages and homes. Taínos had a profound impact on how Europeans viewed the Americas and Indians. Many Arawak (the Taíno language) words entered Spanish and English, including "canoe" and "hammock." The word "Taíno" means "good" or "noble" in Arawak. Taínos used it to distinguish themselves from Caribs, who inhabited most of the Lesser Antilles. Taínos told Columbus that Caribs were a vicious warlike people who ate their enemies. Columbus later had a violent encounter with Caribs, which in his mind reinforced what the Taínos told him. An account of Columbus's first voyage distinguished between "good noble" Indians and violent savage ones. It circulated widely in Europe and molded European perceptions of Indians, including the belief that many were "cannibals"—a corruption of the word "Carib."

Columbus touted Española as a paradise. It had gold and a large population that farmed and lived in villages. After spending a few weeks along the island's north coast,

Columbus loaded two ships with gold, chilies, tobacco, a canoe, a hammock, and seven Taínos. He left 39 men behind, sailed north, and discovered winds that blew east. Columbus reached Spain in March 1493 and headed to Barcelona to brief Ferdinand and Isabel and display the Taínos. He arrived to learn that a published account of his trip had beaten him there by two weeks. By December, versions of the story sold in Paris, Florence, and Rome. Columbus insisted that he had reached Asia and that Japan and China could not be far beyond. Pope Alexander VI believed that he had found people who required evangelization and awarded Spain sovereignty over the lands Columbus had visited. This sat poorly with the Portuguese. In 1494, Spain and Portugal signed the **Treaty of Tordesillas**, by which they divided the world between them. The Americas, excepting Brazil, ended up on the Spanish side of the line.

An Italian named **Giovanni Caboto** was visiting Spain when Columbus returned. Like Columbus, he had lobbied the monarchs of Portugal and Spain to sponsor a

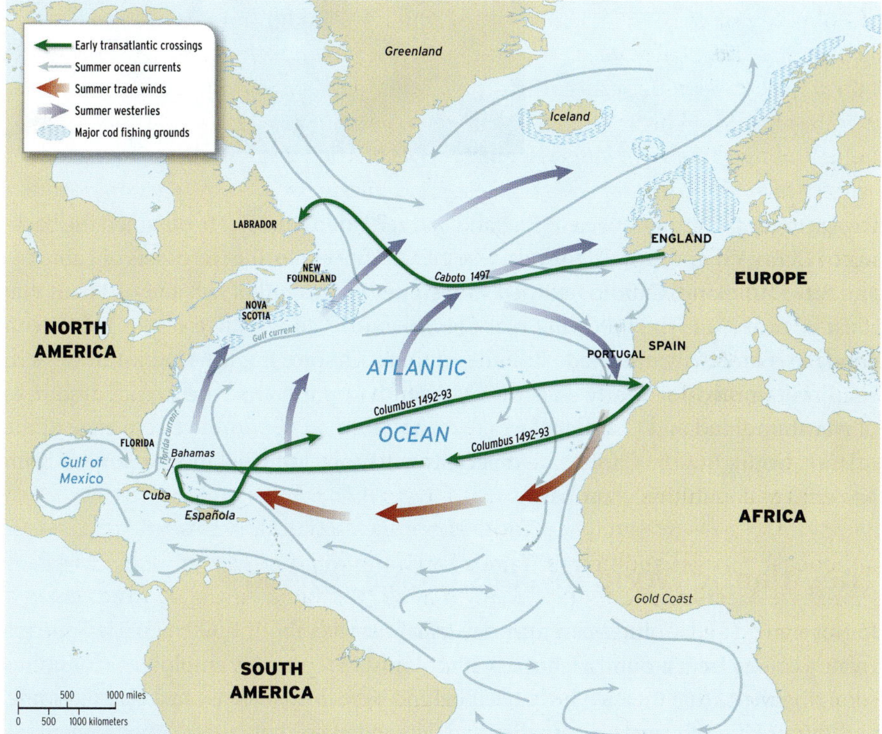


**Map 1.4**

**Summer Winds and Currents, Fishing Banks, and Two Early Transoceanic Crossings of the North Atlantic** Mariners who sailed the Atlantic needed a good understanding of the ocean's winds and currents to navigate it successfully. Columbus and Giovanni Caboto were the first to learn how to return to Europe from the Americas. Note the major cod fishing grounds where cold and warm currents collided.

This view of Seville, attributed to Alonso Sánchez Coello and painted in the late 1550s, captures the city's status as Spain's main gateway to the Americas. In the foreground an expedition prepares to set off for the Americas.

voyage to Asia. Caboto moved to England and settled in Bristol. He obtained the backing of Henry VII and crossed the ocean in 1497. After exploring the coasts of Labrador and Newfoundland, Caboto returned with stories of seas full of fish and of a land that must be near Asia. The following year Caboto embarked with five vessels laden with goods to trade. Only one made it home, without Caboto. English interest in western ventures dimmed for nearly a century. Caboto had publicized the marine resources of Newfoundland and Canada, places that soon formed the northwestern edge of the Atlantic world. But the Caribbean, especially Española, attracted more attention from powerful and ambitious Europeans.

## The Atlantic World Invades the Caribbean

In November 1493, Columbus returned to Española with about 1,500 men. He hoped to create a colony built around a feitoria, with colonists as company employees. Columbus soon discovered that the men he had left behind were dead. Disease had claimed some, and Taínos killed the rest because they had demanded gold or raped Taíno women.

Relations between colonists and Taínos deteriorated as Columbus lost control of his men. They had come to Española for gold and conquest, not a salary. In 1495, colonists provoked a war with most of Española's main caciques. Columbus shipped over 500 Taínos to Spain to show that Española could be profitable. He justified their enslavement on the grounds that they had rebelled. Meanwhile, colonists abandoned the site that Columbus chose. In 1496, they founded Santo Domingo, the first permanent European town in the Americas.

The Spanish squabbled over how much authority Columbus and his brothers could wield and over who had the right to how much Taíno labor and tribute. Colonists wanted to exploit Indians harder. By the late 1490s, Columbus, with royal approval, tried to mollify them by altering the terms of encomiendas. In Spain, encomenderos (holders of encomiendas) held rights to land. In Española an encomendero could demand tribute and service from a designated group of Taínos, above all to mine gold. That did not satisfy Columbus's critics, who in 1500 clamped irons on him and his brothers and sent them to Spain, where Columbus faced charges that he had persecuted his enemies and oppressed Taínos for personal gain. The case against him was dismissed, but Columbus was stripped of his offices. He died in 1506. Two years later, mapmakers named his "discovery" after his friend Amerigo Vespucci, an Italian mariner who had visited the Caribbean.

Columbus's return to Española in 1493 set in motion several developments. First, it ensured the permanence of the "**Columbian exchange**," what historians call the movement of people, plants, animals, and pathogens between the Americas and the rest of the world. One form of exchange, sex between European men and Taíno women, began in 1492. It introduced a strain of syphilis to Europe that quickly mutated into a more virulent and disfiguring form. Since no women accompanied the second expedition, Taíno women became Spanish men's sexual partners, willingly or not. At first, many fathers recognized the children that resulted from such unions and most colonists considered them Spanish. But by the 1530s, the Spanish began to consider them a separate and subordinate group whom they called "mestizos."

Mestizos notwithstanding, colonists hoped to remake Quisqueya into a "Spanish land" by bringing familiar plants and livestock. Wheat, chickpeas, grapes, olives, and sheep, staples of the Mediterranean diet, fared poorly in Caribbean heat and humidity. Because they could not subsist on locally grown grains of European origin, Española's colonists had to eat the unfamiliar cassava whether they liked it or not. European migrants to the Americas received a similar lesson over the next two centuries. They had to learn how to cultivate, prepare, and eat Indian crops to survive, whether they liked it or not.

The cattle and pigs that arrived in 1493 colonized Quisqueya more quickly than the Spanish did. All the cattle that the Spanish introduced to the Americas descended from those they brought to Española between 1493 and 1512. Quisqueya had no natural predators, so colonists let the animals loose to forage. Pigs and cattle soon overran the island. By 1508, authorities sought to protect the conucos that fed Española by permitting hunters to kill feral swine. After 1519, the island's two main exports were hides and sugar from cane, which the Spanish also introduced in 1493. Enslaved West Africans, Spaniards, and Indians herded, slaughtered, and skinned the animals.

Animal and human colonists introduced Taínos to pathogens to which they had little or no immunity and made them more vulnerable to those that had long infected them. Pigs from Columbus's second voyage probably brought influenza to the Americas. Smallpox reached Española by January 1519, the first documented pandemic clearly of European origin to hit the Americas. By then most Taínos had died. Perhaps

GLOBAL PASSAGES

# Cod

In 1497, Giovanni Caboto journeyed to Newfoundland and reported that "the sea there is swarming with fish." Word spread quickly and far. By the 1540s more than one hundred vessels carrying thousands of men left France each year for waters off Newfoundland, Labrador, and Nova Scotia. They wanted cod, which soon comprised over half the fish eaten in Europe.

Cod is a meaty, white-fleshed fish. It prefers waters between 34° and 50° F, where it devours the marine life that thrives wherever warm and cold currents meet on either side of the North Atlantic (Map 1.4). Cod was ideal for a time when people had no refrigeration. Less than 1 percent fat, the fish can be preserved by drying it in the sun and wind.

During the late medieval era, wind-dried cod and ling (a fish related to cod) became Europe's first mass-produced food. At first Scandinavia was Europe's supplier of dried cod. Growing demand pushed fishermen to seek the fish in open water. By 1350, dried cod was Iceland's principal export and a staple on European tables—a cheap, portable, and durable source of protein.

Religion, war, and environmental change boosted demand for cod. Devout Catholics could not eat meat on nearly half the days a year, but they could eat fish. Monarchs provisioned growing armies and navies with cod, largely to save money. Europeans endured frequent crop failures during the "Little Ice Age," a period of global cooling that lasted from 1300 to 1850. They had depleted many of their own coastal fisheries by 1500. In short, a voracious appetite for affordable animal protein compelled Europeans to scour the North Atlantic for cod.

By the early 1500s Europeans swarmed the coast from Labrador to Maine, frequently interacting with Indians. Sometimes they targeted them. In 1501, the Portuguese captain Gaspar Corte-Real enslaved 57 Beothuk on Newfoundland. Twenty-four years later Estevão Gomes took several dozen Abenaki captives to Spain after mapping Maine's coast. Relations between Europeans and the Beothuk, Montagnais, Micmac, and Abenaki were usually guarded but peaceful. Indians soon became discerning consumers of imports. Giovanni da Verrazzano encountered a group of Abenaki in Maine in 1524. They refused to allow his men to land and accepted only "knives, hooks for fishing, and sharp metal" for what they brought to barter. Opportunities for trade increased in the 1540s as cod fishing expanded and French and Basques set up summer camps in Labrador, Newfoundland, and Nova Scotia to salt and dry cod.

Cod was the first American food to enter the daily lives of ordinary Europeans. It took them centuries to accept many foods indigenous to the Americas such as corn or potatoes, but they knew cod and had ventured across the Atlantic to catch

▲

Early modern Europeans fishing and processing cod, 1690s. Just above the legend is a depiction of onshore drying, the most common method for preserving cod in the 1500s and the one that brought European fishermen into regular contact with Indians. Here also is shown the "green" or "wet" method of preserving cod on board ships that developed later.

it. Fishermen were the first Europeans to have regular and sustained contact with North American Indians. From such contact arose a transatlantic trade in animal skins based on Indian labor, one that became a mainstay of North America's economy for centuries. In the early 1600s, word that New England's coast teemed with cod spurred the English to colonize there.

- What prompted Europeans to cross the Atlantic in pursuit of cod?
- What impact did European fishermen's visits have on Indians? What impact did the cod that they caught have on Europe?

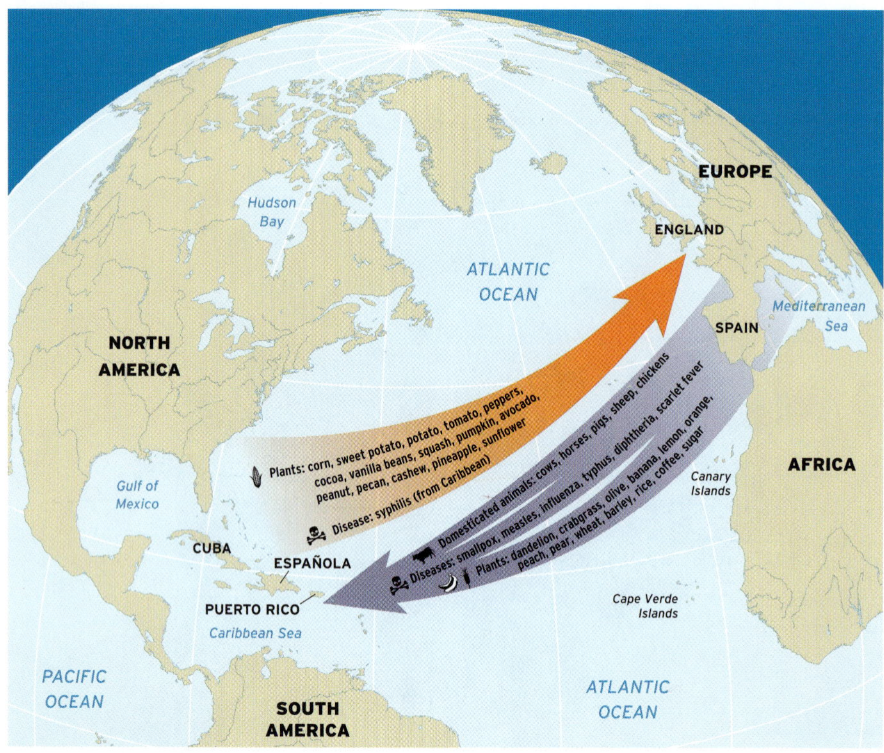


▲ **Map 1.5**

**The Columbian Exchange** Columbus's second voyage established a permanent exchange of plants, animals, and microbes between the Americas and the rest of the world. In some cases it took centuries for Europeans, Africans, and Asians to adopt American crops. The impact of Eurasian microbes on American Indians was immediate and devastating.

400,000 people inhabited Quisqueya in 1492. Spanish officials counted only 11,000 in 1518.

The human toll of Quisqueya's transformation into Española had many consequences. Spaniards stormed the Caribbean in search of new conquests, riches, and slaves. Between 1508 and 1513 they overran Cuba, Puerto Rico, and Jamaica, establishing encomiendas and shipping Taínos to Española. In 1509, Spanish mariners raided the Bahamas. They practically emptied those islands of people in just four years.

The depopulation of the Greater Antilles spurred a missionary-led campaign to end the worst abuses of the conquest. In 1511, the friar Antonio de Montesinos enraged Santo Domingo's elite by delivering a sermon in which he threatened that God would punish them for their cruelty towards Indians. A Montesinos disciple, **Bartolomé de Las Casas**, a priest and former Cuban encomendero, was an even harsher critic of abuse of Indians. He focused his ire on encomiendas and conquistadors, but never questioned Spain's right to rule in the Americas.

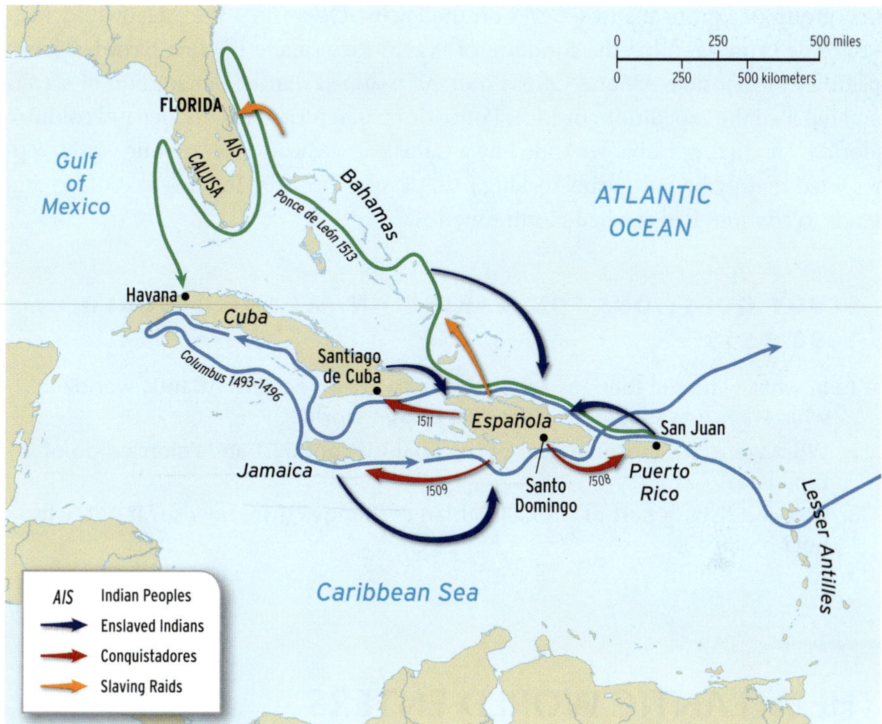


▲ **Map 1.6**

**Española and Spanish Conquests in the Caribbean, 1493–1515** The depopulation of Española's Taínos caused by microbes that the Spanish brought and by Spanish abuses spurred conquistadores and slave raiders to invade nearby islands, a process that led the Spanish to Florida by 1513.

The decimation of the Taíno facilitated the extension of African slavery and plantation agriculture to the Americas. The first shipment of enslaved Africans arrived in Española in 1502. Fourteen years later, a colonist built Española's first functional mill to crush sugar cane, extract the juice, and boil it down to make sugar. During the 1520s Española witnessed the first sugar boom in the Americas. At first most who toiled in the cane fields were enslaved Indians, with artisans from the Canaries, Italy, and Portugal supervising the mills. Genoese merchants financed the first mills and delivered enslaved Africans to the Caribbean, who by the late 1520s had mostly replaced Indians on plantations. As of 1540, 15,000 had been sent to Española and the island had an African majority—some of whom had escaped slavery to found the first free black communities in the Americas. Española remained an important source of sugar to Europe until the 1580s, when sugar production boomed in Brazil.

The devastation of the Greater Antilles led conquistadors to look to the American mainland. The Caribbean was the gateway for invasions of Central America, Mexico, and Florida. An expedition from Española seeking gold and slaves in Panama was the first group of Europeans to set eyes on the Pacific Ocean in 1513. Meanwhile, Juan Ponce de León, who led the conquest of Puerto Rico, made the first recorded European visit to Florida. Ais and Calusa Indians assumed that he led a group of slavers and repelled the expedition. In 1521, Ponce de León returned to conquer and colonize Florida. He died in Cuba, wounded by a Calusa arrowhead. The Atlantic world, represented mainly by Europeans seeking fish, passages to Asia, Indians to enslave, and lands to conquer had reached North America.

**STUDY QUESTIONS FOR MAKING AN ATLANTIC WORLD, 1400–1513**

1. **In what ways did Iberians and Africans create an eastern Atlantic world? In what ways was Columbus a product of that world?**
2. **What were the consequences of the Spanish conquest and colonization of Española?**
3. **Was cod fishing part of the Columbian exchange? If so, how so? If not, why not?**

# THE ATLANTIC WORLD ENTERS NORTH AMERICA, 1513–1565

Knowledge that the Americas had wealthy indigenous empires and that the world's oceans are connected intensified European interest in North America. Mariners mapped the continent's coasts as Spanish-led expeditions invaded its interior in search of Indian empires to conquer and pillage. Experience and Indian resistance soon taught Europeans that there were few riches to be had easily in North America. Nevertheless, the continent became a stage for European imperial rivalries and religious conflicts that led the Spanish to establish the first colony in what would become the United States.

## The Fall of the Mexica

In September 1519, **Hernán Cortés**, leader of a Spanish expedition to Mexico, persuaded the leaders of Tlaxcala to join him against the Mexica. Scholars have long sought to explain how fewer than a thousand Spaniards could have toppled a mighty empire of millions. Most agree that technology and long-term consequences of European agriculture played an indispensible role. But Cortés could not have prevailed without Indian allies like the Tlaxcalans or his translator and advisor **Malintzín**. The Spanish conquest of Mexico was also an Indian conquest of the Mexica.

Cortés acquired Malintzín and 19 other enslaved women from the Chontal Maya in 1519. The Spanish baptized them, renamed them, and parceled them out to provide sexual services. Marina was a Nahua (speaker of Nahuatl, the language of the

Mexica and millions of others in central Mexico). Nahuas soon addressed her as "Malintzín" because no "r" sound exists in Nahuatl and to show her respect as the one who spoke for the powerful strangers. Her knowledge of Nahua culture and politics helped to win allies against the Mexica. Bernal Díaz, a soldier in Cortés's expedition, wrote of Malintzín: "After Our Lord God, it was she who caused New Spain (what the Spanish renamed Mexico after the conquest) to be won."

Malintzín knew that Mexica demands for tribute and captives had alienated many. When the Spanish arrived, Tlaxcala clung to independence, surrounded by city-states allied with or subject to the Mexica (Map 1.7). One Tlaxcalan faction fought the Spanish and lost badly. Thereafter, Tlaxcalans presented themselves as Spain's most loyal allies. Several thousand escorted Cortés when he entered Tenochtitlán in 1519. They suffered the brunt of the casualties when the Mexica reclaimed the city the following year. The Spanish found sanctuary in Tlaxcala and used it as a base to recruit more allies. In 1521, tens of thousands of Tlaxcalans, along with warriors from other Nahua city-states, joined 900 Spaniards in besieging Tenochtitlán and taking the city two months later.

Technology indeed played a key role in the conquest. Horses afforded the Spanish advantages in speed, mobility, and height. They proved especially effective when those who rode them wielded swords and wore armor. Nahua memories of the conquest stressed two forms of technology. One was metal, especially steel blades and armor. The other was the ability of the Spanish to summon help from lands overseas. Ironically, the Spanish maritime network benefitted Cortés even when his superiors did not intend it. Cortés disobeyed the orders of the Spanish governor of Cuba when he chose to embark upon the conquest of the Mexica. In 1520, the governor sent Pánfilo de Narváez and several hundred men to force Cortés to surrender. Cortés persuaded most to defect by promising them a share of the spoils of Tenochtitlán. The Cuban governor's failed plan to control Cortes inadvertently helped him to succeed. When Narváez retreated to Cuba, having lost an eye in battle, the defectors reinforced Cortés's army. They also brought smallpox to Mexico. Lacking immunity to the virus, the people of Tenochtitlán were devastated by the disease after the Mexica managed to expel the Spanish and Tlaxcalans.

Although European technology impressed Nahua peoples, it did not make them think that the Spanish were gods. That notion is mainly a product of two kinds of sources created long after the conquest. One was Spanish narratives written by participants or historians who flattered the Spanish by claiming that Indians took them for gods. The other came from Nahua accounts compiled decades after the fall of Tenochtitlán that sought to explain how the conquest happened. Representing the Spanish as "gods" offered a way to cope with the humiliation of being defeated by a foe whom they vastly outnumbered.

The most important Nahua allies of the Spanish, Malintzín and the Tlaxcalans, retained their ties to the conquerors after the fall of Tenochtitlán. Not long after the Mexica surrendered, Malintzín gave birth to Martín Cortés, Hernán's son. She later married another Spaniard, with whom she had a daughter, Maria. Tlaxcalans continued to act as co-conquerors of the Americas. They claimed to accompany **Francisco de Coronado**

**Map 1.7**

**The Spanish and French Invade North America, 1519–1565** The conquest of Mexico sparked greater European interest in North America. Spanish incursions into the southeast and southwest sought riches and to expand Spain's empire, while France saw North America as a good place to challenge Spanish power.

to New Mexico in 1540 and participated in an aborted Spanish colony in southeastern North America in the early 1560s. Malintzín, Tlaxcalans, and other Indians were crucial in remaking Mexico into New Spain, what Spaniards called Mexico and the territory that they governed from a Mexico City built on Tenochtitlán's ruins.

Efforts to convert Mexico's Indians into Christians also helped to create New Spain. Twelve **Franciscans** arrived in Mexico from Española in 1524. They saw in Mexico a chance to recreate the original Christian communities. Once they had preached the gospel in every language, "The Twelve" believed, Jesus would return to earth, determine who was saved and who was damned, and bring on the end of the world. The eagerness with which Indians sought baptism, sometimes by the thousands at a time, seemed to confirm their vision. In order to convert more Indians, Franciscans and other missionaries burned most of the histories that Nahuas and Maya had written before the conquest and had most of their temples demolished. Franciscans studied Indian languages and wrote detailed accounts of Indian cultures and histories in hopes of facilitating conversion of Indians. They developed a Romanized alphabet for Nahuatl that many Indians soon mastered. In time Franciscans' zeal faded, partly because most Indian converts blended their beliefs and rituals with Christianity. Their successors looked for other Indians to convert. A few decades later, they believed that they had found them in Florida and New Mexico, where Franciscans followed conversion strategies they had learned in Mexico.

The conquest of Mexico triggered more Spanish invasions. In 1532, 160 men led by Francisco Pizarro intervened in a civil war over who should rule the Inca Empire. The intruders took one claimant to the throne, Atahualpa, hostage and ransomed him for enough gold and treasure to fill the room in which they imprisoned him. Pizarro's men then murdered Atahualpa. The Spanish had decapitated the Inca Empire. It took 40 years and the help of Indian allies to conquer it. Silver strikes in Zacatecas, Mexico, and in Potosí (in modern-day Bolivia) in the 1540s ensured that Mexico and Peru became the hubs of the Spanish empire and the main destinations for Spanish immigrants for centuries.

## Invasions of North America and the Rise of Imperial Competition

Dreams of conquering wealthy Indian empires and of finding quicker routes to Asia lured Europeans to North America between the early 1520s and the early 1540s. Explorers in the service of Spain and France mapped the coasts. Spanish and French

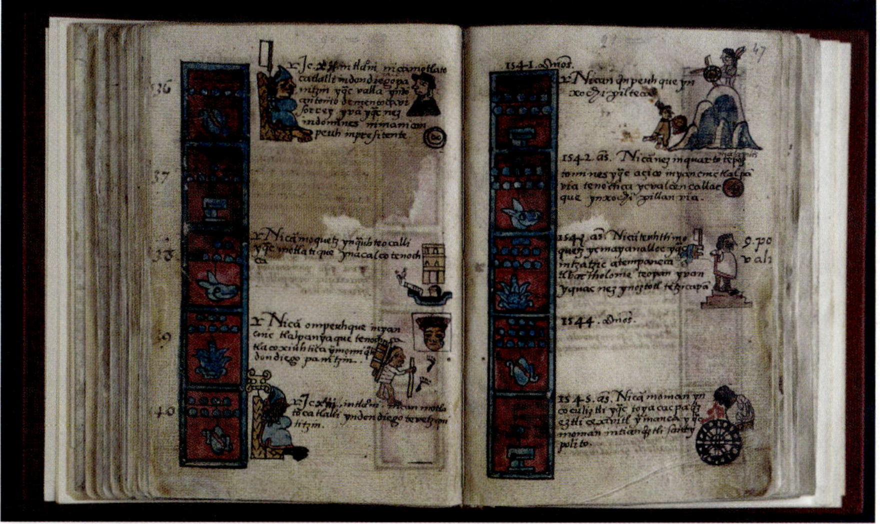

The Tenochca journey north. Over a thousand Indians from Mexico accompanied Coronado to the southwest, including many Tenochca. The entry for 1539, recorded as "39" and as the glyph "[year] 8 ácatl [reed]," reads: "[It was] at this time they departed for the new land; the Tenochca went." Note the figure with a walking stick beside the inscription.

entrepreneurs tried to establish outposts in the southeast and northeast. Meanwhile, three Spanish-led expeditions invaded the interior. Indians rebuffed every incursion.

Europeans first charted the Gulf of Mexico and then began to map the eastern seaboard. Most sought a channel to the Pacific, a possible North American counterpart to the one that Ferdinand Magellan's fleet had used to pass through South America in 1520 and to circumnavigate the globe two years later, a journey that proved that the oceans are connected. Meanwhile, the small fleet of Juan Rodríguez Cabrillo hugged the California coast in the early 1540s (Map 1.7). The voyages exposed more Indians to Europeans, as traders or as captors, laying a foundation for more intensive migration and exchange while furnishing Indians with information to resist European invasions.

Meanwhile, three groups of conquistadors pushed into the southeast and southwest. The leader of the first, Pánfilo de Narváez, lost Mexico to Cortés in 1520. Hernando de Soto, who commanded the second, was an officer to Pizarro. Francisco de Coronado headed the third expedition, which followed a model established by the conquest of Mexico. Most of the nearly 2,000 men whom Coronado led into the southwest and onto the Great Plains were Mexican Indians. None of the expeditions found riches or a powerful empire. Indians did not ally en masse with the Spanish as Nahuas had against the Mexica. Instead, the invaders quickly exhausted whatever welcome they received.

Indian resistance ensured that such incursions failed. News of the invaders travelled far and fast. Indians repeatedly deflected them with tales that the gold and riches they sought were somewhere else. The greedy Spanish took the bait and invariably got lost, far from reinforcements. Indians controlled the flow of information, especially because the Spanish had to depend on Indian interpreters whose loyalty they often doubted. Coronado's men met an enslaved Indian whom they called El Turco (The Turk) at Pecos Pueblo. He led the expedition to Quivira, a town on the Great Plains where, he promised, the Spanish would find what they wanted. Quivira turned out to be a modest Wichita village. Coronado had El Turco garroted. The expedition, adrift on the plains, spent months trudging back to New Mexico. Coronado retreated to Mexico, leaving behind some Indians, two friars whom the Pueblo soon killed, and bad will. De Soto turned to Juan Ortiz for counsel until his death left the Spanish practically rudderless.

Ortiz and four other members of the Narváez expedition survived only because they won the trust of Indians by adopting their customs. **Álvar Núñez Cabeza de Vaca** (Narváez's second-in-command) led the four, who included Esteban, a North African slave, Esteban's master, and another man. They fled Florida on makeshift rafts and washed ashore in Texas, where the Karankawa enslaved them. The Karankawa later freed the four, who walked inland in search of Mexico, posing along the way as healers and winning a large group of followers. Indians led them to Mexico in 1536, eight years after they arrived in Florida. The captives found an eager audience in Mexico City, where colonists heard tales that riches awaited them to the north. Such stories spurred Coronado to invade New Mexico and stumble through the southern plains.

Esteban and Cabeza de Vaca sought to capitalize on what they had learned from their ordeal in different ways. Esteban guided an expedition north in 1539 and is said to have died in a hail of arrows. Cabeza de Vaca wrote about his journey and tried to apply its lessons elsewhere in the Americas. His narrative, published in Spain in 1542, was the first European book to focus exclusively on North America and the first to describe a colonist's captivity among Indians. Cabeza de Vaca advocated peaceful and cooperative relations between Spaniards and Indians. He also tried to practice what he preached. Cabeza de Vaca was appointed governor of portions of what is today Argentina, Uruguay, and Paraguay in 1540. His men revolted and sent him back to Spain four years later.

Indians also scuttled two initiatives to colonize North America between 1526 and 1543. "Francisco de Chicora," seized on the southeast Atlantic coast by Spanish slavers, was instrumental in the rise and demise of the first European settlement in what is today the mainland United States. Francisco took revenge on his captors by accompanying Nicolás Vázquez de Ayllón, Española lawyer and sugar planter, to Spain. There, he spun stories of his homeland that captivated Ayllón and the royal court. In 1526, Ayllón, Francisco, and 600 colonists, including some African slaves, landed in South Carolina. Francisco deserted, as did the other Indians Ayllón brought as interpreters. The colonists moved to present-day Georgia and founded **San Miguel de Gualdape**, the first European settlement in today's mainland United States. Disease and cold killed Ayllón and many others as the survivors split into factions. Only 150 returned to Española.

A similar fate befell the first French effort to colonize North America. In 1534, **Jacques Cartier** entered the Gulf of St. Lawrence seeking precious metals, gems, and a passage to the Pacific. He encountered Iroquoian speakers from the village of Stadacona. Cartier took two of the Indians, Domagaya and Taignoagny, back to France to learn French. He returned the following year, sailed up the St. Lawrence River, and returned the two men to Stadacona. The villagers, hoping to monopolize access to French goods, tried to dissuade Cartier from proceeding upriver. Cartier ignored them and proceeded to Hochelaga, a village on the site of present-day Montreal. Iced in until April 1536, several French died of scurvy before Domagaya showed them how to brew a tea from cedar bark and needles that contained the vitamin C that they needed. Five years later, Cartier led colonists to Canada, where they erected a fort. By 1543, the French left after suffering harsh winters and two more bouts with scurvy. It added insult to injury that samples that Cartier had carried to France and touted as gold and diamonds turned out to be worthless.

Indians turned back European invasions at a profound cost. The French returned to Stadacona and Hochelaga in the late 1500s to find them abandoned. Disease and warfare had forced their residents to flee. De Soto's expedition accelerated the decline of Mississippian chiefdoms. Spaniards returned to the southeast interior in the 1560s to find most towns deserted. By the early 1700s, only the Natchez followed Mississippian ways closely. Other descendants of the peoples whom de Soto plagued would in time become the Choctaw, Chickasaw, and Creek.

Some Europeans concluded that there was little to justify interest in North America. Upon learning where Cartier was headed, Charles V remarked that Canada was "of no value, and if the French take it, necessity will compel them to abandon it." In effect, he had accepted a 1533 papal decree that excluded lands that were unknown to Europeans when Pope Alexander VI granted the Americas to Spain and Portugal in the 1490s. Conquest and occupation, not papal mandates, would thereafter be required to stake claims that other European powers might respect. In the 1560s other French, many of them enemies of the pope, tried to colonize Florida.

## Religious Reformation, Imperial Rivalries, and Piracy

In the 1550s, European rivalries in the Americas became linked to religious conflict in Europe. It began in 1517 when a monk named **Martin Luther** nailed his *Ninety-five Theses* to the door of a church in Germany. He challenged the propriety and ability of church officials to confer forgiveness of sins and salvation upon others. Only personal faith, Luther argued, could save one's soul. Those who concurred came to be known as Protestants for their protests against the Catholic Church's authority.

**Protestantism** was part of a broader reform movement that swept Christianity in western Europe in the 1500s. All reformers, Protestant or Catholic, held that church members should be more pious and know basic Christian doctrine. They agreed that Christians should reject folk beliefs that reformers considered pagan superstition or even satanic. Most demanded that government enforce religious conformity. Protestants denied the authority of the pope and the Catholic Church on the grounds that both were corrupt and violated God's will. They believed that the Bible should be accorded more authority, that its verses should be made more accessible by translating them from Latin into languages such as English or German. Defying Catholic doctrine, Luther asserted that faith mattered more than deeds for salvation. Protestants differed, sometimes violently, on matters such as infant baptism; the degree to which they should reject Catholic ritual, iconography, and theology; how they should govern their churches; and what was the proper relationship between church and state.

Three versions of western European Christianity's reformation played a key role in conflicts over the Americas. One was the Catholic Reformation, which brought new organizations to win converts, renewed insistence on religious orthodoxy, and bolstered Spanish determination to uphold Catholicism. In 1534, Ignatius Loyola, a Basque priest, founded the **Society of Jesus**. One main goal of the Jesuits, as they were popularly known, was to make new converts overseas and in Europe. By 1550, they operated in India and Brazil. Meanwhile, the Spanish proclaimed themselves Catholicism's staunchest defenders and Protestantism's worst enemy.

By the late 1550s England had become Spain's enemy, largely on religious grounds. In 1534, Parliament passed the **Act of Supremacy**, which abolished papal authority over England and made King **Henry VIII** head of the **Church of England**. The new church retained features of Catholic hierarchy such as bishops as well as much Catholic ritual and iconography. After Henry's successor, Edward VI, died in 1553, Henry's Catholic daughter Mary came to power. She married Philip, soon to be king of Spain, and tried to impose Catholicism on England by having prominent Protestants executed. Mary died in 1558. Henry's Protestant daughter **Elizabeth I** succeeded her and reinstated the **Church of England** as the official faith. Elizabeth's religious moderation satisfied most English, but alienated a minority who sought to purge England of all vestiges of Catholicism. Critics labeled them "puritans."

**Puritans** followed the teachings of **John Calvin**, a theologian based in Geneva. He argued that God had already determined who would be saved or damned. People might recognize God's elect by their professions of faith that God had saved them and by their conduct. Calvin thought that a body composed of ministers and elders should oversee church affairs and that local officials should uphold religious orthodoxy. By 1560, **Calvinism** had spread to England, Scotland, the Netherlands, Germany, and France, where its followers were known as **Huguenots**.

France and Spain fought a series of wars starting in the 1520s. French kings authorized private vessels to seize Spanish ships and sell their cargoes. Such **privateers**, many of them Huguenots, began to prowl the Caribbean in the 1530s, capturing ships laden with gold and silver and raiding Spanish settlements. When peace came, some privateers continued to operate without official license as corsairs or pirates. Spain responded in the 1540s by starting to provide military escorts for vessels travelling to and from the Caribbean. By the 1550s, Huguenots challenged Iberian claims to the Americas. War broke out again in 1551, and the Caribbean remained a war zone even after the two powers signed a treaty eight years later. The toll on Spanish America and on Spain's coffers was immense. Between 1556 and 1561 French privateers and pirates made off with more than half of the royal revenues from Spanish America.

As Huguenots attacked Spanish shipping, bloodier religious violence in France encouraged them to seek refuge. Admiral Gaspard de Coligny, a Huguenot who financed privateers, directed the founding of a colony in Brazil in 1555. The Portuguese destroyed it five years later. Florida seemed a good alternative. It was relatively safe and most Spain-bound ships rode the Florida Current up the peninsula's coast. Florida could be an ideal base for French who sought to get rich and wound Catholicism's most militant champion.

## The Founding of Florida

By the early 1560s winds, currents, shoals, religion, and piracy had made the Florida peninsula a global crossroads. Florida Indians had endured countless Spanish slaving raids and four Spanish colonization ventures. Ais and Calusa Indians had also absorbed hundreds of people who were left behind or whose ships had run aground or sunk and salvaged the wrecks, trading the gold and other items that they recovered with other Indians. Soon Florida became the first European battleground for North America and the first permanent European outpost in the mainland United States.

In 1562, the French Admiral Coligny sent Huguenot captain Jean Ribault and 150 men, mostly Huguenots, to North America to establish a colony. Ribault quickly returned to France. The men he left behind built a fort in present-day South Carolina. They soon alienated their Guale hosts and most abandoned the colony. In 1564, another Huguenot fleet under the command of René de Laudonnière arrived with 300 colonists, including Jacques Le Moyne, hired to paint illustrations of Florida to promote the colony in France. They erected Fort Caroline near present-day Jacksonville. The Saturiwa welcomed them until the French began to demand more food than they were able or willing to provide. Colonists saw that the Saturiwa had silver and gold, which suggested that there were mines inland. Many left to find them, unaware that the precious metals had come from shipwrecks. Meanwhile, other French commandeered vessels and sailed off to prey on Spanish shipping.

The Spanish monitored developments in Florida. Pedro Menéndez de Avilés, who had escorted several fleets across the Atlantic, battled French privateers and corsairs, and knew eastern North America's coastline well, thought that the future of the Spanish Empire hung in the balance. If the French had a base in Florida, Menéndez argued, pirates could attack the Spanish at will. Worse, Menéndez warned **Philip II**, French colonists might forge alliances with Florida Indians and convince African slaves in Cuba and Española to rebel. Philip appointed Menéndez governor of Florida and subsidized his expedition of 800 soldiers, mariners, and colonists.

They landed near a Timucuan village on the feast-day of Saint Augustine. Seloy, the village chief, permitted them to found **St. Augustine**, calculating that the Spanish were a better risk than the French. Over the next three months, the Spanish seized Fort Caroline. Menéndez executed most of the French on grounds that they were pirates and Protestant heretics. Laudonnière and Le Moyne escaped. In the 1580s each

## TIMELINE PREHISTORY–1565

**c. 13,000 BCE**
Nomadic hunters from East Asia enter Alaska and migrate south and east

**c. 6000–8000 BCE**
Na-Dene speakers cross Bering Sea into Alaska

**c. 7000 BCE**
Peoples in central Mexico begin to cultivate the ancestor of corn

**c. 3000 BCE**
Aleuts' and Inuits' ancestors begin to arrive in Alaska

**c. 1500 BCE**
Southwestern peoples begin to cultivate corn

**c. 700 CE**
Mississippian chiefdoms emerge in Mississippi River Valley and in southeast

Bow and arrow has spread throughout North America

**c. 900–1300**
Anasazi culture peaks in southwest

**c. 1100–1200**
Cahokia reaches its zenith

**c. 1200–1300**
Drought plagues Indian peoples in Mississippi Valley, Plains, and southwest

**c. 1200–1400**
Na-Dene-speaking ancestors of Navajos and Apaches arrive in southwest

**c. 1300**
Drought and raids compel Anasazi to abandon towns in Southwest

**1300s**
Cahokia abandoned

**c. 1400**
Iroquois Great League of Peace and Huron confederacy founded

**1415**
Portuguese forces capture Ceuta in North Africa

**1419–1420**
Portuguese begin to colonize Madeira islands

**1440s**
Portuguese begin to cultivate sugar cane on Madeira islands

**1441**
Portuguese mariners launch Atlantic slave trade

**1442–1456**
Series of papal decrees authorize Portuguese conquests in Africa and Atlantic slave trade

**1445**
Portuguese establish feitoria (fortified trading post) at Arguim

**1469**
Marriage of Isabel and Ferdinand unites the kingdoms of Castile and Aragon, creating the foundation for modern Spain

**1487**
Bartolomeu Dias navigates past Cape of Good Hope

**1492**
**January** Muslim forces surrender Granada, completing Iberian Christians' reconquest of the peninsula

**April** Christopher Columbus contracts with Ferdinand and Isabel to sail west across Atlantic

**August**Columbus's expedition departs Spain

**October 12** Columbus's expedition makes landfall in the Bahamas

**1493**
**January** Columbus departs Española for Spain

**March** Columbus returns to Spain

**November** Columbus returns to Española and introduces cattle, pigs, and sugar cane to the Americas

**1494**
Treaty of Tordesillas divides most of world into territories claimed by Spain or Portugal

**1496**
Santo Domingo, first permanent European settlement in the Americas, founded on Española

published an account that perpetuated the myth that eastern North America contained precious metals, animating English readers who dreamed of riches like those the Spanish enjoyed.

The founding of St. Augustine signaled that Europeans and Africans were in North America to stay. The colonial history of what would become the mainland United States had begun, more than 70 years after Spaniards and Taínos first met in the Bahamas.

## STUDY QUESTIONS FOR THE ATLANTIC WORLD ENTERS NORTH AMERICA, 1513–1565

1. What explains the conquest of the Mexica?
2. Europeans became very interested in North America in the 1520s and lost interest two decades later. Why?
3. How did religious changes in Europe and piracy lead to the founding of St. Augustine?

**1497**
Giovanni Caboto explores Newfoundland on behalf of England

**1498**
Portuguese mariner Vasco da Gama arrives in India

**1502**
First cargo of enslaved Africans arrives in Española

First record of European women arriving in Americas

First recorded shipment of North American cod to Europe arrives in England

**1508–1513**
Spanish conquer Puerto Rico, Jamaica, and Cuba

**1509–1513**
Spanish slaving raids depopulate Bahamas and likely start targeting Florida

**1513**
Juan Ponce de León leads first recorded European visit to Florida

**1518**
**December** First recorded smallpox epidemic reaches the Americas

**1519–1522**
Voyage originally led by Ferdinand Magellan circumnavigates globe

**1519**
**February** Spanish expedition led by Hernán Cortés reaches Yucatán Peninsula

**October** Spanish-Nahua forces enter Tenochtitlán

**1521**
**July** Spanish-Nahua forces conquer Tenochtitlán

**1524**
First Franciscan missionaries arrive in Mexico

**1526**
Spanish colonists found and abandon San Miguel de Gualdape in Georgia

**1528–1536**
Spanish expedition led by Pánfilo de Narváez and completed by Álvar Núñez Cabeza de Vaca becomes first European group to enter interior of what is today the United States

**1532**
Spanish expedition launches conquest of Peru

**1539–1543**
Spanish expedition led by Hernando de Soto invades southeastern North America

**1540–1542**
Spanish expedition led by Francisco Vázquez de Coronado invades southwestern North America and southern Great Plains

**1542–1543**
Spanish expedition led by Juan Cabrillo explores California's coast

**1540s**
Spanish begin to exploit silver deposits in Mexico and Bolivia

**1558**
"Elizabethan Settlement" brings religious peace to England

**1550s to early 1560s**
French privateers and pirates step up attacks on Spanish shipping in Caribbean

**1562–1565**
French attempt to establish colonies in southeastern North America

**1565**
**September** Spanish forces defeat French and found St. Augustine, Florida

## Summary

- By 1500 the circulation of people, goods, and ideas within North America helped Indians to settle the continent, transform its landscape, and create hundreds of diverse societies capable of adapting to political, social, and environmental change.
- In the 1400s Europeans and Africans created networks that accelerated and increased the flow of people, goods, and ideas between them, led them across the Atlantic, and enabled Europeans to colonize the Caribbean and establish a foothold in the Americas by the 1510s.
- In the 1520s new conquests and new knowledge spurred Europeans to explore North America's coasts and invade its interior, efforts that Indians successfully resisted until the 1560s, when imperial rivalries and religious conflicts led Spain to begin colonizing Florida, altering the relationship between North America and the world.

## Key Terms and People

**Act of Supremacy** *36*
**astrolabe** *16*
**Atlantic slave trade** *19*
**Atlantic world** *6*
**Cabeza de Vaca, Álvar Núñez** *34*
**Caboto, Giovanni** *24*
**Calvin, John** *37*
**Calvinism** *37*
**Cartier, Jacques** *35*
**Church of England (Anglican Church)** 36
**Columbian exchange** *25*
**Columbus, Christopher** *21*
**Coronado, Francisco de** *31*
**Cortés, Hernán** *30*
**Elizabeth I** *36*
**encomienda** *18*
**epic of Deganawidah** *14*
**feitoria** *19*
**Ferdinand of Aragon** *18*
**Franciscans** *32*
**Henry VIII** *36*
**Huguenots** *37*
**Huron Confederacy** *14*
**Iroquois League** *14*
**Isabel of Castile** *18*
**kachina** *10*
**Las Casas, Bartolomé de** *28*
**Luther, Martin** *36*
**Malintzín** *30*
**Mississippian societies** *10*
**mourning wars** *15*
**Narváez, Pánfilo de** *3*
**Philip II of Spain** *38*
**privateer** *37*
**Protestantism** *36*
**Puritans** *37*
**reconquista** *18*
**St. Augustine, Florida** *38*
**San Miguel de Gualdape** *35*
**Society of Jesus (Jesuits)** *36*
**Soto, Hernando de** *3*
**Treaty of Tordesillas** *23*

## Reviewing Chapter 1

1. In what ways did environmental changes shape Indian life before 1565?
2. Europeans had conquered Mexico, Central America, and much of South America by 1565. But they had conquered none of North America north of Mexico. Why?
3. "A whole chapter devoted to events before 1565 in a U.S. history textbook! What for? It was so long ago and nothing much happened." Please take issue with this statement, using specific examples from this chapter.

## Further Reading

Abulafia, David. *The Discovery of Man: Atlantic Encounters in the Age of Columbus.* New Haven and London: Yale University Press, 2008. An excellent synthesis that places the European "discovery" of the Americas within the context of the formation of the Atlantic world.

Fagan, Brian. *Fish on Friday: Feasting, Fasting, and the Discovery of the New World.* New York: Basic Books, 2006. Ties growing European demand for fish to religious and political changes in Europe and presents fishing as key to European expansion across the North Atlantic and into North America.

Northrup, David. *Africa's Discovery of Europe, 1450–1850.* New York: Oxford University Press, 2002. A concise overview of relations between Europeans and Africans that emphasizes African perspectives and motives.

Pauketat, Timothy R. *Cahokia: Ancient America's Great City on the Mississippi.* New York: Viking, 2009. Brings together the latest historical and archeological scholarship on the premiere example of a Mississippian chiefdom in one compact and readable package.

Reséndez, Andrés. *A Land So Strange: The Epic Journey of Cabeza de Vaca: The Extraordinary Tale of a Shipwrecked Spaniard Who Walked across America in the Sixteenth Century.* New York: Basic Books, 2007. A beautifully written account of Cabeza de Vaca's journey that strives to capture Indian as well as Spanish perspectives on a North America that was about to change drastically as a result of Spanish incursions.

Townsend, Camilla. *Malintzín's Choices: An Indian Woman in the Conquest of Mexico.* Albuquerque: University of New Mexico Press, 2006. A sensitive account of Malintzín and her world that explains how and why so many Nahuas chose to join Cortés in attacking the Mexica, an act that enabled the Spanish to conquer Mexico.

# Visual Review

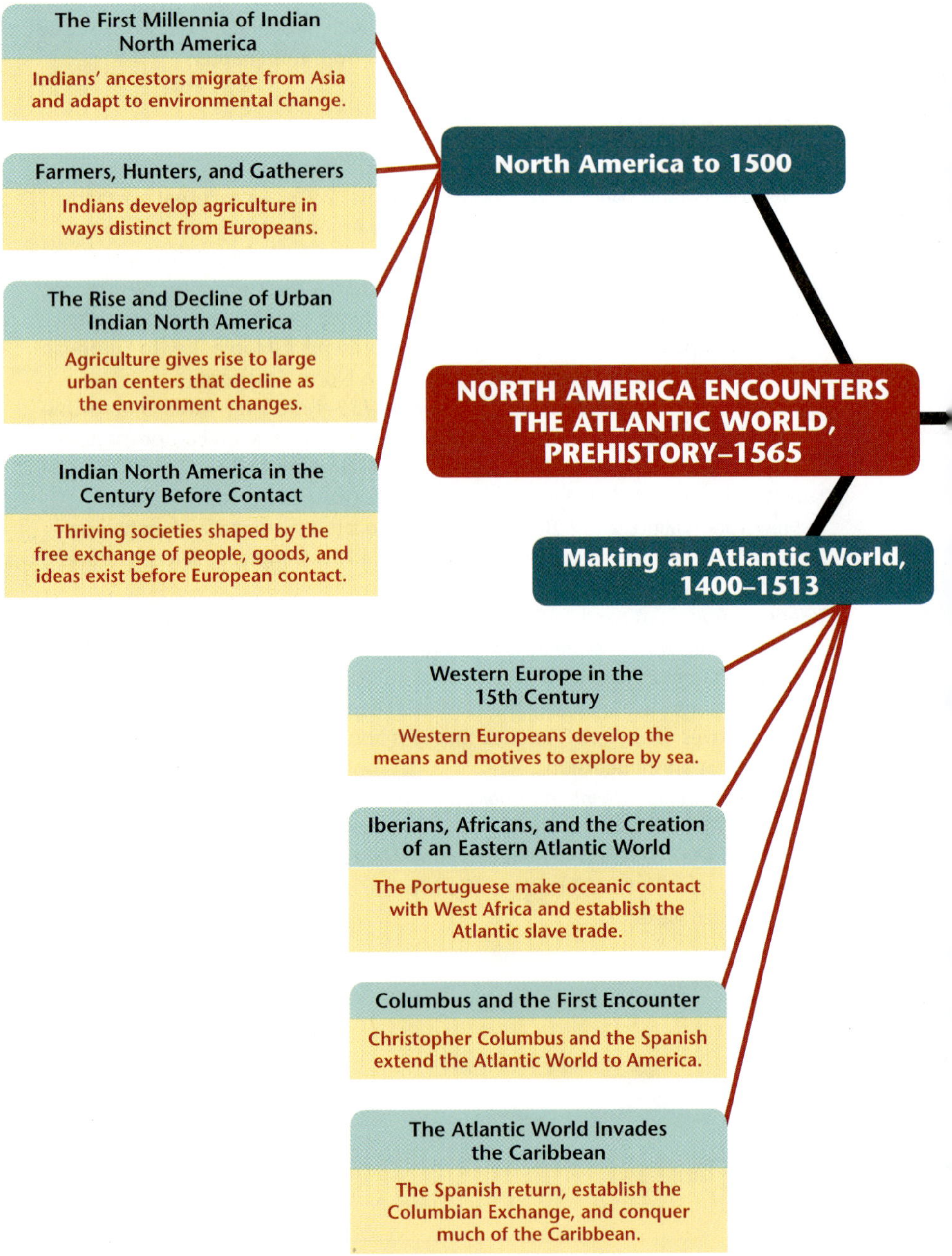

**NORTH AMERICA ENCOUNTERS THE ATLANTIC WORLD, PREHISTORY–1565**

## North America to 1500

**The First Millennia of Indian North America**
Indians' ancestors migrate from Asia and adapt to environmental change.

**Farmers, Hunters, and Gatherers**
Indians develop agriculture in ways distinct from Europeans.

**The Rise and Decline of Urban Indian North America**
Agriculture gives rise to large urban centers that decline as the environment changes.

**Indian North America in the Century Before Contact**
Thriving societies shaped by the free exchange of people, goods, and ideas exist before European contact.

## Making an Atlantic World, 1400–1513

**Western Europe in the 15th Century**
Western Europeans develop the means and motives to explore by sea.

**Iberians, Africans, and the Creation of an Eastern Atlantic World**
The Portuguese make oceanic contact with West Africa and establish the Atlantic slave trade.

**Columbus and the First Encounter**
Christopher Columbus and the Spanish extend the Atlantic World to America.

**The Atlantic World Invades the Caribbean**
The Spanish return, establish the Columbian Exchange, and conquer much of the Caribbean.

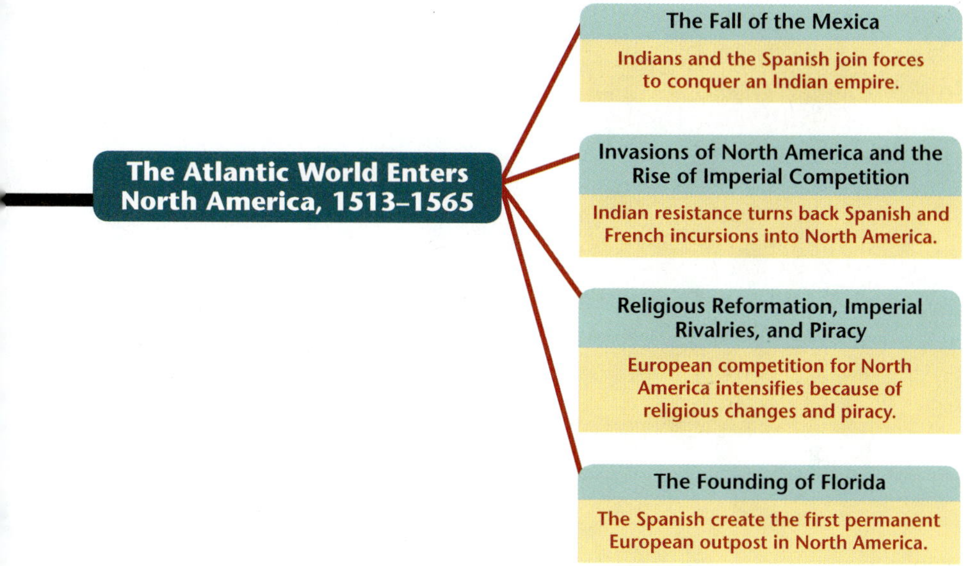

**The Atlantic World Enters North America, 1513–1565**

**The Fall of the Mexica**
Indians and the Spanish join forces to conquer an Indian empire.

**Invasions of North America and the Rise of Imperial Competition**
Indian resistance turns back Spanish and French incursions into North America.

**Religious Reformation, Imperial Rivalries, and Piracy**
European competition for North America intensifies because of religious changes and piracy.

**The Founding of Florida**
The Spanish create the first permanent European outpost in North America.

Their gre
Corne newl
Their sitting at meate
The place of solemne prayer
wherin the Tombe of their Herounds standeth.
SECOTON.
A Ceremony in th
strange iestures and

# 2 Colonists on the Margins

## 1565–1640

In 1616, the **Virginia Company of London** again found itself in dire financial straits. Nine years had elapsed since **Jamestown's** founding and the firm had yet to turn a profit. Reports from Virginia of hard winters, starving colonists, and frequent hostilities with Algonquian Indians of Tsenacommacah, the chiefdom that claimed the land on which the English were building Jamestown, scared off investors. The company badly needed good publicity. Perhaps a celebration of a special visit in 1616 would provide some.

An Algonquian "princess," her English husband, their infant son, and an Indian priest had arrived in London. The "princess" Matoaka was better known by one of her nicknames, **Pocahontas** or "playful one." She was the daughter of **Powhatan**, the paramount chief of Tsenacommacah. Pocahontas had been baptized, a fact that the Virginia Company trumpeted to assure nervous English observers that it could convert Algonquians into anglicized Christian subjects. The visit was important to the Virginia Company's well-being, so the hosts had every reason to make the Indians' stay in London as pleasant as possible.

Instead, the English deeply offended their Algonquian guests by repeatedly deviating from protocols that Algonquians normally followed with their allies. Pocahontas reprimanded **John Smith**, a former colonist who initiated relations between Jamestown and Tsenacommacah and who Pocahontas believed should have known better: "You did promise Powhatan what was yours should be his, and he the like to you." She addressed Smith as "father," using the language of kinship to indicate that they were allies and request his assistance. Pocahontas reminded Smith that he had called Powhatan "father, being in his land a stranger, and by the same reason so must I do you." For eastern Algonquians, fathers were not stern authority figures. Instead, uncles, especially maternal ones, were the male disciplinarians to children. Algonquian fathers

*Algonquian village of Secotan* by John White

### CHAPTER OUTLINE



*continued on page 49*

# America in the World

Pequot War pitted English colonists and Algonquian allies against Pequots (1636–1637).

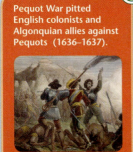

The Mayflower Compact established English governing values in the North America (1620).

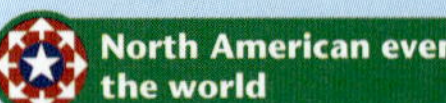

North American event that influenced the world

International event that influenced North America

Event with multinational influence

Conflict

The "Great Migration" accelerated English colonization of New England (1630–1642).
The Massachusetts Bay Colony legalized slavery, the first English colony to do so in North America (1641).
The Virginia Company founded Jamestown, the first permanent English outpost in North America (1607).

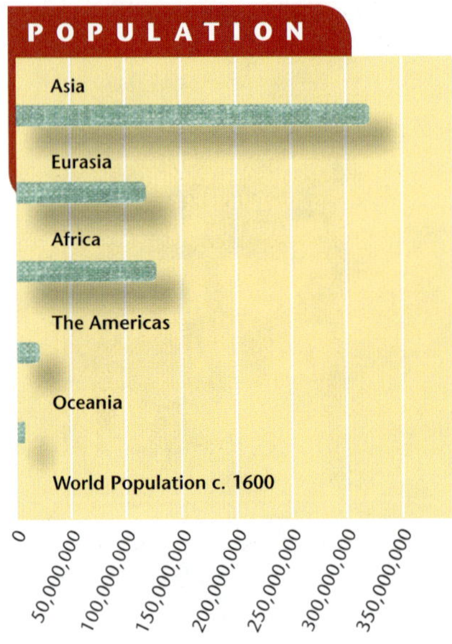


behaved more like what the English would consider indulgent uncles. Uttamatomakkin, the Indian priest, exploded when Smith told him that he had just met **James I**, king of England and Scotland. Uttamatomakkin could not believe it. A paramount chief would have offered him a gift. James did not. "You gave Powhatan a white Dog, which Powhatan fed as himself," he scolded Smith, "but your King gave me nothing, and I am better than your white Dog."

The English had to obey their own social and cultural norms, especially in England. Smith, a commoner, could not allow a princess to call him "father." His English peers and social superiors would find that unseemly and presumptuous. Smith might have explained to Uttamatomakkin that a king outranked everyone in his realm. Subjects normally paid him tribute, and James certainly considered Pocahontas and Uttamatomakkin his subjects.

Despite the offense its representatives caused its Algonquian guests, the Virginia Company reaped good publicity from their visit. Pocahontas, however, fell ill, died, and was buried in England in 1617. Her husband **John Rolfe** returned to Virginia, leaving their son Thomas behind for his kin to raise and educate. Uttamatomakkin also sailed home to tell a grieving Powhatan what he had learned from his visit. Meanwhile, thousands of English poured into Tsenacommacah, most of them to burn the woods and plant tobacco amidst the ashes and charred stumps. Soon hundreds would die at the hands of Tsenacommacah warriors.

The first European settlers clung to the edge of an Indian continent. Their survival usually depended on how well they met Indian needs and heeded Indian ways. The Spanish created North America's first permanent European colonies by intimidating and converting Indians. The French also evangelized Indians, but emphasized cooperation and commerce rather than coercion. English and Dutch colonists expended far less effort on making Christians of Indians and far more on resettling their lands. The strategic alliances that colonists forged with Indians linked North American networks to those that extended across the Atlantic. By the early 1640s, Europeans' ability to draw on their overseas ties enabled their colonies to take root despite often fierce Indian resistance.

## CONQUEST BEGINS AND TRADE EXPANDS, 1565–1607

The conquest and colonization of what became the United States began as what we today call Latin America expanded north. Spanish soldiers and friars struggled to colonize Florida and expand Mexico by conquering New Mexico. An unlikely kingdom, England, emerged as Spain's main European rival in North America. Meanwhile, European fishermen flooded northeastern North America with goods that intensified competition among Indians and began to change their cultures.

**CHAPTER OUTLINE**

*continued from page 45*



## Spain Stakes Claim to Florida

After founding St. Augustine and defeating the French, Pedro Menéndez had an ambitious vision for Florida. The Spanish, supported by a network of coastal garrisons, could protect sea lanes and salvage shipwrecks more easily. The governor hoped that Indians, awed by Spanish might, would become allies and subjects. Jesuit missionaries arrived in 1566 to cement Hispanic-Indian alliances by converting Florida Indians and sending chiefs' sons to Havana to be schooled alongside sons of prominent Cuban colonists. Menéndez also planned a road between his capital, Santa Elena, founded in today's Georgia in 1566, and the mines of Zacatecas in Mexico so that the Spanish Empire could move silver overland and bypass the pirate-infested Caribbean.

Little of his vision became reality. Menéndez ran out of money and lost interest in Florida once he became governor of Cuba in 1567. He had also badly underestimated the distance between Georgia and Mexico. Two expeditions headed west to launch his far-fetched plan. They built small garrisons along the way and returned to Santa Elena. Indians killed off or absorbed each.

Indian resistance and European attacks nearly finished off Florida too. Timucua and French soldiers teamed up to destroy one Spanish fort. Santa Elena and St. Augustine, the last outposts standing by 1574, barely weathered repeated Indian attacks. Thirteen years later the Spanish abandoned Santa Elena and retreated to a St. Augustine that had just been destroyed by an English raid led by Francis Drake. Enslaved Africans owned by **Philip II**, King of Spain, assisted recovery efforts, which included construction of a stone fort like those the Spanish were building in their major Caribbean ports to protect them from their European foes. St. Augustine, Florida's only Spanish settlement, had but 500 residents in 1600 who subsisted mainly on food shipped from Havana.

Franciscan friars pursued Indian converts outside St. Augustine. They replaced the Jesuits in 1573, the same year that Philip II issued the **Royal Orders for New Discoveries**. He decreed that missionaries should play the principal role in exploring, pacifying, and colonizing new territories. Philip also mandated that baptized Indians should live on missions and be hispanized, that is, learn to speak Spanish, keep livestock, cultivate European crops, and use European tools to master European crafts. **Franciscans** began to intensify their efforts in 1595, focusing on Timucua and Guales along the Georgia coast.

Two years later, Guales rebelled. The Franciscans insisted that was because they had barred a chief's heir from having more than one wife, a traditional sign of his authority. Guales killed nearly all the friars before Spanish-Timucua raids compelled some chiefs to surrender in 1600. Within four years, the southernmost mission had

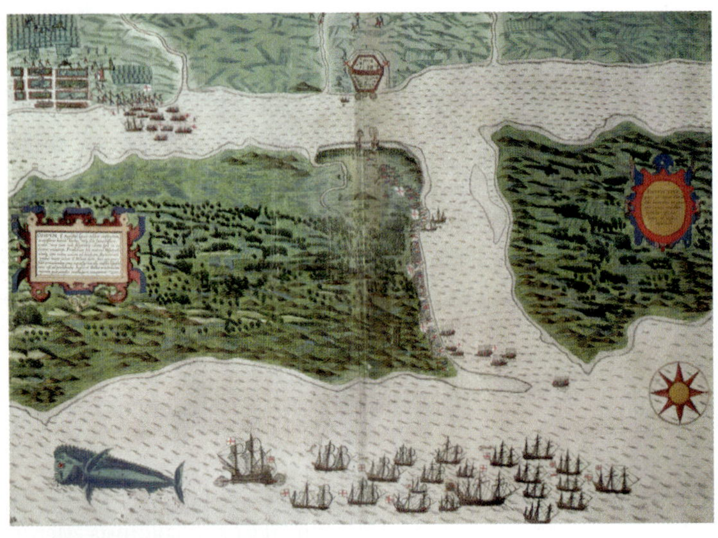

Francis Drake sacks St. Augustine, 1586. War between Spain and England in the 1580s accelerated English attacks on Spanish American colonies. St. Augustine, besieged by English forces, is at the upper left, while more English ships lurk in the Atlantic. Drake, then en route to Roanoke, had raided Santo Domingo and Cartagena before attacking St. Augustine.

reopened. Guales soon paid tribute to the Spanish by sending corn and laborers to St. Augustine.

The Timucua remained indispensible Spanish allies. In 1612, the Franciscan friar Francisco de Pareja published a Spanish-Timucuan catechism and confessional in Mexico City. It was the first printed dictionary of an Indian language spoken north of Mexico. Pareja wrote it to help priests reinforce Catholic doctrine by asking converts pointed questions about their sexual activities, hunting and healing practices, and whether they still followed what Pareja condemned as "superstitions."

The Spanish Empire considered abandoning Florida, but Franciscan lobbying, geography, and competition from other European powers saved the colony. In 1608, Philip III declared that the Spanish would remain in Florida, partly to monitor English colonists in Virginia and to ensure that American silver flowed across the Atlantic to pay for wars in Europe. Virtually no one chose to move to Florida. The poor but strategically located colony scraped by on royal funding and Indian labor.

## New Spain into the Southwest

As Florida's Indians held Spanish colonists at bay, Pueblo Indians in what is today New Mexico faced a series of Spanish-led invasions. Franciscans sought souls, while colonists drawn north from central Mexico by silver strikes in and around Zacatecas sought riches. In 1581, a small group of friars and soldiers arrived and renamed the

Indian pictograph of Spaniards on horseback. Indians drew this image on the walls of Cañón del Muerto. Note how prominently the artist(s) displayed horses and the lances that their riders wielded. The figure in black with a white cross is probably a missionary.

region New Mexico. Pueblos endured three more Spanish incursions before an expedition led by **Juan de Oñate** arrived in 1598.

Visions of the conquest of Mexico motivated Oñate to conquer New Mexico. His father was the first European to discover the Zacatecas silver mines. Oñate was married to Isabel Tolosa Cortés Moctezuma, granddaughter of Hernán Cortés and great-granddaughter of Moctezuma. He even reenacted the conquest of Mexico. Tlaxcalan soldiers composed part of the small army that marched into New Mexico under a banner bearing an image of "Our Lady of the Remedies," as the Spanish did when entering Tenochtitlán. Twelve friars accompanied Oñate, symbolizing Jesus's 12 disciples and the 12 Franciscans who launched the conversion of Mexico.

Pueblos were still nursing the wounds that they had endured from previous Spanish-led invasions, so they decided to receive Oñate peacefully. A delegation of Pueblo chiefs came to his camp and pledged loyalty to Philip II. The chiefs knelt before Oñate and the head friar, kissed the hand of each, and attended Mass.

New Mexico's conquerors won little glory or wealth, but they spilled plenty of Pueblo blood. Spanish soldiers, frustrated that New Mexico had few of the riches that Mexico did, plotted mutiny. Pueblos offered them scarce food and clothing as gifts; the soldiers considered them tribute. When they did not get what they wanted, they extorted, raped, and murdered. Acoma's residents fought back, killing eleven Spanish soldiers. Oñate's men slaughtered 800 Acomas, including 300 women and children. They enslaved 500 women and children. Every Acoman man over age 25 had one foot cut off. Such brutality dissuaded most Pueblos from challenging Spanish authority for decades.

New Mexico served as a base for Spanish expeditions in the region. Three of them searched for the Pacific. The last, in 1604–1605, found it by marching through Arizona and following the Colorado River to the Gulf of California.

Oñate wanted to reach the Pacific in part because the Spanish were considering a California outpost to facilitate trade with East Asia and ward off European rivals. In 1565, Spanish mariners discovered a route from the Philippines to Acapulco. The journey took four to five months, so mariners needed a port to stop for repairs and provisions. The Mexican-Filipino trade was lucrative. Mexican silver bought Chinese silks and porcelain in Manila. Sebastián Vizcaíno explored California's coast in 1602–1603 and concluded that Monterey Bay would best harbor a Spanish port. But New Spain's viceroy decided that a California base would lure English and French smugglers to a remote place that they would otherwise ignore. As a result, Spain showed little interest in California until the 1760s.

**▲ Map 2.1**

**European Invasions of the Southwest and Southeast, 1565 to c. 1610** Florida and New Mexico were the first European outposts in North America. European colonization of what is today the United States began from the Caribbean and Mexico and was oriented toward those regions. Note the location of Roanoke, chosen largely to give English privateers better access to Spanish shipping leaving the Caribbean and sailing up Florida's coast.

The viceroy also wanted to abandon New Mexico, which he considered a money pit. Disgruntled colonists who had returned to Mexico blamed Oñate for their troubles. Friars charged that Oñate interfered with their mission and accused him of adultery and abusing Indians. The viceroy demanded Oñate's resignation, and years later he stood trial in Mexico City. Convicted of adultery and of abusing Indians, priests, and colonists, Oñate was banished from New Mexico and went into exile in Spain.

Franciscan lobbying prevented Spain from abandoning New Mexico. In 1608, Philip III decreed that Spain would stay and that the royal treasury would pay the friars' bills and those of New Mexico's government. He sent a new governor, who ruled from Santa Fé, founded in 1610. New Mexico remained a poor remote satellite of Mexico that drew few Spanish immigrants. As in Florida, friars held most of the power as they dispersed to found missions among Indians.

## England Enters Eastern North America

Three European powers contested Spanish claims to North America and the Caribbean during the last quarter of the sixteenth century: France, the Netherlands, and England. The French and Dutch were wealthier and better able to finance colonizing ventures than the English, but faced religious and political strife at home. Civil wars between Catholics and Huguenots (French Calvinist Protestants) convulsed France between 1562 and 1580. France did not enjoy peace until 1598, when Henry IV became king and granted limited toleration to Huguenots with the **Edict of Nantes**. The Dutch, under direct Spanish rule since 1519, rebelled in the 1570s, an effort led by Calvinists. The two sides did not negotiate a cease-fire until 1608.

By contrast, England enjoyed relative political stability that helped it to emerge as Spain's main rival in the West Indies and North America. Elizabeth I's moderate policies had ended domestic religious strife and enabled the English to focus on other challenges. England's population nearly doubled from three million to around five million between 1500 and 1650, but its economy could not create enough jobs to keep pace. To make matters worse, prominent landlords fenced off **commons** (lands previously open to all residents) to graze sheep and grow grain. This accelerated the concentration of land ownership, pushed those of more modest means off the land, and increased unemployment.

Meanwhile, some English merchants pursued new markets by obtaining licenses for monopolies on commerce with Eastern Europe, the Mediterranean, or Asia. The Muscovy Company formed in 1555 to operate in Russia. Its success encouraged the creation of the Levant Company to trade with the Middle East and the East India Company. These **joint-stock companies** offered a model for financing colonial ventures. Investors bought shares, hoped to earn dividends, and limited their risk if the firm failed. Joint-stock companies later owned and directed English colonies in Virginia, Plymouth, and Massachusetts Bay.

England's renewed interest in the Americas focused first on the Caribbean and on diverting the Spanish Empire's wealth into English hands. John Hawkins led three expeditions from West Africa to the Caribbean to smuggle enslaved Africans to Spanish colonists in the 1560s. The last ended in 1568 when Spanish vessels destroyed two of Hawkins's ships. The English largely abandoned the Atlantic slave trade until the 1640s and instead focused on seizing Spanish ships and raiding Spanish colonies. When England and Spain went to war in 1585, Elizabeth licensed privateers (privately-owned armed ships) to attack Spanish vessels and divide the spoils. Privateers boosted the English economy; the goods that they seized accounted for up to 10 percent of England's imports during the 1590s. After James I became king of England in 1603, he made peace with Spain and temporarily halted privateering.

Some English touted colonization as a way to oppose Spain and Catholicism and solve many of England's social and economic problems. In the 1570s English forces conquered more of Catholic Ireland, which soon lured thousands of land-hungry English colonists and investors such as **Walter Raleigh** who hoped to profit from their labor. The translation and publication in 1583 of Bartolomé de las Casas's writings fueled belief in a "**Black Legend**" of the Spanish conquest in which Spaniards indiscriminately slaughtered Indians, tyrannized them, and imposed Catholic "superstition" on them. Raleighcited las Casas often and claimed that the English would deliver Indians from Spanish and Catholic "tyranny" and convert them into grateful subjects and Protestants. In 1584, Richard Hakluyt the Younger asserted that American colonies would wound Spain and create jobs for English migrants who would grow or extract commodities that English and European consumers wanted to buy.

Privateering and opposition to Spain led to England's first sustained attempt to colonize North America. Investors wanted a coastal base a safe distance from St. Augustine so that privateers could safely sail the Caribbean most of the year. To that end Raleigh sent an expedition to present-day North Carolina in 1584. The explorers recommended Roanoke on the Outer Banks and brought home two Indian men, **Manteo** and Wanchese, to learn English. They taught the scientist **Thomas Harriot** to speak Carolina Algonquian. The following year Raleigh sent a hundred men, including Harriot and the painter **John White**, who were to study the area and its peoples. Their flagship ran aground and seawater ruined their food supply. The English pressed Roanoke Indians for food, but they had little to spare. Convinced that Roanokes would attack, the colonists killed the Roanoke chief Wingina and stuck his head on a pole. Drake arrived in 1586, having just torched St. Augustine in hopes of preventing a Spanish attack on Roanoke. Panicked colonists swarmed aboard his ships.

Raleigh did not give up on the colony, sending a second group composed mostly of families in 1587. Manteo accepted baptism and Governor John White named him lord of Roanoke. Envisioning that colonists would govern the area's Indians through Manteo, White returned to England. War with Spain kept the English from returning to Roanoke until 1590. They found the colony abandoned and a post with the word "CROATOAN" (probably the name of the island where Manteo's people lived) carved into it. The "lost" colonists likely became Algonquian adoptees who lived on North Carolina's Outer Banks or moved north to Chesapeake Bay. Meanwhile, most English interest in colonization stayed focused on Ireland, which attracted far more English migrants than North America did until the 1640s.

Events at Roanoke and English interpretations of them established key patterns in English colonization of the Americas. The display of Wingina's severed head belied Raleigh's assertion that the English would be kinder and gentler colonists than the Spanish. So did subsequent events that indicated that the English often saw the Spanish as models to emulate. But the English presentation of themselves as more humane than the Spanish took root. It still shapes how many in the United States view the nation's colonial past and distinguish it from Latin America's.

## Imports and a Changing Indian Northeast

Long before St. Augustine's founding, Indians in eastern Canada had regular contact with Europeans fishing offshore for cod. By 1580, as many as 20,000 Europeans journeyed across the North Atlantic and back each year. More ships sailed between Europe and Canada than between Spain and its American colonies during the late 1500s. Europeans traded glass beads, metal tools, kettles, and woolen cloth to Indians for small quantities of furs. The imports circulated among Indians via established routes that stretched hundreds of miles inland.

In the early 1580s French merchants began to specialize in acquiring beaver pelts from the St. Lawrence Valley. They sought to meet growing demand in Europe for felted

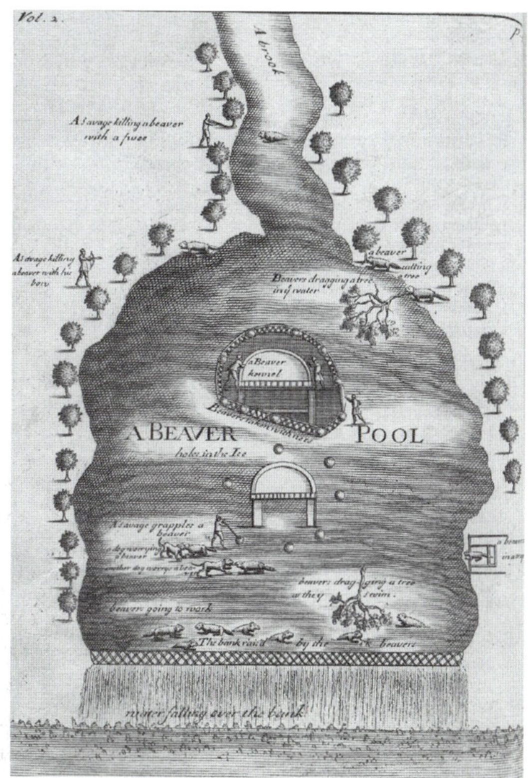


This illustration shows the various ways that Indians hunted beaver and some of the animal's habits, such as how it constructs dams. Beaver pelts were New France's chief export. Trade in them was key to relations between European colonists, their descendants, and Indians in northern North America well into the 1800s.

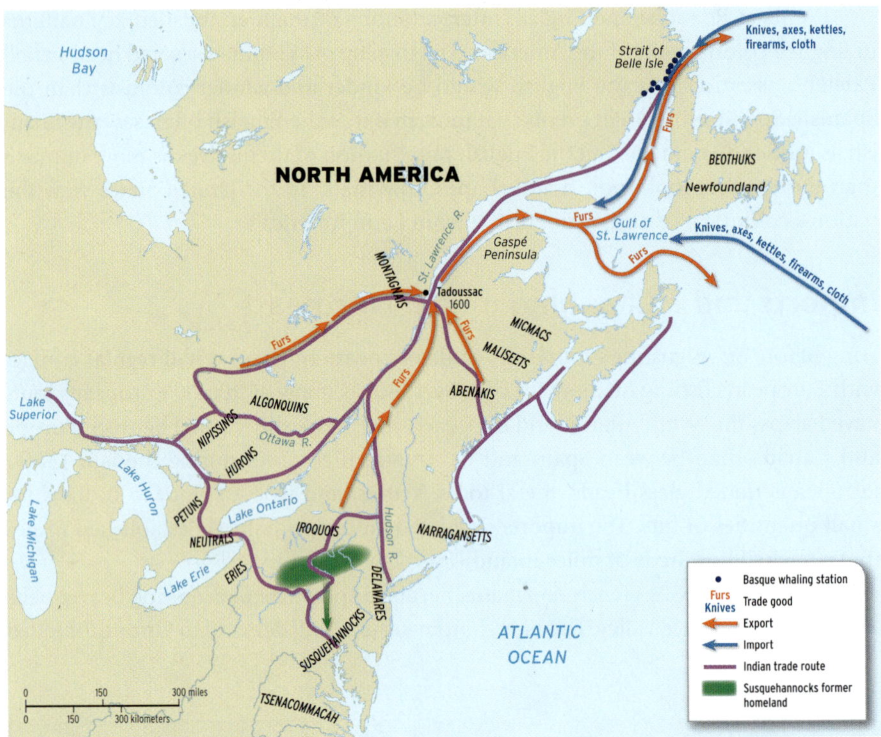


**Map 2.2**

**Trade in the Indian Northeast, c. 1580–1607** The St. Lawrence River Valley and the Indian trade routes that ran through it helped to make the region the chief entry point for European goods into North America. The Huron Confederacy, located at the intersection of many trade routes, had a relatively easy time acquiring imports, while the Iroquois League's peoples, whose lands lay outside those routes, had far more difficulty.

beaver hats. Indian men were happy to bring more pelts; they found beaver less taxing to hunt than other fur-bearing animals. The **fur trade**, like the fishing and whaling industries that gave rise to it, ensured that the St. Lawrence River remained the main gateway for European goods into North America well into the 1600s.

The imports initially reinforced traditional Indian beliefs and practices. Before 1600, relatively few Indians had steady access to such goods, so they seldom used or viewed them in ways that Europeans did. Instead, Indians incorporated imports into their world on their own terms. Few brass or copper kettles remained intact for long; most were broken apart and the pieces put to other uses. Many were reworked into arrowheads, while others became amulets that chiefs wore to display their connection to sources of such valued items. Copper and brass, along with iron goods and glass beads, accompanied prominent people to their graves, indicating the spiritual power that Indians believed infused such objects.

Although Indians assimilated most new goods in traditional ways, trade with Europeans brought important changes. Susquehannocks moved south to the Lower

Susquehanna Valley to escape the Iroquois and be closer to goods that trickled north from Chesapeake Bay. The region's two main Iroquoian-speaking confederacies, the Iroquois (the Seneca, Cayuga, Onondaga, Oneida, and Mohawk) and the Huron, operated in more coordinated and concerted ways, partly to secure better access to trade routes and deny the same to each other. By the 1570s, Mohawks and Oneidas were at war with Montagnais and Algonquins, who funneled imports inland. That gave Iroquois foes an advantage: better weapons. Brass arrowheads outperformed stone-tipped ones. They were lighter, easier to aim, and penetrated wooden armor. As late as 1610 the Iroquois still fought with stone-tipped hatchets, spears, and arrowheads and found themselves on the losing end of a regional arms race.

By then, more Indians with direct and steady access to European goods used them as their manufacturers intended. The imports made life easier, especially for women. Steel axes simplified gathering firewood, and metal kettles were more durable and versatile than ceramic or wooden ones. Refashioning woolen cloth into traditionally-styled garments took less work than it did to dress skins and furs.

Indians in the northeast gradually became more dependent on such imports. By the early 1600s Montagnais had stopped building birch bark canoes and instead bought French-made longboats. Micmacs, who lived too far north to grow corn or much else themselves, became so devoted to gathering beaver pelts that they required French imports to eat. Their situation was an extreme example of the future that awaited most Indians who ventured too far into the Atlantic marketplace.

### STUDY QUESTIONS FOR CONQUEST BEGINS AND TRADE EXPANDS, 1565–1607

1. **In what ways did the Spanish colonization of Florida and New Mexico differ? In what ways did Indian responses to Spanish colonization differ in Florida and New Mexico?**
2. **By what means and for what reasons did England become Spain's chief rival in North America?**
3. **What impact did the fur trade and trade goods have upon Indians in the northeast?**

## EUROPEAN ISLANDS IN AN ALGONQUIAN OCEAN, 1607–1625

Algonquians from the St. Lawrence River to Chesapeake Bay cautiously welcomed the thousands of strangers who arrived between the 1600s and 1620s and began to occupy their lands. A minority of them spoke French or Dutch, came in small numbers to the lands of the Algonquins, Montagnais, and Mahicans, and devoted themselves to trading with their Algonquian neighbors. The vast majority of the foreigners spoke

English and staked claim to large quantities of land, which they soon divided among themselves and began to farm. Most of these disembarked in Tsenacommacah along the estuaries of Chesapeake Bay. The rest landed in Massachusetts Bay in territory claimed by Wampanoags. All the newcomers depended on Algonquian-grown corn and Algonquian knowledge to survive their first years in North America as well as trade with Algonquians and other Indians to make their colonies financially viable. But the English decided rather quickly that they needed Algonquians less than they needed Algonquian land. Their refusal to honor Algonquian ways led to wars with Tsenacommacah and tension along the shores of Massachusetts Bay.

## Tsenacommacah and Virginia

In May 1607, 144 English colonists founded Jamestown on a marshy triangle of land that jutted into the James River. The Virginia Company of London's royal charter gave it exclusive rights to colonize from New England south to Virginia. Its directors and investors hoped to turn a quick profit. But the hardships of establishing a new colony and the lack of gold or anything else of value in the area dimmed English hopes. Hunger, disease, and cold claimed all but thirty-eight Jamestown residents by the spring of 1608.

Peoples of Tsenacommacah watched warily as they tried to determine the strangers' motives. Tsenacommacah had expanded over the previous four decades under the leadership of Wahunsonacock. As Powhatan (paramount chief) he had used diplomacy, marriage, intimidation, and warfare to gain the allegiance of other Algonquian bands and collect tribute from them. By the time the English strangers arrived, Tsenacommacah included almost all Algonquians who lived in Virginia's tidewater region and it was still growing.

Powhatan decided to incorporate Jamestown into Tsenacommacah. In December 1607, warriors seized John Smith, one of the colony's leaders, and delivered him to Powhatan. Powhatan's nine-year-old daughter Pocahontas helped to stage Smith's mock execution. As most Americans know the story, Pocahontas demonstrated her love for Smith by throwing herself on top of him to save his life. Powhatan probably intended the event to symbolize the death of Smith's former identity and the Jamestown leader's rebirth as a chief who led another village that paid Powhatan tribute.

Smith either did not understand or refused to accept the role. Neither did his superiors in the Virginia Company, who believed that Tsenacommacah was subject to Virginia and James I and not the other way around. Powhatan saw no reason to submit to the English, who subsisted on corn that Tsenacommacah's women grew. Warriors attacked Jamestown shortly after John Smith departed in October 1609, initiating nearly five years of intermittent warfare that starved Jamestown. When Smith left, there were 490 colonists. When Thomas Gates arrived as governor in May 1610, only 60 remained.

Pocahontas helped Powhatan monitor events in Jamestown by acting as his emissary and keeping lines of communication open. In 1613, colonists took her hostage. **John Rolfe**, a prominent immigrant, fell in love with her, and the following year, Pocahontas, only sixteen, married Rolfe and was baptized as Rebecca. The

**▲ Map 2.3**

**European Islands in an Algonquian Ocean, 1607–1626** An Algonquian-speaking world surrounded the European outposts at Quebec, New Netherland, Plymouth and Virginia, sustained them, and sometimes threatened them. Algonquian-made wampum enabled a regional trade that benefitted New Netherland and New England. Virginia's encroachments on Tsenacommacah, driven mainly by a tobacco boom, led to two bloody wars, one in 1622 and the other in the 1640s.

marriage halted the war between Tsenacommacah and Virginia and bought the colony some time.

Meanwhile, officials on both sides of the Atlantic concluded that only drastic action could save the colony and the Virginia Company. In 1612, the firm tried to

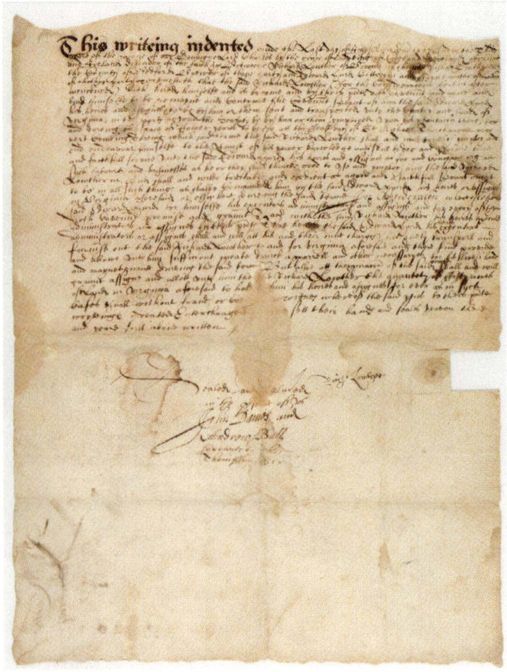
This writing indented

Indentured servant agreement between Richard Lowther and Edward Lyurd, 1627. By this indenture (contract), Lowther agreed to serve a Virginia plantation owner for four years, after which he was to receive 50 acres of land. Lowther differed from most English indentured servants who went to the Americas in that he signed his indenture, an indication that he was probably literate.

lure more investors by putting governance in stockholders' hands. In Virginia, reforms focused on breaking English dependence on Indians. Gates and his successor, Thomas Dale, both military men, put Jamestown under martial law. Dale tried to make Jamestown more self-sufficient by renting land to former company servants in exchange for one month of service and some of the corn that they harvested. Meanwhile the company's defenders in England pleaded that it would take time to turn a profit.

The Virginia Company never earned one, even though colonists learned to cultivate tobacco, a valuable export crop that enabled Virginia to survive. Smoking had a bad reputation in England. In 1604, James I condemned smokers, who aped "the barbarous and beastly manners of the wild, godless, and slavish Indians." But colonists soon imitated Indians by growing tobacco. In 1611, John Rolfe planted seeds of a sweeter-smelling variety of West Indies tobacco that he obtained in England. Virginia began to export tobacco three years later as the English learned how to cure it, probably with help from Pocahontas.

As Virginia colonists adopted tobacco, they adapted English labor systems to meet their needs. In England, families or magistrates regularly bound adolescents and young adults as **indentured servants**. In Virginia, indentured servants, most of them men between 18 and 26 years old, agreed to serve from three to seven years in exchange for passage overseas. They mainly did the hard work of growing, harvesting, and curing tobacco and could be bought and sold against their will. The Virginia Company encouraged immigration and the colony's expansion by creating a headright system in 1617. It promised 50 acres of land for every free adult who went to Virginia and another 50 for each servant imported.

Two years later, company officials sent 90 young women to become planters' wives. They hoped that married men would stay rather than return to England. Persuading English women to emigrate proved a challenge. A shortage of labor and the tobacco boom compelled colonists to put English women, be they servants or wives, to work in the fields, an arrangement that fit Algonquian gender norms but violated those of the English.

The need for labor also led Virginia colonists to purchase Africans. In 1619, the privateer *White Lion* brought the first unfree Africans to enter English North America. At first, colonists considered some Africans to be slaves and others to be indentured servants whom they freed after completing their terms. African slavery emerged gradually over the course of decades in Virginia.

The most significant changes to Virginia Company policy came in the late 1610s when officials decided to let colonists own land and govern themselves. The right to own land drew tens of thousands of men, mostly indentured servants, to Virginia over the next several decades. Land was increasingly scarce in England. To English men, land ownership brought respect, economic independence, and political rights such as serving on a jury, voting, or holding office. In 1619, the Virginia Company established English America's first representative assembly, the **House of Burgesses**. The firm also replaced martial law with English **common law**, setting in motion the development of county courts. The promise of land ownership lured nearly 4,000 English, the vast majority indentured servants, to Virginia between 1619 and 1622. The fields which they cleared and on which they planted tobacco steadily encroached upon Tsenacommacah.

This alarmed Powhatan's kinsman and successor Opechcancanough, who made plans to finish off the colony. In March 1622 Tsenacommacah warriors stormed Virginia, killing more than one in four colonists. The English counterattacked brutally but the war dragged on for 10 years.

It finished off the Virginia Company, which had never earned a profit and faced charges that its mismanagement had cost thousands of English lives. About 1,200 colonists lived in Virginia in 1622, just one-third the number of immigrants who had arrived in the previous three years. Most succumbed to disease. In 1624, James I revoked the bankrupt company's charter and put Virginia under royal rule. Virginians' refusal to honor Algonquian ways had nearly led to their colony's demise. Thickening ties to the Atlantic world and England, sustained mainly by Europeans' desire to smoke tobacco, ultimately saved Virginia.

## New France, New Netherland, New Indian Northeast

As English immigrants struggled to turn Tsenacommacah into Virginia, the French and Dutch claimed the St. Lawrence and Hudson River valleys, respectively. **Samuel de Champlain** charted the coast from Nova Scotia to Cape Cod for France, established alliances with Micmac and Abenaki, and learned of growing English interest in

GLOBAL PASSAGES

## Angela's Ordeal, the Atlantic Slave Trade, and the Creation of African North American Cultures

In 1625, an African woman named Angela lived in Jamestown. She was one of William Pierce's four "servants" and probably spent most of her time tending to livestock. We do not know when Angela died or if she ever became free. Her life and her world shed light on England's marginal position within the Atlantic slave trade well into the 1600s and on Africans' efforts to create new worlds for themselves in North America.

Angela was probably captured in 1619 during a Portuguese-Imbangala war against the Kingdom of Ndongo in Angola. Her Christian name indicates that Angela was baptized before she and about 350 others boarded the *São João Bautista*, one of the Portuguese-registered vessels that ferried the vast majority of Africans to the Americas until 1650. Nearly 700,000 enslaved Africans crossed the Atlantic between 1600 and 1650. More than three-quarters of them departed West Central Africa as Angela did. Most West Central Africans who left between 1616 and 1625 were taken to Brazil and about two in five to Central America or Mexico, Angela's destination. But two privateers, each commanded by an English captain, intercepted the *São João Bautista* in the Gulf of Mexico. A Dutch prince licensed the *White Lion,* and the Duke of Savoy (in Italy) the *Treasurer*. The privateers seized Angela and over 50 others, divided them, and sailed for Virginia. The *White Lion* arrived first and sold 20 people in Jamestown. Fearing that he might be hanged as a pirate in Virginia, the captain of the *Treasurer* headed for Bermuda, which in 1616 became the first English American colony to buy Africans. No one bid on Angela, who landed in Virginia in February 1620.

Angela joined 32 African Virginians and about 900 other colonists. Until 1670, fewer than 5 percent of Virginians were Africans. Angela's background and experience matched those of the first Africans shipped to English and Dutch North America before 1660. Most came as a result of English or Dutch piracy on Spanish shipping (Portugal and Spain were united under Spanish rule between 1581 and 1640). English ships did not transport more than 2,000 Africans across the Atlantic in any decade until the 1640s, when sugar cultivation boomed on Barbados.

Like Angela, most Africans brought to North America before 1660 came from West Central Africa. They spoke one of two closely-related Bantu languages, Kikongo or Kimbundu. Many probably knew some Portuguese too. Most had been baptized and many considered themselves Christian. Among them were Antonio and Isabel,

West Central African leaders often saw baptism as a tool of diplomacy. Here Njinga Mbandi, sister and representative of King Ngola Mbandi of Ndongo, receives baptism during a visit to Angola's Portuguese governor that aimed to end wars that decimated Ndongo and enslaved thousands of West Central Africans, including Angela.

who by 1625 had their son William baptized. A generation later they were free and had become the Johnsons, the most prosperous African American family in English North America, one that owned slaves who grew tobacco. In 1667, their son John bought 44 acres and named the estate "Angola" to honor his parents' origins. About one-quarter of the Africans whose names appear in Virginia's public records between 1635 and 1650 had Iberian names such as Antonio, Manuel, or Maria. Before 1640, most lived and worked alongside at least five other Africans. In short, Angela and other Africans shared much in common that helped them to weather their bondage and sometimes escape it during the first decades of Afro-Virginian history.

- In what ways did the struggle between England and Spain for supremacy in the Americas shape Angela's ordeal and English participation in the Atlantic slave trade?
- In what ways did shared origins in West Central Africa likely shape the lives of Angela and other Africans in early Virginia?

the cod-rich coastal waters of New England. In 1608, perhaps prompted by a failed Virginia Company effort to establish a colony at Sagadahoc in Maine, Champlain founded what became Quebec City. The new French village controlled water access inland. But New France's immediate future looked dim. Only 8 of 28 colonists survived their first Canadian winter.

Indians who forged ties to New France for their own purposes saved the colony. In 1609, Algonquins, Montagnais, and Hurons persuaded Champlain to help them attack the Mohawks. He brought his arquebus, an early musket, which, like other firearms of the time, was wildly inaccurate. With some lucky shooting, Champlain managed to kill three Mohawks. The rest fled, having never seen firearms. Six years later, Champlain cemented an alliance with the Huron Confederacy, longtime Iroquois foe. Hurons became the principal Indian middlemen in New France's fur trade. They and other Indian allies sustained New France's economy.

Champlain lobbied for more support from France, arguing that England and the Netherlands threatened France's claim to the St. Lawrence Valley. But internal political turmoil and the **Thirty Years' War** left France with little money and few people to spare. The Catholic Church proved more receptive. In 1615, four French Récollet priests arrived, followed a decade later by Jesuit missionaries. In 1628, the Company of New France sent 400 colonists to Quebec, but English privateers captured them en route. An English attack the following year forced Champlain to surrender Quebec and send the Jesuits home. They returned when England ceded Quebec to France.

By then, Dutch entrepreneurs had established a colony on the Hudson. In 1609, Henry Hudson sailed upriver in search of a water route to Asia, trading with Algonquians along the way. Five years later, the Dutch founded a trading post, Fort Nassau, now Albany, New York, on Mahican land. Fort Nassau's residents emulated the French by allying with their neighbors. By the early 1620s the Dutch expanded their commercial network to both sides of Long Island Sound and the Delaware Valley.

They did so by catering to Indian beliefs and needs. The Dutch learned of wampum's spiritual and material value to the northeast's Indians. Wampum manufacturing, simplified by imported iron tools that reshaped shells into beads and bored holes through them, soon spread to Narragansett Bay and Long Island Sound. Algonquian women incorporated gathering shells and fashioning them into wampum into their winter routines. Pequots and Narragansett, two peoples well positioned to make wampum, emerged as southern New England's main powers, partly because wampum soon became currency in New Netherland and New England. Meanwhile, Mohawks feared that they might get cut off from the imports that enabled them to fight off their enemies. In 1624, they forced the Mahicans to move, clearing a path between the Iroquois and New Netherland.

Like New France, New Netherland at first was a satellite of its Indian neighbors. In 1621, Dutch officials awarded the **Dutch West India Company** (DWIC) a monopoly on commerce between the Americas, West Africa, and the Netherlands and charged it to establish colonies. The firm focused mainly on the Caribbean and

South America. It sent no colonists to New Netherland until 1624. Two years later, the company purchased Manhattan from Indians and founded its local headquarters, New Amsterdam, on the island to coordinate commerce with Indians. New Netherland remained a low priority for the Dutch West India Company. In 1630, it had just 300 colonists.

## Pilgrims and Algonquians

In 1620–1621, Algonquians watched English immigrants weather their first New England winter. The 102 newcomers called themselves "Pilgrims." Delayed by storms and blown well north of their intended destination—Virginia—they sighted Cape Cod in November. Pilgrims spent a month searching for a suitable site, which they named Plymouth. Some aboard the *Mayflower* argued that the location of their new home nullified the royal charter under which they were to settle and questioned who should govern them. Their leaders responded with the Mayflower Compact, an agreement that all free adult male passengers signed. They promised to obey laws enforced by officials whom they chose. The Pilgrims arrived too late to plant and failed to bring enough to eat. Barely half survived the winter, mainly by devouring corn that Indians had buried.

Plymouth's leaders were religious dissidents from England who had just spent 12 years in the Netherlands. These "Puritans" (as their critics called them) argued that the Church of England was too Catholic. It did not follow God's will as revealed in the Bible; it did not allow believers to choose their own leaders or even whether they wished to belong to the Church of England at all. Puritans believed that Anglican clergy dishonored God by preventing the faithful from disciplining and excluding those who did not believe or practice what the church preached. The Pilgrims who founded Plymouth went a step further. As Separatists, they believed that the Anglican Church could never be reformed; they could only save themselves by leaving it. Pilgrims enjoyed freedom of worship in the Netherlands, but worried that their children would become Dutch or marginalized if they stayed there.

Meanwhile, an epidemic decimated Algonquians who lived near Massachusetts Bay. Fishermen from England and Virginia introduced an unknown disease between 1616 and 1618 that killed up to 90 percent of the peoples who lived nearby. Massasoit, sachem (chief) of the decimated Pokanoket Wampanoags, had to submit to the Narragansetts and pay them tribute. **Tisquantum**, often known as Squanto, paid a higher price. In 1614 an English captain seized him and tried to sell him into slavery in Spain. Tisquantum escaped and somehow made his way to London and Newfoundland. He arrived home in 1619, only to find that disease had killed most of his people, the Patuxet, and scattered the rest.

Eurasian diseases that killed Indians made Plymouth's survival more likely. People felled by the epidemic had buried the corn that saw Pilgrims through their first winter. Colonists did not have to clear land their first spring; Algonquians had done so before they died. As at Jamestown, corn grown by Algonquian women fed Plymouth for its first four years, fruit of an alliance forged with Massasoit in 1621. Massasoit hoped that friendship with Plymouth would allow his people to escape Narragansett control by securing a powerful ally and better access to imported goods. Pilgrims envisioned that Plymouth would become southeastern New England's most powerful village, with Massasoit collecting tribute from other Algonquians as Plymouth shipped beaver pelts to England to pay off company investors. Tisquantum would live in Plymouth and serve as the Pilgrims' guide and interpreter.

Tensions rose as colonists and Indians interpreted the agreement differently. Tisquantum aimed to reconstitute the Patuxet under his leadership by stoking English mistrust of Massasoit, who soon learned that Plymouth's leaders viewed him and his people as subjects. By the summer of 1621, colony officials prohibited Wampanoag social visits and allowed only Massasoit or his designated representative to enter Plymouth. Word of the English-Algonquian war in Virginia led Plymouth colonists to fear a massive conspiracy between Tsenacommacah and New England Algonquian peoples against all English. They embarked on building a fort and sent armed expeditions to nearby villages to extort corn and intimidate their residents. Plymouth soon sought more autonomy from Indians by ending the system of communal production that had been in place since the colony was founded. Ironically, its replacement made Plymouth resemble an Algonquian village. Each family received a parcel to plant, although the land remained company property. Colonists grew corn mostly, with women and children performing much of the field labor. Within two years Plymouth fed itself and had corn left over.

The surplus of corn strengthened the colony. In 1625, its merchants began to exchange corn for beaver pelts with Maine's Kennebec Abenaki. Plymouth also joined the Dutch-Algonquian wampum network. This suited Plymouth well. The best time to ship corn was just after the harvest, when beaver pelts were thinnest. Wampum could be traded anytime, most profitably in late winter and early spring when pelts were thickest.

Still, Plymouth never prospered. In 1627, colonists bought out English shareholders and divided up the livestock and land among male heads of household. They built a relatively obscure society of a few thousand small farmers who scratched out a living on poor soil. But the English had put down roots in New England, an accomplishment that owed much to the Algonquians' intensified contact with Europeans—and with the goods and microbes that they brought to North America.

## STUDY QUESTIONS FOR EUROPEAN ISLANDS IN AN ALGONQUIAN OCEAN, 1607–1625

1. **In what ways did Indians, particularly Algonquians, influence the development of European colonies in eastern North America between 1607 and 1625?**
2. **The stories of Pocahontas and the Pilgrims are two founding myths of the United States. Does viewing their stories from Algonquian perspectives change your understanding of them? Explain.**

# SEEKING GOD, SEIZING LAND, REAPING CONFLICT, 1625 TO C. 1640

As small European outposts grew in three corners of the continent, new patterns emerged and old ones became entrenched. Faith and fear of growing English and Dutch influence moved missionaries in New Mexico and New France to intensify their efforts to convert Indians. Political and religious turmoil in England and western Europe encouraged thousands to seek refuge in New Netherland and in new English colonies in New England and Maryland. Meanwhile, thousands more flooded into Virginia to plant tobacco and seek land. New arrivals who hoped to create a harmonious and prosperous society in New England multiplied rapidly but quickly divided into factions. Heavy immigration and colonial expansion intensified pressure on Algonquians from New England south to Chesapeake Bay, resulting in wars that prompted Indians to think of themselves in new ways.

## Missionaries and Indians in New France and New Mexico

In the late 1620s and early 1630s, Catholic missionaries brought new zeal to their efforts to evangelize Indians in New France and New Mexico. Jesuits served as New France's principal emissaries to Indian allies and the colony's most vocal promoters in France. Meanwhile, Franciscans preached to new groups of Indians on New Mexico's borders while sparring with governors over who should have more power over

Portrait of Father Paul Le Jeune, from an engraving from René Lochon, 1665. Le Jeune served as Jesuit superior in New France from 1632 to 1639. He noted that Montagnais audiences laughed at him because "I pronounce the Indian as a German pronounces French," but were impressed that he could interpret dreams. Le Jeune edited the first 11 editions of the Jesuit Relations.

colonists and Indians. Missionaries studied the cultures of Indians whom they evangelized, but New France's Jesuits proved more willing to meet converts part way than New Mexico's Franciscans.

Jesuits embarked upon two related tasks when they returned to New France in 1632. One was to establish missions among Montagnais and Hurons. The other was to promote their work, seek financial support for it, and recruit colonists. They sought to achieve these goals by gathering reports from Jesuits in New France and publishing them in France. Historians call these narratives, compiled and distributed annually between 1632 and 1673, the *Jesuit Relations*.

Jesuits focused on Hurons, who were easier to reach most of the year because they lived and farmed in large villages. Most Indians who traded with the Hurons spoke their language, so Jesuits who learned it could preach to Huron allies as well. Trade with the French shored up Huron power, particularly against the Iroquois. That was why Huron leaders had to accept Jesuit missions.

Jesuits found Hurons to be grudging hosts, partly because the priests often behaved like rude and annoying guests. At first, Jesuits demanded that converts become culturally French. They expected Indians to renounce their faith in dreams as revelations of the future and become monogamous. Hurons often brushed aside pleas to change their ways by responding "[s]uch is the custom of our country." To Hurons, Jesuits, with their short hair and beards, looked beastly, smelled bad, could neither hunt nor fight, and labored to speak their language. Christian concepts such as sin or eternal punishment after death did not exist in Huron religion. Most Hurons found the promise of a heaven that excluded kin who were not Christian repellent. Jesuits' practice of baptizing dying infants and children led many Hurons to conclude that the priests were sorcerers.

Despite these conflicts, the Huron valued their alliance with France and spared Jesuit lives. Hurons also admired many Jesuit qualities. Unlike other French men, the priests cared little about land, pelts, or sex with Indian women. Rigorous education had trained Jesuits to be skillful debaters who could hold their own in council meetings. Jesuits often showed a warrior's stoic courage in the face of captivity, torture, and death. They also seemed to possess special powers. Their ability to read and write at first astonished Indians. Astronomical charts enabled the priests to predict solar and lunar eclipses. Perhaps most importantly, Jesuits possessed some immunity to diseases that ravaged Indians.

Epidemics and Jesuits' increasing willingness to compromise with converts saved their missions to the Huron. A smallpox outbreak in 1640 pushed over 1,000 Hurons to seek baptism. Many hoped that the sacrament would heal or spare them. Jesuits soon tried to build upon beliefs that Catholics and Hurons shared, such as the power of prayer and the immortality of souls. They created prayer books and catechisms in the Huron language and employed Huron assistants to explain doctrine. Relatively few Hurons identified themselves as Christians; only 500 did so in 1646. But Jesuits established a foothold in Huron territory, sealing the alliance between that confederation and New France and making themselves targets for Iroquois warriors.

As Jesuits prepared to reenter New France, Franciscans in New Mexico expressed a renewed sense of optimism. Eight friars arrived in 1629 and promptly founded missions among the Acoma, Zuni, and Hopi. The head of New Mexico's missions, Fray **Alonso de Benavides**, eagerly anticipated the conversion of Na-Dene speaking peoples who lived on the Pueblo world's borders called Apache "enemy" by the Pueblos. In 1630, Benavides published a report in Madrid that argued for a spiritual conquest launched from New Mexico toward the Atlantic coast to win allies for Spain and shield Indians from Protestant "heresies" that the English and Dutch had brought to North America. The report won a wide audience in Europe but did little to change Spanish policy.

Benavides celebrated that thousands of Pueblos lived within New Mexico's missions, but misinterpreted why many did. Life outside the missions was hard. Spanish officials often seized corn from Pueblos who did not live on missions, disrupting trade with Indians who supplied bison and other game in exchange for Pueblo corn. Missions offered cattle, pigs, and sheep for butchering, as well as some protection from Apache raids and Spanish governors.

These benefits came at a price. Mission Indians endured campaigns to remake them into hispanized Christians. Friars confiscated and destroyed their religious symbols, and built crosses over **kivas**—the sacred cave-like structures in which Pueblos reenacted their creation and honored their gods. Friars undermined systems of Pueblo authority. They adopted the role of Pueblo hunting chiefs by supplying livestock and meat to baptized Indians. Franciscans targeted children for baptism and catechization, luring them with gifts of seed and livestock and taking on the role of both parents as their providers and protectors. They inverted Pueblos' gendered division of labor to match Hispanic norms by compelling men to build homes and women to weave. Pueblo peoples were traditionally **matrilineal** (social identity descended from the mother), but Pueblo women lost their exclusive rights to land, seeds, and children to men wherever missions took deep root.

By the early 1640s, Pueblos found themselves besieged by Apaches. The Spanish introduced horses to Pueblo peoples, who began to trade them to the Apaches in 1601. Horses facilitated Apache raids and reinforced Apache ways by making them more mobile and facilitating their hunts. Growing herds of Apache horses exhausted pastures, forcing Apaches to move more often, strengthening each band's autonomy, and encouraging more raids on Pueblos and colonists. Meanwhile, the Diné, whom the Spanish at first called "Apaches Navaju," traded and raided for sheep as well as horses. Raising sheep and weaving wool soon became central to Navajo culture and the foundation of the Navajo economy.

Indians also raided New Mexico to avenge kin captured and enslaved by Spanish-led incursions. Governor Luis de Rosas saw Indian slavery as a way to profit from his office. Some slaves worked in colonists' households, others in Rosas's textile factory in Santa Fé to make blankets to trade to Plains peoples. The rest were sold to Mexican mines. In 1638, Rosas attacked Plains Apaches, killing 100 and enslaving as many. Apaches retaliated by raiding the lightly defended colony, leaving the disease-ravaged Pueblos weaker and hungrier. About 80,000 Pueblos lived in 150 towns in 1598. By 1640, fewer than half as many inhabited just 43 towns.

## Migration and the Expansion of Dutch and English North America

Heavy immigration between the mid-1620s and 1640 caused New Netherland and English colonies in the Chesapeake, New England, and the Caribbean to grow rapidly. Demand for labor in North America and the West Indies, recruitment by company officials, and events in Europe and the South Atlantic rim channeled migrants across the Atlantic. Political and religious conflict in England prompted the creation of two new mainland colonies, Massachusetts Bay in 1629 and Maryland in 1634, founded to provide a haven for Puritans and Catholics, respectively. The new colonies attracted thousands of migrants who helped to anchor English claims to North America.

By contrast, the Dutch West India Company did relatively little to promote New Netherland to prospective colonists. The firm's directors considered the Hudson River valley a northern outpost of a global Dutch empire that by the early 1640s linked New Netherland to south and southeast Asia, northeastern Brazil, Angola, and the West Indies. Few Dutch had reason to leave Holland, where they enjoyed a prosperous economy, low unemployment, and religious toleration.

As a result, New Netherland became a Dutch colony composed mostly of people who were not Dutch. In 1629, the DWIC encouraged private investment by offering patroonships, large land grants along the Hudson, to those who brought at least 50 immigrants with them. In 1638, a group opposed to company rule left New Netherland, settled near what later became Philadelphia, and recruited colonists from Sweden. Susquehannocks protected them in exchange for imported goods. In 1640, the DWIC issued a **Charter of Freedoms and Exemptions**. It granted 200 acres to whoever brought five adults to New Netherland, and it promised prospective colonists religious freedom and local self-governance, guarantees that lured English Puritans from Massachusetts to eastern Long Island. New Netherland became the most ethnically—and religiously—diverse colony yet seen in North America. In 1644, the French Jesuit Isaac Jogues visited New Amsterdam and heard 18 languages spoken on its streets.

New Netherland also grew because African bondage took root there sooner than in English North America. Africans and their American-born children comprised 30 percent of New Amsterdam's 100 residents in 1638 and 20 percent of nearly 2,000 in 1664. The DWIC's ties to Africa, Brazil, and the Caribbean and its need for labor, largely to build and maintain fortifications and conduct commerce, helped to create such a large black population. In 1648, the DWIC ended its monopoly over the African slave trade to and from New Netherland, but remained the colony's largest importer and buyer of Africans.

New Amsterdam's Africans created the first urban African American community north of St. Augustine. Like their peers in Virginia, New Amsterdam's Africans shared similar origins and experiences. In 1644, 11 men petitioned company director **Willem Kieft** for their freedom. He permitted them to work for themselves and live where they wished, but Kieft required that the men pay the DWIC and bind themselves and their children to serve the company. Such "**half-freedom**" exemplified the discrimination that New Amsterdam's Africans confronted. But many Africans and African Americans earned real freedom. By 1664, one in five in New Netherland had done so.

Although DWIC reforms enabled New Netherland's population to increase rapidly, the Dutch failed to keep pace with the English. The number of people who lived in New Netherland nearly doubled between 1638 and 1643 to 2,000. By 1664, the colony had 10,000 residents. But Virginia had 40,000 and New England 50,000.

Unlike Holland or France, emigrants departed England, Wales, and Scotland in droves. Most went to Ireland. Between 1560 and 1640, 70,000 English and Welsh and 30,000 Scots moved to the island seeking to benefit from English conquests. Migration to America soared during the 1630s. Thousands went to five colonies (St. Christopher, Barbados, Nevis, Providence Island, and Antigua) that the English had recently founded in the West Indies. Thousands more left for the tobacco fields of Maryland and Virginia. Meanwhile, 13,000 headed for New England in the most concentrated and targeted movement of people across the Atlantic and into North America yet. The wave of immigrants during the 1630s swelled the population of English North America and the West Indies from 9,500 in 1630 to 54,000 ten years later. English colonists vastly outnumbered their French, Dutch, and Spanish counterparts from then on, giving England a huge advantage over its European rivals in North America.

Most English who went to the Chesapeake or the West Indies were young single men who sought economic independence. Landless and unemployed, they poured into London and other cities seeking work. Tobacco planters, who desperately needed labor, lured such men to the colonies. One in four died of malaria or another disease within a year of landing in the Chesapeake, but those who survived their American servitude stood a good chance of becoming landowners. About half the men who left London for Maryland or Virginia in 1635 and can be traced in colonial records managed to acquire land. The immigrants entered a colonial world in which men vastly outnumbered women; most died young, and few were American born. This increased demand for servants and increased survivors' chances of owning land and enjoying upward social mobility. With so many men available, English women could be choosier about whom they wished to marry. Those who outlived their husbands owned a large share of land in the Chesapeake colonies and often attracted many suitors.

An array of forces pushed people out of England and drew them to Puritan colonies in America during the 1630s. A worsening economy in eastern England in the 1620s made migration look more attractive. **Charles I**'s decision to suspend Parliament in 1629 cut off the main avenue for peaceful expression of dissent. Some Puritan leaders and London merchants organized the **Massachusetts Bay Company** in 1629 and recruited emigrants by promising them the opportunity to create godly communities in America. So did the Providence Company, which in 1630 launched a colony on Providence Island off the coast of Central America to which it soon tried to lure New England Puritans. Some 3,000 people fled for New England in 1635 after William

Laud became Archbishop of Canterbury, Anglicanism's second highest-ranking official after the monarch, and targeted Puritan reformers.

Those who moved to New England prospered and multiplied. Almost all adult English men there owned land during the 1600s. The number of colonists in New England grew 66 percent during the 1640s, almost entirely through births, largely because women and children comprised a large share of migrants during the 1630s. White women in New England on average gave birth to eight children (compared to seven in England) and more of them reached adulthood. Most of those American-born children knew their grandparents; most people lived past age 60. Such rapid population growth put additional strain on southern New England's Algonquians and made it harder to achieve the social harmony that Puritans sought to create in America.

## Dissent in the City upon a Hill

In 1630, Massachusetts Bay Colony's first governor, **John Winthrop**, articulated the principles upon which he and his fellow Puritans would build a new society. He reminded them that they had entered into a **covenant** with God that required them to translate their faith into actions that obeyed God's will as revealed in the Bible. If colonists stayed united and honored their word to God and one another, they would set the standard for others to follow. "We shall be as a city upon a hill," Winthrop exhorted, "the eyes of all people are upon us." But if colonists violated the covenant, they would invite divine wrath upon themselves and "open the mouths of enemies to speak evil of the ways of God." God, Winthrop argued, had charged them to create a new and godly England in America for the whole world, especially England, to see and emulate.

Winthrop drew deeply from Calvinist beliefs. His shipmates thought that each congregation should decide how it should operate and who should belong to it. Church members should be those whom God had designated for salvation, those who truly believed in God and acted accordingly. Winthrop and most who accompanied him argued that they could still reform the Anglican Church from within, but had to move to New England to do so. There the faithful could honor their covenant with God by purging their churches and communities of sin.

To sustain their "city upon a hill," Massachusetts Bay Puritans tried to ensure that only God's elect were church members and that God's elect held political power. To accomplish the first goal, they developed a "**conversion test**" in the 1630s. Prospective members had to appear before those already deemed elect, testify to their relationship with God, and offer proof that God had saved them. Members judged whether candidates had received saving grace and merited full admission to their congregation. Only the godly could keep a godly society godly, so in 1631 the Massachusetts Bay General Court, composed partly of the colony's elected assembly, made all adult male church members eligible to vote and hold office, whether they owned land or not. Five years later, men who were not church members were barred from voting or holding office, a form of exclusion adopted nowhere else. Other Puritans did adopt the conversion test, which spread from Massachusetts Bay through New England and then to England.

Religious convictions also led Massachusetts Bay Puritans to create a well-educated society. All believers merited direct access to God's will as written in the Bible, so they needed to know how to read. Persecution of Puritans in England meant that New England had to supply its own ministers. In 1636, reformers founded Harvard College to educate colonists' sons and train ministers. Harvard operated Anglo America's first printing press, which rolled off its first publication in 1639. By 1647, six towns had started grammar schools and a new law mandated that every community with more than 100 households have one. A college, a printing press, and an educated public positioned New England Puritans to generate ideas and broadcast them to the Anglo-Atlantic world.

Reforms inspired by Puritanism also reshaped marriage and family life. Puritans in North America made marriage, a sacrament within the Church of England, a civil ceremony. That made it easier for couples to divorce, although few did. Courts regularly addressed domestic violence and prosecuted male offenders. Authorities also granted parents more power over children. In 1647, Massachusetts Bay became the first place in the Anglo-Atlantic world to give parents power over whom their adult children could marry. New laws empowered fathers and husbands most of all. The Body of Liberties of 1641, akin to a bill of rights, stipulated that "[n]o man shall be deprived of his wife or children" unless he broke a law enacted by the General Court.

As Massachusetts Bay's founders labored to make a model English society, they also proclaimed that they would convert Algonquians and live alongside them peacefully. A campaign to convert Indians did not begin until the mid-1640s. Instead, Puritans imagined that they would set examples that would encourage their Indian neighbors to become Christian and adopt English ways, including English gender norms. In 1634, William Wood published *New England's Prospect* to encourage more Puritans to sail to New England. He cast Algonquian men as lazy tyrants who did little but hunt as they "forced" Algonquian women to grow corn, trap lobsters, and build wigwams—all "man's" work in English eyes. English women, Wood thought, offered good role models for Algonquian women. Meanwhile, John Winthrop argued that Algonquians did not deserve their lands because they did not cultivate or develop them permanently. English who farmed, grazed livestock, claimed land as personal property, and erected permanent structures on it had a far more legitimate claim, he insisted.

To Winthrop's chagrin, Indians' rights became a controversial issue, largely because the minister **Roger Williams** made it one. Williams forged ties to Wampanoags and Narragansetts and began to learn their dialects of Algonquian. He authored a tract that argued that the patent Charles I gave the Massachusetts Bay Company did not entitle colonists to Indian land. Massachusetts Bay leaders condemned Williams and had his work burned. Williams threw fuel on the fire. He even wrote Charles I to criticize the patent that he had issued to Massachusetts Bay. The colony's officials responded by banishing Williams in 1636. He moved to Narragansett Bay, founding Providence on land that Narragansetts granted him.

There Williams established the principle of separation of church and state in English America. Today we see this concept as a way to keep religion out of government. Williams's separatist views led him to the opposite conclusion. Use of government power to compel conformity of belief, he argued, corrupted religion. Authorities instead should allow what Williams called "soul liberty," the freedom to believe and

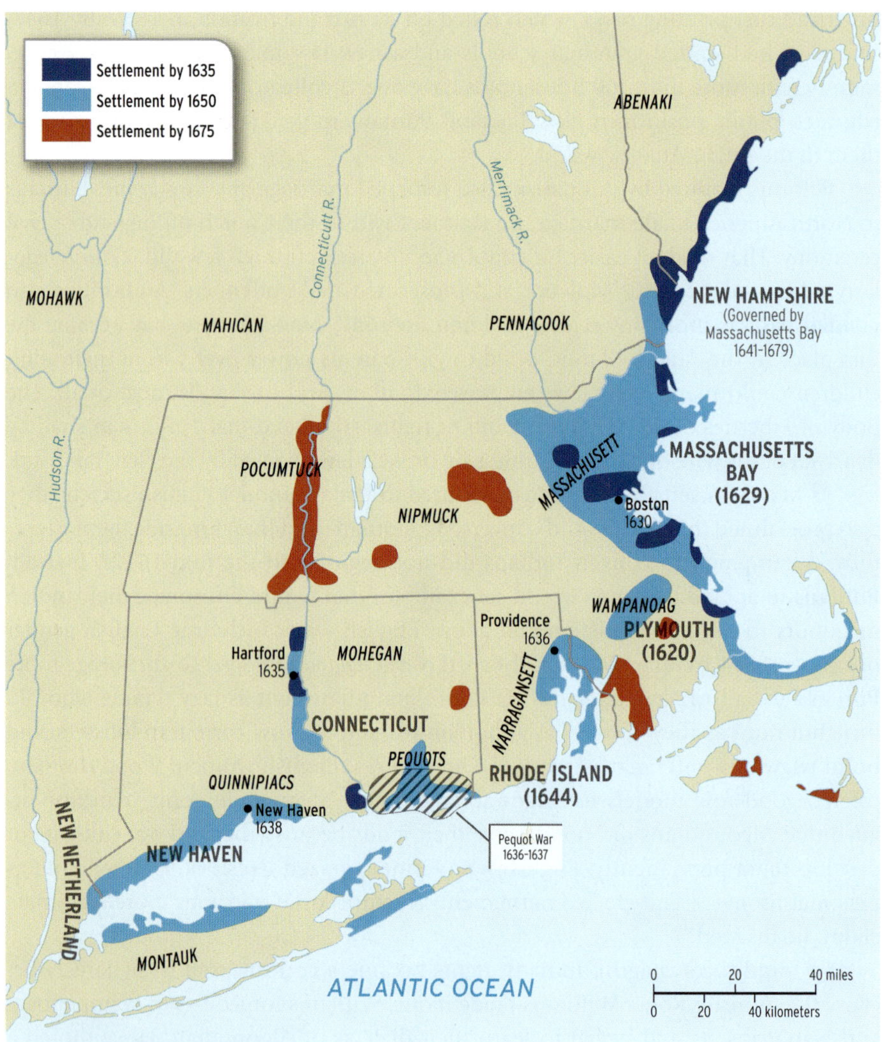


**Map 2.4**

**Colonization of New England, 1635–1675** Religious dissent among Puritans and their habit of migrating as families accelerated English invasions of lands that belonged to Algonquian peoples. Connecticut, New Haven Colony, and Rhode Island, all colonies founded by dissenters who left Massachusetts Bay, expanded rapidly after 1635, a process enabled partly by the Pequot War.

worship as one wished. Williams practiced what he preached by co-founding the Americas' first Baptist church in 1639. He also maintained close ties to Algonquians that protected Providence and enabled him to author an Algonquian-English dictionary. Providence became the first of four English towns, each founded by Massachusetts Bay exiles, that joined to form Rhode Island in 1644.

**Anne Hutchinson** was, after Williams, Rhode Island's second most notorious resident. She was 43 when she sailed to Boston with her husband and 11 children and was admitted to a congregation. Hutchinson soon began to hold meetings for women at her home at which she reviewed the sermons of John Cotton, a Boston minister. Before long Hutchinson, her adversaries charged, was preaching her own views and insisting that good works had no bearing on salvation or on others' knowledge of it. Her enemies, Winthrop among them, abhorred her alleged emphasis on faith alone as evidence of salvation. It challenged how Massachusetts Bay Puritans determined church membership and who should exercise political power. By developing her own theology and preaching it, Hutchinson usurped the job of ministers. She had also claimed a public role that magistrates thought belonged to men alone. Hutchinson faced two trials, one in civil court in 1637, the other in church court in 1638. The first ruled that she be exiled. At the second, a minister admonished her: "You have stept out of your place, you have rather been a Husband than a Wife and a preacher than Hearer; and a Magistrate than a Subject." Hutchinson recanted her views before heading for Rhode Island. Dozens followed her there.

Puritans' tendency to resolve disputes through exile or migration accelerated colonial New England's expansion in the 1630s. The founders of Hartford, Connecticut, considered the criteria for church membership in Massachusetts Bay too restrictive

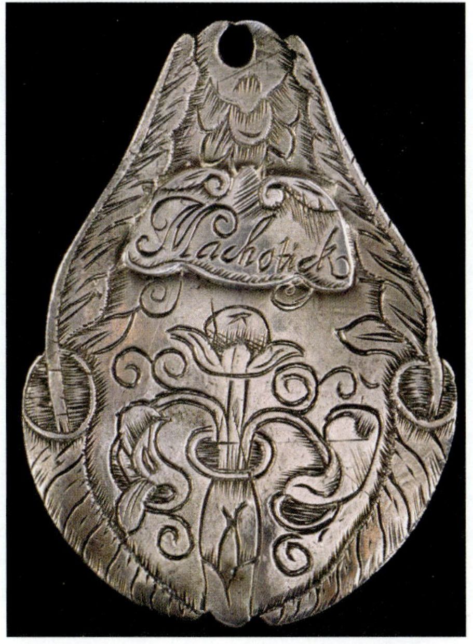


Silver badge given to the "king of the Machotick Indians," Virginia, c. 1662–1677. The 1646 treaty between Tsenacommacah and Virginia required Indians to wear a striped coat to enter English territory. In 1662, Virginia required Indians to carry metal passports. Chiefs needed a silver badge like this one presented to the chief of the Machodoc. Other Indians had to use copper badges.

and thought that its congregations had too much power over government. By contrast, the founders of New Haven Colony left Massachusetts Bay because they considered its union of church and state too loose and permissive. They constructed a theocracy in which ministers made the rules. Rhode Island, Connecticut, and New Haven were all fruits of the tension between individual conscience and conformity within Puritanism. Their creation put even more pressure on Algonquians.

## Colonist-Algonquian Wars

Wars, triggered mainly by immigrant demand for land, erupted between colonists and Algonquians in New Netherland, New England, and Virginia between 1636 and 1644. Each resulted in the decimation, relocation, or subjugation of Algonquians who lived on the borders of English and Dutch North America.

New Netherland generally enjoyed amicable relations with Munsee-speaking Algonquian peoples of the lower Hudson Valley until Willem Kieft arrived in 1638 to oversee Dutch West India Company operations. He aggressively acquired land north and east of Manhattan. Colonists who resettled those areas turned cattle and pigs loose to forage and devour crops that Munsee women planted. Kieft fanned Munsee resentment by demanding tribute to bolster New Amsterdam's defenses. Indians,

### TIMELINE 1555–1648

**1555**
English merchants found Muscovy Company to trade with Russia

**1565**
Spanish mariners discover route from Philippines back to western North America

**1573**
Philip II of Spain issues Royal Orders for New Discoveries

**1580s**
French merchants establish trade in beaver pelts with Indians in Canada

**1585**
English launch colony at Roanoke

**1586**
Sir Francis Drake attacks and destroys St. Augustine

**1587**
English abandon Roanoke colony

**1597–1601**
Guales rebel against Spanish in Florida

**1598**
Spanish forces conquer New Mexico

Edict of Nantes grants tolerance to France's Huguenots

**1601**
Apaches begin to acquire horses from Pueblo peoples

**1602–1603**
Sebastián Vizcaíno explores and maps coast of California

**1607**
**May** Employees of Virginia Company found Jamestown

**December** Tsenacommacah warriors take John Smith captive

**1608**
Spanish officials decide to remain in Florida and New Mexico

French colonists found Quebec

**1609–1613**
First Virginia-Tsenacommacah war

**1609**
French colonists ally with the Montagnais, Algonquin, and Huron against the Mohawks

Henry Hudson sails up river that bears his name and founds New Netherland

**1610**
Santa Fé, New Mexico founded

**1614**
Virginia planters begin to export tobacco

**1616**
Bermudans purchase first unfree Africans brought to English America

**1616–1618**
Disease decimates Algonquians along New England coast

**1618**
Virginia Company permits colonists to own land

Thirty Years' War begins in Europe

**1619**
Virginia planters purchase first shipment of unfree Africans to mainland English North America

Virginia Company permits colonists to establish first representative assembly in English North America

**1620**
**November** Adult male Pilgrims sign Mayflower Compact

**December** Pilgrims found Plymouth Colony

**1621**
Dutch West India Company founded and charged to govern New Netherland

**1622–1632**
Second Virginia-Tsenacommacah War

provoked by the Dutch militia, attacked Staten Island in 1641. The war raged for four years, forcing colonists to seek shelter within New Amsterdam and claiming the lives of Anne Hutchinson and thousands of Munsees. Indians soon vacated most of the lower Hudson Valley and western Long Island.

As war raged around Manhattan, another conflict engulfed Virginia and Tsenacommacah. The colony's expansion, driven by English immigrants and their desire for more land for tobacco, provoked Opechancanough's warriors to attack in 1644. They killed 500 colonists. Virginia militiamen retaliated by storming Algonquian villages and massacring their inhabitants. Two years later, they captured Opechancanough and killed the elderly paramount chief. Officials forced his successor Necotowance to sign a peace treaty that declared that his people were English subjects. Indians could no longer enter English communities without passes. Necotowance and those under his authority had to return guns, Africans, and runaway Indian servants. Thomas Rolfe, Pocahontas's son, fought for Virginia. His service earned him an appointment to run a fort in Chickahominy territory, a position that enabled him to acquire hundreds of acres.

The most complex conflict pitted Pequots against Massachusetts Bay, Connecticut, Narragansetts, and Mohegans. Pequot control over the wampum trade and access to European goods antagonized Mohegans, who were then Pequot tributaries, and

**1622**
Dutch merchants create of wampum industry

**1624**
James I puts Virginia under direct royal rule

Colonization of St. Christopher, first permanent English colony in the West Indies, begins

**1625**
Jesuits arrive in New France

**1626**
New Amsterdam (now New York City) founded

**1627**
English begin to colonize Barbados

**1628**
English begin to colonize Nevis

**1629**
English Puritans found Massachusetts Bay Colony

**1630–1642**
More than 13,000 English emigrate to New England in "Great Migration"

**1630**
Providence Island Company forms and begins to plan colonization of Providence Island in Caribbean

**1632**
Publication of Jesuit Relations begins

English begin to colonize Antigua

**1633**
French-Huron alliance renegotiated to require Jesuit missions within Huron Confederacy

**1634**
Maryland founded

**1635**
Connecticut founded

**1636**
Roger Williams banished from Massachusetts Bay and founds Providence, Rhode Island

Suffrage in Massachusetts Bay restricted to adult male church members

Harvard College founded

**1636–1637**
Pequot War in New England

**1637**
New Haven Colony founded

**1638**
Anne Hutchinson banished from Massachusetts Bay

**1639**
Printing press at Harvard, English America's first, begins operating

**1640**
Dutch West India Company issues Charter of Freedoms and Exemptions for New Netherland

**1641**
Massachusetts Bay becomes first English North American colony to recognize slavery as a legal institution

**1641–1643**
Miantonomi attempts to organize Indian alliance against New England

**1641–1645**
Kieft's War rages in New Netherland

**1643**
United Colonies of New England forms

**1644–1646**
Third Virginia-Tsenacommacah War

**1648**
Thirty Years' War ends in Europe with Treaty of Westphalia

Dutch independence recognized

Narragansetts. A smallpox epidemic weakened Pequots, who fretted as Narragansetts and Mohegans negotiated with Massachusetts Bay leaders. They saw war with Pequots as a way to unite a fractious society and slake demand for land.

The **Pequot War** erupted in 1636. Its bloodiest chapter came in May 1637, when an English-Narragansett-Mohegan force surrounded a Pequot village populated by hundreds of women, children, and elderly men. The Indian allies set fire to the village, and the English shot whoever fled. Only a handful of Pequots survived the English onslaught. This appalled the Narragansett warriors, who complained that English warfare "is too furious, and slays too many men." English and Algonquian forces mopped up Pequot resistance over the next few months. They executed many Pequot men and permitted a small autonomous community of Pequots to remain in their homeland.

Colonists and Indians divided the remaining Pequots. Narragansetts and Mohegans adopted or executed some; colonists bound the rest as servants or sold them into slavery in the West Indies. They shipped a few Pequots to the Puritan colony on Providence Island, where officials described them as "the Cannibal Negroes brought from New England." In exchange New England received enslaved Africans. Massachusetts Bay soon became English North America's first colony to legalize slavery. The 1641 Body of Liberties sanctioned slavery for "lawful Captives in Just Wars, (and such strangers) as willingly sell themselves or are sold to us," a definition that in most colonists' eyes included the Pequots.

English and Algonquians drew different lessons from the war. Most immigrants rejoiced; it opened more land and demonstrated English might. Indians responded in a variety of ways. In 1638, Quinnipiacs, outnumbered by residents of New Haven Colony, agreed to surrender most of their land and confine themselves to a reservation. Mohegans, led by **Uncas**, concluded that it was better to side with the English than fight them. Narragansetts found the new balance of power disturbing. They had expected the war to confirm them as southern New England's largest power. Instead, the English claimed land, influence, and Pequot captives that Narragansetts considered rightfully theirs and treated them as subjects.

The Narragansett sachem **Miantonomi** was particularly offended. By the early 1640s, he had concluded that the English had become too powerful for one Indian nation to contain, so he began to recruit Mohawks and Algonquians throughout southern New England and Long Island to ally against the foreigners. In 1642, Miantonomi urged that Montauks join his cause and see themselves as nearly all English saw them, as *Indians* first and foremost, who shared more in common with each other than they did with the newcomers. He explained, "we must be one as they are, otherwise we shall be all gone shortly." If Indians did not unite, the Narragansett sachem predicted, hungry livestock and the voracious English appetite for land would ruin the world that Indians had made and claim Indians as casualties.

Miantonomi's words fell mostly on deaf ears among the Indian peoples he had hoped to reach, but colonists paid rapt attention. In 1643, Massachusetts Bay, Plymouth, Connecticut, and New Haven formed the **United Colonies of New England** for their mutual defense. Its commissioners urged Uncas to capture Miantonomi, who was killed while in Mohegan custody later that year. Uncas had played, and would continue to play, a role similar to that which Massasoit filled for Plymouth in the 1620s. To most Mohegans, that seemed the best way to meet the challenges they faced. Some Narragansetts chose a different path. They teamed up with Rhode Islanders, excluded from the United Colonies, to take their case straight to Charles I. In a 1644 letter, Canonicus and Pessacus, Miantonomi's uncle and brother, requested protection from English colonists as his loyal subjects and as their equals. Charles was then facing a rebellion in which most Puritans on both sides of the Atlantic sought to overthrow him. He could not have paid the petition much mind. Still, like Miantonomi's proposition, it was a novel way in which Indians employed imported ideas in a bid to regain control over a world that three generations earlier had been entirely theirs.

### STUDY QUESTIONS FOR SEEKING GOD, SEIZING LAND, REAPING CONFLICT, 1625 TO C. 1640

1. **England's North American colonies grew more rapidly than New Netherland or New France. Why? What impact did such rapid growth have on Indians?**
2. **Would Angela's life have been significantly different had she arrived in New Amsterdam rather than Jamestown? If so, how so? If not, why not?**

## Summary

- The Spanish Empire initiated the colonial era of what became the mainland United States by clinging to Florida and New Mexico, while England emerged as Spain's main rival in North America and the Northeast's Indians became more integral participants in Atlantic trade networks.
- In 1607, English, French, and Dutch immigrants began to colonize small areas on the Atlantic coast in lands dominated by Algonquians, with whom they had tense relationships usually marked by mutual misunderstanding and from whom they sought land, knowledge, and goods to send overseas for profit.
- Missionary activity among Indians in New Mexico and New France intensified after 1625, as did English, Dutch, and African migration to North America, which led to the creation of new colonies, the expansion of older ones, and greater demands on Indians that led to war and the subjugation of some Algonquian peoples by the 1640s.

## Key Terms and People

**Benavides, Alonso de** *69*
**Black Legend** *54*
**Champlain, Samuel de** *61*
**Charles I** *71*
**Charter of Freedoms and Exemptions** **70**
**common law** *61*
**commons** *53*
**conversion test** *72*
**covenant** *72*
**Dutch West India Company (DWIC)** **72**
**Edict of Nantes** *53*
**fur trade** *56*
**half-freedom** *70*
**Harriot, Thomas** *54*
**House of Burgesses** *61*
**Hutchinson, Ann** *75*
**indentured servants** *60*
**James I** *48*
**Jamestown** *45*
**joint-stock company** *53*
**Kieft, Willem** *70*
**kiva** *69*
**Manteo** *54*
**Massachusetts Bay Company** *71*
**matrilineal** *69*
**Miantonomi** *78*
**Oñate, Juan de** *51*
**Pequot War** *78*
**Philip II** *49*
**Pocahontas** *45*
**Powhatan** *45*
**Raleigh, Walter** *54*
**Rolfe, John** *48*
**Royal Orders for New Discoveries** **49**
**Smith, John** *45*
**Thirty Years' War** *64*
**Tisquantum** *65*
**Uncas** *78*
**United Colonies of New England** *78*
**Virginia Company of London** *45*
**White, John** *54*
**Williams, Roger** *73*
**Winthrop, John** *72*

## Reviewing Chapter 2

1. In what ways did the movement of people, goods, and ideas shape North America between 1565 and the 1640s?
2. Cultural differences were mainly responsible for conflicts between Europeans and Indians. Is this statement correct? If so, why? If not, why not?
3. In what ways did religion influence events in North America between 1565 and 1640?

## Further Reading

Brewer, Holly. *By Birth or Consent: Children, Law, and the Anglo-American Revolution in Authority*. Chapel Hill: University of North Carolina Press, 2005. A fascinating account that accords a central role to Puritans in the shaping of modern Anglo-American concepts of rights, be they children's, spouses', or parents' rights.

Calloway, Colin G. *One Vast Winter Count: The Native American West before Lewis and Clark*. Lincoln and London: University of Nebraska Press, 2003. An overview of Indian history from the arrival of humans to the early 1800s that focuses on southwestern and Plains peoples and how they adapted to European invaders.

Games, Alison. *Migration and the Origins of the English Atlantic World*. Cambridge, Mass.: Harvard University Press, 1999. Tracks English men and women who migrated through London in the 1630s to North America and the Caribbean and examines how they fared in their new homes.

Kupperman, Karen Ordahl. *The Jamestown Project*. Cambridge, Mass.: Belknap Press of Harvard University Press, 2007. A comprehensive history published on the 400th anniversary of the founding of Jamestown which argues that early Virginia provided a successful model to the English for how to colonize the Americas.

Townsend, Camilla. *Pocahontas and the Powhatan Dilemma*. New York: Hill and Wang, 2004. A sensitive account of Pocahontas and her world that clearly spells out the challenges that English colonization posed for her and for Tsenacommacah's residents.

Van Zandt, Cynthia J. *Brothers Among Nations: The Pursuit of Intercultural Alliances in Early America, 1580–1660*. New York: Oxford University Press, 2008. A pathbreaking exploration of the ties that Europeans and Indians forged to one another and of the significance of such ties for early European efforts to colonize eastern North America.

# Visual Review

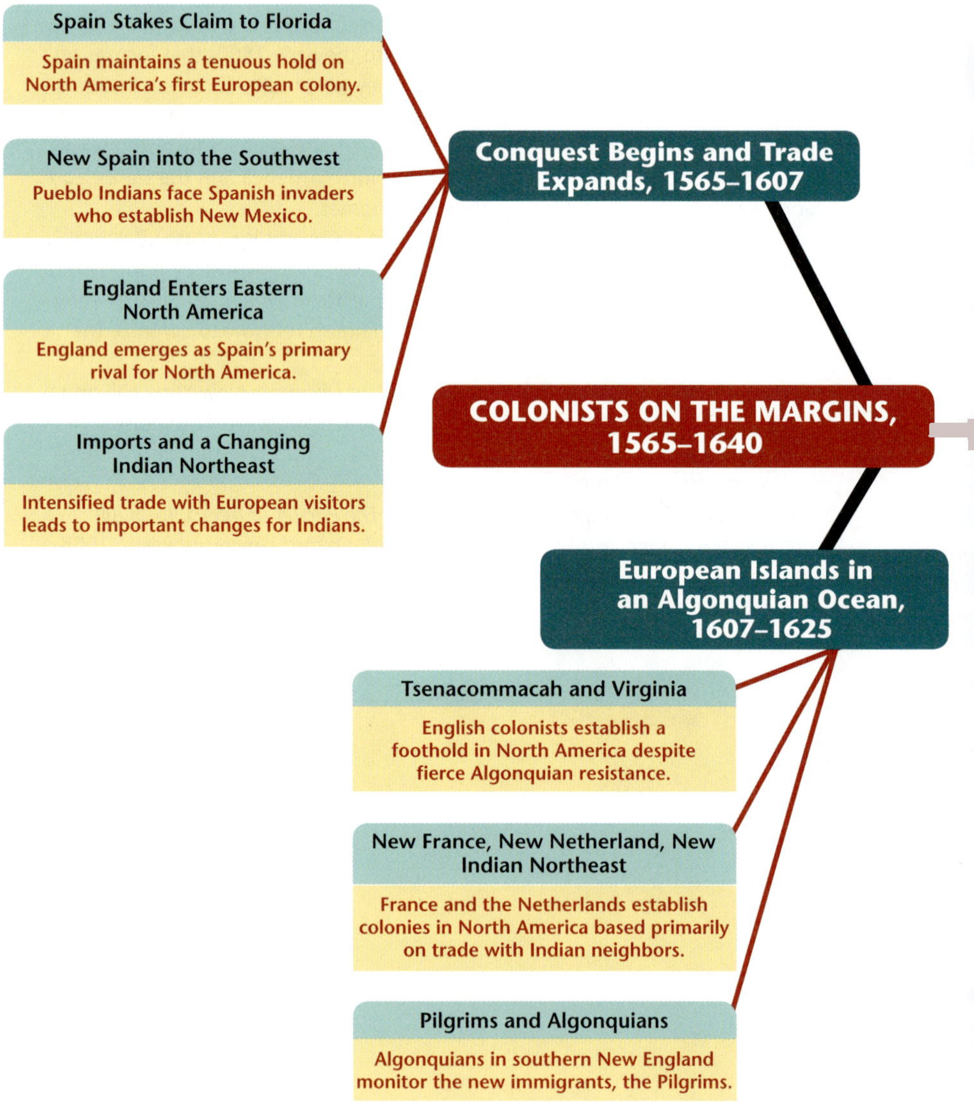

## COLONISTS ON THE MARGINS, 1565–1640

### Conquest Begins and Trade Expands, 1565–1607

**Spain Stakes Claim to Florida**

Spain maintains a tenuous hold on North America's first European colony.

**New Spain into the Southwest**

Pueblo Indians face Spanish invaders who establish New Mexico.

**England Enters Eastern North America**

England emerges as Spain's primary rival for North America.

**Imports and a Changing Indian Northeast**

Intensified trade with European visitors leads to important changes for Indians.

### European Islands in an Algonquian Ocean, 1607–1625

**Tsenacommacah and Virginia**

English colonists establish a foothold in North America despite fierce Algonquian resistance.

**New France, New Netherland, New Indian Northeast**

France and the Netherlands establish colonies in North America based primarily on trade with Indian neighbors.

**Pilgrims and Algonquians**

Algonquians in southern New England monitor the new immigrants, the Pilgrims.

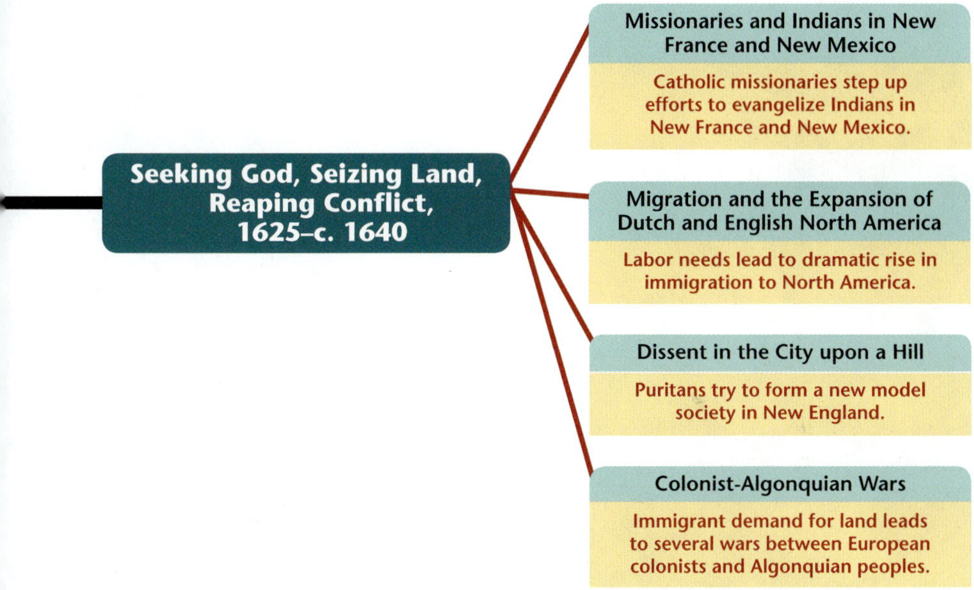

**Seeking God, Seizing Land, Reaping Conflict, 1625–c. 1640**

**Missionaries and Indians in New France and New Mexico**

Catholic missionaries step up efforts to evangelize Indians in New France and New Mexico.

**Migration and the Expansion of Dutch and English North America**

Labor needs lead to dramatic rise in immigration to North America.

**Dissent in the City upon a Hill**

Puritans try to form a new model society in New England.

**Colonist-Algonquian Wars**

Immigrant demand for land leads to several wars between European colonists and Algonquian peoples.

# 3 Forging Tighter Bonds

## 1640 to the 1690s

"Who is the father?" the midwife demanded of Anne Orthwood, an indentured servant who was in the throes of labor in the summer of 1664. The young woman identified him as John Kendall, one of Virginia's most prominent men and her former master. Orthwood gave birth to twins before suffering an agonizing death, probably from an infection she contracted during childbirth. One baby died. The other, Jasper, faced a hard life. John Kendall denied he was the father. County officials agreed, but did not want taxpayers to foot the bill for raising Jasper, so they found Kendall legally responsible for his son's care. Kendall soon bound Jasper out to a friend who owned a nearby plantation. For the next 22 years, Jasper worked as an indentured servant. In 1686, he sued for his freedom, won, and then disappeared from local records.

Anne Orthwood's path to an early grave and Jasper's passage through servitude to freedom resulted from deep changes taking place in Virginia between the 1660s and 1680s. Anne was born into poverty and a fatherless home in Bristol, England. In 1662, she joined a torrent of nearly 30,000 English streaming to Virginia and Maryland during the 1650s and 1660s to work as servants. Their labor, and that of a slowly increasing population of enslaved Africans, more than doubled Virginia's tobacco exports during the

◄ Elsje (Rutgers) Schuyler Vas, 1723, attributed to Gerardus Duyckinck I

**CHAPTER OUTLINE**

# America in the World

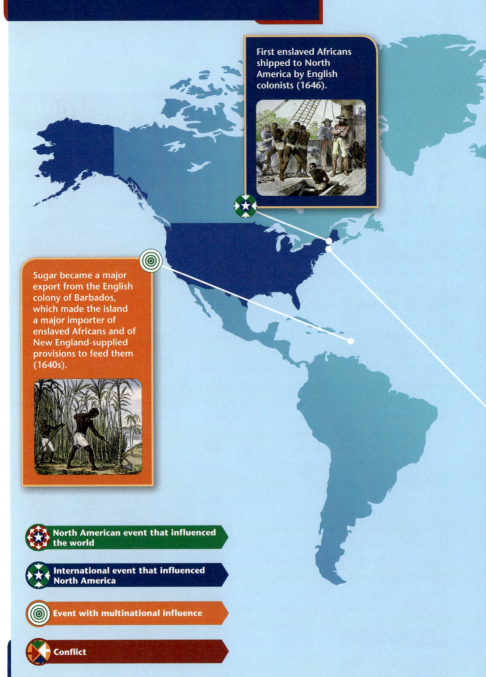

First enslaved Africans shipped to North America by English colonists (1646).

Sugar became a major export from the English colony of Barbados, which made the island a major importer of enslaved Africans and of New England-supplied provisions to feed them (1640s).

North American event that influenced the world

International event that influenced North America

Event with multinational influence

Conflict

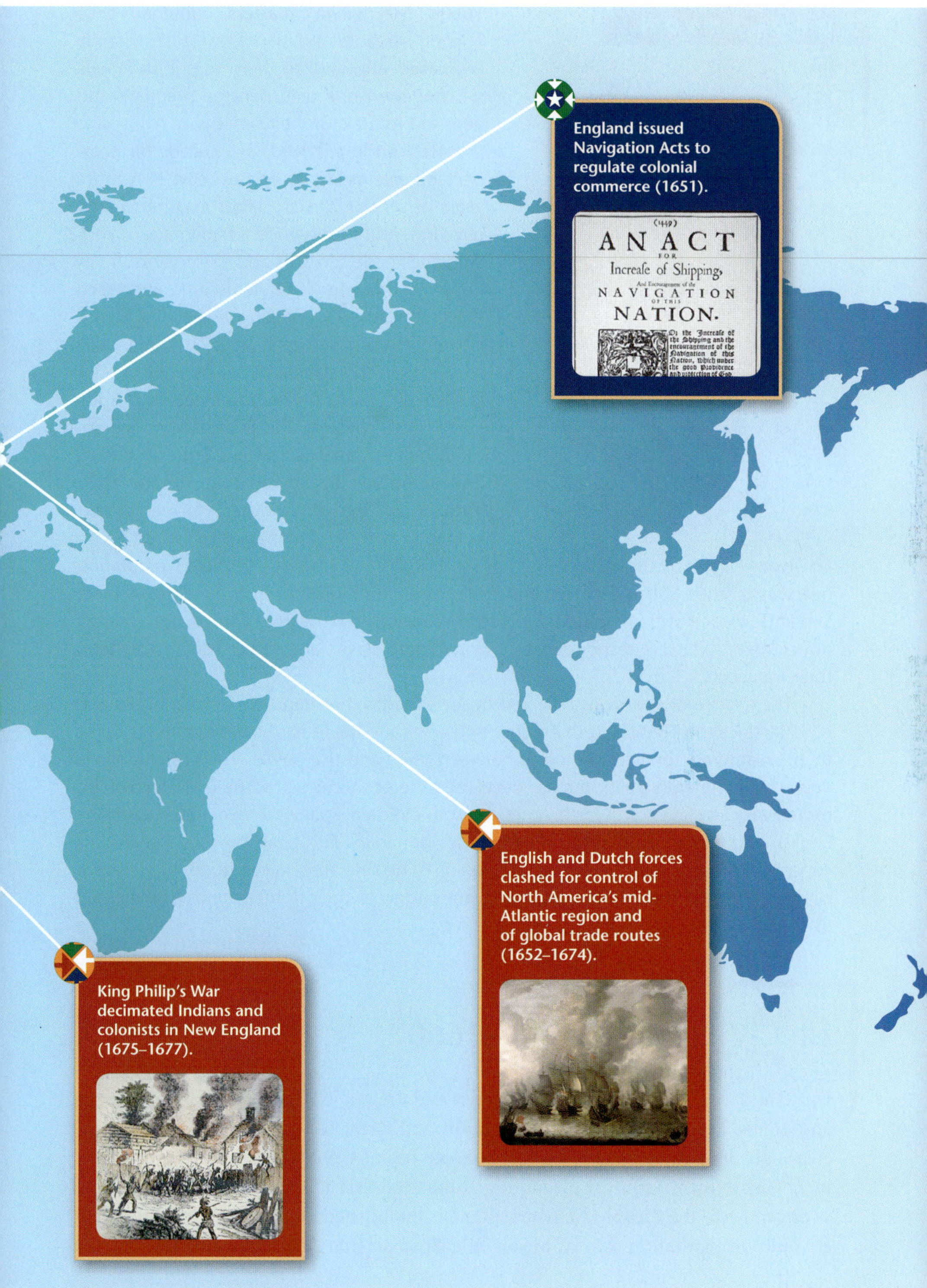
England issued Navigation Acts to regulate colonial commerce (1651).
(1449)
AN ACT
FOR
Increase of Shipping,
And Encouragement of the
NAVIGATION
OF THIS
NATION.
English and Dutch forces clashed for control of North America's mid-Atlantic region and of global trade routes (1652–1674).
King Philip's War decimated Indians and colonists in New England (1675–1677).

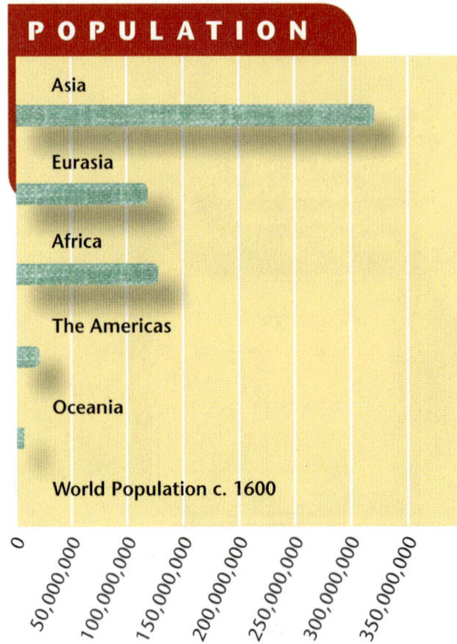


1660s. Meanwhile, masters tightened their grip on servants and slaves. In 1662, Virginia lawmakers empowered them to punish female servants like Anne who became pregnant and deprived masters of their services.

Had Anne survived, she faced the prospect of several lashes and at least two more years of servitude. Hard labor and harsh laws gave indentured servitude a bad image in England and made servants and ex-servants in Virginia resentful. In 1672, legislators addressed these concerns by enacting a law that emancipated male bastards at age 21, three years sooner than the standards set by English poor law. Jasper's lawsuit was a direct result. Despite his master's protests that English poor law entitled him to Jasper's services until he turned 24, Anne's son based his claim on the 1672 Virginia law that his mother's former master helped to write and managed to escape bondage two years early. But the change in the law did not improve Virginia's reputation overseas or calm sullen servants and ex-servants. Immigration from England slowed. Servants, ex-servants, and slaves joined a rebellion that nearly toppled the colony's government. Masters responded by buying more slaves and fewer servants to tend their tobacco.

The Orthwoods' ordeals reflected major changes that had taken place locally and globally since the 1640s. North America's colonies and the Indian societies that bordered them weathered conflicts and crises between 1640 and the 1690s. Their resolution redrew the continent's political map, developed the economies of some English colonies, rooted African slavery in North American soil, checked Spanish power, and made the English and French empires North America's dominant European powers. Indians still controlled most of North America. But colonists, be they free, in servitude, or enslaved, claimed and held more of the continent, due largely to their tighter bonds to the world overseas.

## UNCIVIL WARS, 1640–1660

Death and violence gripped North America and the Anglo-Atlantic world in the 1640s and 1650s. Epidemics ravaged the Iroquois and Great Lakes peoples, fueling an increasingly destructive cycle of warfare between Indians. A civil war in England echoed in English North America, prompting some colonists to fight and others to forge stronger ties to the Caribbean, where planters established English America's first society built on plantation slavery. Meanwhile, Spanish friars expanded mission systems in Florida and New Mexico, sparking Indian rebellions and sharper conflicts with those colonies' governors.

## Smallpox and War Plague the Great Lakes

The arrival of thousands of Dutch and English colonists in the 1630s, many of whom carried the smallpox virus, enabled the disease to take root in northeastern North America. The first epidemic struck in 1633, followed by another six years later. The virus killed a disproportionate number of Indians between the ages of 15 and 40, the people who usually did most of the farming, hunting, and caring for children, the sick, and the elderly. Traditional Indian remedies worsened the epidemics. By the early 1640s, epidemics had probably killed more than half the population of the Iroquois, reducing it to around 10,000. They ravaged the league's peoples and their Indian neighbors over the next 30 years.

Grief and rage at the toll that smallpox took set the Iroquois and their neighbors on the warpath. The epidemic of 1639–1640 launched a conflict between the Iroquois and Huron that raged for nine years. Some historians call it the "**Beaver Wars**" because

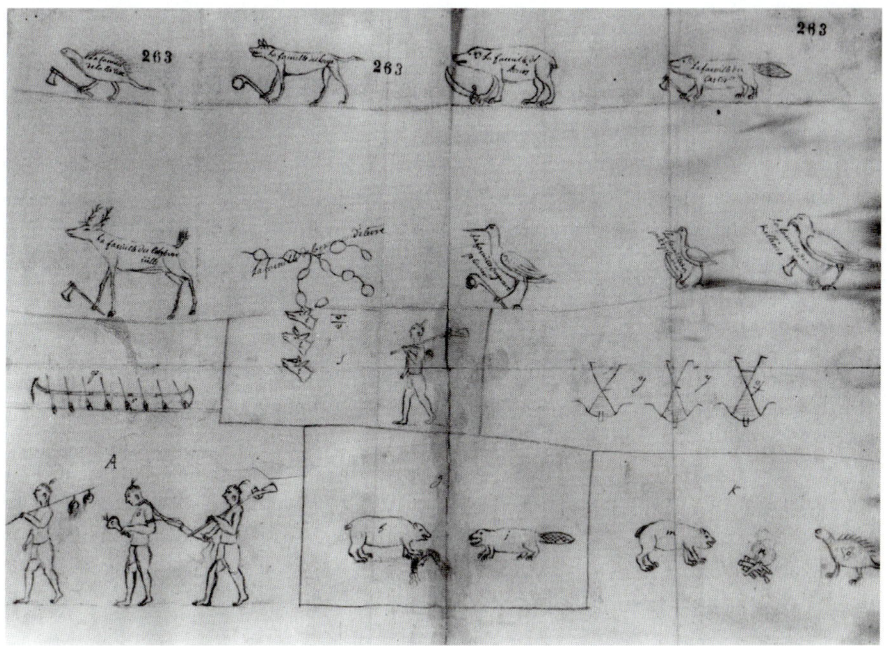


French drawing of an Iroquois (probably Seneca) tree bark carving depicting a mourning war raid. Each member of the war party drew the totem animal of his clan, each holding a weapon. The three upside down figures at center right indicate that the warriors killed two men and one woman. At bottom left one warrior carries two scalps, while the other watches over a captive.

control of hunting grounds was often the combatants' objective. Hunters had already emptied much of New England, New York, and Pennsylvania of beaver, whose pelts bought firearms, hatchets, and other imports that enabled Indians to defend themselves and live better.

Indians needed better access to pelts, but replacing the kin claimed by disease and violence mattered far more to them. Indeed, the Iroquois waged "mourning wars" principally to take their Algonquian- or Iroquoian-speaking neighbors (such as Hurons) captive. Most Indians in eastern North America usually targeted children, adolescents, and women—groups considered most likely to acculturate—for adoption. Men taken prisoner, deemed least likely to accept life in captivity, were often symbolically incorporated in a different way. The torture inflicted on them allowed captors to assuage their grief and avenge the loss of loved ones. The captive demonstrated his manhood by meeting his excruciating death stoically.

By contrast, captives adopted into a clan usually assumed the place, and often the name and identity, of a loved one who had died. Such strangers became kin, but it did not mean that they assimilated completely. Jesuit missionaries to the main Onondaga village in the 1650s and 1660s organized three separate congregations, two for captives and one for native-born Onondaga. In many Iroquois villages, two in three residents might be adoptees.

A steady supply of Dutch firearms from New Netherland enabled the Iroquois to outgun most of their Indian foes from the 1630s into the 1660s. The Huron, long allied with the French, and the Indians who sheltered them were perhaps the mourning wars' biggest losers. The Iroquois ended the "Beaver Wars" by storming two Huron towns and a Jesuit mission and killing hundreds in 1649. Hurons who evaded captivity fled north and west, while the Petuns, closely associated with the Huron, sought shelter among other Iroquoian-speaking peoples—the Neutrals and the Eries. Iroquois warriors overwhelmed each as the refugees streamed west to Wisconsin. There they regrouped to form a new people, the Huron-Petuns or Wyandot, in the 1650s and 1660s alongside thousands of Algonquians, also forced to flee their homelands by epidemics and Iroquois raids. Together the refugees plotted revenge against the Iroquois.

In just one generation the Great Lakes region and the Iroquois were transformed. Microbes and mourning wars had depopulated a vast area that stretched from the Great Lakes south to the Ohio River and east to the Susquehanna River. The once-mighty Huron Confederacy had become a diaspora, with most of its people living in captivity within the Iroquois longhouse.

## English Civil Wars and the Remaking of English America

Across the Atlantic, the English divided into those who believed that Charles I was their supreme leader and those who insisted that **Parliament** was. In 1642, the factions took up arms against each other. Most Puritans sided with Parliamentarians, who in 1649 tried Charles, beheaded him, and proclaimed that England had become a commonwealth. Four years later, the Puritan general **Oliver Cromwell**, commander

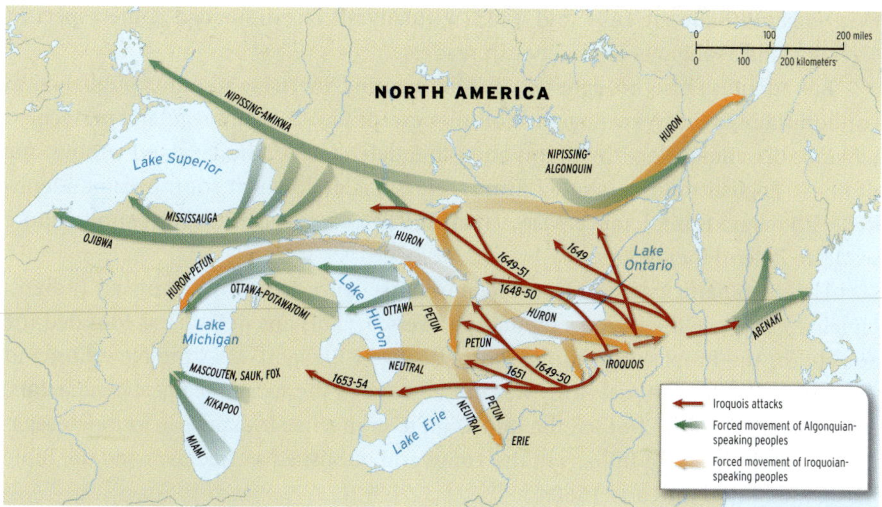


▲ **Map 3.1**

**Iroquois Mourning Wars and the Dispersal of Great Lakes and New England Peoples, 1648–1653** The Iroquois League's mourning wars took their greatest toll on nearby Indian peoples between 1648 and 1653. This map shows peoples claimed or dispersed by Iroquois attacks and where those who escaped Iroquois raids sought refuge. Refugees who headed for Quebec were usually Christian converts.

of the New Model Army, staged a military coup and named himself Lord Protector. Cromwell died in 1658 after trying to appoint his son to succeed him. By then the English had tired of political instability. Most acclaimed the ascent of Charles's son and heir, **Charles II**, to the throne in 1660, an event that finally ended the **English Civil War**.

England's civil war roiled Maryland between 1645 and 1647. The colony's royalist governor, Leonard Calvert, ended the conflict by leading an invasion from Virginia. Calvert, soon on his deathbed, named Margaret Brent executrix of his will. She later served as local representative for Calvert's heir. Brent belonged to a prominent family, so she commanded respect from everyone in the colony. In 1648, she tried to fulfill the duties of her office by demanding the right to speak and vote in Maryland's Assembly. The governor denied Brent's request because of her sex.

Leaders of six colonies, including Maryland and Virginia, responded to news of Charles's execution by declaring allegiance to his son. Barbados and Virginia offered refuge to royalists fleeing England. In 1652, a Commonwealth fleet forced Virginia governor **William Berkeley** to accept England's new rulers before its commander removed him from office.

In New England, England's civil war brought long-awaited opportunities and unforeseen challenges. Reformers in England sought an alternative to Anglicanism. In the early 1640s many thought that New England might offer one, a prospect that delighted Massachusetts Bay leaders. London printers published over 20 works about

New England between 1641 and 1643. Virtually all recommended some aspect of New England's religious life to English readers.

But attention also brought unwelcome scrutiny. In 1644, accounts published in London claimed that New England colonies except Rhode Island regularly persecuted religious dissenters. Roger Williams and other defenders of Rhode Island wrote some of them. English opinion shifted against New England, which soon became identified with religious intolerance. Massachusetts Bay leaders responded by penning more works to defend themselves.

They also participated in New England's first concerted effort to convert Indians, largely to improve the region's reputation overseas. Puritans in England founded the Society for the Propagation of the Gospel in New England, later the **New England Company**. The New Model Army was initially one of the society's largest benefactors. The missionary **John Eliot** led the campaign to evangelize Indians. He founded separate towns for baptized Indians in the 1650s and published a catechism and the Bible in Algonquian in the early 1660s.

Eliot's work generated good press in England, but it did not make New England's union of church and state more appealing to English reformers seeking an alternative to the Church of England. When the English Civil War began, New England's orthodox leaders rejoiced that their vision of a godly society might be transplanted in England. By 1649, developments across the Atlantic had dashed such hopes.

Events in England also helped give rise to colonial North America's first witch scare. As many as 200,000 people in Europe, at least three in four of them women,

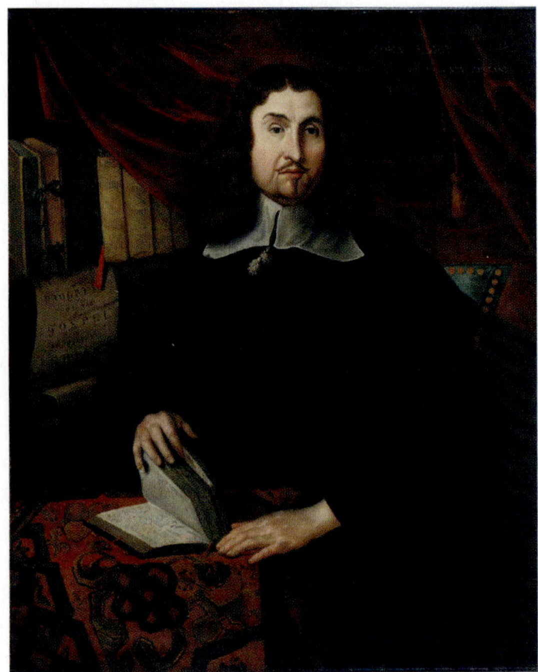

John Eliot, 1659. Eliot led the campaign to convert Indians in New England. He began to organize "praying towns," separate communities for Christian Indians, during the 1650s and later translated the Bible into the Massachusetts dialect of Algonquian. Eliot also lobbied vociferously against the Indian slave trade that arose during King Philip's War.

were accused of witchcraft during the 1500s and 1600, and 60,000 were executed. Witch hunts peaked in England in the mid-1640s, particularly in East Anglia, birthplace of many New Englanders. Connecticut prosecuted and executed its first witch in 1647. In all, 79 New England colonists, 61 of them women, were accused of witchcraft; 33 were tried, and 15 were executed between 1647 and 1663.

Some accused witches belonged to a new egalitarian sect that originated in England during the Civil War. Its members called themselves the **Society of Friends**. Their enemies knew them as "Quakers" because their bodies "quaked" when they encountered God. Friends preached that people would find little of God's will in biblical verses, ministers' sermons, or formal services. Instead, God had given everyone an "inner light"—an innate ability to determine what God wanted for them and for the world. Friends preached and practiced pacifism, did not remove their hats upon

"The Quakers Meeting." The Society of Friends offended many English for several reasons, significant among them their willingness to permit women to speak during church services. This mezzotint, produced in the late 1600s, intended to satirize Quakers by showing them in meeting as a woman stood on a box and preached to them.

meeting someone who outranked them socially, and addressed superiors in familiar terms, using "thee" or "thou" rather than the formal "you." They also created separate and autonomous governing structures for men and women and permitted women such as Mary Dyer to preach and serve as missionaries.

Such beliefs and practices brought Quakers persecution on both sides of the Atlantic, especially in most of New England. Massachusetts Bay officials executed four Quakers between 1659 and 1661, Mary Dyer among them. Quakers publicized such persecution as they lobbied English authorities to revoke New England colonies' charters.

The English Civil War created bigger headaches for New England's leaders. The war halted the stream of migrants into New England and set it in reverse. One in seven who sailed to New England between 1630 and 1642 returned to England. Cromwell recruited some New England ministers to lead congregations in parts of Ireland that the New Model Army conquered. He also tried to lure New Englanders to colonize Jamaica, seized by English forces in 1655.

New England colonists had reason to seek a better life elsewhere. The English Civil War had provoked a full-blown economic depression. New England ran a large trade deficit with English merchants. The savings of thousands of English immigrants had provided the funds that bridged New England's trade gap during the 1630s by paying for what colonists imported from England. When the migrants stopped coming in the early 1640s, so did the money.

Colonists had to find other ways to earn income and produce some of what they could no longer afford to import. English migrants to New England were among the Atlantic world's best-educated people and many had skills to process what the region's fields, forests, and seas offered. Axe-wielding men cut into massive forests, furnishing local and Caribbean carpenters with wood. The English Civil War sharply reduced the number of English vessels that fished off New England's coast, so crews of colonists filled the breech. They caught and salted cod, packing the fish in locally crafted barrels. New England-made ships ferried the fishermen into the sea and back.

The English Civil War profoundly altered colonists' participation in Atlantic networks. The conflict accelerated the development of New England's shipbuilding industry. By the early 1640s New England-built ships, sailed by colonists, took salted fish, salt pork, horses, and timber to Spain, Portugal, and the West Indies. New England shipyards soon employed thousands exporting vessels to England. Thousands more found work sailing the Atlantic or pulling cod from it.

New England vessels also began to transport enslaved Africans. In 1646, a ship arrived in Boston from West Africa carrying the first enslaved Africans whom mainland English colonists brought across the Atlantic. Authorities charged the captain with kidnapping and repatriated his victims at public expense. The region's engagement in the Atlantic slave trade and its ties to the Caribbean prompted Rhode Island to outlaw lifelong slavery in 1652. The bill's authors noted that "there is a common course practiced among English men" to buy Africans so that "they may have them for service or slaves forever." Antislavery views did not prevail. By the 1670s, Boston merchants were buying small numbers of enslaved people in Madagascar and selling them in the Caribbean and North America.

Necessity compelled New England to lay the foundation of a diverse economy. Heavy immigration was the region's economic lifeline in the 1630s. Colonists' trade with other North American colonies, Europe, and the West Indies sustained them a generation later. To John Winthrop, such ties seemed heaven sent. Just as Massachusetts Bay seemed about to go bankrupt, "it pleased the Lord to open to us a Trade with Barbados."

## Planters and Slaves of the Caribbean

In 1627, English colonists splashed ashore on Barbados. Thirteen years later, Barbados, just 144 square miles, had as many English as Virginia. By 1680, it was England's wealthiest and most populous colony. The vast majority were enslaved Africans who toiled and died in the sugar cane fields that blanketed the island.

At first it looked as if Barbados might become a smaller version of Virginia without Indians, a place where English grew tobacco on small farms staffed with white indentured servants. Two features soon distinguished Barbados from Virginia. In 1636, the governor declared that all Africans and Indians brought to the island were to be considered slaves unless they had a contract that said otherwise. Planters also began to grow export crops other than tobacco and earn higher profits from them. These included cotton and indigo, source of a brilliant blue dye. The new crops enabled planters to buy more laborers, expand their estates, and experiment with cultivating sugar cane. Their success made them look like good credit risks to London merchants, who issued planters loans to purchase land, enslaved Africans, and the expensive machinery that processed cane into sugar.

Planter ambition, English credit, and the exertions and expertise of thousands of enslaved Africans transformed Barbados. The Dutch West India Company, which then ruled much of northeastern Brazil, most likely shipped Brazilian slaves who knew how to make sugar to Barbados. By the early 1660s, cane covered 60 percent of the island. Barbados soon replaced Brazil as the Americas' biggest supplier of sugar to Europe.

The sugar boom tied Barbados and New England together. Cane fields and mills' need for lumber and fuel to boil cane juice down to sugar claimed most of the island's trees. New England forests provided wood to build and repair mills, and barrels made from New England oak held molasses and sugar that Barbados exported. New England's fields, meadows, and coasts fed Barbadian workers and allowed the majority of them to produce sugar and little else. The more land and labor devoted to cane, the less remained for growing food on Barbados.

The sugar boom of the 1640s accelerated the rise of African slavery and the decline of indentured servitude on Barbados. The more that planters demanded cane, the worse Barbados looked to English servants. Why would anyone choose to leave England and endure years of drudgery in a cane field, especially if most good land was already owned by masters? Young men in London feared that they might be "Barbadosed"—bound and sent away against their will. Many likened servitude to slavery, a natural association, given the rapidly growing numbers of enslaved Africans sentenced to the cane fields and a 1657 Barbados law that barred servants from leaving plantations without a pass from their masters. Servants, many of them Irish prisoners of war, rebelled in 1647, making enslaved African labor look more desirable to planters. In England, members of Parliament criticized the treatment of English servants in Barbados, adding to the planters' interest in enslaved African labor. The sugar boom made England a major participant in the Atlantic slave trade and it created English America's first slave society. In 1672, Charles II chartered the **Royal African Company** and gave it a monopoly over commerce, including the Atlantic slave trade, between Atlantic Africa and the English Empire. Enslaved Africans were already the majority on Barbados and had been for at least a decade.

Most Africans met an early grave. Few had families; planters preferred to buy young men because they considered them better workers. They also calculated that it was cheaper to import people than to ensure that those whom they already enslaved lived longer and healthier lives. Their arithmetic turned cane fields into killing fields. Only the Atlantic slave trade sustained the black majority on Barbados and elsewhere in the English West Indies.

Tighter control of enslaved people and white solidarity sustained planter rule. Barbados legislators sought both by enacting English America's first slave code in 1661. The code prescribed different treatment and different levels of protection before the law for enslaved Africans and white servants. It deputized free white men to police

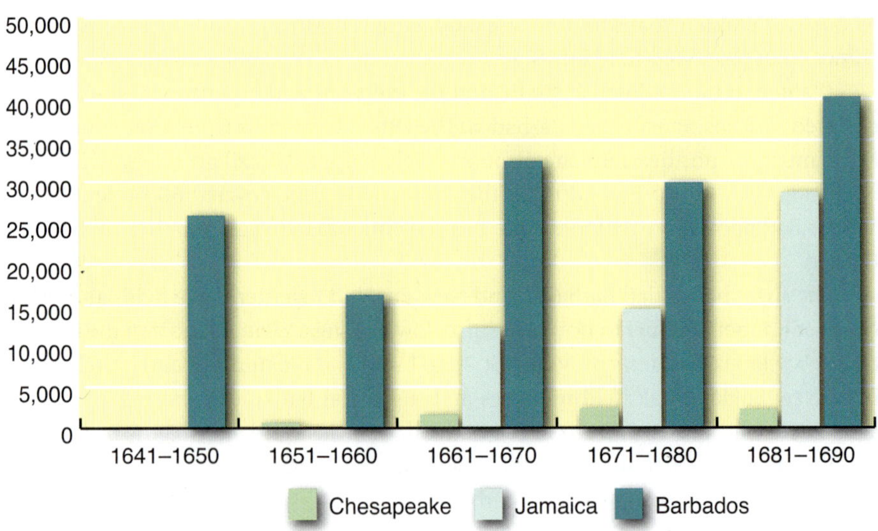


**Figure 3.1**

**Enslaved Africans disembarked in the Chesapeake Colonies, Barbados, and Jamaica (estimated), 1641–1690** More enslaved Africans by far went to the English Caribbean than to English colonies in mainland North America. Over 20 times as many went to Barbados as to Virginia and Maryland between 1641 and 1690, partly because so many died young and overworked in the island's cane fields.

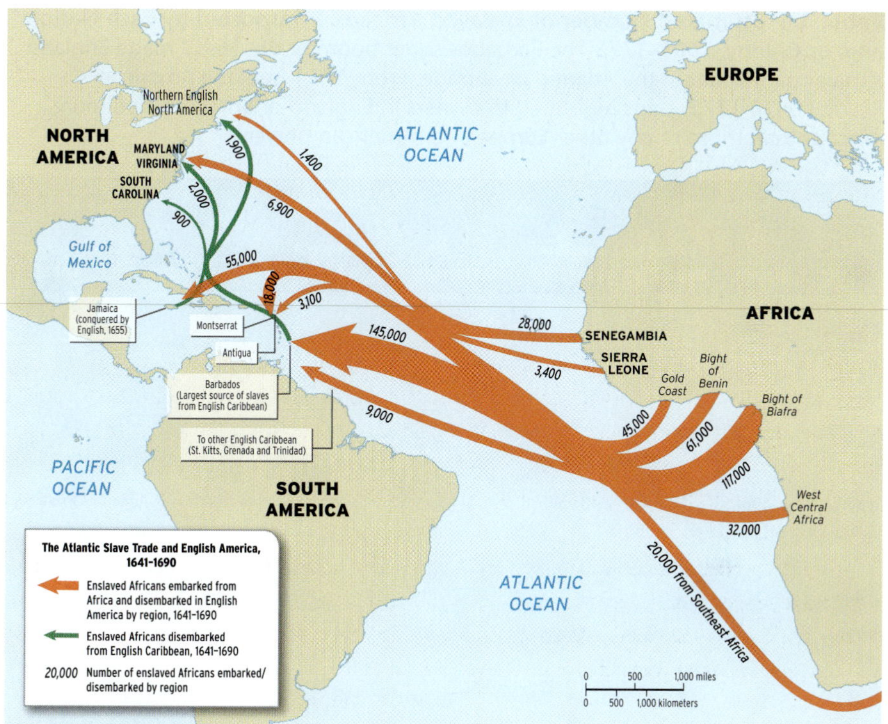


**Map 3.2**

**The Atlantic Slave Trade and English America, 1641–1690** Nearly one enslaved African in four died while crossing the Atlantic to English America between 1641 and 1690. Over half of those who survived the journey landed in Barbados. That island and others in the English Caribbean sent at least 5,000 enslaved Africans to England's mainland North American colonies.

slaves' movements and encouraged them to whip those found without a pass from their masters. The **Barbados slave code** became one of the most influential pieces of legislation in the Anglo-Atlantic world. Many English colonies duplicated portions of it. Four copied it completely, including South Carolina and Georgia.

## Church and Indians in the Southeast and Southwest

In 1633, Spanish friars established the first mission among Apalachee Indians in the Florida Panhandle. Their initiative answered a long-standing invitation from Apalachee chiefs who thought that better relations with the Spanish would bring them more power, prestige, and better access to imports. Growing trade with a St. Augustine that needed Apalachee-grown corn also prompted the gesture.

Unconverted Apalachee and their Chisca allies set seven missions ablaze and drove the Spanish out just 14 years later. Spanish soldiers and Timucua warriors recruited from missions retaliated, attacking an army of thousands. The two sides fought

**Table 3.1 Estimated Number of Enslaved Africans Transported by Each Nation and/or Colony, 1601–1775** The Barbados sugar boom of the 1640s made England a major participant in the Atlantic slave trade. From 1651 until the American Revolution in 1775, ships registered to owners in England or Britain carried more Africans than those of any other European or American power.

| | Spain | Portugal/ Brazil (c) | England/ Britain | Netherlands | British North America (c) | France | Denmark | Totals |
|---|---|---|---|---|---|---|---|---|
| 1601–1625 | 83,496 | 267,519 | 0 | 1,829 | 0 | 0 | 0 | 352,843 |
| 1626–1650 | 44,313 | 201,609 | 33,695 | 31,729 | 824 | 1,827 | 1,053 | 315,050 |
| 1651–1675 | 12,601 | 244,793 | 122,367 | 100,526 | 0 | 7,125 | 653 | 488,064 |
| 1676–1700 | 5,860 | 297,272 | 272,200 | 85,847 | 3,327 | 29,484 | 25,685 | 719,674 |
| 1701–1725 | 0 | 474,447 | 410,597 | 73,816 | 3,277 | 120,939 | 5,833 | 1,088,909 |
| 1726–1750 | 0 | 536,696 | 554,042 | 83,095 | 34,004 | 259,095 | 4,793 | 1,471,725 |
| 1751–1775 | 4,239 | 528,693 | 832,047 | 132,330 | 84,580 | 325,918 | 17,508 | 1,925,314 |
| Totals | 150,509 | 2,551,028 | 2,224,947 | 509,172 | 126,012 | 744,387 | 55,525 | 6,361,580 |

Note: Places that were colonies between 1601 and 1775 are designated above with (c).

to a stalemate. When a smaller Spanish-led force returned, the decimated Apalachee surrendered. They handed over those whom the Spanish believed had led the rebellion. Some were hanged; the rest were sentenced to toil in St. Augustine. Florida's governor also demanded that Apalachee chiefs send laborers to the Spanish town, just as Timucua and Guales did.

The Apalachee integrated into Florida's economy with tragic results. In 1655, an epidemic followed the road that linked Apalachee, Timucua, and St. Augustine, spread largely by Indians forced to transport goods or work in the Spanish town. It devastated Apalachee towns already reeling from Spanish demands for tribute and labor. By mid-century, Apalachee's population plummeted from 30,000 to 10,000. At most 2,500 Timucua and 2,000 Guales survived the epidemic.

Many Timucua could take no more. In 1656, rumors of an English raid led the governor to order Apalachee, Guale, and Timucua chiefs to muster warriors and march to St. Augustine's defense. Lucas Menéndez, a Timucua chief who nursed grievances against the governor, refused to go. He persuaded some of his peers to attack Spanish colonists, but spare friars who ran the missions. Unlike Guale insurgents in 1597 or the Apalachee in 1647, Timucua chiefs accepted missions as integral to their world. They killed or drove off most colonists and communicated with letters written in a

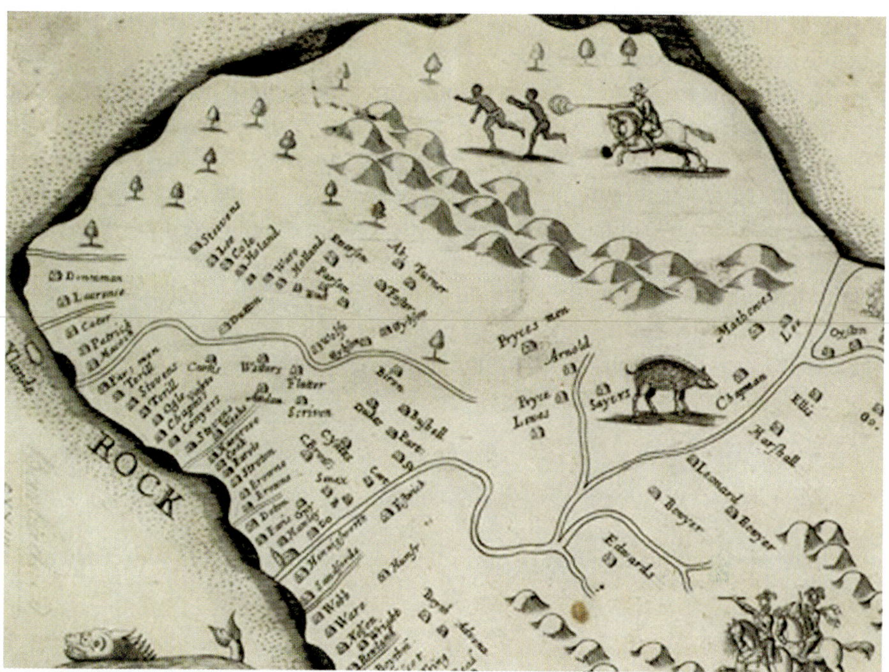


Here two enslaved African fugitives flee a white pursuer. The image illustrates a map that accompanied a history of Barbados written by Richard Ligon, who visited there in the late 1640s. In 1661, Barbados enacted English America's first slave code, much of which addressed the capture and punishment of runaways.

Timucuan alphabet that friars had taught them. Executions and sentences of forced labor in St. Augustine ended the **Timucua revolt**. The Apalachee helped the Spanish regain control. Spanish soldiers and friars regathered the Timucua into missions strewn along the road between Apalachee and St. Augustine. Their forced resettlement depopulated even more of north Florida. Spanish ranchers replaced them with cattle.

The Timucua revolt gave friars the upper hand in their struggle with Florida governors. It rankled them that governor Diego de Rebolledo ridiculed their efforts to reform Indian cultures. In 1658, friars had Rebolledo summoned to Spain to stand trial for using his office to abuse Indians. By 1675, 11,000 Indians lived in missions, most of them in Apalachee. Florida's mission system and the friars would never be more powerful.

Tensions between friars, officials, and Indians also roiled New Mexican politics. Small revolts in Taos in 1639 and in Tewa villages in 1650 temporarily allied church and state, as did rumors of a conspiracy between Pueblos and Indians of northern Mexico. Cultural and linguistic differences made it hard for Pueblos to unite. Taos rebels sought refuge among Apaches, while leaders of the Tewa uprising were hanged and their suspected sympathizers sold into slavery. After a 1643 decree imposed a heavier tribute burden on the Pueblos, many left New Mexico, and as exiles, they helped to organize Apache raids on the colony.

The cease-fire between Franciscan friars and governors ended in the late 1650s. The new governor, Bernardo López de Mendizábal, thought the friars had too much power. He outlawed use of involuntary Indian labor at missions. Many Pueblos resented friars' often brutal attempts to strip them of their beliefs. Friars charged that the governor undermined them by siding with village chiefs and medicine men and encouraging polygamy and ceremonial dances. Reacting to a drought that began in 1660, Pueblos revived **katsina** dances to make the rains return, rituals that friars labeled devil worship. Franciscans had Mendizábal arrested and taken in chains to Mexico City. They did the same to his successor, securing their dominance over New Mexico.

### STUDY QUESTIONS FOR UNCIVIL WARS, 1640–1660

1. **What impact did the English Civil War have on North America and the West Indies?**
2. **In what ways and for what reasons did Indian life change between 1640 and 1660?**

# NEW IMPERIAL ORDERS, 1660–1680

The 1660s heralded a new order for colonial English and French North America. New monarchs launched reforms and waged wars intended to forge integrated empires from scattered North American and Caribbean colonies. Conquest brought a large, diverse, and established population of colonists who were not English under English rule for the first time. Meanwhile, political and social changes in the Chesapeake and a new Barbadian colony in Carolina rooted plantation slavery in North America.

## English Empire and the Conquest of New Netherland

In 1660, English America learned that England again had a king. Charles II's reign brought enduring changes for colonists and Indians by the time he died in 1685. English entrepreneurs had founded four new colonies, while imperial officials had reorganized three others. New Netherland entered England's empire by conquest, making it the first Anglo-American society in which authorities governed large numbers of settled Europeans who were not English. All colonists faced an empire that sought to tighten oversight of their internal affairs and their commerce overseas.

Charles II and his ministers followed precedents set during the English Civil War. They established a committee modeled after one that the interregnum government created to supervise colonial affairs. It helped to interpret and enforce the **Navigation Acts** (Table 3.2), a series of laws that began to go into effect in 1651 that permitted

**Table 3.2 Navigation Acts** As English authorities began to see colonies as a key source of wealth, they began to regulate American colonists' commerce with Atlantic markets. Here are some of the most important laws, known as the Navigation Acts.

| Year Legislation Passed | Key Provisions and Outcomes |
|---|---|
| 1651 | All goods sent to England from America, Africa, or Asia must be carried in vessels owned and staffed by Englishmen or English colonists<br>Dutch merchants barred from English colonies<br>Provokes First Anglo-Dutch War |
| 1660 | Only vessels owned by Englishmen and operated by crews that were at least three-quarters English may dock in colonial ports<br>Stipulated list of "enumerated goods" including sugar and tobacco, which had to be shipped to England before they could be taken elsewhere |
| 1663 | Most non-English goods headed for English colonies must first be shipped through England and taxed there |
| 1673 | Colonists required to pay duties on enumerated goods shipped to England<br>Customs agents appointed and stationed in every colony to collect duties |
| 1696 | Extends system of vice-admiralty courts from England to colonies to clamp down on smuggling and enforce Navigation Acts |

free trade within England's empire but restricted commerce with people outside it. The Navigation Acts indicated American colonies' growing importance to England. English merchants applauded them, but the reaction among colonists was mixed. On the positive side, the laws guaranteed markets for their goods and services, as well as freedom to trade within the English empire. The Navigation Acts also empowered colonial merchants to compete for the business of moving goods about the Anglo-Atlantic. Nevertheless, colonial planters and merchants chafed at the regulations. Planters thought the laws deprived them of markets by levying duties on tobacco and sugar and by requiring that those commodities, designated as "enumerated goods," be unloaded in England before proceeding to European markets. Merchants objected that European imports destined for English North America also had to pass through England before being shipped across the Atlantic, an arrangement that they believed unfairly favored their English counterparts.

English officials looked to the Navigation Acts to sever English colonists' thickening ties with Dutch merchants. Massachusetts Bay grudgingly ceased trade with New Netherland during the **First Anglo-Dutch War** (1652–1654), but quickly resumed it when peace came, even though the first Navigation Act of 1651 clearly barred commerce with the Dutch. Dutch merchants also transported enslaved Africans to English colonies, especially when the English Civil War disrupted Anglo-Atlantic trade. In 1663, Charles II awarded the predecessor of the Royal African Company a monopoly on English trade with Africa, a concession that included the Atlantic slave trade. The company's attacks on Dutch shipping and forts in West Africa sparked the **Second Anglo-Dutch War** (1664–1667).

In North America that war began when a small English fleet won New Amsterdam's surrender without firing a shot. The city and New Netherland became New York in August 1664, taking on the title of Charles's brother **James, Duke of York**. Commander Richard Nicolls promised Dutch colonists a New York that would resemble New Netherland. The **Articles of Capitulation** granted Dutch residents religious liberty, freedom from military conscription, property rights, and free trade and freedom of movement within the English empire. The Articles also allowed the Dutch to continue following their inheritance customs. New York's English rulers considered these privileges that they might revoke. Dutch New Yorkers saw them as rights.

England's grip on New York was tenuous. In 1673, a Dutch fleet conquered the colony. A peace treaty returned the colony to England a year later, but the English were alarmed at New York's quick capitulation to the Dutch. London officials briefly discussed using force to remove Dutch settlers to make way for English immigrants, but James instructed governor Edmund Andros to exact retribution by other means. In 1675, he prosecuted eight Dutch merchants who refused to swear allegiance to England. Seven faced charges that they were foreigners who traded illegally in New York.

Their trials accelerated the Anglicization of many Dutch elites in New York City. They calculated that cooperation with English officials and intermarriage with English colonists was the best way to secure their status. Assimilation was not a one-way street. Few English women moved to New York, so many English men married Dutch women, who incorporated them into their families, churches, and communities. New York's English adopted Dutch words such as cookie, stoop, and boss.

Dutch vocabulary enriched American English partly because much of New York's "Dutch" majority strove to become more "Dutch" in the wake of English conquest. The Dutch Reformed Church assumed a more prominent role in New York than it had in New Netherland. Another way for Dutch colonists to assert a Dutch identity was to continue to divide their estates in Dutch ways. This gave Dutch women more power than English women had. Dutch inheritance law permitted women to keep property that they brought to a marriage, favored husbands and wives writing wills together, left estates in widows' hands rather than their children's, and divided estates equally between sons and daughters. These practices eroded gradually during the early 1700s, first in New York City, and a generation later in the areas along the Hudson River to the north of the city.

Growing English domination of New York's public life during the 1680s alienated many Dutch and widened political divisions. Dutch who lived upriver resented the growing power of Manhattan's wealthy Anglo-Dutch merchants. So did most of the city's artisans, Dutch and English, who saw a small number of well-connected men conspiring with officials to issue regulations that threatened their livelihood. In 1689, this brew of class and ethnic tensions boiled over as political instability wracked the Anglo-Atlantic world and war erupted with France.

## Quebec and the Expansion of French America

In 1665, as New Yorkers adjusted to their first year of English rule, a regiment of some 1,000 French troops landed in Quebec. The arrival of North America's first standing army doubled the number of men in New France. **Louis XIV**'s minister **Jean-Baptiste Colbert** considered the regiment crucial to his plan to reform France's empire. He, like his English rivals, believed that colonies existed mainly to provide raw materials to the kingdom that founded them and protected markets for its manufactures—a philosophy called **mercantilism**. To accomplish these goals, Colbert aimed to repopulate Canada, increase royal control over New France, diversify the colony's economy, and better integrate it into French Atlantic trade networks.

First the French had to curb Iroquois raids. That was the regiment's job. All the Iroquois except the Mohawks favored peace with New France, partly because England's conquest of New Netherland curtailed their supply of firearms. In 1666, the French launched their third and final invasion of Mohawk country, looting and torching dozens of longhouses and two years' worth of food stores. Under the treaty the Mohawks accepted with New France and its Indian allies, the Iroquois agreed to admit Jesuits. Soon Iroquois villages, especially the Mohawks, divided into those who favored hosting priests and those who did not.

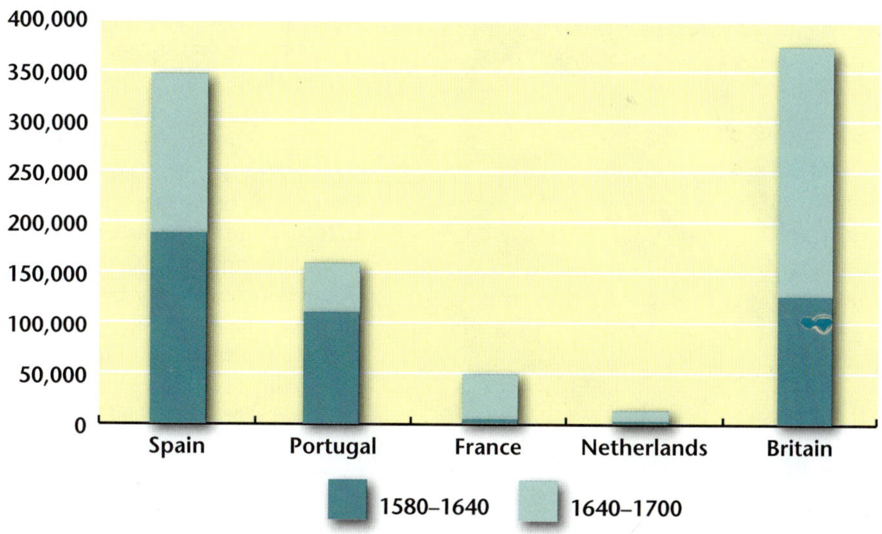


▲ Figure 3.2

**European emigration to the Americas, 1580–1700** Between 1580 and 1700, England sent more Europeans to the Americas than any of its rivals. Nearly half the European migrants to the Americas between 1640 and 1700 were English. The majority of English went to mainland North America, where the populations of English colonies dwarfed those of European rivals.

GLOBAL PASSAGES

# Global Catholicism, Indian Christianity, and Catherine/Kateri Tekakwitha

A young Mohawk woman died in April 1680. Father Claude Chauchetière called her Catherine, her baptismal name. His superior Pierre Cholenec gave Catherine last rites and claimed that he saw her pock-marked face clear after she died. Both men wrote a biography of Catherine. Chauchetière advised ill French colonists to pray for her help. Catherine soon won a regional following. Three hundred years later the "Mohawk saint" had an international one consisting largely of Catholic clergy and American Indians. Pope John Paul II beatified Catherine in 1980, the first step on the path toward sainthood.

This bronze statue of Kateri Tekakwitha by Estella Loretto, a Jemez Pueblo sculptor, stands in front of the Cathedral Basilica of St. Francis of Assisi in Santa Fé. Unveiled in 2002 to mark the cathedral structure's 150th anniversary, it testifies to the devotion for Kateri Tekakwitha in New Mexico.

In 1656, an Algonquin captive living in the Mohawk village Gandaouagué gave birth to Tekakwitha. Smallpox scarred the girl's face when she was six and killed her mother and brother. When war with New France broke out, the village residents fled. Peace required that they accept Jesuits. One baptized Tekakwitha on Easter Sunday in 1676, giving her the name of Catherine. She moved to Kahnawake, a village peopled mostly by Christian Mohawks located near Montreal. Kin awaited her there. Tekakwitha joined other devout women who practiced celibacy and inflicted pain on themselves, becoming a group leader shortly before she died at the age of 24.

Jesuits viewed Catherine and her peers as women who had almost ceased to be Indian, but they saw themselves as Catholic and Iroquoian. Baptism, a ritual in which one assumed a new identity to join a community, had Iroquoian analogs. So did abstaining from sex, burning or whipping oneself, and plunging into an icy pond. Jesuits interpreted these as acts of penance for sins. Tekakwitha and her circle could see them as preparation for possible torment, in this world or the next, and as a means to spiritual transcendence.

Chauchetière promoted Catherine's power to work miracles rather than her melding of Catholic and Indian beliefs. Tekakwitha's remains were exhumed in 1684 and buried in a mission chapel to accommodate pilgrims, almost all of whom were French Canadians. Chauchetière's biography of Catherine collected dust in France for nearly two centuries. In 1717, Jesuits published a short version of Cholenec's work in France to counter critics who argued that Jesuits in China had adapted too much to local customs. They thought it vindicated their belief that non-European converts could become saintly. Seven years later a Spanish-language edition of Cholenec's narrative surfaced in Mexico City to boost a campaign to found a convent exclusively for Indian women.

A campaign to beatify Catherine Tekakwitha began in the 1880s in the United States with strong support from Catholic bishops who believed that her beatification might counter rampant anti-Catholic prejudice by showing that Catholicism was "native" to American soil. The number of publications devoted to Tekakwitha's life surged over the next century. Many of them called her "Kateri" rather than "Catherine" Tekakwitha. In 1939, a group of white missionaries founded the Tekakwitha Conference in Montana to promote her beatification.

Meanwhile, Tekakwitha earned a following among Indian Catholics, who took control of the Tekakwitha Conference in the 1970s. Indian devotees revere Kateri Tekakwitha as someone who was fully Catholic and fully Indian. Support for her canonization is strong in New Mexico within "Kateri Circles" that Indian women have formed in affiliation with the Tekakwitha Conference. Kateri Circles see Tekakwitha as a role model whose faith empowered her to transcend suffering. **Catherine/Kateri Tekakwitha** in life journeyed between upstate New York and Quebec. Accounts of her life, death, faith, and example have circled the world, attracted a global following, and inspired Indians in the United States.

- In what ways have Catholic clergy and Indians portrayed the life of Tekakwitha since her death? In what ways have those portraits differed? What might account for such differences?

- Tekakwitha and Pocahontas chose to participate in colonial societies that profoundly altered their worlds. Are their lives, and the choices that they made, comparable? Explain.

By 1677, fear of the French prompted the Iroquois to forge a set of interlocking alliances with English colonies from New England south to Maryland. Under this "**Covenant Chain**," the league claimed to speak for Indians to their east and south. Iroquois League peoples indicated how much the French mattered to them by adopting a Mohawk term, Onontio ("Big Mountain"), a play on the name of a previous French governor, to address any French governor. Great Lakes Indians soon did likewise to show their respect and oblige Onontio to protect them and furnish them with trade goods.

After securing a tense peace, French officials focused on resettling New France. Colbert noted how colonization with families seemed to enhance English power and he wanted to emulate it. He directed officials to recruit male servants and young women, who would become wives in a society in which white men vastly outnumbered white women.

Wars in Europe and budgetary constraints stopped the flow of immigrants by the mid-1670s. New France's population reached 10,000 and grew mainly by natural increase thereafter. On average in New France women married at 22. They gave birth to more children than women in France did, and more of their children survived to adulthood. France's population barely grew during the 1700s, whereas New France's practically doubled every generation.

Aside from more native-born French Canadians, New France attained few of Colbert's goals. It developed into a modest colony of landlords, tenants, and peasants that still depended on furs to pay for imports. Colbert envisioned that Canadian-built ships would ferry fish, provisions, and timber to France's Caribbean colonies and return with sugar, rum, and molasses. New England, for reasons of climate, geography, and demography, outcompeted New France in the French West Indies. Its merchants provided more goods more cheaply as well as access to a far bigger colonial market. French colonists in the West Indies agreed, to the chagrin of French and English officials.

Few French immigrants and dependence on the fur trade resulted in a sprawling French claim to the interior of North America that was impossible to defend without Indian allies. New France's predicament was partly a consequence of its treaty with the Iroquois, which improved French access inland. Robert Cavalier de La Salle won approval to sail down the Mississippi and establish trading posts along the way. He reached the river's mouth in 1682, claimed the area that it drained for France, and named it Louisiana after Louis XIV. In the 1670s fur traders and missionaries founded posts at Michilimackinac and Sault Sainte Marie, strategic points overlooking exits from Lakes Michigan and Superior, respectively. Michilimackinac served as a base for fur traders headed west. They often married Algonquian women to claim kin status among the Indians with whom they did business. Both posts attracted refugees of the Iroquois mourning wars and bolstered French ties to those peoples. Competition from the north made these French outposts necessary after the **Hudson's Bay Company** formed in England in 1670. The English, who offered more goods at better prices than the French, attracted Cree Indians who brought pelts to Hudson's Bay outposts. A struggle soon began between England and France for North America's interior.

## Chesapeake Servitude, Mainland Slavery

As the English tried to remake New Netherland into New York and the French attempted to transform New France, Maryland and Virginia experienced drastic changes. These contributed to, and were accelerated by, **Bacon's Rebellion**—a complex set of events in 1675–1676 that involved war between colonists and Indians as well as a civil war in which whites of every social rank and enslaved Africans joined to topple Virginia's governor. By the early 1680s, Virginia resembled Barbados. It too had become a society dependent on slavery and founded on the principle of white supremacy.

Plantation slavery and racial consciousness emerged gradually and together in the Chesapeake. In 1643, Virginia legislators enacted their first law that discriminated explicitly on the basis of race by designating men and African women, but not white women, as taxable field laborers. The legal status of people of African descent remained ambiguous into the 1660s. Many were considered indentured servants. A few gained freedom, owned land, and even held slaves. A 1668 law, however, compelled free black women to pay a tax, compounding the burden on struggling black families (Table 3.3).

Virginia lawmakers built most of the legal foundation for the perpetual enslavement of Africans during the 1660s. They laid one cornerstone in 1662 by declaring that a child's legal status should follow that of the mother. This broke with English law and gender norms, under which a child inherited legal status from the father. Worse, it made slavery heritable and in the masters' eyes remade enslaved women into commodities valued for their production and reproduction. This encouraged masters to abuse enslaved women sexually and it emasculated enslaved fathers. Legislators laid another cornerstone in 1667 by resolving that slaves who had been baptized and had converted to Christianity did not have legal grounds to sue for freedom.

Although masters enjoyed new powers, they did not immediately purchase many more slaves. In 1670, the 2,000 enslaved Virginians formed 5 percent of the colony's population. Enforcement of the Navigation Acts barred Dutch vessels from bringing Africans to the Chesapeake, and the Royal African Company did not license ships to trade directly with Virginia until 1678. Still, around 6,000 Africans were sent to Chesapeake Bay between 1660 and 1690. Much of the slow but steady growth of the region's enslaved population just before Bacon's Rebellion also owed to trade with the West Indies, where planters obtained slaves in exchange for grain and meat (Map 3.2).

The gradual expansion of African slavery in the Chesapeake was tied to changes in indentured servitude and to the region's reputation in England. In the late 1650s and early 1660s the number of servants who came to Virginia, three in four of them men, surged as their prospects declined in Barbados (Figure 3.3). But soon Chesapeake planters had trouble finding servants at a price that they were willing to pay. Improving job prospects in England kept many at home, as did reports of what awaited servants across the ocean. As with Barbados, news from the Chesapeake likened servitude to slavery.

Women and men experienced servitude differently. Recruiters told women in England weighing whether to cross the Atlantic that they would not have to work in

**Table 3.3 Selected Key Legal Developments Concerning Slavery and Race in English America, 1635–1696** Slavery and racism emerged gradually and together in English America during the 17th century. Here are some of the key legal milestones in that process, one in which Barbados played a key role.

| Year | Colony | Key Provisions |
|---|---|---|
| 1635 | Barbados | Governor declares that all Africans and Indians brought to the island to be considered slaves unless they have a contract that says otherwise |
| 1641 | Massachusetts Bay | Legalizes slavery within the colony |
| 1643 | Virginia | Women of African descent and all men made subject to tithe to support Church of England |
| 1661 | Barbados | First comprehensive slave code in English America, setting model for other colonies to follow |
| 1661 | Virginia | Indentured servants who run away with slaves to serve time that slave missed as well as time that they missed |
| 1662 | Virginia | Child's legal status to follow that of the mother rather than the father |
| 1664 | Maryland | Slavery defined as a lifelong legal condition |
| 1665 | New York | New English Assembly, composed largely of migrants from New England, recognizes slavery as lifelong condition |
| 1667 | Virginia | Denies that baptism provides legal grounds to sue for freedom |
| 1670 | Virginia | Indians taken captive outside colony and imported to serve for life; those captured within colony to serve 12 years (if children) or until age 30 |
| 1679 | New York | Enslavement of Indians prohibited |
| 1680 | Virginia | Enslaved blacks barred from carrying arms, gathering (particularly for feasts and burials), or leaving plantations without a pass from their master |
| 1691 | Virginia | Whites barred from marrying blacks, mulattos, or Indians; children born of unions between English women and black men to become servants; mothers to pay fine, become servants, or have their servitude extended<br>Masters owed compensation if their runaway slaves are killed while being captured<br>Freed people ordered to leave colony |
| 1692 | Virginia | Special courts created for trying slaves accused of crimes |
| 1696 | South Carolina | Establishes first comprehensive slave code, modeled after that of Barbados, in English North America |

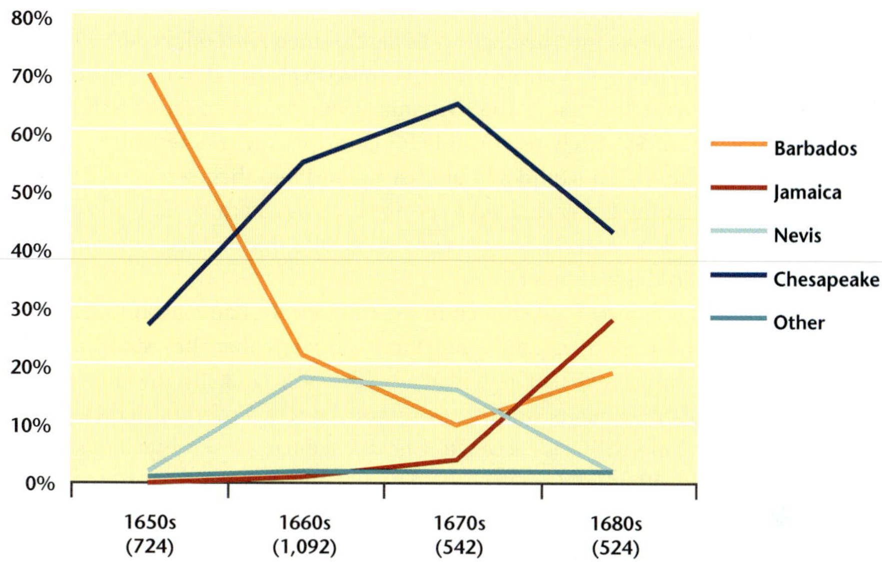


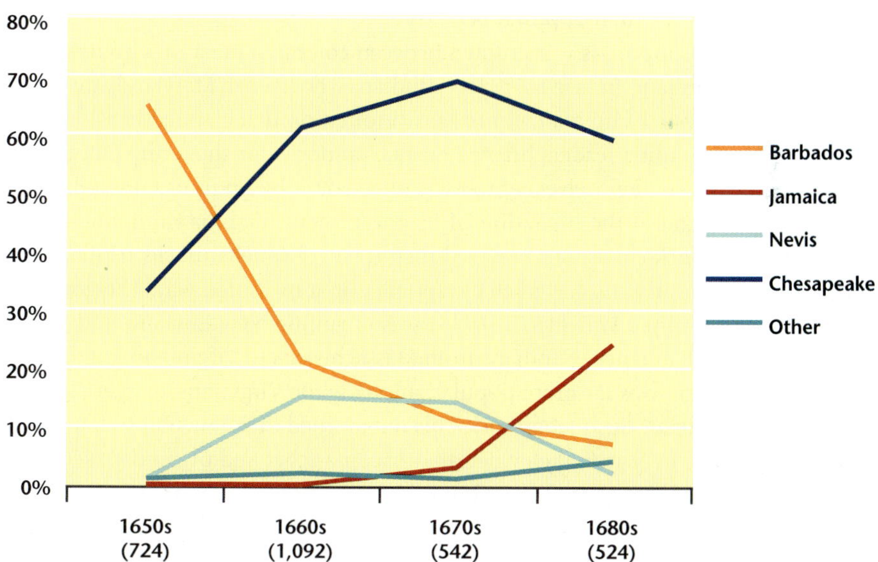


▲ **Figure 3.3**

**Migration of male and female indentured servants to English America, 1654–1686** These figures, based mainly on indentures recorded in Bristol, England, show that some two-thirds of indentured servants headed to Barbados in the 1650s. The Chesapeake colonies became the main destination for the next two decades for male servants and for the next three decades for female servants, including Anne Orthwood.

the tobacco fields and that they could pick a husband in a society teeming with eligible bachelors. The first claim was usually a lie. The second carried some truth. Female servants could find suitors, but they had to beware of men who might lure them to bed with promises of marriage and then leave them to deal with the consequences of pregnancy. Making matters worse, a 1662 Virginia law made female servants, frequent targets of sexual advances, solely responsible for compensating masters for time lost by pregnancy and labor. That could add at least two years to their servitude. If a servant mother died and the father dodged responsibility for paternity, her child had to become an indentured servant. This is the fate that befell Anne and Jasper Orthwood, whose story introduced this chapter.

Before the 1660s, young English men in the Chesapeake had reason to fear that they would not survive their servitude. But they also knew that they stood a good chance of owning land, even if it might not be the best land. By the mid-1670s, however, wealthy planters, many of them close associates of Governor Berkeley, had claimed most good land with easy access to Chesapeake Bay. Ex-servants and sons of small planters could either work as tenants or hired hands—or move to the colony's borders and risk Indian attacks.

Berkeley also made powerful enemies, none more prominent than **Nathaniel Bacon**. The English aristocrat arrived in 1674, certain that his high birth entitled him to high office. Berkeley agreed, appointing Bacon to his council. Bacon believed that he had a more legitimate claim to power than did those who surrounded Berkeley. He took charge of a faction that opposed Berkeley.

Bacon gained support as war erupted between colonists, most of whom wanted Indian land, and Indians. In July 1675, Doeg Indians who lived in Maryland attempted to collect a debt from a Virginia colonist, a confrontation that claimed lives on both sides. Chesapeake militia leaders blamed Susquehannocks for sheltering Doegs. The Susquehannocks were themselves refugees, pushed south by Iroquois raids, who had resettled in Maryland at the invitation of its government. Virginia militiamen murdered Susquehannock chiefs and besieged their town. Susquehannocks retaliated by raiding Virginia in early 1676. Berkeley responded in a measured way. The governor knew that **King Philip's War** (1675–1676) was engulfing New England and feared that an anti-English alliance of Indians from Massachusetts to Virginia might form.

Bacon's solution was far more popular among white Virginians—target all Indians. Rather than pursue Susquehannocks, his men turned their guns on Indians who lived among them. In May Berkeley declared Bacon a rebel and organized elections. The governor's forces captured Bacon, but newly elected burgesses asked that Berkeley pardon him. He did, reseating Bacon on the council but refusing to authorize Bacon to attack any Indians he wished. Bacon's followers took up arms and drove Berkeley from Jamestown. The governor's supporters soon gained the upper hand. Bacon, desperate to save himself, promised freedom to servants and slaves of Berkeley loyalists. About 250 slaves, 1 in 10 who then lived in Virginia, joined white servants and ex-servants to storm and torch Jamestown as Berkeley fled for his life. Charles II authorized Berkeley to offer freedom to servants and slaves who sided with him. The governor declined, calculating that it would alienate planters. Some of his allies thought otherwise. One persuaded hundreds of servants and slaves to surrender by promising them freedom, a ruse that effectively ended the rebellion.

Bacon's Rebellion remade Virginia's borders and its politics. Susquehannocks straggled north, where many submitted to the Iroquois. Charles II appointed a commission to investigate matters in Virginia. It concluded that high taxes, vulnerability to Indian attack, official corruption, and concentration of land ownership sparked the uprising. The king, increasingly dependent on revenues raised from duties on tobacco, needed a stable Virginia, so he dismissed Berkeley.

The rebellion accelerated the entrenchment of slavery and of white supremacy. Planters fretted that a resentful white underclass might develop, so increasing numbers of them opted to purchase enslaved Africans rather than indentured servants. Consequently, Virginia's black population grew to 5,000 by 1698, when slaves comprised at least half the colony's unfree workers. New laws passed between 1680 and 1691 hardened racial distinctions and empowered masters and officials to exert more control over slaves and free blacks. In 1691, Virginia prohibited interracial marriage, punished white women for giving birth to interracial children, and required that anyone who was manumitted (freed) to leave the colony within six months or the person who freed them would be fined (Table 3.3). Unlike Barbados, Maryland and Virginia retained a white majority. They formed the northern edge of a rim of societies based on African slavery that extended south to Carolina, the Caribbean, and Brazil.

## The Creation of South Carolina

When Charles I was executed in the English Civil War, Sir John Colleton, one of his greatest supporters, fled England to become a Barbados planter. In 1663, Charles II rewarded his loyalty by granting the exclusive right to colonize land between Virginia and Florida to a group that Colleton headed. The planter and his partners named the colony "Carolina" to honor the king.

Carolina's proprietors envisioned that colonists would pay them to use their land and live peacefully alongside Indians. They promised land grants for each immigrant, including enslaved ones, to each household head who paid for their passage, as well as religious toleration and a representative assembly. Colonists were to bring the gospel to nearby Indians and leave most trade with Indians beyond Carolina's borders to the proprietors.

In 1669, Carolina's proprietors, helped by their secretary, **John Locke**, laid out their principles in the Fundamental Constitutions. They asserted proprietors' exclusive right to negotiate land concessions from Indians, stated explicitly that conversion to Christianity would not deliver slaves from bondage, and declared that free white men were to have absolute authority over enslaved Africans. The Fundamental Constitutions never took effect because colonists rejected them, even though most had lobbied for such powers over slaves.

Carolina colonists embraced slavery so tightly in part because so many of them came from Barbados. After 1660 thousands of English left Barbados for other parts of English America, and many took slaves with them. Barbados profoundly influenced the development of the new colony. Barbadians founded Carolina's first permanent colonial settlement in 1670 and comprised most of the 1,300 people of European descent who moved to South Carolina over the next two decades. Land drew most, whether they were sons of prominent planters who feared that their status would erode if they stayed on Barbados, or young men, craftsmen, or small planters who decided that they would never succeed there. Barbadians helped to craft North America's first comprehensive slave code in 1696. They also oriented Carolina's economy toward the West Indies, which needed food and labor. White Carolinians or enslaved ones reared cattle and pigs and grew corn and peas, while Indians sent enslaved captives for export to the Caribbean.

This encouraged contact with a group of recent arrivals whom colonists called the Westo. They were probably Iroquoian speakers whom the Iroquois pushed south in the 1650s. By 1670, the Westo had carved out a foothold along the Savannah River. Their targets included other Indians, Spanish missions, and English colonists. In 1674, a band of Shawnee, the Savannah, brokered a treaty between the Westo and Carolina. Carolina needed secure borders and trade, while the Westo feared that their archenemy the Cherokee might ally with Virginia. They needed a more convenient source of imported goods, especially weapons, without which the Westo faced exodus or captivity.

So began a lucrative English trade in enslaved Indians from southeastern North America. Westos raided what is today coastal Georgia to seize Yamasees, a newly formed people who had migrated there to seek refuge, and attacked other foes, including the Cherokee. Soon Carolina leaders decided that the Westo had outlived their usefulness. Westo raids alienated too many other Indians, so colonists teamed up with the Savannah to kill or enslave most Westos. Ironically, Yamasees became allies to South Carolina in the 1680s and would remain so for three decades, supplying Indian slaves to the colony.

Carolina's growing dependence on trafficking in Indian slaves alarmed the colony's proprietors in England. In 1680, they ordered that no allied or friendly Indians within 200 miles of Carolina be enslaved. That left a huge loophole for colonists to exploit. Three years later, proprietors created a licensing system to ensure that only enslaved Indians captured in "just wars" were exported, but their agents did not enforce it. By the 1690s, the Indian slave trade exacerbated tensions between the English and Spanish, depopulated vast areas, and accelerated the transformation of the region's Indian politics.

## Metacom and the Algonquian Battle for New England

Most New England colonists dreaded the news of Charles II's coronation. Their association with the losers of the English Civil War jeopardized their colonies' precarious legal standing. Although few Puritan dissidents fled England for Massachusetts Bay, the colony endured a wave of assaults on its legal right to exist. Quakers launched many of them, as did colonists in New Hampshire and Maine who did not want Massachusetts to govern them. Nor did Indians, who petitioned Charles II as loyal subjects who deserved protection from disloyal colonists headquartered in Boston.

Political uncertainty fed a growing sense of crisis in New England in the 1660s and 1670s. Some took defeat in the English Civil War as a sign that they had lost God's favor. Worse might befall them, they feared, as the generation that founded New England began to die off. Were they worthy, they wondered, of the founders' legacy? A growing number of ministers told them, in sermons called **jeremiads**, that they were not and never would be unless they changed their ways and honored God as their parents had. In 1662, New England ministers, terrified that they might lose future generations, declared that they would baptize children of parents who were not church members. Critics rejected this as a **"Half-Way" Covenant** that resembled Anglicanism too closely. Meanwhile, church membership rates plummeted. Worse, as ministers and magistrates saw matters, most new members were women, who could not vote. That, they feared, might break the bond between church and state and endanger everyone.

Meanwhile, some New England colonists seized opportunities to forge new ties to England. In 1661 John Winthrop, Jr., became a charter member of the **Royal Society** of London for the Promotion of Natural Knowledge, known as the Royal Society, a group that advocated scientific inquiry. Its founders believed that people glorified God and bolstered faith by studying the natural world.

Colonists like Winthrop sent specimens to London, corresponded with Royal Society fellows, and published in the society's journal. They subscribed to Royal Society journals and lent them to others. Winthrop donated New England's first telescope to Harvard, where others used it to observe comets in the 1680s. Their work informed the thought of Isaac Newton and prompted Puritan minister Increase Mather to organize the Boston Philosophical Society in 1683, the first organization to promote science in Anglo-America. The group, modeled on the Royal Society, soon disbanded, but its members and their peers maintained ties to the London organization.

Colonists who joined scientific networks used science to distinguish themselves from Indians and assert their Englishness. Winthrop and his American peers claimed that their engagement with science demonstrated their superiority to "superstitious" Indians who, they claimed, were incapable of such intellectual work. This reassured colonists who feared that life or birth in America made them seem inferior in the eyes of English across the Atlantic.

Algonquian peoples in southern New England were far more worried about their future. They had become the minority, forced to accommodate immigrants who had arrived only a generation earlier. Economic and environmental changes left them no choice. The more colonists traded overseas, the less they needed Indians. In 1661, a mint opened in Boston. Within a year most New England colonists stopped using wampum as currency. Southern New England Indians increasingly found that they could only pay their debts with land. The more land they sold, the less they had for hunting and fishing. Multiplying herds of English-owned cattle and pigs threatened to overrun what remained in Indian hands. The livestock spread seeds of plants that colonists considered weeds, ate many of the same plants as deer, and devoured Indian plots of corn, beans, and squash. Indians who faced famine countered such invasions by filing suits in colonial courts or by killing and eating the invading livestock.

Algonquian tried to adapt by selectively adopting English ways. If colonists could let livestock loose and hunt them, why couldn't Wampanoags and Narragansetts? Algonquians decided that pigs suited them best; they required less care than cattle. Colonists objected because keeping pigs would discourage Algonquian men from replacing women in the fields and becoming husbands of the soil and of their households as English men were. Colonists also refused to share public grazing lands with Indians. In 1669, Portsmouth, Rhode Island officials forced Massasoit's son, the Wampanoag sachem **Metacom** (whom they called Philip), to remove his pigs from "Hog Island." Metacom sought coexistence. Colonists rejected it.

Metacom responded by organizing an Algonquian alliance to confront the English. The hanging of three Wampanoags, convicted in Plymouth of murdering a Christian Indian, ignited King Philip's War (1675–1676). It claimed thousands of lives and became the bloodiest conflict, on a per capita basis, in Anglo-American history. Indian attacks terrified colonists and destroyed 25 English towns. Massachusetts Bay leaders made plans to evacuate most of the colony and shelter colonists behind a ring of wooden ramparts a few miles from Boston.

Medallion presented to Christian Indian soldiers serving with Massachusetts forces during King Philip's War, 1676. Christian Indians helped New England win King Philip's War and secure release of captured colonists. Massachusetts Bay officials gave this medallion to Christian Indian soldiers for their service (to quote the inscription on the back of the medallion) "in the present Warr with the Heathen Natives of this Land."

Indians, regardless of which side they chose, suffered most from the war. English-led attacks compelled most to flee inland and keep moving, leaving them hungrier and more vulnerable to cold and disease. New York's governor persuaded Mohawks to side with the English, deny Metacom's pleas for help, and raid his allies. Both sides considered Christian Indians suspect. Massachusetts Bay soldiers rounded up and exiled most to a bleak island in Boston Harbor, where many died or were enslaved illegally. Other Christian Indians negotiated the release of English captives or fought alongside colonists. One shot Metacom, while another beheaded and quartered his corpse in August 1676. Metacom's head, stuck atop a post, remained on display in Plymouth for years. His wife and their nine-year old son were jailed in Plymouth. She was not heard from again, but he joined hundreds of Algonquians who were enslaved and put on a boat, most likely headed to the West Indies.

Metacom's death did not end the war. Algonquians in northern New England continued to raid boats and towns in New Hampshire and Maine. The attacks revived traumatic memories for colonists, who were unleashing a torrent of published works about King Philip's

War that were read on both sides of the Atlantic. One, by **Mary Rowlandson**, a minister's wife whom Indians had captured, was published in Massachusetts and London in 1682. It became the second best-selling book in New England after the Bible. We know little about how southern New England's Algonquians understood the conflict, but we know what it meant for them. Most who survived the war became captives, refugees, or struggled to remain autonomous peoples surrounded by colonists who increasingly pretended that they did not exist.

**STUDY QUESTIONS FOR NEW IMPERIAL ORDERS, 1660–1680**

1. **Wars between colonists and Indians erupted across eastern North America in the 1660s and 1670s. Why? Did the conflicts share one underlying cause or did each have distinct origins? Explain.**
2. **Slavery arrived in South Carolina and developed in Virginia and Barbados. In what ways did this difference matter in the development of each place?**
3. **Why did royal power increase within the English and French empires during the 1660s? What impact did royal reforms have on North America?**

# VICTORIOUS PUEBLOS, A NEW MID-ATLANTIC, AND "GLORIOUS" REVOLUTIONS, 1680 TO THE 1690S

The 1680s brought revolutions to the Spanish southwest and the Anglo-Atlantic world that resulted in civil wars, social turmoil, and imperial conflicts throughout North America. Pueblo Indians began the decade by driving the Spanish from New Mexico, but spent the next dozen years disputing what they should do with their independence. New English colonies emerged in the mid-Atlantic, each committed to religious freedom that attracted thousands of immigrants from other parts of English America, the British Isles, and western Europe. The overthrow of another English king in 1688 triggered revolts in three colonies and the first of many wars between England, France, and Indians for control of eastern North America.

## The Pueblo War for Independence

On an August evening in 1680, Pueblo messengers departed Taos. **Popé**, a medicine man whom Spanish friars had recently whipped for practicing "idolatry," dispatched them to alert other towns that a planned uprising would begin in two days. New Mexico's diverse Indians were mostly united against Spanish rule. As their rebellion began, Pueblo and Apache warriors slaughtered horses and mules to constrict colonists' mobility before storming missions and Spanish towns. Within two weeks, 1,400

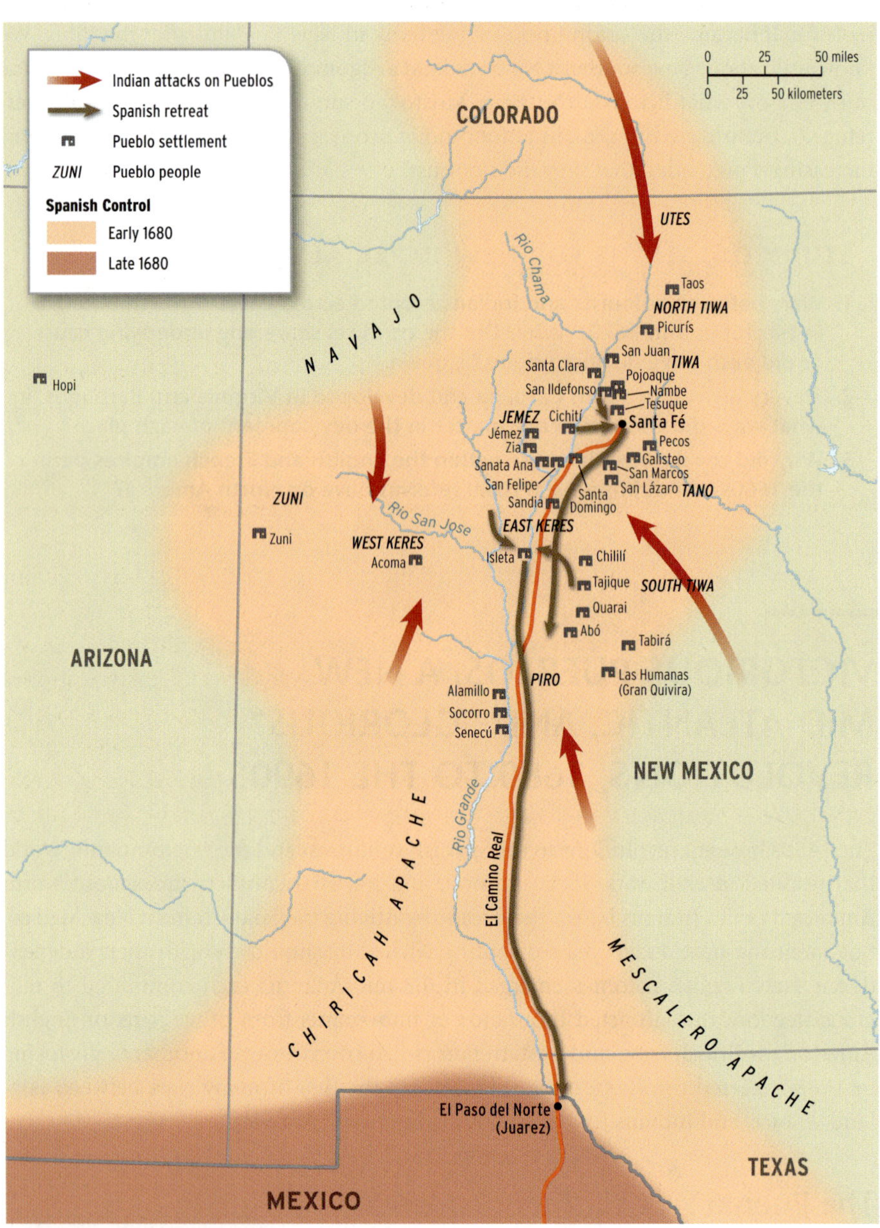


**Map 3.3**

**Pueblo War for Independence** The Pueblo War for Independence, organized largely by Popé of Taos Pueblo, drove the Spanish out of New Mexico in 1680. Colonists sought refuge in El Paso del Norte (today's Ciudad Juárez, Mexico). They did not return for a dozen years.

colonists, with 500 Indian slaves in tow, abandoned New Mexico, leaving behind hundreds of dead, including over 20 friars. Pueblos had waged the most successful war for independence in North American history to date.

A number of factors prompted the war. Approximately 100,000 Indians lived in New Mexico when the Spanish conquered the region in 1598. By 1680, 17,000 remained. The southwest had endured a severe drought for two decades. Navajo and Apache raids in the 1670s worsened food shortages. Spanish demands for tribute and for sex from Pueblo women became even more onerous in such trying times. In 1675, the Spanish cracked down on Pueblo rituals, especially on those that beseeched katsinas to bring rain, fertility, and prosperity. That may well have been the final provocation.

It seems that it was for Popé. The medicine man considered the Pueblo gods as the war's real leaders, and himself as their instrument. Popé claimed the gods had punished Pueblos for having adopted the ways of their foreign oppressors. Pueblos, Popé insisted, could end their suffering by ridding themselves of the Spanish and all that they brought and returning to their preconquest beliefs. Only then they would they regain the favor of katsinas and other gods, who would restore the era of peace and prosperity that Pueblos enjoyed just after their creation.

That idyllic time did not return. Most Pueblos wanted the Spanish gone, but disagreed on what should happen once they left. Many men celebrated the end of monogamy, one of the friars' most hated impositions, by seeking a different or an additional wife. Pueblos restored kivas to reenact their creation, while many destroyed churches, crosses, and images of Jesus Christ and the Virgin Mary. Popé's allies rejected their Christian names for native ones and punished those who spoke Spanish or invoked Jesus or Mary. The most zealous sought to reject what the Spanish had brought, regardless of its usefulness. Spanish tools were to be cast aside and broken. Indians were to plant only corn and beans as their ancestors had and "burn the seeds which the Spaniards sowed." For many Pueblos, this went too far. Spanish tools had become integral to their lives. So had peaches, beef, and pork. All these they saw as "native" to their New Mexico. So were Jesus and the Virgin Mary, who many had incorporated into the pantheon that created and sustained their ancestors.

Such differences fed conflicts that erupted almost as soon as the Spanish fled. The drought and Apache raids continued, as violence broke out within some towns between supporters and opponents of Popé's reforms. Warriors stormed granaries of neighboring communities, and nearly all Pueblo towns fell victim to Ute raids.

Popé died in 1692, just as the Spanish were launching their reconquest of New Mexico. They feared that growing French interest in Texas and Louisiana threatened Spanish control of northern Mexico and the silver that flowed from that region. New Mexico's new governor Diego de Vargas also believed that the Pueblo victory had sustained a wave of Indian rebellions across northern Mexico and inspired new ones.

Many Pueblos had decided that they preferred a future under Spanish rule to one without it. According to some Pueblo accounts, a delegation representing several towns invited the Spanish to return. Popé's successor Tupatú initiated peace talks and offered to join the Spanish against Pueblo holdouts. Vargas toured nearly two dozen towns, bullying most into submission. After returning to El Paso, he mustered several hundred men, most of them New Mexico refugees, and returned to Santa Fé in late 1693.

Vargas found the town in enemy hands. It took the Spanish and their Pueblo allies two days to take it. It took nine more months to conquer most of the towns that refused to accept Spanish rule. In 1696, a Pueblo raid killed over 25 colonists and friars. Vargas forced Indian allies to attack holdout towns and compel those in hiding to surrender, finally bringing the **Pueblo War for Independence** to an end. Hundreds of Pueblos fled, seeking shelter among Hopis and Navajos.

## A More Multicultural Mid-Atlantic

As Pueblos governed New Mexico, Indians whom the English called the Delawares watched thousands of Europeans stream into their lands. England staked claim to the area by conquering New Netherland, which gave Charles II more opportunities to reward supporters. In 1664, he granted title to land between the Hudson and Delaware rivers to two Carolina proprietors, John Berkeley and George Carteret, who named their venture New Jersey. Twelve years later, Berkeley sold his share to a London-based group of Quakers, an act that split the colony into East and West Jersey. **William Penn**, one of England's most famous Quakers, was a West Jersey booster whose father was an admiral and a royal advisor. Charles repaid a debt to the deceased father and sought to rid England of the dissenting son by granting land west of the Delaware to Penn. He named it Pennsylvania. New Jersey and Pennsylvania roughly followed models set by New Netherland and Carolina, with proprietors promising European immigrants religious freedom. In 1665, New Jersey's original proprietors also promised them a representative assembly and free trade within the English Empire, all of which attracted English from New England and eastern Long Island. Soon Barbadians came, some with as many as 30 enslaved Africans. East Jersey's proprietors recruited hundreds of Scots after taking on Scottish partners in 1683. Each group of free immigrants settled among their own, creating an ethnic and religious quilt that barely cohered politically. The only issue that united the 7,000 Europeans who lived in East Jersey in 1700 was hatred of **quitrents**, an annual fee that proprietors demanded for use of land that colonists had cleared, built on, and believed should be entirely theirs.

The Quaker proprietors of West Jersey and Pennsylvania assiduously recruited immigrants. In 1682, about 2,000 Quakers landed in Pennsylvania, followed by another 6,000 over the next three years. By 1700, Pennsylvania had 18,000 colonists, who hailed from all over the British Isles and central Europe. Quakers lured fellow believers from Scotland, Ireland, Wales, and northern England. Penn had pamphlets printed in German and Dutch to advertise Pennsylvania's religious freedom, cheap land, and low taxes. Much of the colony's rapid population growth owed to American-born children, for many immigrants came as families. They usually settled near others who spoke and prayed as they did. That simplified childrearing, especially for Quaker parents who had sailed across the Atlantic to nurture their children's inner light.

A new model city, Philadelphia, linked Pennsylvania to the Atlantic world. Founded in 1682, the town had 2,000 residents by 1700. Penn hoped that Philadelphia would avert the fate of London, where crowded dwellings let fire and plague

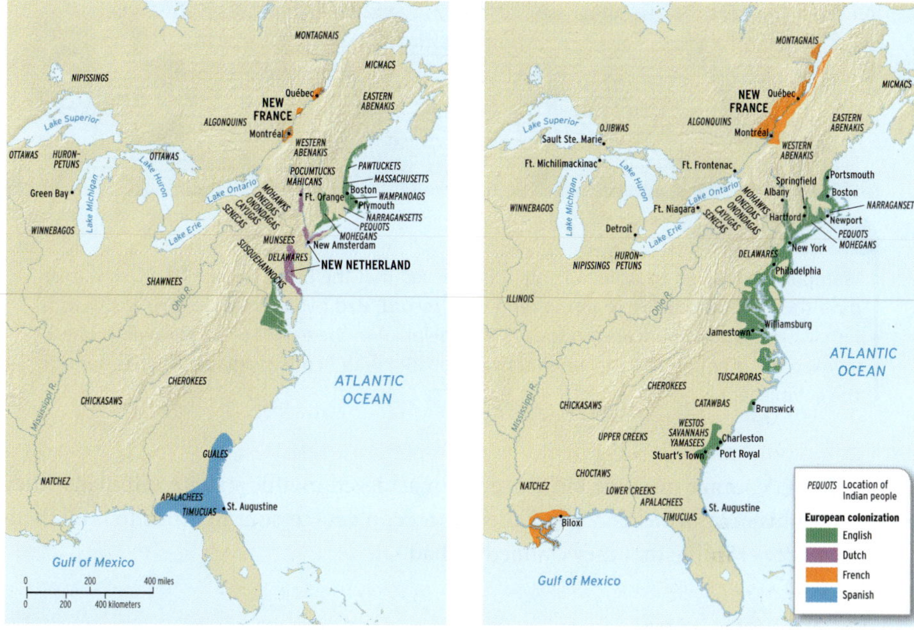


▲ **Map 3.4**

**Eastern North America, 1660 and 1700** The English conquest of New Netherland in 1664 and the founding of colonies in New Jersey, Pennsylvania, Delaware, and the Carolinas enabled the English to stake claim to and to resettle most of the eastern coast of North America from Maine to South Carolina by 1700.

spread easily. He oriented the city on a grid, with wide streets, room between low-rise homes to allow air to circulate and contain fires, and open space set aside for parks. The Philadelphia that emerged reflected little of his vision. Land speculators and the artisans, shopkeepers, and indentured servants who streamed in made a dense urban environment of Penn's model city. So did merchants' ties to ports throughout the English Atlantic, which spurred more immigration and anchored a growing trade in flour and other provisions to the West Indies.

Links to the West Indies helped slavery take root in Pennsylvania, even as some there expressed opposition to slavery. In 1688, a group of four Germantown Quakers petitioned the local Quaker meeting to end the colony's participation in the Atlantic slave trade and bar slavery within it. Neither the Germantown Meeting, forced to consider North America's first antislavery statement, nor a superior meeting to which it forwarded the petition, decided the matter. By 1700, some 3,000 Pennsylvanians, one in six, were enslaved and of African descent.

Unlike in Carolina, Pennsylvania's leaders cultivated amicable relations with Indians. This owed partly to Quaker principles of pacifism and justice. Penn negotiated land concessions with Delaware leaders personally, learned their language, and bought land from them on terms that they found agreeable. The Delawares saw such transactions as a way to maintain ties to Pennsylvania's rulers, whose support they

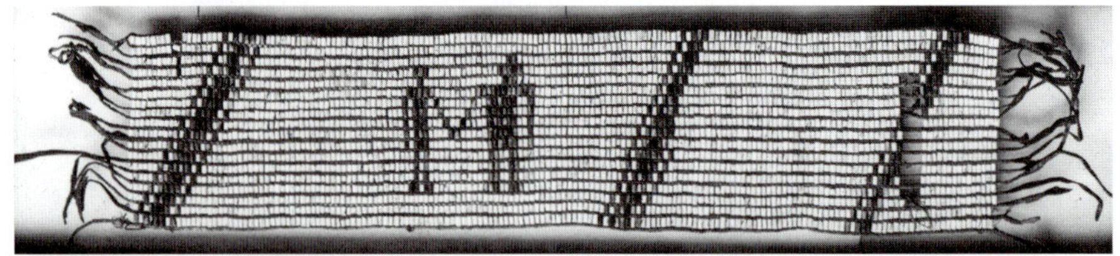

Wampum belt given to William Penn. It is believed that the Lenni Lenape (the Delawares) gave this wampum belt to Penn to represent, record, and commemorate their treaty with him at Shackamixon (located in today's Philadelphia) in the early 1680s. Delawares often invoked the memory of Penn when they negotiated with Pennsylvania authorities during the colonial era.

needed to counter Iroquois influence. Penn achieved mythic status for Indians. They invoked his memory as they negotiated with Penn's successors and tried to hold them to the lofty example that they claimed he had set.

## English North America's "Glorious" Revolutions

In 1689, colonists in English North America hailed their new sovereigns William and Mary by taking up arms against their local leaders. When Charles II died in 1685, his brother James II became king of England. The next three years brought bitter disputes between James and the Parliament over whose authority was supreme and over the king's embrace of Catholicism. When James suspended Parliament, his opponents feared the king would ally with France's Louis XIV to impose Catholicism and deprive them of liberty and property. Louis' persecution of Protestants fanned such fears. In 1685, he revoked the Edict of Nantes, which, in 1598, had granted French Protestants (known as Huguenots) liberty to practice their faith in Catholic France. Over 100,000 Huguenots fled France. Many sought refuge in England, while over 2,000 journeyed to Massachusetts, New York, and South Carolina.

The Huguenots' ordeal incensed James's enemies in England. In 1688, they asked Prince William of Orange, Dutch husband of James's Protestant daughter Mary, to intervene. A few months later he did, backed by an army of 15,000. Parliament declared the throne vacant after James fled to France and then invited William and Mary to occupy it. The victors trumpeted James's abdication as a peaceful and bloodless "**Glorious Revolution**" that preserved English liberty, even though mob attacks and pitched battles claimed thousands of lives in England, Scotland, and Ireland over the next two years.

Colonists had reasons to bid James good riddance. He hit planters' pockets by raising duties on sugar and tobacco, which made those goods more expensive and decreased demand for them. The king's fervent Catholicism added to colonists' alienation throughout Anglo America, but reforms that James imposed on them generated the most opposition, particularly in Massachusetts Bay. He created the **Dominion of New England** in 1685. It united eight contiguous colonies, from New England to New Jersey, under one governor, Edmond Andros, who dissolved representative assemblies, reduced town meetings to once a year, enforced the Navigation Acts, and barred Puritan congregations from using taxes to pay ministers. Most unsettling of all, the Dominion jeopardized land titles and required that their holders pay a quitrent on land that they had once owned outright.

Colonists in Massachusetts Bay, New York, and Maryland responded to news of events in England with violence. In April 1689, around 2,000 armed militiamen descended on Boston. Andros, guarded by 14 soldiers, surrendered. In May, New York militias, inspired by events in Boston, mutinied, forcing the lieutenant governor into exile. In Maryland, a group called the Protestant Associators demanded that the governor and his council proclaim William and Mary as monarchs of England. They refused, so the Associators overthrew the governor and council and put them under house arrest. Maryland law soon barred Catholics and Quakers from holding office.

In New York, rebels led by **Jacob Leisler** seized power in the name of William and Mary. They targeted the Anglo-Dutch mercantile elite and Dutch Reformed clergy who supported English rule. Leisler's opponents portrayed him to officials in London as a tyrannical demagogue and his faction as dominated by Dutch. Leisler held power as New Yorkers waited nearly two years for a replacement to arrive, who Leisler refused to accept. He was convicted of treason and hanged in 1691. Leisler's rule and conflicting memories of it haunted New York politics for a decade.

Ironically, colonists who rebelled to protest royal authority helped to strengthen it. Maryland's Protestant Associators curtailed proprietary power and received a governor appointed by the king. So did Massachusetts Bay. Its leaders had lobbied hard to revive their old charter and regain their autonomy. Massachusetts's 1691 royal charter gave it authority over Plymouth but curbed religion's influence over politics. Property holding replaced church membership as one key qualification to vote.

## North America's Hundred Years' War Begins

William and Mary's coronation triggered war in Europe and North America. In 1690, rebels in New York and New England sought to demonstrate loyalty to their monarchs and defend Protestantism by planning an invasion of Canada, an initiative that ended in fiasco and mutual recrimination. Canadian Mohawks and Abenakis, backed by the French, raided New York and northern New England, torching English towns and taking captives as colonists barricaded themselves behind ramparts and heavy wooden doors. **King William's War** (1689–1697) marked New England's second devastating conflict in a generation. It struck when many were unsure of who had the right to govern them or on what terms. Massachusetts Bay still lacked a charter, so its rulers had no clear legal sanction to act.

In Salem, the terror of Abenaki attacks and uncertainty over who was in charge fed a panic that resulted in the execution of 20 and the accusation of nearly 200 on charges of witchcraft. The scare began in 1692 when Betty, the nine-year-old daughter of minister Samuel Parris, developed pains for which no doctor could find a physical cause. Tituba, an Arawak Indian from Guyana whom Parris purchased in Barbados and brought to New England, tried to end Betty's suffering by baking a cake that contained the girl's urine and feeding it to a dog. Popular belief held that the dog, whose form the witch had taken, would name the witch. Tituba was among the first women arrested. Her testimony convinced investigators that there were indeed witches in Salem who had made a pact with Satan. That, they thought, could explain the Abenaki raids that compelled refugees to seek shelter in the town and the symptoms that afflicted people, particularly young females, who implicated others, mostly women. Magistrates stopped prosecuting when a growing number of the accused were prominent figures rather than socially marginal ones—and when they began to doubt the evidence presented to them.

The Salem witch scare was one of the last in the northern Atlantic world. Scotland suffered one in the late 1690s that was sparked by similar factors, including fear of invasion. Similar developments ended that scare, although with far less carnage than in Salem. A judge who presided over the Salem witch hunt, Samuel Sewall, apologized for his conduct a few years later. Tituba recanted her confession and was sold to someone who paid her jail fees.

King William's War had far bigger repercussions for Indians. It widened divisions within the Iroquois as anti-French Mohawks joined aborted English invasions of Canada. In 1693, French forces, guided by Canadian Mohawks, invaded Mohawk country, torched three towns, and headed north with 300 captives. Iroquois leaders concluded that the English would never honor their promises of assistance and looked to negotiate peace with New France. Meanwhile, New France's governor encouraged Huron-Petuns and Algonquians to avenge the Iroquois raids that in the 1640s and 1650s had

## TIMELINE 1640–1696

**1640s**
Sugar boom begins on Barbados

**1642**
English Civil War erupts

Puritan migration to New England halts

**1646**
First colonial ship carrying enslaved Africans to North America docks in Boston

**1647**
Apalachee rebellion in Florida

**1649**
Charles I beheaded; England becomes a commonwealth

Iroquois attacks destroy Huron Confederacy

Predecessor of New England Company founded to promote conversion of New England Algonquians

**1651**
First Navigation Act to regulate commerce of English colonies

**1652–1654**
First Anglo-Dutch War

**1652**
Rhode Island outlaws lifelong slavery for Europeans and Africans

**1656**
Timucua rebel in Florida

**1660**
Monarchy restored to England with crowning of Charles II

**1661**
Barbados legislators create colonial English America's first comprehensive slave code

Royal Society of London founded and colonists admitted as members

**1662**
Virginia lawmakers decide that children should inherit their legal status from mothers rather than fathers

**1663**
Proprietors receive English royal charter to Carolina

Company of Royal Adventurers to Africa (antecedent of Royal African Company) granted monopoly to ship enslaved Africans to English North America and West Indies

**1664–1667**
Second Anglo-Dutch War

**1664**
**August** English forces conquer New Netherland from Dutch Empire and rename it New York

**1666**
**September** French raid on Mohawk Country

**1667**
**June** Mohawks join rest of Five Nations in peace treaty with New France

**1669**
Fundamental Constitutions of Carolina written

**1670**
First permanent English settlement in South Carolina

Hudson's Bay Company founded

**1672–1674**
Third Anglo-Dutch War

**1673**
**July** New York captured by Dutch and renamed New Netherland

**1674**
**October** Dutch return New York to English control

forced them from their homelands. King William's War ended in 1697 for Europeans and colonists. It raged four more years for most Indians and decimated the Iroquois. Its diplomats thereafter strove for neutrality in the conflicts between the two European empires that claimed parts of the northeast.

The Iroquois tried to stay out of what became a second Hundred Years' War between England and France. It began in 1689 and ended in 1783 when the American Revolution did. For the Boston minister Cotton Mather, King William's War gave New England a new sense of purpose. He considered the region a shield that defended the English world and Protestantism against France and Catholicism. For English and French colonists, the war made their corner of the world seem more important to their rulers across the Atlantic. That forged even tighter bonds between North America and the European empires that claimed more of it.

## STUDY QUESTIONS FOR VICTORIOUS PUEBLOS, A NEW MID-ATLANTIC, AND "GLORIOUS" REVOLUTIONS, 1680 TO THE 1690S

1. **What impact did the Glorious Revolution have on North America?**
2. **New York, New Jersey, Pennsylvania, and Carolina all became part of the English empire as a result of Charles II's coronation. Did these colonies have anything else in common? Please support your answer with specific examples.**

**1675**

**June** King Philip's War begins in southern New England

**July** Doeg Indian raid into Virginia sparks Bacon's Rebellion

**September** King Philip's War spreads to northern New England

**1676**

**August** King Philip's War ends in southern New England

**October** Bacon's Rebellion ends

**1677**

**April** English colonies and the Iroquois League establish the Covenant Chain

**August** King Philip's War ends in northern New England

**1680**

**August** Pueblo war for independence drives Spanish from New Mexico

**1681**

Charles II grants Pennsylvania to William Penn

**1682**

Mary Rowlandson's captivity narrative published

Philadelphia founded

Robert Cavalier de La Salle arrives at mouth of Mississippi River, claims its watershed for France, and renames area Louisiana

**1685**

James II crowned King of England

Dominion of New England established

**1688**

"Glorious Revolution" in England

James II forced to abdicate throne

William and Mary crowned King and Queen of England

**1689**

Revolts inspired by "Glorious Revolution" overthrow governments of Massachusetts Bay, New York, and Maryland

**April** Dominion of New England terminated

**1689–1697**

King William's War

**1691**

Massachusetts granted new royal charter

**1692**

**January** Salem witch crisis begins

**August** Spanish forces begin to reconquer New Mexico

**1693**

**May** Salem witch crisis ends

**1696**

**November** Spanish complete reconquest of New Mexico and end Pueblo war for independence

## Summary

- Political instability gripped North America between 1640 and 1660 as Iroquois raids decimated their Indian foes; New England responded to civil war in England by diversifying its economy and forging ties to Barbados, English America's first slave society; and friars claimed more power in Florida and New Mexico.
- Between 1660 and 1680 the founding of South Carolina and war in Virginia entrenched slavery and white supremacy in an English North America enlarged by the conquest of New Netherland, scarred by warfare with Indians, threatened by expanding French claims, and governed by a new king who sought more control over colonial affairs.
- The 1680s and 1690s brought an Indian struggle for independence in New Mexico, the establishment of multicultural colonies in Pennsylvania and New Jersey, and more political instability in the English Atlantic world that sparked the first of many conflicts between the English and French empires and posed new challenges for Indians.

## Key Terms and People

**Articles of Capitulation** *102*
**Bacon, Nathaniel** *110*
**Bacon's Rebellion** *107*
**Barbados slave code** *97*
**Beaver Wars** *89*
**Berkeley, William** *91*
**Catherine/Kateri Tekakwitha** *105*
**Charles II** *91*
**Colbert, Jean-Baptiste** *103*
**Covenant Chain** *106*
**Cromwell, Oliver** *90*
**Dominion of New England** *120*
**Eliot, John** *92*
**English Civil War** *91*
**First Anglo-Dutch War** *101*
**Glorious Revolution** *120*
**Half-Way Covenant** *113*
**Hudson's Bay Company** *106*
**James, Duke of York (James II)** *102*
**jeremiad** *113*
**katsinas** *117*
**King Philip's War** *110*
**King William's War** *121*
**Leisler, Jacob** *121*
**Locke, John** *111*
**Louis XIV** *120*
**mercantilism** *103*
**Metacom/Philip** *114*
**Navigation Acts** *100*
**New England Company** *92*
**Parliament** *90*
**Penn, William** *118*
**Popé** *115*
**Pueblo War for Independence** *118*
**quitrent** *118*
**Rowlandson, Mary** *115*
**Royal African Company** *96*
**Royal Society** *113*
**Second Anglo-Dutch War** *102*
**Society of Friends/Quakers** *93*
**Timucua revolt** *99*

## Reviewing Chapter 3

1. Environmental change played as big a role in shaping politics and economics in North America and the Caribbean between 1640 and the 1690s as disease or religion did. Does this chapter support this claim? Please use specific examples to support your answer.
2. Was the Pueblo war for independence a unique event in the history of colonial North America up to the 1690s? If so, why? If not, why not?
3. In what ways did patterns of migration to, from, and within North America change between 1640 and the 1690s? What role did politics and North America's tighter bonds to the Atlantic world play in shaping migration?

## Further Reading

Greer, Allan. *Mohawk Saint: Catherine Tekakwitha and the Jesuits.* New York: Oxford University Press, 2005. A superb account of Tekakwitha, Iroquois conversion to Christianity, and the challenges that she and other Mohawks faced during the mid- to late-17th century.

Gutiérrez, Ramón A. *When Jesus Came, the Corn Mothers Went Away: Marriage, Sexuality, and Power in New Mexico, 1500-1846.* Stanford, Calif.: Stanford University Press, 1991. Now more than twenty years old, but still the best account of Spanish colonization and Spanish-Pueblo relations in New Mexico.

Menard, Russell R. *Sweet Negotiations: Sugar, Slavery, and Plantation Agriculture in Early Barbados.* Charlottesville and London: University of Virginia Press, 2006. An excellent explanation of the causes and consequences of the Barbados sugar boom.

Pagan, John Ruston. *Anne Orthwood's Bastard: Sex and Law in Early Virginia.* New York: Oxford University Press, 2003. A carefully crafted study of gender, indentured servitude, and the rise of an "American" body of legal thought in mid-17th century Virginia.

Pestana, Carla Gardina. *The English Atlantic in an Age of Revolution, 1640–1661.* Cambridge, Mass., and London: Harvard University Press, 2004. Presents the English Civil War as a transatlantic event that profoundly remade the English Empire.

Pulsipher, Jenny Hale. *Subjects Unto the Same King: Indians, English, and the Contest for Authority in Colonial New England.* Philadelphia: University of Pennsylvania Press, 2005. Explores English-Algonquian relations and their relationship to English imperial politics during the 17th century.

# Visual Review

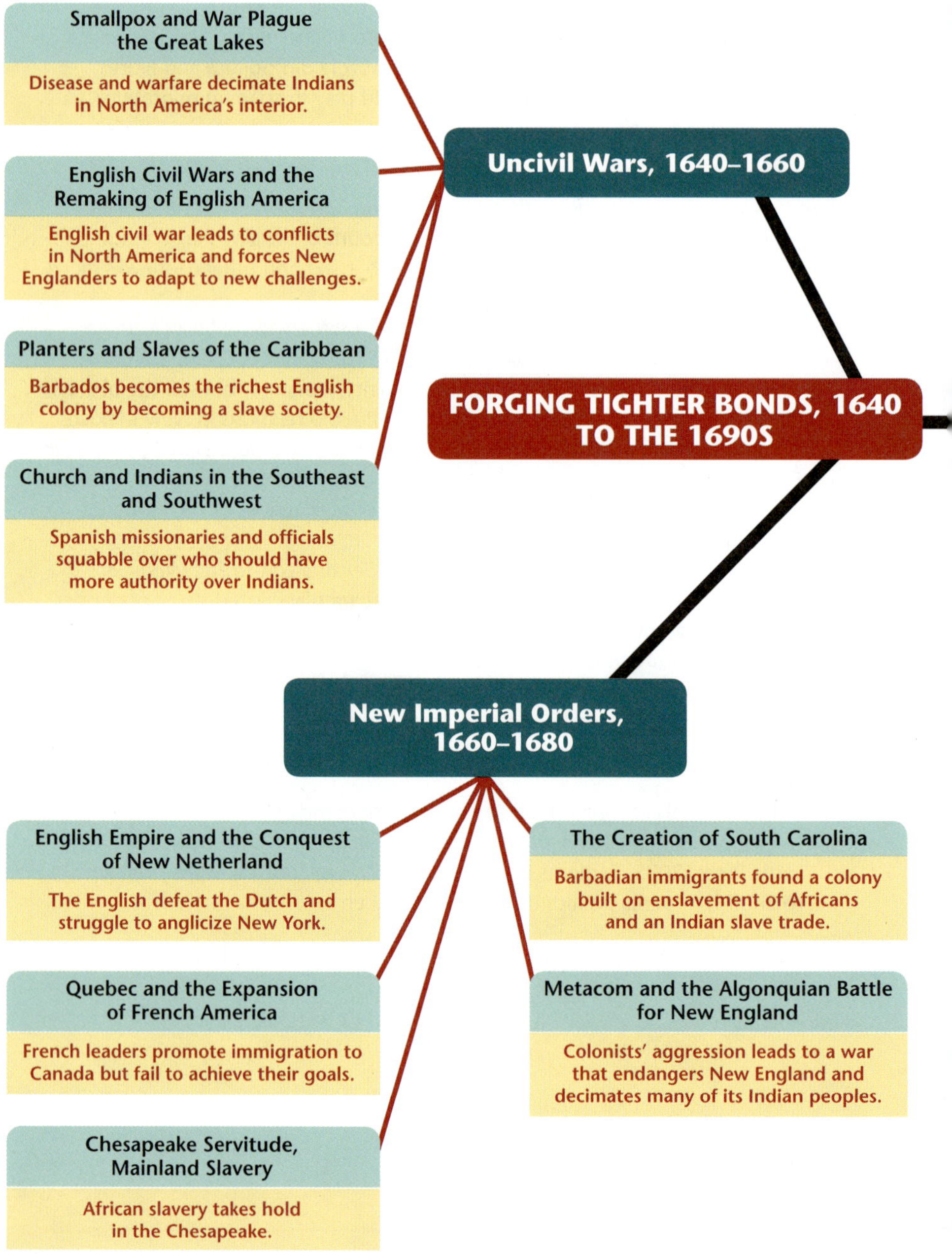

## FORGING TIGHTER BONDS, 1640 TO THE 1690S

### Uncivil Wars, 1640–1660

**Smallpox and War Plague the Great Lakes**

Disease and warfare decimate Indians in North America's interior.

**English Civil Wars and the Remaking of English America**

English civil war leads to conflicts in North America and forces New Englanders to adapt to new challenges.

**Planters and Slaves of the Caribbean**

Barbados becomes the richest English colony by becoming a slave society.

**Church and Indians in the Southeast and Southwest**

Spanish missionaries and officials squabble over who should have more authority over Indians.

### New Imperial Orders, 1660–1680

**English Empire and the Conquest of New Netherland**

The English defeat the Dutch and struggle to anglicize New York.

**Quebec and the Expansion of French America**

French leaders promote immigration to Canada but fail to achieve their goals.

**Chesapeake Servitude, Mainland Slavery**

African slavery takes hold in the Chesapeake.

**The Creation of South Carolina**

Barbadian immigrants found a colony built on enslavement of Africans and an Indian slave trade.

**Metacom and the Algonquian Battle for New England**

Colonists' aggression leads to a war that endangers New England and decimates many of its Indian peoples.

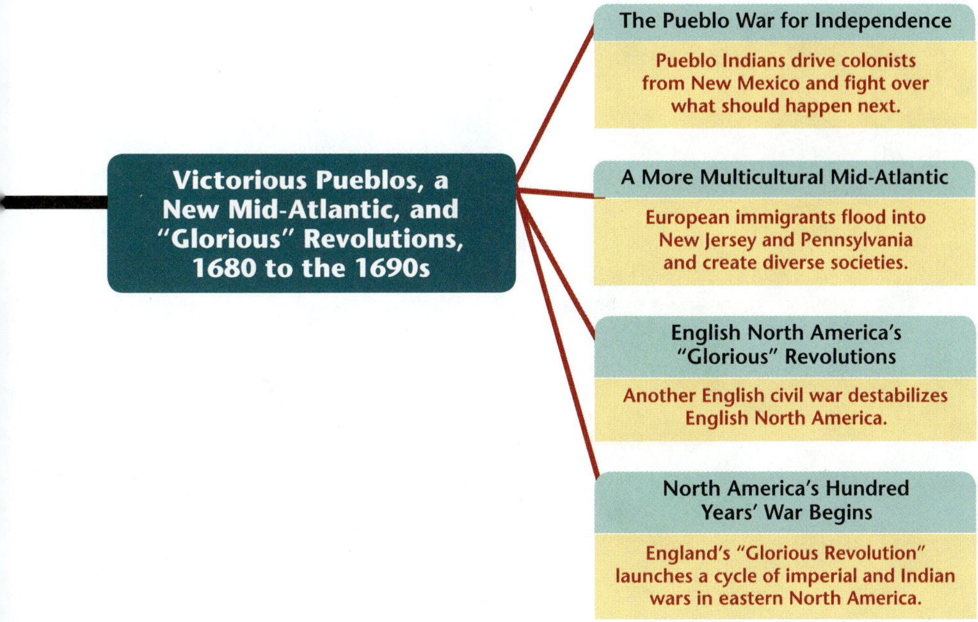

**Victorious Pueblos, a New Mid-Atlantic, and "Glorious" Revolutions, 1680 to the 1690s**

**The Pueblo War for Independence**

Pueblo Indians drive colonists from New Mexico and fight over what should happen next.

**A More Multicultural Mid-Atlantic**

European immigrants flood into New Jersey and Pennsylvania and create diverse societies.

**English North America's "Glorious" Revolutions**

Another English civil war destabilizes English North America.

**North America's Hundred Years' War Begins**

England's "Glorious Revolution" launches a cycle of imperial and Indian wars in eastern North America.

# 4 Accelerating the Pace of Change

## c. 1690–1730

CHAPTER OUTLINE



This entire colony," a Louisiana priest complained in 1717, "is a veritable Babylon." Five years later, a French military officer saw corruption and disorder everywhere, from the governor down to the smugglers, pirates, soldiers, sailors, convict servants, slaves, runaways, and Indians who slogged through the muddy streets of New Orleans. "In short," he reported, Louisiana "is without religion, without justice, without discipline, without order, and without police."

This was not news to those who ran France and its empire. They had literally tied France's fortunes to the success of Louisiana and deeply regretted it. In 1717, Philippe, the Duc d'Orléans, handed control of the colony and the French economy to John Law, a brilliant Scottish financier. D'Orléans hoped that Louisiana could produce tobacco, ending France's dependence on a supply imported from the Chesapeake via England, and he was confident that Law would deliver. Law devised a pyramid scheme in which his firm, eventually named the Company of the Indies, sold shares to French investors to finance the colonization of Louisiana. He guaranteed that they would earn huge profits and assured his superiors that Louisiana would soon fill royal coffers drained by decades of European warfare.

The price of company stock initially soared as the firm used the proceeds to send thousands of enslaved Africans, French

Tee Yee Neen Ho Ga Row (Hendrick Tejonihokarawa)

# America in the World

Fox Wars pitted Fox Indians against French-allied Indians and French colonists, decimating the Fox (1712–1735).

The French colonized Louisiana, building Fort Biloxi (1699) and New Orleans (1718).

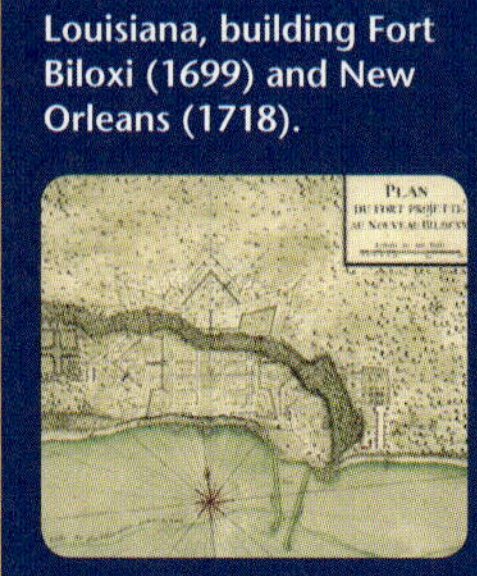

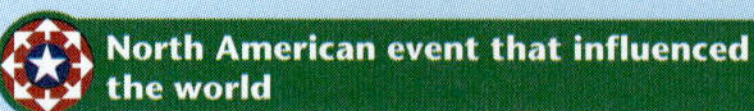

North American event that influenced the world

International event that influenced North America

Event with multinational influence

Conflict

Treaties between Indian nations and French and English empires stabilized northeastern North America for over a generation (1701).
Les Gens du Saulx
Les Gens dela Montagne
Boom in rice cultivation increased demand for African slaves (1720s).
The Yamasee War imperiled the British colony of South Carolina (1715–1716).

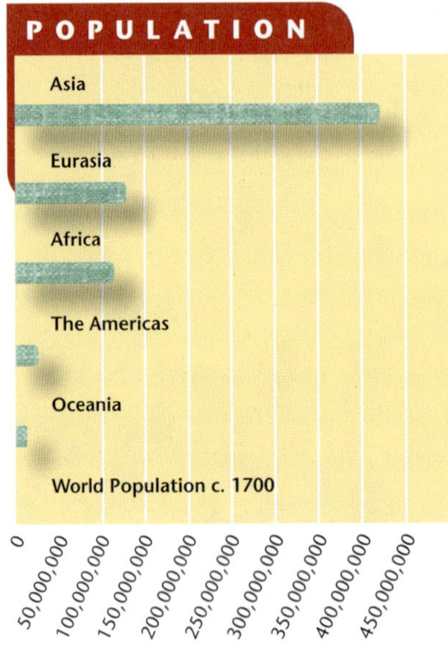


convict servants, and Germans to the banks of the Lower Mississippi. Meanwhile, urban planners envisioned that New Orleans—founded in 1718, named after the Duc, and built strategically on the site of an Indian portage between the Mississippi and Lake Pontchartrain—would become a model French city. A hurricane imperiled that dream by swamping New Orleans in 1722. The Company responded by having its slaves erect levees and dig canals to divert water from the town.

By the time the flood inundated New Orleans, enthusiasm for Louisiana had dried up in France. In 1720, the value of Company of the Indies stock plummeted and the "**Mississippi Bubble**" burst. A disgraced John Law fled France; he died poor in Venice nine years later. The company that he abandoned abruptly halted shipments of food to Louisiana, leaving colonists to starve. The Company of the Indies limped along for another decade. In 1731, its directors handed Louisiana back to **Louis XV**, who, unlike his great-uncle the

A French view of Louisiana, c. 1720. This fanciful scene (the Gulf Coast has no mountains; few Mexican Indians visited Louisiana) shows what French officials and investors hoped Louisiana would become: a magnet to lure trade from Mexico to the French Empire. Instead, the colony's ports, especially New Orleans, became magnets for smugglers who dodged French regulations.

Duc d'Orléans, practically forgot that it existed. But the unsavory reputations of Louisiana and New Orleans stuck. Some 13,000 Europeans and Africans, most of them brought in chains, had come to Louisiana since 1717. Only 6,000 remained 15 years later. Few people arrived over the next three decades. Largely cut off from direct contact with the Atlantic and virtually autonomous from the French Empire, a small group of American-born merchants made New Orleans the smuggling capital of the northern Gulf of Mexico. Meanwhile, Louisiana became a small and poor colony with an American-born black majority. Even so, it anchored French claims to North America's interior, extended European influence deep into Indian country, and accelerated the pace of changes already underway on the continent.

From the 1690s to 1730 European empires staked bigger claims to North America as colonial expansion, warfare, and wider dissemination of European goods eroded Indian power. Heavier immigration, a transatlantic Protestant movement that sought more pious believers and new converts around the world, and stronger political bonds overseas altered how colonists in British North America viewed each other, the British Empire, and the Atlantic world. A growing native-born elite empowered and informed by its ties to Atlantic networks led efforts to classify colonists by race, diversify British North America's economy, and distinguish themselves from newly arrived and poorer colonists.

# TURMOIL IN INDIAN NORTH AMERICA

In 1700, Indians comprised the vast majority of North Americans. One hundred years later, Europeans, Africans, and their descendants vastly outnumbered Indians, due largely to events that altered and often convulsed Indian North America between the 1690s and 1730. Diffusion of goods, especially horses and guns, promoted violence among Indians from the Rockies east to the Appalachians, stoking an Indian slave trade that moved captives across the continent and altered Indian politics, particularly in the southeast. The founding of new colonies in Texas and Louisiana accelerated these developments, empowering some neighboring Indian peoples at the expense of others and extending European claims into the interior. Meanwhile, the power of Indians along the southeastern Atlantic coast and in the Northeast waned as wars sapped their strength and imports and colonists began to flood into their lands.

## Horses and Violence on the Northern Plains

In the early 1700s, Indians of the northern Great Plains and Great Basin encountered new peoples and goods. From the North and East came French fur trappers and British traders bearing firearms. From the South and West came Indians mounted on horses.

Saukamappee, a young Cree adopted by the Blackfeet, witnessed these changes. He was a young man when the Blackfeet first saw horses. Sometime around 1730 Shoshone warriors wielding stone clubs and mounted on *Misstutin* (literally "big dogs" to the Blackfeet) slaughtered their stunned foes. Blackfeet soon acquired horses through trade or theft. Within a generation they became a fully equestrian people who introduced horses to the Cree. In return, the Cree provided firearms that enabled Blackfeet to gain the upper hand over Shoshone (Map 4.1).

Crees and Shoshones played crucial roles in transforming the region. Cree men carried pelts to Hudson's Bay Company outposts, taking away firearms, knives, and twisted ropes of Brazilian-grown tobacco. The Cree traded the imports to Indians to their south and west. Shoshones occupied the northern end of an Indian network that funneled horses along the Continental Divide and across it. Horses reached the Shoshone around 1700 thanks, according to Shoshone oral traditions, to the Comanche. In turn, Shoshones supplied horses to Indians who lived on the Columbia Plateau,

▲ **Map 4.1**

**Horses and Guns Enter the Great Plains, c. 1600 to c. 1770** Horses spread more rapidly on western trade routes along the Rockies than they did in the Great Plains. French traders, many of them from Louisiana, played a crucial role in introducing firearms to Plains peoples, as did the Hudson's Bay Company.

who incorporated them into their seasonal migration as they fished for salmon, hunted bison, and gathered berries and roots.

Indians' desire to acquire horses intensified trade in Indian slaves. Shoshones raided the Blackfeet partly to replace people taken for sale to Spanish colonists in the Southwest. Pawnee villages in Nebraska served as way stations for captives from the Southwest and Northern Plains. The Illinois and Osage sold some who ended up in the Great Lakes or South Carolina. Others went to New Mexico.

The advent of the horse and growing commercial ties to colonists encouraged Plains peoples to further exploit captive Indians. Female captives often had the dirty and smelly task of processing beaver pelts and buffalo hides for trade, a job that exemplified the empowerment of Plains Indian men at the expense of Indian women. Marriage established a Comanche man's claim to independence, but he could not wed until he had acquired enough prestige through hunting, warfare, and capturing a foe's horses and people. Women and children made the best captives, partly because they were most easily assimilated.

By 1706, horses had carried Comanches from their Great Basin homeland to areas rich in bison herds on the southern plains (Map 4.1). Their arrival on New Mexico's border recast relations between Indians, Hispanic colonists, and Spanish officials. So did the coming of French colonists to Texas in the 1680s.

## Indians and Hispanics Forge a New Southwest

In 1685, the French began to construct a fort near the Gulf coast. Spanish officials fretted that they might win over Indian customers and imperil Mexican silver mines and Spanish commerce in the Gulf. The French challenge and the Pueblo war for independence spurred the Spanish to establish a mission and presidio (a fort) within the Hasinai Confederacy, a group of Caddoan-speaking towns in eastern Texas and western Louisiana, in the early 1690s. The Spanish knew the Hasinai as "the Kingdom of Tejas," the Caddo word for ally.

By 1693, the Caddo forced the Spanish to leave, largely because the newcomers would not follow Caddo gender norms. Caddo delegations to other peoples normally included women and children to convey peaceful intentions. The Spanish party that founded Texas was composed entirely of men, but it marched under a banner that depicted the Virgin Mary, symbolic leader of the Spanish campaign to evangelize Texas. The Hasinai interpreted the strangers' display of a woman's image as a sign of peace. But Spanish soldiers soon began to prey on Caddo women, so the Hasinai threw them out. The Spanish were unlike the French men who had arrived a decade earlier. They came alone rather than in heavily armed groups, and they married Caddo women who afforded them full membership in a society organized around matrilineal clans.

Failure to obey Caddo ways and an inability to meet Hasanai demand for imported goods continued to curb Spanish influence. In 1716, the Hasinai permitted construction of a presidio and missions. The Spanish hoped that the new outpost, Los Adaes, would curb French influence. Caddo welcomed the Spanish as long as they behaved well and provided an alternative source of goods. Spanish officials tried to honor Caddo values by recruiting families to settle near the presidio and mission, but found few takers. The Spanish abandoned the mission in the late 1720s. The Hispanic colonists who stayed behind traded horses to the nearby French post at Natchitoches for food and firearms. The Hasanai prospered by supplying Louisiana with livestock and French goods, particularly firearms, to Indians to their north and west.

The Spanish turned their attention to south Texas. In 1718, they founded missions and a presidio at San Antonio de Béjar, today's San Antonio. The small village attracted diverse bands of Indians from the lower Rio Grande Valley who, like the Spanish, sought protection from Plains Apaches. Apache raids on San Antonio were so frequent that local officials begged for more colonists to help defend it. Their pleas fell on deaf ears until 1731, when 55 colonists arrived, increasing San Antonio's Hispanic population to 300 and that of Texas to 500.

Comanches helped to ensure that San Antonio remained a Hispanic island in an Indian ocean. Apaches raided San Antonio and New Mexico partly to replace horses stolen by Comanches and Utes. Apaches also attacked New Mexico to avenge colonists' enslavement of hundreds of their kin. Some had been taken in Spanish-Pueblo raids; others were bought from Utes and Comanches, who also traded Apaches to the Pawnee.

Slaving raids also had a profound impact on the Navajo, who had offered refuge to hundreds of Pueblos who fled the Spanish reconquest of New Mexico. Refugees' weaving skills bolstered an economy that increasingly depended on raising sheep and weaving wool into blankets and textiles. Navajos sometimes raided New Mexico for sheep. Spanish-Pueblo incursions between 1705 and 1709 took Navajo captives and forced the Navajo to leave Spanish livestock alone. Ute raids gave the Navajo more reason to seek peace with New Mexico.

Growing Navajo dependence on sheep had profound environmental and social consequences. By the 1720s, sheep had overgrazed canyons in northwestern New Mexico, which prompted the Navajo to move west in search of fresher pastures. Raising sheep also threatened to divide Navajo society into those who owned large flocks and those who did not. Rustling outsiders' flocks offered a way for poorer men to acquire sheep and ease tensions among the Navajo.

Colonists and Pueblos in New Mexico also found ways to compromise. After the reconquest, Pueblos accepted Spanish rule, helped to defend the colony, and joined in Spanish slaving raids in exchange for more autonomy and Spanish protection from Indian foes. Governors still required Pueblo men to construct public buildings, maintain irrigation systems, and work Spanish officials' fields, while Pueblo women performed domestic labor, ground wheat and corn, and baked bread. But Indian leaders of each town determined who should serve when. Pueblo dignitaries and medicine men, not missionaries, chose town leaders, and friars intervened less frequently in Pueblo society. Hispanics and Pueblos had settled into an uneasy alliance, largely as a consequence of the Pueblo war for independence and Apache and Comanche raids.

## Indians, the French, and the Making of Louisiana

In 1699, the French claimed the mouth of the Mississippi River by building a fort at Biloxi. They quickly learned how much they depended on Indians. Colonists needed Indians to feed them, defend them, and trade with them. Indians noted that a disproportionate share of the first colonists of Louisiana and Illinois, then part of Louisiana, were French Canadians who knew Indian ways. Many became kin by marrying Indian women and settling in Indian towns.

The French arrived at a propitious moment for the Choctaw, who lived farther from English and Spanish sources of imported goods than most of their enemies did. By the 1690s they were frequent targets of Chickasaw slaving raids sponsored by South Carolina colonists. This encouraged the Choctaw to affiliate with Louisiana's French colonists, but it did not ensure their friendship. In 1711, the colony's governor, fearful that the English might lure the Choctaw to their side, declared the Choctaw "the key to this country," which required that the French furnish them with "cloth to clothe them and weapons to defend themselves."

The French alliance with the Choctaw would prove vital to the survival of Louisiana. The area's last surviving Mississippian culture, the Natchez, occupied a bluff with

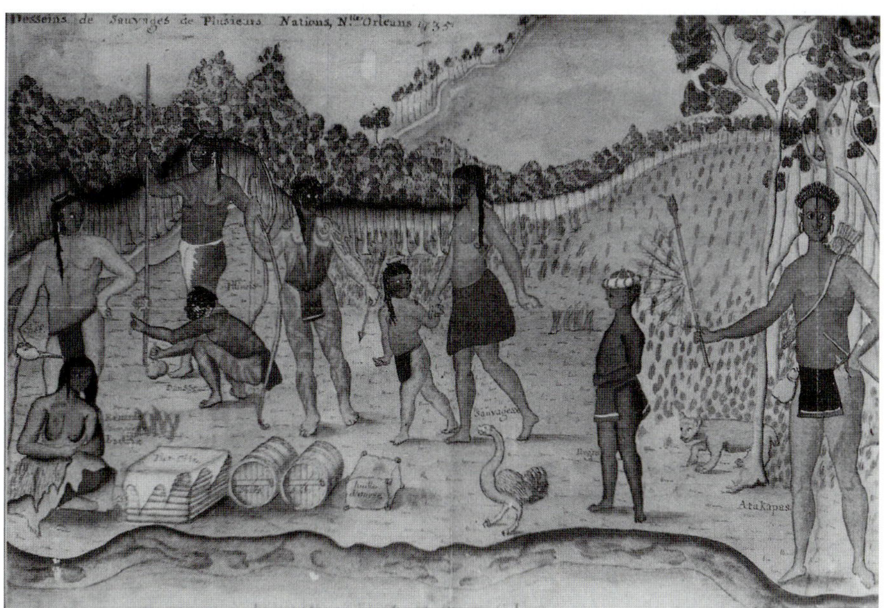


Indians and Africans on a New Orleans levee, 1730s. An enslaved Fox woman, barrels of liquor, and bundles of deerskins occupy the foreground. An enslaved African boy and an Attakapas hunter stand to the right. He holds a calumet (peace pipe), used in Indian diplomatic rituals throughout the region. The scene indicates Louisiana's dependence on Indians and Africans.

rich soils that offered protection from floods. For the French, it was an ideal place for establishing tobacco plantations. Tensions flared between the **Natchez** and the French as colonists imported African slaves to begin growing tobacco in the 1720s. The Natchez resented French incursions into their lands and their own growing dependence on French goods. Natchez warriors and African slaves struck back one morning in 1729. They killed over 200 colonists and captured nearly 300 African slaves and 50 white women and children. Choctaw warriors enabled French colonists to win the **Natchez War** and suppress Louisiana's enslaved Africans. French officials handed three Africans who had joined the Natchez over to the Choctaw, who burned them to death.

The war made a diaspora of the Natchez and brought political change to Louisiana. Hundreds of Natchez were enslaved and sold to sugar planters in Saint Domingue. Louisiana's governor, exasperated by his dependence on Indians, complained that "[t]he least little nation thinks itself our protector." He requested more troops so that he could compel Indians to respect him, but instead lost his job. Louis XV, fed up with bad news from Louisiana, took control of the colony in 1731, and then mostly ignored what happened there.

## Indians, Empires, and the Remaking of the Southeast

Although South Carolina did not depend on Indians as much as Louisiana did, the colony needed them to supply two exports: deerskins and slaves. Indian hunters provided deerskins, which Europeans often used instead of cowhides. Indian warriors captured people and enslaved them. Some enslaved Indians whom English colonists shipped from Carolina, mainly to the West Indies, had trudged from as far as the Northern Plains and Southwest, but most came from southeastern peoples allied with France or Spain whom English-sponsored warriors had seized.

Slaving raids spread disease that killed thousands and fed violence that engulfed the Indian southeast. Dozens of South Carolina soldiers accompanied thousands of Indians, most of them Creek, in a wave of attacks on Apalachee missions in northern Florida. They slaughtered hundreds, enslaved thousands, and reduced Florida's missions to ashes between 1702 and 1706 (Map 4.2). Five years later, the Tuscarora, kin to the peoples of the Iroquois League, retaliated for slaving raids and colonists' encroachment on their lands by attacking farms and towns in North Carolina. South Carolina sent troops to assist, but Catawbas, Yamasees, and Cherokees comprised most of the force that killed or enslaved about 1,000 Tuscarora and won the **Tuscarora War** (1711–1713).

Peoples who suffered slaving raids often split apart. Some Tuscaroras stayed in North Carolina after the war ended. About 2,000 others found shelter alongside the Iroquois. Some mission Apalachees relocated near St. Augustine for protection and to shore up its defenses. Others sought refuge among other Indians in present-day Georgia and Alabama. Some Indians fled deep into Florida, with Indian slave raiders in hot pursuit, or boarded ships headed for Cuba.

The British Caribbean was probably the main destination for Indian slaves, though some remained in South Carolina, where they comprised 15 percent of the

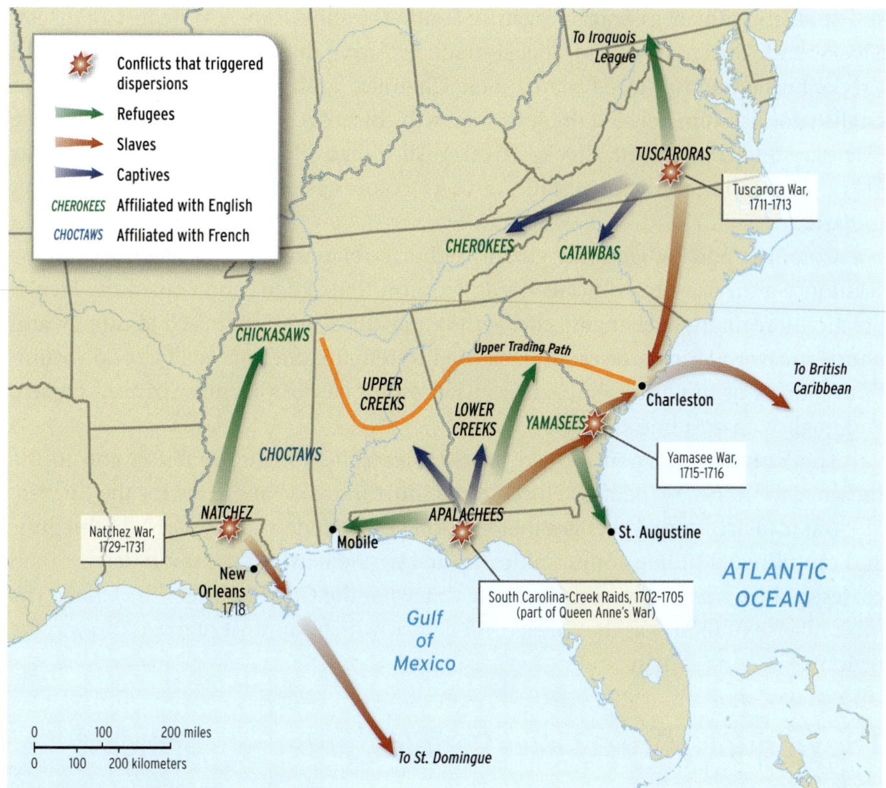


**Map 4.2**

**War, the Indian Slave Trade, and the Dispersal of Southeastern Indian Peoples, c. 1700–1730** Epidemics, demand for Indian slaves, and English and French invasions of Indian lands devastated the Southeast's Indian peoples. This map charts the movements of four peoples—the Apalachee, the Tuscarora, the Yamasee, and the Natchez—dispersed by conflicts with European colonists and Indians affiliated with them.

population in 1708. Others were sold to New England, New York, and Virginia. Colonists in those regions bought them because they were cheaper than Africans, although they soon developed a reputation as "malacious, surly, and revengeful," according to a 1712 Massachusetts law that barred their entry. Other New England colonies followed suit.

Meanwhile, South Carolina had developed a bad reputation among its Indian neighbors. So many Indians left Charleston in chains that the port exported more slaves than it imported until 1715. Cherokees, Creeks, and Chickasaws felt cheated by traveling English traders licensed by the colony. The Yamasee were particularly resentful. They had been allies to South Carolina for three decades, but by the early 1710s, Yamasees were deeply indebted to English merchants, mainly because they no longer had direct access to deerskins and Indian slaves. English planters coveted Yamasee lands and dreamed of growing rice on them.

In 1715, Indian grievances against South Carolina turned violent. Cherokees, Creeks, and Chickasaws killed English traders visiting their villages as Yamasees and Creeks burned and pillaged plantations. Cherokee and Chickasaw dependence on English goods ultimately led them to side with colonists, a decision that brought the Cherokee into conflict with Creeks. The English-Indian alliance won the **Yamasee War** (1715–1716), but not before it killed 1 in 16 colonists and took a far greater toll on Indians.

Colonists and Indians struggled to stabilize relations in the wake of such devastation. South Carolina officials fixed prices on trade goods and copied the French practice of regularly exchanging gifts with Indian allies, who promised to capture and return runaway African slaves. Indians tried to remain autonomous by seeking multiple sources of imports, while Creeks used diplomacy to play the Spanish, French, and English against one another.

The Yamasee War transformed the Southeast. It brought an abrupt end to the Indian slave trade, as Indians refused to conduct more slaving raids for the English. The war also accelerated changes that had long been underway. By 1720, multiethnic and multilingual Indian communities, united by the need for common defense, had coalesced into new political entities: the Catawba, the Cherokee, the Chickasaw. The most diverse of these was the Creek confederacy, which for most of the 1700s was the region's foremost Indian power.

## The Iroquois, Great Lakes Peoples, and the Northeast

As war roiled the Carolinas and Louisiana, Indian politics in the Northeast and Great Lakes stabilized, thanks largely to two treaties signed by the Iroquois, known together as the "**Grand Settlement of 1701**." In one, the Iroquois, decimated by King William's War, agreed to cease hostilities with Great Lakes peoples and exchange captives with them. The French guaranteed the Iroquois hunting and trading rights west to Detroit, which the French founded in 1701. In the other, the Iroquois retained the right to trade at Albany. The league also promised to remain neutral in future Anglo-French wars.

Conflict over trade with Great Lakes peoples and factionalism within the Iroquois League nearly unraveled the "Grand Settlement." The French had hoped that they would be able to monitor relations between the Iroquois and the Ottawa, Potawatomi, Wyandot, and Ojibwa, thousands of whom accepted a French invitation to resettle near Detroit. This brought these French allies closer to sources of British goods such as coarse woolen cloth, blankets, and kettles, which tended to be cheaper, more abundant, and better suited to Indian tastes than similar French imports. The most direct path to those British goods was through the Iroquois, who in 1707 granted Great Lakes Indians permission to travel to Albany. As trade dried up at Montreal, the French intervened in the Iroquois League's internal affairs, enraging a large faction of Mohawks.

Those Mohawks decided to take sides in **Queen Anne's War** (1702–1713), a conflict between Britain, France, and Spain fought largely to determine whether relatives of France's king Louis XIV should be allowed to sit on the throne of Spain. In 1709,

Mohawks agreed to join an invasion of Canada that British officials later canceled. The following year, three Mohawks and a Mahican traveled to London, where the "Four Indian Kings" (as the London press called them) met Queen Anne to lobby for a British invasion of Canada. Their efforts initially bore fruit. In 1711, Britain sent over 5,000 troops across the Atlantic, the largest British military force yet to reach the Americas, to join New England and New York militiamen in an attack on New France. A storm off the coast of Canada ran nine ships aground, claiming over 700 lives and prompting the British to scuttle the mission, much to many Mohawks' dismay.

By 1717, the Iroquois agreed that neutrality was their best course. Tuscaroras driven north by British colonists helped to maintain that consensus, especially after the Iroquois admitted them to their league in 1722. The Iroquois directed their wars for captives at peoples such as the Catawba and Cherokee and negotiated with British colonies to ensure that their warriors could travel freely to and from the Southeast.

Meanwhile, the French struggled to keep the Iroquois from taking sides in wars in the Great Lakes that involved their Indian allies. Peoples friendly to the French sought to drive a wedge between the Fox, whose Wisconsin territory was near rich sources of pelts, and the French, fearing that a French-Fox alliance would deprive them of trade goods. Skillful diplomacy and "gifts" of Fox slaves persuaded the French to side against the Fox in three wars (1712–1716, 1723–1725, and 1728–1735). The Fox numbered several thousand when the **Fox Wars** began, but only a few hundred when the wars ended. The rest escaped to Iowa or were killed, adopted by their enemies, or enslaved by the French. Some Fox slaves deemed too dangerous were sent to the West Indies.

The role that Fox captives played in sealing the alliance between New France and its Indian allies underscores how important Indian captives were to regional diplomacy. In 1705, Ottawas, at the request of the French, atoned for a raid on the Iroquois by seizing Sioux and sending them to the Iroquois for adoption. New France's governor ransomed Indian captives from western allies and traded them to free New England colonists whom Abenakis and Canadian Mohawks had seized during Queen Anne's War.

Peace between the Northeast's three main powers—the British, the French, and the Iroquois—displaced weaker Indians. By 1722, Pennsylvania officials accepted Iroquois claims that they spoke for Delawares and Shawnees. The arrangement enhanced Iroquois power, partly because it provided the league's peoples an alternative source of British goods. But Delawares and Shawnees had their lands in eastern Pennsylvania sold out from under them. They headed west, where they began to upset the region's delicate balance of power in the 1740s.

The stability that the Iroquois enjoyed came at a high cost. The league's peoples could no longer mask their dependence on Europeans. In the 1720s the Iroquois permitted the French and British to construct rival forts and trading posts near Lake Ontario. These diverted western Indians' trade and flooded Iroquois villages with cheap alcohol, eliciting requests that the sale of rum be banned west of Albany. Meanwhile, New York encroached on Mohawk country. The colonization of the Iroquois, the Northeast's preeminent Indian power for generations, had begun.

**STUDY QUESTIONS FOR TURMOIL IN INDIAN NORTH AMERICA**

1. In what ways did horses and guns change life for Indians on the Northern Plains and in the Southwest?
2. What impact did the Indian slave trade have on North America?
3. What was the Great Settlement of 1701? By what means and at what cost did it bring political stability to northeastern North America?

# MIGRATION, RELIGION, AND EMPIRES

Indians' grip on eastern North America weakened in part because tens of thousands of enslaved Africans and European immigrants flooded in. The newcomers, particularly the Africans, provoked a backlash from white colonists that entrenched racism throughout colonial North America. Massive immigration, along with thickening transatlantic ties among Protestants who sought American converts and a more powerful British empire, bound North America more tightly to the Atlantic world.

## The Africanization of North America

Colonial North America expanded rapidly in the early 1700s, largely as a result of its Africanization. More Africans landed in North America in the first decade of the eighteenth century than had done so between 1565 and 1690. Enslaved Africans comprised the majority of immigrants to North America between 1691 and 1730.

The intensification of the Atlantic slave trade destabilized African politics and coincided with major economic changes in Africa. In 1704, a popular movement erupted in West Central Africa that sought to end years of civil war between competitors for the throne of Kongo and halt the flow of thousands of captives into the Atlantic slave trade. King Pedro crushed the rebellion five years later and sold most of the rebels whom his forces captured into slavery. Meanwhile, gold production tailed off near the Gold Coast in the late 1600s. Warring states in the region needed to pay for firearms and gunpowder to equip armies, so the streams of captives sent to the coast widened. The Gold Coast exported over 330,000 people between 1690 and 1730, one-third of them in the 1720s.

Most captives suffered alienation long before boarding a slave ship. Separated from kin and village, captives were viewed as disgraced outsiders by the peoples through whose lands they passed. In many coastal communities, residents understood Atlantic enslavement as a kind of witchcraft that literally turned those taken away into commodities such as gunpowder. Captives endured a long voyage across the Atlantic, shackled together and confined below deck. About one in five did not survive it. Merchants and captains, especially of British ships, gradually improved survival rates over time, earning bigger profits.

Enslaved people came to North America from all parts of Africa that participated directly in the Atlantic slave trade, but North American colonies remained a relatively small market for the Atlantic's vast and rapidly growing slave trade (Map 4.3). Most Africans brought to North America between 1691 and 1730 departed from Senegambia or the Bight of Biafra (Table 4.1). Even though North American colonists bought enslaved Africans in unprecedented numbers, they purchased 5 percent of the Africans exported to the Americas and 10 percent of those carried in British ships (Map 4.3).

Although more than two-thirds of the Africans shipped to North America between 1691 and 1730 arrived in Virginia or Maryland, the market for them extended to all the British and French colonies. South Carolina and Louisiana began to import Africans in large numbers in the 1720s (Table 4.2). Over 3,000 enslaved Africans disembarked in northern British colonies between 1691 and 1730, including hundreds who arrived in New York from Madagascar in the 1690s. Another 6,000 arrived in New England, New York, and Pennsylvania via the West Indies.

Expanded cultivation of tobacco particularly stoked North American demand for enslaved labor. Tobacco exports from Maryland and Virginia to Britain nearly tripled

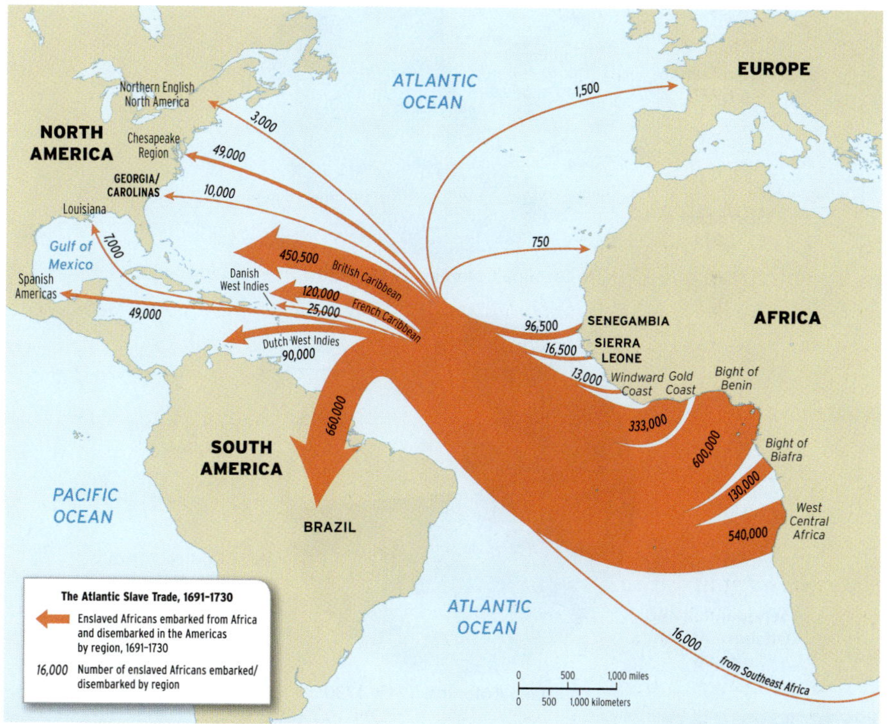


▲ **Map 4.3**

**The Atlantic Slave Trade, 1691–1730** This map provides a broad American perspective on the Atlantic slave trade. About 69,000 enslaved Africans landed in North America between 1691 and 1730, about two times as many as between 1641 and 1690. More than half arrived in the 1720s. But over 95 percent went elsewhere in the Americas, mostly to the Caribbean or Brazil.

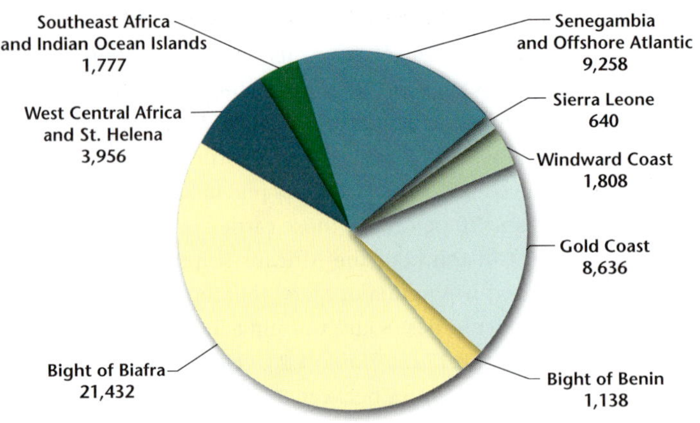


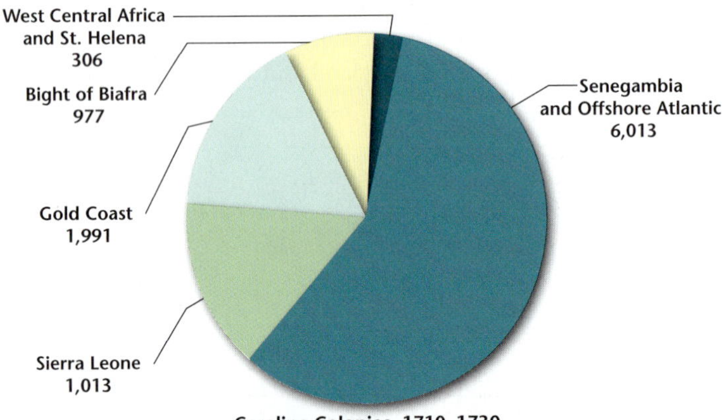


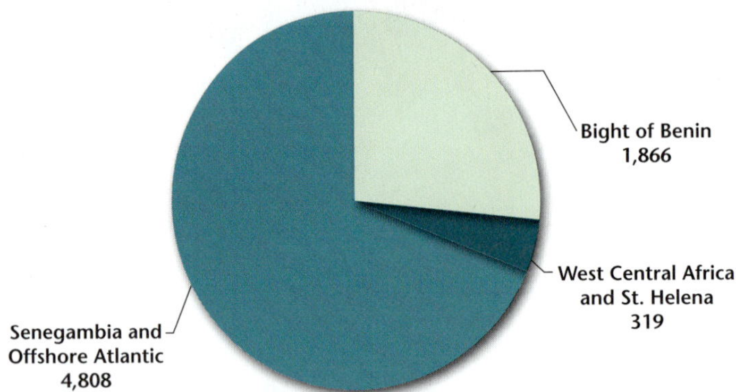


▲ **Figure 4.1**

**Regional origins of enslaved Africans disembarked in regions of North America (estimated), 1692–1730** Enslaved Africans sent from ports in the Bight of Biafra composed nearly half of those brought directly to the Chesapeake colonies between the 1690s and 1730, while those who left Africa from Senegambia comprised the majority of those sent directly from Africa to South Carolina and Louisiana.

**Table 4.1** **Regional Origins of Enslaved Africans Disembarked in North America (Estimated), 1692–1730**

| | Senegambia and Offshore Atlantic | Sierra Leone | Windward Coast | Gold Coast | Bight of Benin | Bight of Biafra | West Central Africa and St. Helena | South-east Africa and Indian Ocean islands | Totals |
|---|---|---|---|---|---|---|---|---|---|
| 1692–1700 | 2,299 | 0 | 0 | 0 | 0 | 2,924 | 0 | 1,461 | 6,684 |
| 1701–1710 | 3,213 | 0 | 0 | 3,423 | 872 | 5,295 | 231 | 96 | 13,131 |
| 1711–1720 | 2,811 | 311 | 0 | 2,851 | 739 | 4,393 | 220 | 1,355 | 12,679 |
| 1721–1730 | 11,756 | 1,342 | 1,808 | 5,458 | 1,393 | 9,797 | 4,434 | 851 | 36,838 |
| Totals | 20,079 | 1,653 | 1,808 | 11,731 | 3,004 | 22,410 | 4,885 | 3,763 | 69,332 |

**Table 4.2** **Enslaved Africans Disembarked in North America by Region (Estimated), 1692–1730** Over two-thirds of enslaved Africans who crossed the Atlantic directly to North America between 1692 and 1730 landed in the Chesapeake colonies, particularly in Virginia, a result of the switch from indentured to enslaved labor and of efforts to sustain increases in tobacco production as cheaply as possible.

| | Mainland North America | | | | | |
|---|---|---|---|---|---|---|
| | Northern British North America | Chesapeake | Carolina | Louisiana | Other | Totals |
| 1692–1700 | 1,461 | 5,223 | 0 | 0 | 0 | 6,684 |
| 1701–1710 | 96 | 12,808 | 227 | 0 | 0 | 13,131 |
| 1711–1720 | 823 | 9,025 | 2,223 | 607 | 0 | 12,679 |
| 1721–1730 | 709 | 21,588 | 7,851 | 6,386 | 304 | 36,838 |
| Totals | 3,090 | 48,645 | 10,301 | 6,993 | 304 | 69,332 |

between 1705 and 1730. Louisiana imported thousands of Africans between 1717 and 1731 as planters tried and failed to make the colony a tobacco exporter that could compete with the Chesapeake and Brazil.

Meanwhile, the expansion of rice cultivation made South Carolina a major destination for enslaved Africans. Carolina planters began to grow the crop in the 1690s, and by the 1720s, the knowledge, skill, and labor of thousands of recently arrived Africans enabled South Carolina to export millions of pounds of rice a year.

Regional differences shaped Africans' new lives in North America. The Chesapeake was a white world. Slaves did not comprise 20 percent of Virginians until 1710. Chesapeake planters bought so many Africans from different parts of the continent that it was hard for slaves to find a common language other than English. The presence of more American-born slaves meant that there were more enslaved black women in the Chesapeake than anywhere else in North America, so relatively more enslaved men could find partners and start families. By contrast, South Carolina and Louisiana had African majorities by the 1720s. Most who arrived in both colonies during that decade came from Senegambia, increasing the odds that they would meet someone who spoke their language or shared their memories of Africa. African men vastly outnumbered black women in both colonies. This made it harder to start families than in the Chesapeake and made authorities in South Carolina leery of exporting enslaved African women.

Even so, similarities in Africans' experiences of enslavement outweighed such regional differences. Colonists considered Africans dangerous and brutish, partly because they did not speak or understand English or French. As many as one in four succumbed to disease and died within a year of arrival. Most who survived had trouble starting families. Enslaved men outnumbered women in North America before 1730, largely because women comprised fewer than one-third of the Africans who arrived between 1690 and 1730. For many Africans, North American slavery brought an early grave and profound social isolation.

Sir Hans Sloane obtained this drum in Jamaica while visiting there in the early 1700s and noted that it had come from Virginia. Someone brought the drum from Africa to Virginia, where enslaved Africans likely used it for funeral rites that helped them forge a sense of kinship and community.

Africans combated alienation by adapting beliefs and practices of their homelands, many of which centered around honoring their dead. For most Africans death initiated the soul's journey from the material world to the realm of spirits and ancestors. Those who died without kin risked becoming ghosts doomed to haunt the living. Only a proper funeral assured that the soul reached its proper destination and found peace, so friends and neighbors acted as kin to the deceased. They sponsored funeral processions, followed by singing, dancing, drumming and feasting, to celebrate the soul's arrival to its resting place. These rituals alarmed colonists. Virginia officials feared that nighttime funerals would enable slaves to conspire and tried to ban them in the 1680s. Graves testify to how Africans honored their dead. Tobacco pipes often accompanied those buried in Virginia during the early 1700s, a practice common in West Africa.

Some Africans violently resisted enslavement. In 1712, some four dozen slaves set fire to a building in New York City and attacked the whites who came to extinguish the blaze, killing nine and injuring several more. Officials hanged 20 slaves, burned 3 at the stake, and hoisted 1 in chains until he starved to death. Investigators concluded that the rebels, many from the Gold Coast, sought "to destroy all the White[s] in order to obtain their freedom." The rebels prepared for battle as if they had been in Africa by binding one another to secrecy "by Sucking the blood of each Others hands," while some rubbed a powder on their clothing in the belief that it would make them invulnerable.

Meanwhile, Virginia masters had nightmares of slave conspiracies. They claimed to have uncovered six between 1709 and 1731. In 1729, a dozen runaways tried to create a sanctuary for themselves. Governor William Gooch ordered it destroyed to save Virginia from "a design which might have proved as dangerous" to whites "as is that of the Negroes in the Mountains of Jamaica." By likening the runaways to Jamaican **Maroons**, fugitives from slavery notorious among slave owners in the Anglo-Atlantic world, Gooch understood them as participants in a form of resistance long common in the Caribbean and Brazil.

Many British colonists, alarmed by the rapidly growing numbers of Africans among them, tried to restrict the Atlantic slave trade. In Boston judge **Samuel Sewall** and merchant **John Saffin** debated the slave trade as the 18th century dawned. Sewall charged that the Atlantic slave trade was immoral and that it endangered whites because Africans took the place of "Men that might make Husbands for our Daughters" and would "remain in our Body Politick as a kind of extravasat [alien] Blood." Saffin countered with Anglo-America's first militant defense of the Atlantic slave trade and slavery. The Bible and the Atlantic world provided examples, he insisted, which indicated that God had decreed that some were to rule while others were "to be born Slaves, and so to remain during their lives." Pennsylvania lawmakers responded to the 1712 New York revolt by imposing a tax on each imported slave. Eleven years later, Virginia legislators imposed a duty on imported Africans to strengthen their militia against possible slave rebellions.

## The "Naturalization" of Slavery and Racism

The tens of thousands of enslaved people brought to North America between the 1690s and 1730 accelerated the growth of slavery in the British colonies and Louisiana. So did the births of thousands of children to enslaved women. Meanwhile, British colonists and French imperial officials, alarmed by a rapidly growing black population, enacted laws that codified slavery and enshrined racism throughout North America.

African and African American women in the Chesapeake raised the first large generation to be born into slavery in North America. In the early 1700s, an American-born slave woman could expect to give birth to nine children, six of whom might survive past age four. By the 1730s, the Chesapeake colonies were home to the first enslaved population composed mostly of native-born people of African descent in the history of the Americas.

Chesapeake masters' desire to cut costs helps to explain why they promoted the growth of slave families. Chesapeake Bay was farther from Africa than any other major market for enslaved Africans, which increased what Chesapeake masters paid for those brought directly from Africa. An enslaved African faced a high chance of dying soon after arrival and had to learn basic English to understand commands. Anglo-American masters also believed that American-born slaves were more intelligent, better suited for skilled labor, and less likely to rebel than Africans. Maryland and Virginia planters also encouraged the formation of slave families by buying more African women during the 1720s.

The growth of slavery spurred the creation of slave codes throughout colonial North America. In 1726, Pennsylvania became the last British colony founded during the 1600s to pass a comprehensive slave code. Meanwhile, Louisiana colonists mostly ignored North America's first imperially mandated slave code. In 1724, Louis XV extended the **Code Noir**, first issued in 1685 to cover the French West Indies, to Louisiana. Like its predecessor, the Louisiana Code Noir directed masters to provide slaves with a minimum amount of food and clothing as well as access to religious instruction. Slaves were to be baptized and married; married slaves had the right to stay together. Virtually all these provisions went unenforced. The new Code Noir afforded free people of color in Louisiana many rights that free whites enjoyed, among them to petition officials and testify in court. But the 1724 Code Noir discriminated against free people of color by banning interracial marriages and imposing fines on parents of mixed-race children. French officials hoped to ensure that Louisiana would not become like the French Caribbean, where a growing population of mixed-race people gave those islands a bad reputation in Europe.

The Code Noir was part of another wave that swept North America in the 1690s and early 1700s—the desire to draw a clear color line. Discouraging private **manumissions** was one way to limit the ranks of free blacks. By 1729, every northern British colony had made slaveholders financially responsible for freeing their slaves by requiring them to post bonds to ensure that freed people would not become a burden on taxpayers. Unlike Virginia, or South Carolina after 1722, northern British colonies did not require that freed people leave after manumission. Nor did they bar entry to free blacks.

The new laws made life harder for free blacks. The slave codes of New York and New Jersey prohibited anyone freed after they took effect from owning real estate. Pennsylvania's slave code empowered local officials to sentence free black "loiterers" to at least one year's service and make indentured servants of children born to free black women. Virginia and South Carolina disenfranchised black men in the 1720s and Virginia reimposed a tax on free black women.

Prohibitions on interracial sex were crucial to guarding the color line. In 1705, Massachusetts outlawed marriage between people of African and European descent. Virginia's slave code of that year decreed that unwed white mothers of biracial children should pay a fine or serve a five-year indenture, while free whites who chose to wed a black partner were to be fined and spend six months in prison. North Carolina criminalized interracial sex for white women in 1715.

The press reinforced the color line. In 1718, *The Boston News-Letter* published a story in which a white vigilante in Connecticut sliced off the genitalia of a black man who he claimed was about to rape a white woman. The paper's editors celebrated his deed, which they thought sent an unmistakable message to "all Negroes meddling with any White Woman."

## European Immigrants and Imperial Expansion

Most Europeans who came to North America between 1690 and 1730 did so voluntarily, with the vast majority going to British colonies. Thicker commercial, personal, and institutional ties between British North America, Britain, and German-speaking Europe helped to determine who went where and when they arrived. So did political changes, including the **Act of Union**, which created the United Kingdom by merging the kingdoms and parliaments of England and Scotland in 1707.

The Act of Union opened a British empire fully to Scots. A Scot in New York, Samuel Vetch, touted the expansion of British North America as a way to knit the new United Kingdom together. He led a transatlantic campaign that involved the "Four Indian Kings," which advocated using British soldiers to conquer Canada and colonizing Nova Scotia with Scots. Soldiers from New England and Britain conquered Nova Scotia for the British Empire during Queen Anne's War, but most of it remained in the hands of French Acadians and Micmacs for decades. The 1,300 Scots who landed in North America between 1710 and 1730 mostly settled elsewhere, but they had a greater impact on British colonies than their numbers would suggest (Table 4.3). Many royal governors were Scots. Scottish doctors trained at the University of Edinburgh dominated the ranks of elite physicians in British North America and linked the colonies to scientific networks in Britain and Europe.

Immigrants from southern Ireland and Ulster (Northern Ireland) comprised a much larger stream of people to North America between 1690 and 1730. Most migrants from southern Ireland came as indentured servants and landed in the Chesapeake colonies or Pennsylvania. Ulsterite migration was largely a byproduct of that region's linen trade. The **Linen Act of 1705** encouraged the export of Irish linen to North America. In turn, linen manufacturing in Northern Ireland boosted demand for flaxseed (the source of linen) that New England and Pennsylvania farmers grew. Overdependence on linen, rent increases, and crop failures between 1718 and 1729 prompted thousands of Ulsterites to set sail to North America (Table 4.3). Passages were relatively inexpensive, so most Ulster migrants could pay their own way and travel as families. Most settled in Pennsylvania, some after living in New England. In

**Table 4.3 Estimated European Migration to British North America by Ethnic Group and Compared to Enslaved African Migration, 1700–1729** Over two-thirds of migrants who arrived in English/British North America between 1700 and the 1720s were enslaved Africans. The vast majority of European immigrants were not English, the first time that had happened in the history of English/British colonization of the Americas.

| Decade | Germans | Ulster Irish | Southern Irish | Scots | English | Welsh | Other | Africans | Total |
|---|---|---|---|---|---|---|---|---|---|
| 1700–1709 | 100 | 600 | 800 | 200 | 400 | 300 | 100 | 12,900 | 15,400 |
| 1710–1719 | 3,700 | 1,200 | 1,700 | 500 | 1,300 | 900 | 200 | 10,500 | 20,000 |
| 1720–1729 | 2,300 | 2,100 | 3,000 | 800 | 2,200 | 1,500 | 200 | 30,500 | 42,600 |
| TOTALS | 6,100 | 3,900 | 5,500 | 1,500 | 3,900 | 2,700 | 500 | 53,900 | 78,000 |

Note: "Germans" refers to German speakers, not to people who came from what is today Germany. "Africans" refers to people brought via the Atlantic slave trade from Africa who disembarked in British North America. "British North America" does not include Nova Scotia or the Caribbean.

1730, a return to prosperity halted the exodus from Ulster. It resumed when the Irish economy soured.

Meanwhile, thousands of Germans headed for North America. They came in three waves. The first arrived between 1683 and 1709, mainly to escape religious persecution. They came from many parts of German-speaking northern and central Europe and sailed for Philadelphia, drawn by William Penn's promises of religious freedom, pamphlets published in German, or letters from kin or from fellow believers who had already emigrated. The second wave of German immigration occurred between 1709 and 1714 and hailed mainly from what is today southwest Germany, an area ravaged by Queen Anne's War. Most migrated to New York or North Carolina as participants in large planned colonization ventures, one of which sparked the Tuscarora War. The third wave was the largest and deepest. Triggered primarily by overpopulation and land scarcity, it also originated mainly in southwest Germany and lasted from 1717 until 1775. Like Ulsterites, most Germans settled in Pennsylvania, while a small number went to Louisiana in the 1720s.

British colonists had mixed reactions to the Ulsterite and German immigrants. In New England, the minister **Cotton Mather** at first celebrated Ulsterite immigration as a way to bolster local defenses against French and Indian foes. He soon changed his mind, declaring that the Presbyterian newcomers had "most indecently and ingratefully given much disturbance to the peace of our churches." In Pennsylvania, James Logan, provincial secretary in the late 1720s, saw an invasion "by those shoals of foreigners the Palatines and strangers from the North of Ireland that crowd

# The State of the *Palatines*,

FOR

# Fifty Years paſt to this preſent Time.

CONTAINING,

I. An Account of the Principality of the Palatinate; and of the *Barbarities* and Ravages committed by Order of the French King upon the Inhabitants; *Burning* to the Ground a great Number of their moſt Famous Cities, and throwing the *Bones* of Emperors, Princes and Prelates, out of their Tombs, *&c.*

II. The Caſe of the Palatines, Publiſhed by themſelves, and Humbly Offered to the Tradeſmen of England. VVith a Liſt of them, and the Trades which the Men are brought up to.

III. The Humble Petition of the Juſtices of *Middleſex* to Her *Majeſty* on their *Behalf*, with Her *Majeſties* Order thereupon, and an Abſtract of the *Brief* graciouſly Granted for their Subſiſtence.

IV. A Letter about Settling and Employing them in other Countries.

V. A Proclamation of the States-General for Naturalizing all Strangers, and receiving them into their Country.

VI. Laſtly, Their preſent Encamping at Camberwell and *Black-heath*, in many Hundred Tents, by Her *Majeſties* Grace and Favour, till they can be otherwiſe diſpos'd of, and how they Employ themſelves; with their *Marriages*, *Burials*, *&c.* Alſo the great Kindneſs their Anceſtors ſhew'd to the Engliſh Proteſtants in the bloody Reign of Queen *Mary*.

Palatine refugee camp in London, 1709. Some 15,000 Germans fled war-torn areas of the Rhine Valley for London, lured by rumors that they would be resettled and granted land in North America. Many ended up in refugee camps like this one located near London, from which they were transported to North Carolina and upstate New York.

in upon us." He worried that the Irish might soon "make themselves Proprietors of the Province," while the Germans might ensure that "these colonies will in time be lost to the Crown."

Although most Europeans chose to sail to North America, thousands came against their will. The Spanish, British, and French empires sent convicts to work in their colonies. Many of the hundreds who went to Florida in the early 1700s had been prisoners in Spanish and Mexican jails. English officials sentenced Scottish and Irish rebels to servitude in North America or the West Indies on various occasions during the 1600s. A similar fate befell some 500 Scots who in 1715 participated in the **Jacobite Rebellion** against the crowning of **George I**. The governor of South Carolina purchased some and sent them to fight the Yamasee War.

Worries about surging crime led Parliament to make colonial servitude a tool of Britain's criminal justice system. The **Transportation Act of 1718** mandated exile to North America for seven years to life for those convicted of crimes ranging from theft to receipt of stolen goods to capital felonies. Most convicts sent to North America committed property crimes. A few were violent offenders. At least 3,000 came from Britain and Ireland by 1730, the first of 50,000 to be transported to North America before 1775.

Convicts played a significant role in the colonization of Louisiana. Most Europeans who went to Louisiana before 1763 arrived between 1717 and 1721 and were indentured servants, bound to serve the Company of the Indies for three years, or prisoners. Few chose to go to Louisiana, partly because most who did died young en route or alongside a bayou. In 1726, Louisiana census takers counted 2,300 Europeans, including 300 indentured servants. Five years later, there were 2,000. Immigration to French Louisiana was brief and concentrated. Europeans did not return in significant numbers until Spain took charge of the colony in the 1760s.

European immigration left a profound mark on North America. It helped France cling to the middle of the continent. Immigration benefitted British North America most, as Ulsterite and German migrants pushed its borders outward. The new arrivals also reinforced British colonists' ties to an Atlantic Protestant network that had mobilized partly to counter what it perceived as a global Catholic threat.

## Pietism and Atlantic Protestantism

In 1710, Cotton Mather, New England's most prominent minister, published *A Discourse Concerning Faith and Fervency*. Mather urged readers to pray for "a plentiful Effusion of the Holy Spirit on the world. Then will Converting work go forward among the Nations." A London printer published Mather's work in 1713. It was one of his contributions to **Pietism**, a Protestant movement that linked North America, Britain, the Netherlands, and central Europe. Pietists promoted the personal piety of believers and the evangelization of all, including American Indians and enslaved Africans.

Pietism drew from many sources. These included English Puritanism, Anglicanism, and Dutch Calvinism. Pietism took its name from a Lutheran reform movement initiated by the German pastor **Philipp Jakob Spener**. In 1670, Spener began to hold small gatherings called *collegia pietatis* ("gatherings for piety") which reflected his conviction that church reform depended on the spiritual renewal of each believer. Universal practice of personal piety would trigger Christ's return to Earth, an event that Spener argued would destroy the Catholic Church. Pietists affiliated with Germany's University of Halle sustained and expanded on Spener's work. August Hermann Francke, a professor of theology, helped to make Halle a center of Pietism.

Halle and the Church of England played crucial roles in spreading Pietism's principles overseas. Francke's teachings influenced many German and Dutch pastors in New York, New Jersey, and Pennsylvania, while Francke and other Halle faculty corresponded with Cotton Mather. Meanwhile, Anglican reformers in London founded two societies to promote the Church of England in America. In 1699, the **Society for Promoting Christian Knowledge** (SPCK) formed, publishing and disseminating Bibles and tracts to cultivate personal piety. The **Society for the Propagation of the Gospel in Foreign Parts** (SPG) was founded in 1701. It focused on sending missionaries to North America and the West Indies.

The SPG devoted much of its attention to enslaved Africans. But SPG missionaries persuaded few masters that conversion would make for more obedient slaves. Men like Francis Le Jau in South Carolina usually blamed planters for their lack of success, claiming that they unduly limited access to slave audiences. But SPG advocates did not realize or did not acknowledge that their own message often discouraged Africans. Le Jau required slaves seeking baptism to swear that they were not doing so to press masters to free them. African men had to promise to abandon **polygamy**. Missionaries also requested that enslaved converts devote part of each Sunday to attend services, the day they customarily had for themselves and one that they often spent trying to grow more food.

Some Anglicans confirmed masters' worries about the risks of evangelizing slaves. In 1729, James Blair, a Virginia clergyman, noted that some slaves converted because they believed that "Christianity will help them to their freedom." The following year some slaves claimed that George II had "ordered all those slaves free that were Christians." By linking conversion to Christianity and royal authority to their yearning for freedom, these slaves articulated an African American political ideology that resurfaced in the 1770s.

Puritan ministers and SPG missionaries evangelized Africans and African Americans in northern cities. In 1693, Cotton Mather founded the Society of Negroes in Boston. Mather invited slaves to meet at his home every Sunday, where he preached against drunkenness, stealing, or disobedience to masters. Mather further promoted evangelization of slaves by publishing *The Negro Christianized* in 1706. Meanwhile, Elias Neau, SPG missionary to New York City, operated a school that attracted as many as 1 in 10 black New Yorkers. Few attended more than three times, but many who never returned kept the catechism books that they had been given, hoping to learn to read.

The visit of the "Four Indian Kings" to London encouraged English Pietists to pay more attention to Indians. Indian disinterest ensured that SPG missions fared poorly.

GLOBAL PASSAGES

## New York, Madagascar, and Indian Ocean Piracy

Around 1680 pirates began to leave the Caribbean, their base for over a century, to dodge naval patrols and find easier pickings. By 1690, a base in Madagascar gave them easy access to the Red Sea and Indian Ocean. Pirates often targeted a fleet that sailed between India and Mocha, an Arabian Peninsula port on the Red Sea that exported coffee and welcomed Muslim pilgrims who then proceeded overland to Mecca.

New Yorkers helped to establish European piracy in the Indian Ocean. Like other North American port cities, New York welcomed pirates, who needed food, clothing, alcohol, and ship repairs and paid for them with scarce gold and silver. During the 1680s New York merchants had learned that they could reap even bigger profits by shipping supplies to the Indian Ocean and charging pirates for the convenience.

Economic and political changes intensified New York's ties to Indian Ocean piracy in the early 1690s. King William's War disrupted New York's economy, and the high unemployment that followed tempted some mariners to turn or return to piracy. After the colony's new governor, Benjamin Fletcher, took office in 1692, he granted pirates refuge, often using his official powers to designate them "privateers" and line his own pockets. Fletcher's Council consisted largely of merchants who traded with pirates. One councilor, Frederick Philipse, employed an agent in Madagascar who sold clothing, naval stores, firearms, ammunition, and liquor to pirates and local rulers. The local rulers handed war captives over to pirates, who sold them to Philipse's agent along with gold, silver, spices, and Indian textiles they had stolen. Rum sold in Madagascar for up to 30 times what it cost in New York, while slaves could be bought in Madagascar for a fraction of the price on Africa's

The same was true for most New England ministers who worked under the auspices of the New England Company, although Experience Mayhew's pastoral work among Wampanoag on Martha's Vineyard was an exception. Company leaders trumpeted Mayhew's deeds by publishing an account of them in London in 1727.

Such Pietists hoped to show an Anglo-Atlantic audience that New England and the New England Company were responding to French Jesuits' efforts among the Abenaki in Maine. New England, they contended, was a key front in the battle to preserve British and Protestant liberty from French and Catholic tyranny. That struggle, British North Americans believed, also bound them more tightly to the British empire and to the monarchs who headed it.

Atlantic coast. Philipse shipped hundreds of Madagascar slaves to New York during the 1690s.

Events in the Indian Ocean, London, and New York severed New Yorkers' ties to Madagascar. Pirate attacks on ships belonging to subjects of India's Mughal Empire created a crisis for the **East India Company** (EIC) and England. Mughals imprisoned company employees and threatened to throw the EIC out. Meanwhile, Parliament passed the East India Act in 1698 to cement the firm's monopoly on English commerce in the Indian Ocean. London officials also cracked down on piracy by recalling Fletcher. His replacement, the Earl of Bellomont, denounced piracy as "not only injurious to the Honour of his Majesty, and the English Nation, but also highly prejudicial to the Trade of England." Bellomont ordered that illicit cargoes be confiscated. Some local officials defied him by helping to smuggle illegal goods into town. Philipse sent a ship to Delaware Bay to meet a vessel arriving from Madagascar. It offloaded most of the contraband and headed to Hamburg to sell it. The EIC and pirates claimed three of the four ships that city merchants sent to Madagascar in 1698. Philipse tried to sneak East Indian cargo into New York, but officials confiscated it. He was removed from the Council. Philipse died in 1702, leaving over 90,000 acres of land, city real estate, slaves, and a small fleet, a fortune built largely on trade with pirates.

Two important precedents had been set. Ties between colonial merchants and pirates could be cut and imperial officials had demonstrated that they would act on the EIC's behalf against colonists' interests. In the 1770s, that became a major issue for colonists who drank tea provided by the EIC.

- Why did New Yorkers help to establish European piracy in the Indian Ocean? Why did English officials seek to sever their ties to Indian Ocean pirates in the 1690s?
- What relationship did the campaign to cut New York's ties to Indian Ocean pirates have to the British empire's broader war on piracy during the 1700s?

## Imperial Authority and Colonial Resistance

Starting in the late 1600s, royal supervision of colonial British North America intensified, as did imperial efforts to regulate its economy. Colonists tried to skirt rules that they deemed contrary to their interests and promoted those that they thought served them well. In the process, their ties to their monarchs, the British empire, and the Atlantic world grew stronger.

Royal authority played a bigger role in British colonists' lives in many ways. Monarchs began to appoint governors for New Jersey, Nova Scotia, South Carolina, and North Carolina between 1702 and 1729, bringing 9 of the 13 British mainland colonies under royal rule. By the 1720s many colonists' homes contained mass-produced images of British royalty. Celebrations of royal holidays dotted the calendars of major port towns, which by 1740 staged at least six such events a year. The most raucous was November 5th, Pope's or Guy Fawkes Day. It commemorated the discovery of a Catholic plot to blow up Parliament. **Pope's Day** processions featuring the display (and sometimes burning) of papal effigies were common in port towns by the late 1690s. In 1702, Bostonians added an effigy of the **Pretender**—the Catholic Stuart who claimed the British throne and whose loyalists in Britain launched the 1715 Jacobite Rebellion—to the festivities, a practice that spread throughout British North America. Colonists' enthusiasm for such rituals expressed their growing desire to be recognized as Britons who were loyal subjects and partners in a global battle against what they saw as a Catholic menace.

As British colonists celebrated their monarchs, imperial officials claimed more power over their commerce. In 1696, William III created the **Board of Trade**, an advisory council charged to oversee colonial matters. The act testified to the colonies' growing significance to England's economy. In 1700–1701 colonists in British North America and the West Indies comprised just over 10 percent of the market for what England exported and almost 20 percent of the value of what it imported. The Board of Trade implemented the **Navigation Act of 1696** to tighten regulations on colonial trade and established **vice-admiralty courts** in the colonies to enforce the law.

Between 1700 and 1730, the Royal Navy and the vice-admiralty courts waged a war on piracy that colonists increasingly supported. Pirates had long found shelter in colonial ports as good customers who often paid in scarce silver or gold. But doing business with pirates became less appealing after Parliament passed the first effective empire-wide law to combat piracy in 1700. It mandated the death penalty for those

Hanging of Major Stede Bonnet. Bonnet was a Barbadian planter who turned to piracy in 1717, preying on shipping along the Atlantic coast of North America and in the Caribbean. Captured along the North Carolina coast, he was convicted by Charleston's vice-admiralty courts and executed in 1718.

convicted of piracy or for aiding and abetting pirates. The growth of piracy was, in part, a consequence of policies that followed the end of Queen Anne's War. As the Royal Navy was demobilized, mariners' wages were cut, and thousands lost their jobs. Many turned to piracy. They increasingly targeted ships belonging to colonial merchants. Some pirates, driven from the Bahamas, sought sanctuary in North Carolina. Their leaders included Edward Teach, better known as Blackbeard. In 1718, a fleet of British, Virginia, and South Carolina vessels killed Teach and captured many of his associates, who were tried, convicted, and hanged. A similar fate befell hundreds more as colonial officials, naval officers, and vice-admiralty judges throughout North America tightened the noose on piracy. By the late 1720s, the British empire had won the war on piracy, making the Atlantic safer for commerce that its leaders considered legitimate.

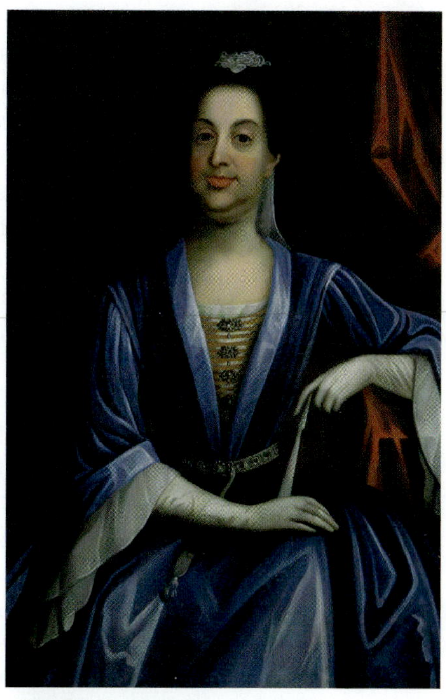

Putative Portrait of Edward Hyde, Viscount Cornbury. Cornbury, governor of New York, acquired many enemies there. Some spread rumors in England that Cornbury wore women's clothing publicly. This portrait was painted in England, probably in the early 1700s, and is most likely of a woman. Decades later people in England began to claim that it was of Cornbury.

Securing raw materials for the Royal Navy that defeated the pirates also proved to be a challenge. As Britain's forests receded from overcutting, its shipbuilders became dependent on timber and naval stores (tar, pitch, and turpentine—used mainly to preserve and waterproof ships) from Sweden and Russia. The Navy especially needed timber for ship masts. Vast forests of white pine in Maine and New Hampshire seemed the solution to their problem. A series of laws enacted between 1691 and 1729 barred New England lumbermen and mill owners from cutting down and exporting mature white pines that the Royal Navy wanted to reserve for its masts. Colonists, often aided by corrupt officials charged with enforcing the conservation policies, dodged the regulations. The Royal Navy had better luck at encouraging colonists to make naval stores by offering them financial incentives. By 1717, North America made over half of England's tar and pitch.

The challenges facing imperial officials illustrate key developments in the relationship between Britain and its North American colonies. Colonists could defy or ignore laws that they found onerous, often with the complicity of those charged to enforce them. Historians have called this arrangement "**salutary neglect**" and claim that it characterized the colonial-imperial relationship into the 1760s. Colonists also kept tabs on events in Britain, forged ties to prominent figures there, and often steered policies and politics to suit their purposes.

Factions of colonists enlisted contacts in London to fight local political battles, often targeting royal governors. One campaign centered around Edward Hyde, Viscount Cornbury, governor of New York and New Jersey. Cornbury's efforts to consolidate imperial authority and strengthen the Church of England won him enemies on both sides of the Atlantic: prominent colonists, members of the Whig Party in England, and Dissenters, English Protestants who were not Anglicans. Between 1707 and 1709 three colonists asserted, probably falsely, that Cornbury had often appeared in public in New York dressed in women's clothing. He was removed from office, his reputation in England in tatters.

Colonists' transatlantic lobbying undermined many royal governors and helped to make the tone and style of colonial politics resemble those of England. Royal governors faced obstacles that executives in Britain did not. Too many male colonists owned land and had the right to vote. They elected assemblies composed of wealthy men who jealously guarded their powers to tax and budget and frequently deprived governors of funds. Such bodies increasingly viewed themselves as mini-Parliaments obliged to defend and preserve what they understood to be British liberties against what they deemed arbitrary executive power. Colonists professed adoration for kings and queens, but they often showed contempt for those whom monarchs appointed to govern them.

### STUDY QUESTIONS FOR MIGRATION, RELIGION, AND EMPIRES

1. **In what ways and by what means did slavery and racism expand in North America during the early 1700s? In what ways did enslaved Africans adjust to their new lives in North America?**
2. **What impact did Pietism and growing royal authority have on British North America?**

## LAYING FOUNDATIONS IN BRITISH NORTH AMERICA

Unprecedented levels of involuntary immigration and thickening ties to transatlantic networks transformed colonial North America. Colonial British North America's economy grew and diversified, financing the emergence of a native-born elite that could more easily imitate its English peers because a communications revolution kept colonists abreast of events across the Atlantic and within the colonies.

## An Industrious Revolution

By 1730, colonists in British North America had laid a foundation for the economic development of what would become the United States by intensifying old activities and developing new ones in response to overseas and domestic markets. Households diversified the range of goods that they produced and services that they provided. Their Anglo-American version of a transatlantic "**industrious revolution**" enabled colonial British North America to take significant steps toward industrialization and created market-oriented societies that relied more heavily on enslaved labor and devalued the voices and skills of white women.

The English Civil War had forced New England colonists to pursue a wider variety of ways to earn a living to narrow the region's trade deficit. Most continued to scratch out a living on small farms while others fished or cut timber for export. Migration to areas recently conquered from or ceded by Indians enabled New England to accommodate a growing and mostly native-born population—86,000 strong by 1690—and enabled the majority of households to be economically independent. A cycle of wars with French Canada and its Indian allies between 1689 and 1727 made life on the frontier harder. Meanwhile, the region's population soared to over 200,000 by 1730.

New Englanders responded by working harder and diversifying their labor. This was particularly true in coastal or densely populated areas. Fishermen journeyed further out to sea to catch more cod, which they processed on board rather than returning immediately to port. Whalers began to pursue their prey into the deep ocean. Meanwhile, more young men left home in hopes of becoming financially independent sooner. Some toiled on neighbors' farms, while others took up a trade such as blacksmithing, tanning, or shoemaking. Female labor supported young men who sought to become independent and older men who wanted to remain independent. Women and girls who churned butter, grew vegetables, and operated a growing number of spinning wheels in rural New England often secured a household's place in an expanding market economy.

Two developments marked the commercialization of New England's economy. One was use of paper money, introduced to ease the scarcity of coin. Massachusetts first issued paper money in 1690 as an emergency measure to finance wartime spending. By 1712, its government declared that paper could be used to pay private debts. Prominent Boston merchants and their creditors in England feared that debtors would repay loans, pegged to the value of silver or gold, with paper that would become worthless. Paper money soon became one of the most controversial issues in colonial politics, dominating several Massachusetts elections between 1719 and 1741.

The other key development was the growth of manufacturing. Shipbuilding soared during the late 1600s and early 1700s in port cities and towns. The imperial wars that ravaged New England's borders fed demand for ships throughout the Anglo-Atlantic. Shipyards created work for loggers and millworkers as well as for carpenters,

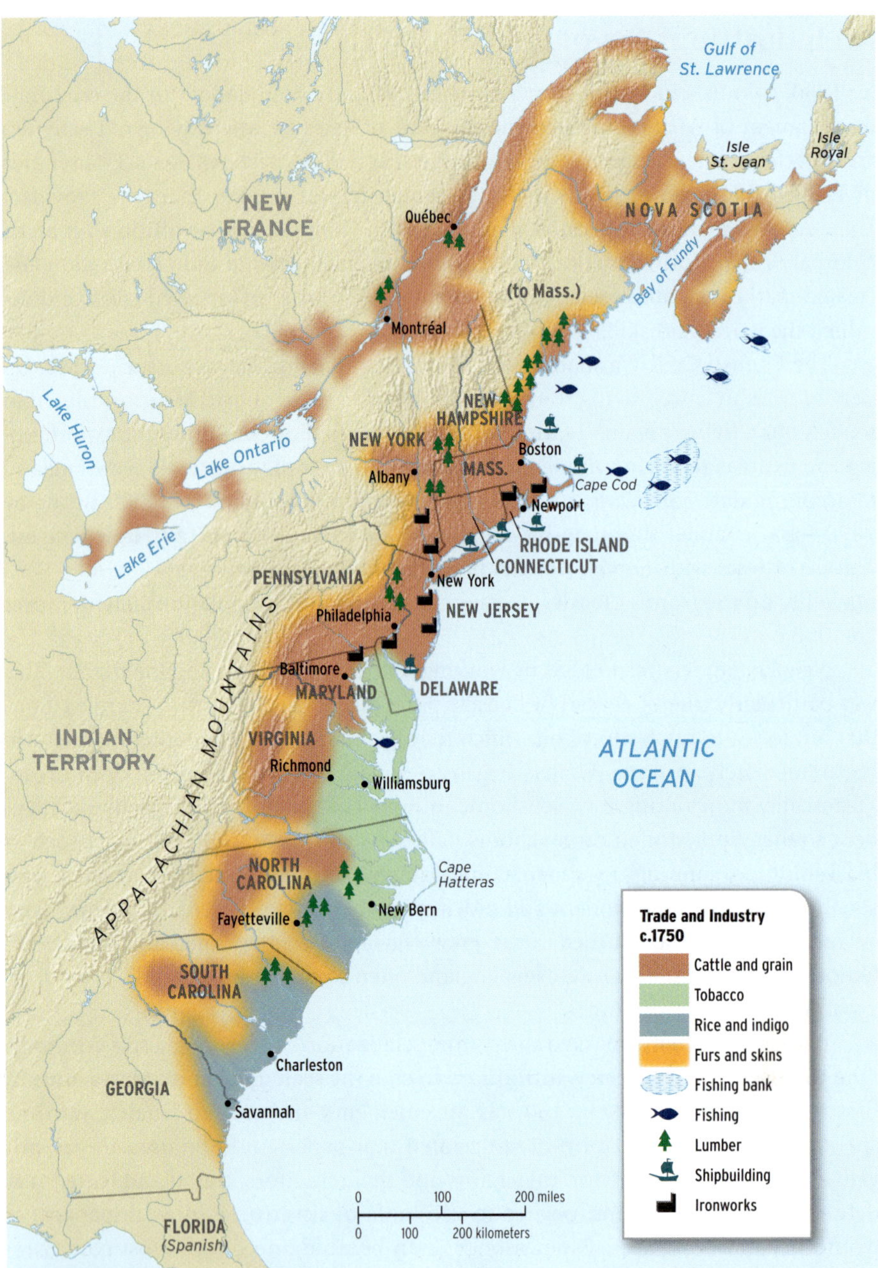


**Map 4.4**

**The Economy of British North America, c. 1750** The industrious revolution of the late 1600s and early 1700s made British North America a major supplier of ships, iron, rice, and naval stores to Atlantic markets and rapidly expanded grain and meat exports, much of which went to the Caribbean, Spain, or Portugal.

joiners, and caulkers who crafted vessels and kept them seaworthy. Investors bought shares in ships; local firms insured them; and thousands of local men sailed them. By the early 1700s New England shipbuilders competed with peers in New York and Philadelphia. Colonists built the vessels that plied the Atlantic seaboard, linking the mainland to the West Indies. By the Revolution, one-third of the ships known to the insurer Lloyd's of London had been launched from North America.

In the Chesapeake colonies, diversification was a response to dependence on tobacco. Overproduction and war kept tobacco prices low between 1680 and 1720, so plantations and small farms cultivated more wheat and raised more livestock. Abundant rivers and bigger grain harvests encouraged investment in water-powered mills to grind grain into flour. Clusters of mills provided nuclei for new towns such as Norfolk and Baltimore.

Diversification brought an early form of industrialization. By the 1720s, planters and English investors were operating iron furnaces and forges near the shores of Chesapeake Bay. Ironworks demanded enormous amounts of land, capital, and labor. The iron business attracted planters in part because it could employ indentured servants and slaves all year round. Colonial ironmasters soon discovered that they had a bigger market locally than overseas. By 1750, the center of iron manufacturing shifted north to Pennsylvania. By the Revolution, British North America made one-seventh of the world's raw iron and was its third-largest producer, an accomplishment that owed largely to thousands of slaves who staffed ironworks.

Enslaved labor played an indispensable role in the development of British North America's economy. Slaves enabled the expansion of tobacco production in the Chesapeake and the exponential increase in rice production in South Carolina. By the 1730s enslaved men, almost all American born, filled many skilled positions in ironworks in the Chesapeake. They were part of a growing contingent of enslaved tradesmen on plantations and in port cities as planters and urban artisans looked to cut costs. Such opportunities sharpened inequality among slaves, as trades remained virtually off-limits to African-born men and to women.

Meanwhile, white women found themselves increasingly cast to the sidelines of the economy and the legal system. The diffusion of paper money and growing use of promissory notes facilitated economic growth that encouraged households, especially those headed by men, to borrow from distant creditors as well as neighbors. This development effectively excluded married women and most widows from a growing share of economic activity. So did changes in the legal system. During the early 1700s courts began to demand formal pleas of parties to civil cases, increasing the need for costly lawyers, who understood such procedures. The number of lawsuits soared during the first half of the 1700s, especially to collect debts. Women's participation in such cases declined, even as their voices carried less weight in court. Fewer wives helped to draw up wills, and fewer widows administered husbands' estates.

The expansion and diversification of British North America's economy also widened the gap between rich and poor. Most of the benefits ended up in the hands of those best positioned to profit from Atlantic ties, urban merchants and large planters. They used their growing fortunes to distinguish themselves from other colonists.

## A Creole Elite Pursues Gentility

Starting around 1660, England's merchants began to build stylish townhouses in cities, while its gentry, lesser aristocrats, remodeled country houses or built new ones according to the latest fashions. New standards of beauty, speech, dress, body carriage, and personal conduct accompanied changes in housing. Three decades later, British North America's wealthiest strove to be genteel, modeling themselves on their English counterparts, and by the early 1700s, an American-born elite adopted and adapted transatlantic norms of **gentility**. By the Revolution, colonists who wished to be considered gentlemen and ladies—prominent merchants and planters, clergy, professionals, judges, and officials—were expected to follow the rules of "polite society."

Three developments heralded gentility's arrival in British North America and helped to disseminate it. One was the courtesy book. Intended principally for children and adolescents, courtesy books instructed readers on codes of conduct. Authors sought to inculcate deference to social rank, control over one's body, and regard for others' feelings. "Polite" people were gracious, elegant, and restrained individuals who did not offend or embarrass others.

Another sign of gentility was drinking tea, which the East India Company purchased in China and shipped to Britain. Around 1690 women of means in England began to gather in the parlors of urban townhouses and country estates to converse and drink tea. Etiquette required that hostesses buy a teapot, containers for sugar and cream, tongs, teaspoons, cups, and saucers as well as tea and sugar. By the 1720s, white women of means in the colonies had made "tea tables" the principal vehicle for spreading ideas about manners and taste.

The mansion house also hastened and symbolized the rise of gentility in North America. Some wealthy Boston merchants marked their rising social status by building huge homes of brick during the 1710s, while their Philadelphia peers commissioned country estates to which they retreated during summers, when epidemics often raged in town. The stateliest mansions were built for wealthy Virginia planters. Men such as **William Byrd II** began to replace their wooden homes with brick mansions during the 1720s. Although wood was cheaper, brick expressed a sense of permanence and identification with the English gentry.

The Virginia mansions differed from the homes they replaced in many ways. They contained several rooms and were two stories rather than one. The first floor provided the stage for wealthy planters to host dinners and dances that displayed their gentility. The mansions were designed to conceal the labor that sustained their privileged inhabitants. Kitchens and laundries, operated mainly by enslaved women and supervised by planters' wives, were moved to separate buildings. By the mid-1700s, Virginia's great houses commanded the landscape around them. Erected on bluffs and surrounded by landscaped gardens, the mansions trumpeted their owners' wealth and power.

The mansions reflected a more assertive and native-born Chesapeake elite. By the 1690s a clear majority of the region's prominent families were American born. Elites laid out new capitals at Annapolis in the 1690s and Williamsburg a decade later, housing the institutions of provincial government in stately brick buildings. In 1693 they chartered the College of William and Mary, in hopes that it would mold what one of them called "a set of better polished patriots."

Members of Virginia's plantocracy expressed pride in overseeing their estates. William Byrd II thought that his mastery of others, especially slaves, legitimated his claim to belong to a colonial gentry that was the equal of England's, even though few English gentry owned slaves. "Like one of the patriarchs," he wrote, "I have my flocks and my herds, my bond-men, and bond-women," whose labor allowed him to "live in a kind of independence." Byrd's vigilance kept "all my people to their duty, to set all the springs in motion, and to make every one draw his equal share to carry the machine forward."

## The Anglo-Atlantic's Communications Revolution

In 1690, Byrd's father complained of Virginia, "We are here at the end of the World, and Europe may be turned topsy turvy ere we can hear a Word of it." Forty years later, fewer in British North America would have shared his frustration. A communications revolution had accelerated and broadened the flow of information across the Atlantic and about British North America.

The communications revolution had many intertwined components. The number of ships that traveled between England, North America, and the West Indies increased sharply, with the total number entering Boston harbor nearly tripling between 1688 and 1730. Intercolonial coastal trade grew even more spectacularly. Heavier maritime traffic disseminated information more quickly and conveniently.

Printed information reached more people, as colonists began to publish their own newspapers. In 1704, *The Boston News-letter* became British North America's first established newspaper. Its publisher, John Campbell, was Boston's postmaster, which enabled him to get the paper to rural subscribers and boost demand for postal services. Campbell modeled his paper after *The London Gazette*. *The News-Letter* provided little local coverage, focusing mainly on foreign news that interested merchants.

Campbell soon had competitors. In 1719, James Franklin, who had learned printing in London, launched *The Boston Gazette*. Two years later, Franklin founded *The New-England Courant*, giving Boston three weeklies. By 1735, New York City had two newspapers, Philadelphia two, and Virginia and South Carolina one each. Boston had five, more than any English-speaking city except London.

Colonial newspapers provided a forum for debating matters of local interest, especially as publishers vied for readers. The *Courant* immediately took sides in the biggest controversy raging in Boston—whether residents should be inoculated against smallpox, after an epidemic had struck the city. Cotton Mather advocated inoculation to Boston's physicians, nearly all of whom countered that deliberately exposing people to smallpox would fan the epidemic. *The Courant* sided with them and poked fun at ministers like Mather, "Who like faithful Shepherds take care of their *Flocks*,/ By teaching and practising what's Orthodox,/Pray hard against *Sickness*, yet preach up the POX!" Franklin published editorials by the Scot William Douglass against inoculation. An alumnus of the University of Edinburgh's medical school, he was the only

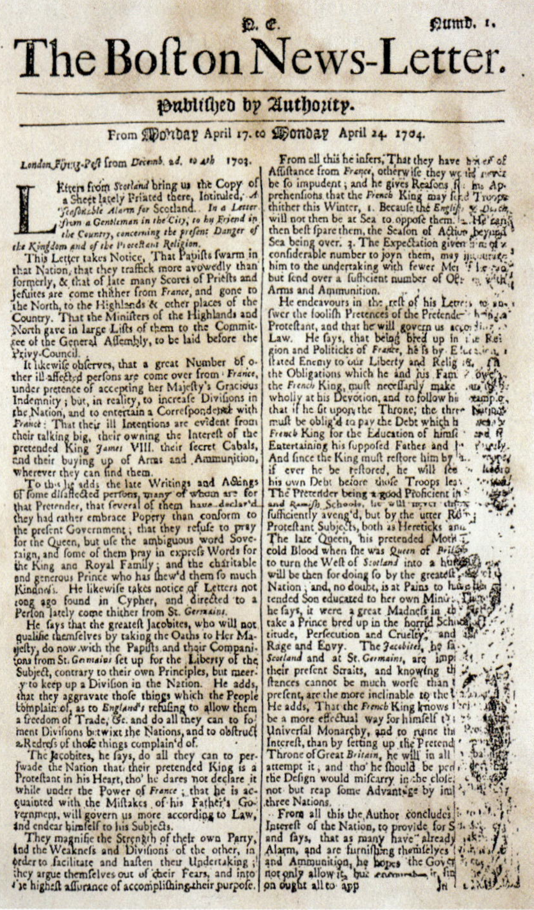

N. E. Numb. 1.

# The Boſton News-Letter.

Publiſhed by Authority.

From Monday April 17. to Monday April 24. 1704.

*London Flying-Poſt* from *Decemb.* 2d. *to* 4th 1703.

LEtters from *Scotland* bring us the Copy of a Sheet lately Printed there, Intituled, *A Seaſonable Alarm for* Scotland. *In a Letter from a Gentleman in the City, to his Friend in the Country, concerning the preſent Danger of the Kingdom and of the Proteſtant Religion.*

This Letter takes Notice, That Papiſts ſwarm in that Nation, that they traffick more avowedly than formerly, & that of late many Scores of Prieſts and Jeſuites are come thither from *France*, and gone to the North, to the Highlands & other places of the Country. That the Miniſters of the Highlands and North gave in large Liſts of them to the Committee of the General Aſſembly, to be laid before the Privy-Council.

It likewiſe obſerves, that a great Number of other ill-affected perſons are come over from *France*, under pretence of accepting her Majeſty's Gracious Indemnity; but, in reality, to increaſe Diviſions in the Nation, and to entertain a Correſpondence with *France*: That their ill Intentions are evident from their talking big, their owning the Intereſt of the pretended King *James* VIII. their ſecret Cabals, and their buying up of Arms and Ammunition, wherever they can find them.

To this he adds the late Writings and Actings of ſome diſaffected perſons, many of whom are for that Pretender, that ſeveral of them have declar'd they had rather embrace Popery than conform to the preſent Government; that they refuſe to pray for the Queen, but uſe the ambiguous word Soveraign, and ſome of them pray in expreſs Words for the King and Royal Family; and the charitable and generous Prince who has ſhew'd them ſo much Kindneſs. He likewiſe takes notice of Letters not long ago found in Cypher, and directed to a Perſon lately come thither from St. *Germains*.

He ſays that the greateſt Jacobites, who will not qualifie themſelves by taking the Oaths to Her Majeſty, do now with the Papiſts and their Companions from St. *Germains* ſet up for the Liberty of the Subject, contrary to their own Principles, but meerly to keep up a Diviſion in the Nation. He adds, that they aggravate thoſe things which the People complain of, as to *England's* refuſing to allow them a freedom of Trade, &c. and do all they can to foment Diviſions betwixt the Nations, and to obſtruct a Redreſs of thoſe things complain'd of.

The Jacobites, he ſays, do all they can to perſwade the Nation that their pretended King is a Proteſtant in his Heart, tho' he dares not declare it while under the Power of *France*; that he is acquainted with the Miſtakes of his Father's Government, will govern us more according to Law, and endear himſelf to his Subjects.

They magnifie the Strength of their own Party, and the Weakneſs and Diviſions of the other, in order to facilitate and haſten their Undertaking; they argue themſelves out of their Fears, and into the higheſt aſſurance of accompliſhing their purpoſe.

From all this he infers, That they have [illegible] of Aſſiſtance from *France*, otherwiſe they would never be ſo impudent; and he gives Reaſons for his Apprehenſions that the *French* King may ſend Troops thither this Winter, 1. Becauſe the *English* & *Dutch* will not then be at Sea to oppoſe them. 2. He can then beſt ſpare them, the Seaſon of Action beyond Sea being over. 3. The Expectation given [illegible] of a conſiderable number to joyn them, may [illegible] him to the undertaking with fewer Men [illegible] but ſend over a ſufficient number of Officers with Arms and Ammunition.

He endeavours in the reſt of his Letter to anſwer the fooliſh Pretences of the Pretender [illegible] a Proteſtant, and that he will govern us according [illegible] Law. He ſays, that being bred up in the Religion and Politicks of *France*, he is by Education [illegible] ſtated Enemy to our Liberty and Religion. [illegible] the Obligations which he and his Family owe [illegible] the *French* King, muſt neceſſarily make [illegible] wholly at his Devotion, and to follow his example [illegible] that if he ſit upon the Throne; the three Nations [illegible] muſt be oblig'd to pay the Debt which h[illegible] *French* King for the Education of himſ[illegible] and ſ[illegible] Entertaining his ſuppoſed Father and h[illegible] And ſince the King muſt reſtore him by [illegible] if ever he be reſtored, he will ſee [illegible] his own Debt before thoſe Troops lea[illegible] The Pretender being a good Proficient in [illegible] and *Romiſh* Schools, he will never [illegible] ſufficiently aveng'd, but by the utter R[illegible] Proteſtant Subjects, both as Hereticks an[illegible] The late Queen, his pretended Moth[illegible] cold Blood when ſhe was *Queen of Brit*[illegible] to turn the Weſt of *Scotland* into a hu[illegible] will be then for doing ſo by the greateſt [illegible] Nation; and, no doubt, is at Pains to ha[illegible] tended Son educated to her own Mind[illegible] he ſays, it were a great Madneſs in th[illegible] take a Prince bred up in the horrid Sch[illegible] titude, Perſecution and Cruelty, and [illegible] Rage and Envy. The *Jacobites*, he ſa[illegible] *Scotland* and at St. *Germains*, are imp[illegible] their preſent Straits, and knowing th[illegible] ſtances cannot be much worſe than [illegible] preſent, are the more inclinable to the [illegible] He adds, That the *French* King knows [illegible] be a more effectual way for himſelf t[illegible] Univerſal Monarchy, and to ruine th[illegible] Intereſt, than by ſetting up the Pretend[illegible] Throne of Great *Britain*, he will in all [illegible] attempt it; and tho' he ſhould be perſ[illegible] the Deſign would miſcarry in the cloſe, [illegible] not but reap ſome Advantage by im[illegible] three Nations.

From all this the Author concludes [illegible] Intereſt of the Nation, to provide for S[illegible] and ſays, that as many have already [illegible] Alarm, and are furniſhing themſelves [illegible] and Ammunition, he hopes the Gover[illegible] not only allow it, but encourage it [illegible] on ought all to app[illegible]

This is the first issue of *The Boston News-Letter*, the first newspaper to be published continuously in British North America. The phrase "Published by Authority" indicates that the paper served as an official organ of the Massachusetts government. This issue was just two pages, one sheet printed on both sides.

doctor with a university degree in town. The *Courant* persuaded Boston officials to halt inoculation, but James Franklin made powerful enemies who had him arrested in 1723 after he refused to obey an order to clear future issues of the paper with Massachusetts officials before publishing them. James's younger brother Benjamin began to publish the *Courant* later that year. The paper folded in 1726, but not before demonstrating that there was a market for local political controversy and that newspapers could fill it.

Colonial newspapers connected readers to literary innovations and political debates in Britain. Here too the *Courant* played a key role. The Franklins borrowed features from London's *The Spectator*, such as mixing literary essays with news reports

*The Coffeehous Mob*, from Edward Ward, *Vulgus Britannicus; or, The British Hudibras* (1710). Coffeehouses were public spaces where men shared information, did business, and discussed politics. Note the newspapers and pamphlets on the table in the foreground. Some, including this image's creator, thought that coffeehouses enabled "vulgar" people like the patron who is hurling his coffee at another to spread gossip and disorder.

and running editorials that used fictitious names to conceal the author's identity. The *Courant* reprinted many of *Cato's Letters*. These essays, written by John Trenchard and Thomas Gordon and first published in *The London Journal*, defended civil liberties and implored readers to remain vigilant against political corruption. Reprints of *Cato's Letters* fueled colonists' protests against British imperial reforms in the 1760s.

Colonial newsprint connected colonists to one another. Newspapers became a common means by which masters tried to stop servants and slaves from fleeing for their freedom. Newspapers also reported on events in other colonies. Colonial newspapers still focused on news from Britain and Europe, gleaned mainly from London papers, but their attention to affairs elsewhere in British North America made colonists more aware of one another and set the stage for coverage of intercolonial events such as the religious revivals of the 1730s and 1740s.

The growth of new kinds of social and commercial space also helped to circulate ideas. The most common was the tavern. By the 1720s, there was one licensed tavern for every 100 residents of Boston, New York, and Philadelphia. People gathered in taverns to share news as well as drink. Taverns began to serve two other purposes. Colonists separated themselves by social class as taverns increasingly catered to patrons of a particular income level. By 1730, men of shared interests formed private clubs that met in taverns.

Meanwhile, coffeehouses sprang up in colonial cities. The first in the Anglo-Atlantic world opened in Oxford, England, in 1650. London had several hundred by 1700, more than any other city except Istanbul. The first coffeehouse in the colonies opened in Boston in 1676, and by 1724, every major port city in British North America had at least one. Coffeehouses were places for men to do business and to get the latest information on local and global events, some by reading newspapers or listening to others read them aloud.

Coffeehouses were also places to receive mail from overseas, but security was a problem. In 1718, Boston's postmaster warned that letters deposited in coffeehouse mailbags might be "Opened, Imbezled or Detained." He requested that captains of ships headed for Britain collect mail at the post office. The communications revolution had brought the Atlantic world closer together and made British North American colonists more engaged participants in it.

## STUDY QUESTIONS FOR LAYING FOUNDATIONS IN BRITISH NORTH AMERICA

1. **How and why did British North Americans diversify their economies? What were the consequences of commercialization and diversification?**
2. **In what ways did ideas and practices in England influence society and culture in British North America?**

## TIMELINE 1676–1731

**1676**
First coffeehouse in English North America opens in Boston

**1690–1693**
Hasinai Confederacy ejects Spanish soldiers and missionaries attempting to stake claim to Texas

**1690**
Massachusetts Bay Colony issues paper money

**1693**
College of William and Mary founded

**1694**
University of Halle founded in Germany

**1696**
English imperial authorities create Board of Trade to monitor colonial affairs

Vice-admiralty courts created to enforce England's Navigation Acts in American colonies

**1698**
Anglicans found Society for Promoting Christian Knowledge (SPCK)

Monopoly of Royal African Company on English Atlantic slave trade ends

**1699**
French begin to colonize Louisiana by building fort at Biloxi

**1700**
Bostonian Samuel Sewall publishes *The Selling of Joseph* condemning the Atlantic slave trade as immoral

Parliament mandates death penalty for piracy or for aiding and abetting pirates

**1701**
Church of England creates Society for the Propagation of the Gospel in Foreign Parts (SPG)

Iroquois reach "Grand Settlement" treaties with English and French empires and France's Indian allies

Detroit founded

Boston merchant John Saffin responds to Sewall with militant defense of Atlantic slave trade and slavery

**1702–1713**
Queen Anne's War erupts, pitting Austria, Holland, and Britain against France and Spain

**1702–1706**
English and Indian raids virtually destroy Spanish Florida's mission system

**1704**
*Boston News-Letter* becomes first continuously published newspaper in British North America

**1705**
Linen Act permits export of Irish linen to English North America

**1706**
Comanche complete migration from Great Basin to southern Plains

**1707**
Act of Union joins kingdoms of England and Wales and Scotland to form the United Kingdom

**1709**
Indian slavery legalized in New France

## Summary

- Horses, guns, and other imported goods diffused more widely among Indians, stoking conflict among Indians, expanding an Indian slave trade, and eroding Indian power in the Northeast and Southeast.
- Unprecedented levels of African and European immigration, a growing transatlantic Protestant network, and a mightier British empire expanded the borders of colonial North America, entrenched slavery and racism throughout eastern North America, and bound British colonists more tightly to the Atlantic world.
- British North America's economy grew and diversified, helping a native-born elite to form and encouraging the development of communication networks that accelerated and expanded the flow of ideas within the Anglo-Atlantic world.

**1709–1714**
Wave of German war refugees arrives in British North America

**1710**
Four Indian "kings" visit London to lobby for a British invasion of New France

British forces capture Port Royal, Acadia

**1711–1713**
Tuscarora War in North Carolina

**1711**
British scuttle invasion of Quebec

**1712–1716**
First Fox War

**1712**
Slave rebellion in New York City

North Carolina separates from South Carolina and becomes royal colony

**1713**
Treaty of Utrecht ends Queen Anne's War; British empire wins claim to Gibraltar, Hudson Bay, Nova Scotia, St. Kitts, and Newfoundland

**1714**
George, Elector of Hanover, crowned George I of the United Kingdom

**1715**
Jacobites in Scotland rebel against crowning of George I

**1715–1716**
Yamasee War in South Carolina, ending that colony's Indian slave trade

**1718**
Transportation Act approves exile of British convicts to North America as servants

First wave of Ulster emigration to North America begins

New Orleans founded

San Antonio de Béjar founded, establishing a permanent Spanish settlement in Texas

**1720s**
Rice cultivation booms in South Carolina, increasing demand for enslaved Africans

**1722**
Tuscarora admitted to Iroquois League

**1723–1725**
Second Fox War

**1724**
Louis XV modifies Code Noir and extends it to Louisiana

**1728–1735**
Third Fox War

**1729**
First wave of Ulster immigration to North America ends

**1729–1730**
Natchez War in Louisiana

**1731**
Louis XV assumes control of Louisiana from Company of the Indies

## Key Terms and People

**Act of Union** *149*
**Board of Trade** *156*
**Byrd, William, II** *162*
**Code Noir** *148*
**East India Company (EIC)** *155*
**Fox Wars** *141*
**gentility** *162*
**George I** *152*
**Grand Settlement of 1701** *140*
**industrious revolution** *159*
**Jacobite Rebellion** *152*
**Linen Act of 1705** *149*
**Louis XV** *133*
**manumission** *148*
**Maroons** *147*
**Mather, Cotton** *150*
**Mississippi Bubble** *132*
**Natchez War** *138*
**Navigation Act of 1696** *156*
**Pietism** *152*
**polygamy** *153*
**Pope's Day** *156*
**Pretender, the** *156*
**Queen Anne's War** *140*
**Saffin, John** *147*
**salutary neglect** *157*
**Sewall, Samuel** *147*
**Society for Promoting Christian Knowledge (SPCK)** *153*
**Society for the Propagation of the Gospel in Foreign Parts (SPG)** *153*
**Spener, Philipp Jakob** *153*
**Transportation Act of 1718** *153*
**Tuscarora War** *138*
**vice-admiralty courts** *156*
**Yamasee War** *140*

## Reviewing Chapter 4

1. "The circulation of people and goods between 1690 and 1730 eroded Indian power and increased that of colonists in North America." Does the evidence presented in this chapter support this statement conclusively? If so, how so? If not, why not?
2. In what ways did North Americans adjust to growing imperial influence between 1690 and 1730? What role did the flow of ideas across the Atlantic play in determining how colonists in British North America saw themselves and their relationship to the British empire?

## Further Reading

Barr, Juliana. *Peace Came in the Form of a Woman: Indians and Spaniards in the Texas Borderlands.* Chapel Hill and London: University of North Carolina Press, 2007. An excellent account of Spanish-Indian relations in 18th century Texas in which Indians compel colonists to conform to their ways of diplomacy.

Dawdy, Shannon Lee. *Building the Devil's Empire: French Colonial New Orleans.* Chicago and London: University of Chicago Press, 2008. Explains how New Orleans, through the actions of its residents and the ways that French officials perceived those actions, acquired its seedy reputation.

Gallay, Alan. *The Indian Slave Trade: The Rise of the English Empire in the American South, 1670–1717.* New Haven: Yale University Press, 2002. A prize-winning exploration of the Indian slave trade's impact on southeastern North America's Indians and on English colonization and imperial expansion.

McConville, Brendan. *The King's Three Faces: The Rise and Fall of Royal America, 1688–1776.* Chapel Hill and London: University of North Carolina Press, 2006. An iconoclastic view of British North American politics which argues that colonists regarded British monarchs highly until just before the American Revolution.

Richter, Daniel K. *The Ordeal of the Longhouse: The Peoples of the Iroquois League in the Era of European Colonization.* Chapel Hill: University of North Carolina Press, 1992. A masterful account of how the Iroquois resisted and adapted to colonization over the course of two centuries.

Smallwood, Stephanie E. *Saltwater Slavery: A Middle Passage from Africa to American Diaspora.* Cambridge, Mass.: Harvard University Press, 2007. A sensitive and haunting portrait of the Atlantic slave trade focused on trying to fathom its meaning and the meaning of enslavement to those who endured them.

# Visual Review

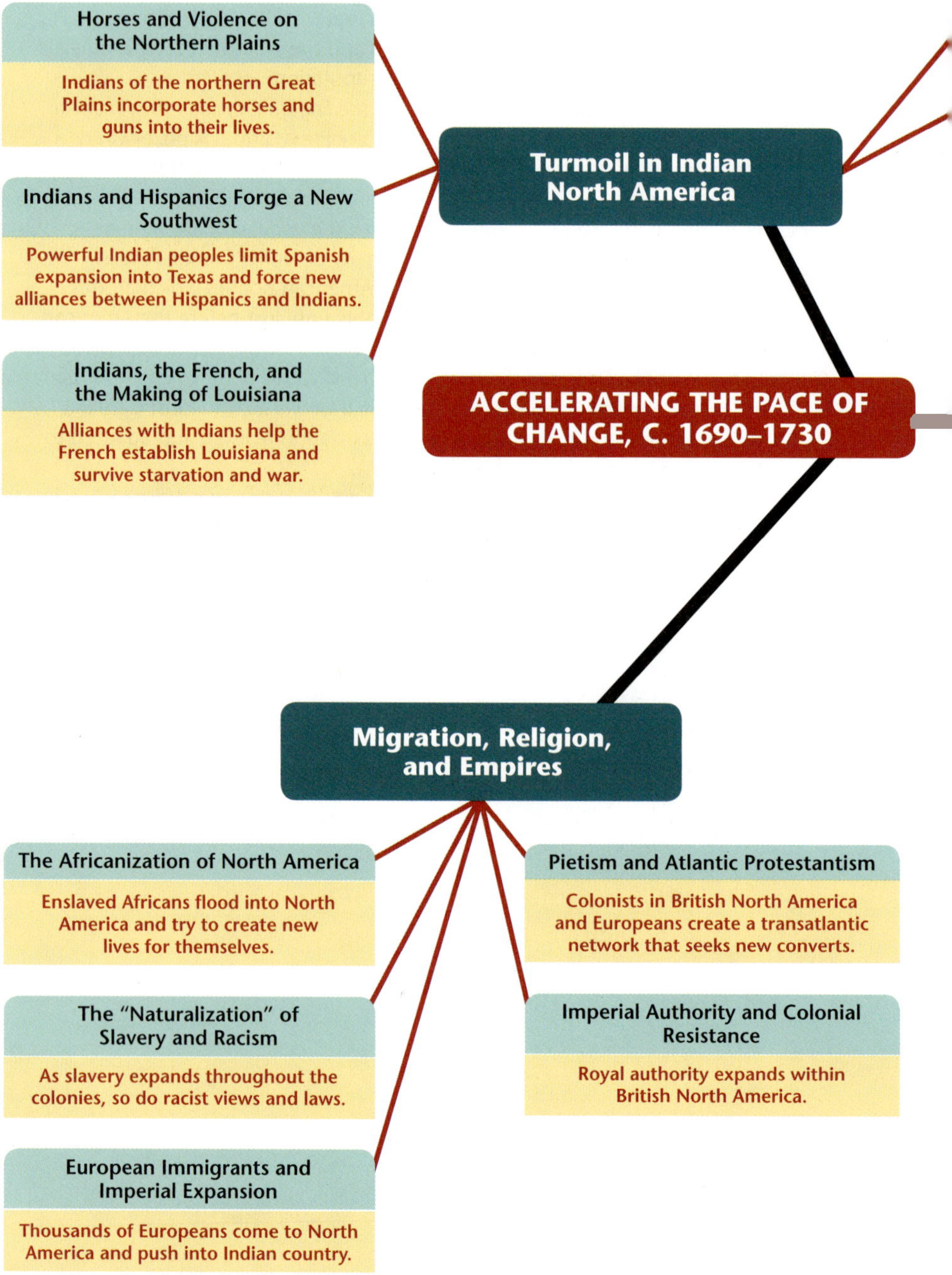

**ACCELERATING THE PACE OF CHANGE, C. 1690–1730**

## Turmoil in Indian North America

**Horses and Violence on the Northern Plains**

Indians of the northern Great Plains incorporate horses and guns into their lives.

**Indians and Hispanics Forge a New Southwest**

Powerful Indian peoples limit Spanish expansion into Texas and force new alliances between Hispanics and Indians.

**Indians, the French, and the Making of Louisiana**

Alliances with Indians help the French establish Louisiana and survive starvation and war.

## Migration, Religion, and Empires

**The Africanization of North America**

Enslaved Africans flood into North America and try to create new lives for themselves.

**The "Naturalization" of Slavery and Racism**

As slavery expands throughout the colonies, so do racist views and laws.

**European Immigrants and Imperial Expansion**

Thousands of Europeans come to North America and push into Indian country.

**Pietism and Atlantic Protestantism**

Colonists in British North America and Europeans create a transatlantic network that seeks new converts.

**Imperial Authority and Colonial Resistance**

Royal authority expands within British North America.

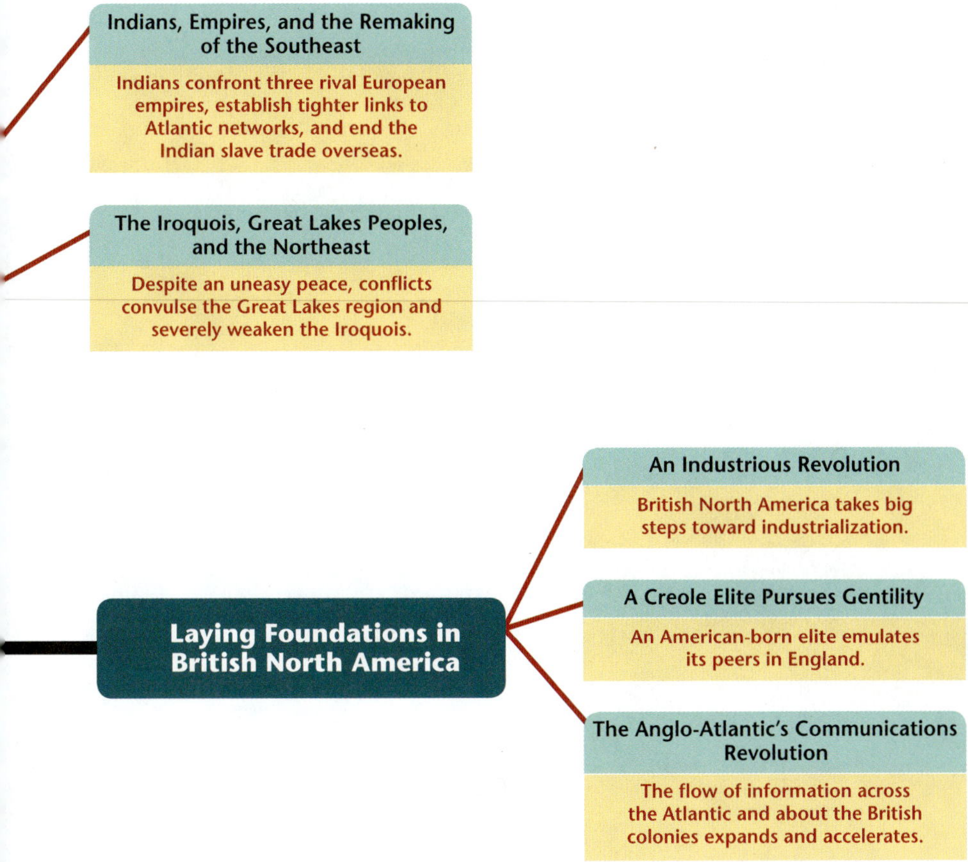

**Indians, Empires, and the Remaking of the Southeast**

Indians confront three rival European empires, establish tighter links to Atlantic networks, and end the Indian slave trade overseas.

**The Iroquois, Great Lakes Peoples, and the Northeast**

Despite an uneasy peace, conflicts convulse the Great Lakes region and severely weaken the Iroquois.

**Laying Foundations in British North America**

**An Industrious Revolution**

British North America takes big steps toward industrialization.

**A Creole Elite Pursues Gentility**

An American-born elite emulates its peers in England.

**The Anglo-Atlantic's Communications Revolution**

The flow of information across the Atlantic and about the British colonies expands and accelerates.

# 5 Battling for Souls, Minds, and the Heart of North America

## 1730–1763

In August 1763, 50 people boarded a ship in St. Augustine, Florida, heading to Havana, Cuba. Most had come to Spanish Florida after escaping slavery in South Carolina or Georgia or had parents who did. Now Britain claimed Florida as spoils of its victory over Spain and France in the Seven Years' War. Fearing enslavement if they stayed, Captain Francisco Menéndez and his neighbors in **Gracia Real de Santa Teresa de Mose** (the first free black town in what is today the United States) again sought liberty by fleeing south.

Few on board knew better than Menéndez how precarious freedom could be. Born in Africa in 1703 and later enslaved, he won his freedom at age 35 by serving in the Spanish military for over a decade. In 1740, Menéndez commanded a contingent of free black soldiers who helped to save St. Augustine from British forces. Believing that his deeds in battle merited a royal commission and a salary from King Philip V, Menéndez resolved to go to Spain to make his case in person. He became a privateer to pay his way across the Atlantic, but never made it to Spain. In 1741, a Boston-based privateer captured and tortured Menéndez. The ship's captain renamed Menéndez "Don Blass" and took him to the Bahamas, where the British vice-admiralty court condemned him to slavery. Somehow Menéndez managed to get free, for by 1759 he again led the militia of Gracia Real de Santa Teresa de Mose.

Menéndez and his family tried to settle in San Agustín de la Nueva Florida, a new town created near Havana for 84

Portrait of George Whitefield by John Wollaston, oil on canvas, c. 1742

America in the World
British colonists' defiance of the Molasses Act increased tensions with imperial officials that eventually led to the American Revolution (1733).
Albany Congress secures Iroquois League neutrality and reaches agreement for common defense of British colonies in impending war with France (1754).
North American event that influenced the world
International event that influenced North America
Event with multinational influence
Conflict

King George's War spurred flood of German emigrants to British North America (1749–1754).
British books of fiction—such as the scandalous novel *Pamela*—bolstered a robust reprinting and publishing industry in the British colonies (1742).
The Seven Years' War nearly bankrupted Britain and resulted in more and higher taxes to which colonists objected, setting in motion events that led to the American Revolution (1763–1764).

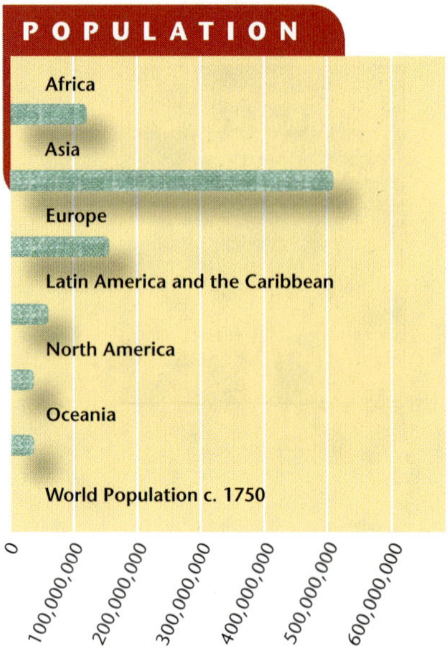

**POPULATION**



Florida families. Spanish authorities gave each household land, provisions, tools, and an enslaved African. Most Floridians soon abandoned the struggling town. So did Menéndez and his family, who went back to Havana.

Francisco Menéndez navigated many of the dramatic changes that profoundly altered North America and the Atlantic world between 1730 and 1763. Rapid expansion of British North America, largely through the immigration of enslaved Africans like Menéndez, fed conflicts with Indians and rival European empires. Menéndez won his freedom in one of these wars, but lost it in the next. Meanwhile, as British colonists' demand for imported goods grew and their participation in transatlantic intellectual and religious networks became more vocal, a global war for empire broke out, due largely to events in North America that British colonists had set in motion. Britain's resulting win of all of North America east of the Mississippi forced Menéndez and his neighbors from their homes to preserve their freedom.

# IMMIGRANTS AND INDIANS

African and European immigration to British North America surged between 1730 and 1775, elevating tensions within colonies that absorbed tens of thousands of newcomers. As immigrants and native-born colonists headed west, they displaced Indians, upsetting a precarious balance of power in eastern North America. Meanwhile, new Indian powers arose on the Great Plains as imperial warfare and slave unrest convulsed the southeast, New York, and the West Indies.

## Immigrants in Chains

The population of colonial British North America soared from 900,000 in 1730 to 2.5 million 45 years later (Figure 5.3). Immigrants directly accounted for 40 percent of that growth. By the American Revolution, most people in British North America were immigrants or first-generation colonists.

Most who came to North America between 1730 and 1775 arrived in chains. Over 200,000 came from Africa, accounting for just over half the 400,000 enslaved Africans who came directly from Africa to what became the United States (Figure 5.1). Demand for enslaved Africans in North America still paled beside that elsewhere in

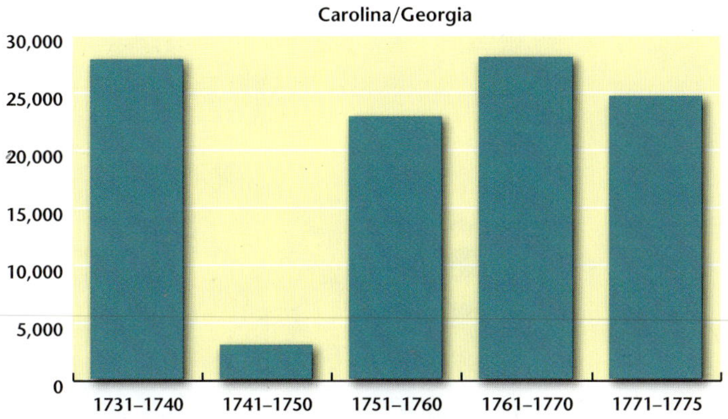


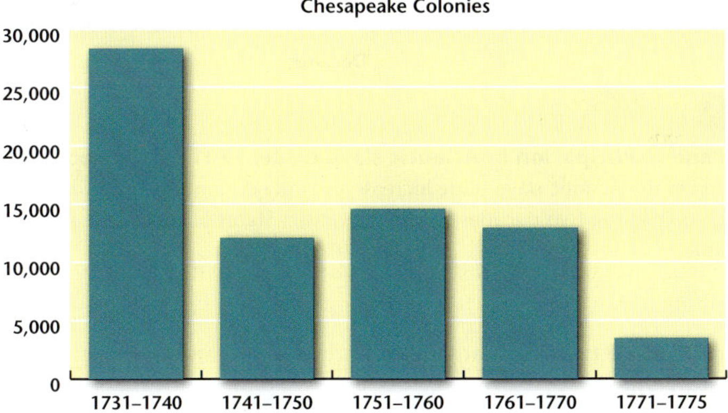


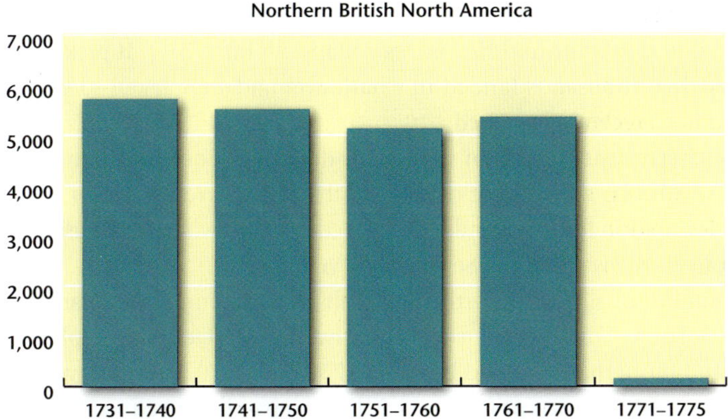


▲ **Figure 5.1**

**Estimated numbers of enslaved Africans who disembarked in North America by region, 1731–1775** After 1750 South Carolina and Georgia became the main North American destinations for enslaved Africans, especially after Georgia legalized slavery. Declining demand for enslaved Africans in the Chesapeake owed largely to natural increase in the region's enslaved population. Note the steady demand for enslaved people in northern colonies.

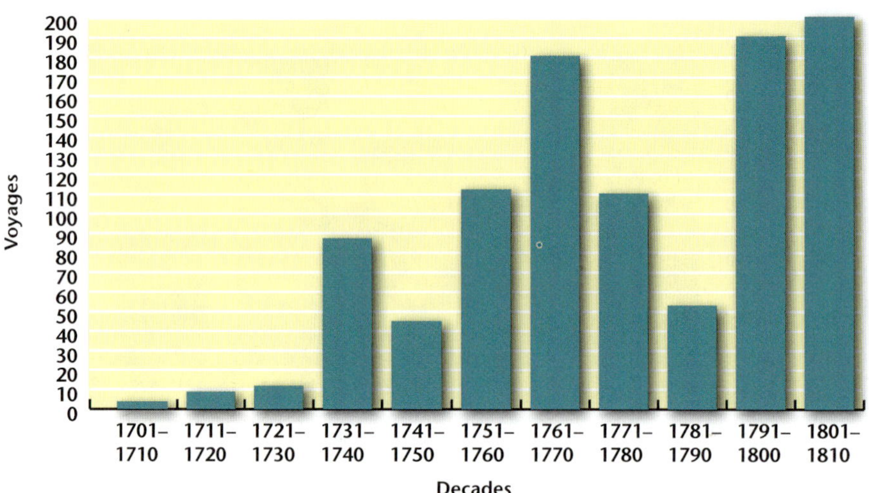


▲ **Figure 5.2**

**Rhode Island participation in Atlantic slave trade, 1701–1807** Rhode Islanders' participation in the Atlantic slave trade increased sharply during the 1730s. It peaked in the 1760s and again in the two decades before the United States outlawed the Atlantic slave trade in 1808.

the Americas. Nearly twice as many disembarked in Jamaica, the British empire's biggest Caribbean colony.

Most enslaved Africans entered North America through South Carolina or Virginia. Demand for enslaved labor in South Carolina plummeted during the 1740s as wars raged in the Atlantic and rice prices collapsed (Table 5.1). It picked up again in the 1760s, when thousands landed in Charleston and were taken to Georgia, where slavery had been recently legalized.

By contrast, only two African slave ships docked in Louisiana between 1730 and 1763. A few Africans entered the colony via the French West Indies. Louisiana again became a destination for thousands of enslaved Africans when Spain assumed control of the colony in the wake of the Seven Years' War.

The number of slaves in northern British colonies increased sharply. The black population of New York, New Jersey, Pennsylvania, and Delaware tripled and that of New England more than doubled between 1730 and 1770. Few enslaved northerners arrived directly from Africa prior to 1740, but instead had lived in the Caribbean or in another mainland colony.

Slavery in northern colonies differed markedly from slavery in the South. Unlike slaves in the South, most of whom lived and worked on plantations, most northern slaves lived in or near a city, particularly Boston, New York, Philadelphia, or Newport. During the 1740s one Bostonian in nine was enslaved, as was one New Yorker in five. One Rhode Island household in seven owned at least one slave in 1774; some owned as many as 20. Most enslaved northerners were men and lived

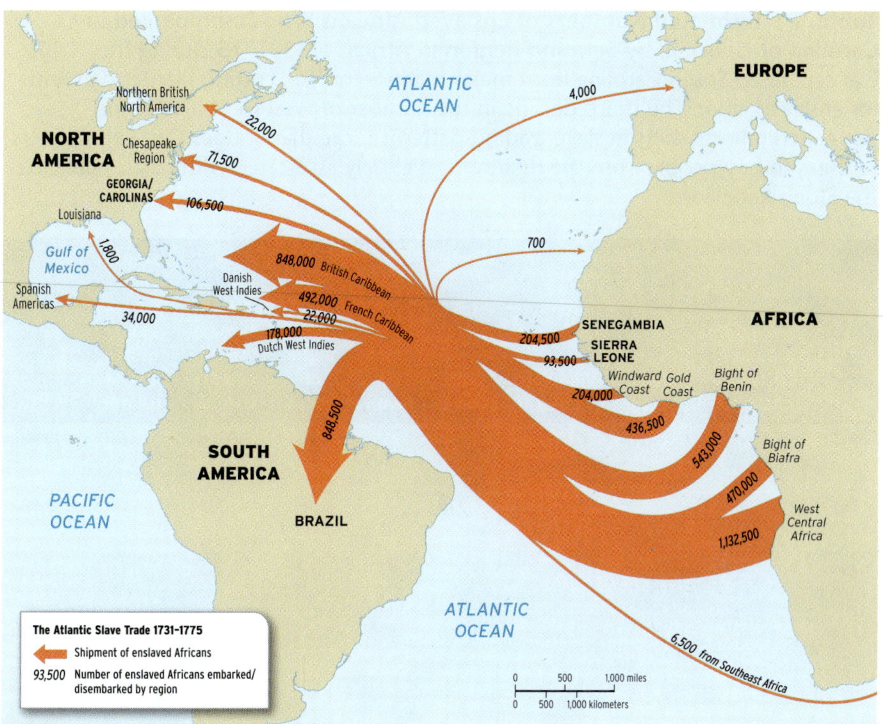


▲ **Map 5.1**

**North America and the Atlantic Slave Trade, 1731–1775** Demand for enslaved Africans continued to surge throughout the Americas after 1730. Nearly three times as many enslaved Africans landed in mainland North America between 1731 and 1775 as in the previous 40 years, with the majority landing in South Carolina or Georgia rather than the Chesapeake colonies.

with at most one other slave, making it harder to establish families or an autonomous culture. Still, black New Englanders, free and enslaved, staged annual Election Days to choose a "king" or "governor" by the 1750s. Their peers in New York and New Jersey did likewise in Pinkster celebrations. Africans in the Caribbean and Brazil had long staged similar events.

The growth of slavery in northern colonies owed partly to colonists' greater participation in the Atlantic slave trade. In the 1730s Rhode Island merchants began to invest heavily in shipping and selling Africans (Figure 5.2). Four decades later they controlled 70 percent of British North America's colonial slave trade and their vessels had transported nearly 60,000 Africans across the Atlantic. Rhode Islanders' ability to supply New England rum to suit African tastes prompted Gold Coast merchants to seek their business. Once they had secured their human cargoes, more than two in three Rhode Island-based crews set sail for the Caribbean.

Tens of thousands of British and Irish convicts also came to North America against their will after 1730. They made up nearly one-fourth of British migrants and

**Table 5.1 Estimated Numbers of Enslaved Africans Who Disembarked in Carolina or Georgia, by Sending Region in Africa, 1731–1775** During the 1740s war separated South Carolina from major markets for rice, cutting planter demand for enslaved labor. The sharp decline in the number of West Central Africans purchased reflects shifts in slave trading patterns more than it does Carolina planters refusing to buy people from the region most closely associated with participants in the Stono Rebellion.

| | Senegambia and Offshore Atlantic | Sierra Leone | Windward Coast | Gold Coast | Bight of Benin | Bight of Biafra | West Central Africa and St. Helena | Southeast Africa and Indian Ocean islands | Totals |
|---|---|---|---|---|---|---|---|---|---|
| 1731–1740 | 3,469 | 0 | 0 | 447 | 0 | 5,582 | 18,362 | 0 | 27,860 |
| 1741–1750 | 769 | 0 | 330 | 219 | 0 | 1,378 | 287 | 0 | 2,982 |
| 1751–1760 | 7,369 | 2,559 | 1,525 | 2,655 | 529 | 4,724 | 3,183 | 311 | 22,856 |
| 1761–1770 | 7,367 | 5,028 | 4,352 | 3,368 | 698 | 1,476 | 5,754 | 0 | 28,044 |
| 1771–1775 | 7,611 | 4,848 | 3,386 | 4,877 | 1,117 | 150 | 2,638 | 0 | 24,627 |
| Totals | 26,585 | 12,435 | 9,594 | 11,566 | 2,345 | 13,311 | 30,224 | 311 | 106,370 |

Potter family of Matunuck, Rhode Island, c. 1740. Here the Potter family of southern Rhode Island poses with an enslaved boy who is serving them tea, linking their aspirations to gentility with slavery. Rhode Island's enslaved population grew more than six times between 1720 and 1750, due partly to local merchants' growing participation in the Atlantic slave trade.

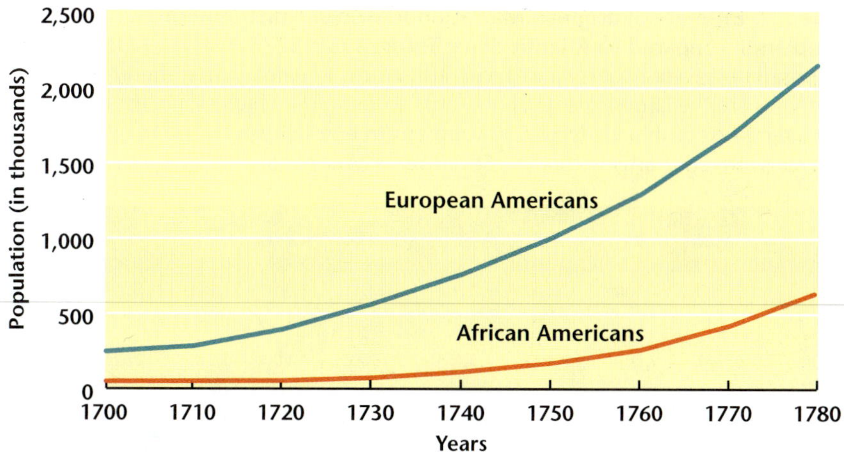


▲ **Figure 5.3**

**Population of mainland British North American colonies that became part of the United States, 1700–1780** Between 1700 and 1750, the population of British North America more than doubled, and it doubled again by the American Revolution, by which time one in five colonists was African or African American. Natural increase rather than immigration directly accounted for most of this rapid population growth.

the majority of English migrants to North America between 1700 and 1776. Population growth, rising crime rates, and more severe laws in England increased the number of convicts shipped to North America. In 1731, a pamphlet published in London defended the convict trade as "Draining the Nation of its offensive Rubbish without taking away their Lives."

Over 90 percent of convicts did their time in the Chesapeake. They were cheap: a male convict could be bought for about one-third of what a young enslaved African man might cost in the 1760s, but buying convicts was risky because they tended to run away more often than other servants or slaves. Sometimes they were violent. But convicts were inexpensive and social pariahs, so many masters and overseers treated them with impunity.

Not all colonists welcomed the arrival of England's convicts. Among them was **Benjamin Franklin**, who campaigned vociferously against the transportation of convicted felons to the colonies. Franklin's newspaper *The Pennsylvania Gazette* focused on convicts' crimes during the early 1750s. Franklin once suggested that colonists retaliate for the convict trade by exporting rattlesnakes to England, signing the essay "Americanus." He spoke to a British North America built largely on a transatlantic trade in people in chains.

## The Making of Irish and German America

Ireland was the second largest source of immigrants to British North America between 1730 and 1775, with over half arriving after 1750 (Table 5.2). Most Irish who

**Table 5.2 Estimated European Migration to British North America by Ethnic Group and Compared to Atlantic Slave Trade, 1730–1775** Enslaved Africans comprised the majority of migrants to British North America during the 1730s and they were the largest group of migrants entering the colonies in each decade thereafter. Most of the nearly 30,000 Germans to enter British North America during the 1750s arrived shortly before the Seven Years' War began.

| Decade | Germans | Ulster Irish | Southern Irish | Scots | English | Welsh | Other | Africans | Total |
|---|---|---|---|---|---|---|---|---|---|
| 1730–1739 | 13,000 | 4,400 | 7,400 | 2,000 | 4,900 | 3,200 | 800 | 60,700 | 96,400 |
| 1740–1749 | 16,600 | 9,200 | 9,100 | 3,100 | 7,500 | 4,900 | 1,100 | 21,600 | 73,100 |
| 1750–1759 | 29,100 | 14,200 | 8,100 | 3,700 | 8,800 | 5,800 | 1,200 | 38,200 | 109,100 |
| 1760–1769 | 14,500 | 21,200 | 8,500 | 10,000 | 11,900 | 7,800 | 1,600 | 51,600 | 127,100 |
| 1770–1775 | 5,200 | 13,200 | 3,900 | 15,000 | 7,100 | 4,600 | 700 | 31,000 | 80,700 |
| Total | 78, 400 | 62,200 | 37,000 | 33,800 | 40,200 | 26,300 | 5,400 | 203,100 | 486,400 |

Note: "Germans" refers to German speakers, not to people who came from what is today Germany. "Africans" refers to people brought via the Atlantic slave trade who disembarked in British North America. "British North America" does not include Nova Scotia or the Caribbean.

migrated between 1730 and 1763 were young, single, male, and indentured servants. Families from Ulster (Northern Ireland) who paid their own way across the Atlantic dominated Irish immigration from 1763 to the Revolution. Crop failures and slumping demand for linen in 1739 sparked a wave of emigration to North America over the next two years. The promise of better opportunities, particularly land ownership, led thousands more to follow.

Most landed in Philadelphia or in New Castle, Delaware, where demand for indentured servants was high. Commercial ties linked those ports to Ireland. Most ex-servants who concluded their terms headed for Pennsylvania's and New Jersey's frontiers, where land was cheaper. Ulsterites, later known in North America as Scots Irish, who had paid their own way went west immediately. After 1750, more of them landed in Pennsylvania and trekked south to western Maryland, Virginia's Shenandoah Valley, Piedmont North Carolina, and South Carolina's Upcountry. Thousands followed the Great Wagon Road, on which construction began in 1730, from Philadelphia to the southern backcountry.

▸ Map 5.2

**Race, Ethnicity, and the Colonization of British North America, c. 1775** European immigration and the Atlantic slave trade made an ethnic and racial mosaic of colonial British North America. The colonies were even more diverse than this map suggests, for it shows the largest group in each area, which often was not the majority. Most Scots arrived after the Seven Years' War.

Predominant Immigrant Groups 1775
English
Scots-Irish
Highland Scots
Dutch
French
German
African
J Jews
S Swedes
W Welsh
FH French Huguenots
Québec
Montréal
MAINE
NEW HAMPSHIRE
MASSACHUSETTS
Boston
FH
Albany
NEW YORK
CONNECTICUT
Newport
RHODE ISLAND
FH
New York
FH
PENNSYLVANIA
Philadelphia
J
NEW JERSEY
W
S
S
Baltimore
DELAWARE
MARYLAND
VIRGINIA
FH
Richmond
Williamsburg
NORTH CAROLINA
FH
New Bern
Fayetteville
SOUTH CAROLINA
FH FH
J
Charles Town
GEORGIA
J
Savannah
ATLANTIC OCEAN
FLORIDA
0 100 200 miles
0 100 200 kilometers

Along the way the Irish encountered thousands of Germans. Absolutist princes, high taxes, compulsory labor, and scarcity of land pushed over 70,000 Germans, mainly from the Palatinate (the region bordering the Rhine River) to North America between 1730 and 1775. The prospect of owning land, lower taxes, and religious freedom lured them across the Atlantic in numbers that alarmed German authorities. In 1768, Joseph II, emperor of Austria, tried to curb emigration to North America by ordering that no one from his empire could relocate there.

Most Germans landed in Philadelphia, where nearly 35,000 docked between 1749 and 1754. A network of merchants that formed in the 1730s and linked the Rhineland, Rotterdam, London, and Philadelphia delivered them. Before the 1750s, most German immigrants had come as families. Many had kin who wrote them about North America and helped them adjust to their new lives. After the 1750s, most German immigrants were single men who became "**redemptioners**," indentured servants who paid for their passage across the Atlantic by selling their services when they landed. In 1775, 1 in 10 colonists spoke German, as did 1 in 3 Pennsylvanians.

The influx of Germans alarmed many colonists, particularly Franklin. He referred to them as "Palatine Boors" who threatened to make Pennsylvania "become a Colony of *Aliens*, who will shortly be so numerous as to Germanize us instead of our Anglifying them, and will never adopt our Language or Customs, any more than they can acquire our Complexion." Such views, printed in London in 1755, came back to haunt Franklin.

That was partly because Germans comprised over 90 percent of naturalized British subjects in the mainland colonies. The **Plantation Act of 1740** allowed non-Catholic aliens who resided for at least seven years in British North America, received communion in a Protestant church, swore allegiance to George II, and paid two shillings to become citizens. An average laborer could earn that in a day. The law also permitted Jews in the colonies to naturalize by excusing them from the religious requirement.

Political controversies in Pennsylvania and the English- and German-language press spurred thousands of Germans to become naturalized British subjects. Most German voters traditionally supported the Assembly Party, which kept taxes low, did not demand military service of them or their sons, and opposed the colony's proprietor Thomas Penn, who sought to increase rents and land prices. In 1755, Christopher Saur published essays in his newspaper *Pennsylvanische Berichte* and in his annual almanac in which he likened Penn to the feudal lords who had exploited his readers back in Germany. Ten years later, over 2,600 Germans applied for naturalization just before an election that turned on whether Pennsylvania should be governed by the king or the Penns, who had recently made it easier to own land. Many new German voters and a sizable number of more established Germans, appalled by what Franklin had written about Germans in the 1750s, sided with the Penns. Franklin and others in the Assembly Party lost their elections and left the colony's assembly.

Heavy immigration accelerated the expansion of British North America and sparked debates on who could be considered British and who belonged in the colonies.

( 10 )

geſtrengen Herrn beliebt machen. Die Ueberſetzung ſo im erſten Blat gedruckt, iſt recht nach dem eigentlichen Sinn und Verſtand der Worte und des gantzen Satzes von ſechs Männern überſetzt, ſo beyde Sprachen verſteken. Um denen **Lockvögeln** unſere Unpartheylichkeit zu zeigen, ſolget hier der gantze Satz in engliſch und teutſch.

| | |
|---|---|
| And ſince Detachments of Engliſh from Britain ſent to America will have their Places at home ſo ſoon ſupplied and increaſe ſo largely here; why ſhould the Palatine Boors be ſuffered to ſwarm into our Settlements and by Herding together, eſtabliſh their Language and Manners to the Excluſion of ours. | Und weñ die Schaaren von Engländern, welche man von Brittanien nach America abgeſchickt hat, in ihrer eigenen Heimath ſo bald wieder aufgefült werden, nach dem ſie hier gelandet ſind, ſich ſelbſt ſo zahlreich fortpflanzen: warum leyden wirs, daß die teutſchen Baurentölpel in denen Landſchaften die wir angebauet haben, überall ſo lange herum ſtreichen, bis ſie endlich wie eine Heerde von ihrem eigenen Gezüchte ſich zuſammen lagern und ihre eigene Sprache und Sitten unter ſich beybehalten, damit die unſren niemahls aufkommen mögen. |

Nun mag es ein jeder nach belieben ſelbſt überſetzen, ſo gut erkan, daß weiß ich gewiß, daß niemand einen Ehren Titel oder eine Lobrede daraus machen wird. Der Leſer kan ſelbſt urtheilen ob dieſe **Lockvögel** ſamt ihren Helfſern und Helffers-Helffern, Verſetzer oder Verfälſcher ſind.

Ich will ein wenig erklären, was das engliſche Wort Boor vor eine Bedeutung hat. Unter denen Engländern

German printers in Pennsylvania made a point of broadcasting Benjamin Franklin's insulting "Palatine Boors" comment and translating it into German during charged elections in the mid-1760s. Here is an example from a German-language newspaper published in Philadelphia in 1764.

The labor of thousands of enslaved Africans accelerated the expansion of Virginia and Georgia and extended plantation agriculture to new areas. Meanwhile, thousands of German and Irish immigrants flooded into Pennsylvania and spilled into the southern backcountry. Resentful Indians, whom the new immigrants had pushed aside, watched from beyond the Appalachians, as did other Indians who feared that soon they might also lose their homelands.

## Indians in Motion

The world of Indians who lived between the Rockies and the Appalachians changed even more rapidly as more people and imports flowed into North America after 1730. Massive European immigration meant exile for some eastern peoples. Wider diffusion of horses and guns enabled the rise of new Indian powers on the Great Plains as Indians in the southeast continued to adjust to life alongside three rival European empires.

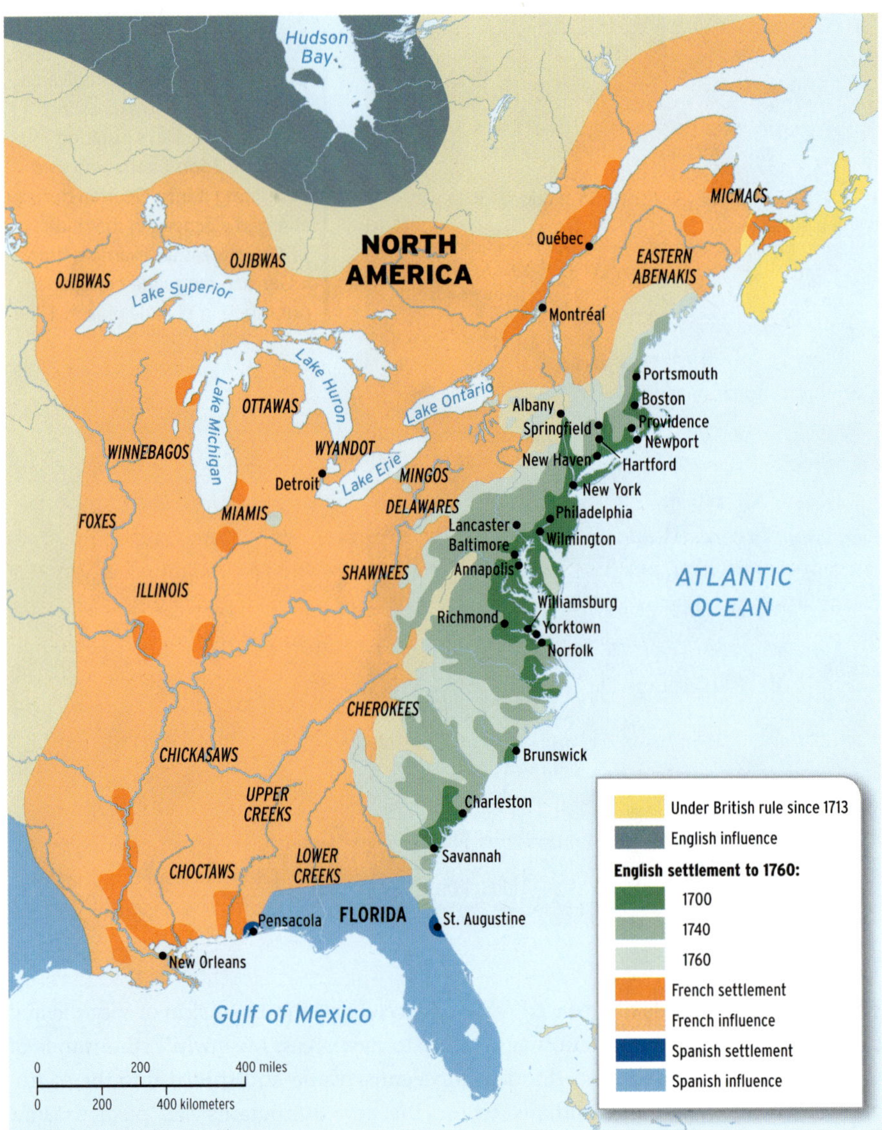


**Map 5.3**

**Political Map of Eastern North America, Mid-18th Century** Most Indians in the Ohio Valley who chose to take sides between the French and British preferred the French. British colonization, focused on control of land and exclusion of Indian peoples, expanded rapidly between 1700 and 1740, particularly in Pennsylvania and Virginia. Note the westward exodus of Delawares and Shawnees from Pennsylvania.

Few Indians suffered more from displacement by immigrants than Delawares. A 1736 treaty between Pennsylvania and the Iroquois League awarded the Iroquois the right to speak for all Indians who lived between them and Philadelphia. A year later Pennsylvanians tricked Delaware leaders into the "Walking Purchase." Delawares thought they had agreed to sell no more land than what one man could walk in a day and a half through the woods. Colonial officials sent runners along cleared and marked paths to claim 1,200 square miles of the Delawares' land. The Iroquois brushed aside Delaware protests that Pennsylvania had tricked them. Many Delawares trudged to Ohio, where they settled alongside Shawnees, many of whom also had been exiled from Pennsylvania. The refugees, now beyond the reach of colonists and the Iroquois League, seethed as they pondered what they had lost.

Meanwhile, horses and guns continued to transform life for Indians on the Great Plains. By 1760, virtually all Plains peoples had horses and most had firearms (Map 4.1). Wider incorporation of horses encouraged more peoples to become nomadic and focus on hunting bison. This meant more work for women and for enslaved captives, who had to process the hides.

The dispersal of horses and guns encouraged more violence and led to the rise of three powers, the newest of which was the Sioux. Teton and Yanktonais Sioux gradually entered the Great Plains from Minnesota in the late 1600s, partly to hunt bison to eat, but mainly to hunt beaver to trade to the French for firearms and other imports. As these Sioux depleted local stocks of beaver, they headed west, displacing less well-armed peoples such as the Omaha, Cheyenne, Missouri, and Iowa. They also began to acquire horses and incorporate them into their routines. By the 1740s Teton, Yankton, and Yanktonais Sioux had reached the Missouri River, where Mandans, Hidatsas, and Arikaras, well-armed agricultural peoples who had large herds of horses, impeded their expansion. Two decades later the western Sioux had become fully equestrian while still maintaining good access to firearms. The mobility that horses afforded the Sioux enabled them to dodge smallpox epidemics that devastated horticultural villagers such as the Arikaras, Hidatsas, and Mandans. By the time Lewis and Clark arrived in 1804, the Sioux dominated the northern Great Plains.

Meanwhile, the Osage had become the main power on the east-central Plains. Their location between the Missouri and Arkansas Rivers enabled Osages to deny Indian peoples to their west and south access to supplies of trade goods from the French, including firearms. French colonists in Illinois had to maintain good relations with the more powerful and populous Osage, who sent them mules and Indian slaves.

Comanches were the most powerful group of Indians to emerge in North America in the 1700s. Spanish law denied Comanches access to firearms in New Mexico, so they obtained them from the French. In return, Comanches offered bison hides, captives, mules, and horses. By the 1750s, Comanche raids forced Spanish colonists and longtime Indian foes to patch over their differences. Apaches sought shelter within Spanish missions in Texas but found little there. Fear of Comanches led Spanish colonists to ally with Utes to secure New Mexico's northwestern border, which extended violence and slaving raids well into the Great Basin as Utes funneled captives to New Mexico. So did Comanches, who brought Indian slaves and French guns to New Mexican trade fairs.

Southeastern Indians confronted a different situation. The Yamasee and Natchez wars left two principal Indian powers: the Choctaw and the Creek confederacy. The conflicts also accelerated the depopulation of the region. This allowed the population

Apache pictograph, Rattlesnake Canyon, Texas. Comanche raids forced many Apaches to seek shelter in Spanish missions, where they came under friars' supervision. Resentful Apaches who fled the missions painted the mission church as a friar whose upraised arms suggest church towers and whose hands are crosses. Note the arrow piercing the friar's body.

of white-tailed deer to explode just as bovine epidemics struck Britain and western Europe. Creek and Choctaw men hunted deer and sent their skins to merchants in Louisiana, South Carolina, and Georgia to fill demand for hides in Europe. English traders lured the Choctaw to supply more deerskins by selling them liquor and getting them into debt. Meanwhile, South Carolina officials attempted to persuade the Choctaw to abandon their long-standing alliance with the French and side instead with the British. Their efforts, and the concerted French response to them, led to a bloody civil war among the Choctaw in the late 1740s. Environmental change, trade, and rivalries between European empires destabilized Indian societies and the Southeast.

## Slave Resistance, the Southeast, and the Greater Caribbean

In 1733, a group of English entrepreneurs led by **James Oglethorpe** founded Georgia. The colony's trustees hoped to free British debtors from prison and redeem them through the hard work of establishing a new society, offer sanctuary to Europe's persecuted Protestants, and convert Indians, particularly those allied with the British. In addition, the trustees envisioned Georgia as a buffer between South Carolina and Florida, where hundreds who fled enslavement sought freedom among the Spanish and their Indian allies. That goal, and Oglethorpe's belief that slavery corrupted whites by encouraging them to be lazy, led the trustees to outlaw slavery in 1735.

Georgia's ban took shape as the Spanish encouraged slaves to flee South Carolina. In 1738, Florida's governor granted freedom to all fugitive Carolina slaves who

Medal of St. Christopher, Florida. Archeologists found this at the site of Gracia Real de Santa Teresa de Mose. St. Christopher, patron saint of travelers and of Havana, Cuba, is carrying Jesus over water. African beliefs that they would return to Africa after death may have encouraged Mose residents to identify with St. Christopher.

reached the colony. A few months later he licensed Gracia Real Santa Teresa de Mose, a town near St. Augustine, composed largely of people who had escaped slavery in South Carolina. The men of Mose, led by Francisco Menéndez, formed a militia to defend St. Augustine. The governor and Mose residents followed a precedent set in the Caribbean in the late 1500s in which Spanish officials allowed blacks who had escaped slavery to form towns in exchange for assurances that residents would defend the Spanish.

In 1739, offers of sanctuary in Florida helped to spark the **Stono Rebellion** in South Carolina, the largest and bloodiest slave revolt in colonial British North American history. A group of slaves who had recently arrived from Kongo, were baptized Catholics, and likely had military experience in Africa, led the revolt. Rebels burned homes and killed over 20 whites as they headed for Florida. It took whites a month to restore order.

The Stono Rebellion was part of a wave of slave revolts and conspiracies that rocked the West Indies and eastern North America between 1733 and 1741. Some arose from a network maintained partly by enslaved Africans and African Americans that linked eastern North America and the West Indies. The first revolt occurred in the Danish Virgin Islands. Akwamu slaves from Africa's Gold Coast took control of the island of St. John, where they hoped to establish a kingdom and enslave everyone who was not Akwamu. Three years later, Gold Coast slaves conspired to stage a similar revolt in Antigua. In 1739, Jamaica's **Maroons**, fugitives from slavery or their descendants, forced the British to sign peace treaties. Finally, rumors that slaves had plotted with foreign agents to commit arson, kill whites, and turn New York over to

Spain convulsed the city in 1741. Officials interrogated nearly 200 people, banished more than 70, and executed 4 whites and 30 slaves. Among the latter was Will, present at the St. John revolt and the Antigua conspiracy. "Will was very expert at Plots," sneered a judge who oversaw the New York trials, "for this was the third Time he had engaged in them."

War between the British and Spanish empires influenced events in South Carolina and New York. Parliament declared war on Spain in 1739, ostensibly to defend British commerce and mariners from a Spanish crackdown on smuggling in the Caribbean, after someone displayed what some claimed was the severed ear of Robert Jenkins, a British ship captain. The **War of Jenkins' Ear** (1739–1742) had two main American theaters—the Caribbean and southeastern North America—and was the first conflict in which large numbers of British colonists left North America to fight. British officers recruited 3,500 volunteers from New Hampshire south to North Carolina to help besiege Cartagena, Colombia, where hundreds died of disease.

Meanwhile, British and Spanish forces, along with thousands of Indians, faced off in the southeast. Troops under Oglethorpe's command failed to take St. Augustine, thanks partly to Mose's militia. The Spanish and their Indian allies invaded Georgia and were driven back to Florida. Georgia had shielded South Carolina from Florida, while Spain's policy of sheltering fugitives from British slavery had shored up Florida's defenses.

The War of Jenkins' Ear led to many changes. It and King George's War, what colonists called a 1744–1748 conflict between the British and French empires, cut South Carolina off from Spain and the Mediterranean, key markets for rice. This precipitated a recession that encouraged planters to diversify their crops. Many experimented with indigo, which yielded a blue dye that British textile firms imported from the Spanish and French Caribbean. An imperial bounty (bonus) on indigo initiated in 1749 helped to make it South Carolina's second most valuable export. After peace with the Spanish empire was restored, many South Carolina planters moved to Georgia. They argued strenuously that the region's climate and malarial swamps necessitated the exploitation of Africans, who, they claimed, were naturally suited to withstand both better than whites. In 1750, Georgia's trustees legalized slavery.

## STUDY QUESTIONS FOR IMMIGRANTS AND INDIANS

1. **In what ways did unfree and free immigration alter North America between 1730 and the 1760s?**
2. **In what ways did the movement of goods and people change Indian societies and Indian politics?**
3. **Was the impact of the movement of people different on southeastern North America than it was on North America as a whole? Please explain, using specific examples.**

# MINDS, SOULS, AND WALLETS

In the 1730s, colonists in British North America began to participate in new ways in transatlantic intellectual, commercial, and religious networks. The most educated of them embraced and practiced science, while thousands flocked to sermons delivered by people who brought evangelical Christianity to both sides of the Atlantic and converted thousands of blacks and Indians. Nearly everyone in eastern North America eagerly purchased British imports, as thickening ties to transatlantic and continental networks transformed how colonists and Indians thought of themselves and of their relationships to one another and to the world.

## North Americans Engage the Enlightenment

After 1730, colonists became fully engaged in the ideas of the **Enlightenment**. This philosophical movement attracted intellectuals in Britain, continental Europe, and the Americas; celebrated the use of reason as the key to progress; and disseminated knowledge via international communication networks. Enlightenment participants saw themselves as part of a collective effort to improve humanity. They tried to determine a system of universal laws that governed nature and the development of human societies. Most viewed science as critical to discovering and understanding such laws, and most considered arbitrary authority, whether wielded by clergy or monarchs, an impediment to progress that must be challenged.

Expansion of the newspaper industry kept colonists informed on distant developments. The number of newspapers published in British North America rose from 5 to 22 between 1728 and 1760. By the early 1740s, a number of changes had occurred in the newspaper business. Printers began to produce them in southern colonies, which helped to reinforce their role as brokers for the purchase of servants and slaves, as well as for the return of runaways. Colonists began to accept newspapers as legitimate vehicles for political dissent. In 1735, John Peter Zenger, who printed the *New York Weekly Journal* at the direction of James Alexander, went on trial for libeling New York's governor and was acquitted. The verdict set a precedent that people had the right to monitor leaders' actions and challenge them in print in order to preserve liberty. Newspapers also devoted more attention to North American affairs. Coverage of religious revivals and wars alerted readers to events in neighboring colonies and led many to identify more closely with one another and the British Empire.

The creation of more colonial colleges also facilitated the exchange of ideas. Clergy founded five between 1746 and 1766. They are today the University of Pennsylvania, Columbia, Princeton, Rutgers, and Brown. Most were established to train ministers, but all offered a secular and practical curriculum to students of all Christian denominations, following a model provided by Scottish and Dissenting (Protestant but not Anglican) institutions of higher education in Britain. The colleges trained a

To British colonists, the most significant event of King George's War occurred when colonial soldiers besieged and captured the French fortress and town of Louisbourg in Canada. Newspapers like this issue of the *Pennsylvania Gazette* kept readers in the colonies abreast of developments at Louisbourg.

*PHILADELPHIA, June 6. 1745.*

As the *CAPE-BRETON* Expedition is at present the Subject of most Conversations, we hope the following Draught (rough as it is, for want of good Engravers here) will be acceptable to our Readers; as it may serve to give them an Idea of the Strength and Situation of the Town now besieged by our Forces, and render the News we receive from thence more intelligible.

PLAN of the Town and Harbour of *LOUISBURGH.*



EXPLANATION.

1. The Island Battery, at the Mouth of the Harbour, mounting 34 Guns,-----Pounders. This Battery can rake Ships fore and aft before they come to the Harbour's Mouth, and take them in the Side as they are passing in.
2. The Grand Battery, of 36 Forty two Pounders, planted right against the Mouth of the Harbour, and can rake Ships fore and aft as they enter.
3. The Town N. East Battery, which mounts 18 Twenty four Pounders on two Faces, which can play on the Ships as soon as they have entered the Harbour.
4. The Circular Battery, which mounts 16 Twenty-four Pounders, stands on high Ground, and overlooks all the Works. This Battery can also gaul Ships, as soon as they enter the Harbour.
5. Three Flanks, mounting 2 Eighteen Pounders each.
6. A small Battery, which mounts 8 Nine Pounders. All these Guns command any Ship in the Harbour.
7. The Fort or Citadel, fortified distinctly from the Town, in which the Governor lives.
8. A Rock, called the Barrel.

T The Center of the Town. L The Light-House.

Every Bastion of the Town Wall has Embrasures or Ports for a Number of Guns to defend the Land Side.

The black Strokes drawn from the several Batteries, shew the Lines in which the Shot may be directed.

*CAPE-BRETON* Island, on which *Louisburgh* is built, lies on the South of the Gulph of *St. Lawrence*, and commands the Entrance into that River, and the Country of *Canada*. It is reckon'd 140 Leagues in Circuit, full of fine Bays and Harbours, extreamly convenient for Fishing Stages. It was always reckon'd a Part of *Nova-Scotia*. For the Importance of this Place see our *Gazette*, No. 858. As soon as the French King had begun the present unjust War against the English, the People of *Louisburgh* attack'd the *New-England* Town of *Canso*, consisting of about 150 Houses and a Fort, took it, burnt it to the Ground, and carried away the People, Men, Women and Children, Prisoners. They then laid Siege to *Annapolis Royal*, and would have taken it, if seasonable Assistance had not been sent from *Boston*. Mr. *Duvivier* went home to *France* last Fall for more Soldiers, *&c.* to renew that Attempt, and for Stores for Privateers, of which they proposed to fit out a great Number this Summer, being the last Year unprovided: Yet one of their Cruisers only, took 4 Sail in a few Days, off our Capes, to a very considerable Value. What might we have expected from a dozen Sail, making each 3 or 4 Cruises a Year? They boasted that during the War they should have no Occasion to cut Fire-Wood, for that the Jackstaves of English Vessels would be a Supply sufficient. It is therefore in their own NECESSARY DEFENCE, as well as that of all the other *British* Colonies, that the People of *New-England* have undertaken the present Expedition against that Place, to which may the *GOD OF HOSTS* grant Success. *Amen.*

To be SOLD,
By publick Vendue, on the *12th* Instant,
in *New-York*,

THE *French* Prize Ship *VALIANT*, Burden about 300 Tons, mounting 12 Four Pounders, with all her other Tackle and Apparel.

growing number of American-born doctors, lawyers, and merchants. Nine alumni of the College of New Jersey (now Princeton) attended the Constitutional Convention in 1787, including James Madison.

Beyond the walls of the colonies' colleges, libraries brought ideas swirling about the Atlantic world to colonists. In 1731, Franklin and other members of the Junto, a mutual aid society, formed the Library Company of Philadelphia, which lent books to members. By the 1750s, many towns had lending libraries. Many of the books patrons checked out offered self-improvement: advice on how to become a better farmer, public speaker, or bookkeeper.

Novels, the most popular type of books borrowed from colonial libraries, encouraged readers to think of themselves as part of an Anglo-Atlantic world. Authors such as Daniel Defoe began to publish novels in Britain in the early 1700s. Relatively few colonists read them before 1740. Most early novels focused on women's marriage and career choices in an emerging commercial society in which families afforded daughters less guidance or protection, above all from grasping, lustful, or deceitful suitors. Some novelists, including Samuel Richardson, offered moral instruction. In 1742, his most popular work, *Pamela: Or, Virtue Rewarded*, was the first novel to be published in North America, two years after it appeared in Britain. It told the story of a servant girl who resists her employer's efforts to seduce her. Her virtue so impresses him that he asks her to marry him. *Pamela* evoked negative reactions from some female readers, but most seem to have identified with Pamela for having honored her parents' wishes and her principles while attracting a husband.

Meanwhile, more British North Americans became ambitious and noteworthy scientists. They continued the practice, begun in the 1660s, of providing firsthand accounts of local plants and animals and shipping specimens overseas. John Bartram and his son William toured eastern North America, gathered many of its plants into a botanical garden, and published accounts of their travels. Cadwallader Colden studied botany, maintained a horticultural garden, and furnished European contacts with seeds and seedlings. His daughter Jane inherited the garden, made hundreds of detailed observations of American plants, and became the Anglo-Atlantic's first widely acclaimed female botanist.

Benjamin Franklin was the 18th century's most famous American-born person in Europe, principally because of his science. He focused on electricity, long considered little more than a curiosity. Franklin designed experiments that led to inventions like the lightning rod, proving that scientific experiments could yield practical benefits. He also developed a set of general laws that seemed to govern how electricity worked and did so under controlled conditions resembling those in nature. His discovery helped Franklin get elected to the Royal Society of London in 1756.

Franklin's reception overseas as a first-rate scientist who also was an American made him an exception. European scientists generally saw their American peers as suppliers of specimens and firsthand observations of North American nature, but did not think them capable of ascertaining laws that governed the universe. Such disdain led some colonial scholars to assert that as Americans they were best qualified to explain and depict American flora and fauna. They began to speak of the emergence of a distinctly "American Philosophy," discussions that led Franklin and John Bartram to organize North America's first intercolonial scientific society in Philadelphia in 1743. Twenty-five years later, it merged with a rival to become the **American Philosophical Society**, with Franklin as president.

## Becoming a Consumer Society

Most British North Americans did not read *Transactions* or frequent libraries, but almost everyone bought the British goods that filled shops. By the 1750s, most white families proudly displayed British-made ceramic teapots and teacups, china, and silverware in their homes. "[O]ur Beds, our Tables and our Bodies are covered" with British-made cloth, commented one colonial pamphlet of that decade. In 1773, North Americans bought 26 percent of manufactured goods exported from Britain, almost five times as much as in 1700. Per capita consumption of British exports increased 50 percent in the colonies between 1720 and 1770, largely because British industry and Anglo-Atlantic shipping networks offered colonists an unprecedented number and variety of goods to choose from. Their expanding choices as consumers led colonists to redefine their relationships to one another and to the British Empire.

Drinking tea, a sign of refinement and gentility to British on both sides of the Atlantic, helped usher in the consumer revolution. One writer asserted in 1734 that

Here Susanna Truax poses at ease with imported possessions. Her striped dress is made of British cloth. On the table behind her are a teapot, a full tea cup on a saucer, and a bowl with sugar cubes, all testament to her participation in colonial Anglo-America's consumer revolution.

New Yorkers had to "have their tea tho their families want bread." Ten years later, a customer at a Maryland tavern demanded more respectful service because his wife "drank tea twice a day" at home. Even Indians drank tea. In 1750, a Seneca chief hosted two missionaries, who were surprised to be served the beverage on a tea table.

British innovation stoked demand for tea, textiles, and other goods. A growing supply and array of goods made in Britain increased competition among manufacturers, lowering prices. Stoneware goods at midcentury were fired at higher temperatures to hold scalding liquids. That stimulated tea consumption. In the 1730s British textile manufacturers began to assemble pattern books for export merchants who shipped them to colonial clients who, in turn, used them to learn what was fashionable. In the 1740s representatives (factors) of mercantile houses headquartered in Glasgow began to set up shop in Virginia to compete with large planters for the business of small farmers, producers of two-thirds of the colony's tobacco. Small planters sold tobacco at the "Scotch stores," selected from a wide variety of goods, and bought on long-term credit. This decreased the influence of planter elites who had long controlled their access to Atlantic markets. Colonial merchants and shopkeepers spurred demand by extending credit to customers. In the major port cities of New England and the mid-Atlantic, wholesale merchants imported goods and shipped many of them to retailers in the countryside. The retailers bought on credit and sold the imported goods on credit to their rural customers, who paid their debts with what they made, grew, or raised. Retailers had those products hauled or shipped to wholesalers in the major port cities, who in turn sold many of them to the West Indies or southern Europe for specie or bills of exchange to pay creditors in Britain. Ships built by colonists and raw materials such as whale oil or naval stores like tar or pitch also helped colonial merchants balance their accounts with British merchants.

Ads in newspapers indicate that British North America was becoming one interconnected market. Colonists could buy the same goods almost everywhere at the same time. Archeological studies reveal that colonists who shared a socioeconomic bracket bought virtually the same goods wherever they lived. A growing network of small coastal vessels carried imports from merchants in northern cities to small ports in the south.

African Americans also bought imports. Enslaved men who lived in or near Charleston, especially tradesmen, often sold their time and expertise to whites. Enslaved ironworkers in the Chesapeake had access to the overwork system, under which they earned the market rate in cash or credit for work that exceeded their daily or weekly quotas. By 1750 most low country South Carolina plantations had implemented the **task system**. Like the overwork system, the task system assigned enslaved adults a daily or weekly work quota. Once they met it, they could tend their own gardens, raise chickens, or weave baskets. Slaves could sell what they made or grew. Their earnings enabled them to buy hats or cloth from which they made garments or had

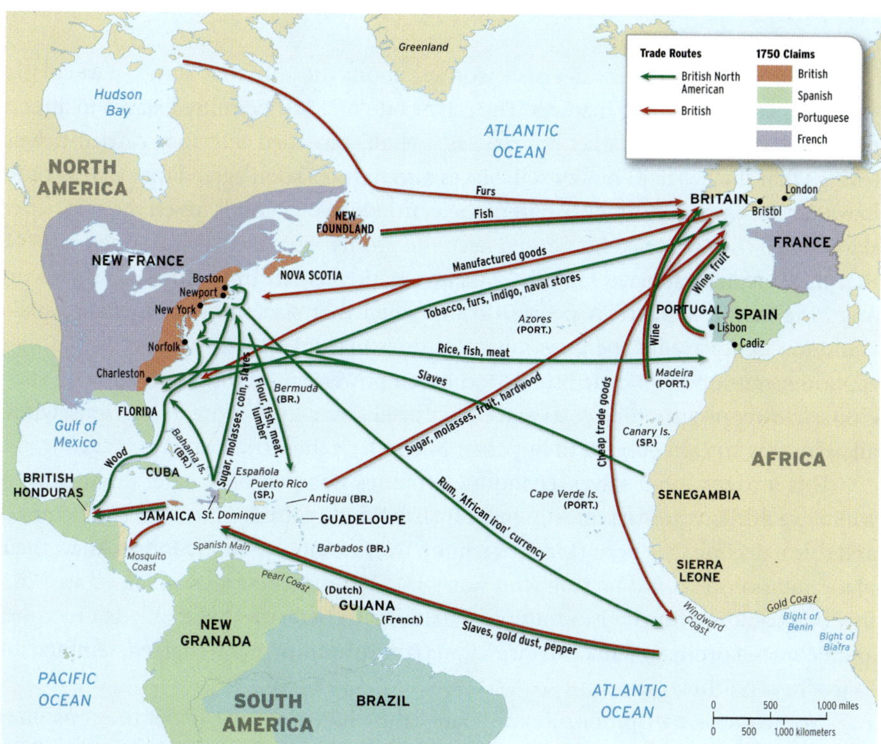


**Map 5.4**

**British-Atlantic Trade, c. 1750** By 1750, British North America was integral to British Atlantic commerce. Colonists' trade with Spain, Portugal, and the Caribbean helped them foot the bill for the manufactured goods that they imported from Britain.

them tailored. Such attire displayed the fruits of their labor and distinguished them from slaves who wore the standard clothing that masters distributed.

Slaves had unequal access to opportunities to earn income. Those who had marketable skills, worked for an industrial enterprise, or lived in or near a city enjoyed advantages that most who worked the fields or lived in more remote areas did not. Slaves who labored under the **gang system**, commonly used to tend tobacco, had less autonomy than those who worked under the task system. Men accounted for the vast majority of skilled slaves and had more chances than women did to earn money. Enslaved women dominated public markets in Charleston and Savannah, where they sold slave-grown produce and slave-made handicrafts, replicating a gendered division of labor long common in Africa and the Caribbean.

Authorities failed to stymie the rise of an autonomous slave economy. Artisans feared that the hiring of enslaved men threatened their livelihood, while other whites insisted that hiring of slaves was a security risk. In 1740, just after the Stono Rebellion, such arguments prevailed as South Carolina legislators prohibited slaves from hiring themselves out and fined those who hired them. Eleven years later Charleston officials acknowledged how unrealistic such laws were by licensing enslaved men to work as porters, laborers, fishermen, or craftsmen and setting rates to eliminate bargaining between slaves and employers.

South Carolina authorities also worried about the role that slaves, particularly women, played in public markets. The slave code of 1740 permitted slaves to attend the Charleston public market on masters' behalf, provided that they carried tickets listing what they were to buy or sell. Slaves and masters soon agreed that slaves could hawk masters' produce and use part of the earnings to buy goods, resell them to other slaves when they returned home, and keep the profits. A market clerk claimed in 1741 that the "insolent abusive Manner" of slave marketers left him "afraid to say or do Anything in the Market." A petition complained that slaves who ran market stalls could too easily evade "the government of their masters." Many masters fretted that economic autonomy afforded slaves too much power, but permitted it anyway. They enjoyed lower provisioning costs and encouraged slaves to be more industrious, while allowing few to earn enough to buy their freedom or their children's.

This anxiety about slaves' economic activities was part of a larger discussion in which wealthier colonists, mostly men, insisted that consumerism had led to moral and social decline. The poor (black or white), women, and youth no longer knew their place and no one could be sure who was who. A commentator complained in 1765 that one could no longer use clothing to distinguish between those "of great Fortune, and People of ordinary Rank." Conspicuous consumption, many charged, tempted all to live beyond their means.

Women took a disproportionate share of the blame for the ills of the consumer revolution. Some women hurled the blame back at men. In 1746, one noted in a Boston newspaper that male readers had called tea "a Female Luxury." She retorted that her male friends were as "great *Tea-Sots* as any of us."

North America's growing significance to Britain led imperial officials to seek more control over the colonial economy. Between 1732 and 1764 Parliament enacted laws that tightened regulations on colonial manufacturing and restricted what British

**Table 5.3 Key Laws Regulating British North America's Manufacturing, Trade, and Monetary Supply, 1732–1764** Imperial officials marked British North America's growing importance to Britain as a market for British goods and as a potential competitor for British manufacturers by crafting new regulations in the mid-1700s. Many colonists resented these laws, sentiment that fed their resistance to imperial reforms in the wake of the Seven Years' War.

| Name of Legislation | Year Passed | Key Provisions |
|---|---|---|
| Hat Act | 1732 | Barred colonists from producing beaver felt hats for export to other British colonies to protect British manufacturers |
| Molasses Act | 1733 | Imposed prohibitively high duty on sugar and molasses imported to British North America from French and Dutch Caribbean to protect British West Indies planters |
| Iron Act | 1750 | Barred colonists from building more rolling or slitting mills, which made hoops, tire iron, and nails that colonists usually imported from Britain |
| Currency Act | 1751 | Prohibited colonial governments from issuing more paper money, except in cases of emergency |
| Sugar Act | 1764 | Modified regulations issued under Molasses Act and bolstered their enforcement<br>First overt tax raised by Parliament in British America<br>Yielded more revenue than any imperial tax levied on British America prior to American Revolution |
| Currency Act | 1764 | Outlawed printing of paper money in colonies |

North Americans could export or import, particularly from the French and Dutch Caribbean (Table 5.3). Meanwhile, British lawmakers and imperial officials constricted colonists' ability to set their own monetary policies, measures that delighted merchants and other lenders in England.

Some colonists thought that such regulations signaled that Britain discounted their importance to the empire. In 1751, Franklin responded to the Iron Act by asserting that colonists' growing consumption of British goods should lead imperial officials to see them as fellow Britons who were partners in forging the empire's future. Seven years later, Franklin explicitly connected consumer choice and personal liberty. He asked, "Would you not say that you are free, have a Right to dress as you please, and that such an Edict . . . would be a Breach of your Privileges, and such a Government tyrannical?" In the 1760s and 1770s, thousands of colonists linked liberty and consumer choice by boycotting British imports to protest imperial reforms that they considered tyrannical.

## Revivals and the Rise of Evangelical Christianity

In 1741, Hannah Heaton, a 20-year-old Connecticut woman, attended a sermon. Years later, she recalled how it had transformed her life: "It seemed to me I was a sinking down in to hell. I thot the floor I stood on gave way and I was just a going but

GLOBAL PASSAGES

## The Birth of Methodism

John Wesley, a missionary for the Society for the Propagation of the Gospel, arrived in Georgia in 1736. While at Oxford University, Wesley, his brother Charles, and **George Whitefield** belonged to a student group whose members called themselves "**Methodists,**" due partly to their habit of rising early to plan how they would budget their time that day. Brought to Georgia by family friend James Oglethorpe, Wesley was to minister to Anglicans and convert Chickasaws, British allies against the Choctaw and French. But he crossed the Atlantic with one main goal: to save his own soul, an outcome that he tied to work among Indians.

Wesley did not convert any Chickasaws, but the two years that he spent in Georgia shaped him and Christianity profoundly. He gathered two dozen Savannah parishioners into "a sort of little society" that met weekly "to instruct and exhort one another." Wesley also paid regular visits to colonists near Savannah who lacked a pastor; a prototype of the itinerant preaching and circuit system that later characterized Methodism. Wesley became familiar with Moravianism in Georgia, kept close ties to Moravians after he returned to London, and visited the Moravian settlement in Germany. He later adapted Moravian rituals that became Methodist hallmarks: watch nights (midnight vigils), love feasts (quasi-sacramental meals), and letter days, on which believers communicated their spiritual accomplishments to peers far away. Wesley fused the Moravian concept that one could convert instantly and Anglicanism's precept that salvation was attainable to all who sought it. Enthusiastic preaching increased Methodism's popularity, particularly among working people in

then I began to resign and as I resigned my distress began to go off till I was perfectly easy quiet and calm . . . it seemed as if I had a new soul & body both." Heaton had participated in revivals that gripped most of British North America in the 1730s and 1740s and flared again in the south during the 1750s and 1760s.

Heaton remembered a time when religion became more important to residents of British North America. Ministers filled churches and preachers lured thousands to outdoors sermons with emotional messages of damnation and redemption delivered in simple and direct language that anyone could understand. The preachers brought evangelical Christianity to North America. They sought converts by stressing personal piety and the relative equality of all believers before God and one another. Most discounted adherence to ritual and reason and denied that formal education and theological training were the best claim to spiritual authority. Expression of such beliefs opened deep divisions within colonial Christianity and led colonists to identify more closely with fellow believers in other colonies and across the Atlantic.

Britain and North America. Wesley disliked the style until he read Jonathan Edwards' account of a revival in Massachusetts.

Like the Moravians, Wesley eagerly sought converts among slaves, but he later parted ways with the Moravians by becoming a militant opponent of slavery. Wesley visited Carolina plantations and soon conceived the outlines of what became Methodist practice for evangelizing enslaved people: target "the planters who were most receptive to his message," learn which slaves "were best inclined and understood English," and travel between plantations. Organized Methodism came to the Americas in Antigua around 1760. Preachers targeted enslaved people for conversion. In 1766, Robert Strawbridge built North America's first Methodist preaching house in Maryland. He recruited Jacob Toogood, a slave, to preach. Wesley drew from the works of the Pennsylvania Quaker **Anthony Benezet** for "Thoughts Upon Slavery," an essay that he published in 1774. Wesley denounced colonial slavery as "the vilest that ever saw the sun." The following year, his disciple Thomas Rankin was probably the first Methodist in North America to oppose slavery publicly, telling a Maryland audience that "the sins of Great Britain and her colonies had called aloud for vengeance," including "the dreadful sin of buying and selling the souls and bodies of the poor Africans." Methodists were among the new nation's sharpest critics of slavery until southern Methodists reconciled themselves to slaveholding in the early 1800s.

- In what ways did movement of people and ideas shape the development of Methodism?
- What impact did John Wesley's visit to North America have on the course that Methodism took when adherents began to seek converts in North America?

In many ways, Hannah Heaton's spiritual awakening and that of thousands of other colonists was a legacy of Pietism, which celebrated the exchange of ideas and techniques across ethnic, national, and denominational lines and promoted the evangelization (the conversion to Christianity) of Africans and Indians. The United Brethren knitted these strands of Pietism together. Revived in Germany in 1727 on the estates of Count Nicolaus Ludwig von Zinzendorf, the Brethren, better known as **Moravians**, sought to create closed, economically autonomous, sex-segregated communities in which Christian liturgical rituals and piety infused daily life. Georgia hosted the first Moravian community in British North America in the 1730s. By the mid-1750s, most Moravians, including a new influx who were fleeing persecution in Germany, had settled in Pennsylvania or North Carolina. Although there never were many Moravians, they played a key role in the development of Anglo-Atlantic Christianity by pioneering evangelizing techniques and sharing them with British and colonial **revivalists**.

Colonists filled leading roles in the transatlantic awakening, none more so than **Jonathan Edwards**, a Massachusetts minister. He merged Pietism with an emotional style of preaching and brought both to orthodox New England Puritanism. Edwards's charged sermons sparked a revival, an outpouring of religious enthusiasm, in the Connecticut River Valley in the 1730s. Edwards demanded that listeners repent and practice what they professed or face eternal damnation. Edwards broadcast news of his labors to an Anglo-Atlantic audience. Word of his deeds spread to Britain, prompting George Whitefield, an Anglican pastor, to tour British North America.

Whitefield was probably the first transatlantic celebrity. Colonists, who had read newspaper accounts of Whitefield's revivals in England and Wales, feverishly anticipated his visit. Thousands came to his outdoor sermons in Philadelphia in 1739, and the tour itself garnered an unprecedented level of coverage of colonial events in North American newspapers (Map 5.5).

In part, public interest was so great because revivalists generated enormous controversy. Critics directed fire at the enthusiasm that revivalists expressed and elicited and at their disdain for authority. Revivalists also sparked conflicts within denominations and between established ministers and itinerants, touring preachers who did not oversee a congregation. One faction within each denomination cast revivalism as irrational, too egalitarian, and too disrespectful of trained ministers. Traditional Presbyterian ministers were known as the "Old Side," while ministers who advocated revivalism belonged to the "New Side." Meanwhile, New England Congregationalists split into "Old Lights" and "New Lights." In 1742, Old Light supporters in Connecticut targeted itinerants by passing a law that declared that "any *Foreigner* or *Stranger*" who preached without permission from settled ministers was to be considered "a *vagrant*" and banished from the colony. In the 1740s and early 1750s German Lutheran and Reformed ministers in Europe and North America targeted Moravians, largely because their preaching and attentive ministry attracted Germans in New Jersey and Pennsylvania who had no Lutheran or Reformed pastor to serve them. Such campaigns sometimes led to violence against Moravian missionaries.

Moravians also drew fire because they disobeyed gender norms. Hundreds of Moravian women in Germany and North America served as eldresses, teachers who instructed women and men, overseers, deaconesses, or itinerant missionaries. The "choir system" by which Moravian communities segregated the sexes allowed women autonomy and challenged the model of the male-dominated nuclear family. Moravian hymns and imagery attributed some feminine characteristics to Christ. Moravian theology spoke of the Holy Spirit as "Mother."

Other revivalists also empowered women. Women's voices echoed loudly in New Light congregations that formed in New England during Baptist revivals in the 1730s and 1740s as well as in many Baptist churches in Pennsylvania. Women disciplined others for sexual misconduct, theft, and improper preaching. Women's votes helped to select some ministers, choose deacons, and admit new members. In 1764, Morgan Edwards became minister of a Baptist congregation in Philadelphia and refused to consult women when selecting elders. This provoked Joanna Anthony to pen a letter

▲ **Map 5.5**

**George Whitefield's First American Tour, 1739–1741** Whitefield preached to huge audiences in every English colony, some of which he visited multiple times. He died in 1770, having completed 15 preaching tours of Scotland, 3 of Ireland, and 7 of North America. But his first American tour was by far his most famous.

to the congregation. It was the first time "we ever knew of sisters being treated with such contempt in that church," she protested. "We know our former rights and we beg to know who had a right to deprive us of them."

Morgan Edwards and his allies soon prevailed. Revivalists and evangelical sects had long faced charges that they afforded women too much power, which encouraged irrational behavior. In 1742, Old Light minister Charles Chauncy claimed that revivalists' "frightful language . . . has its intended effect upon one or two weak women," whose "shrieks catch from one to another, till a great part of the congregation is affected." As evangelical congregations took root, women's influence within them ebbed.

Even so, the ideals of the awakening and evangelical Christianity promoted egalitarianism and skepticism toward established authority. Baptists, Methodists, and Presbyterians who evangelized Virginia in the 1760s and 1770s challenged the notion of a hierarchical, official, taxpayer-supported religion to which all must at least theoretically belong. Their efforts shaped James Madison's and Thomas Jefferson's views concerning the separation of church and state. Evangelicals helped to reconceive the relationship of the individual to the community and to society, so that people could decide for themselves to which community they wished to belong. Finally, revivalists drew Africans, African Americans, and Indians to Christianity.

## African, African American, and Indian Awakenings

Many blacks and Indians proved receptive to evangelical Protestantism, largely because preachers reached out to them with messages that they found attractive. Moravians were the first evangelicals in the Americas to target Africans and African Americans for conversion, establishing their first mission in the Danish Virgin Islands in 1732. Moravian outreach to Africans and African Americans spread from the Virgin Islands to the British West Indies, Pennsylvania, and New Jersey. They preached racial equality among believers but submission to masters, some of whom were Moravian church officials.

Like Moravians, George Whitefield considered enslaved Africans and African Americans his spiritual equals and he exhorted masters to practice what he preached. In 1740, Whitefield convinced the South Carolina planter Jonathan Bryan to build a school for black students. Bryan and his kin soon led a local movement to evangelize slaves. Like Moravians, Whitefield reconciled himself to slavery. He advocated its legalization in Georgia and later became a slave owner. That did not diminish Whitefield's importance to some black converts. His death in 1770 moved **Phyllis Wheatley** to publish her first poem, which circulated through the colonies via newsprint.

A number of factors encouraged more slaves and free blacks to convert to Christianity. Charismatic sermons and services lured black audiences and kept them as congregants. So did the willingness of evangelicals, especially Baptists and Methodists, to permit blacks, be they enslaved or free, to preach and become leaders.

Demographic changes helped to spread evangelical Christianity among Africans and African Americans. The growing numbers of **creole** (American born), English-speaking slaves lowered linguistic and cultural barriers to conversion, including the share of animist or Muslim Africans who might ostracize converts. By the American Revolution, just 1 in 3 enslaved people in South Carolina and fewer than 1 in 10 in Virginia was African. Nearly all lived in cabins for families, which had replaced dormitory-style group or communal quarters by the 1740s and gave them more privacy to worship as they wished.

Similarities between evangelical and African rituals and worldviews attracted black converts. The beliefs and practices of Methodists and Separate Baptists resembled those of many West Africans. Separate Baptists and Methodists saw the conversion experience as the chief means of entry into the church community. For Separate Baptists, that rite of passage, ritually confirmed by baptism, delivered the convert into the world anew: a "rebirth" in Christ. This was akin to West and West Central African initiation rituals associated with the symbolic death and rebirth of initiates in which a ritual bath marked rebirth and preceded return to ordinary life. African beliefs that the world would return to an idyllic past found confirmation in Separate Baptists' and Methodists' acceptance of all converts as spiritual equals.

Meanwhile, Indians in eastern North America experienced two distinct forms of religious awakening. One owed mostly to the work of colonists and European missionaries. Moravians established five mission towns for Indians between the 1740s and 1760s, the most significant of them in Pennsylvania. They baptized hundreds of Mahicans and Delawares, particularly women and children. Moravian women's participation in evangelization encouraged such conversions, as did similarities between Moravian and Indian beliefs. Moravians and Indians believed that dreams offered revelation and required careful interpretation. Indian women also found Moravians' portrayal of the Holy Spirit as Mother attractive. Mahican and Delaware Moravians afforded their male kin better access to colonial networks and served to bridge Christian and non-Christian Indian communities.

Meanwhile, missionaries and itinerants won Indian converts in New England. In 1753, Eleazar Wheelock, a New Light Congregational minister, founded a free school in Connecticut for Indian children who, he envisioned, would become agents of spiritual and cultural transformation among their peoples. Another New Light minister, James Davenport, converted many Narragansetts in the 1740s. They soon built a separate church, led by Samuel Niles, the first Narragansett minister, in which they practiced a form of Christianity that resembled their traditional beliefs. It emphasized visions rather than Scripture, guided by ministers who lacked a formal education.

Narragansett Christians in part reacted to discrimination that Indians confronted in New England. By the mid-1700s, most Old Lights and Anglicans had black and Indian worshippers sit in separate pews or galleries. Indians at Wheelock's school faced a worsening situation. In 1769, Wheelock persuaded the Earl of Dartmouth to grant land in New Hampshire for a new Indian school. Dartmouth College soon began to admit white boys, who drove out Indian pupils in 1776.

Samson Occom's life captured the dilemmas of Christian Indians' Great Awakening. Occom, a Mohegan, converted in 1740 after hearing a James Davenport sermon. He graduated from Wheelock's school, was ordained a Congregational minister, and moved to a reservation to work as a pastor and schoolteacher. In 1765, Occom toured Britain to raise funds for Wheelock's school. Three years later, Occom published an autobiography in which he explained how and why he had converted to Christianity. He also charged that his superiors overworked and underpaid him because "I am a poor Indian. I Can't help that God has made me So; I did not make my self so." Occom remained a committed minister, but came to conclude that Indians could only realize Christianity's egalitarian potential by separating themselves from whites.

Other Indians experienced a religious awakening in which converts rejected Europeans and their ways. Such "nativists" concluded that Indians could regain spiritual and political power only by rejecting most of what Europeans had brought, including Christianity, manufactured goods, and alcohol. In 1737, Shawnees and Onondagas spoke of a vision that God had "driven the wild animals out of the country" to punish Indians for killing game to trade it for alcohol. Some had come to believe that Indians were a race distinct from Europeans and Africans and so should reject Christianity. These views particularly resonated in Upper Susquehanna and Ohio valley towns composed largely of Delawares and Shawnees exiled from Pennsylvania.

The Delaware **Neolin** was the most influential figure in this Indian awakening. In 1761, he urged that Indians "learn to live without any Trade or Connections with the White people" and renounce "all the Sins & Vices" that Indians had learned from them. Once Indians cut their dependence on trade goods, "then will the great Spirit . . . give us strength to conquer our enemies." Neolin's words found receptive ears, especially among Indians alienated by British traders and fearful that British colonists, on the verge of winning the Seven Years' War, would soon invade their lands. The Ottawa **Pontiac** claimed that they inspired him to besiege the British at Detroit in 1763, the first salvo in a war between Indians, British soldiers, and colonists that engulfed the Great Lakes and the Ohio Valley for three years.

Neolin's message, the events that helped to produce it, and the ways in which many Indians heeded it were products of the confluence of peoples, goods, and ideas within North America. A movement born of refugees displaced by colonial expansion, nativism borrowed from Christianity to resist evangelization, reject the consumer revolution that was transforming British North America, and defend Indians' political and cultural independence. By the early 1750s Indians knew that the Ohio Valley, whether they had claimed it since time immemorial or had recently been forced to move there, had become the focal point of the struggle between the British and French for supremacy in North America.

## STUDY QUESTIONS FOR MINDS, SOULS, AND WALLETS

1. **What impact did the circulation of goods and ideas have on British North America? In what ways did the flow of goods and ideas shape how colonists related to one another and to the British Empire?**
2. **What was the relationship between spiritual awakening and the movement of goods and ideas in North America between 1730 and 1763? Did the relationship between such awakening and flows of goods and ideas change depending on whether one was white, black, or Indian? Explain.**

# NORTH AMERICA AND THE FIRST WORLD WAR FOR EMPIRE, 1754–1763

In 1754, skirmishes between British colonists, the French, and Indians in western Pennsylvania erupted into a world war. North America became the focus of British and French aims and the cause of war between the two empires. The conflict, often known as the French and Indian War in the United States and the **Seven Years' War** in Europe, transformed North America politically and socially. Victory made Britain eastern North America's dominant power and sparked new tensions between imperial officials, colonists, and Indians.

## The Road to World War

In the 1740s, the delicate balance of power between the British and French, the Iroquois, and Indians of the Great Lakes that had long kept the peace in the Ohio Valley tottered. Immigration to British North America and colonial expansion pushed Indians, mostly Delawares and Shawnees, into the Ohio Valley and beyond the reach of the Iroquois. In 1744, the Iroquois League ceded claims to the Ohio Valley to Virginia with the Treaty of Lancaster. By early 1745, Virginia had granted over 300,000 acres to a group of land speculators composed mainly of well-connected planters who soon called themselves the **Ohio Company of Virginia**. After King George's War ended, the Ohio Company sent surveyors to map the area and traders to sell to Indians. They found plenty of takers; the British offered a wider array of goods at better prices than the French.

French officials responded by staking their claim to the Ohio Valley. The Ohio River and its northern tributaries linked Quebec, Illinois, and Louisiana, so British control of the region would effectively cut French North America in two. In 1749, a French expedition planted lead plates bearing the fleur-de-lis, the symbol of Louis XV, along the Ohio River, in a bid to stake claim to the area. The French had more effective ways to assert influence. One was a staple of French and Indian diplomacy: distribute subsidized trade goods to recruit Indian allies from the Great Lakes to attack Indians with ties to traders bearing British goods. Another was new: build a chain of forts to halt British encroachment. Soldiers completed the last and most important of these, Fort Duquesne, site of today's Pittsburgh, in 1754.

Construction of French forts provoked panic among British colonists and imperial officials. In June 1754, representatives of seven colonies and of the Iroquois League met at Albany in a bid to keep the Iroquois from siding with the French and create a plan to coordinate defense of the participating colonies. The **Albany Congress** dissuaded the Iroquois from becoming French allies, but did little to unite colonial governments that prized their autonomy. A few months earlier, Virginia's government had entrusted **George Washington** with the command of 200 men and sent them west to build Fort Necessity. It was to shadow Fort Duquesne and block the way to

Maryland and Virginia. Washington had little military experience and had been put in charge of poorly trained soldiers and an underfunded operation.

He also proved to be a poor diplomat to Indians, most of whom were inclined to stay out of the conflict or side with the French because the British had thousands of land-hungry colonists and seemed to pose the greater threat. Washington had few Indian allies. Those he had, most prominent among them Tanaghrisson, an adopted Catawba captive whom the Iroquois League had appointed to supervise Shawnees, Delawares, and Mingoes in Ohio, refused to heed him. In May 1754, Tanaghrisson and warriors under his direction killed and scalped a French officer and a dozen French soldiers who had surrendered to Washington. Two months later French and Indian forces overran Fort Necessity, killing 30. The humiliated survivors trudged east as French soldiers torched what remained of British claims in the Ohio Valley. The war for the heart of eastern North America had begun.

## The Course of War

For three years the war went badly for Britain and its colonies. Word of Washington's defeat prompted officials in London to send two regiments of British soldiers under the command of Edward Braddock. Braddock and his army, accompanied by Washington and colonial militiamen, headed for Fort Duquesne. Braddock's incompetent diplomacy drove most Indians to the French. In July 1755, the British approached the Monongahela River, marching down a narrow road in orderly columns. Their French, French Canadian, and Indian foes, concealed behind trees or rocks, attacked from all sides. The British colonists sensibly aped their enemy's tactics or fled. Braddock and the British regulars did neither. Their European tactical training equated standing one's ground with valor and courage. It got nearly 1,000 of them killed or wounded at the Monongahela, including Braddock. Only one field aide, Washington, escaped the battle unscathed. The debacle exposed Pennsylvania, Maryland, and Virginia to Indian raids, triggering political turmoil in Pennsylvania as victims and fearful colonists clamored for protection.

The battle at the Monongahela underscored Indians' importance to French strategy. So did subsequent defeats inflicted on British and provincial troops in New York, a key battleground. Only one British official, William Johnson, appointed in 1755 to the newly created post of Indian Superintendent for the Northern Colonies, managed to recruit Indian allies and persuade them to fight. Johnson was married to a Mohawk woman, so he could call on the Mohawks for help. They answered his pleas once before following an Iroquois League recommendation to stay out of the war.

By 1758, three developments turned the tide in the British empire's favor. The French lost most of their Indian allies. Canadian soldiers and militiamen, along with Canada's governor-general Pierre de Rigaud Vaudreuil, argued that France should rely on Indians to raid British colonies and force them to seek peace. The commander of French forces, the **Marquis de Montcalm**, insisted that such a policy would never work because Indians fought primarily to loot, gather captives, and go home. At first, the Canadians' view prevailed. In 1757, nearly 2,000 Indians, including about 1,000 from the Great Lakes and further west, helped to besiege Fort William Henry. Montcalm negotiated the surrender of the British and provincial garrison and promised it safe passage to a nearby British fort. Montcalm behaved as if he were fighting in Europe and dealing with a defeated foe. His Indian allies, denied even the weapons that their enemy had handed over, reminded him that he was in America by killing nearly 200 provincial soldiers and camp followers and taking away hundreds. Montcalm and Vaudreuil, eager to save face with British peers and with Indians, ransomed over 200 captives at the French Crown's expense. But the damage was done. Great Lakes warriors did not heed French requests for help in large numbers again, particularly as the French proved increasingly unable to supply them with the firearms and other goods that they needed.

Meanwhile, new British leaders plotted a different course. In 1757, **William Pitt** assumed charge of war policy as anxiety gripped Britain. The war had recently spread to Europe, where a superior French army threatened to defeat Britain's main allies, Hanover and Prussia. In response, Pitt decided to leverage British assets to strike at French weaknesses. Large payments to Hanover and Prussia, financed by British taxpayers, would enable them to continue fighting. The Royal Navy, the world's mightiest, would raid French ports, disrupt France's oceanic supply lines, and seize its outposts in Africa, India, and North America. Pitt hoped to tie down French forces in Europe and force France to sacrifice its colonies and the revenue they generated. By the time Pitt resigned in 1761, his plan had succeeded brilliantly. His successors were left to determine how to pay for it.

British victory in North America came largely because tens of thousands of colonists took up arms. In 1758, they comprised almost of half of the nearly 50,000 men who British commanders sent into battle. Provincial leaders recruited most in a matter of months, partly because Pitt changed a policy that had rankled colonists. Before 1758 no provincial field officer, even a general, could rank higher than captain while serving with a regular unit. Thanks to Pitt's reforms, provincial majors, colonels, and generals were considered peers of British officers of the same rank.

The British military advantage in North America arose from differences in how the English and French had colonized North America since the early 1600s. Massive immigration, high birthrates, and intensive resettlement of Indian lands gave the British a much larger potential fighting force in North America than the French. Their model of colonization—minimal and sporadic immigration, with extensive territorial claims backed by Indian alliances—could not match the British, who fielded twice as many troops in North America than the French. France counted on Indian allies to make up the difference. Once most Indians abandoned the war, British victory was a matter of time.

In 1758, Anglo-Americans won four key victories, three through combat and one through Indian diplomacy. They took Louisbourg, key to France's naval defense of Canada, in July. A few weeks later a force composed mainly of colonists captured Fort Frontenac, the key supply post to French forts and Indian allies to the west. An agreement concluded at the Treaty of Easton in October secured peace with Ohio Indians, above all the Delawares, in exchange for promises to bar colonization of their lands.

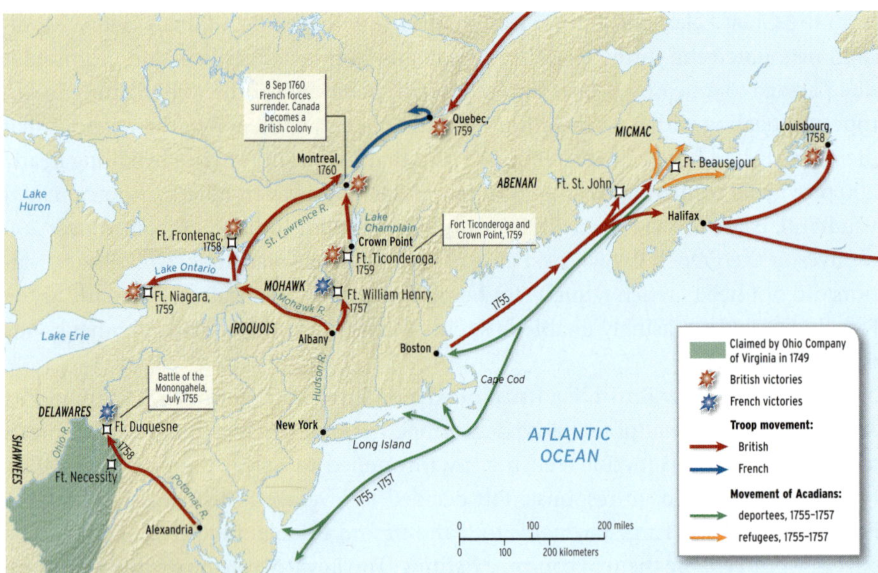


▲ **Map 5.6**

**The Seven Years' War in Northeastern North America, 1754–1760** Together the Ohio Valley, upstate New York, and Canada comprised the bloodiest battleground of the Seven Years' War in North America. Here are the principal battles discussed in the text and when they occurred, as well the routes that Acadian deportees and refugees took after the British invasion in 1755.

With their supply lines cut and most Indian allies gone, French soldiers blew up Fort Duquesne. Anglo-Americans built a replacement and named it Fort Pitt.

French and Canadian forces retreated to Canada to await an Anglo-American invasion. It arrived in the summer of 1759, when troops commanded by **James Wolfe** besieged the city of Quebec. In September they scaled the cliffs that guarded the city and engaged Montcalm's army. Within a day, the Anglo-Americans had won, though Wolfe and Montcalm died in battle. In April 1760, French forces surrounded Quebec, but British reinforcements soon broke the siege and effectively completed the conquest of Canada by taking Montreal in September. The war between European and Euro-American combatants in North America had ended.

By then, the war outside Europe had shifted to the West Indies and Asia. The British captured Guadeloupe in 1759 and Martinique three years later. Only Saint Domingue, the wealthiest plantation colony in the Americas, and Guyana remained of France's once-vast American empire. Between 1759 and 1761 the British East India Company won battles in India and took Pondicherry, the French base of operations there. In 1762, Spain entered the war on France's side. Britain retaliated by conquering Havana and Manila, capital of the Philippines.

In February 1763, Europeans agreed to end hostilities among themselves under the terms of the **Treaty of Paris**, but the war continued for many Indians. One thing

Benjamin West, *The Death of General Wolfe*, 1770. West, a Pennsylvanian, painted this 11 years after British forces captured Quebec. It is highly allegorical; only the officer clutching the flag could have been with Wolfe when he died. British colonists found West's work compelling. They purchased thousands of copies, an indication of their eagerness to identify as Britons.

was clear. The British were the dominant European power in North America and the West Indies and seemed on their way to becoming the world's mightiest empire.

## New Divisions

The Seven Years' War opened new divisions in North America. The terms of the Treaty of Paris transformed eastern North America's political geography. France surrendered North America, swapping Canada for the return of Guadeloupe. France had lured the Spanish into the war by agreeing to cede Louisiana to them. The Treaty of Paris awarded control of that colony to Spain, which traded Florida to the British in order to regain control of Havana. The British Empire claimed almost all of North America east of the Mississippi.

For the vast majority of Indians west of the Mississippi the new European division of North America changed little. In 1764, Spanish officials founded St. Louis to bolster their claim to the region, reap more profits from Indian trade, and clamp down on the Indian slave trade. Competition from British and French Canadian traders offered Indians of the upper Mississippi and Missouri river valleys better access to trade goods.

Most Indians who lived between the Mississippi and the Appalachians confronted a new challenge. They could no longer play two strong European rivals against one another as many had for decades. Worse, the more populous empire, the one that grew through intensive resettlement of Indian lands, had won and its colonists wanted their land. Indians had two stark choices: accept British rule and gradually cede their lands or take up arms. Most who agreed with Neolin and Pontiac opted to fight. Their success prompted the British to issue a decree in October 1763 that barred colonists from crossing the Appalachians, a decision that only widened divisions between imperial officials and colonists.

The Seven Years' War elevated tensions between colonists and the empire for which they had proudly fought. To most British officials, the war's prosecution and steep costs demonstrated that they needed more control over colonial affairs, including tighter regulation of commerce. For colonists, particularly veterans, the war offered an often unsettling view of the British empire. At least one-third of service-eligible men in Massachusetts fought in the Seven Years' War. New England soldiers often saw British commanders as despots too eager to use the whip to maintain authority and British regulars as debauched sinners whose wickedness might cause New Englanders to lose God's favor in a war that they considered an epic struggle against Catholicism. British officers and regulars considered themselves military professionals and considered colonists undisciplined and unruly. Nor could the British fathom colonists' attitude toward military service as voluntary and contractual. This did not, however, make colonial veterans incipient revolutionaries. For years, their service made them identify more strongly as Britons and subjects of George III. But it also gave them perspectives and skills that some later drew on to resist imperial policies that they believed threatened their British liberties.

The war's prosecution also widened divisions among colonists. In 1756, many Quakers withdrew from Pennsylvania politics to protest the provincial government's decision to support the war and dodge accusations that Quaker legislators had not budgeted enough to defend the colony adequately. Some left politics as part of a broader campaign for Quaker spiritual renewal, which required that Friends renounce activities that compromised core Quaker values.

A few Quaker reformers, particularly **John Woolman** and Anthony Benezet, targeted slavery. In 1753, Woolman denounced slaveholding as a violation of Quaker values. Benezet likened the Atlantic slave trade to Indians' taking of white captives during the Seven Years' War. In 1758, the Philadelphia Yearly Meeting decided that Quaker monthly meetings should punish buyers and sellers of slaves. Woolman observed that many participants thought that "liberty was the negro's right," but the Philadelphia Monthly Meeting did not bar members from owning slaves until 1776. Meanwhile, Benezet lobbied against the Atlantic slave trade, recommending in 1771 that Britain outlaw it. Benezet's writings, and the relationships that he formed with

Thomas Davies, *View of the Plundering of and Burning of the City of Grymross.* Many Acadian who escaped removal at the hands of British and British North American soldiers sought refuge in present-day New Brunswick. From there some Acadian waged guerrilla warfare against the British. In 1758, British forces destroyed many Acadian settlements, including Grimrose ("Grymross" above), and deported their residents.

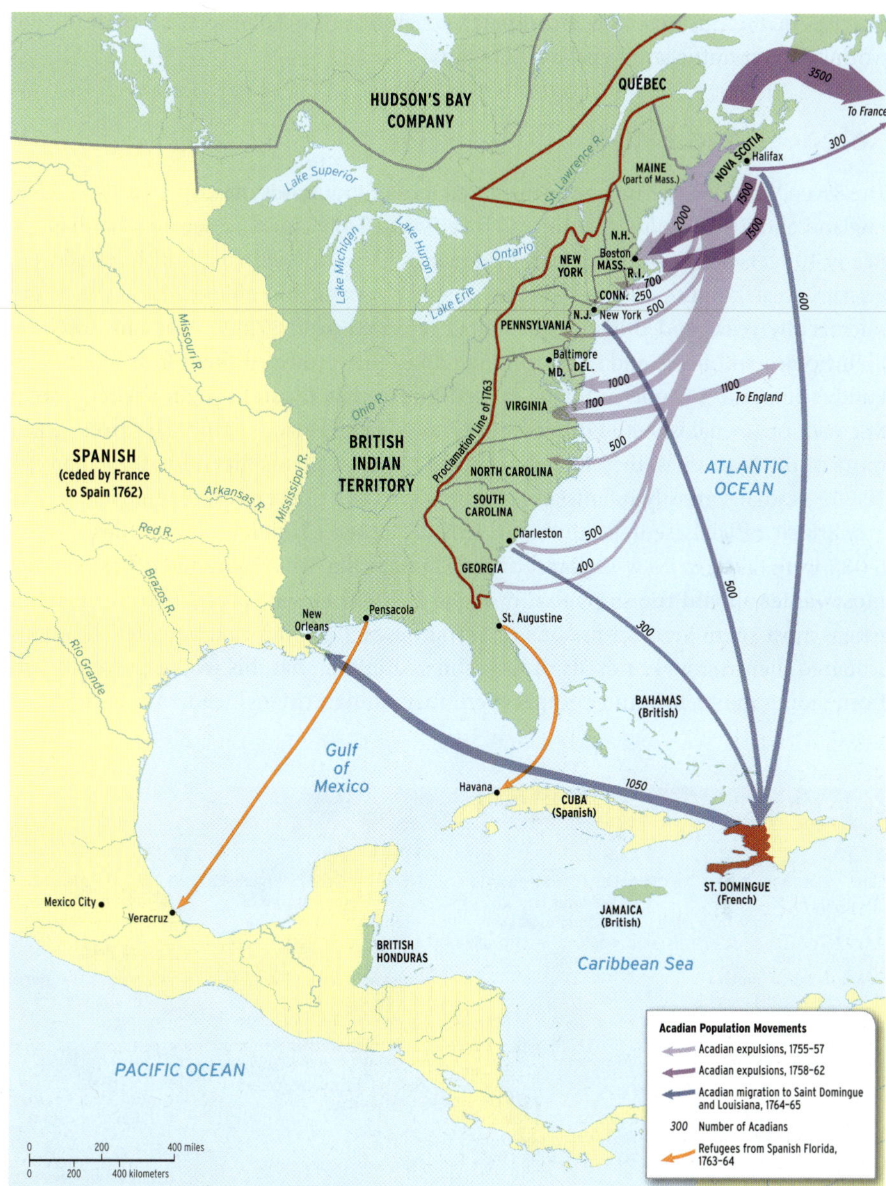


▲ **Map 5.7**

**Colonial Refugees and Exiles of the Seven Years' War, 1755–1765** British victories in the Seven Years' War forced thousands of colonists to leave their homes. This map shows the movement of Acadian deportees and refugees, thousands of whom began to relocate to Louisiana in 1765, as well as those of Hispanic, African, and Indian Floridians, who fled British Florida for Cuba or Mexico.

activists in Britain, exported a campaign to abolish the Atlantic slave trade to the world's largest trafficker in enslaved Africans.

## Refugees and Exiles

The Seven Years' War permanently displaced tens of thousands of people. In 1755, New England and British soldiers stormed Nova Scotia. They aimed to secure what had for nearly 40 years been a British colony by deporting Acadians, who the British feared were a security risk because they were Catholic, spoke French, and often had kin ties to the Micmac. By year's end British soldiers had removed nearly 7,000 Acadians, torching their homes and fields and destroying the dikes that protected them from the Bay of Fundy's high tides. Some Acadians evaded British custody and sought shelter among Micmacs or Abenakis, while others moved to French Canada. As British forces seized more of the Maritimes, they forced out most of the Acadians they found. As many as 10,000 Acadians, mostly infants and children, died as a direct result of removal.

British officials sent Acadians to 9 of the other 13 mainland colonies. Nearly 5,000 were taken to New England or the Chesapeake, where Virginia officials made most winter aboard the ships that brought them. They sent over 1,000 to England, where most spent years in prisons or workhouses. Colonies that accepted Acadians scattered them across hundreds of townships, thinking that this would prevent them from aiding the French and compel them to assimilate. Many Acadian families were

### TIMELINE 1727–1765

**1727**
Junto founded in Philadelphia

**1731**
First subscription library in British North America founded in Philadelphia

**1732**
Parliament passes Hat Act

**1733**
James Oglethorpe founds Georgia as colony to reform English debtors

Parliament passes Molasses Act, placing duties on molasses imported to British colonies from French Caribbean

**November** Gold Coast slaves rebel and seize control of most of St. John, Danish Virgin Islands

**1734–1735**
Jonathan Edwards leads religious revival in Massachusetts

**1735**
John Peter Zenger acquitted of seditious libel in New York, establishing precedent for principle of freedom of the press

**1736**
Slave conspiracy in Antigua results in execution of 88 slaves

**1737**
Pennsylvania's proprietor makes "Walking Purchase" from Delawares

**1738**
Gracia Real de Santa Teresa de Mose, a free black town, founded in Florida

**1739**
**September** Stono Rebellion in South Carolina

**1739–1742**
War of Jenkins' Ear between British and Spanish Empire

**1739–1741**
Evangelist George Whitefield completes first tour of British North America

**1740**
Parliament passes Plantation Act, streamlining naturalization procedures in British American colonies

South Carolina legislators enact new slave code

**1741**
Slave conspiracy rumored, and suspected conspirators tried and executed, in New York City

Moravians arrive in Pennsylvania and establish settlements at Bethlehem and Nazareth

**1742**
*Pamela*, first novel published in British North America

**1743**
Precursor to American Philosophical Society founded in Philadelphia

**1744–1748**
King George's War between British and French empires

**1745**
Massachusetts troops capture Louisbourg, Canada, from French

**1746**
College of New Jersey (later Princeton) founded

**1749–1754**
End of King George's War spurs flood of German emigrants from Rhineland to North America

**1750**
Parliament passes Iron Act

Georgia's Trustees legalize slavery in colony

broken apart, as most of their children in Massachusetts and Maryland became indentured servants. In the 1750s, Boston, New York, and Philadelphia newspapers printed notices of Acadians seeking to reunite with parents or children. Most Acadians preferred to leave British America if they could not return to Nova Scotia. Most thought that the next best option was to go to France or a French colony. Over 1,000 Acadians sailed to Saint Domingue, resettled there by the French government. Nearly half of them left for Louisiana, where French officials remained in charge until 1766. There they began to call themselves Cajuns.

As Acadians dreamed of an American refuge, thousands of Floridians sailed away. British officials told free residents of Spanish Florida that they could stay and accept assurances of freedom of religion and respect for their property rights or sell what they owned and leave. Most left. Nearly 3,000 headed to Cuba between August 1763 and January 1764. They included Francisco Menéndez, his neighbors, and hundreds of Canary Islanders and Catalan soldiers who had recently arrived to defend Florida from the British. Hundreds of south Florida Indians also went to Cuba, while Floridians who fled Pensacola sought refuge in Mexico. In Cuba one in five Floridians died of disease or hunger within three years of arrival. Pleas for help to the Spanish Crown yielded only a pension to Cuban women who had been wives, widows, or daughters of Floridians in 1763. Memories of such suffering ran deep among Cuba's Florida exiles. Most refused to return when Spain regained control of Florida as a reward from the United States for supporting the American Revolution.

**1753**

Reverend Eleazar Wheelock admits Indians to Moor's Charity School in Connecticut, predecessor of Dartmouth College

**1754**

**June–July** Albany Congress reaches treaty with Iroquois League and discusses potential union of British mainland colonies

**July** Seven Years' War begins, triggered by combat in western Pennsylvania between Virginia militia commanded by George Washington and French-Indian alliance

**1755**

**July** British and provincial forces under command of General Edward Braddock defeated at Battle of Monongahela

**October** 7,000 Acadians deported from Nova Scotia to British mainland colonies

**1756**

**May** Britain officially declares war on France

**1757**

British Prime Minister William Pitt revamps British war strategy

**August** French forces capture Fort William Henry but alienate Indian allies

**1758**

**May–July** British and provincial forces besiege and capture Fort Louisbourg

**August** British forces capture Fort Frontenac

**October** Treaty of Easton makes peace between British authorities and Ohio Indians

**November** French forces blow up Fort Duquesne to prevent British capture of it

**1759**

**June–September** British forces under the command of Gen. James Wolfe besiege and conquer city of Quebec

**1760**

**September** British forces capture Montreal, effectively ending war between British and French in North America

**October** George II dies; his grandson George III becomes king of Britain

**1762**

Spain declares war on British Empire; British forces capture Havana

**1763**

**February** Treaty of Paris ends Seven Years' War: France cedes Louisiana to Spain; Spain cedes Florida to Britain; France cedes Canada, most of North America between Appalachians and Mississippi River, and four Caribbean islands to Britain

**May** Pan-Indian alliance led by Pontiac (Ottawa) attacks Detroit to prevent British resettlement of Ohio Valley and Great Lakes region

**October** George III issues Royal Proclamation barring colonists from settling west of Appalachians

**1765**

Acadians begin to move to Louisiana

## STUDY QUESTIONS FOR NORTH AMERICA AND THE FIRST WORLD WAR FOR EMPIRE

1. What explains French success early in the Seven Years' War? What explains the British empire's victory in the conflict?
2. What new divisions did the Seven Years' War create in North America? Why did some of those divisions result in the movement of thousands from or within North America?

## Summary

- Record levels of free and unfree immigration accelerated population growth in British North America and fostered political and cultural tensions within the colonies.
- British North American colonists, white and black, became vital consumers of imported goods and important participants in Atlantic intellectual and religious networks in ways that changed their understanding of who they were, while new Indian powers arose on the Great Plains and Indians in the Ohio Valley strove to reject the ways of the Euro-American world.
- The Seven Years' War resulted in a British victory that altered North America's political map, creating new divisions within North America and forcing thousands to leave.

## Key Terms and People

**Albany Congress** *205*
**American Philosophical Society** *193*
**Benezet, Anthony** *199*
**creole** *202*
**Edwards, Jonathan** *200*
**Enlightenment** *191*
**Franklin, Benjamin** *181*
**gang system** *196*
**Gracia Real de Santa Teresa de Mose** **173**
**Maroons** *189*
**Marquis de Montcalm** *206*
**Methodists** *198*
**Moravians (United Brethren)** *199*
**Neolin** *204*
**Oglethorpe, James** *188*
**Ohio Company of Virginia** *205*
**Pitt, William** *207*
**Plantation Act of 1740** *184*
**Pontiac** *204*
**redemptioners** *184*
**revivalists** *199*
**Seven Years' War (French and Indian War)** *205*
**Stono Rebellion** *189*
**task system** *195*
**Treaty of Paris** *208*
**War of Jenkins' Ear** *190*
**Washington, George** *205*
**Wesley, John** *198*
**Wheatley, Phyllis** *202*
**Whitefield, George** *198*
**Wolfe, James** *208*
**Woolman, John** *210*

## Reviewing Chapter 5

1. Indians play a smaller role in this chapter than they did in previous chapters of *American Horizons*. Why?
2. "North America's relationship to the global circulation of people, goods, and ideas intensified between 1730 and 1763 but did not change fundamentally during that period." Do you agree? Explain, using specific examples from this chapter.
3. British North Americans considered themselves more British in 1763, even though they had never been more American. Why?

## Further Reading

Breen, T. H. *The Marketplace of Revolution: How Consumer Politics Shaped American Independence.* New York: Oxford University Press, 2004. Details colonial Anglo America's consumer revolution and links it to the American Revolution.

Faragher, John Mack. *A Great and Noble Scheme: The Tragic Story of the Expulsion of the French Acadians from Their American Homeland.* New York: W. W. Norton, 2005. An evocative overview of Acadian removal and of what happened to Acadians after they were expelled from their homeland.

Landers, Jane. *Black Society in Spanish Florida.* Urbana and Chicago: University of Illinois Press, 1999. Sharply contrasts slavery and freedom in Florida while under Spanish rule with slavery and freedom in the English colonies and in the states that bordered Florida.

Merritt, Jane T. *At the Crossroads: Indians and Empires on a Mid-Atlantic Frontier, 1700–1763.*Chapel Hill and London: University of North Carolina Press, 2003. Examines intercultural relations between Indians and European colonists in Pennsylvania in ways that are sensitive to gender as it explains why some Indians converted to Christianity while others rejected it.

Parrish, Susan Scott. *American Curiosity: Cultures of Natural History in the Colonial British Atlantic World.* Chapel Hill and London: University of North Carolina Press, 2006. Explores and explains how British colonists' participation in scientific investigation of the natural world reinforced racist thought and helped to create an American identity.

Waldstreicher, David. *Runaway America: Benjamin Franklin, Slavery, and the American Revolution.* New York: Hill and Wang, 2004. A concise and engagingly written account of Franklin and the evolution of his views on slavery, focused on his activities as an entrepreneur and politician.

# Visual Review

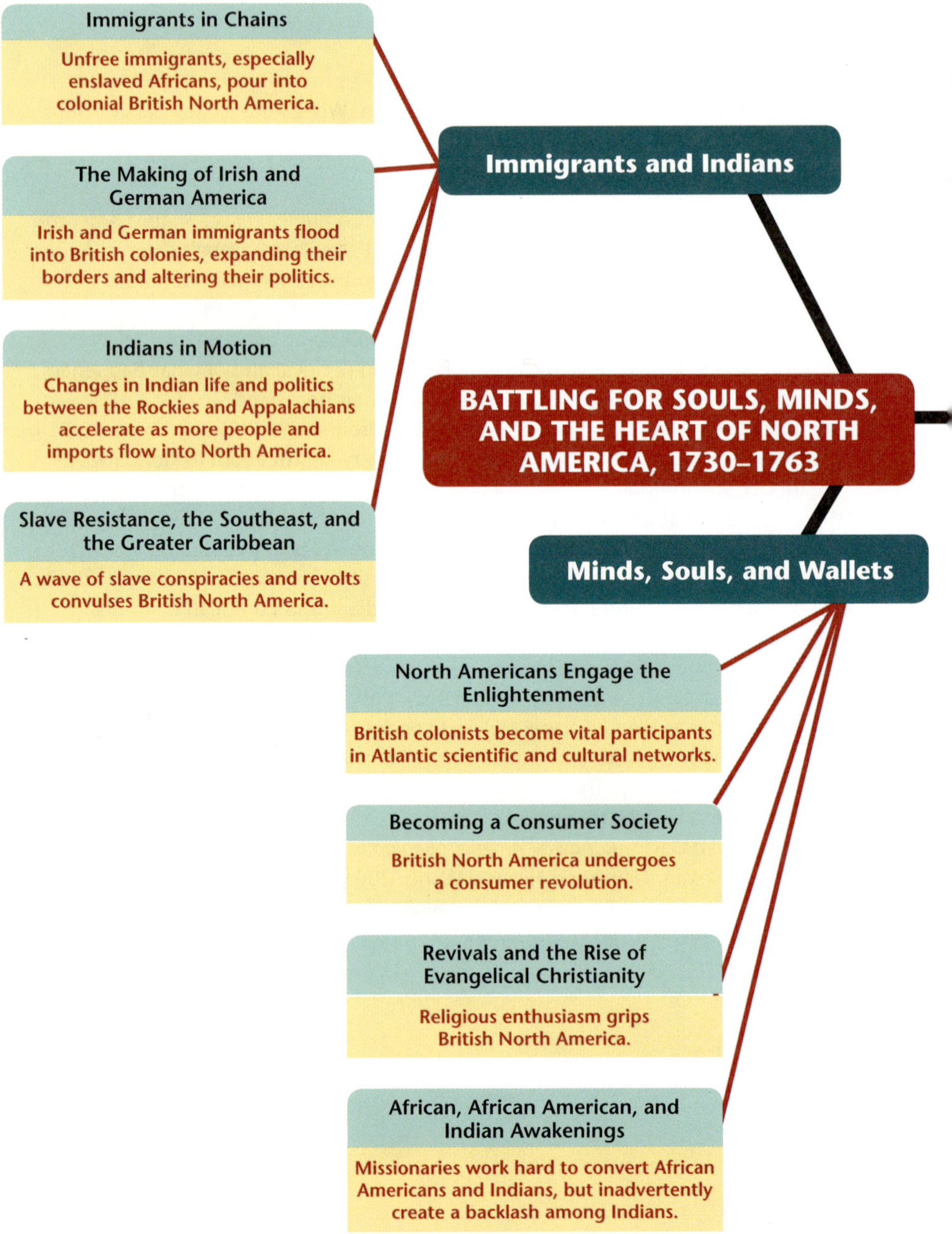

## BATTLING FOR SOULS, MINDS, AND THE HEART OF NORTH AMERICA, 1730–1763

### Immigrants and Indians

**Immigrants in Chains**

Unfree immigrants, especially enslaved Africans, pour into colonial British North America.

**The Making of Irish and German America**

Irish and German immigrants flood into British colonies, expanding their borders and altering their politics.

**Indians in Motion**

Changes in Indian life and politics between the Rockies and Appalachians accelerate as more people and imports flow into North America.

**Slave Resistance, the Southeast, and the Greater Caribbean**

A wave of slave conspiracies and revolts convulses British North America.

### Minds, Souls, and Wallets

**North Americans Engage the Enlightenment**

British colonists become vital participants in Atlantic scientific and cultural networks.

**Becoming a Consumer Society**

British North America undergoes a consumer revolution.

**Revivals and the Rise of Evangelical Christianity**

Religious enthusiasm grips British North America.

**African, African American, and Indian Awakenings**

Missionaries work hard to convert African Americans and Indians, but inadvertently create a backlash among Indians.

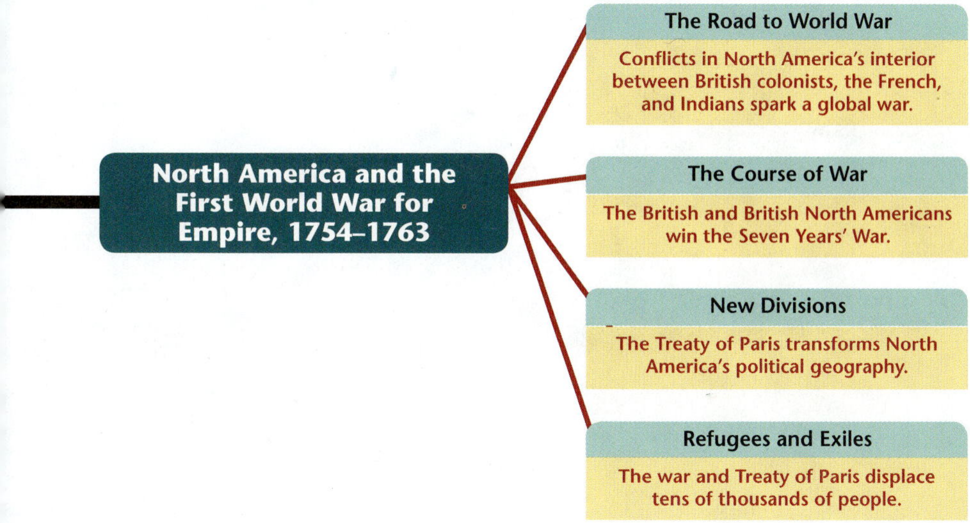

**North America and the First World War for Empire, 1754–1763**

**The Road to World War**

Conflicts in North America's interior between British colonists, the French, and Indians spark a global war.

**The Course of War**

The British and British North Americans win the Seven Years' War.

**New Divisions**

The Treaty of Paris transforms North America's political geography.

**Refugees and Exiles**

The war and Treaty of Paris displace tens of thousands of people.

# 6 Empire and Resistance

## 1763–1776

On December 31, 1775, Major General **Richard Montgomery** was killed while leading a failed invasion of Quebec by American Continental Army soldiers. Montgomery attacked the Canadian capital city in an effort to salvage the American invasion that had stalled during a tough winter. The Continental Congress had hoped to force concessions from the British government by invading Canadian colonies. Instead, Montgomery died, and his fellow American commander **Benedict Arnold** led a miserable retreat back to New England.

Montgomery was immediately hailed as a hero and martyr to the American cause of liberty. The Continental Congress authorized a public funeral in Philadelphia and built a monument to his memory. American artist John Trumbull painted a heroic image of Montgomery's death that directly referenced a famous painting of the idolized British general James Wolfe, who had died in an attack on Quebec in the French and Indian War and was immortalized by British painter Benjamin West. Even in fighting the British, Americans looked to British examples to define images of heroism.

Richard Montgomery was born into an aristocratic Dublin family, attended Trinity College, and joined the British army in time to fight against the French in Canada during the French and Indian War. He rose through the ranks from 1757 to 1763, serving in Canada, New York, Barbados, Martinique, and Cuba. By the end of the war, he was a respected captain in the British Army, one of the men who enforced the reach of the British empire with military power.

Growing disgruntled with the military hierarchy, Montgomery

*The Death of General Montgomery in the Attack on Quebec, December 31, 1775* by John Trumbull, oil on canvas, 1786

### CHAPTER OUTLINE



*continued on page 223*

# America in the World

The Revolutionary War began at the Battles of Lexington and Concord (1775).

British soldiers killed five men in the "Boston Massacre," heightening tensions in the colonies (1770).

The Declaration of Independence announced that the United States of America was independent of Britain (1776).

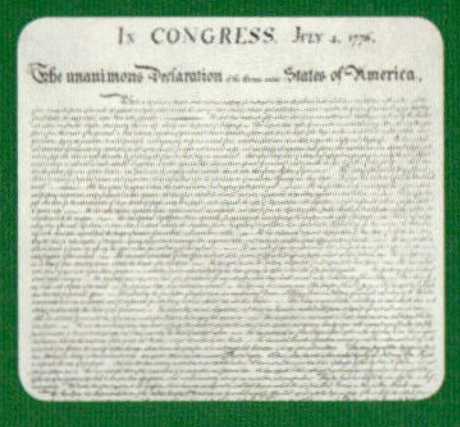
IN CONGRESS, JULY 4, 1776.

The unanimous Declaration of the thirteen united States of America,

U.S. event that influenced the world

International event that influenced the United States

Event with multinational influence

Conflict

The Boston Tea Party was an early act of insurgence by colonial resistance leading to the American Revolution (1773).
The British Stamp Act led to growing discontent in the colonies (1765).

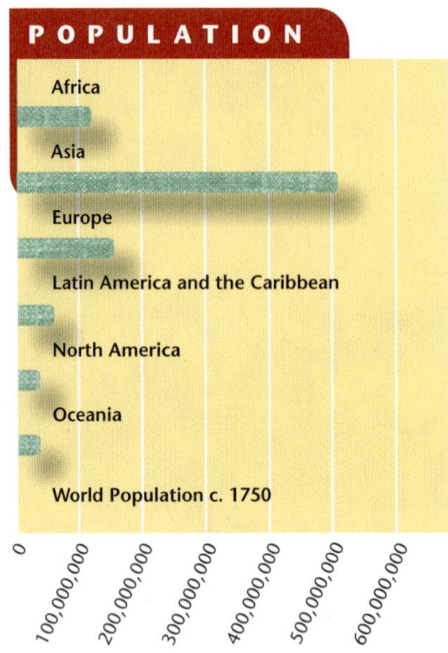


moved to New York in 1773, where he married Janet Livingston, a member of one of the colony's wealthiest families. Montgomery was elected to the New York legislature, where he voiced his opposition to British crackdowns on the colonies. Montgomery was a natural choice to be appointed a commander when the Continental Army formed in June 1775. When Montgomery was killed in Quebec, this time fighting *against* the British Army, he was one of the most experienced and promising military commanders in the American army.

As an American hero who until recently had been a British army officer, Richard Montgomery was in many ways the perfect symbol of how resistance began to undermine the British empire in North America between 1763 and 1775. Many American colonists had strong ties to Britain or had recently emigrated like Montgomery, and they mostly considered themselves obedient subjects of the British crown at the end of the French and Indian War. Yet, the series of British taxes and government restrictions imposed on the colonies after the war convinced many Americans that the time had come to throw off imperial control. British military presence in North American heightened the tension.

Between 1763 and 1776, both the British and Spanish empires sought increased control over their North American imperial subjects. North Americans, many of whom like Montgomery had cast off old identities to feel more "American," challenged European control. Spain was able to maintain control and spread its empire, but in the British case, a cycle of protest and reaction would lead to a full-scale war and to the United States of America declaring its independence.

## ENGLISH AND SPANISH IMPERIAL REFORM

The French and Indian War ended in 1763, won by two newly crowned kings. George III became king of Britain in 1760, while Charles III was crowned in Spain in 1759. Both kings won substantial new colonial territory from France in the war, and substantial financial burdens along with it. Besides an estimated £140,000,000 in war debt, it cost Britain about £300,000 per year to defend the North American territories in local conflicts over religion, land, and Indian-colonist relations. British and Spanish officials both began attempting to recover some of these costs from the profits of the colonies themselves, as well as trying to calm conflicts. The new policies from new kings unleashed many unintended consequences in North America.

## Transatlantic Trade as an Engine of Conflict

Each region of the British colonies had its own economic character, but trade was central to all of them. New England shipbuilding and lumber equipped the navy that policed much of the rest of the British empire and provided barrels for the rum trade, and New England fishermen fed European countries with 240 million pounds of cod and mackerel each year. The Mid-Atlantic colonies added iron production, fur trading, and shipbuilding to their trade in agricultural products, and Quaker and Jewish merchants relying on transatlantic religious and kinship networks grew especially prosperous. The Chesapeake colonies of Maryland and Virginia produced tobacco, while the Carolinas and Georgia contributed pine tar, indigo,

**CHAPTER OUTLINE**

*continued from page 219*

Portrait of George III. George III assumed the throne of Great Britain in 1760, during the Seven Years' War, and he reigned as king longer than any previous British monarch, until 1820. The beginning of George III's reign was marked by the British defeat of the French in the Seven Years' War, but his keen regard for royal privilege was soon tested by the American Revolution.

and rice. Merchants in every colony also engaged in the slave trade. Britain sought to monopolize the trade of colonial commodities with Continental Europe and with Spanish and French colonies in the Caribbean. Despite the high level of American colonists' exports, they imported 30 percent more.

Since the 1660s, the British Parliament had imposed a series of controls and taxes on colonial trade through a series of **Navigation Acts**. But crown and parliamentary officials had not strictly enforced the laws. Colonial assemblies and colonial merchants had by the 1760s become accustomed to governing themselves on trade matters. Trade in the British colonies was so lucrative that even though smuggling ran rampant, the government enjoyed sufficient revenue to encourage a policy of salutary neglect (ignoring infractions of the Navigation Acts, as long as the government still made hefty profits). The colonial population doubled from 1 million in 1750 to 2 million in 1770, and Great Britain made good money both importing from and exporting to that growing population.

As transatlantic trade grew, so did North American cities. By 1775, Boston, New York, Newport, Philadelphia, and Charleston held more than 9,000 people, and each was a fast-growing commercial center. These cities, and a host of smaller ones, housed the legal, political, and financial institutions that facilitated imperial trade. Boston, Philadelphia, and New York all experienced a sharp growth in poverty during the 1750s and 1760s. Urban trade and the close contact between people from different ends of the social spectrum (from slaves to artisans to merchants and imperial officials) would help to make colonial cities major centers of political mobilization in the 1770s.

The great debts incurred by the British in the Seven Years' War caused British officials to renew their interest in North American trade when George Grenville became prime minister, first lord of the treasury, and chancellor of the exchequer in April 1763. Grenville enacted a series of policies that changed the course of colonial policy and touched off colonial resistance. Grenville sought to lower the domestic tax burden in England by raising revenues from the colonies. He moved to enforce and expand trade regulations and invested new power in colonial customs officials, who were supposed to be collecting duties under the 1733 Molasses Act, which often went unpaid.

## Grenville's Program

Grenville moved the Sugar Act through Parliament in 1764. It was designed to raise greater revenue through strict enforcement of trade taxes on the American colonies, even as it lowered many trade duties imposed by previous legislation. The Sugar Act increased taxes and controls not only on sugar but also on coffee, coconuts, whale fins, silk, and animal hides. The act also forbade American colonists from importing rum from any non-British source. Many colonists openly smuggled molasses from Spanish and French Caribbean islands to avoid paying tax revenues, and smuggled goods were often much cheaper than legal ones. Grenville established a new vice-admiralty court at Halifax, Nova Scotia, to seize any ships caught smuggling goods between the British American colonies and the French West Indies. Grenville's legislative

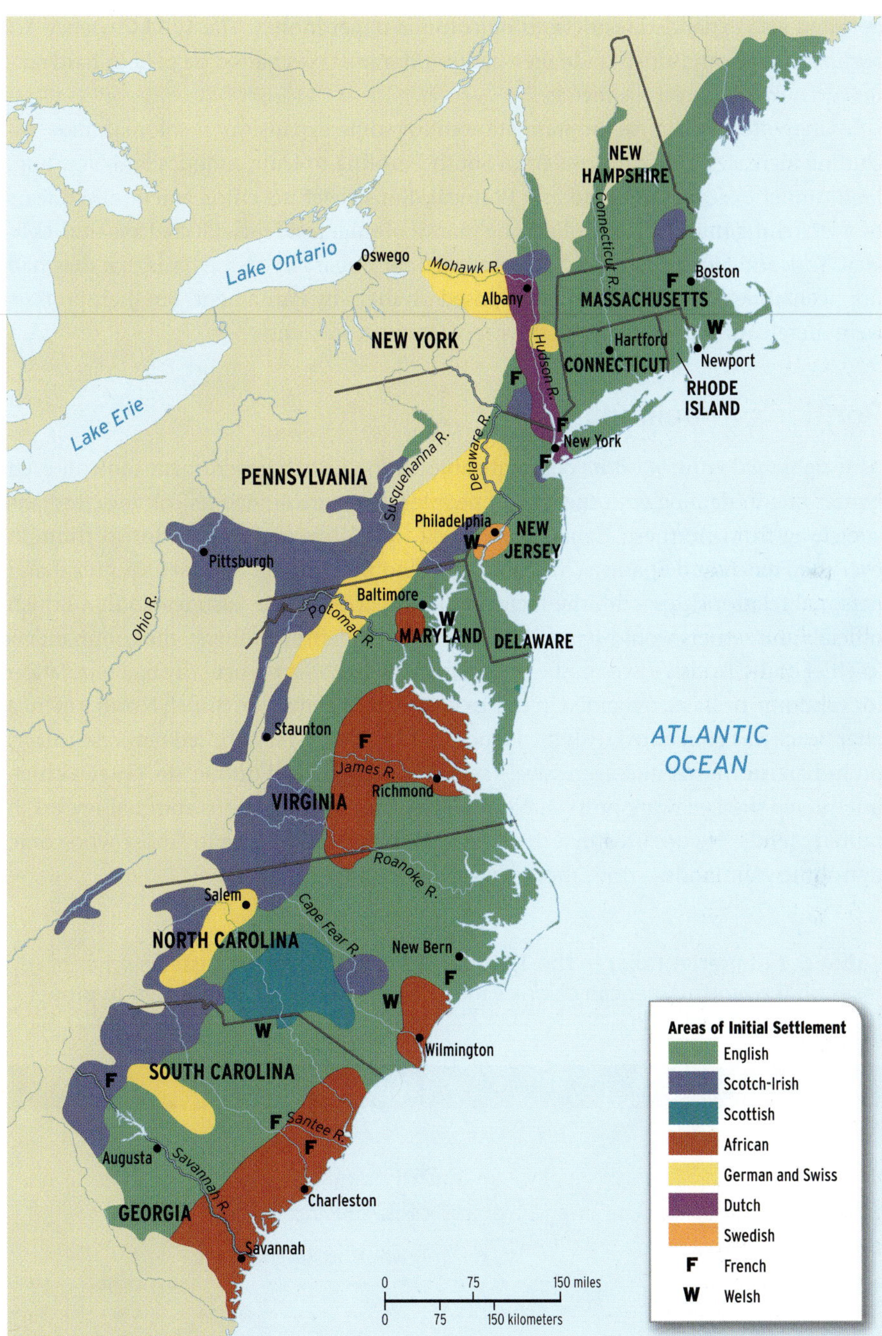


▲ **Map 6.1**

**Ethnic Diversity in the British Colonies, c. 1770** The British colonies in North America were marked by an unusually high level of ethnic and racial diversity.

program also expanded restrictions on colonial paper money. The 1764 Currency Act required that both British trade merchants and trade taxes had to be paid in hard currency, backed by precious metals.

Grenville's legislative program allowed for some expansion in colonial trade, including increases in rice exports from South Carolina to Latin America and New England timber exports to Ireland and Portugal. But stricter tax enforcement raised fears of overarching imperial control among many colonial residents. Elected assemblies in New York and North Carolina both protested the Sugar Act on the basis that they had not been allowed to vote for taxes imposed on them by Parliament. But their protests were merely mild precursors of stiffer resistance yet to come.

## Pontiac's Rebellion

As it tightened control on its colonial subjects, the British government took an even harder line in dealing with the Indian peoples who surrounded its colonies. Indians stretching from northern Canada to Florida were dismayed by the British triumph over the French and Spanish in 1763. Many had better trade, as well as political and personal relationships, with the French than the British. They also feared that British officials and settlers would seize additional land. Sir Jeffrey Amherst, the commander-in-chief of the British forces in the imperial war who had a particularly bad reputation for subduing Indians, remained in charge as governor general of British North America after peace was concluded with the French in 1763. Amherst imposed new restrictions on Indian fur traders and aggressively seized Seneca lands. **Pontiac**, the Ottawa chief, interpreted the Delaware prophet **Neolin**'s message of indigenous spiritual revival in military terms. He declared that the creator mandated resistance to "those who come to trouble your lands,—drive them out, make war upon them."

**Table 6.1 Imperial Taxes in the 1760s and 1770s** Parliament passed a series of taxes on the North American colonies that sparked resistance and helped to propel the American Revolution.

| Year | Legislation |
|---|---|
| 1764 | Sugar Act |
| 1765 | Stamp Act |
| 1766 | Declaratory Act |
| 1767 | Townshend Revenue Acts |
| 1773 | Tea Act |
| 1774 | Coercive or Intolerable Acts<br>Boston Port Bill<br>Massachusetts Government Act<br>Administration of Justice Act<br>Quartering Act<br>Quebec Act |

Pontiac did just that in the spring of 1763. He gathered forces from different groups of Ohio Valley and Great Lakes Indians who wished to keep British settlers from the land between the Allegheny Mountains and the Mississippi River and to drive British military forces back east of the Alleghenies. Beginning in May, Pontiac assaulted Detroit while his allied Potawatomie, Miami, Huron, Mingo, Ojibwa, and Shawnee forces attacked 11 different British forts and a number of settler communities. The 3,500 warriors allied to Pontiac were well matched against a roughly equal number of British troops. Pontiac's forces captured most of the forts they attacked, but by Fall their food and ammunition supplies ran low—and many were afflicted with smallpox, in part spread by British troops who traded infected blankets intentionally.

In October 1763, the government in London tried to deal with the rising violence by sending reinforcements and through royal pronouncement. King George III issued the **Proclamation of 1763** that prohibited almost all settlement west of the Appalachian Mountains and restricted land sales to the east. But many British settlers simply ignored the Proclamation and continued to settle in western territories occupied by Indians. Pontiac and many of his supporters concluded a peace agreement

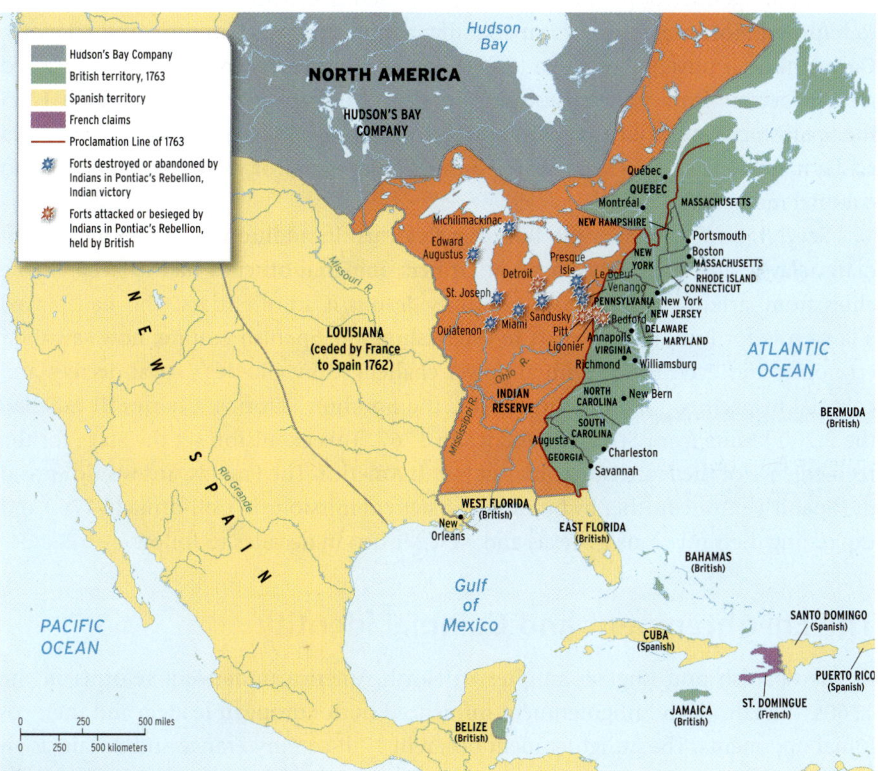


**Map 6.2**

**North America in 1763** This map shows the line drawn in the Proclamation of 1763 and depicts the major clashes during Pontiac's Rebellion.

with the British in 1766, while thousands of settlers poured into their territories by the mid-1770s.

## Bourbon Reforms

The Spanish government was more successful at centralizing control and reforming its empire in North America after 1763. In the peace of 1763 that settled the global war for empire, Spain acquired the French territory west of the Mississippi River and the city of New Orleans, but traded possession of Florida to Britain in exchange for Havana, Cuba, which the British had occupied in 1762. Charles III (a member of the Bourbon dynasty that took control of the Spanish crown in the 1710s) and a close group of reforming bureaucrats influenced by ideas of the Iberian Enlightenment sought to rebuild central imperial control over North and South America. The Bourbon Reforms (as their actions came to be called) also aimed to increase Spanish crown revenues and control over institutions of the Catholic Church.

Charles III appointed José de Gálvez as Minister of the Indies, and Gálvez immediately sought to reduce the authority of Creole families who governed the mixed-race and indigenous populations in Spanish America. Gálvez and other officials tried to reform almost every area of imperial life: administrative, economic, and religious. Gálvez himself travelled to Cuba and Mexico to impose new regulations that raised greater revenue from trade customs, mining, and Indian tribute payments. In 1765 the Spanish crown broke up colonial trade monopolies long enjoyed by Seville and Cádiz merchants and increased taxes on the larger group of merchants allowed into colonial markets.

Several groups resisted the Bourbon Reforms. In addition to unrest among Indians, slaves, and mixed-race peasant farmers, imperial officials had to keep Creole elites from striking against royal authority. Jesuits, Catholic friars who had played a large role for hundreds of years in establishing the Spanish empire, now saw their economic and even their spiritual power challenged by Charles's royal decrees and colonial inspectors. When Jesuits resisted the Bourbon Reforms, Charles III expelled the 2,200 Jesuits from Spanish America in 1767. This expulsion set the stage for the reemergence of the Franciscan order in North America. The Franciscans would spread the Spanish empire further by building a system of missions in California in 1769 and expanding their missions in Texas and New Mexico in decades to follow.

## The Enlightenment and Colonial Identity

As the Spanish and English empires in North America underwent reforms in the 1760s, the European Enlightenment influenced both European leaders and their colonial opponents. The Enlightenment began in 17th-century France and Britain as an intellectual movement that emphasized the powers of reason, observation, and experience to explain the natural and social worlds. The ideas of Enlightenment thinkers influenced social and economic reform, science, philosophy, and social and political theory. Principles of human rights and individualism circulated in books, pamphlets, and newspapers throughout North America, especially in the British colonies. The works of English politician and philosopher **John Locke**, especially his *Two Treatises on Government* (1690), argued that governments must protect the rights of individuals to pursue life, liberty, and property. The French writers who most influenced British North Americans were Voltaire and Montesquieu, whose *Spirit of the Laws* (1748) became a well-read guide on how to create a republic, a representative government with separation of powers.

Most British American colonists in 1763 saw themselves as part of the empire of British liberty, a view enhanced by Enlightenment principles. They believed that the British government was a bastion of liberty and property rights, and they revered the powerful check that Parliament could provide on royal authority in the British system of mixed government. American colonists became fascinated with British writers who extolled more radical forms of republican government, such as Algernon Sidney, John Trenchard, and Thomas Gordon. Their republican ideas influenced colonists who viewed parliamentary and royal crackdowns on the colonies as threats to liberty. Spanish Bourbon reformers were influenced by Montesquieu and by Spanish Enlightenment thinkers to apply rationalist principles to their reform efforts.

Americans who opposed British taxes during the imperial crisis called themselves "Whigs" after the opposition political party in England that stood against excesses of centralized royal power. Learned Americans, interested in pursuing and promoting enlightened scientific knowledge founded the American Philosophical Society in Philadelphia in 1769. Benjamin Franklin and several other founders of the American Philosophical Society would soon become leaders of colonial resistance to Britain.

### STUDY QUESTIONS FOR ENGLISH AND SPANISH IMPERIAL REFORM

1. **In what ways were British and Spanish colonial reforms similar? In what ways were they different?**
2. **Why did Pontiac's Rebellion help lead to the Proclamation of 1763?**

## STAMP ACT AND RESISTANCE

When the British Parliament and Prime Minister Grenville imposed direct taxes on American colonists in 1764 and 1765, they galvanized colonial protest movements. Americans were used to taxing themselves, and they objected to change. The 1765 **Stamp Act** inaugurated a new era of resistance in the British colonies. Maryland lawyer Daniel Dulany urged his fellow colonists during the Stamp Act crisis: "Instead of moping . . . and whining to excite compassion; in such a situation we ought with spirit, and vigour, and alacrity, to bid defiance to tyranny." Many British North Americans heeded his call to defiance, and Parliament faced a resistance movement more widespread and coordinated than any they had seen before.

## Parliamentary Action

In the months leading up to the Stamp Act's passage in March 1765, at least eight colonial assemblies sent petitions to Parliament in protest. But Grenville was determined not only to raise funds but also to assert imperial authority. The bill assessed, for the first time, a unified tax that would fall on all British colonists across boundary lines. Grenville argued before Parliament that Americans were "virtually" represented in that body.

The Stamp Act taxed paper, shipping and legal documents, playing cards, dice, newspapers, pamphlets, almanacs, and calendars. Although the tax was approximately 30 percent lower than similar taxes within Great Britain, the amount mattered little to those who objected to what they saw as a change in Parliamentary authority, from the regulation of trade to direct taxation of colonists. To enforce the taxes, the British government appointed stamp "distributors" in each colony to collect the taxes.

## Protest and Repeal

When word of the Stamp Act reached the colonies, the Virginia House of Burgesses adopted resolutions of protest proposed by **Patrick Henry**. Virginia's Royal Governor, Francis Fauquier, dissolved the assembly rather than let protest get out of hand. The stamp distributors themselves provided a target for colonial resistance to the Stamp

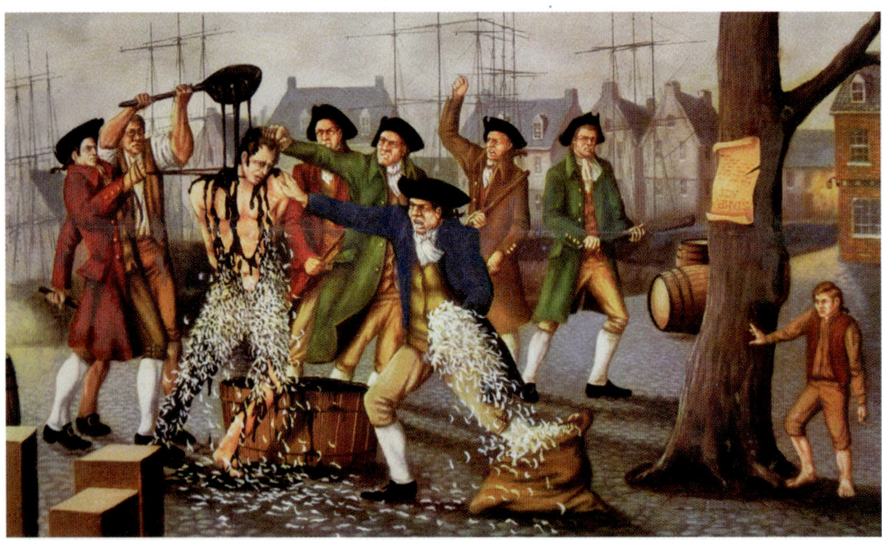

This engraving shows colonial protestors tarring and feathering a stamp collector as part of a protest against the Stamp Act. No stamp collectors were personally tarred and feathered during the protests, but the painful tactic was used occasionally against government supporters. Boston stamp collector Andrew Oliver did have his home destroyed by a mob.

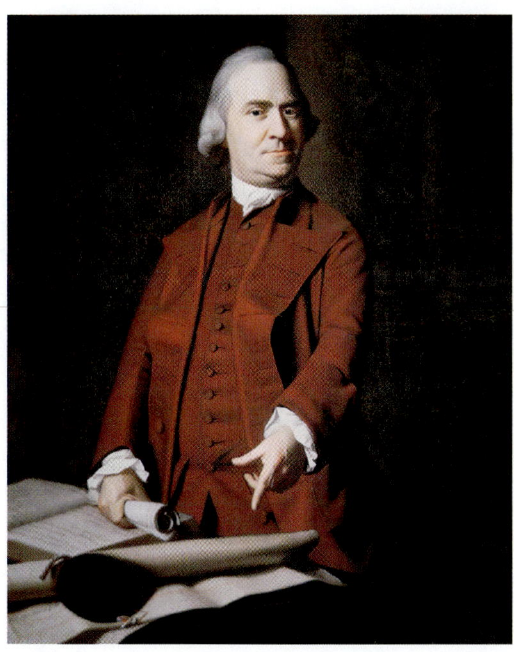

Samuel Adams was a member of the Boston Town Meeting and the Massachusetts House of Representatives when he began to coordinate protests to increased British taxation and colonial control in the 1760s. Credited as one of the founders of the "Sons of Liberty," Adams circulated letters to other colonies calling for solidarity and protest against British authority. He became a member of the Continental Congress, and later served as governor of Massachusetts in the 1790s.

Act. In August 1765, after Andrew Oliver, the brother-in-law of Massachusetts Royal Lieutenant Governor Thomas Hutchinson, agreed to become the Stamp Distributor in that colony, a crowd in Boston hanged him in effigy from what became known as "liberty tree." A crowd led by a poor shoemaker, Seven Years' War veteran **Ebenezer MacIntosh**, then attacked Oliver's office and his house. The following day, Oliver resigned his post as stamp tax collector.

Serious crowd violence against British authority spread. In Boston, residents attacked officials of the royal admiralty courts and destroyed the house of Lieutenant Governor Hutchinson. Groups of Stamp Act protesters soon began calling themselves "**Sons of Liberty**." The Sons of Liberty coordinated crowd actions, petitions, pamphlets, and consumer boycotts, and spread awareness of colonial protests between colonies. One of leaders of the Boston Sons of Liberty, **Samuel Adams**, claimed that British subjects would have pursued the same strategies if they "thought their essential Unalienable Rights . . . invaded by Parliament."

In addition to popular protest, first the Virginia House of Burgesses and then other colonial assemblies passed legislation opposing the Stamp Act. The Massachusetts legislature called on other colonies to appoint delegates to a meeting in New York in October 1765. Twenty-seven delegates from nine colonies met for two weeks and passed a series of resolutions insisting that although colonial subjects owed allegiance to king and parliament, they were "entitled to all the inherent rights and liberties of his natural born subjects within the kingdom of Great-Britain." The Stamp Act Congress also protested in petitions to the British against taxation without representation, while acknowledging obedience to legislation governing imperial trade. The actions of the Stamp Act Congress demonstrated an unprecedented level of cooperation among colonies and a strong resolution to resist taxation.

In the midst of the Stamp Act protests, George III replaced Grenville as prime minister, appointing the Marquis of Rockingham in July 1765. Rockingham, who aligned himself with the **Whig Party** in Parliament, faced the immediate challenge of how to quell the unrest. The commander of British military forces in the colonies, General **Thomas Gage**, told the government that he lacked the time, resources, and troops to militarily subdue the opposition. In addition to resisting the Stamp Act through crowd action against tax collectors and legislative protest, colonists in British America also began to organize localized boycotts of British trade goods. Rockingham faced a difficult choice in Parliament, especially after Whig leader **William Pitt** declared that Parliament had no right to tax the unrepresented colonists. Rockingham realized that enforcement of the tax had become impossible. On March 1, 1766, Parliament repealed the Stamp Act.

## Empire and Authority

Although Parliament repealed the Stamp Act, Britain retained its authority to tax the colonies. The debate over repeal prompted discussion in both Parliament and in the colonies about the nature and limits of British sovereignty. Worried that Americans would take the wrong message from the repeal of the Stamp Act, Parliament passed the Declaratory Act. This new act reasserted the British right to control the colonies and pass laws "in all cases whatsoever," a phrase that echoed a declaratory act used to emphasize English control of Ireland in 1719. British commentators also stressed that the king's royal authority united all subjects of the crown throughout the empire, and most Americans agreed in 1766. Even protestor John Dickinson wrote that Americans admired their "excellent prince" in whose "good dispositions they could confide."

Apart from the Stamp Act, tensions inside the colonies provoked conflicts over imperial authority. In several colonies, conflict between eastern and western inhabitants over land rights, political representation, and Indian policy caused trouble for imperial officials. Pontiac's War had increased tensions, particularly in Pennsylvania. In 1763 and 1764, a group of armed men in western Pennsylvania calling themselves the "Paxton Boys" attacked Susquehannock Indians (also known as Conestoga) who had been guaranteed protection by the crown and by the royal government in Philadelphia. **Benjamin Franklin** negotiated a compromise when 600 armed westerners marched on the capital to protest the Paxton Boys' indictment. In the following years, groups of armed "regulators," farmers from western North Carolina, marched against imperial officials who tried to enforce taxes and legal judgments against them.

This kind of unrest led Parliament to pass the first Quartering Act in 1765, authorizing British military forces to be permanently housed in the colonies—at the expense of colonists. In the midst of their resistance to the Stamp Act, many colonists refused to comply with the requirement that they house and feed British troops. Despite disorder in cities and the countryside, most colonists resented the idea that they should be compelled to house British troops.

**STUDY QUESTIONS FOR STAMP ACT AND RESISTANCE**

1. **Why did the colonial resistance movement continue, despite the Stamp Act's repeal?**
2. **In what ways did resistance to British taxation cause British North Americans to work together?**

# CONSUMER RESISTANCE

Britain was expanding as a consumer society by the mid-eighteenth century, and many American colonists wanted to emulate the British taste in clothing, furniture, and housing styles. Tied to the British empire through education, trade, and reverence for English liberty, Americans also found themselves deeply enmeshed in a common world of goods and the credit relationships that enabled their circulation. Ironically, this developing consumer society in the colonies also provided a powerful new strategy of resistance during the rising tensions of imperial conflict after 1765. During the 1760s, the American population grew by an astonishing 40 percent, and between 1700 and 1770 the per capita American expenditure on British goods grew by 20 percent. These growth trends meant that American consumers held enormous economic clout. When they began collectively to exercise that clout to protest British control and taxation, they helped accelerate an imperial crisis.

## Townshend Duties

In June 1767, the British Parliament passed a new series of taxes that emphasized their resolve to legislate for the colonies "in all cases whatsoever," as the Declaratory Act stated. The annual cost of keeping troops in North America reached £700,000 (over $76 million today). Whig Chancellor of the Exchequer, Charles Townshend, ushered a new series of taxes through Parliament known as the "**Townshend Acts**" or "Townshend Duties." These taxes hit a variety of commodities central to the transatlantic colonial trade: tea, paper, lead, glass, and paint. The acts also continued a previous tax on molasses, the essential product used to manufacture rum, although at a lower rate.

Along with the new taxes, Parliament continued to press for stricter enforcement of trade duties. The British treasury department created an American Board of Customs in Boston staffed by royal appointees. Vice-admiralty courts were established at Boston, Philadelphia, and Charleston and granted the authority to try and fine smugglers without any local jury. The British government also centralized government oversight of the colonies, and instructed colonial governors to impose control over elected colonial assemblies. The presence of British troops in major American cities, under the terms of the 1765 Quartering Act, emphasized that military power might be used to enhance this new centralized imperial control. When the New York assembly refused to enforce the Quartering Act, Parliament passed a restraining act that suspended its legislative authority until it complied.

## The Non-Importation Movement

Colonists who opposed British taxation immediately responded to the Townshend Duties by renewing their collective action. By October 1767, when news of the acts spread, men and women in Boston and elsewhere had started to discuss boycotting British imports. By the time the new taxes went into effect in November 1767, many American colonists had already pledged to avoid purchasing British goods and vowed to make do with their own homemade items and homespun cloth. By the spring of 1768 the non-importation movement had spread from Boston to New York, Philadelphia, Charleston, and other port cities. John Dickinson argued in his very popular 1768 pamphlet series *Letters from a Farmer in Pennsylvania* that Parliament could regulate trade but that colonists would not submit to Parliamentary taxation of any kind. Samuel Adams drafted a petition to King George III, passed by the Massachusetts legislature in January 1768 and subsequently endorsed by Virginia and other colonial assemblies, that protested "taxation without representation" and called for colonies to coordinate their resistance.

Britain largely ignored the petitions and protests by colonial assemblies throughout 1768, and so the non-importation movement spread. In 1769, groups in several colonies signed formal non-importation agreements, called "associations," and the Sons of Liberty and other organizations who had protested the Stamp Act reemerged. Several colonial governments, including the Boston Town Meeting and the Connecticut, New Jersey, and New York assemblies passed resolutions supporting non-importation. Non-importation drastically reduced the trade of sugar into the North American colonies and increased hardship where sugar was produced in the West Indies, causing thousands of enslaved people to starve. But the British continued to ignore the boycotts.

While broadly based, the non-importation movement fostered bitter disputes between those who supported the Parliamentary taxes and the boycotters. People caught selling or trying to buy British goods in major cities found themselves punished by angry crowds; several Boston newspapers even published violators' names on the front page.

## Men and Women: Tea and Politics

The non-importation movement brought men and women together politically as they opposed imperial authority. Boycotts invested women's everyday activities of purchasing, preparing, and consuming commodities such as tea with political meaning. Tea drinking had become an important part of many white women's social rituals by the mid-1700s, linking American women to the British importers who traded tea from India and China to North America. As one Boston newspaper predicted in November 1767, "The cost of consuming foreign tea is very expensive in this colony . . . to lay an extensive tax on its consumption, would be very disagreeable to the Ladies."

Polished mahogany tea tables like this one became the setting for genteel socializing in elite American homes, where men and women drank tea, displayed their fine china and silver, and held conversations. While the tea and china were imported, tables like this one were often made in the colonies by master furniture makers.

Male supporters of the non-importation movement appealed to women in speeches and newspaper articles to participate in the boycotts, and several women also wrote to newspapers appealing for the "Daughters of Liberty" to act. Female shopkeepers were among those who signed public pledges not to sell freshly imported British goods, and city women made a show of drinking only coffee or home-brewed herbal tea. Other women conspicuously wore only home-spun fabric and held spinning bees to raise supplies of homemade textiles.

By the end of 1769, the British government realized that the Townshend duties had failed. The taxes had brought in less than £20,000, while British merchants had lost more than £700,000 in business. The new British ministry, headed by Lord North, decided in 1770 to repeal all of the Townshend duties except for the tax on tea, which would continue "as a mark of the supremacy of Parliament." The non-importation movement quickly faded with the repeal of the other Townshend duties, but the legacy of political mobilization would live on.

## The Boston Massacre

While the Townshend duties were in place, harsh resistance to them in Boston particularly vexed the British government, and they responded by sending British soldiers to keep order in that city. Beginning on October 1, 1768, the first of 4,000 British soldiers arrived to police Boston, a city of just 15,000. The soldiers, stationed around the city in private residences due to the Quartering Act, often clashed with local citizens. Soldiers also competed for seasonal jobs with poor working people of Boston, many of whom were also active in the Whig resistance. Tensions heated up in 1770 when a customs official killed 11-year-old Christopher Seider in late February, sparking mob action and a skirmish between Boston rope workers and British soldiers on March 3.

GLOBAL PASSAGES

## Crowd Action, Violence, and State Authority

The Boston Massacre sparked outrage in Massachusetts and other British North American colonies, but it was not the only occasion in the 1760s and 1770s when soldiers killed protestors. Crowd actions to enforce community standards of behavior, mob violence, and political protests were relatively common around the Atlantic World in the 18th century. Sometimes, such as in cases of food riots or crowd actions against houses of prostitution, such protests could actually reinforce governmental authority, but government officials always ran the risk that crowds could get out of control. 18th-century governments lacked police forces for the most part and often used military forces to enforce civic order. In the 1760s and 1770s, with the mechanisms of imperial control changing—especially following the French and Indian War—British and Spanish officials increasingly used violence to reassert state authority and squelch dissent.

The Spanish government used military force to end a revolt in Louisiana in 1768. Spain had been slow to take control over Louisiana after the French ceded it in 1763, and the first Spanish governor, Don Antonio de Ulloa, did not assume office in New Orleans until 1766. No one in the city's mix of French, German, Indian, and free and enslaved African settlers wanted to submit to Spanish authority—especially the city's elites, whose extensive trade and smuggling Ulloa tried to control. Prominent citizens of New Orleans, led by several French settlers, revolted in October 1768, demanded that Ulloa leave the colony, and tried to rejoin the French empire. Spain responded by sending a new governor, General Alexandre O'Reilly, with 2,000 troops to put down the revolt. O'Reilly swiftly seized the protest leaders, tried them, confiscated their property, imprisoned many, and executed 12 men by firing squad. The Louisiana revolt was the largest in North America until that point, and it prompted the biggest imperial military crackdown in North America prior to 1774.

In London, when the radical printer and member of parliament John Wilkes was arrested in 1763 for libeling King George III in his newspaper, Wilkes's supporters responded with a wide range of protests. Wilkes fled to Paris, but he returned to

Tensions boiled over on March 5, 1770, in the incident that became known as the **Boston Massacre**. A crowd began to harass a British sentry, and when eight soldiers came to his aid, the crowd began throwing rocks and snowballs at them. The soldiers responded by firing into the crowd. Five working men were killed, including a runaway slave named Crispus Attucks. Following the skirmish, public opinion against the British

Britain in 1768 and was again elected to Parliament. However, he was seized by the government in May and imprisoned in London. On May 10, the opening day of Parliament, as many as 20,000 people gathered outside the king's Bench Prison to support Wilkes. When a judge read the Riot Act—outlawing violence—he was pelted with stones. Soldiers fired into the crowd, and other armed guards pursued rioters around the city as violence spread. More than seven people were killed and scores wounded in what became known as the St. George's Field Massacre. The memory of these killings fueled political opposition in England for decades, and the cause of "Wilkes and Liberty" also became popular with rebellious North American colonists.

British officials were also willing to use military force outside major cities like London and Boston. In Ulster, Ireland, Britain used military force against members of the "Hearts of Oak" movement, which protested road taxes and rising farm rents in the 1760s. The British did so again when the "Hearts of Steel" protested landowner fees in the 1770s. When western North Carolina "Regulators" protested the Stamp Act, abuses by local tax officials, and other economic grievances, Royal Governor William Tryon cracked down. After protests took place in Hillsborough, North Carolina, in 1770 and 1771, the colonial assembly passed a "Bloody Act" outlawing riots. When Regulator protestors again gathered at Alamance Creek in May 1771, Tryon attacked them with North Carolina militia forces, and men were killed on both sides of the battle. Tryon also executed several Regulator leaders for treason before he left to become royal governor of New York.

Enforcing government authority, especially in far-flung colonies, was a careful balancing act for both Britain and Spain in the 1760s and 1770s. Using military forces to control rebellion could restore order, as it did in Spanish New Orleans. But it could also spawn resentment that might further threaten control, as the British would learn in North America.

- In what ways did the Wilkesite protests in England resemble the British colonial protests in North America? In what ways were they different?
- How would you compare the Spanish crackdown in New Orleans in 1768 to the Boston Massacre? What do the differences reveal about British and Spanish colonial authority?

soldiers ran high, especially after silversmith **Paul Revere** published an inflammatory engraving of the incident depicting the British soldiers as cruel murderers. **John Adams** and **Josiah Quincy, Jr.**, Boston lawyers who were loyal to the Whig cause but believed in fair trials, helped to acquit the British commander, Captain Preston. Only two of the soldiers were found guilty of manslaughter, and they were lightly punished and released.

The BLOODY MASSACRE perpetrated in King Street BOSTON on March 5th 1770 by a party of the 29th REGT
BUTCHER'S HALL
Engrav'd Printed & Sold by PAUL REVERE BOSTON
Unhappy BOSTON! ſee thy Sons deplore,
Thy hallow'd Walks beſmear'd with guiltleſs Gore:
While faithleſs P—n and his ſavage Bands,
With murd'rous Rancour ſtretch their bloody Hands;
Like fierce Barbarians grinning o'er their Prey,
Approve the Carnage, and enjoy the Day.
If ſcalding drops from Rage from Anguiſh Wrung
If ſpeechleſs Sorrows lab'ring for a Tongue,
Or if a weeping World can ought appeaſe
The plaintive Ghoſts of Victims ſuch as theſe;
The Patriot's copious Tears for each are ſhed,
A glorious Tribute which embalms the Dead.
But know, FATE ſummons to that awful Goal,
Where JUSTICE ſtrips the Murd'rer of his Soul:
Should venal C—ts the ſcandal of the Land,
Snatch the relentleſs Villain from her Hand,
Keen Execrations on this Plate inſcrib'd,
Shall reach a JUDGE who never can be brib'd.
The unhappy Sufferers were Meſs. SAML GRAY, SAML MAVERICK, JAMS CALDWELL, CRISPUS ATTUCKS & PATK CARR
Killed. Six wounded; two of them (CHRISTR MONK & JOHN CLARK) Mortally


Paul Revere published this propagandistic engraving of the Boston Massacre in 1770. It shows British soldiers shooting down unarmed civilians in front of the Boston Custom House, which Revere relabeled as "Butcher's Hall." Revere was one of the best engravers in Massachusetts, and his work helped to spread outrage.

## STUDY QUESTIONS FOR CONSUMER RESISTANCE

1. **Why did North American colonists use non-importation as a resistance strategy against British taxation?**
2. **In what ways did protests mobilize elite white women and poorer men and women?**

# RESISTANCE BECOMES REVOLUTION

Between 1770 and 1776, resistance to imperial change turned into a full-on revolution. After a short cooling-off period at the beginning of the 1770s, colonial protests threatened to turn violent. Eventually, that violence would be channeled into organized revolutionary warfare. How could the colonists fight a war with Britain and still remain part of the British empire?

## Boston Tea Party and Coercive Acts

Although the formal associations that organized boycotts during the non-importation movement faded away after 1770, the tax on tea remained, and many colonists who feared the next Parliamentary move continued to avoid drinking tea. Beginning in Boston, and then spreading to every colony, groups of men formed Committees of Correspondence to provide networks of communication between Whigs in different colonies. The committees were in place when Parliament passed the Tea Act in March of 1773, granting the East India Company a monopoly on the North American tea trade. The monopoly lowered the price of tea, but it did not remove the tax. This legislation reawakened popular protest, as Whigs quickly planned resistance against tea agents.

In several port cities, to avoid protests, government officials persuaded ship captains to leave port without unloading the East India Company tea. But in Boston in December 1773, Governor Thomas Hutchinson refused to allow the tea ships to leave without unloading their cargo of tea. On December 16, Samuel Adams and other Sons of Liberty organized a mass meeting in Old South Meeting House, where they denounced the tea shipments as instruments of British tyranny. That evening, 30–60 men disguised as Mohawk Indians stormed the tea ships and dumped 90,000 pounds of tea into Boston Harbor. The "**Boston Tea Party**" mobilized Bostonians and spread strenuous tea resistance to other colonies. Protestors burned a tea ship in Annapolis, Maryland; Princeton University students destroyed tea and effigies of Thomas Hutchinson; and new tea boycott associations formed—including one among the women of Edenton, North Carolina.

The destruction of property in the tea protests shocked Parliament, which quickly sanctioned Massachusetts in a series of 1774 laws dubbed the "**Coercive Acts**" or the "Intolerable Acts" by Whig colonists. Lord North told the House of Commons that "We are now to establish our authority, or give it up entirely"—and not even those in Parliament who favored the colonists' cause, such as Edmund Burke, were ready to relent. The Coercive Acts closed the port of Boston and reorganized the Massachusetts government, altering its colonial charter to put more authority in the hands of royal appointees. The acts also imposed royal control over local courts; authorized troops to be forcibly billeted in private houses and buildings; and installed the British Army commander, Thomas Gage, as the new colonial governor. In addition to these Coercive Acts, Parliament also passed the Quebec Act in 1774—which further

This engraving shows the Boston Tea Party or "The Destruction of the Tea" as it was sometimes known, as imagined by the print firm of Currier and Ives in the 1840s. The depiction of the incident shows how the Tea Party has been a popular subject of popular imagination since the end of the 18th century. Though the protesters did disguise themselves as "Mohawk Indians," the effect was likely not as complete as depicted here.

frightened Protestant New Englanders by expanding royal control in Canada and endorsing official Catholicism.

## Empire, Control, and the Language of Slavery

The Coercive Acts galvanized political opposition inside Massachusetts, and Whigs soon organized a new boycott movement. The crackdown on Massachusetts also energized Whigs in many other colonies, who feared similar repressive action. Philadelphians began to call for a meeting to issue colonial petitions to the king—the highest and last authority who might redress their grievances. After Virginia's royal governor dissolved the House of Burgesses, the legislative body met illegally at a tavern in Williamsburg to endorse a new boycott and to echo the call for a continental congress to coordinate protests.

**Thomas Jefferson** argued that Parliament sought to subdue the colonies through "a series of oppressions," and he expressed a vision of the British engaged in "a deliberate systematical plan of reducing us to slavery." Jefferson's use of the word "slavery" signaled the fear that many colonists had of being deprived of their traditional liberties. The term was used by a range of Americans who shared that fear. During the boycott movement, **Abigail Adams** referred to tea as "this weed of Slavery." Her husband, Massachusetts lawyer John Adams, wrote that England, "once the land of liberty—the school of patriots—the nurse of heroes, has become the land of slavery." This language of slavery indicated how deeply many Whigs had come to fear the British government and what they viewed as the corruption of the British system.

American colonists were not blind to the irony of calling themselves "slaves" to the British government while many colonists actually owned African American slaves. In fact, they intentionally used the term "slavery" to indicate a subordinate, degraded position with which they were intimately familiar. Many of the leaders of the Revolutionary movement, especially in colonies like Virginia where the institution of slavery was strong, had social prestige because of inherited wealth based on slave ownership and slave labor. Virginian **George Washington** wrote during the controversy over the Coercive Acts, "The crisis is arrived when we must assert our rights or submit to every imposition, that can be heaped upon us, till custom and use shall make us as tame and abject slaves, as the blacks we rule over with such arbitrary sway." In every colony, African American slaves lived beside free men and women, and that reality made political "slavery" all the more fearsome as the British asserted their power.

## Mobilization

Parliament had intended the Coercive Acts to cut off Massachusetts from the other colonies, to isolate radicals and stop their rebellion. Instead, the acts roused sympathy for Massachusetts and prompted Whigs in far-flung colonies to unite more than ever before. In September 1774, representatives of 12 colonies met in a Continental Congress at Philadelphia. Jamaica and other Caribbean colonies opposed the Coercive Acts, but their assemblies took no action to join the Continental Congress—since Caribbean planters served in and had more direct access to Parliament than did their neighbors to the north. The **First Continental Congress** proceeded to appeal to King George III to check abuses of Parliamentary authority. The Congress even discussed colonial independence, although very few delegates openly supported it.

An angry King George urged Parliament to impose even more control on the colonies to break what he deemed "disobedience to the law." Committees in all thirteen British North American colonies organized for public defense. In Boston, Thomas Gage and his British had all but shut down the city. Local militias in Massachusetts and Connecticut went on alert to respond quickly (as "**minute men**") to possible British military action, after Gage's forces captured a powder cache in Charlestown in September 1774. In the early months of 1775, Edmund Burke and other sympathetic members of Parliament tried unsuccessfully to get the North government to make concessions to the colonists.

## War Begins

Early in 1775, General Gage decided to crack down on Whig activities in Concord, Massachusetts, where the dissolved colonial assembly met illegally and where he suspected colonists had a stockpile of weapons and gunpowder. On the evening of

April 18, 1775, Gage assembled 700 of his 3,500 red coats (as British soldiers were nicknamed) on Boston Common and readied them to be transported into the countryside. Whig activists Paul Revere and William Dawes rode out of Boston to warn the militiamen at Concord and nearby Lexington and to warn radical leaders Samuel Adams and John Hancock to leave Lexington, where they had fled under threat of arrest. In the early morning of April 19, Captain John Parker's company of militia in Lexington skirmished with British soldiers led by Major John Pitcairn on Lexington Green. Eight militia men were killed in the opening battle of the Revolutionary War.

Later that morning, five miles away in Concord, the local militia, now reinforced by other men from the surrounding countryside, engaged British regulars in a larger battle at the North Bridge. After the battle, the British soldiers made their way back to Boston along the winding 16-mile rural road. They came under fire from the woods, as hundreds of Massachusetts militia troops sniped at the regulars. Gage's troops holed up in Boston, awaiting reinforcements, as more than 10,000 colonial militia forces surrounded the city over the next month. Colonists up and down the eastern seaboard celebrated resistance to the British Army.

The Second Continental Congress convened on May 10, 1775, just one day after **Ethan Allen**, with assistance from men commanded by Benedict Arnold, had captured the British Fort Ticonderoga. As the British planned their next move, the Continental Congress set about organizing a Continental Army, and on June 15 they chose as its commander George Washington, whose genteel Virginia heritage and military experience made him stand out among the delegates. Even before Washington could assume command, the Battle of Bunker Hill took place on June 17. Major General William Howe, who had arrived in Boston with reinforcements, ordered an attack on the heights at Charlestown, across the Charles River from Boston. The Americans fortified Breed's Hill, which they misidentified as Bunker Hill, and met the better-equipped regulars who streamed up the Hill in three waves of attack to try and capture the heights. Although the colonial forces retreated to end the battle, they claimed victory in proving they could hold up against greater numbers of well-trained soldiers. The British also suffered their heaviest casualty rate of the entire war: Of 2,500 soldiers, 228 died and 826 were wounded.

For the remainder of the year, the British remained in Boston plotting their next move, as Washington and the Continental Congress worked to organize and equip the Continental Army. Two expeditions, one led by **Philip Schuyler** and Richard Montgomery, the other by Benedict Arnold, set out for Canada late in the year, but both ended in disaster. By January 1776 Montgomery was killed and no groundswell of support emerged for the American cause in Canada. In Virginia, Governor Dunmore offered freedom to slaves and indentured servants who joined the British against the Americans, and in December he led a force of British regulars, escaped slaves, and loyalists in a battle against a Virginia Continental Army regiment outside of Norfolk. Dunmore's force was defeated, he fled the colony, and many of the slaves who had joined his cause when he promised them freedom were sold back into bondage in the Caribbean.

**STUDY QUESTIONS FOR RESISTANCE BECOMES REVOLUTION**

1. **How did Boston play a key role in the imperial crisis that moved British colonists toward independence?**
2. **What British and North American actions caused colonial resistance to escalate into warfare?**

# DECLARING INDEPENDENCE

With the Revolutionary War well under way, the British empire in North America reached its breaking point. As the first six months of the Revolutionary War unfolded, the Second Continental Congress began seriously to consider the possibility of declaring independence from Great Britain, even though colonies had never before tried such a bold maneuver.

## The World's First Declaration of Independence

Even through the first months of the Revolutionary War, many Whigs had continued to pledge allegiance to the king. In July 1775 the Continental Congress sent an "**Olive Branch Petition**" to George III seeking his intervention to settle the conflict, but by spring 1776, Congress fielded petitions from colonial committees and assemblies calling for independence. In May 1776, the City of London petitioned George III to approach his colonies peacefully, but the king responded that the colonists had "brought upon themselves" the trouble "by an unjustifiable resistance to the constitutional authority of this Kingdom." When the king rejected peace, even moderates like Philadelphia's Robert Morris conceded that a "declaration of Independency" was probably inevitable.

Virginia's delegation to the Continental Congress, headed by Richard Henry Lee, proposed a motion to declare independence from Great Britain on June 7, 1776. After debate over whether independence would bring aid from France and Spain, Congress delayed voting on the resolution until the beginning of July to give colonial committees and assemblies time to endorse the idea. A Congressional subcommittee, which included John Adams and Thomas Jefferson, worked on the motion that would declare the separation of the colonies from the British empire. Jefferson wrote the declaration, with some editing by Adams and Benjamin Franklin. The Continental Congress voted for independence on July 2, and the following day a large British fleet commanded by General William Howe bearing a rejuvenated British army force landed outside New York City.

The **Declaration of Independence**, issued by Congress on July 4, 1776, was the first document of its kind in world history. Many colonies, assemblies, and legislative

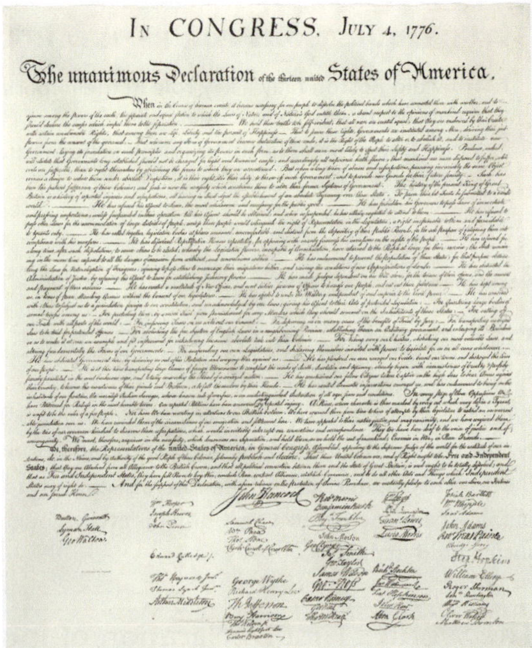
IN CONGRESS. JULY 4, 1776.

The unanimous Declaration of the thirteen united States of America,

The Declaration of Independence. The Continental Congress took a huge risk by issuing the Declaration of Independence in July 1776. No colony in the history of the world had ever declared its independence and asserted its right to become a nation. Success depended on the reaction of the rest of the world and on the ability of the Americans to win their revolutionary war.

bodies had in previous centuries put forth declarations concerning rights and privileges, and this document drew on many historical precedents that defined the British sense of rights and liberty. But never before had a group of colonies listed its grievances, declared itself to be an independent state, and asserted its own sovereignty. The Declaration began with a sweeping statement about rights that put a new twist on the Enlightenment ideas of John Locke: "We hold these truths to be self-evident, that all Men are created equal, that they are endowed by their Creator with certain unalienable Rights, that among these are Life, Liberty and the Pursuit of Happiness." The Declaration enumerated violations of the rights of colonists.

The Declaration appealed to "the rest of mankind" to recognize that the United States was free and independent of the British empire. The Declaration of Independence itself, however, would not be sufficient to guarantee the success of the United States. The Revolutionary War intensified and offered a military test for the new nation that would last several more years.

## Establishment of Comandancia General of the Interior Provinces

By contrast to the British Empire, which seemed very close to losing its North American colonies altogether, Spanish officials were able to bring more area in North America under their control through the Bourbon Reforms. José de Gálvez visited Mexico in the 1760s, and by the 1770s many of his plans for California, New Mexico, and other areas of North America were bearing fruit. Franciscan friars Gaspar de Portolá, Father

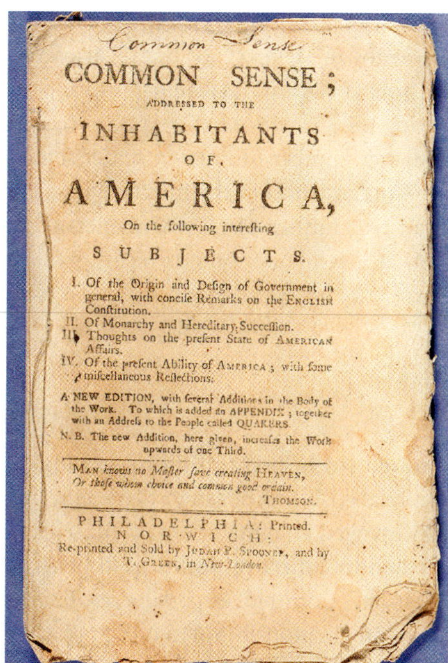
Common Sense

COMMON SENSE;

ADDRESSED TO THE

INHABITANTS

OF

AMERICA,

On the following intereſting

SUBJECTS.

I. Of the Origin and Deſign of Government in general, with conciſe Remarks on the ENGLISH Conſtitution.

II. Of Monarchy and Hereditary Succeſſion.

III. Thoughts on the preſent State of AMERICAN Affairs.

IV. Of the preſent Ability of AMERICA; with ſome miſcellaneous Reflections.

A NEW EDITION, with ſeveral Additions in the Body of the Work. To which is added an APPENDIX; together with an Addreſs to the People called QUAKERS.

N. B. The new Addition, here given, increaſes the Work upwards of one Third.

MAN knows no Maſter ſave creating HEAVEN,
Or thoſe whom choice and common good ordain.
THOMSON.

PHILADELPHIA: Printed.
NORWICH:
Re-printed and Sold by JUDAH P. SPOONER, and by T. GREEN, in New-London.

Thomas Paine was an English radical who had come to America in 1774, in part because he supported the American protests against Parliament. His immensely popular 1776 pamphlet *Common Sense* advocated independence and helped to gain public acceptance for that tactic among the patriot population. Paine also supported the American war effort with other pamphlets such as "The Crisis." Later in the 1780s, he moved to France and became an important figure in the French Revolution.

Junípero Serra, and Fernando de Rivera y Moncada established a string of missions and presidio forts stretching from southern to northern California by 1774. Juan Bautista de Anza (later the governor of New Mexico) set the stage for further growth in the California mission system in 1774 when he opened a new land route from Mexico and brought an infusion of colonists and livestock to Northern California. José de Gálvez had put forth a plan in the 1760s to break the northern part of New Spain off from Mexico and bring it under direct crown control, and he got the chance to implement his plan when Charles III appointed him Secretary of the Indies in January 1776.

Mission Dolores. Father Junípero Sera founded the Misíon San Francisco de Asís (now knows as Mission Dolores) in 1776 as part of the effort by the Franciscans to spread the Spanish mission system to the north in California from the 1760s to the 1780s.

Charles III issued a royal order on August 22, 1776, that created the Comandancia General of the Interior Provinces. The Spanish colonies north of Mexico were formed into a semi-autonomous territory for military defense, trade expansion, and crown administration. Teodoro de Croix, a French-born Spanish official who later served as viceroy of Peru, was appointed as the first governor of the Interior Provinces. Croix was ordered to coordinate with the Spanish viceroy in Mexico City, but he also exercised autonomous authority in many areas. Croix and Anza pursued aggressive policies against native peoples, for example playing the Comanche and Apache against one another, and sought to control the increasing number of Russian settlers entering Spanish territory. The organization of the Comandancia of the Interior Provinces helped the California mission system to spread even further. The Comandancia set in motion the development of Northern Mexico as a semiautonomous region. Unlike the British, Spain maintained ultimate authority, and independence movements were postponed for several decades.

## Ideology and Resistance

In the British colonies, the Independence movement helped to solidify ideological changes that had been underway since the imperial crisis first began in 1763. Elite colonists who supported the Whig cause formally invoked Enlightenment political ideas, but ordinary men and women who participated in collective protest also believed in the importance of "liberty" and "representation." Committees passing resolutions and crowds rioting against tax collectors or boycott violators found that their place as consumers in the markets of the Atlantic world empowered their political views.

Techniques of resistance in the 1760s and early 1770s—pamphlet writing, riots, destruction of property, crowd actions to enforce community standards, burning enemies in effigy, petitions—were all familiar to the British. Crowds in England and Ireland regularly used these methods throughout the first three quarters of the 18th

### TIMELINE 1763–1776

**1763**

**February 10** The Treaty of Paris ends the Seven Years' War

**May** Pontiac's Rebellion begins when Ottawa forces lay siege to Ft. Detroit

**October 7** George III forbids settlement west of the Appalachian mountains in the Proclamation of 1763

**1764**

**April 5** Parliament revises the Navigation Acts and passes the Sugar Act

**April 19** The Currency Act curtails colonial paper money

**1765**

**March 22** Parliament passes the Stamp Act, which taxes legal documents, printed matter, and other paper goods

**May 15** The Quartering Act requires colonists to house and pay for British troops

**May** The Virginia House of Burgesses protests the Stamp Act and urges other colonies to join the opposition

**October 19** The Stamp Act Congress meets in Philadelphia

**1766**

**March 18** The Stamp Act is repealed, but the Declaratory Act stresses that Parliament can tax the colonies in "all cases whatsoever"

**July** A treaty concludes Pontiac's rebellion

**1767**

Charles III expels the Jesuits from New Spain for opposing his Bourbon Reform program

**July** Parliament suspends the New York legislature for refusing to comply with the Quartering Act

**November** John Dickinson's *Letters from a Farmer in Pennsylvania* begin to appear in newspapers

**November 20** The Townshend Duties tax a new range of colonial products

**1768**

**January** Massachusetts legislature petitions George III to protest "taxation without representation"

**1769**

**July 16** Father Junípero Serra founds his first mission church at San Diego de Alcalá

**1770**

**March 5** Five men are killed by British soldiers in the "Boston Massacre"

**April** Parliament withdraws all of the Townshend Duties, except for the tax on tea

**1772**

**October** The Boston Town Meeting urges Committees of Correspondence to form across the British colonies

**1773**

**April** Parliament passes the Tea Act, seeking to bolster

century to protest suppression of their political heroes, high food prices, taxes, and changes in foreign policy. Tens of thousands of people in England petitioned the government and took to the streets between 1763 and 1774 to protest the persecution of radical printer John Wilkes, who was denied his duly elected seat to Parliament during that period. Cries of "Wilkes and Liberty!" could be heard in the streets of London and Middlesex, but also in Charleston, New York, and Boston—where the Sons of Liberty and other American protestors linked their own movement to the Wilkesite cause.

British American colonists fit into a transatlantic tradition of protest, but only they turned their efforts into a full-blown movement for political independence and into a revolutionary war. In the move for independence, Whig Americans rejected not just the actions of the British government, but British control altogether. They moved from hoping that the king would protect them from excess Parliamentary control to rejecting the monarchy. They became Americans.

## Taking Stock of Empire

In 1776, Spain was expanding its North American empire just as the British empire in North America crumbled. New Spain stretched as far north as the presidio and Mission Dolores in San Francisco, and the Bourbon reforms increased crown control over extensive territory north of Mexico. British imperial reforms had achieved the opposite result. After successive attempts to raise revenue from the colonies, and successive resistance in return, thirteen British colonies declared independence from the British crown and formed the United States of America. Certainly not everyone in the British North American colonies supported independence, but for the time

the profits of the East India Company

**December 16** 90,000 pounds of East India Company tea is thrown into Boston Harbor at the Boston Tea Party

**1774**

**March 31** Parliament closes the port of Boston and suspends the Massachusetts legislature

**September** The First Continental Congress meets at Philadelphia

**October** The Continental Congress forms a Continental Association to coordinate non-importation

**October 7** Parliament passes the Quebec Act

**1775**

**March 23** Patrick Henry delivers his "Give me liberty or give me death" speech in the Virginia House of Burgesses

**April 19** The Revolutionary War begins at the Battles of Lexington and Concord

**May** American forces capture Fort Ticonderoga

**May** The Second Continental Congress meets in Philadelphia

**June 15** Congress forms the Continental Army and appoints George Washington as commander

**June 17** The Battle of Bunker Hill

**November** The governor of Virginia offers freedom to slaves who will join his fight against rebellious colonists

**December 31** Richard Montgomery killed in the unsuccessful American attack on Quebec

**1776**

**January** Thomas Paine's *Common Sense* is published

**March 17** British forces evacuate Boston

**July 4** Congress issues the Declaration of Independence, creating the United States of America being the Whigs who supported the actions of the Continental Congress seemed to have the upper hand.

### STUDY QUESTIONS FOR DECLARING INDEPENDENCE

1. **On what grounds did the Declaration of Independence base its justification of separation from Great Britain?**
2. **How did British colonial protests finally result in a revolutionary ideology by 1776?**
3. **How did the Spanish government consolidate control over increasing territory in North America in the mid-18th century?**

## Summary

- Both the British and Spanish governments sought more centralized control over their North American colonies following the Seven Years' War, in part to raise revenue.
- The 1765 Stamp Act inaugurated a stiff opposition movement in the British North American colonies and touched off a decade-long debate over Parliament's authority to tax the colonies.
- Between 1767 and 1770, American men and women politicized consumerism by fighting British taxation through a series of non-importation movements.
- Between 1770 and 1776, British imperial authorities cracked down on colonial resistance, especially in Massachusetts, and touched off a revolutionary war.
- In 1776, Congress declared independence from Great Britain and created the United States of America, and the Spanish imperial government created the Comandancia General of the Interior Provinces.

## Key Terms and People

**Adams, Abigail** *240*
**Adams, John** *237*
**Adams, Samuel** *231*
**Allen, Ethan** *242*
**Arnold, Benedict** *219*
**Boston Massacre** *236*
**Boston Tea Party** *239*
**Coercive Acts (Intolerable Acts)** *239*
**Declaration of Independence** *243*
**First Continental Congress** *241*
**Franklin, Benjamin** *232*
**Gage, Thomas** *232*
**Henry, Patrick** *230*
**Jefferson, Thomas** *240*
**Locke, John** *229*
**MacIntosh, Ebenezer** *231*
**minute men** *241*
**Montgomery, Richard** *219*
**Navigation Acts** *224*
**Neolin** *226*
**Olive Branch Petition** *243*
**Pitt, William** *232*
**Pontiac** *226*
**Proclamation of 1763** *227*
**Quincy, Josiah, Jr.** *237*
**Revere, Paul** *237*

**Schuyler, Philip** *242*
**Sons of Liberty** *231*
**Stamp Act** *229*
**Townshend Acts** *233*
**Washington, George** *241*
**Whig Party** *232*

## Reviewing Chapter 6

1. How did the circulation of people, goods, and ideas between Europe and North America help lead to the American Revolution?
2. Compare the consequences of British and Spanish imperial reforms in the mid-1700s.

## Further Reading

Armitage, David. *The Declaration of Independence: A Global History.* Cambridge: Harvard University Press, 2007. This excellent, short book examines the global influences on the Declaration of Independence and how the Declaration has influenced other countries' independence movements ever since. The volume also contains copies of various declarations of independence from around the world from 1776 to 1993.

Breen, T. H. *The Marketplace of Revolution: How Consumer Politics Shaped American Independence.* New York: Oxford University Press, 2004. Breen argues that American colonists forged a shared identity as consumers that empowered them and led to their political organization during the imperial crisis.

Elliott, J. H. *Empires of the Atlantic World: Britain and Spain in America, 1492–1830.* New Haven: Yale University Press, 2006. This sweeping history contrasts the development of the British and Spanish colonies in North America over the course of more than 300 years. Elliott's book provides a good basis to compare how England and Spain dealt with resistance in the 1760s differently.

Fenn, Elizabeth. "Biological Warfare in Eighteenth-Century North America: Beyond Jeffrey Amherst." *Journal of American History* 86 (March 2000): 1552–1580. This important article examines the claims that British general Jeffrey Amherst intentionally traded smallpox-infected items with Pontiac's warriors and places the act in the context of other acts of germ warfare in the 18th century.

Young, Alfred F. *The Shoemaker and the Tea Party.* Boston: Beacon Press, 1999. Young traces the life story of shoemaker George Robert Twelves Hewes, who participated in the Boston Tea Party, and looks at how his memories of resistance and revolution shaped history into the 1830s. Young also charts the history of the term "Boston Tea Party," and looks at what the term tells us about the use of historical memory in U.S. culture.

# Visual Review

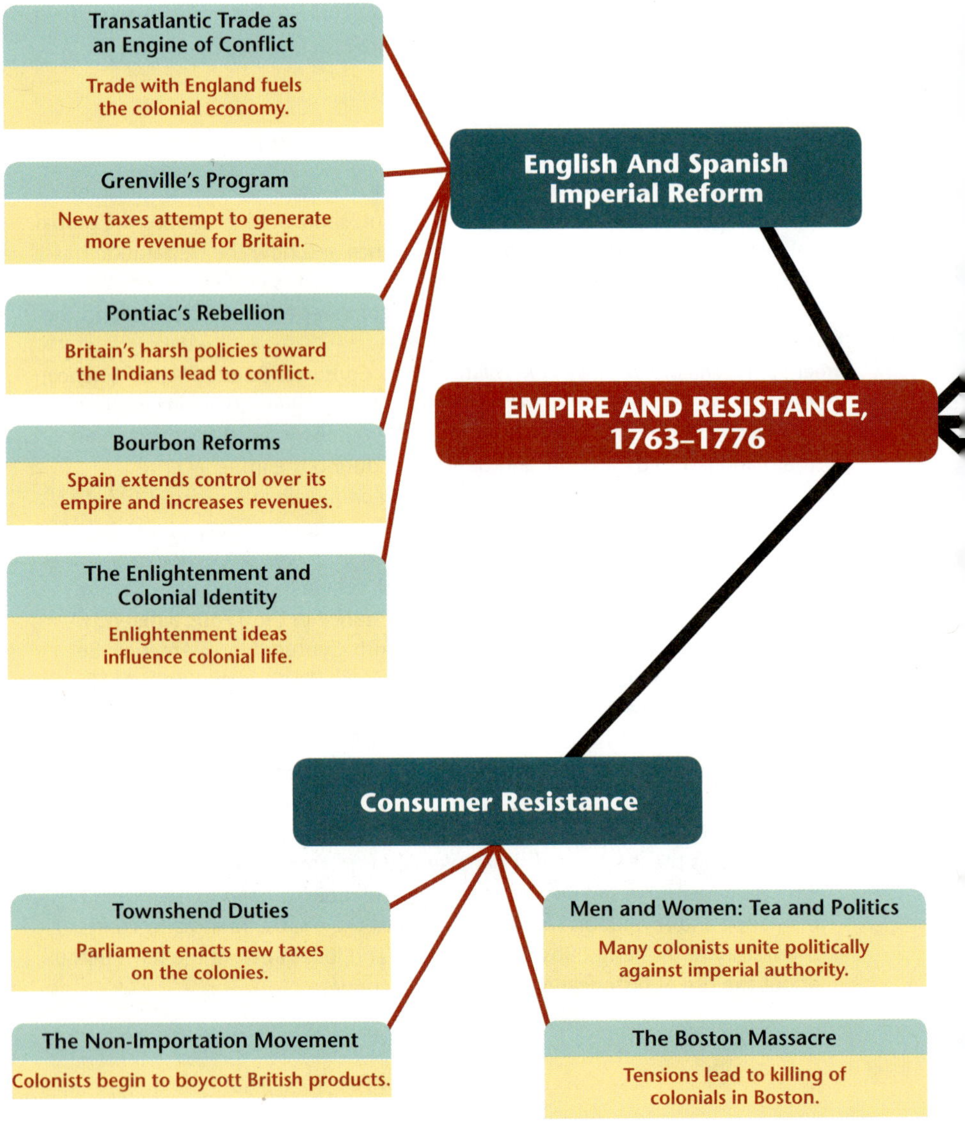

**EMPIRE AND RESISTANCE, 1763–1776**

## English And Spanish Imperial Reform

**Transatlantic Trade as an Engine of Conflict**
Trade with England fuels the colonial economy.

**Grenville's Program**
New taxes attempt to generate more revenue for Britain.

**Pontiac's Rebellion**
Britain's harsh policies toward the Indians lead to conflict.

**Bourbon Reforms**
Spain extends control over its empire and increases revenues.

**The Enlightenment and Colonial Identity**
Enlightenment ideas influence colonial life.

## Consumer Resistance

**Townshend Duties**
Parliament enacts new taxes on the colonies.

**The Non-Importation Movement**
Colonists begin to boycott British products.

**Men and Women: Tea and Politics**
Many colonists unite politically against imperial authority.

**The Boston Massacre**
Tensions lead to killing of colonials in Boston.

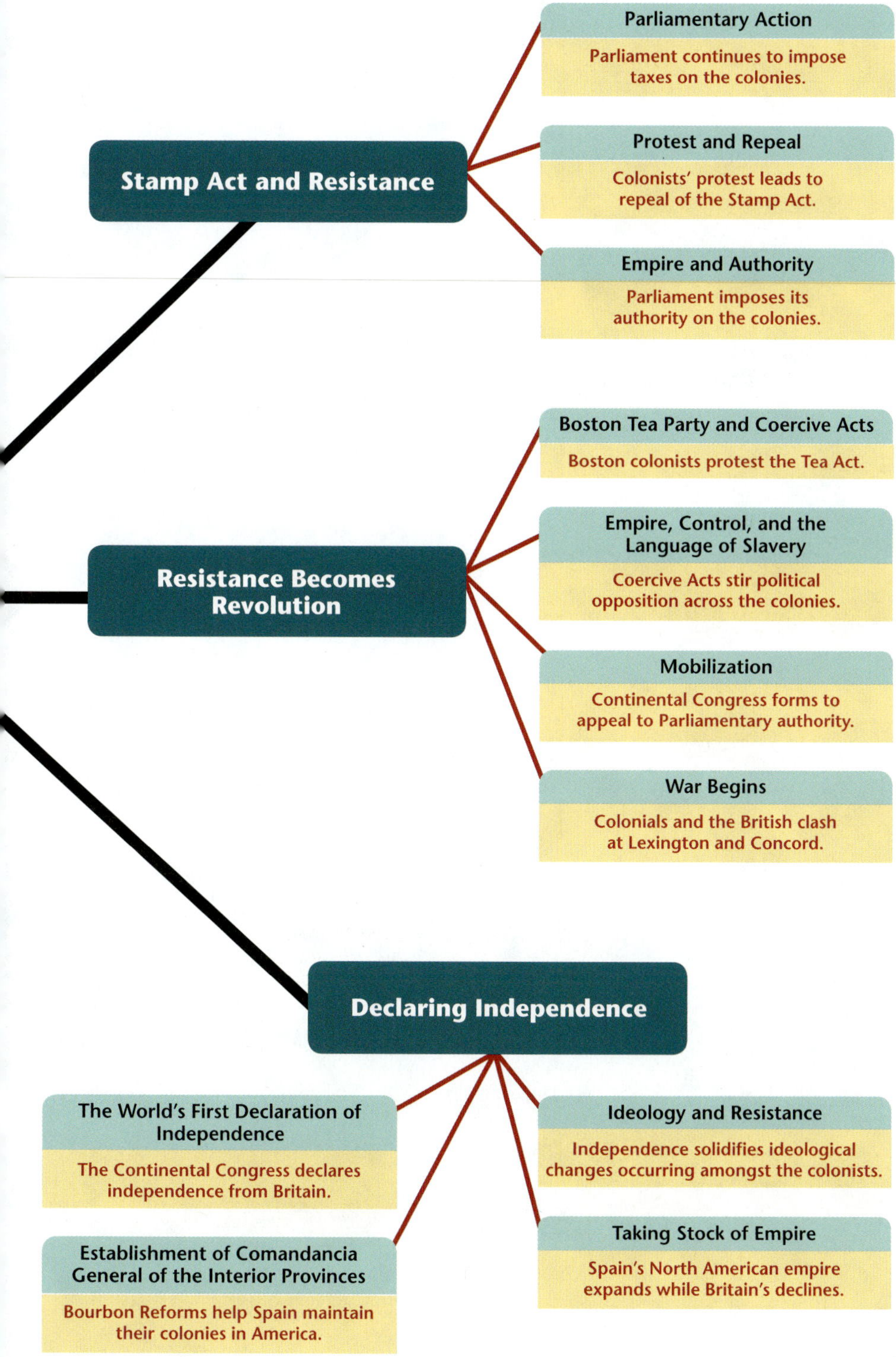

## Stamp Act and Resistance

**Parliamentary Action**
Parliament continues to impose taxes on the colonies.

**Protest and Repeal**
Colonists' protest leads to repeal of the Stamp Act.

**Empire and Authority**
Parliament imposes its authority on the colonies.

## Resistance Becomes Revolution

**Boston Tea Party and Coercive Acts**
Boston colonists protest the Tea Act.

**Empire, Control, and the Language of Slavery**
Coercive Acts stir political opposition across the colonies.

**Mobilization**
Continental Congress forms to appeal to Parliamentary authority.

**War Begins**
Colonials and the British clash at Lexington and Concord.

## Declaring Independence

**The World's First Declaration of Independence**
The Continental Congress declares independence from Britain.

**Establishment of Comandancia General of the Interior Provinces**
Bourbon Reforms help Spain maintain their colonies in America.

**Ideology and Resistance**
Independence solidifies ideological changes occurring amongst the colonists.

**Taking Stock of Empire**
Spain's North American empire expands while Britain's declines.

# 7 A Revolutionary Nation

## 1776–1789

When Benjamin Franklin arrived in Paris on December 21, 1776, thousands of people turned out to catch a glimpse of him. Franklin was visiting to court French assistance for the American fight against Great Britain, France's traditional enemy. Franklin hoped to convince the French to support the American Revolution, because, as he declared,"' Tis a Common observation here that our Cause is the *Cause of all Mankind*; and that we are fighting for their liberty in defending our own." French king Louis XVI was not sure that he wanted to support the Americans in their Revolution, nor was he, as Europe's most absolutist king, convinced that French "liberty" was at stake. But Franklin's personal popularity grew so quickly by the beginning of 1777 that the French government could not ignore American diplomacy.

Franklin was the most famous American in Europe. His scientific experiments and publications had endeared him to French aristocrats and intellectuals, particularly to *philosophes* (Enlightenment philosophers) like Voltaire and Rousseau and to the physiocrats who were interested in economic philosophy. The Comte de Chaumont invited Franklin to live at his estate just outside Paris, and fashionable aristocrats sought Franklin as a party guest. Franklin dressed simply and often wore a fur hat to project a rugged American image. Franklin's face appeared on paintings, engravings, statues, jewelry, candy boxes, dishes, and handkerchiefs. Franklin wrote his daughter that "your father's face [is] as well known as that of the moon." John Adams later wrote that "There was scarcely a peasant or a citizen,

*George Washington*, 1780 by Charles Willson Peale, c. 1779–1781

**CHAPTER OUTLINE**



*continued on page 257*

# America in the World

The U.S. Constitution established a democratic example for the world (1789).

The Articles of Confederation legally established the United States, facilitating resistance to Britain (1777).

To all to whom

The state supreme court declared slavery unconstitutional in New Hampshire, an early abolitionist victory (1783).

U.S. event that influenced the world

International event that influenced the United States

Event with multinational influence

Conflict

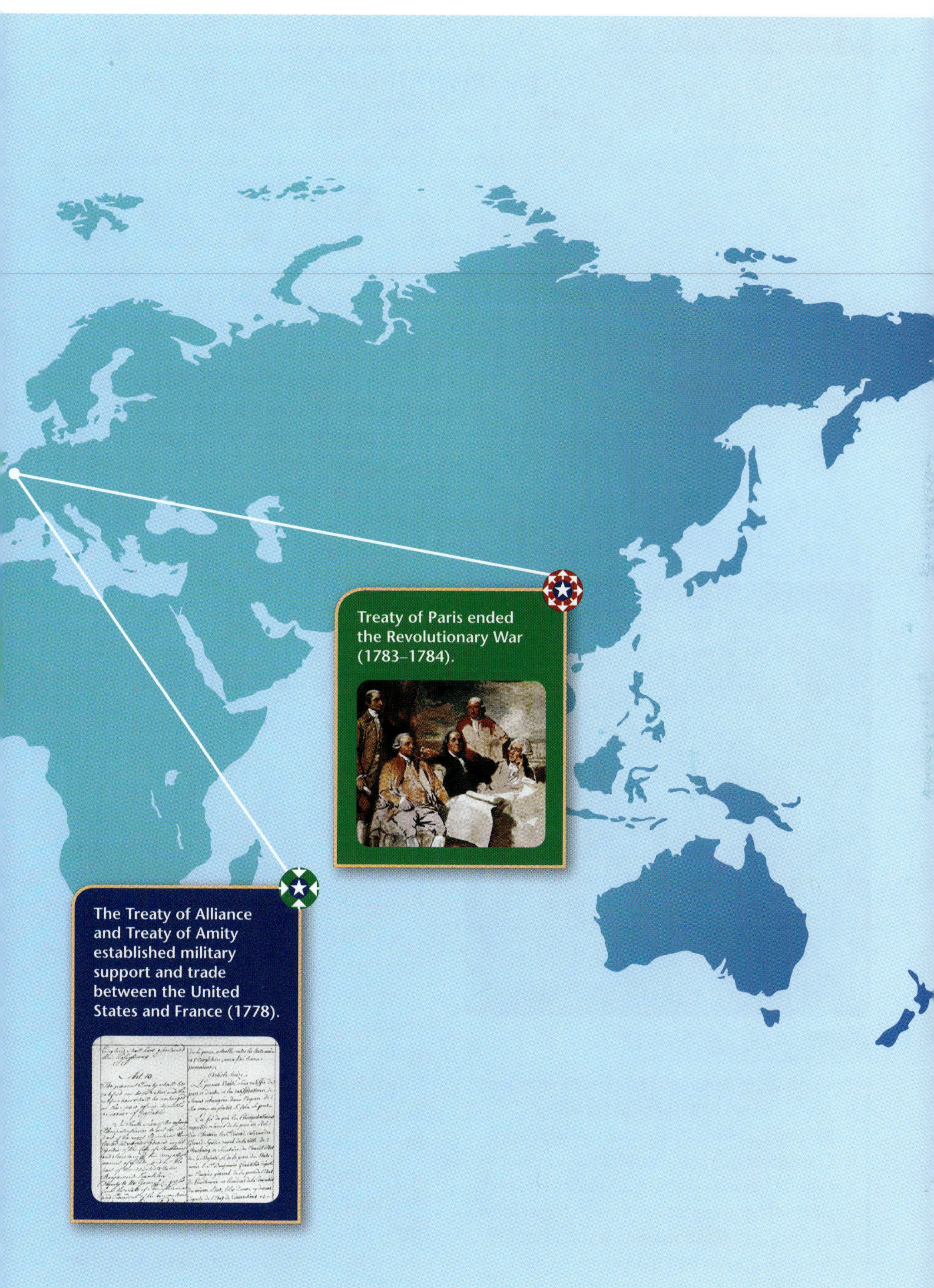
Treaty of Paris ended the Revolutionary War (1783–1784).
The Treaty of Alliance and Treaty of Amity established military support and trade between the United States and France (1778).

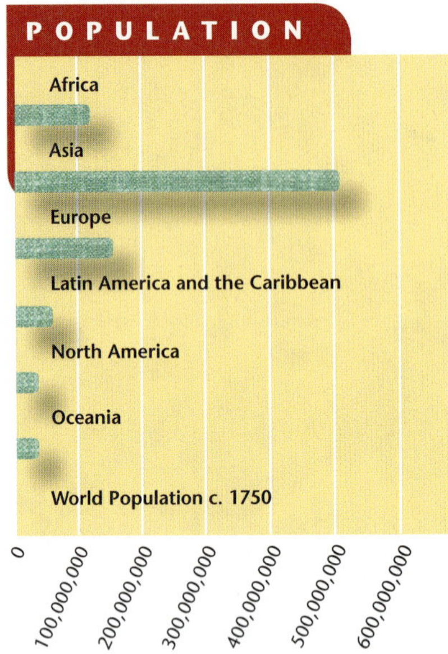


a valet de chambre, coachman or footman, a lady's chambermaid nor a scullion in the kitchen who was not familiar with Franklin's name."

Franklin left the United States for France just a few months after signing the Declaration of Independence and with the experience of having lived for almost 20 years in Britain, representing colonial interests to the British crown. This about-face represents the American feeling that they had to use any method they could to gain foreign assistance for the Revolutionary War, even as France and other European powers waited to see whether Americans could win. Between 1776 and 1789, the United States relied on foreign help as it secured its independence from Great Britain and struggled to form stable state and national governments. But Americans, like Franklin, also believed that their Revolution offered a new vision of liberty to the rest of the world.

This portrait of Benjamin Franklin, commissioned by the American Philosophical Society in 1789, depicts him as a learned man of science. Documents about and pieces of his invention—the lightening rod—lie on the table before him, as a bolt of lightning strikes outside his window. Franklin's scientific knowledge was one of the bases of his great international reputation.

## THE REVOLUTION TAKES ROOT

Following the Declaration of Independence in 1776, the United States became a sovereign nation, and each of the 13 states also established new forms of revolutionary government. The Declaration stated that it had become necessary for "one people to dissolve the political bands which have connected them with another," but in reality many loyalists, Quakers, royal officials, and other American inhabitants did not cut ties to Britain or express instantaneous allegiance to the new United States. The new nation would have to exert authority over these doubters, but it might never get that chance if it could not win the ongoing war with Great Britain. The United States faced five more years of warfare and the challenge of convincing the rest of the world that it was capable of governing itself and worthy of recognition.



## Ideology and Transatlantic Politics

The American revolutionaries expressed a set of political and social values that gave meaning to their actions. In their writings and in the state and national governments they established, patriots expressed an ideology of republicanism, which mixed classical Roman governmental ideals with the values from the European Enlightenment.

American revolutionaries rejected monarchy and established themselves as citizens of a representative republic. Republicanism emphasized liberty and guarded against any tyrannical exercise of governmental power—such as the colonists perceived in the conflict with Britain leading up to the Revolutionary War. James Madison wrote after the Revolutionary War that "we may define a republic to be . . . a government which derives all its powers directly or indirectly from the body of the people." But republicanism meant more than just a form of government, since it also implied much about how citizens should relate to one another and to the forms of power in society. Revolutionaries believed that in order for a voluntary republic to flourish, its citizens must show civic virtue, a disinterested care for the common good. Ideally, instead of being governed by hereditary aristocracy and patronage, as one revolutionary put it, "all offices lie open to men of merit, of whatever rank or condition."

Because of their belief in republicanism, many American revolutionaries also believed that the future worldwide cause of liberty and the happiness of "the great family of mankind" rested on the success of their movement. This belief in their own role in world history put some revolutionaries in an awkward situation, since they still had to gain European support for the war against Great Britain. John Adams, the Massachusetts politician who was sent to Europe as a diplomat and to negotiate foreign loans, firmly believed that America, as the depository of republican virtue, faced political danger in dealing with European monarchies. Adams desired good commercial and diplomatic relations with France, the Netherlands, and Spain, but he feared that "America has been the Sport of European Wars and Politicks long enough." Americans were in the paradoxical situation of needing help from European monarchs to win their own antimonarchical war—and thereby to guarantee the existence of their republic, which they believed could transform the world.

## Trying Times: War Continues

Both British and American military commanders exercised caution in their approach to the Revolutionary War between 1776 and 1778. As a result, neither side gained a distinct strategic advantage. Each side won important battles, but neither was willing or able to attempt to inflict a crushing defeat on the other. As long as the revolutionary spirit and independence movement survived, it would take a monumental British effort to make the United States lose the war. The revolutionaries, although they enjoyed the support of about 70 percent of the white population in America, could not be assured of a victory.

Briefly turning his attention south, British army commander **Sir William Howe** ordered his forces to evacuate Boston in March 1776. Nine British warships bearing seven regiments of soldiers, commanded by General **Lord Cornwallis**, arrived off the coast of South Carolina. There they joined **Sir Henry Clinton**'s forces in an attack on Charleston that revolutionaries narrowly rebuffed at the Battle of Sullivan's Island on June 28, 1776. British naval forces commanded by Admiral Sir Peter Parker sailed back north—headed for New York and Halifax.

In September 1776 William Howe and his brother Admiral **Sir Richard Howe** used their 32,000 British and German mercenary troops—dubbed "Hessians" by the Americans—to launch an attack against American commander General George Washington's forces at Long Island. The Howes' forces defeated the American army and militia troops in a series of battles stretching from Brooklyn Heights to White Plains, New York, through the fall. Although missing several chances to destroy the Americans, they managed to occupy New York City for the rest of the war. General Cornwallis's force chased Washington across New Jersey. Then, in the first week of December, Washington fled with his troops into Pennsylvania. Cornwallis left Hessian troops to watch the Americans across the Delaware, and returned to New York to go into winter quarters.

Thomas Paine correctly described the American military predicament when he declared in his pamphlet *The Crisis* on December 19, 1776, that "these are the times that try men's souls." Washington, who had received some state militia reinforcements, decided to cross the Delaware again and launch a surprise attack on the Hessian camp at Trenton, New Jersey, late on Christmas night. The unconventional attack was successful, but also seemed to confirm that Washington was most successful when he avoided open European-style battles. Washington's victory at the Battle of Trenton, which he followed with a victory over some of Cornwallis's forces at the Battle of Princeton on January 3, 1777, represented two of his few early successes.

General Washington had trouble taking advantage of the successes at Princeton and Trenton. American forces were plagued by spotty militia performance, expiring enlistments, and severe conflict with local loyalists.

In the fall of 1777, Washington tried to defend the U.S. capital at Philadelphia, but Howe defeated him in a series of battles in and around Brandywine, Pennsylvania. Washington's force survived, but it was not clear whether American troops could beat the British in open battle. Congress was forced to flee Philadelphia, which Howe occupied in September. After losing a close contest at Germantown on October 4, Washington retreated and prepared to enter winter quarters at Valley Forge, Pennsylvania.

▲ **Map 7.1**

**Major Revolutionary War Battles, 1775–1778** This map shows the locations of major battles in the first four years of the Revolutionary War and also depicts areas of particular loyalist and patriot strength.

Further north, the British government sent Major General John Burgoyne in early 1777 to Canada with another plan to invade New England and recapture Fort Ticonderoga. His mixed force of British, Hessian, Canadian militia, Loyalist, and Indian troops made slow progress after capturing Fort Ticonderoga at the beginning of July. American commander Major General **Horatio Gates** dealt Burgoyne's troops a blow at Freeman's Farm on the Hudson River in September. After receiving reinforcements, Gates won an even bigger battle at Saratoga, New York, on October 7, forcing Burgoyne to surrender his entire 6,000-man army to Gates, who had proved that American forces could inflict decisive defeat. Victory in the battle of Saratoga was one of the most significant moments in the entire Revolutionary War.

## Alliance with France

The Battle of Saratoga was the turning point of the Revolutionary War because it helped to convince France to form an alliance with the United States. The French foreign minister, the **Comte de Vergennes**, had authorized secret aid to the American revolutionaries since May 1776. Sympathetic aristocrats and merchants sent money and supplies. The playwright Caron de Beaumarchais, for example, set up the trade company Hortalez & Cie. to secretly funnel aid to the United States. From 1776 onward, the French supplied over 90 percent of the gunpowder used by the American military. Vergennes personally wanted to ally with the United States, but he had not been able to build political support for the move. Now, the news of the decisive American victory at Saratoga gave Vergennes all he needed to support the United States openly against France's enemy, Great Britain. Spain continued to drag its feet, but the French moved forward with an alliance.

The French government granted the United States diplomatic recognition at the end of 1777. In February 1778, France and the United States signed a Treaty of Amity and Commerce and a Treaty of Alliance, in which France promised "not to lay down their arms until the Independence of the United States shall have been formally or tacitly assured." Congress ratified both treaties on May 4, 1778, creating the first diplomatic alliance in American history. In April 1778, the **Comte d'Estaing** sailed for America with a fleet of 16 French warships and 4,000 troops. Early in 1778, George Washington despaired that the American military was in a "distressed, ruinous, and deplorable condition," and he feared defeat "if a remedy is not soon applied." Patriots hoped that French aid would bring just such a remedy.

### STUDY QUESTIONS FOR THE REVOLUTION TAKES ROOT

1. **In what ways did the battle of Saratoga represent a key turning point in the Revolutionary War?**
2. **Why did the American revolutionaries have to seek and accept aid from European monarchies?**

# THE STRUCTURE OF AUTHORITY

One cause of George Washington's despair over future prospects was the uncertain and unstable organization of the American government and military—which French aid could only partially address. While winning a war, the United States had to build an effective governmental structure. The Second Continental Congress had directed the early operations of the war and had declared independence from Great Britain, but by the time it ratified the treaty with France, it still operated under no formal constitutional authority. It took the Congress more than 16 months to draft the **Articles of Confederation** and several more years for all the states to ratify it. Although the Continental Army expressed clear allegiance to civilian Congressional authority, it had its own internal organizational difficulties—especially regarding supply and the coordination of army and militia forces and enlistments. Even though many states were better organized, what would determine their relationship to one another and to Congress?

## State Governments

In May 1776, even before the Continental Congress adopted the Declaration of Independence, it instructed individual colonies to begin drafting state constitutions. Whigs, who had been governing in practice without constitutional authority in many colonies, and who had been directing some war operations, decided to focus their energies on written constitutions that would define state power. In many cases, state constitutions as written documents (different from the unwritten British constitution), grew out of royal charters and other colonial decrees. By the end of 1776, 11 of 13 states had all drafted state constitutions, and Georgia and New York completed theirs the following year.

Every state established itself as a representative republic that derived sovereignty from the people, who would demonstrate their consent through voting. Each state established a balance between executive, legislative, and judicial powers, in keeping with the political idea of **separation of powers** articulated by the French Enlightenment philosopher the Baron de Montesquieu. Most states kept a judicial system similar to their colonial structures. Having cast off colonial governors who represented royal authority, however, most states limited the power of state governors and established advising governor's councils that were appointed by the elected legislatures. Many states also implemented term limits and frequent elections for their governors. Almost every state established a two-house legislature, with a Roman-style senate that could act as a brake on any "excessively" democratic actions taken by the lower house. Some states enlarged their legislatures, to grant more representation to western areas that were filling up with settlers, and five states directly tied representation to population size, a very new concept. All states except for Massachusetts and Connecticut abolished established state religions, although most still required government office holders to be Christian.

Despite similarities, some states were clearly more democratic than others. Pennsylvania had no governor at all and established a unicameral legislature with strict term limits that proportionally represented the population and was elected by all free men over 21 who paid taxes. Maryland's revolutionary planter elites defined a government in which only the lower house of the legislature was popularly elected, with a powerful governor, and that had high property-holding qualifications for officeholders, who served long terms. In all the states, even the least democratic, new ranks of men such as artisans began to assume offices and responsibilities that would never have fallen to them in the stricter hierarchical days of colonial government.

## Articles of Confederation

Soon after declaring independence, Congress realized that it needed to form a legitimate national government. A committee charged with the task of creating a national constitution delivered a draft of the Articles of Confederation to Congress in 1777, although deep disagreements among the states delayed full ratification until four years later. The Articles proposed a national government for "The United States of America," but it was a very weak government.

As North Carolina Congressman Thomas Burke wrote, "the United States ought to be as One Sovereign with respect to foreign Powers, in all things that relate to War or where the States have one Common Interest." The Articles limited centralized power and reserved decision making in most other areas to the states. Congress had no power to tax citizens of the states, which contributed to severe national financial problems. Congress controlled the military and the war-making power, but the Articles directly forbade the sustaining of a military force once the war ended. Each state exercised one collective vote under the Articles, and to change most national policies required nine votes out of thirteen. Only a unanimous vote could change any provision of the actual Articles.

## Military Organization

One of the most important parts of the traditional limiting of power in republican society was the restraint of the military power and its subordination to civilian authority. When the first Continental Congress authorized the creation of the Continental Army in June of 1775, commissioned officers, and appointed George Washington as commander in chief, it built in several weaknesses to prevent the military from assuming too much power in society. Americans viewed militias, in the words of the Virginia constitution, as "the proper, natural, and safe defense of a free state." But militias could never be effective enough to win a war against the British military, so the United States had to create an army and a navy.

Congress initially restricted enlistments in the Continental Army to one year, but after problems recruiting new men became apparent, Congress authorized three-year terms and began to pay enlistment bounties in 1777. By 1779, Congress allowed men to enlist for the duration of the war and paid bounties as high as $200. Before 1777, Continental officers recruited their own men, but after that date, Congress imposed recruiting quotas on each state, and states relied on conscripts and militia forces to fill the army ranks. Historians estimate the number of American men in arms during the Revolution at between 250,000 and 350,000, at least 10 percent of the total American population.

Volunteer state militias provided men to the Continental Army, but they also continued to fight alongside army forces throughout the war. While militia units were often less disciplined and less organized in battle, they did contribute to troop strength and success, especially after the war turned south after 1778. Militia forces' volunteer status was supposed to restrain military authority and connect the military to revolutionary values. Many men who enlisted in the revolutionary military, especially at the beginning of the war, expressed a strong allegiance to the revolutionary cause, but economic incentives—wages and enlistment bounties—also influenced the decision to join the Continental Army. The average soldier was in his late twenties. European officers serving with the Continental Army marveled at the success of common men, like shoemakers, who became American officers.

The Continental Congress oversaw military affairs using a series of executive committees, but Congress also granted George Washington "full, ample, and complete" powers to direct the army as he saw fit. Both enlisted men and officers suffered from Congress' inability to guarantee adequate supplies to military forces. Congress lacked funds, struggled with guaranteeing food and shoes to troops, and did not provide consistent uniforms until 1781. During the brutal winter of 1777–1778, one quarter

This painting of the Continental encampment at Valley Forge in the winter of 1777–1778 shows the bleak challenge faced by the soldiers living there. Twelve thousand men were stationed at Valley Forge, where they faced near starvation, disease, and terribly cold weather. Thousands died of pneumonia and typhoid fever, and thousands more were listed as "unfit for service."

GLOBAL PASSAGES

## International Officers in the American Revolutionary Military

For some in Europe, the financial and military support provided by their governments was not enough to help the American cause. Many European military men volunteered to join the American military directly as officers. These international military volunteers brought with them a range of advantages: connections to politicians and military establishments in Europe, personal financial resources, military skill, and knowledge. Several noted American officers, like Richard Montgomery and **John Paul Jones**, were born in Britain. But officers from Continental Europe further enhanced the cache of the American military forces and increased international approval for the American Revolution. As the lead American diplomat in France, Benjamin Franklin actively recruited Europeans to join the Continental Army. As most European officers were drawn from the aristocracy, Franklin's personal popularity among the upper crust proved useful in that regard. Several of these men proved to be vital to the American war effort.

**Tadeusz Kosciuszko**, a graduate of the Polish Royal School and the French school of engineering and artillery. He was commissioned as colonel of engineers in 1776 and played a key role in designing the fortifications at West Point and entrenchments at Saratoga. Kosciuszko served out the war, and was made a brigadier general in 1783. Also important to American engineering was Chevalier **Louis Duportail**, who served most of the war as a brigadier general and chief of army engineers. Benjamin Franklin recruited **Friedrich Wilhelm von Steuben**, an impoverished former Prussian staff officer who became inspector general of the Continental Army during the winter at Valley Forge, where he drilled American troops into shape. He

of the 10,000 American soldiers who wintered at Valley Forge, Pennsylvania, died, partly because of poor food and shelter. Some judged the winter encampment of 1780 at Morristown, New Jersey, to be even worse. Hard conditions made it all the more remarkable that the mutiny of the Pennsylvania line in January 1780 marked one of the only large-scale troop revolts of the war.

## Diplomacy and International Finance

Foreign credit was the main engine of war finance. The United States sent a series of envoys to European countries, particularly Britain's rivals, seeking recognition and funding, which would prove vital to the cause. France, Spain, and the Netherlands all sought was one of Washington's most effective aids. Less effective was **Casimir Pulaski**, a Pole who commanded American cavalry and later his own elite corps as a brigadier general in the Continental Army until he was killed in 1779.

The most famous French volunteer, **Marie-Joseph-Paul-Yves-Roch-Gilbert du Motier, Marquis de Lafayette**, joined the American cause when he was only 19 years old along with his friend, the highly capable Johan de Kalb (who was also a French spy) in 1777. Both men were commissioned majors general. Lafayette fought ably, returned to France for a year to gather French government support before rejoining the Americans, and played a major role in the defeat of Cornwallis at Yorktown in 1781.

Many of the foreign officers in the Continental Army who were not killed during the war (as de Kalb and Pulaski were) participated in revolutionary and independence movements in Europe in subsequent decades. Although aristocrats, Lafayette, Duportail, and other French supporters of the American cause joined the French Revolution when it began in 1789. Most of them were later persecuted in the Revolution's more radical phase, including Lafayette, who was imprisoned by French forces in Austria. Kosciuszko led several campaigns in the Polish independence movement against Russia during the 1790s. Lafayette and von Steuben were given American citizenship and land grants in thanks for their American service. Several European officers, including von Steuben, retired in the United States. Both Kosciuszko and Lafayette returned to the United States after the War, and Lafayette's extended tour in 1824–1825 was one of the largest events commemorating the American Revolution during the first 50 years after the war.

- How might the willingness of these officers to serve in the American military have influenced opinion in Europe in favor of the United States?
- Does the service of men like Lafayette and Kosciuszko in European revolutionary movements indicate that the American Revolution influenced Europe?

to gain advantage over the British by aiding the United States, although they extended aid with varying levels of enthusiasm. The United States could not have continued the war effort without French assistance. Over the course of the war, the French lent the United States approximately $7 million and gave more than $2 million in outright gifts.

Other European countries also took an interest in the war, which German poet Christoph Wieland called "the greatest political event of the 1770s, and perhaps . . . of the entire century." The Spanish had sent some money and supplies but had largely held the United States at arm's length—in part because they did not wish to see colonial independence movements spread into Spanish America. However, Spain declared war on Britain in April 1779. The Spanish governor of Louisiana and East Florida **Bernardo de Gálvez** captured several British forts along the Mississippi River and at Mobile and Pensacola, indirectly helping the American war effort. In January 1780, **John Jay** arrived in Madrid seeking Spanish diplomatic recognition, but the prediction by the French foreign minister that "Spain . . . will interest herself very little in the Americans" proved true. Spain never formally recognized American independence during the war—although the Spanish government did agree to open trade between the United States and Cuba and to loan the United States $170,000. The trade with Cuba was particularly significant, given that it replaced much of the prohibited U.S. trade with the British West Indies and provided the United States access to hard currency.

When the British captured neutral ships from several countries trading with the United States in 1780, Russian empress **Catherine the Great** responded by forming the League of Armed Neutrality to protect neutral shipping, although Russia never formally recognized the United States during the Revolution. Sweden, Denmark, Portugal, the Netherlands, and Sicily all joined the League—tying up British naval resources and attempting to open further U.S. trade. The Dutch were friendliest to the American cause, who had allowed a smuggled arms trade to the revolutionaries since before 1777. A few months after all of the Dutch provinces and Prince William V formally recognized the United States, American envoy John Adams convinced Dutch bankers to loan the United States $2 million in July 1782.

**STUDY QUESTIONS FOR THE STRUCTURE OF AUTHORITY**

1. **What difference did foreign aid make to the American Revolution?**
2. **How did the ideology of republicanism affect government and military authority in the United States during the American Revolution?**

# SECURING INDEPENDENCE

With the French as allies, American revolutionaries had high expectations that the war would be winnable, but the road ahead was not easy. The focus of the military conflict shifted to the seas and into the southern states. Bitter social divisions there helped to intensify the fighting. Loyalists held onto their British identities, even as they were forced to fight their neighbors or leave their homes. African Americans assessed how to maximize their own potential for freedom in the midst of wartime chaos. Indian nations tried to decide whether their future interests lay with the British or the unknown United States. Nothing seemed easy during the last years of the Revolutionary War, but one thing was certain—the United States would cease to exist if it did not win the war.

## War at Sea

The most immediate impact of French assistance came in the naval war. As early as the first year of the war, the United States established a navy and an ambitious shipbuilding program, with several states also fielding their own naval forces. Although

John Paul Jones commanded the USS *Bon Homme Richard*, a warship loaned to the United States by France and named in honor of Benjamin Franklin's *Poor Richard's Almanac*. Jones battled the British ship HMS *Serapis* off the coast of Yorkshire, England, in September 1779, and his capture of the British navy vessel helped to convince the French to increase their support for the naval war against Britain.

the U.S. Navy succeeded in several early small attacks, no American navy could hope to defeat the British Navy—the strongest and best-equipped sea force in the world—that was blockading the northern U.S. coastline. Instead, American ships focused on disrupting British operations and harassing commercial shipping. Captain **Nicholas Biddle**, a former member of the Royal Navy, successfully raided British ships in the West Indies in 1777. Basing his U.S. naval operations in France, former Scotsman Captain John Paul Jones successfully raided the Scottish coastline and the Irish Sea. Jones cemented his reputation in September 1779 when he defeated the British frigate *Serapis* in a thrilling battle, taking the ship as a prize after declaring "I have not yet begun to fight!" During the course of the Revolution, the U.S. government commissioned over 2,000 privateers, which threatened and captured British trade ships and tied up British naval forces.

French entry into the war changed naval combat by diverting British attention away from the main fight in America and forcing them to commit to naval warfare in the English Channel, the Mediterranean, the Caribbean, and off the coast of India to defend their empire. The French concentrated most of their forces on the Caribbean islands that they had lost to the British in the Seven Years' War. The French admiral

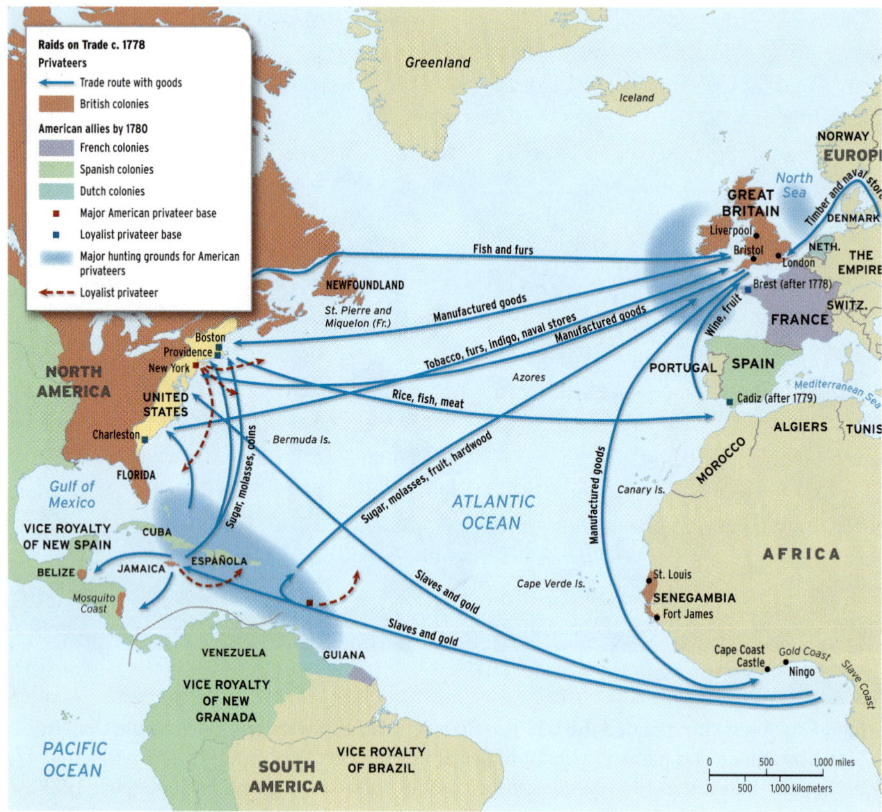


▲ Map 7.2

**Revolutionary War Battles in the Caribbean** Much of the hottest naval warfare in the Revolutionary War took place around the Caribbean, where countries battled to control trade and tried to wrest control of islands away from one another.

Comte d'Estaing arrived with his fleet in the summer of 1778, and after botching an attack on British-controlled Newport, Rhode Island, he sailed for the West Indies. The British captured St. Lucia in December 1778, but the French captured and held the island of Grenada.

With Caribbean battles underway, the French sent naval help to North America. D'Estaing failed to oust the British from Savannah in September 1779. In 1780 and 1781, French naval assistance proved more effective. Commodore **Marquis de Ternay** carried 5,500 French army troops under the Comte de Rochambeau to reinforce the Continental Army in July 1780, and in October 1781, the French admiral **Comte de Grasse** added his fleet to the fight at Yorktown.

## War in the South

Britain's cabinet war ministers, led by **Lord George Germain**, shifted the focus of their ground efforts to the south in 1778. On March 8, 1778, British cabinet officials replaced commander Sir William Howe with Sir Henry Clinton, whom they ordered to abandon Philadelphia to prepare for the naval warfare and attacks on the Carolinas and Georgia. As Clinton tried to evacuate his army from Philadelphia back to New York, he ran up against George Washington's army. In winter quarters at Valley Forge, Washington's troops had suffered from bad weather and a lack of food and clothing, but they had also been strengthened by the training and drill offered by the new inspector general of the army, the Baron von Steuben. U.S. and British forces clashed at Monmouth, New Jersey, on June 28, 1778, and although Clinton's army escaped, only a poor performance from Washington's second-in-command Charles Lee kept the Americans from crushing the British Army.

The South saw much of the worst fighting between patriots and loyalists of the entire war. The British invaded Georgia, and easily captured Savannah in December 1778. Support from loyalists, thousands of runaway slaves, and some Cherokees helped subdue the patriot civilian population, and the British were able to recapture the Georgia state government. The patriot defeat in South Carolina was even more disastrous. The British sent forces over land to surround Charleston, and British Generals Clinton and Cornwallis fought "storm, rain, hail, snow, and . . . waves" to sail to Charleston with additional troops. They bottled up American commander Major General **Benjamin Lincoln** in the City of Charleston, and Lincoln was forced to surrender the city and his entire army on May 12, 1780. Clinton returned to New York, and he left Cornwallis in charge of putting down further resistance in South Carolina and pushing into North Carolina. In the following months, the backcountry of South Carolina witnessed brutal clashes between loyalist/British detachments and patriot militias. In 1780 British lieutenant colonel **Banastre Tarleton** acquired a bloody reputation by destroying property, killing prisoners, and keeping the rebels off balance.

Without consulting General Washington, and against his wishes, Congress appointed Horatio Gates to command the Continental Army's Southern Department. Gates's command proved disastrous when he dispatched a small force to Camden, South Carolina, without properly positioning his militia support or assessing the opposing forces. Cornwallis crushed the Americans at Camden, and they retreated in disarray. Gates himself rode as fast as he could all the way to Hillsboro, North Carolina. But the bitter defeat did little to change the course of the war, as rural skirmishes persisted and Cornwallis continued to wait for his expected mass uprising of loyalists. Instead, many white southerners began to support the Americans out of anger when the British shielded runaway slaves.

After Camden, Congress removed Gates from command and replaced him with Nathanael Greene, who had been Washington's first choice for a southern commander and was probably the finest strategist in the American military. Although his army was in poor shape, Greene took heart from the victory of American militia forces at Kings Mountain, South Carolina, on October 7. Greene divided his army into four parts and kept British and loyalist forces on the run through the Carolina backcountry. Greene, and his able sub-commander **Daniel Morgan**, who bested Tarleton at Cowpens in January 1781, engaged Cornwallis in three open battles that year at Guilford Courthouse, Hobkirk's Hill, and Eutaw Springs. The Americans lost all three battles, but they inflicted terrible damage on Cornwallis's combined forces. Greene's strategy

▲ **Map 7.3**

**Major Revolutionary War Battles, 1779–1783** Although the Revolutionary War was mostly concluded after Cornwallis's surrender at Yorktown in 1781, skirmishing continued until the Treaty of Paris in 1783 ended the conflict.

inflicted some of the heaviest casualties of the war on Cornwallis, who moved into Virginia and marched toward Yorktown.

## Loyalists: Resistance and Migration

The loyalist population on the whole played a large role in the British war effort. Loyalists, dubbed "Tories" by the revolutionaries, made up almost 20 percent of the total population of the United States during the war. Loyalists expressed different notions of "liberty" than those put forth by the revolutionaries, and they held onto British colonial identity and notions of obedience in the midst of conflict. Several ethnic or religious minority groups who relied on crown protection remained loyal, although they did not constitute a majority in any state: Germans in the Mid-Atlantic, Anglicans in New England, landholders in the Hudson Valley, Scotch-Irish immigrants in the southern backcountry, and Dutch settlers in New Jersey.

Estimates of the number of loyalists who fled the United States for England, Canada, and the West Indies during and immediately after the war reach as high as 80,000, or 1 out of every 40 people in the United States. Many who emigrated were wealthy before the war, and loyalists had millions of dollars' worth of land and personal property seized by states and by Congress. An estimated additional 20,000 African American slaves ran away from their masters and sought British protection during the war, including some who emigrated to Canada, Nova Scotia, and Sierra Leone after the war. White and black loyalists who resettled in other parts of the British Empire sometimes helped to shore up imperial control, but they also faced inconsistent treatment. Black emigrants to Canada achieved freedom, but many slaves who took the British up on their offer of protection and freedom were instead re-enslaved in the West Indies.

Loyalists found it difficult to return to their former homes—even after the war ended. Even groups who were merely ambivalent about the war and tried to remain neutral, such as Pennsylvania Quakers who objected because of their religion, found it difficult to reintegrate into American society.

## Indian Warfare

Indian populations in North America were also torn apart by the Revolutionary War. It seemed as though the United States might be even less generous toward Indians than Great Britain had been, but not all Indian peoples aligned themselves with the British. Religion, trade, political calculations, and personal relationships influenced which way Indian peoples cast their support, and divisions existed, even within tight-knit kinship groups. Some native peoples also used the Revolution as an opportunity to try and advance their own regional interests, such as when **Joseph Brant** led Mohawk and other Iroquois troops against Pennsylvania and New York frontier settlers in the "Border War" of 1777–1779. The Iroquois attacks, particularly on the Wyoming Valley, Pennsylvania, were long remembered for their brutal force.

Brant, a respected commander, could not unite the powerful Six Nations entirely in favor of the British. Some Oneida and Tuscarora peoples in New England joined the American army at Valley Forge. The Oneida played a decisive role in the American victory at the Battle of Oriskany in 1777. By the end of the war, most other Iroquois groups had joined Brant in his support for the British, especially after American major general John Sullivan pursued a scorched-earth campaign against them in New York in the summer of 1779.

The United States was not as generous to many Indian groups who offered their support, notably pushing the Delaware into the arms of the British after failing to follow the terms of an alliance signed at Pittsburgh in 1778. Other Delaware who refused to take sides were forced to abandon their lands in Ohio. The Shawnee tried to remain neutral, but by the time the war was over many Shawnee warriors fought for the British in an attempt to hold onto Ohio frontier lands. American troops attacked Cherokee lands in 1776, 1780, and 1781, and many Cherokee aligned themselves with loyalist militias in the brutal fighting in the Carolinas and Georgia in 1780 and 1781.

## African Americans at War

Like Indians, not all African Americans adopted the same stance toward the Revolutionary War. But those men who were able to participate—either on the American or the British side—often managed to change their social status as a result. African Americans constituted a small but significant percentage of Revolutionary fighters on land and water, and in some battles—such as the 1778 battle at Monmouth, New Jersey—black men fought on both sides.

▲ This painting depicts the British surrender at the Battle of Yorktown in 1781, the last major campaign of the Revolutionary War. In the image, American General Benjamin Lincoln accepts the sword of surrender from British General Cornwallis's subordinate officer. Artist John Trumbull painted a larger version of this image inside the rotunda of the U.S. Capital building.

African American men served in the British infantry and navy, and many runaway slaves worked as spies and laborers for British forces. Some African Americans who fled colonial masters to join the British military were freed from slavery and resettled in Canada after the war. Others who were re-enslaved in the West Indies continued their military service by becoming part of the British West Indian Regiments that fought in the Napoleonic Wars in the 1790s.

Service in the American military often presented a path to personal freedom, and many black men and women did support the patriot cause from its beginning. Although George Washington initially banned blacks from the Continental Army, the need for troops forced him to abandon this policy within months, and in some areas black men made up as much as 25 percent of American fighting forces. Many slaves from northern states enlisted, and their state governments sometimes purchased their freedom from their masters, whom they replaced in service. Some, like the Concord, Massachusetts, slave Richard Hobby, joined the American military when their masters were away from home. Even in southern states, some slaves and many free black men enlisted in the American army and militias. Both Massachusetts and Rhode Island set up separate, black militia units, but for the most part black and white men served together in integrated companies. Black Revolutionary War veterans would also help aid the antislavery cause after the war.

## Peace and Shifting Empires

The final phase of the Revolutionary War began when British general Cornwallis entrenched his troops in Yorktown, Virginia, in August 1781. General Washington learned of Cornwallis's move and realized that Yorktown's position on the Chesapeake Bay made it vulnerable. He also learned that the Comte de Grasse would soon arrive with his French squadron. So Washington boldly marched almost his whole army, accompanied by French forces under the Comte de Rochambeau, from New York to Virginia to link up with Nathanael Greene's southern troops. By the end of September, the American forces surrounded Yorktown and laid siege to Cornwallis's force. For almost two weeks, the American and French forces pounded Cornwallis's men with artillery fire and pushed them back toward the Chesapeake coast with carefully executed skirmishes. Under increasing pressure, Cornwallis realized he had no escape, and on October 19, 1781, he had a subordinate, General Charles O'Hara, surrender his entire army.

When British prime minister Lord North heard the news of Yorktown, he reportedly exclaimed, "Oh God! It is all over!" The British government decided to pursue peace negotiations. A preliminary peace agreement was concluded in Paris in November 1782 without any input from French officials. Although French foreign minister Vergennes had no hand in the negotiations, he was impressed with the Americans' diplomacy, and he negotiated a separate peace with Britain and convinced the Spanish to do the same. The Netherlands also concluded a separate treaty. American negotiators Franklin, John Jay, John Adams, and **Henry Laurens** successfully played French and British interests against one another when they concluded final negotiations with Britain and signed the final Treaty of Paris on September 3, 1783.

The terms of the Treaty of Paris were favorable to the United States. The treaty recognized American independence and established borders stretching from the Great Lakes down the Mississippi River to the 31st parallel. Britain granted American fishing rights off Nova Scotia, and Congress agreed to honor all war debts, to restore confiscated loyalist property, and to disallow any retribution against British supporters. Britain's Native American allies were incensed that Britain had negotiated away land rights to the United States without consulting or involving them. The British and Americans agreed to free passage on the Mississippi, but the Spanish objected and blocked free trade on the river in 1784. In their separate peace negotiations, France, Spain, and Britain swapped possession of several Caribbean islands, and Britain traded control of East and West Florida to Spain in return for Gibraltar. Although the British dragged their feet enforcing parts of the Treaty of Paris, the agreement nonetheless concluded the first-ever successful colonial war of independence, and guaranteed the existence of the United States of America.

### STUDY QUESTIONS FOR SECURING INDEPENDENCE

1. **How did divisions inside the United States shape the course of the Revolutionary War?**
2. **What were the immediate consequences of the Treaty of Paris?**

# RESTRUCTURING POLITICAL AND SOCIAL AUTHORITY

By winning the Revolutionary War, patriots gained the chance to make their experiment with republican government and their commitment to liberty permanent. But Americans faced obstacles to the peaceful refashioning of power and society. How could loyalists be reintegrated into society? What consequences did republican liberty hold for subordinate people in society? Could the states govern harmoniously and share power with Congress? How would Americans pay the crushing debts incurred during the war? Would economic changes brought on by the war continue as the United States struggled to become successful in commercial trade?

## Power in the States

During the years of demobilization from the Revolutionary War, Congress and the states were still negotiating their power relationships. Under the Articles of Confederation, Congress tried to coordinate national policy, but states exercised great power directly over their citizens. Several states, including Massachusetts, ratified less democratic constitutions in the 1780s. States gradually repealed laws against the return of loyalists, although many loyalists, especially in northern states, never regained all the property they had lost in the war. The southern states generally restricted loyalists less, but a series of debates raged over whether prewar debts owed to wealthy loyalists would have to be honored.

The states all had to deal with political tensions unleashed by what John Jay called the "rage for emigrating to the western country," which sometimes worsened clashes between states. Western inhabitants, many of whom were veterans lured west by land bounties handed out for wartime service or by land investment companies, demanded increased representation of western areas in state legislatures. South Carolina, North Carolina, Georgia, and Virginia all moved their state capitals to towns that lay further west, partly because of the shift in population. States also clashed with one another over rival land claims. Virginia peacefully ceded western territory to Congress in 1784, but border conflicts raged between Pennsylvania and Connecticut and between Pennsylvania and Virginia. New York and New Jersey engaged in an all-out trade war between 1783 and 1787.

The states' massive war debts and their shared national war debt made conflicts over land and representation even more difficult. Congress could not agree on how to finance these debts, but legislation in 1785 promised the states future repayment. Robert Morris, who directed national finances until 1785, wanted the states to grant Congress the power to tax, which would keep debt in national hands and enhance centralized power. But on a national level, the states could not even agree to grant Congress the power to impose a small impost tax. Southern states, especially Virginia, owed particularly large debts, which they might never be able to pay. By 1786, New York was the first of several states that began to assume national debts directly, which threatened to weaken the national government even further.

## Economic Change

A dizzying mix of new economic opportunities and crises emerged in the postwar years. Devalued paper currency that Congress had printed during the war created inflation and conflicts between Congress and state governments, who were required to pay contributions to the war effort in hard currency (silver and gold) after 1781. States also printed their own forms of paper currency throughout the 1780s, which caused further inflation. Prices declined after the war, and they did not return to their prewar level until 1789. Because Congress lacked the power to tax, state governments assessed property taxes and duties on trade goods. Congress defaulted on foreign and domestic loan payments after the war, because it simply lacked funds.

The United States expanded foreign trade after the Revolution, but European powers still tried to restrict some international commerce. The government had relied on the war to open Caribbean and European trade routes. Britain closed its Caribbean island colonies to American trade, and both France and Spain left high duties in place on American-Caribbean trade. As a result, port cities such as Boston, Philadelphia, Newport, and Charleston faced slow recovery from the war, and their economies were severely depressed throughout the 1780s. The West Indies had comprised America's largest outlet for trade in foodstuffs, and the crippling of that trade both decreased farm income and stimulated greater trade within the United States. A few merchants

These are just a few examples of the paper currency printed by various states during and after the Revolution. Widespread trade of state paper notes, and even paper certificates printed by banks or land companies, helped contribute to inflation and economic uncertainty during the period.

who gained special Spanish trade permission enriched themselves by trading flour and other products to Cuba. Americans continued to import far more than they exported, a fact that further exacerbated the shortage of hard currency.

## Women and Revolution

Many women had participated directly in the Revolutionary War. As many as 20,000 accompanied the Continental Army as camp followers. These women, many of whom were related to soldiers, played vital roles cooking, doing laundry, and giving medical care to the troops. Other camp followers probably served direct military roles: bringing water to cool artillery pieces or even occasionally picking up weapons themselves. The most notable example of a fighting woman was **Deborah Sampson Gannett**, who disguised herself as a man and twice enlisted in the Continental Army. Wealthier women organized by **Esther DeBerdt Reed** and **Sarah Franklin Bache** formed the Ladies' Association of Philadelphia, which raised funds and distributed clothing to needy soldiers in 1781.

Although American women had contributed mightily to the war effort, they had little direct political influence and no political power in the new republic. But the Revolution did cause some shifts in white women's roles based on republican values. Historians use the term "republican motherhood" to describe the social expectation that women would contribute to the republic by raising their children—especially their sons—to be good citizens. In a society that was struggling to define itself according to the civic virtue demanded of a liberated citizenship, women could also exert broader influence over society and culture in a way that had political consequences. As the patriot women who had participated in the boycott movements before the Revolution had learned, women could also exert some degree of influence through their consumer choices.

Women's support for the patriot cause and their special role in spreading republican ideology did not translate into their direct inclusion in American politics. New Jersey allowed a small number of independent, property-holding women to vote for a time, but for the most part formal political participation was a male privilege. Many states liberalized divorce laws following the Revolution to allow women to separate from abusive or runaway husbands, although **coverture** laws still meant that married women could not own property. Patriot women lost confiscated property if their husbands were loyalists because state laws did not recognize that they could possess separate political identities.

## Racial Ideology and Questioning Slavery

The Revolutionary notion that "all men are created equal" pushed antislavery efforts forward in many northern states. But slavery thrived elsewhere, and African Americans still faced constant racism and resistance to their full participation in American society.

Some black American veterans, like Prince Whipple of New Hampshire, used their Revolutionary military experience to argue generally on behalf of African American freedom. Whipple and other African American men petitioned the New Hampshire legislature in 1779 to end slavery "for the sake of justice, liberty, and the rights of mankind." In 1783, New Hampshire adopted a state constitution that included a Declaration of Rights that ended slavery in the state.

BROTHER PRINCE HALL
WARRANTEE WORSHIPFUL MASTER, AFRICAN LODGE 459 A. L. 5784, A. D. 1784
FOUNDER OF COLORED FRATERNITY OF FREE AND ACCEPTED MASONS
BOSTON, MASS.
RAISED TO MASTER MASON


Although early biographical details of Prince Hall are hard to authenticate, he most likely was a former slave who served in the Massachusetts militia during the Revolutionary War. After the war, he became one of the most prominent free black men in Boston, where he worked to end slavery in Massachusetts and to better the lives of African Americans. He is depicted here in his role as the founder of the first black Masonic lodge in the United States, African Lodge No. 1 in Boston, an organization that also worked for black emancipation and betterment.

Before the Revolution, some Quakers and Mennonites had argued against the institution of slavery. After the war, Revolutionary ideology, black military heroism, and continued petitions by African Americans helped to expand the antislavery cause. Vermont's state constitution became the first to outlaw slavery in 1777, and a successful lawsuit by slaves who invoked the rights guaranteed by the Massachusetts 1780 constitution ended slavery there a few years later. Pennsylvania, and several other northern states, passed laws that gradually outlawed slavery by granting freedom to slaves once they reached a certain age. This gradual approach allowed the institution to linger into the 1820s in New York and New Jersey. In the states stretching from Maryland to the south, the institution of slavery survived and even intensified after the Revolution. Delaware, Maryland, and Virginia legislatures allowed individual slave owners to free their slaves for a time in the 1780s, but by the turn of the century fear of slave rebellion ended that practice. The American Revolution's emphasis on liberty aided some African Americans to claim rights and freedoms, but slavery survived and promised to divide the country along regional lines in the future.

**STUDY QUESTIONS FOR RESTRUCTURING SOCIAL AND POLITICAL AUTHORITY**

1. **In what ways did the Revolutionary War change the social roles of some women and African Americans?**
2. **Why was the economy in the post-Revolutionary United States so unstable?**

# A FEDERAL NATION

Many average Americans had fought for liberty in the Revolutionary War, but they were suffering in the postwar economic chaos. Everyone agreed that the economy and the state and national governments were deeply troubled. But they did not agree on which solutions would preserve the liberty that had been so hard won in the Revolutionary War: some favored a stronger central government, and others looked to the states for solutions. The creation of the U.S. Constitution was a victory for those who wanted more centralized power, but the concept of **federalism** also insured that the states would remain powerful. A new politics arose based on the concept of **popular sovereignty**, the notion that the people could consent to granting power to both state and federal governments without giving up their rights as the true source of authority in American society.

## Debt and Discontent

The uncertain economic system in the United States following the Revolutionary War caused hardship and unrest among a variety of poor farmers and a variety of veterans and artisans, who owed great debts or were owed money by the government. While governmental leaders worried that the Articles of Confederation provided too little national tax power, poor men and women felt simultaneously squeezed by heavy state taxation. The poor faced a variety of other economic challenges, starting with the newly inflated prices. Both taxes and private debt payment often required hard currency, but many poor people had little access to anything other than devalued paper money or the direct trade of farm goods. Although excess paper money hurt them by causing inflation, the poor relied on it.

By 1785, as the number of people imprisoned for the inability to repay debts rose above 1,000 in each state, debtors from New Hampshire to Massachusetts to Virginia began to organize themselves to oppose state and county enforcement of debts. Taking lessons from the pre-Revolutionary political protest movements, debtors petitioned state legislatures for the redress of their grievances and to demand the reinstatement of paper currency. Debtors were angry that their hard currency payments often went to repay land speculators who held state war bonds.

With state legislatures slow to respond, several groups took stronger action and resorted to protests and armed actions to close down county courts. Armed groups tangled with sheriffs seeking to seize property from debtors in Virginia, Pennsylvania, Delaware, New Jersey, New York, and Massachusetts. The largest armed insurrection came when Revolutionary veteran Daniel Shays organized protestors in Western Massachusetts in 1786 into an armed resistance movement. Denied the right to assemble to protest creditors and tax collectors, Shays' supporters threatened violence. In December 1786, they shut down courts in Springfield, Massachusetts, and a month later they marched against the state arsenal in that city. Massachusetts governor Benjamin Lincoln called out the state militia to put down **Shays' Rebellion**, and Daniel Shays himself fled to Canada.

Lincoln also appealed to Congress for help in suppressing Shays' Rebellion. Although the rebellion ended before Congress responded, a number of national leaders seized the opportunity to call for enhancing the power of the national government. George Washington agreed with his friend John Jay in 1786 that "our affairs are drawing rapidly to a crisis." Elites and politicians worried that popular uprisings like Shays' Rebellion could spread or get out of control. A small meeting in Annapolis, Maryland, in September 1786 solidified conversations among nationalists like James Madison and Alexander Hamilton, who thought the time had come to change the Articles of Confederation. The Annapolis Convention issued a call for all the states to send delegates to a new convention in Philadelphia the following summer.

## Constitutional Convention

Instead of merely changing the Articles of Confederation, the Philadelphia convention proposed an entirely new U.S. Constitution. It was, perhaps, not surprising that delegates to the Constitutional Convention moved beyond amending the Articles of Confederation, since they largely came from the elite, creditor class of merchants, lawyers, and plantation owners who believed that the weakness of the national government and the popular unrest threatened social order. They also rose above those interests to create a great political document that has become the longest-lasting written constitution for any government in the world. Every state but Rhode Island sent delegates to meet in Philadelphia in May 1787. Some of the most prominent leaders of the Revolution—George Washington, Benjamin Franklin, James Madison, and John Dickinson—came together to shape a new national government for the United States.

The convention elected George Washington presiding officer and agreed to meet in secret. Although the delegates tried hard to keep news of their deliberations from leaking out, we know much about what took place because of their written communications and the careful notes James Madison kept of their oral debates.

All of the proposals and counterproposals that the delegates debated fit within the conception of republicanism—the new national government would surely confirm the United States as a representative republic. They clashed over how to balance regional and economic interests within that representation, and though the delegates generally agreed that they needed to restrain volatile popular democracy, they did not agree on the structures that would best do that. In the first several days of debate, Edmund Randolph introduced James Madison's Virginia Plan, which proposed a two-house national legislature chosen according to proportional representation, a judicial branch, and a president elected by the legislature. Madison strongly advocated for the Enlightenment idea of **balance of powers** that would put authority in different branches of government, providing checks and balances against one another. Many states with small populations disliked Madison's plan, but it proved a useful starting point for debate. William Paterson, a New Jersey delegate, proposed a rival New Jersey Plan, that would keep more of the state power in the Articles of Confederation by retaining a unicameral legislature with equal state representation, but which would have greater financial power. On July 16, the delegates adopted what became known as "The Great Compromise" between the Virginia and New Jersey plans and decided to form a bicameral legislature: A House of Representatives would be tied to proportional representation, and a Senate would represent each state equally. Creating this form for Congress allowed the Convention to balance the interests of small and large states.

After the legislature was settled, other compromises followed. The delegates created the electoral college to elect the president as a way to give power to the states and to restrain popular democracy. They also designated that the House of Representatives would stay quite small (as compared to the total population) in an effort to further insulate it from popular passions. Delegates to the convention largely tried to avoid the thorny issue of slavery, but they could not sidestep discussing the institution altogether. After difficult debate, the delegates decided that three-fifths of slaves, or "other persons" as the final document phrased it, would be counted in the population for representation, although the convention never discussed direct citizenship rights or political status for the slaves themselves. The three-fifths compromise ensured that southern states, where the majority of slaves lived, would exercise strong political influence in the first decades of the republic. Delegates also agreed to restrict Congress from outlawing the international slave trade until 1808.

Near the end of the convention, Virginian George Mason proposed the inclusion of a bill of rights, a written guarantee of civil liberties, within the Constitution. Many delegates, despite their desire for a more powerful central government, still had a fear of too much national power infringing the rights of individuals. Several state constitutions contained such guarantees, but the majority of delegates did not think they were necessary. Several delegates, such as Marylander **Luther Martin**, were so upset by the exclusion of a bill of rights that they disavowed the work of the convention and opposed the Constitution. The Philadelphia Convention closed on September 17, 1787, and it remained to be seen whether such opposition would prevent the Constitution from being ratified.

## Ratification

The new U.S. Constitution would be ratified by specially elected conventions, not by the state legislatures, a majority of which would probably have opposed ratification outright. The Constitution was set to go into effect when nine of the 13 states ratified it. The Constitution's supporters, who dubbed themselves "Federalists," faced off against a very loose coalition of opponents, subsequently dubbed "Antifederalists." Federalist leaders, including Alexander Hamilton, John Jay, James Madison, and **John Marshall**, had impressive financing, coordination, and access to newspaper and pamphlet publishers. They also counted among their ranks the most famous national and international revolutionaries: George Washington and Benjamin Franklin. The Federalists won converts in cities and seaports interested in commerce and trade, and from creditors who favored strong government power. The Antifederalists—including Samuel Adams, Elbridge Jerry, Patrick Henry, George Mason, Richard Henry Lee, George Clinton, and Mercy Otis Warren—were much less organized and much more wary of centralized power. Some Antifederalists objected to the lack of rights protection in the Constitution; others favored weak national power or direct democracy.

The political skills of the Federalists were on display as they easily won ratification in Delaware, Pennsylvania, and New Jersey by the end of 1787. Georgia and Connecticut each ratified the document in January 1788. In February, Massachusetts

Mercy Otis Warren, a sharp thinker and prominent resident of Boston, supported the revolutionary cause by publishing, anonymously, poetry and plays during the war. After the war, she opposed the U.S. Constitution on the grounds that it created too much centralized government power. She continued to broadcast her Antifederalist opinions in her 1805 three-volume *History of the Rise, Progress, and Termination of the American Revolution.*

ratified the Constitution by a narrower margin, but only after proposing amendments and making Federalists promise that they would agree to add a bill of rights later.

As the ratifying conventions continued, the newspaper and pamphlet war between the Federalists and Antifederalists intensified. Madison, Hamilton, and Jay anonymously published the "Federalist" essays, sometimes called the **Federalist Papers**, which offered wide-ranging arguments in favor of ratification. Their words, republished in books, pamphlets, and newspapers in many states debating ratification, helped to shape convention politics and became some of the most enduring and popular political commentaries in American history. Madison, Hamilton, and Jay applied Enlightenment political theories to the U.S. context, and argued that the constitution was necessary. Madison, in particular, also took a new era of politics into account when he argued in essays 10 and 51 that the Constitution could balance the behavior self-interested Americans, who were not necessarily always guided by republican virtue.

By narrow margins, Maryland and South Carolina ratified the Constitution in the spring of 1788. When New Hampshire ratified it on June 21, 1788, the Constitution technically went into effect, since nine states had completed the process. But it was unlikely that the new government would ever take shape without the support of the large and influential states of New York and Virginia. On June 23, Virginia gave its assent, delivering along with ratification 20 proposed amendments and support for a future bill of rights. On June 26, New York followed suit. North Carolina rejected ratification in August, only subsequently voting for ratification in November when it was clear the document would go into effect. Rhode Island held out its ratification until May 1790.

At the conclusion of the Constitutional Convention in September 1787, Benjamin Franklin, less than a year away from his own death, rose to urge his fellow delegates to sign the new Constitution. He claimed that the document would "astonish our enemies, who are waiting with confidence to hear that our councils are confounded . . . and that our states are on the point of separation." Franklin declared, "I consent, Sir, to this Constitution because I expect no better and because I am not sure that it is not the best.

## TIMELINE 1776–1789

### 1776

**July** Congress issues the Declaration of Independence

**September** British occupy New York City

**December 25** Battle of Trenton, NJ

### 1777

**January 3** Battle of Princeton, NJ

**September 11** Battle of Brandywine, PA

**September 19** Congress flees Philadelphia

**September 26** The British occupy Philadelphia

**October 4** Battle of Germantown, PA

**October 17** John Burgoyne surrenders his British army to Horatio Gates after losing Battle of Saratoga

**November** Congress submits the Articles of Confederation to the states

**December 17** The Continental Army enters winter quarters at Valley Forge, PA

### 1778

**February** Treaty of Alliance and a Treaty of Amity and Commerce between France and United States

**March** France formally recognizes the United States

**June 17** France declares war on Great Britain

**June 18** British evacuate Philadelphia

**December 29** British seize control of Savanna, GA

### 1779

**August** American forces defeat Iroquois leader Joseph Brant

### 1780

**March** Spanish governor Galvez captures Mobile from the British

**May 12** British capture Charleston, SC

**August 16** Battle of Camden, SC

### 1781

**January 1** Members of the PA line mutiny

**January 17** Battle of Cowpens, SC

**March 15** Battle of Guilford Courthouse, NC

**September 8** Battle of Eutaw Springs, SC

**October 19** Cornwallis surrenders his army to the United States

### 1782

**April** The Netherlands recognize the United States

### 1783

**January** France and Spain make peace with Britain

**Table 7.1 When the States Ratified the U.S. Constitution** Although the U.S. Constitution went into effect in 1789, it took longer for every state in the union to ratify the document.

| Date of Ratification | State |
|---|---|
| December 1787 | Delaware<br>New Jersey<br>Pennsylvania |
| January 1788 | Connecticut<br>Georgia |
| February 1788 | Massachusetts |
| April 1788 | Maryland |
| May 1788 | South Carolina |
| June 1788 | New Hampshire<br>Virginia |
| July 1788 | New York |
| November 1789 | North Carolina |
| May 1790 | Rhode Island |

The opinions I have had of its errors, I sacrifice to the public good." That very notion of republican sacrifice for "the common good" had motivated many of those who fought in the Revolution. Conflicts during the war and developments in postwar society had proven that more struggle was necessary to find out whose version of "the public good" would reign in American government. And, as Franklin reminded the other convention delegates, much of the world would be watching to see if the United States of America could succeed.

Massachusetts Supreme Court declares slavery unconstitutional in that state

**September 3** Treaty of Paris ends the Revolutionary War

**1784**

**January** Congress ratifies the Treaty of Paris

**June** Spain forbids American trade on the Mississippi River

**1786**

**September** Annapolis Convention calls for amending the Articles of Confederation

**1787**

**January** Shays' Rebellion is put down by the Massachusetts militia

**February** Congress calls for a convention to amend the Articles of Confederation

**May 25** Constitutional Convention convenes in Philadelphia

**September 17** Constitutional Convention closes

**October** *The Federalist* papers first published

**December 7** Delaware ratifies the U.S. Constitution

**December 12** Pennsylvania ratifies the U.S. Constitution

**December 18** New Jersey ratifies the U.S. Constitution

**1788**

**January 2** Georgia ratifies the U.S. Constitution

**January 9** Connecticut ratifies the U.S. Constitution

**February 6** Massachusetts narrowly ratifies the U.S. Constitution

**March** Constitutional ratification fails in Rhode Island

**April 28** Maryland ratifies the U.S. Constitution

**May 23** South Carolina ratifies the U.S. Constitution

**June 21** New Hampshire ratifies the U.S. Constitution (technically fulfilling its ratification)

**June 25** Virginia ratifies the U.S. Constitution

**June 26** New York ratifies the U.S. Constitution (virtually guaranteeing it will succeed)

**August 2** Constitutional ratification fails in North Carolina

**1789**

**January 1** The U.S. Constitution takes effect

## STUDY QUESTIONS FOR A FEDERAL NATION

1. **What factors led to the calling of the Constitutional Convention?**
2. **In what ways and for what reasons did Federalists and Antifederalists disagree so strongly over what form of government would protect republicanism?**

## Summary

- The American Revolution centered around the best way to protect "liberty" and republican government, although not everyone in society agreed on how to do so.
- European help, especially from France, was absolutely essential to the American victory in the Revolutionary War, which was an international conflict.
- The ideology of republicanism built in some weaknesses to the American military, but American military forces performed surprisingly well against British troops and their allies.
- The Revolutionary War caused changes in the social roles and power of Native American groups, African Americans, and white women.
- During and after the Revolutionary War, finance and economic difficulties dramatized power struggles within the states and between the states and the U.S. national government.
- The U.S. Constitution created a new government based on new ideas of federalism and popular sovereignty, while at the same time seeking to restrain somewhat the forces of popular democracy.

## Key Terms and People

**Articles of Confederation** *261*
**Bache, Sarah Franklin** *276*
**balance of powers** *280*
**Biddle, Nicholas** *267*
**Brant, Joseph** *271*
**Catherine the Great** *266*
**Clinton, Sir Henry** *258*
**Cornwallis, Lord** *258*
**coverture** *277*
**Duportail, Louis** *264*
**Estaing, d', Comte** *260*
**federalism** *278*
**Federalist Papers** *282*
**Gálvez, Bernardo de** *265*
**Gannett, Deborah Sampson** *276*
**Gates, Horatio** *260*
**Germain, Lord George** *268*
**Grasse, Comte de** *268*
**Howe, Sir Richard** *258*
**Howe, Sir William** *258*
**Jay, John** *266*
**Jones, John Paul** *264*
**Kosciuszko, Tadeusz** *264*
**Lafayette, Marquis de, Marie-Joseph-Paul-Yves-Roch-Gilbert du Motier** *265*
**Laurens, Henry** *273*
**Lincoln, Benjamin** *269*
**Marshall, John** *281*
**Martin, Luther** *281*
**Morgan, Daniel** *269*
**popular sovereignty** *278*

**Pulaski, Casimir** *265*
**Reed, Esther DeBerdt** *276*
**separation of powers** *261*
**Shays' Rebellion** *279*
**Steuben, Friedrich Wilhelm von** *264*
**Tarleton, Banastre** *269*
**Ternay, Marquis de** *268*
**Vergennes, Comte de** *260*

## Reviewing Chapter 7

1. How did the United States win independence from the world's most powerful empire?
2. Why did the United States win the Revolutionary War?
3. How did the circulation of people, goods, and ideas across the Atlantic Ocean complicate and contribute to the American victory in the Revolution?

## Further Reading

Gould, Eliga H., and Peter S. Onuf, eds. *The American Revolution in the Atlantic World.* Baltimore: Johns Hopkins University Press, 2005. This volume of essays presents a multifaceted look at the American Revolution in the context of Atlantic world history. It includes 15 essays on social, political, military, and cultural history stretching from the imperial crisis through the ratification of the Constitution.

Higginbotham, Don. *The War for American Independence.* Boston: Northeastern University Press, 1983. This book is the best one-volume military history of the American Revolution. It explains how the United States won the war, with European help, despite organizational and strategic disadvantages.

Holton, Woody. *Unruly Americans and the Origins of the American Constitution.* New York: Hill and Wang, 2007. Holton argues in this book that although the framers of the U.S. Constitution feared the middling and lower sort, the Constitution was nonetheless shaped by the desires and interests of people in the states who participated in the ratifying conventions. The conventions were much more democratic than the Constitutional Convention.

Jasanoff, Maya. *Liberty's Exiles: American Loyalists in the Revolutionary World.* New York: Alfred A. Knopf, 2011. Jasanoff's book traces the fate of white Loyalists, Indians, and African Americans who supported the British during the American Revolution as they were exiled to Britain and the British empire including Canada, Sierra Leone, India, and Australia.

Kerber, Linda K. *Women of the Republic: Intellect and Ideology in Revolutionary America.* Linda Kerber examines women's participation in the American Revolution and how the Revolution then changed gender roles, especially for women. Kerber coined the term "republican motherhood" to describe the political importance given to white women's family duties in the aftermath of the Revolution.

Wood, Gordon S. *The Radicalism of the American Revolution.* New York: Alfred A. Knopf, 1992. This book traces the ideological shifts that accompanied the United States, making it a country first shaped by republicanism and then by a growing sense of the importance of democracy. Wood argues that the American Revolution was much more radical than it is usually given credit for being.

# Visual Review

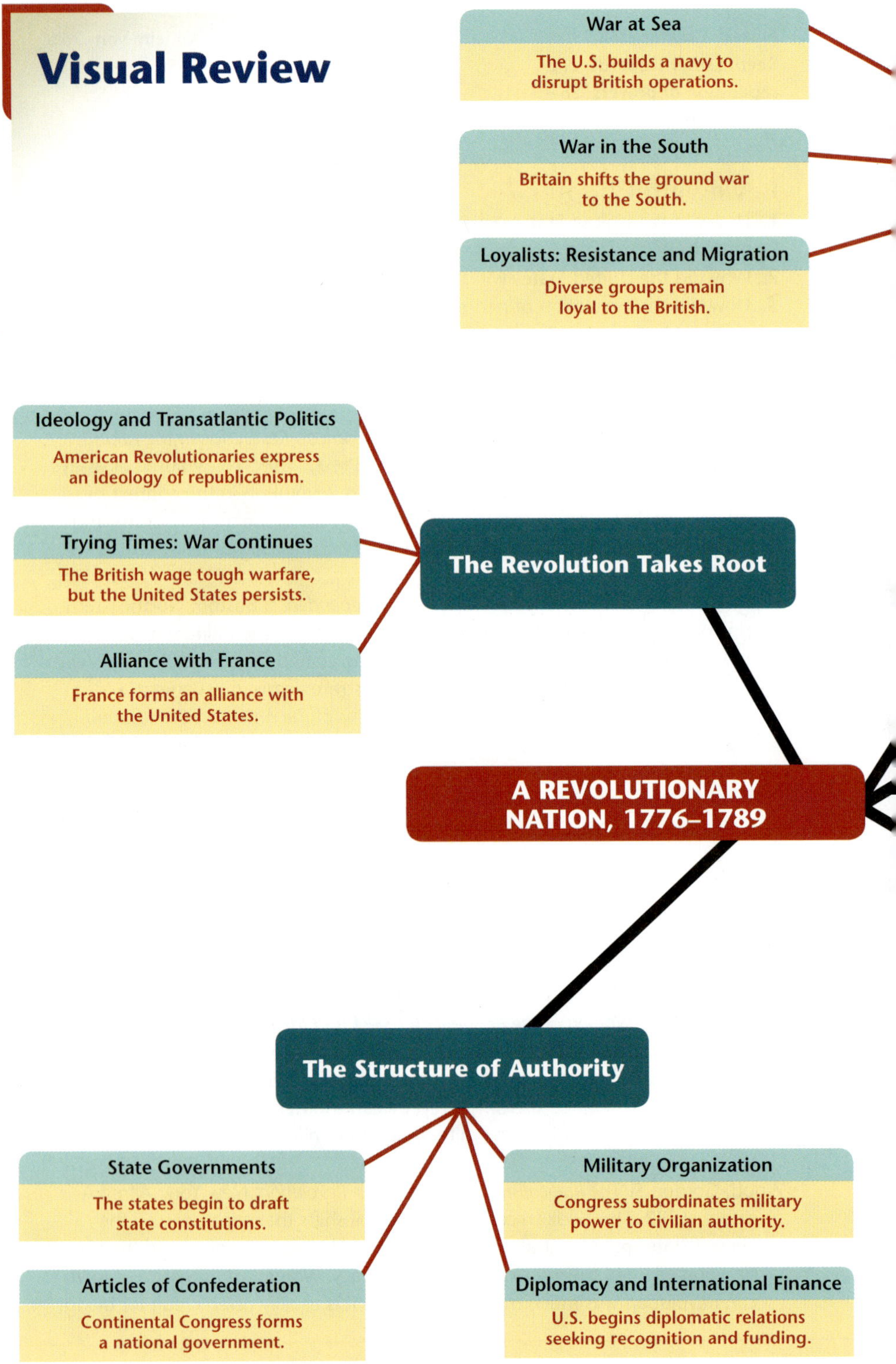

**War at Sea**
The U.S. builds a navy to disrupt British operations.

**War in the South**
Britain shifts the ground war to the South.

**Loyalists: Resistance and Migration**
Diverse groups remain loyal to the British.

**Ideology and Transatlantic Politics**
American Revolutionaries express an ideology of republicanism.

**Trying Times: War Continues**
The British wage tough warfare, but the United States persists.

**Alliance with France**
France forms an alliance with the United States.

**The Revolution Takes Root**

**A REVOLUTIONARY NATION, 1776–1789**

**The Structure of Authority**

**State Governments**
The states begin to draft state constitutions.

**Military Organization**
Congress subordinates military power to civilian authority.

**Articles of Confederation**
Continental Congress forms a national government.

**Diplomacy and International Finance**
U.S. begins diplomatic relations seeking recognition and funding.

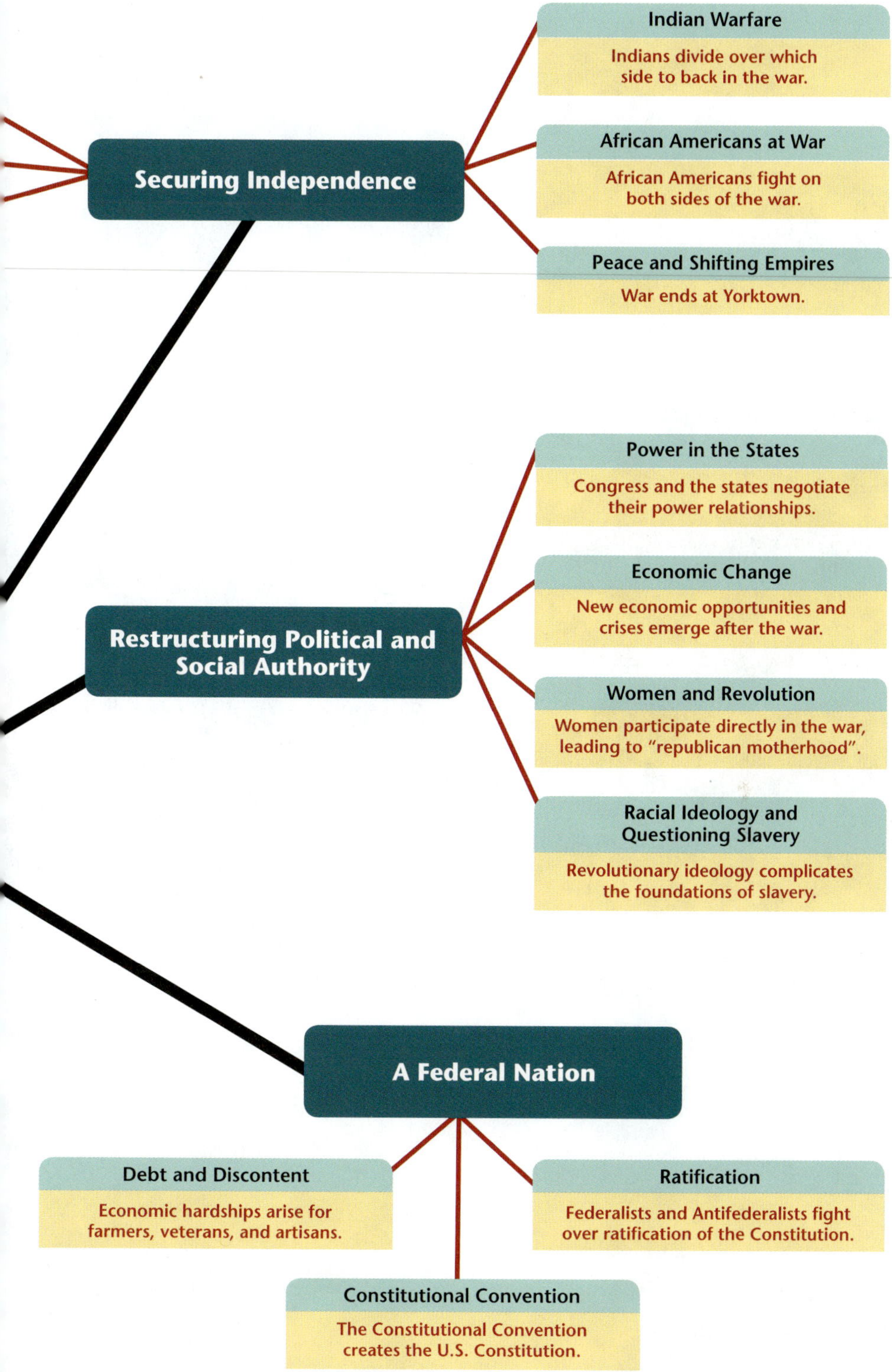

## Securing Independence

### Indian Warfare
Indians divide over which side to back in the war.

### African Americans at War
African Americans fight on both sides of the war.

### Peace and Shifting Empires
War ends at Yorktown.

## Restructuring Political and Social Authority

### Power in the States
Congress and the states negotiate their power relationships.

### Economic Change
New economic opportunities and crises emerge after the war.

### Women and Revolution
Women participate directly in the war, leading to "republican motherhood".

### Racial Ideology and Questioning Slavery
Revolutionary ideology complicates the foundations of slavery.

## A Federal Nation

### Debt and Discontent
Economic hardships arise for farmers, veterans, and artisans.

### Ratification
Federalists and Antifederalists fight over ratification of the Constitution.

### Constitutional Convention
The Constitutional Convention creates the U.S. Constitution.

# 8 A New Nation Facing a Revolutionary World

## 1789–1815

In April 1793 the French Revolutionary government sent **Edmund Charles Genet** on a diplomatic mission to convince the United States "to assist in every way the extension of the empire of liberty." Genet was to cement the 1778 French alliance with the United States and seek help in France's newly declared war on Great Britain, Spain, Austria, and Prussia.

Genet hoped also to sign a new commercial treaty with the United States, to use the United States as a staging ground to outfit privateers, to expel Britain and Spain from Canada and Louisiana, and to recruit U.S. citizens for French military service. The Girondins—a republican political group that controlled Revolutionary France early in 1793—hoped that Genet would build on the financial relationship France and the United States had forged during the American Revolution. But they misunderstood U.S. politics and President Washington's desire to keep the nation neutral.

As Genet traveled from South Carolina to the U.S. capital at Philadelphia, he defied American officials who wished him to keep a low profile. He received an enthusiastic welcome, however, from crowds of men and women who demonstrated their support for the French Revolution by cheering, displaying French symbols, and attending banquets and balls in his honor. Genet openly encouraged people to oppose Washington's Proclamation of Neutrality in the European war, issued two weeks after his arrival. He hatched a secret plan in Georgia to mobilize backcountry Americans against

◂ Général Toussaint Louverture (1743–1803)

**CHAPTER OUTLINE**



*continued on page 293*

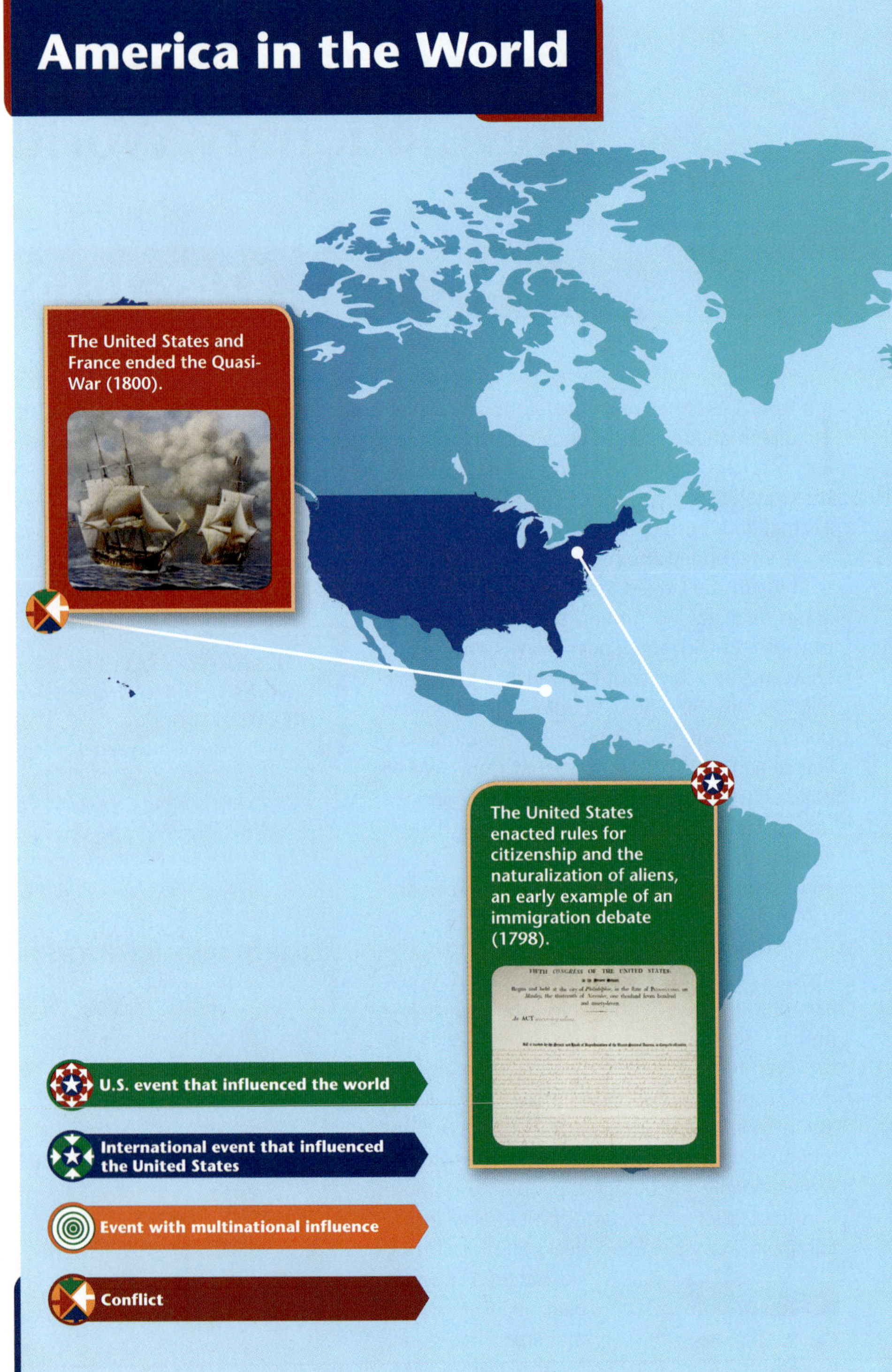
America in the World
The United States and France ended the Quasi-War (1800).
The United States enacted rules for citizenship and the naturalization of aliens, an early example of an immigration debate (1798).
FIFTH CONGRESS OF THE UNITED STATES
U.S. event that influenced the world
International event that influenced the United States
Event with multinational influence
Conflict

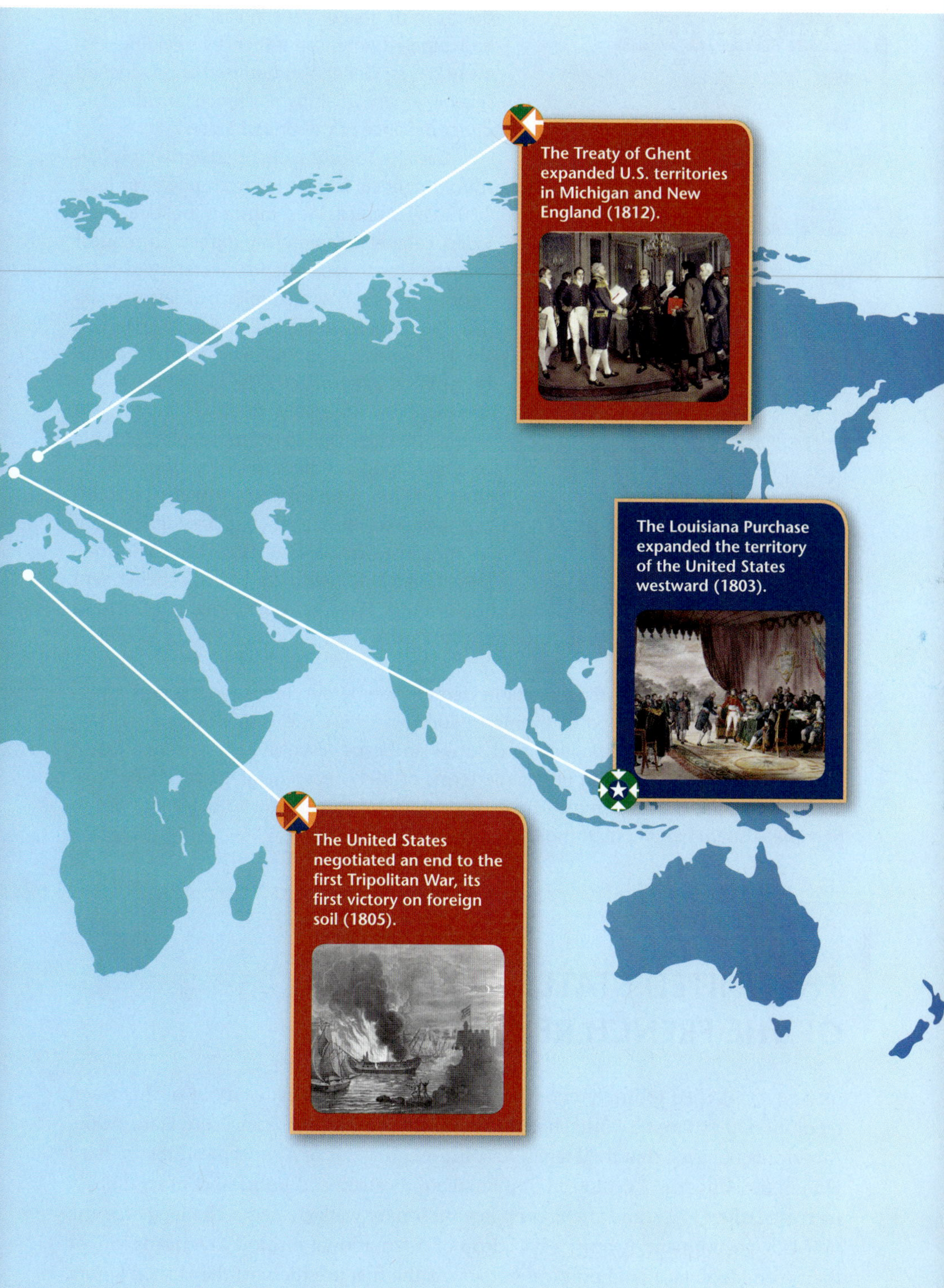
The Treaty of Ghent expanded U.S. territories in Michigan and New England (1812).
The Louisiana Purchase expanded the territory of the United States westward (1803).
The United States negotiated an end to the first Tripolitan War, its first victory on foreign soil (1805).

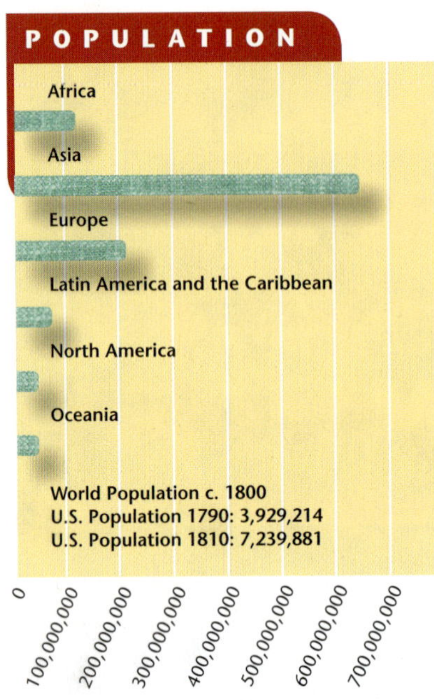


the Spanish government in East Florida, which had angered American settlers by shielding runaway slaves. Genet also outfitted and launched several American ships as French privateers in direct defiance of the United States.

Genet's fortunes changed when his Girondin political faction fell from power in June 1793. By August Washington's politically divided cabinet unanimously agreed to request that the French recall Genet. Secretary of State Thomas Jefferson wrote diplomatic letters making the request, while still trying to maintain the U.S. relationship with France that he and his political allies prized. The Girondins' rivals, the Jacobins, agreed to recall Genet, to help ensure that the United States would continue to export food to France. In the spring of 1794 the new French government threatened to arrest and execute Genet, but President Washington instead allowed the man who had threatened U.S. neutrality to avoid being sent home to the guillotine. Genet settled in New York State, where he married Cornelia Clinton, one of his political supporters and the governor's daughter, and lived quietly until his death in 1834.

The controversy over Genet's actions demonstrated how connected the new American nation continued to be to events in Europe—where the French Revolution was dramatically changing the political and social landscape. Even as U.S. citizens tried to become accustomed to living under the terms of their new federal constitution, revolutionary change in France meant that the new nation would have to be careful not to become ensnared in global turmoil.

## THE UNITED STATES IN THE AGE OF THE FRENCH REVOLUTION

As Americans tried to implement the government that had evolved out of their own revolution, they faced a world changed by revolutions in both France and Haiti. Many Americans believed that the French Revolution grew out of a concept of liberty, hard won in the American Revolution. But French radicalism and political conflict quickly increased after 1793, and the French Revolutionary wars created a challenge for the new U.S. government. Against a backdrop of international turmoil Americans fought their own ideological and political battles. As the first president of the United States, George Washington wanted to remain neutral in the European wars, but taking such a position was not always easy. Conflicts in Europe helped to fuel the growth of the first U.S. political parties, which reflected deep disagreements among Americans about how their new government should work. In a revolutionary world, how would Americans manage their own political and social change?

**CHAPTER OUTLINE**

*continued from page 289*



## The New Nation and the New Revolution

Initially, Americans believed that the 1789 French Revolution was linked to the ideals of the American Revolution, especially as expressed in the Declaration of Independence. When the Estates General, the third estate of the French legislature, formed the National Assembly in June 1789 and street fighting escalated after the storming of the notorious Bastille prison in Paris in July, the American minister to France, Thomas Jefferson, looked on approvingly. At first, American friends such as the Marquis de Lafayette took a hand in shaping a new French government. King Louis XVI fled the capital, and in August the Estates General issued the Declaration of the Rights of Man and of the Citizen, declaring "Men are born and remain free and equal in rights." As Jefferson left France to take up his post as the first U.S. Secretary of State, he thought that American liberty was taking root in Europe. Most Americans supported the French Revolution in its early stages.

Events soon weakened U.S. support. The execution of the royal family in 1793; the execution or imprisonment of leaders beloved by Americans, such as Lafayette; and France's bid to spread revolutionary republicanism through warfare soon divided U.S. opinion. During "the Terror" in France hundreds of people judged to be political enemies of "the people" were executed by guillotine—actions that many, like John Adams, viewed as far too radical. To many members of the American elite, the French seemed to endorse a dangerous excess of equality and democracy. But others, such as Jefferson himself, continued to view France as a new beacon of liberty.

In an already contentious domestic political scene, Americans could not avoid conflict over the French Revolution and its social and political consequences. If the French based their revolution on American liberty, was the United States susceptible to the same kind of "Terror"? Would the French situation affirm or disrupt American politics? Would the French abolition of slavery in its Caribbean colonies in 1794 affect the United States? Attorney General Edmund Randolph wrote to President Washington that he worried about the "ardour of some, to transplant French politics, as fresh fuel for our politics."

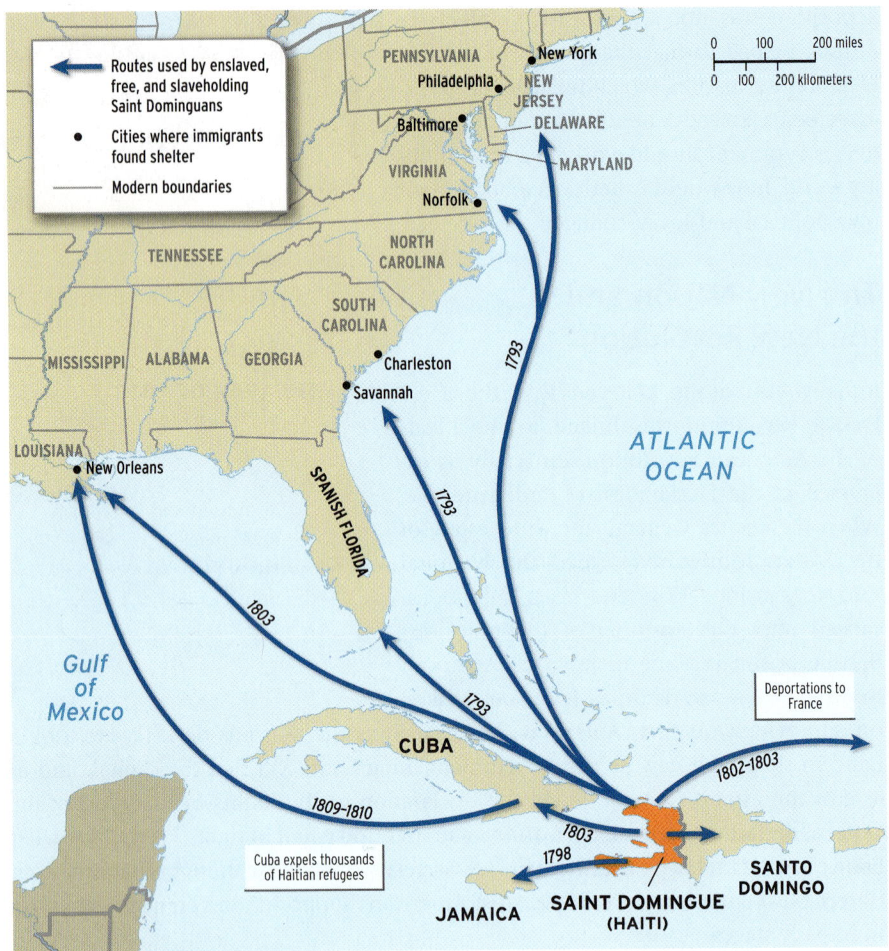


▲ **Map 8.1**

**Migration out of Saint Domingue/Haiti, 1793–1809** Thousands of people fled or were forcibly removed from the island of Saint Domingue during the Haitian Revolution. Many, including slave owners, slaves, and free people of color, ended up in U.S. cities.

## The Rise of Party Tensions

When the U.S. electoral college met for the first time in February 1789, it unanimously chose George Washington as president. His personal prestige and heroism in the Revolutionary War meant that Americans trusted him to direct the expanded powers given to the federal government by the new Constitution. John Adams, the respected Massachusetts statesman and former American Minister to Great Britain, was elected the first vice president.

Despite the unanimity of support for Washington, both the cabinet and Congress remained divided during his first term. Congress was dominated by merchants, lawyers, and gentlemen who had been strong supporters of the new Constitution. They soon introduced a slate of amendments to the document as the Federalists had promised Antifederalists during the ratification debates in 1788. The 10 amendments, known as the **Bill of Rights**, focused primarily on guaranteeing individual liberties and restraining Congress from inhibiting the press or establishing a state religion; they were ratified by the states in 1791. The old divisions over the Constitution, however, were soon overtaken by a new set of political disagreements regarding the proper uses of federal power and attitudes toward Britain and France.

Two of Washington's cabinet ministers, Secretary of State Thomas Jefferson and Secretary of the Treasury Alexander Hamilton, opposed one another at almost every turn. They headed rival political factions during the 1790s, creating the first political parties in American history, the Federalists and the Democratic Republicans, even though neither side believed in the legitimacy of parties. Federalists, led by the brilliant Hamilton, Washington's former aide-de-camp, favored the strong use of federal power, greater taxation, and keeping direct political power in the hand of educated elites. Federalists thought the United States should restore good relations with Great Britain, and Hamilton was among political leaders most critical of the antiaristocratic "excesses" of the French Revolution. Democratic Republicans, led by Jefferson and James Madison, favored the French and their democratic style. Jeffersonians argued that state governments should continue to check the power of the federal government. Moreover, they rejected Hamilton's plans to encourage commerce and U.S. financial development. Jefferson believed farming to be the base of the ideal developing American economy; in addition, he insisted, in contrast to Hamilton, that democratic politics should include the participation of nonelite white men, especially farmers and artisans.

Federalists and Democratic Republicans clashed over notions of how government power ought to be used. The Federalists envisioned a version of American "liberty" that rested on traditional republican values and elite leadership, while the Democratic Republicans generally favored a more personal notion of democratic "liberty."

One of the first issues that the supporters of Hamilton and Jefferson contended over—the assumption of state Revolutionary War debts by the federal

**Table 8.1 Political Parties in the 1790s** This table contrasts the two political parties that arose in the 1790s.

| Federalist Party | Democratic Republican Party |
|---|---|
| • Favored strong federal government<br>• Favored friendship with the British<br>• Opposed the French Revolution<br>• Power base among merchants, property owners, urban workers in commercial enterprises<br>• Minority party after 1800<br>• Strongest region: New England | • Favored limited federal power<br>• Hostile to Great Britain<br>• Sympathetic to the French Revolution<br>• Power base among southern planters and northern farmers<br>• Majority party after 1800 |

government—also revealed the regional strength of each faction. Jefferson, James Madison, and other southerners opposed the assumption of state debts, not only because they wanted to restrict centralized power, but because many southern states had already paid back their creditors. Hamilton argued that the federal government had to pay the outstanding debts of large states like Pennsylvania and New York to reassure foreign governments of the fiscal power of the United States. In the summer of 1790 the two sides compromised. Congress voted to assume the debts but pacified skeptical southerners by voting to locate the new federal capital city on the Potomac River in the District of Columbia, south of the previous capital in Philadelphia.

In 1790 and 1791 Hamilton's aggressive financial proposals drove the two political factions further apart. Hamilton wanted to encourage economic development by wielding strong federal power that the Democratic Republicans strongly opposed. He issued a report on Public Credit that argued for financing public debt and proposed a series of excise taxes. Hamilton also proposed the creation of a National Bank, supported by federal funds and private shareholders. Although Jefferson and Madison argued that the bank was unconstitutional, Congress chartered it in February 1791. The Democratic Republicans also opposed Hamilton's efforts to impose international tariffs and fund American economic enterprise.

Although neither the Federalists nor the Democratic Republicans were yet highly organized as political parties, they were increasingly open about their opposition. By 1792 each side patronized its own newspaper. Neither side nominated official candidates in elections, but people in towns and countryside could choose allegiances since candidates' sympathies were usually widely known, and many smaller newspapers openly declared support for one side or another.

## Neutrality and Jay's Treaty

Amid infighting and opposition President Washington tried to remain neutral regarding the two developing political parties. By February 1793, however, he grew increasingly concerned that the United States was getting too involved in France's new revolutionary wars. Even Jefferson wanted to keep the United States out of war, but he favored France and was keen to honor the alliance of 1778 between the "sister republics." Hamilton believed that the alliance should be suspended. President Washington issued a Proclamation of Neutrality in the European wars on April 22, just weeks after he had been inaugurated for his second term as president. The goal of the Proclamation of Neutrality was to keep open the rights of U.S. ships to trade with both Britain and France and their Caribbean colonies.

The United States wanted to maintain trade relations with Britain and France, but the nation risked becoming a pawn between the two bigger European powers. The British government ordered the Royal Navy to seize any U.S. ship trading with the French in the Caribbean, and they took hundreds of American merchant vessels as prizes and began to kidnap American sailors and impress them into Royal Navy service. In order to stop these actions, Washington sent Chief Justice John Jay to London to negotiate a treaty with the British government, the terms of which Washington kept secret from the public for months. Thomas Jefferson resigned as Secretary of State at the end of 1793, in part because he believed that Hamilton had influenced Washington to become pro-British.

When the Senate finally debated **Jay's Treaty**, which granted the United States trade rights on the Mississippi, in the British East Indies, and at western forts, French minister to the United States Pierre Adet, U.S. Secretary of State Edmund Randolph, and several state legislatures all opposed it. Opponents of the treaty charged that it was ragingly pro-British. Angry crowds of Americans with French and Democratic-Republican sympathies burned Jay in effigy in city streets. As the Senate narrowly ratified the Treaty in June 1795, President Washington's popularity plummeted.

## The Popular Politics of Rebellion

A series of events in 1794 also tested Washington's popularity and confirmed that domestic politics and trade were intertwined. Part of Hamilton's 1791 program of excise taxes had levied duties on distilled liquor, which threatened Westerners, who could gain more profits by shipping spirits to urban markets than by shipping bulky corn or wheat. Farmers in Virginia, Kentucky, Maryland, North Carolina, and South Carolina refused to pay the taxes. But Pennsylvanians mounted the hottest protest when, in July 1794, crowds attacked tax collector John Neville and burned his house. Within weeks 6,000 protesters, including some members of the Pennsylvania militia, had gathered outside Pittsburgh and threatened more widespread violence against the Whiskey Tax.

The **Whiskey Rebellion** in western Pennsylvania prompted Washington to assert federal power using military force. Hamilton, who was increasingly close to Washington, led 15,000 federalized militia troops from other states into Pennsylvania in September. Widespread violence was avoided, but troops arrested several leaders of the rebellion. The use of federal military power against domestic protesters outraged Democratic Republicans. President Washington, convinced that Democratic Republicans were partly to blame for the unrest, suggested that radical pro-Jefferson political clubs, called Democratic Republican societies, had encouraged protesters. The Whiskey Rebellion revealed deep disagreement over the proper exercise of federal power and the proper role of popular politics. In 1794 some wondered if the Whiskey Rebellion and its suppression might be the beginning of an American version of the French "Terror."

## Indian Warfare and European Power

Federal power was also contested in western conflicts between settlers and Indians, who were trying to navigate between increasingly aggressive U.S. citizens and traditional European enemies and allies. After 1789, the British kept seven forts south of Upper Canada, and they actively traded and negotiated with the Miami, Shawnee, and other tribes in the Ohio region, who frequently clashed with U.S. settlers. The settlement of western lands granted to Revolutionary War veterans also placed increasing pressure on Ohio-region Indian peoples.

The Washington administration sent the small U.S. army, supplemented by western militia troops, to pacify the Ohio country in 1790 and in 1791. General **Josiah Harmar** attacked Miami Town, an Indian-British trade hub, in October 1790. Miami warrior **Little Turtle** surprised Harmar's force with superior numbers and tactics and inflicted a crushing defeat that cost Harmar his job. The following November, Little Turtle organized Miami, Shawnee, and other allied tribal forces, with British logistical support, to resist when **Arthur St. Clair**, governor of the Northwest Territory, led another attack on Miami Town. At the Wabash River, Little Turtle's forces killed more than 600 American soldiers and delivered one of the greatest victories over the United States by Indians over the United States.

In 1794 Washington sent U.S. army forces—this time headed by former Revolutionary War general **"Mad" Anthony Wayne**—to fight against the Shawnee and Miami Confederacy. Wayne commanded almost 4,000 army and militia troops, he built strong forts, and he exploited disagreements over how to respond within the Indian confederacy. In August 1794, Wayne defeated the confederacy at the Battle of Fallen Timbers. The following year he signed the Treaty of Greenville with 12 Indian nations in the Northwest Territory, some of whom signed unwillingly because the treaty granted U.S. settlers access to wide tracts of land. The Battle of Fallen Timbers was a key watershed in Indian history, as it compelled many Indians to accommodate U.S. demands. The British stayed out of the conflict temporarily but stood ready to exploit future tensions as settlement increased.

During the period of calm between the United States and Britain after Jay's Treaty and the Treaty of Greenville, the Spanish, weakened by their involvement in the European wars, feared a combined attack in Florida and Louisiana. In 1795, they sought to reduce tensions with the United States by agreeing to a new treaty. That summer in Madrid, U.S. diplomat Thomas Pinckney negotiated a highly favorable agreement with Spanish prime minister Don Manuel de Godoy, as Godoy sought to settle Spain's war with France to reduce European tensions. **Pinckney's Treaty**—also known as the Treaty of San Lorenzo—opened Mississippi River trade to the United States, provided tax-free markets in New Orleans, settled Florida border issues, and guaranteed Spanish help against southwest Indians. The U.S. Senate unanimously ratified the new treaty in 1796, and it seemed for a moment that the U.S. might have stabilized threats from Indian and European powers.

## STUDY QUESTIONS FOR THE UNITED STATES IN THE AGE OF THE FRENCH REVOLUTION

1. **In what ways did domestic and international events influence partisan conflict during Washington's presidency?**
2. **How did the development of political parties influence American government in the 1790s?**

# PARTY CONFLICT INTENSIFIES

George Washington, battered by his critics but sure that he had successfully stabilized the new republic, decided not to serve a third term as president—setting a precedent that would stand for over 100 years. Despite controversies during his second term, Washington's personal prestige, reputation, and leadership had helped to win the Revolutionary War, establish the Constitution, and ensure the smooth beginnings of the federal government. Many Americans worried about what would follow after his retirement. As he left office in 1796, Washington published a "Farewell Address" warning, "Against the insidious wiles of foreign influence (I conjure you to believe me, fellow-citizens) the jealousy of a free people ought to be constantly awake." He urged Americans to trade with Europe, but to guard against overinvolvement in European politics and "to steer clear of permanent alliances with any portion of the foreign world." Washington also warned against factionalism in U.S. politics, but it soon became clear that the United States could avoid neither international problems nor party politics.

## Adams in Power

John Adams won the presidential election of 1796, despite opposition from fellow Federalist Alexander Hamilton, who thought him insufficiently conservative. States chose members of the electoral college in a patchwork of methods ranging from popular voting to selection by state legislatures, and the electors did not have to reflect popular opinion in their votes. Prior to the ratification of the Twelfth Amendment in 1804, the candidate who received the second highest number of votes in the electoral college was elected vice president. Neither the Federalists nor the Democratic Republicans yet

Sarah Montgomery Thompson embroidered this picture, based on a popular painting, to celebrate George Washington's retirement from the presidency in 1797. The woman in the picture represents liberty; she holds in her hand a pole topped by a cap, both symbols of liberty. Liberty commends George Washington as he points across the Potomac River back to his home at Mount Vernon.

formally nominated candidates for the presidency, and electors from several different states split their votes for a variety of Federalist and Democratic-Republican candidates. As a result Thomas Jefferson received the second-highest vote total and was elected vice president. The fact that the president and vice president led opposing political parties showed how the parties themselves were not yet solidly organized, disciplined entities.

President Adams had to navigate between Jefferson's more democratic party on the one hand and Hamilton's more conservative wing of his own party on the other. In 1796 Federalists also won a slim majority in Congress, and they moved quickly to fill up the federal judiciary with their allies. Although Adams handled crises well, he was never able to match Washington's popularity or to unite the country around Federalist politics.

John and Abigail Adams were the first presidential couple to take up residence in the yet unfinished White House, as the planned city of Washington, DC, became the new U.S. capital in 1799. French planner Pierre L'Enfant, English architects Benjamin Henry Latrobe and William Thornton, and a variety of Irish and African American surveyors and builders worked throughout the 1790s to build a capital city whose design reflected American reverence for Greek and Roman classical ideals.

## Quasi-War with France

As the United States seemed to get caught up in the war between Britain and France, President Adams faced huge pressure to declare war on France. Adams wrote in a 1796 letter, "I dread not a War, with France or England, if either forces it upon Us, but

John Adams and Abigail Adams had a close relationship nurtured by frequent correspondence when they had to be apart. Abigail was one of John's strongest supporters when he was vice president and president, and she resented political criticism of her husband. Both John and Abigail remained strong supporters of Federalist causes for the remainder of their lives.

will make no Aggression upon either, with my free Will, without just and necessary Cause and Provocation." Adams pursued a balancing act of nonaggression throughout his term as president, despite diplomatic and military crises with France and the persistent urging of some other Federalists. In mid-1796 the French decreed that trade ships from countries that remained neutral in their war with Britain would be subject to capture just as British ships were. The British also continued to harass U.S. traders. Tensions rose further during Adams's first few months in office when the French rejected American envoy Charles Cotesworth Pinckney.

Mirrors like this, made from wood or plaster covered in gold leaf, became popular among wealthy, fashionable Americans in the 1790s. Decorating one's home with furniture featuring the bald eagle, a symbol of the United States, was a way to display patriotism and a taste for lavish material goods.

Over the objection of many fellow Federalists, Adams decided to send Elbridge Gerry and John Marshall to join Pinckney in a new diplomatic delegation to France. Emboldened by Napoleon Bonaparte's military victories in western Europe, the French were openly hostile to the Americans when they arrived in October of 1797. In what became dubbed "The XYZ Affair," French officials, identified to Congress and in the American press only by those initials, bullied and humiliated the American diplomats with demands for bribes that insulted U.S. sovereignty. The chairman of the House Ways and Means Committee famously expressed American resistance to French demands when he declared "Millions for defense, but not one cent for tribute!"

Controversy raged throughout 1798 and the Federalist Congress verged on declaring war. Congress fortified the U.S. Navy, and Adams ordered Hamilton to strengthen the still-small U.S. Army. French and U.S. ships fought skirmishes in the Caribbean. In early 1799, as French ships hovered off the coast of America, the two countries seemed to be involved in an undeclared Quasi-War. To deflate tensions, Adams decided to send a new team of diplomats to France in October. Although he managed to avoid an all-out war, he faced criticism from political opponents and from fellow Federalists, who thought he was weak on France.

## Alien and Sedition Acts

President Adams was less successful in his efforts to balance domestic political tensions during the Quasi-War with France. Believing that he had public support, Adams and his allies in Congress passed a series of **Alien and Sedition Acts** during

This cartoon, "Property Protected à la Françoise," lampoons the quasi-war between the United States and France and the XYZ affair. In the image, menacing French figures threaten America, represented by the woman dressed in fashionable clothing with a Native American feathered head dress. The "French Directors" demand private plunder to put in their sack at the point of a sword labeled "French Argument." Meanwhile, John Bull, a character representing Great Britain, sits atop a rock in the background laughing at the conflict.

the summer of 1798. These acts only aggravated political and social conflicts around the country. The three "Alien" acts restricted immigration into the United States and gave the president power to deport anyone thought to be dangerous. The Sedition Law imposed steep fines and prison sentences on anyone found guilty of conspiring to "oppose any measure or measures of the government of the United States" or anyone who spoke or wrote maliciously against the government or the president. Both sets of measures directly targeted Democratic Republicans, who found support among immigrants from Ireland, France, and the Caribbean as well as from radical newspaper editors. The Alien and Sedition Acts backfired.

To many, the Sedition Act seemed like an unconstitutional overreaction to political opposition. Several high-profile newspaper editors, convicted of sedition and imprisoned for writing against the Adams administration, became martyrs who galvanized public support against the Sedition law. In August 1798, Vice President Jefferson secretly drafted resolutions, subsequently passed by the Democratic-Republican controlled Kentucky legislature, denouncing the laws as unconstitutional and arguing that states need not comply with them. James Madison then drafted a similar set of resolutions for Virginia. Other state legislatures, including Massachusetts and Maryland, denounced the Kentucky and Virginia Resolutions as dangerous precedents for state nullification of federal law. Americans entered the election year of 1800 barely at peace with France and fraught with internal division over the practice of political opposition.

## Slave Rebellions: Saint Domingue and Virginia

Anxieties among American elites in the late 1790s also increased because of signs of revolution close to home—especially in the form of slave revolts. In 1791 black slaves in the French colony of Saint Domingue (now the nation of Haiti) on the Caribbean island of Hispaniola revolted against their masters, whom they drastically outnumbered. Led by charismatic former slave **Toussaint Louverture**, the rebels switched to the French revolutionary cause in 1794, after the French government abolished slavery. Louverture, now the governor general of Saint Domingue, bested Spanish and English forces and took over the entire island of Hispaniola for the French; he also pacified the large mixed-race population on the island. By the end of the decade Toussaint ruled Saint Domingue, and many white politicians in the United States were unsettled by the specter of a formerly enslaved black rebel in charge of a major French colony near U.S. shores.

Their fears seemed justified when a Virginia slave named **Gabriel**, emboldened by the Saint Domingue revolt and the political divisions he witnessed inside his state, planned a large-scale revolt to coincide with the 1800 presidential election. Gabriel believed that free blacks and artisans would join his cause, and he planned to carry a banner reading "death or Liberty," a play on Patrick Henry's phrase from the American Revolution, when he marched on the capital at Richmond. Instead, Gabriel and his compatriots were betrayed, and he was tried and executed in October 1800. Virginia legislators imposed harsher slave codes in the aftermath of the rebellion in an effort to crack down on any rebellious slaves who might be inspired by Saint Domingue.

### STUDY QUESTIONS FOR PARTY CONFLICT INTENSIFIES

1. **What diplomatic challenges (both with Europe and with Indian nations) faced the United States during the 1790s?**
2. **In what ways did the Alien and Sedition Acts expose fundamental differences between Democratic Republicans and Federalists?**

# THE "REVOLUTION" OF 1800 AND THE REVOLUTION OF 1804

Thomas Jefferson claimed, "The election of 1800 was as real a revolution in the principles of our government as that of 1776 was in its form." Jefferson referred to the shift in power from the Federalists to his own Democratic-Republican party and his hopes that he might return the United States to the principles of the American Revolution as he and his supporters interpreted them. Because most Americans still believed that politicians should hold disinterested republican values, they still did not openly accept party politics. They practiced them nonetheless, and it seemed remarkable that presidential power could change hands peacefully from one party to another. Jefferson's own power would be tested by the continued tensions from the Anglo-French Wars, now fueled by Napoleon Bonaparte's rise to power in France. Meanwhile, the radical social and political upheaval in Saint Domingue grew until the colony declared its independence as the Haitian republic in 1804. Both "revolutions" would change American politics.

## Jefferson Elected

Jefferson considered the election of 1800 so revolutionary in part because the transfer of power from Federalists to Democratic Republicans took place peacefully. In the immediate aftermath of the Quasi-War with France, many Federalists believed that a pro-French Democratic-Republican victory might lead to all-out civil war in the United States. One Connecticut Federalist predicted that if Jefferson beat Adams for the presidency, "the soil will be soaked with blood, and the nation black with crimes." Although Jefferson served as vice president under Adams, the two men held truly opposite opinions, and Adams had largely ignored Jefferson while they were in office. Adams also faced opposition from Alexander Hamilton and other members of his own Federalist party who were more conservative than he was.

State campaigning and legislative elections leading up to the 1800 presidential race mattered enormously because the states exercised huge influence in the electoral college. Voters exercised little direct choice in the presidential election. In 10 of 16 states, the presidential electors were chosen by the state legislature, and the remaining 6 used a patchwork system in which only some of the presidential electors were chosen by popular vote.

By the time each state had chosen its members of the electoral college, in early December, it was clear that the election would be deadlocked. When the electoral college votes were officially tallied, Adams was defeated for president, but neither Burr nor Jefferson could be declared the winner. Thomas Jefferson and Aaron Burr tied with 73 votes each, and John Adams received 65. The Constitution provided that the candidate with the most votes would become president, while the runner-up would assume the vice presidency, but the Democratic Republicans had failed to plan their electoral voting well enough to have their intended vice presidential candidate, Aaron Burr, come in second. With Burr and Jefferson tied, the Constitution stipulated that the House of Representatives, still ruled by a Federalist majority, would decide the election.

In February 1801 the House met in continuous session to decide the election. Burr refused to concede, and he even considered striking a deal with Federalists to become president. Ultimately, however, after 36 rounds of balloting, Jefferson prevailed, and Burr was elected vice president. Constitutional crisis was averted, and violence never broke out as the Federalists ceded the presidency to the Democratic Republicans.

## Democracy: Limits and Conflicts

As they transitioned into power, the Democratic Republicans wished to erase the Federalist influence in politics: the use of centralized federal power, the turn toward Britain, the public debt, the excise taxes. As the Democratic Republicans believed in agriculture and a democracy built on the power of free, white, property-holding men, they limited the political voice of women and free African Americans, both of whom had made some limited advances under the Federalists. In 1807, for example, the New Jersey legislature disenfranchised property-holding women and free African Americans who had voted for decades, largely because they supported the Federalist party.

The Democratic Republicans exercised power in Congress and in the executive branch during the first decade of the 19th century, but they still had to battle the Federalists in state politics and in the federal judiciary. Among his last acts as president, John Adams filled the federal courts and many other appointed offices with Federalists and nominated moderate Virginia Federalist John Marshall as chief justice of the Supreme Court. Marshall became a strong opponent of the Democratic Republicans as he put his imprint on the Court. In the landmark 1803 case of ***Marbury v. Madison***, Marshall's opinion firmly established the principle of "judicial review," the right of the U.S. Supreme Court to rule on the constitutionality of legislation and executive actions. The case concerned a battle between one of Adams's Federalist appointees and Democratic-Republican Secretary of State James Madison, but in the long run the particulars mattered far less than Marshall's assertion of judicial authority.

The divide between the parties in the United States remained bitter, not the least because neither one was yet convinced of the legitimacy of party politics. In 1801, John Adams called the Democratic Republicans "a group of foreign liars, encouraged by a few ambitious native gentlemen," while most Democratic Republicans held Federalists in no higher regard. Unless personal honor became intertwined with electoral matters—as was the case in 1804 when Vice President Burr killed Alexander Hamilton in a duel over perceived personal insults during the New York governor's race—most battles took place in the realm of politics. Unlike the French or Haitians, Americans in the 1790s did not resort to widespread violence or turmoil to work out their ideological differences.

## Haitian Revolution

The majority of white Americans were shocked as slave rebellion and colonial unrest in Saint Domingue spread into a national revolution by 1804. Although the nation of Haiti declared its independence from France, and Haitians pledged to "live free and independent" in terms familiar to those who had lived through the American Revolution, the new republic did not receive support from the U.S. government. The 1805 Haitian constitution's permanent abolition of slavery, designation of all Haitian citizens as "Black," and declaration that "No white man" would "ever be able to acquire any property" struck most white Americans as far too radical.

Toussaint Louverture, the former slave who ruled the island of Saint Domingue in 1801, fought off a French invasion early in 1802. But later that year French troops

GLOBAL PASSAGES

# Revolutionary Migrations

Thousands of people moved around the Atlantic world as a result of the French and Haitian Revolutions—making migration one of the most important influences of the Atlantic revolutions. Free and slave migrants to the United States from France and Haiti brought with them food, clothing, language, and other cultural traditions that influenced and changed American society.

Tens of thousands of people fled France during the early years of the Revolution there, many of whom were clergy and aristocrats, but the ranks of émigrés (as they were known) also included soldiers, peasants, and even workers and middle-class radicals. Among the thousands who spent at least some time in the United States was the former British radical and American Revolutionary pamphleteer Thomas Paine, who assumed French citizenship in 1792 (the year he published *The Rights of Man*), only to flee back to the United States in 1802. Most French émigrés did not have the choice to return home until at least the 1820s, since the French government confiscated and sold their property and condemned many of them.

Philadelphia, the capital of the United States during the 1790s, became the center of French culture in America during that decade, as scores of French émigrés settled there. Louis Philippe, the future king of France, took part in Philadelphia high society and romanced several American women. The boarding house where members of Congress and Vice President Adams lived was run by a Monsieur Francis. Aristocratic and bourgeois French émigrés in Philadelphia established political clubs, fraternal lodges, cultural societies, and businesses ranging from bakeries to wig shops to bookstores and newspapers.

The slave rebellion in Saint Domingue that became the Haitian Revolution prompted even more migration to the United States: between 1793 and 1809 at least 15,000 slaves, white French colonists, and free people of color fled from the island to America. Most San Dominguan refugees, about two-thirds of them white and one-third of them black, ended up in American port cities (Philadelphia, New Orleans, New York, Boston, Baltimore, and Charleston) because they often escaped on French merchant ships.

The thousands of white slave masters who managed to force their slaves to accompany them from Saint Domingue presented a dilemma for the United States. Slave masters sought loopholes, for example, to the Pennsylvania manumission law that promised freedom after six months to any slave brought to the state. In 1809 Congress voted an exemption to the recent prohibition on international importation of slaves when it allowed white masters to bring more than 3,000 slaves with

The high empire waists, narrow skirts, light material, and embroidery on these dresses show the stylistic influence of French fashion on U.S. women at the turn of the 19th century. The dress in the back was rumored to have been worn by Maryland native Elizabeth Patterson in December 1803 when she married Jerome Bonaparte, Napoleon's brother. The dress caused a scandal because it was so different from previous fashion and because it was so sheer.

them to Louisiana from Cuba, where they had taken refuge after the Haitian Revolution. In 1811 **Charles Deslondes**, a slave brought to Louisiana, led one of the bloodiest and largest slave rebellions in American history.

The United States had also influenced Saint Domingue. Haitian leader Jacques Dessalines was an admirer of the American Revolution, and future Haitian president and king **Henri Christope** had very possibly served among hundreds of mixed-race Saint Dominguans alongside French troops at the Siege of Savannah during the American Revolution. In later decades, hundreds of African Americans would emigrate to Haiti, viewing the island as a bastion of black power and freedom. Their journey formed just part of the complex story of migration across the Caribbean.

- How do you think the migration of tens of thousands of people across the Atlantic and the Caribbean shaped the relationship between the United States and the revolutions in France and Saint Domingue?
- How significant was the decision by Congress to allow Saint Dominguan slaveholders to bring slaves into the United States after the international slave trade had been outlawed?

arrested him and deported him to France, where he died in prison. The French probably planned to reimpose slavery if they could control Saint Domingue. **Jean-Jacques Dessalines**, another former slave and a skilled military commander, took over leadership of the black revolt. In 1802, after a bloody campaign, Dessalines captured the French stronghold of Le Cap Français. He then expelled French troops and most of the remaining white residents who had not already fled or been executed. On January 1, 1804, Dessalines declared Haitian independence.

The new Haitian republic found little support with President Jefferson. White politicians were concerned that American slaves would be encouraged by the successful slave revolt and national revolution in Haiti. Moreover, Jefferson sought good relations with French emperor Napoleon Bonaparte. Several southern states extended repressive laws they had passed in the aftermath of Gabriel's Rebellion. These laws further restricted the rights of free blacks, imposed harsher slave discipline, and forbade slave owners from freeing slaves and slaves from purchasing their own freedom. The Adams administration had encouraged Louverture's efforts against the French, but now Jefferson refused to recognize the independent Haitian republic.

## The Louisiana Purchase

Although Thomas Jefferson supported the limitation of federal government power, as president he exercised great authority in expanding the territory of the United States. In the October 1800 Treaty of San Ildefonso, Spain secretly ceded the entire Louisiana territory, including New Orleans, back to France. More than one-half million Americans living west of the Appalachian Mountains relied on the Mississippi River for their growing agricultural trade, and they worried when Spain closed New Orleans as a precursor to the transfer of power. Jefferson was convinced that development of wide-open land by American small farmers held the key to the country's future, and he wanted to prevent Napoleon from pursuing imperial dreams of his own in North America.

Napoleon, preoccupied with troubles in Haiti and a recent military defeat in Egypt, sought to rebuild strength for the next round of war against Great Britain. As a result, when Jefferson sent Robert Livingston and James Monroe to France to attempt to purchase New Orleans and a portion of West Florida, Napoleon's foreign minister Talleyrand instead offered to sell the entire Louisiana territory.

The Constitution did not directly address whether the federal government could purchase new territory, but after some agonizing Jefferson concluded that the "laws of necessity, of self-preservation, of saving our country when in danger" authorized the purchase. In April 1803 he paid $15 million to purchase the vast Louisiana Territory, which almost doubled the size of the United States. Jefferson argued that this strong use of federal power still fit with his Democratic-Republican vision because it opened so much land for farming and small-scale commerce. The Louisiana Purchase was hailed as a glorious triumph when it was announced on July 4, 1803.

**STUDY QUESTIONS FOR THE "REVOLUTION" OF 1800 AND THE REVOLUTION OF 1804**

1. **How "revolutionary" was Jefferson's election in the "Revolution" of 1800?**
2. **In what ways did slave revolts and the Haitian revolution influence American politics?**

# TRADE, CONFLICT, WARFARE

Jefferson hoped the new Louisiana territory could be developed for U.S. economic growth, as it seemed to offer limitless opportunity for commerce and trade. Between the 1790s and 1807, the United States increasingly defined itself as a commercial nation with a role in the world economy. International trade energized the American economy, but it would also lead the nation into conflict and war in North Africa and Europe. Trade offered economic benefits, but they came with diplomatic entanglements and military conflict.

## Transatlantic and Caribbean Trade

The Anglo-French wars and upheaval in the Caribbean presented both opportunities and obstacles. Following the Revolutionary War the French, British, and Spanish all opened new avenues of trade to Americans, who in the 1790s sought to expand opportunities even further. During the first Anglo-French War (1793–1801) American pursuit of trade as a neutral nation had caused international friction. Americans continued to try to expand trade during the European Peace of Amiens (1801–1803), although their efforts proved difficult. When the Napoleonic Wars resumed in 1803, Americans increasingly found themselves lured into naval conflict.

When the French Revolution first spread into open warfare in Europe, the United States benefited, since the French and British allowed Americans limited neutral trading rights that undermined previous Spanish and Portuguese monopolies. American exports grew from $20.2 million in 1793 to $94 million in 1801. Much of that growth came as the United States became the main trade intermediary between European nations and their Caribbean colonies. Both France and Britain allowed U.S. traders to carry goods to their rival colonies in the Caribbean by way of the United States.

During the period of European peace from 1801 to 1803 American exports again declined to $54 million; at the same time, however, U.S. traders continued to increase their percentage share of the Caribbean re-export trade. Once the Europeans renewed their warfare in 1803, U.S. trade in the Caribbean and Latin America again skyrocketed by 1807 to its highest level ever. Exports peaked at $108 million in 1807. Imports

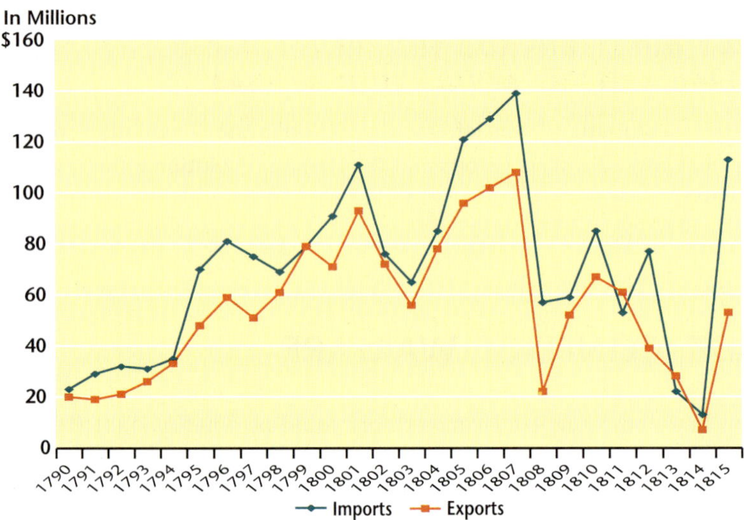


▲ **Figure 8.1**

**Total U.S. imports and exports, 1790–1815** Use this graph to think about the causes and effects of the War of 1812.

increased even more, from $33 million in 1793 to $146 million in 1807—an indication of the growing appetite for European goods.

Americans did move to curtail one area of international exchange in this period—the international slave trade. Although the U.S. Constitution forbade Congress to outlaw the international trade before the year 1808, legislative debate on how to halt the international traffic in slaves began in 1806. Congressional representatives from slave and free states disagreed bitterly over the status of illegally imported slaves and punishments for slave smugglers. The British outlawed their slave trade in 1807, and the U.S. Congress followed by passing a law in March of that year banning the international slave trade as of January 1, 1808. The law was significant, although it did nothing to curtail the growing internal slave trade, and the U.S. population of slaves would skyrocket in coming decades.

Although the European states periodically recognized U.S. neutral trading rights, they also interfered with U.S. shipping on a regular basis. After their 1805 victory over Napoleon at the Battle of Trafalgar, the British denied the United States right to engage in re-export trade with France and began seizing scores of U.S. ships and their cargo. Between 1803 and 1812 the British also detained an estimated 6,000 U.S. sailors and impressed them into the Royal Navy.

## Mediterranean Trade: Barbary Wars

The United States also faced conflict in the Mediterranean. In the 17th and 18th centuries ships from the Barbary states of Algeria, Morocco, Tunis, and Tripoli harassed traders in the Mediterranean and captured foreign hostages. Lacking European protection after the Revolutionary War, the United States sought to contain the Barbary privateers—or pirates, as Europeans and Americans called them—by concluding a series of treaties in the 1780s and 1790s and paying tribute to the Barbary rulers. Congress, and particularly Thomas Jefferson, had been reluctant to pay too much, and Americans continued to be harassed and kidnapped. By the mid-1790s, Algiers alone had sold over 100 American citizens into slavery. The image of Christian Americans serving as captive slaves in exotic Muslim settings, spread by newspaper articles, pamphlets, and books about their captivity, aroused the American public against the practice. When Congress agreed to pay $1 million to Algiers in 1796 to free American captives—a figure equal to roughly one-sixth of the federal budget—the other Barbary leaders raised their demands.

Despite President Jefferson's reduction of the defense budget and the Democratic Republicans' general skepticism of building U.S. naval power, Jefferson proved willing to fight in North Africa. When the Pasha of Tripoli, **Yusuf Qaramanli**, declared war on the United States in 1801, Jefferson imposed a blockade on Tripoli and endorsed a program of shipbuilding. When the U.S. warship *Philadelphia* ran aground off the coast of Tripoli in 1803, the Tripolitans captured all 307 of its sailors and demanded more than $1.5 million in tribute. **Captain Stephen Decatur** and his *Enterprise* crew then slipped into the harbor of Tripoli and burned the *Philadelphia*. **William Eaton**, the U.S. consul to Tunis, invaded the Tripolitan city of Derna with the help of Yusuf Quaramanli's rival, his brother Ahmed. In June 1805 the United States and Tripoli reached a peace agreement that included a new U.S. payment of $60,000 in tribute to ransom the captured American sailors.

Later, Algiers declared war on the United States, but it agreed to a peace treaty after Captain Decatur captured the flagship of the Algerian fleet in June 1815. Despite creative military action, the ongoing Barbary conflicts exposed how weak the United States remained in the world. Only after 1815, when the nation proved it could wage war against Great Britain, did the Barbary states agree to stop demanding tribute payments and allow freer Mediterranean trade.

## Western Discontents

Although the Louisiana purchase had blunted the influence of France inside North America, many U.S. citizens still encountered conflicts with Spain, Britain, and Indian nations. After Vice President Burr was not reelected for a second term, he sought to aggrandize himself with a set of convoluted imperial maneuvers. By 1805, Burr organized western settlers and planned an attack to wrest control of Mexico away from Spain. One of his coconspirators, James Wilkinson, who was both the highest-ranking U.S. army general and a paid Spanish secret agent, revealed the plot to Thomas Jefferson. Burr was captured and tried for treason in 1807, but Chief Justice John Marshall's narrow constitutional interpretation of treason led to Burr's acquittal. Burr fled to England in 1808.

After the 1785 Treaty of Greenville, white American settlers poured into the Northwest Territory, which occupied roughly the area of modern-day Ohio, Indiana, Michigan, and Wisconsin. Population increased so quickly that Ohio reached the required

60,000 residents and became a state in 1803. This status placed additional pressure on the Shawnee and other northwest Indians who had resisted American expansion and worked with the British after the Revolution. **Tecumseh**, who had helped lead the Shawnee against the United States in the 1790s, moved further west to the White River in Indiana, where he established Prophetstown. Tecumseh's brother, **Tenskwatawa**, who was known as "The Prophet," preached a religious revitalization movement that urged Indian peoples to reject the adaptation embraced by tribes like the Cherokee and, instead, to return to traditional ways of life.

In addition to Tenskwatawa's message, Tecumseh used his personal magnetism to build a Pan-Indian movement among differing tribes who all faced American encroachment on their lands. Tecumseh rejected the notion of private land ownership, and he urged other leaders to repudiate past American treaties and to refuse new ones. While Tecumseh was away gathering allies, Indiana territorial governor **William Henry Harrison** attacked Prophetstown and defeated Shawnee warriors at the Battle of Tippecanoe on November 7, 1811. Tecumseh aligned with the British in Canada and awaited the next confrontation.

## European Wars and Commercial Sanctions

International conflict did not seem far off as American tensions with Britain, and to a lesser degree France, built after 1805. With the United States now firmly engaged in transatlantic trade, disaster struck when Britain and France moved to restrict trade and to impose naval blockades on one another. The British agreed to new trade relations with the United States in the **Monroe-Pinckney Treaty of 1806**, but the Democratic-Republican controlled U.S. Senate refused to ratify the treaty. In the summer of 1807 the British ship *Leopard* fired on the U.S. warship *Chesapeake* and impressed several of her sailors—an action that outraged the American public. Britain declared in the November 1807 **Orders in Council** that U.S. ships would have to stop in British ports for licensing and inspection before they could trade with France or French colonies, or they would be seized. The French countered later that year with the Milan Decree, which stated ships would be seized if they complied with the British orders.

The Democratic Republicans controlled large majorities in both houses of Congress, and they first tried to avoid war by imposing commercial sanctions on Britain and France. Congress approved the Embargo Act in December 1807, which cut off all foreign trade. The act hurt European economies, but it did far more damage to the United States. James Madison, Jefferson's Democratic-Republican successor as president, continued to support the notion of controlling international relations through trade sanctions, even though the embargo seemed ineffective. In the Non-Intercourse Act of 1809 Congress reopened trade with countries other than Britain and France. All restrictions were lifted in May 1810 because they were too difficult to enforce.

France was able to exploit the terms of the legislation that replaced the Non-Intercourse Act, known as Macon's Bill No. 2, in order to shift American hostilities decisively toward Great Britain in 1811. Macon's Bill No. 2 reopened trade with France and Britain, but promised to reimpose sanctions on one side if the other agreed to stop harassing ships and recognize U.S. neutral trading rights. In July the French foreign minister, the duc de Cadore, agreed to withdraw sanctions against U.S. shipping. U.S. political opinion then turned against Britain.

**STUDY QUESTIONS FOR TRADE, CONFLICT, WARFARE**

1. **How did American policies toward naval interference by the Barbary states differ from those they applied to Britain and France?**
2. **What were the effects of European warfare on American commerce?**

# THE WAR OF 1812

More than a decade of trying to remain neutral in the wars between France and England had not worked for the United States, and trade sanctions had failed. By 1812, American political ire focused on Great Britain. If the United States refused to fight Britain, would that not compromise its independence hard won in the American Revolution? Perhaps only warfare would give the United States a chance to be taken seriously on the world stage.

## War Declared

President Madison and the belligerent Democratic Republicans in control of Congress, known as the War Hawks, agitated for war against Britain. Kentuckian Henry Clay, the Speaker of the House, and South Carolinian John C. Calhoun led the charge for war. They faced stiff opposition from Federalists, who feared that their largely New England constituents would be hurt by war and a cessation of trade. The British continued to harass American ships, although they repealed the Orders in Council and pledged to stop impressment. Just two days before the repeal, unaware that Britain had acted, the U.S. Congress narrowly voted to declare war.

The United States entered the War of 1812 on June 18, despite the resistance of Federalists and many residents of New England and the Mid-Atlantic states. The War Hawks hoped to guarantee "free trade and sailors' rights," to expel the British from North America, and to pacify Indian nations, such as the Shawnee, who they felt stood in the way of American expansion in the West. The Shawnee and many other Indians aligned themselves with the British, who promised to halt U.S. expansionism.

## Opposition to the War of 1812

Federalist New Englanders spearheaded opposition to the war throughout its duration. In the week after Congress declared war, the severity of party conflict over the war became apparent as terrible rioting broke out in Baltimore, a politically divided city. Alexander Hanson, a Federalist newspaper editor, denounced the war in print as "unnecessary, inexpedient" and as driven by Democratic-Republican personal grudges. In return, a pro-war mob demolished his printing office. After Hanson continued to publish his paper, he was taken into protective custody, but a mob rushed the jail, savagely beat Hanson, and killed former Revolutionary War general James Lingan, who was trying to protect him. City officials did little to stop the violence.

Despite the chilling effect of the Baltimore riots and cries that they were disloyal, Federalists maintained political resistance throughout the war. New England Federalists were free to push their opposition because they still held state majorities. Federalist governors in Rhode Island, Massachusetts, and Connecticut all initially refused to mobilize state militias or have them controlled by federal officers, but eventually most militias did participate. In 1814 delegates from New England states gathered in secret at the Hartford Convention, where they discussed seceding from the union and endorsed the idea that states could nullify federal laws.

## U.S. Offensives in Canada

As during the Revolutionary War, the War of 1812 saw another series of unsuccessful American invasions of Canada. Expelling the British from their largest North American colony would surely grant new land to the United States and deny support to Indian enemies. In 1812, commanding army general Henry Dearborn put forth a plan for a three-pronged attack on Canada.

In July of 1812, Michigan territorial governor William Hull and his troops crossed into Canada at the Detroit River, but their progress stalled, and British general Isaac Brock then laid siege against the American fort at Detroit. In August, Hull surrendered at Fort Mackinac, and he delivered both Detroit and Fort Dearborn, the present-day site of Chicago, to the British. In October of 1812, American forces outnumbered British, Canadian, and allied Indian forces at the Niagara River, but Stephen Van Rensselaer's plans to capture the Queenstown Heights failed because he could not figure out a way to cross the river. Van Rensselear, called "Van Bladder" by his men because he spewed so much hot air in useless speeches, also abandoned plans to attack Fort Erie in November. In addition, General Henry Dearborn's attack on Montreal failed. Problems plagued all three attacks on Canada as coordinating army and militia troops proved difficult.

Secretary of War John Armstrong focused on Canada again in 1813, as Britain and the United States battled for control of the Great Lakes. In April, an American force under Zebulon Pike inflicted a bloody defeat on the city of York, present-day Toronto. Pike's men looted houses and burned government buildings. In the West, British general Henry Proctor, bolstered by Tecumseh's Indian forces, pushed back the Americans by invading Ohio and attacking Fort Meigs. Proctor failed to stop Indian forces from slaughtering American prisoners along the River Raisin, and Tecumseh personally had to intervene. "Remember the Raisin!" became a rallying cry among American troops.

## Tecumseh and Pan-Indian Resistance

General Proctor's second attack into Ohio in July 1813 was actually planned by Tecumseh, the Shawnee leader. Proctor and Tecumseh unsuccessfully attacked Fort Meigs a second time and then went after Fort Stephenson, a small fortification on

**Map 8.2**

**The War of 1812** This map depicts the major battles and campaigns in the War of 1812.

the Sandusky River expertly defended by Kentucky sharpshooters. When Proctor's men lost the engagement, the general blamed Tecumseh and retreated into Canada. Tecumseh urged the British to continue the offensive against the United States, and he compared Proctor to "a fat animal" that puts its tail "between its legs and runs off." Some of Tecumseh's allies grew disillusioned with the British, and the great warrior now fought to hold together his coalition.

A new American army and militia force under the command of former Indiana territorial governor William Henry Harrison and **Richard Mentor Johnson**, a Kentucky congressman, pursued Proctor as he pulled his forces back into Canada. On October 5, 1813, they clashed with Proctor and Tecumseh at the Battle of the Thames near Moraviantown. The American troops routed the British, and although the Indian fighters held out longer, they lost heart when word spread that Tecumseh had been killed. Some of Johnson's militia troops claimed to have cut off pieces of Tecumseh's skin as souvenirs after the battle. It is more likely that Tecumseh's men removed him from the field. Mutilated or not, Tecumseh's death also meant the death of his Pan-Indian resistance movement against the United States.

Although some of Tecumseh's allies immediately ended their British alliance and began to make terms with the United States, others continued to resist in their own ways. Among those who fought in Canada were Little Warrior and other members of the "Red Stick" faction of the Creek nation. Since the 1780s these Red Sticks had resisted the Creek government's moves toward accommodation and their grants of land rights to the United States in Georgia and Alabama. After returning from fighting with Tecumseh in the summer of 1812, the Red Sticks, assisted by the Spanish, ignited a Creek civil war. After Red Sticks destroyed Fort Mims in August, U.S. army troops joined the fight, and General **Andrew Jackson** pursued the hostile Creeks with a vengeance. In November 1813 Jackson defeated the Red Sticks at Tallushatchee and Talladega and then almost completely wiped them out at the Battle of Horseshoe Bend in March 1814. The United States used the opportunity of the War of 1812 to tamp down Indian resistance.

## Naval War

When it entered the War of 1812, no one thought that the United States could match the Royal Navy, the world's most impressive naval fighting force; however, American naval forces did better than expected. Both at sea and on the Great Lakes, the U.S. Navy was initially more impressive than U.S. ground troops. The United States benefited partly because Great Britain's naval attentions were being absorbed by the final

This 1833 engraving by William Emmons shows how Americans continued to be fascinated by the death of Tecumseh at the Battle of the Thames long after the battle in 1813. Richard Mentor Johnson, who claimed to be the man who shot Tecumseh, was elected vice president in part because of that reputation. Tecumseh was revered as a brave enemy whose tragic death nonetheless proved American superiority to Indians.

struggle against Napoleon, but it also relied on some very skilled U.S. commanders. Two impressive early victories came when Captain Isaac Hull's fast USS *Constitution* bested the HMS *Guerriere* off the coast of Boston in August 1812 and when Captain Stephen Decatur's USS *United States* captured the British frigate HMS *Macedonian* as a prize near the Canary Islands in October. In December the USS *Constitution* outmaneuvered the HMS *Java* near Brazil.

Early in 1813, Americans controlled Lake Ontario and successfully repelled a British attack on their naval base at Sackets Harbor. Even more impressive was the September 10, 1813, victory at the Battle of Lake Erie, where **Oliver Hazard Perry** first commanded the *Lawrence* and then, when it became incapacitated, took the helm of the *Niagara* to beat a British fleet of six ships. After the thrilling victory Perry wrote to William Henry Harrison: "We have met the enemy, and they are ours." Later in 1813, U.S. naval victories slowed, however, once the British imposed a stronger blockade on the United States.

## British Offensive

By the end of 1813, after Napoleon's October defeat, the British turned new attention and resources on the United States. The U.S. troops faced more experienced, better supplied, and better commanded British soldiers.

In the north, the British and Americans traded the advantage in 1814. The governor-general of Canada, Sir George Prevost, planned an offensive at Plattsburgh, New York, in September, but he retreated after American naval forces won a decisive victory on Lake Champlain and cut off his supply route. American general James Wilkinson failed in his effort to attack Montreal in October 1813, but fighting continued there the following year. American troops won victories at Chippewa and Lundy's Lane and twice attacked Fort Erie before blowing it up entirely on November 8. The British occupied northern Maine and found the American locals largely sympathetic.

The British offensive on the Chesapeake was far more successful. Congress was slow to fortify Washington, while the British blockaded the coast and invaded Maryland in August. On August 24 British forces massed at Bladensburg, across the Potomac from the capital, and badly defeated U.S. forces. Most of the inhabitants of the capital had been evacuated, and congressional clerks and first lady **Dolley Madison** saved government property and records. The British entered Washington on the evening of August 24 and burned almost every government building, including the White House, before leaving the next day. Then they captured Alexandria, Virginia, without a fight.

The British advance was stopped, however, when they reached Baltimore in early September. Francis Scott Key wrote the poem "The Star-Spangled Banner" after watching the battle of Fort McHenry on September 13. For 25 hours, the British fired over 1,500 rounds, including exploding shells and screaming Congreve rockets, at Fort McHenry. But American forces survived the bombardment with their arms intact, and they repelled the British, who retreated from Baltimore on September 15. When the British left Maryland, they took with them 2,000 runaway slaves, who later resettled in Canada.

## The War Ends

Despite the intense fighting around Washington, DC, the British were anxious to negotiate an end to the American war now that they were at peace with France. The United States and Britain signed the Treaty of Ghent, which ended the War of 1812, on Christmas Eve 1814. The treaty resulted in few dramatic changes from before the war. Britain agreed to evacuate American territory, both sides pledged to make peace with Indian nations, and each side agreed to settle Canadian border issues by future negotiation. Ironically, the treaty made no mention of the prewar naval or trade conflicts that had led to war.

Despite the fact that the Treaty restored things to a prewar status quo, the United States claimed victory. In part, the Americans' claim was based on their most glorious battle, fought at New Orleans just days after the peace treaty had been signed. On January 8, 1815, Andrew Jackson, helped by a group of international and French privateers known as the Baratarian pirates, foiled a British attack on New Orleans. The battle plans of British commander Sir Edward Packenham dissolved in the swamps and fog of the Gulf coast, and Packenham himself was killed as Jackson skillfully defended the city. In this final battle of the war, Jackson seemed to prove that Americans

### TIMELINE 1789–1815

**1789**

**April 30** George Washington inaugurated first U.S. president

**July 14** Crowds storm the Bastille in Paris, beginning the French Revolution

**1790**

**December 6** Philadelphia becomes the U.S. capital city as Washington, DC, is being built

**December 15** Bill of Rights ratified

**1791**

**August 22** Saint Domingue slave rebellion begins

**1793**

**January 21** French King Louis XVI executed

**April 8** "Citizen" Edmund Charles Genet arrives in Charleston, South Carolina

**April 22** George Washington issues Neutrality Proclamation

**1794**

**February 4** France outlaws slavery in its colonies

**September 24** President Washington orders federal military power to put down the Whiskey Rebellion

**November 19** U.S. and British diplomats secretly sign Jay's Treaty

**1795**

**June 24** U.S. Senate ratifies Jay's Treaty with Great Britain

**August 3** United States signs Treaty of Greenville with representatives from 12 Northwest Indian nations

**October 27** Pinckney's Treaty (Treaty of San Lorenzo) opens trade on the Mississippi to the United States

**1796**

**August 19** Treaty of San Ildefonso creates French-Spanish alliance against Great Britain; Spain secretly cedes Louisiana Territory to France

**November 8** John Adams elected president; Thomas Jefferson elected vice president

**1797**

**October 18** French ministers dubbed "X, Y, and Z" demand bribes from U.S. diplomats

**1798**

**April 3** President Adams publicizes the "XYZ Affair"

**June–July** Congress passes the Alien and Sedition Acts

**November 16** Kentucky legislature passes Thomas Jefferson's "Kentucky Resolutions"

**December 24** Virginia legislature passes James Madison's "Virginia Resolutions"

**1799**

**February 9** USS *Constellation* captures the French frigate *L'Insurgente* in the Caribbean

**October 16** President Adams sends a new diplomatic mission to France to avoid open war

**1800**

**August 30** Gabriel's Rebellion betrayed in Richmond, Virginia

**September 30** The United States and France agree to end their Quasi-War

**1801**

**January 20** President Adams appoints John Marshall chief justice of the Supreme Court

**February 17** The U.S. House of Representatives elects Thomas Jefferson President and Aaron Burr vice president after the electoral college is deadlocked

**May 14** Yusuf Qaramanli, the pasha of Tripoli, declares war on the United States

**1802**

**March 25** France and Britain agree to Peace of Amiens, temporarily halting warfare between them

**1803**

**February 24** Supreme Court establishes judicial

Paintings like this one, which glorified Andrew Jackson's victory at the Battle of New Orleans, helped to propel him into politics and to enhance his reputation for heroism. The image also shows in the foreground Kentucky "hunters"—rustic backwoodsmen who fought with Jackson and were revered in popular culture for their deft use of rifles and noted for their buckskin clothing.

review in *Marbury v. Madison*

**May 2** United States and France agree on Louisiana Purchase

**1804**

**January 1** Jacques Dessalines declares the Independence of Haiti

**November 6** Thomas Jefferson reelected president; George Clinton elected vice president

**1805**

**June 4** United States negotiates end to the Tripolitan War and agrees to pay $60,000 in tribute

**October 21** British defeat combined French/Spanish fleet at Battle of Trafalgar; British Admiral Horatio Nelson dies

**1807**

**February 19** Aaron Burr is arrested for plotting against Spain in the American West

**November** British Orders in Council mandate licensing for all neutral traders

**December 13** France extends the Continental System of blockades to neutral powers in the Milan Decree

**1808**

**January 1** Legislation outlawing the international slave trade becomes U.S. law

**December 7** James Madison elected president; George Clinton reelected vice president

**December 22** President Jefferson signs the Embargo Act

**1809**

**March 1** Congress replaces the Embargo Act with the Non-Intercourse Act

**1810**

**May 1** Congress replaces the Non-Intercourse Act with Macon's Bill No. 2

**November 2** President Madison opens trade with France and moves to impose sanctions on Great Britain

**1811**

**January 8** Charles Deslondes leads 150–500 slaves and runaways in a violent rebellion outside of New Orleans

**November 7** William Henry Harrison defeats Shawnee troops at Battle of Tippecanoe

**1812**

**June 18** United States declares war on Great Britain

**July** Several opponents of the War of 1812 killed in Baltimore riots

**December 2** James Madison reelected president; Elbridge Gerry elected vice president

**1813**

**August 30** The Red Sticks rebellion ignites the Creek War

**1814**

**March 27** Andrew Jackson puts down the Red Sticks Rebellion at the Battle of Horseshoe Bend

**August 8** United States and Great Britain begin peace negotiations in Ghent, Belgium

**August 24–25** Washington, DC, burned by the British

**December 24** The Treaty of Ghent, ending the War of 1812, is signed

**1815**

**January 5** New England Federalists meet in Hartford, Connecticut, to discuss their opposition to the War of 1812

**January 8** British defeated at the Battle of New Orleans

**June 30** Algeria agrees to end its war against the United States could best a well-formed European force: the combined British force suffered 2,450 casualties compared to the Americans' 350.

Although the War of 1812 changed little in international politics, the United States emerged with a new set of heroes, including Andrew Jackson and Oliver Hazard Perry. Despite the fact that many of their war plans had failed, the Democratic Republicans gained luster from the war, and the Federalist party was all but destroyed by its opposition to the war and by backlash against the Hartford Convention. Simultaneously, the Napoleonic wars were over, and the United States had proved to its citizens and to the world that it could stand up to Great Britain and survive.

### STUDY QUESTIONS FOR THE WAR OF 1812

1. **What caused the War of 1812?**
2. **How were American politics between 1789 and 1815 influenced by other nations, including Indian nations?**

## Summary

- The federal government and the first clash between political parties in the United States took shape against a backdrop of transatlantic revolution and warfare.
- Men and women in the United States supported the French Revolution at first, but its radicalization after 1793 worsened rifts in American politics.
- The United States was increasingly tied to other parts of the world through trade and migration, but these ties also brought conflict and war with North Africans (The Barbary Wars) and Europeans (the War of 1812).
- Slave revolt in Saint Domingue, which became the Haitian Revolution, influenced U.S. politics, slave revolts, and legal crackdowns on African Americans.
- Indians, both united in a Pan-Indian movement and separately, posed stiff military resistance to the United States.
- As political parties developed, American politics in the 1790s were contentious. The Democratic Republicans had the political upper hand after 1800, but the Federalists continued to oppose them until after the War of 1812.

## Key Terms and People

## Reviewing Chapter 8

1. How did the movement of people between France, Saint Domingue, and the United States influence political events in the 1790s?
2. Did the United States successfully use warfare to increase its territory and/or clout in the world between 1789 and 1815?
3. What signs do you see that the citizens of the United States were developing a national identity between 1789 and 1815?

## Further Reading

Egerton, Douglas R. *Gabriel's Rebellion: The Virginia Slave Conspiracies of 1800 & 1802*. Chapel Hill: University of North Carolina Press, 1993. Egerton argues that the Election of 1800 provided the political context and opportunity for slave rebellion in Virginia. Gabriel's rebellion was also influenced by the revolutions in France and Saint Domingue. Both slave revolts discussed in this work had a great impact on Virginia politics.

Pasley, Jeffrey L., Andrew W. Robertson, and David Waldstreicher, eds. *Beyond the Founders: New Approaches to the Political History of the Early American Republic*. Chapel Hill: University of North Carolina Press, 2004. This book of essays introduces readers to a wide variety of ways to view the politics of the early republic in chapters on everything from fashion to political communication to male social clubs.

Sharp, James Roger. *American Politics in the Early American Republic: The New Nation in Crisis*. New Haven: Yale University Press, 1993. Sharp examines the formation of what he calls the two "proto-parties" in American politics in the 1790s. He argues that the politics of the 1790s must be viewed from the vantage point that Americans did not know whether or how their country would hold together, which increased their sense of crisis over political opposition.

White, Ashli. *Encountering Revolution: Haiti and the Making of the Early Republic*. Baltimore: Johns Hopkins University Press, 2010. White's book examines how the Haitian Revolution affected U.S. politics and society during the formative years of party contest in the United States. White pays particular attention to how refugees from Saint Domingue affected the racial thinking of U.S. citizens.

Zagarri, Rosemarie. *Revolutionary Backlash: Women and Politics in the Early American Republic*. Philadelphia: University of Pennsylvania Press, 2007. Zagarri's book shows how white women participated in the political culture and partisanship of the early American republic. She shows that debates about women's rights started in the late 1780s, even as society at large was moving to restrict women to a more "social" and less political role.

# Visual Review

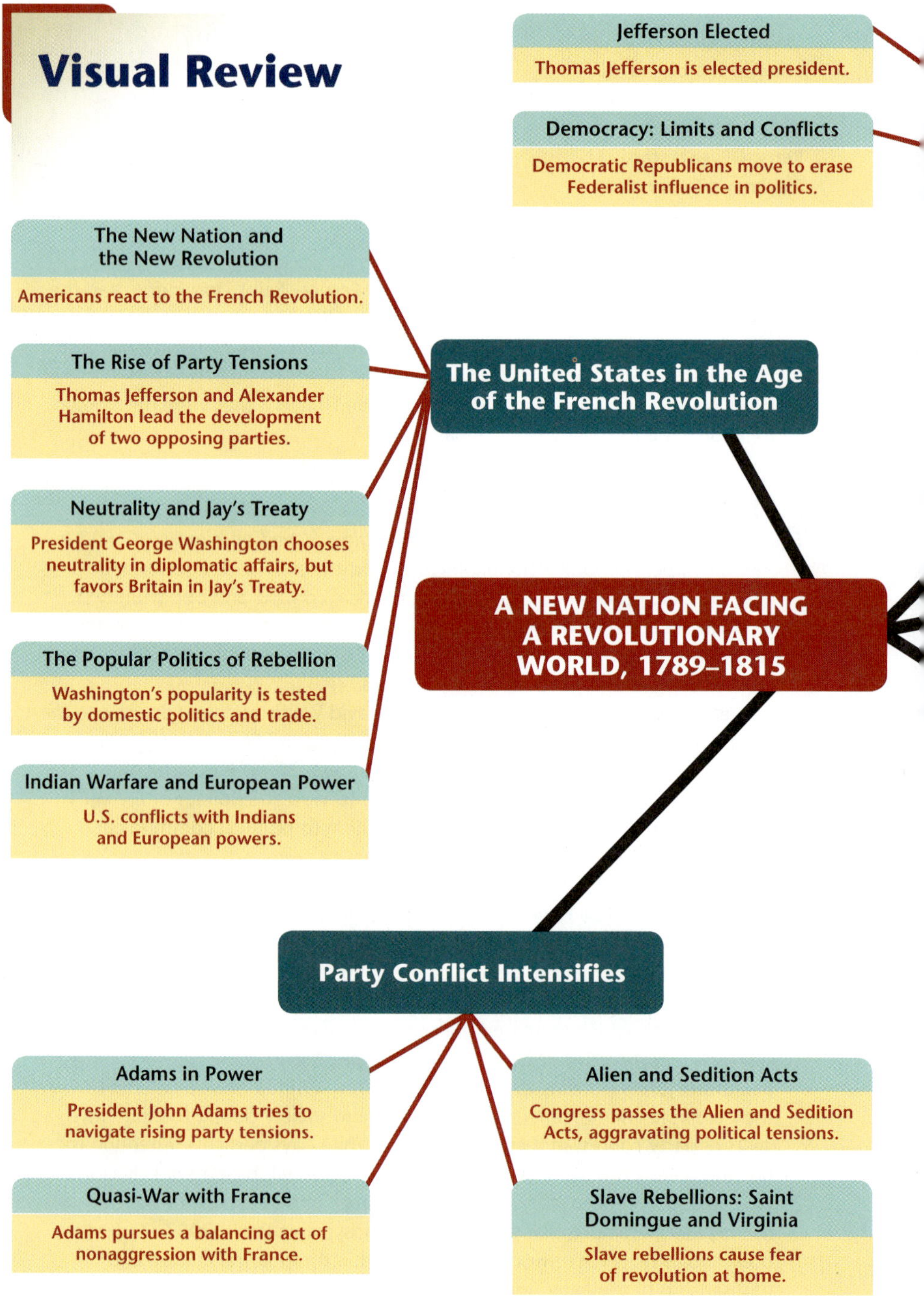

## A NEW NATION FACING A REVOLUTIONARY WORLD, 1789–1815

### The United States in the Age of the French Revolution

**The New Nation and the New Revolution**
Americans react to the French Revolution.

**The Rise of Party Tensions**
Thomas Jefferson and Alexander Hamilton lead the development of two opposing parties.

**Neutrality and Jay's Treaty**
President George Washington chooses neutrality in diplomatic affairs, but favors Britain in Jay's Treaty.

**The Popular Politics of Rebellion**
Washington's popularity is tested by domestic politics and trade.

**Indian Warfare and European Power**
U.S. conflicts with Indians and European powers.

### Party Conflict Intensifies

**Adams in Power**
President John Adams tries to navigate rising party tensions.

**Quasi-War with France**
Adams pursues a balancing act of nonaggression with France.

**Alien and Sedition Acts**
Congress passes the Alien and Sedition Acts, aggravating political tensions.

**Slave Rebellions: Saint Domingue and Virginia**
Slave rebellions cause fear of revolution at home.

**Jefferson Elected**
Thomas Jefferson is elected president.

**Democracy: Limits and Conflicts**
Democratic Republicans move to erase Federalist influence in politics.

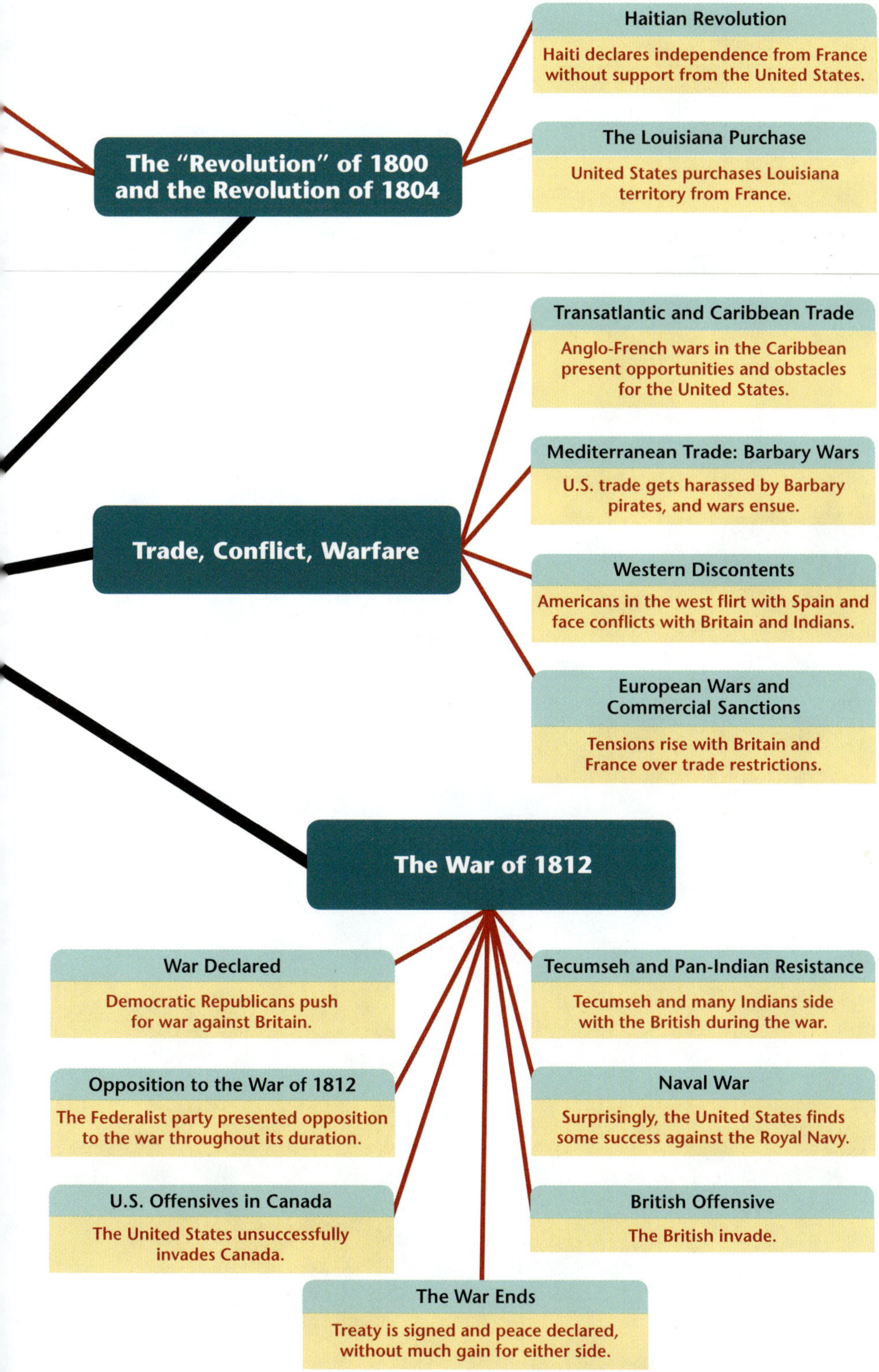

## The "Revolution" of 1800 and the Revolution of 1804

**Haitian Revolution**

Haiti declares independence from France without support from the United States.

**The Louisiana Purchase**

United States purchases Louisiana territory from France.

## Trade, Conflict, Warfare

**Transatlantic and Caribbean Trade**

Anglo-French wars in the Caribbean present opportunities and obstacles for the United States.

**Mediterranean Trade: Barbary Wars**

U.S. trade gets harassed by Barbary pirates, and wars ensue.

**Western Discontents**

Americans in the west flirt with Spain and face conflicts with Britain and Indians.

**European Wars and Commercial Sanctions**

Tensions rise with Britain and France over trade restrictions.

## The War of 1812

**War Declared**

Democratic Republicans push for war against Britain.

**Opposition to the War of 1812**

The Federalist party presented opposition to the war throughout its duration.

**U.S. Offensives in Canada**

The United States unsuccessfully invades Canada.

**The War Ends**

Treaty is signed and peace declared, without much gain for either side.

**Tecumseh and Pan-Indian Resistance**

Tecumseh and many Indians side with the British during the war.

**Naval War**

Surprisingly, the United States finds some success against the Royal Navy.

**British Offensive**

The British invade.

# American Peoples on the Move

## 1789–1824

Anne Royall traveled around the rapidly developing Alabama territory for almost a decade after her husband died in 1812. She traveled in part to avoid legal battles over her husband's will, which relatives had overturned in Virginia in 1819. A widow in her forties, Royall also gathered material for her later career as a high-profile Washington writer, critic, and pioneering woman journalist.

During just one week in January 1818 Royall personally encountered many of the people and forces transforming the southern United States. She saw General Andrew Jackson at a tavern in Melton's Bluff. She wrote to a friend that Jackson, on his way to Florida to subdue the Seminole and the Spanish, was not "handsome" but he was "easy and affable." Royall had heard many stories in Tennessee and Alabama about the military hero Jackson and how he inspired allegiance in his troops. Just days earlier she had visited his nearby cotton plantation on the Tennessee River and described the plantation as "white with cotton and alive with Negroes."

The same week Royall toured an abandoned Cherokee village near Melton's Bluff, occupied until recently by people who had ceded their land to the United States and moved to Arkansas against their wishes. Royall was amazed at the town's civilized quality of life: "Why, these Indians have been like us—cornfields, apple trees and peach trees. Fences like ours." Eleven boatloads of Cherokees camped nearby as they made their way to Arkansas. Royall described

*Black Sawyers Working in front of the Bank of Pennsylvania, Philadelphia* by John Lewis Krimmel

### CHAPTER OUTLINE



*continued on page 329*

# America in the World

John Jacob Astor established fur trading empire, a key northern industry (1808).

The Lewis and Clark expedition led to access to natural resources and territorial expansion (1803).

Andrew Jackson invaded and seized western Florida from Spain (1818).

 U.S. event that influenced the world

 International event that influenced the United States

 Event with multinational influence

 Conflict

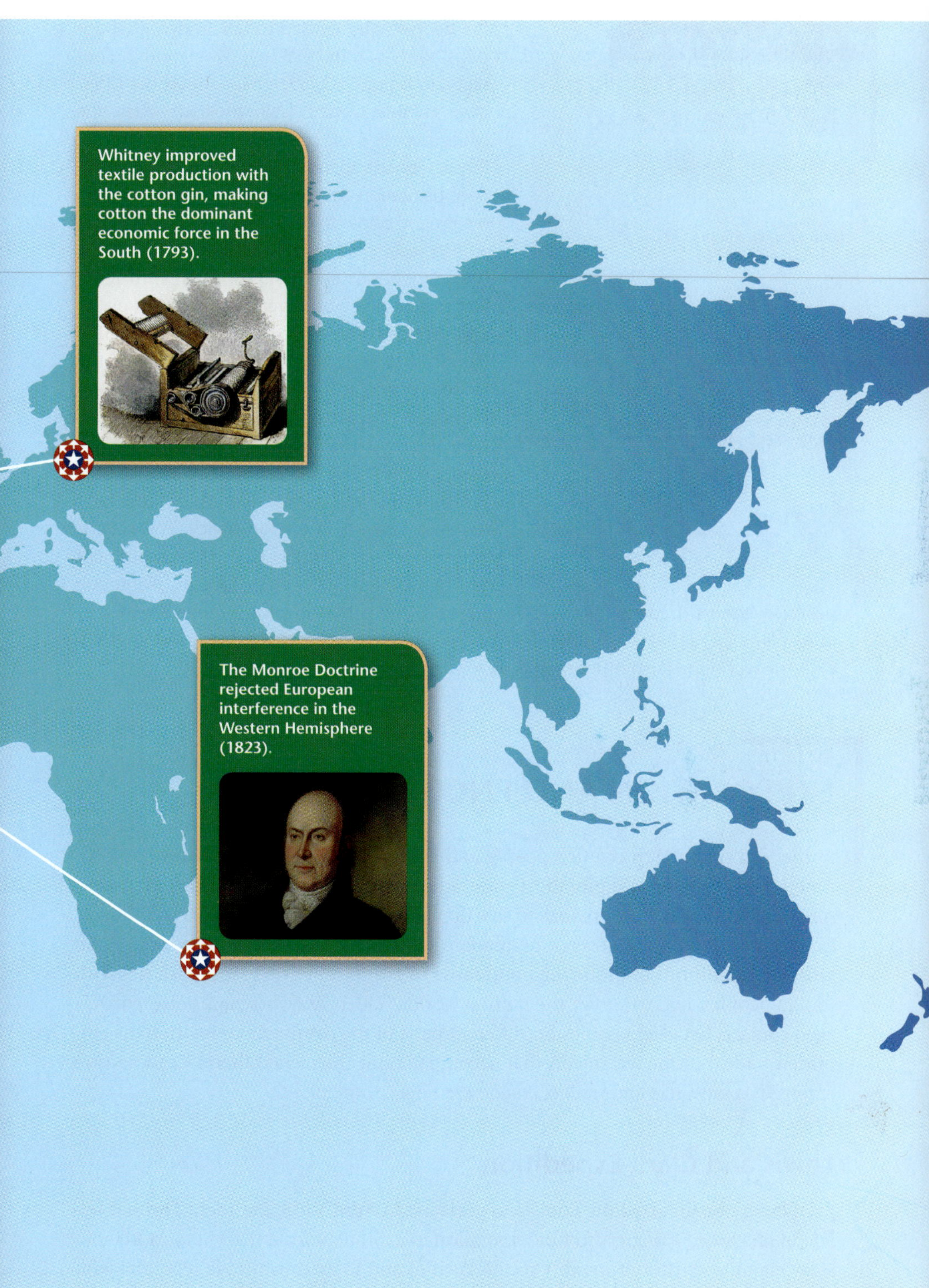
Whitney improved textile production with the cotton gin, making cotton the dominant economic force in the South (1793).
The Monroe Doctrine rejected European interference in the Western Hemisphere (1823).

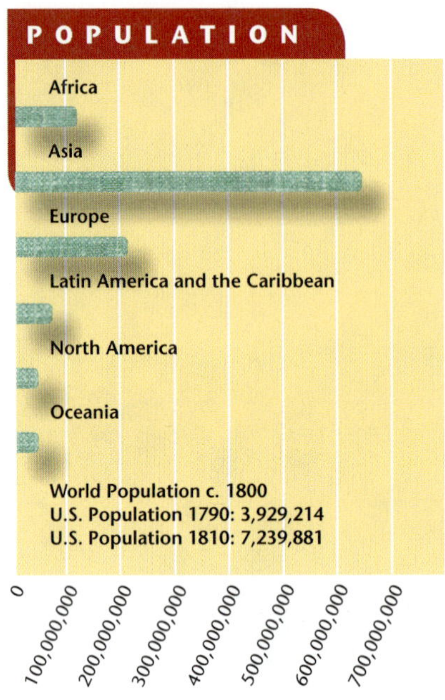


the people, who refused to talk to her, as "poor dogs" and observed that they "were nothing but skin and bones." Royall remarked that the Cherokee chimneys were "still smoking, when the white people took possession" of their homes. Royall's observations of Indian culture, migration, plantation agriculture, and slavery reflected dynamic changes in her society.

In one small area of Alabama, Royall saw the tremendous energy and potential for conflict that could be observed in a thousand places around North America between 1789 and 1824. During that time the physical expansion of the United States and the population movement improved prospects for many but also caused new tensions in the borderlands and with Indian peoples. The United States expanded its horizons through exploration and trade and began a new era in foreign policy. The actions and movements of individuals, both prominent and humble—white women, Indians, plantation slaves, overseers, traders, military commanders, and others like those Anne Royall met in Alabama in 1818—shaped the development of the United States and its relationship with the world in North America and beyond.

## EXPLORATION AND ENCOUNTER

At the turn of the 19th century, people and goods moved across the spaces of North America, as the pace of exploration and trade quickened. Governments on the North American continent were anxious to size up natural resources and prospects for future expansion beyond their areas of permanent settlement. The United States and Spain sent out expeditions to probe the boundaries of North America, to establish ties with Indian peoples, and to survey the natural world. Traders and merchants also encouraged contacts between peoples on different parts of the continent. Many Indians embraced trade, but the expansion that accompanied it threatened them. Competition emerged as explorers and traders crisscrossed the continent.

### Lewis and Clark Expedition

Even before he finalized the Louisiana purchase in April 1803, President Thomas Jefferson had asked Congress to fund a mission to explore beyond the Missouri River to stake claim to territory (possibly to the Pacific) and to establish trade relations with Indian nations. Jefferson appointed his secretary, **Meriwether Lewis**, commander of the expedition. Lewis chose as his fellow "captain" **William Clark**, a retired army lieutenant who was an excellent backwoodsman and cartographer. Lewis and Clark took with them 29 men in what they called their "Corps of Discovery." The Corps included Kentucky hunters, soldiers, French Canadian boatmen, an interpreter, and Clark's slave, York.

**CHAPTER OUTLINE**

*continued from page 352*



Jefferson charged Lewis and Clark to communicate to Indian nations that the United States was now in control of the Louisiana Territory, to observe plants and animals, to make maps, and to explore routes for future trade. In 1804 the Corps, ruled by tight military discipline, traveled up the Missouri River and met with powerful Indian groups: the Teton Sioux (Lakota), the Arikara, and the Yankton Sioux. Much of the area the Corps surveyed beyond the Missouri River was as yet unexplored by Europeans and Americans, and Lewis and Clark benefited from Indian knowledge gained over centuries of trade and warfare throughout the region. They wintered at the Mandan villages—in present North Dakota—where they were joined by French Canadian trader Toussaint Charbonneau and his wife, the Shoshone **Sacagawea**. Sacagawea remained with the expedition, even after she gave birth to a son. Sacagawea provided essential linguistic and geographic skills to Lewis and Clark.

The Corps traveled up the Missouri alternately by foot and by canoe until August, when they crossed the Rocky Mountains and the Bitterroot Mountains. After the very difficult crossings, the party reached the Pacific in November 1805 and established winter quarters at the Columbia River. Setting out again in the spring of 1806, the group split into smaller parties to attempt to find an easier crossing over the Rockies, but by the time they rejoined at the confluence of the Yellowstone and Missouri rivers on August 12, it was clear that they could find no easy overland Pacific trade route. The Corps returned to St. Louis on September 23, 1806.

The Lewis and Clark expedition succeeded in several ways even though it did not establish the easy trade routes that Thomas Jefferson had hoped would expand the U.S. agricultural empire. The explorers observed and catalogued hundreds of species of animals and plants, and their maps and landscape descriptions were of use to future explorers and settlers. Lewis and Clark solidified U.S. claims over much of the Louisiana territory, and they claimed portions of Oregon—as they avoided several military parties sent by the Spanish to try to intercept them. They also established good relations and solid trade ties with several Indian groups, most notably the Mandan and Shoshonis, although many other groups took Lewis and Clark's flashy trinkets and pronouncements that Thomas Jefferson was their new "great father" with a dose of skepticism. The Teton Sioux and the Piegan were notably hostile to the Corps, and the expedition probably narrowly avoided all-out war with these Indian peoples.

Captains Lewis & Clark holding a Council with the Indians Page 17


This idealized illustration of Lewis and Clark holding a council with some of the Indians they encountered on their journey of exploration appeared as an illustration in the 1810 edition of the journal of their travels, a very popular book. The image shows Lewis and Clark as carefully dressed orators who hold the attention of Indian men eager to hear what they say.

## Zebulon Pike

Spain, also skeptical of American power, contested the southwestern boundaries of the Louisiana Purchase. In 1786, the Spanish governor of New Mexico had concluded peace agreements with the powerful Comanche people and had sent explorer Pedro Vial across the southern plains to St. Louis, to find trails and to establish a strong claim on the territory. Although the Spanish government later ceded the Louisiana Territory to France, which sold it to the United States in 1803, neither treaty clearly defined the southwestern territorial border.

U.S. military commanders sent Captain **Zebulon Pike** on an expedition to define the U.S. claim to the southwestern part of the Louisiana Territory. Between August 1805 and April 1806, Pike had journeyed up the Mississippi River to explore the source of the river and to form relationships with northern Indian groups. In 1806, General **James Wilkinson** sent Pike west from St. Louis to establish diplomatic ties with the Osage and Comanche, to try and negotiate peace between traditional enemies the Kansas and Osage, and to explore the Arkansas and Red rivers without antagonizing Spain.

The task proved impossible. Pike survived several rounds of intrigue and desertion by his Osage and Pawnee guides, but when he tried to negotiate with the Pawnee near the Republican River he learned that they had recently been visited by a large Spanish military force under Lieutenant Facundo Melgares. Abandoning most of his plans for Indian treaties, Pike followed Spanish and Indian trails across the Rockies. By January 1807, he was lost, and his expedition strayed to the Rio Grande River—very near to Spanish settlement. The Spanish captured Pike and his men in February 1807. Pike was taken first to Santa Fe and then to Chihuahua for interrogation, and several of his men were imprisoned for two years in Mexico. When Pike was allowed to return to St. Louis in July 1807, he quickly published his journals filled with his observations of the western territory and Mexico, which proved very popular, although President Jefferson never considered Pike's military expedition as significant as Lewis and Clark's scientific and trade exploration. Pike's expedition proved that the United States could not take for granted that it could expand without resistance, even in the Louisiana Territory.

## Plains Indian Peoples

U.S. government officials and settlers, in part tantalized by the maps and exploration narratives published by Pike, Lewis and Clark, and others, increasingly viewed the Great Plains as a desirable location. Indian peoples on the plains were already experiencing changes in their lives. By the 1790s the use of horses for transportation, hunting, and war fighting had taken hold both west and east of the Rockies. Villages of Mandan, Hidatsa, and Arikara on the upper Missouri River acted as centers for trade networks that included Indian tribes and Europeans and stretched from the Great Lakes to the Pacific Ocean. The western Comanches operated another trade center just northeast of the Rio Grande River. By the 1820s, the Mandan and the Arikara found themselves squeezed between U.S. and British fur-trading companies.

Along with increased trade came diseases, including smallpox, measles, and whooping cough. In some areas, mortality rates reached as high as 70 percent in the epidemic outbreaks in the first half of the 19th century.

With their population decreasing, Indian people contested for power. Fights between tribal rivals—notably between the Apache and the Comanche—continued throughout the period. The nomadic Sioux people gained power over village-based groups like the Mandan and Arikara, whose population density caused epidemics to hit them harder. Factions within the Osage desired so badly to keep the advantage provided by the gun trade over their enemies that they agreed in 1808 to cede "50,000 square miles of excellent country" to the United States in return for trade goods. Osage lands became a prime location for Indians forcibly removed from the East after the War of 1812. Plains peoples remained powerful until 1824, but they were beginning to feel pressure from exploration across their lands and growth of the white population.

## Astor and the Fur Trade

Instead of settlement, exploration, or diplomatic engagement, **John Jacob Astor** sought profit in western North America. After emigrating to the United States from Germany in 1784, Astor began his North American Fur Company in New York City in 1785. Undaunted by strict British trade rules, Astor began by selling furs to retailers in New York and Europe. After Jay's Treaty (1794) allowed direct U.S.-Canadian trade, Astor built up his business and increased his inventory. Through the 1790s, most of the fur made into hats and outerwear in the United States still came from Canadian firms, including the Hudson Bay Company and the North West Company, which operated vast networks of semi-independent Indian and mixed-race trappers.

By 1808 Astor had extended his business with a bold move into the newly expanding China trade. He exported wholesale furs to China and received payment in trade goods such as tea and silks that he could sell in North America and Europe for a great profit. In 1808, hoping to take advantage of disruptions in the fur trade caused by the Napoleonic wars in Europe, Astor received a New York state charter and founded the American Fur Company. With his new company Astor planned a network of traders who would deal across North America directly with Indian hunters and enmesh themselves in Indian culture. He hoped to gain market share by expanding his operation through the Great Lakes and all the way to the Columbia River. In 1810, Astor formed a new joint-stock company, the Pacific Fur Company, and in 1811 he sent two expeditions to found a trading post on the Columbia River. From that post, Astoria, he hoped to directly challenge the Russian traders who dominated the Oregon territory.

Astor's plans, however, suffered during the War of 1812. Under threat from the Royal Navy, Astor sold Astoria to the North West Company in October 1813. The American Fur Company survived, and Astor convinced Congress in 1816 to bar British citizens from the fur trade in U.S. territory. Other smaller fur trading companies thrived in the United States—including the Missouri Fur Company cofounded by William Clark—but Astor's business skill and the worldwide scale of his efforts made him one of the richest men in America. Sensing a shift in tastes away from furs and Chinese goods, Astor deftly pulled out of the China trade in 1824 and a decade later moved his fur fortune into New York real estate.

## Asian Trade

Americans had only begun to trade in China in 1784 when financier Robert Morris sent the first American vessel, *The Empress of China*, on a trade mission. Under the command of Captain John Green, it carried a load of ginseng (prized by Chinese men as an aphrodisiac) and other goods. The United States and China did not share diplomatic relations until 1844, but urban merchants quickly built up a significant trade with the port of Canton. During the tensions of the Napoleonic Wars, U.S. traders quickly expanded their business as they exported tea from China. On the eve of the War of 1812, the United States was second only to Great Britain in its share of the trade.

Uninhibited by European monopolies that sought to govern the tea trade, U.S. traders developed relationships with Canton, who controlled the Chinese tea market. After 1802, American merchants also became involved in the growing opium trade into China. Americans proved adept at negotiating the complex system of taxes and bribes in Canton. The Chinese consumed great quantities of American trade products including ginseng, sea otter fur, and seal fur. But American consumers were even more

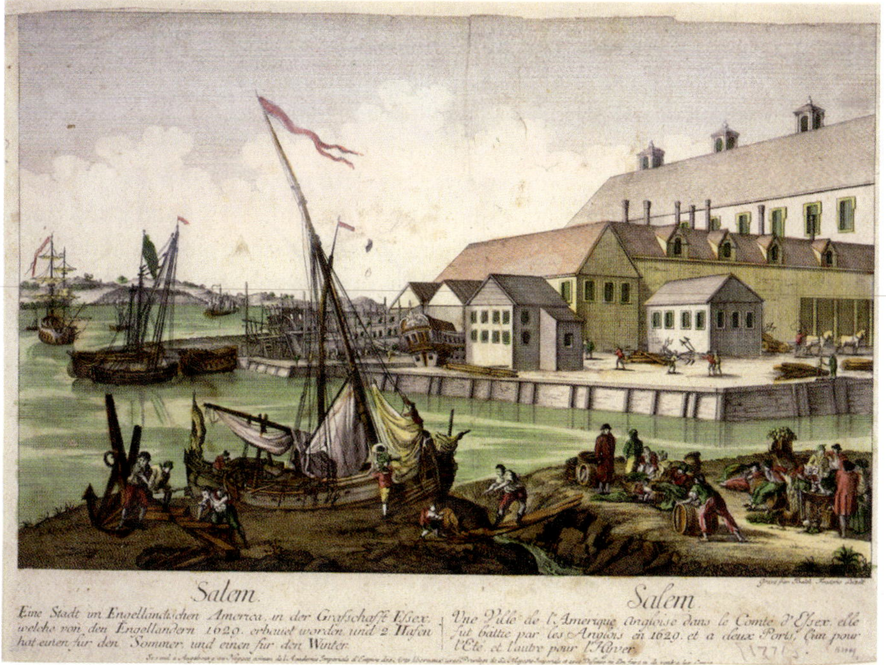

Salem.
Eine Stadt im Engelländischen America, in der Grafschaft Essex welche von den Engelländern 1629. erbauet worden und 2 Hafen hat einen für den Sommer, und einen für den Winter.
Salem.
Une Ville de l'Amerique Angloise dans le Comte d'Essex elle fut battie par les Anglois en 1629. et a deux Ports, l'un pour l'Eté et l'autre pour l'Hiver.


This 18th-century engraving shows the port of Salem, Massachusetts, one of the busiest trading ports in New England. In the 18th century Salem became a home to shipbuilding and cod fishing, and by the turn of the 19th century, it had become a major hub for American trade with Europe, the West Indies, China, Africa, and Russia.

attracted to Chinese products: silk, furniture, porcelain, silverware, wallpaper, hand-loomed cloth, and decorative objects of many varieties. U.S. citizens thought of China as an exotic and uncivilized "far eastern" place, but Chinese goods shaped their tastes and fashions.

Many U.S. merchants who were involved in trade with China also spread into the burgeoning trade with India during the same period. Before 1783, India had been closed to Americans because the British government had allowed the East India Company a monopoly over trade there. But the Treaty of Paris that ended the Revolutionary War opened the way for American trade with India, and during the Napoleonic Wars in Europe, American merchants took advantage of disruptions to European traders to quickly expand their Indian trade. American merchants focused mainly on Calcutta because the Bay of Bengal was the easiest entry point for American ships, which had trouble risking the dangerous seas of the Indian Ocean.

By the 1820s, the trade between Calcutta and New England grew rich, and trade included not only a huge variety of material but also cultural exchanges. Indian cloth, from cotton sheeting to printed chintzes and elaborate silks, was advertised widely in American newspapers as a luxury good. Americans also consumed saltpeter, indigo, ginger, animal hides, and shellac imported in great quantities from Calcutta. Many Yankee traders paid cash for their goods purchased in India, but they also traded to India a smaller amount of American goods—rum, glassware, books, timber, and cigars. In the 1830s, New England traders shifted into trading ice to Calcutta. From the 1830s to the 1850s thousands of tons of ice were exported to India.

Unlike the fur trade in North America, American trade in China and India was rarely accompanied by significant exploration or scientific observation. U.S. merchants gained a foothold in the rich countries of Asia with pure profit in mind. Traders and mariners reported back their impressions of the exotic-seeming East, and both China and India formed part of the American imagination. Asian trade helped fuel American interest in the people, goods, and events far outside U.S. borders.

**STUDY QUESTIONS FOR EXPLORATION AND ENCOUNTER**

1. **In what ways were North American trade and exploration interrelated in this period?**
2. **Describe the balance of power between the United States, Plains Indians peoples, and the Spanish between 1803 and 1815.**

# SHIFTING BORDERS

As nations expanded across North America, political tensions and all-out clashes resulted. The United States expanded south and west as it created new states and struggled to integrate the territory of the Louisiana Purchase. The Spanish pushed north and east, extending the mission system in California and contesting U.S. expansion in the Louisiana territory. The British and Russians expanded their interests on the borders between the United States and Canada. Thousands of Indian groups sought to deal with these developments through both peaceful and warlike means.

## Jeffersonian Agrarianism

In the first quarter of the 19th century, an ideology that valued land and farming underlay much of the energetic movement within the United States. Thomas Jefferson called farmers "the chosen people of God" and referred to agriculture as "the most useful of the occupations of man." Jefferson believed that farmers made the most patriotic, hardworking citizens and thought that farming would form the basis for stable national development and wealth. In Jefferson's idealized vision, the United States would be sustained by a base of independent, white farmers who prized liberty and community. As a prominent Virginian who owned a slave plantation, Jefferson also recognized the role that enslaved black labor would play in creating a class of free and independent white "farmer" plantation owners in slave-holding areas. Almanac

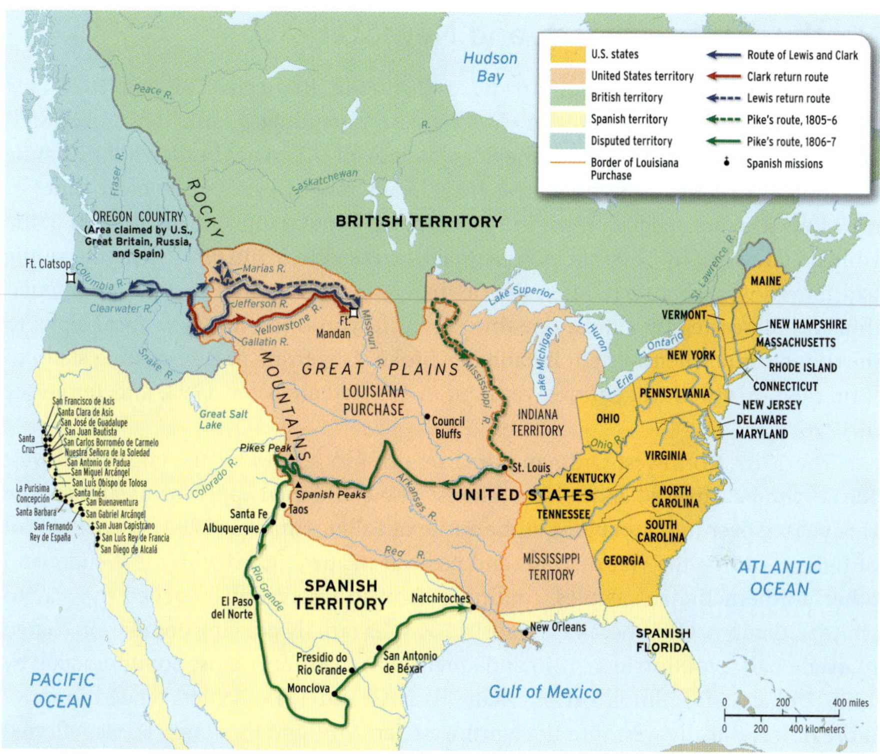


**▲ Map 9.1**

**Exploration and Development in North America, 1803–1810** During the first decade of the 19th century both Spain and the United States tried to spread their influence across North America.

authors, newspaper editors and others embraced Jefferson's view of agriculture and its contribution to a distinctly American character.

Although Jefferson and his compatriots idolized farming, they also admitted that American agriculture would have to be linked to trade and commerce. In the 1790s, Jefferson's Democratic Republicans did not wish to encourage the United States to become a commercial manufacturing country, in contrast to the beliefs of Alexander Hamilton and his Federalist counterparts, but they knew that farmers would have to be able to trade their products to provide a stable national economic base. **Yeomen** and plantation farmers needed at least two things to make this vision of the United States work—land and the ability to market their produce.

Both land and marketability of their produce brought Jeffersonian farmers into contact with people and governments well beyond their national borders. Jefferson's purchase of the Louisiana Territory in 1803 set the stage for the realization of his agrarian ambitions, but the mere purchase of the territory would not guarantee its smooth transition into American farmland.

## Northwest, Southwest, and New States

The U.S. population was both growing and mobile. Between 1789 and 1824 new states joined the United States in waves, as the expanding population moved well beyond the eastern seaboard. For the first time not all U.S. states bordered the Atlantic Ocean. Many settlers in frontier areas had already moved west one or more times in their lives. The first federal census in 1790 counted about 4,000,000 inhabitants of the United States, but by 1800 the number had increased to 5,300,000. So many people had moved west that population density barely increased, even though the population was increasing by almost one-third every 10 years. The first new admissions to the union came when western inhabitants broke away from already existing states to form their own political entities: Vermont in 1791, Kentucky in 1792, and Tennessee in 1796.

The 1787 Northwest Ordinance had set out procedures for the large Northwest Territory to be surveyed and sold to settlers, who could then apply for statehood. The U.S. victory over Indian nations at the Battle of Fallen Timbers (1794), displacement of Indians during the War of 1812, and postwar treaties signed with the Wendat and other northern Indian peoples, confining them to reservations, opened the way to white settlement. Ohio became a state in 1803. Its rapidly growing population soared to over a half a million after 1810 and emerged as the fourth most populous state by 1820. Indiana and Illinois became states in 1816 and 1818. Settlers tended to move more or less directly west into the Northwest Territory, and these new states reflected a mixture of regional cultures that sometimes conflicted.

As migrants from northeastern states flooded into the Northwest Territory—where slavery was prohibited—many Virginians moved into Kentucky and Tennessee, southern Ohio, Indiana, and Illinois. Other inhabitants of the original southern states moved south and west into Alabama and along the Gulf coast to Louisiana, Mississippi, and Arkansas. After Massachusetts native Eli Whitney patented an innovative mechanized cotton gin in 1793, cotton processing became much easier and more profitable, and settlers moved into many southern areas looking for new land for plantations. Land in the Deep South—for instance, in Alabama and Georgia—produced much better cotton than did land further north. U.S. cotton production increased 10-fold between 1800 and 1820. Parts of the Louisiana Territory also lured settlers who hoped to make their fortunes on sugar plantations or in the fur trade.

## The Missouri Compromise

In 1818 the territory of Missouri applied to Congress for admission to the union as a state, the first state west of the Mississippi River. Because the number of free and slave states in the union was precariously balanced and because so many slaves lived in Missouri, the issue of slavery caused controversy as soon as **Henry Clay** presented resolutions to the House of Representatives to admit Missouri to the union. In February 1819, New York congressman **James Tallmadge, Jr.**, introduced amendments to the Missouri statehood legislation that would ban the further introduction of slaves there and would gradually emancipate slaves who already lived in the territory. After vigorous debate, the House of Representatives approved the amendments, but the Senate struck them down. The matter had to be carried over to the next session of Congress.

Antislavery activists across the Mid-Atlantic and New England held meetings and sent petitions denouncing slavery as an evil that could not be allowed to spread. Several state legislatures adopted competing resolutions for and against the admission of Missouri as a slave state. Congress reconsidered Missouri for statehood in December. Congressmen, President **James Monroe**, and others debated constitutional issues such as whether Congress had the right to place restrictions on new states and whether slaves in the Missouri Territory should be immediately counted for representation under the three-fifths clause. These debates also saw some southern politicians using the relatively uncommon argument that slavery was a positive institution, instead of a shameful burden. The spread of cotton agriculture seemed to raise the stakes on the expansion of slavery.

By March 1819, Congress reached a complex compromise. Missouri would be admitted as a slave state and Maine would be admitted as a free state—thereby preserving the balance of slave and free states in Congress. Illinois Democratic-Republican Senator Jesse B. Thomas also proposed an amendment to the Missouri admission bill that he hoped would avoid future conflict by defining a line on the map to determine future slave and free states. The line at 36°30′ latitude drawn across the Louisiana Purchase territory would permit slavery only to its south. Missouri would stand as the exception, since it was north of the line.

In March 1820, Congress approved the Missouri Compromise resolutions. Missouri was fully admitted to the union on February 26, 1821. The Missouri Compromise temporarily tamped down the political controversy over slavery, but Thomas Jefferson predicted future trouble when he wrote that the compromise filled him with "terror" because conflict "is hushed, indeed, for the moment. But this is a reprieve only, not a final sentence."

## African American Migration and Colonization

The Missouri Compromise emphasized a basic fact of U.S. westward expansion between 1789 and 1824: as a group, black people were even more dramatically affected by demographic change and movement than whites. Both the slave population and the free African American population increased during that time. Over 100,000 slaves were imported into the United States between the end of the Revolution and the abolition of the slave trade in 1808. After the legal importation of slaves stopped, the expansion of U.S. territory and strong demand for slaves in new plantation areas stimulated the internal market for slaves, and families were regularly broken apart by sales. Slaves' living conditions usually deteriorated as they were moved into the Deep South. These conditions were symbolized by the coffle—the method of transportation used to move groups of slaves. Groups of up to 30 people in pairs were chained or tied together by metal halters around their necks and then marched over long distances. Once they arrived at cotton or sugar plantations, most slaves faced brutal working conditions.

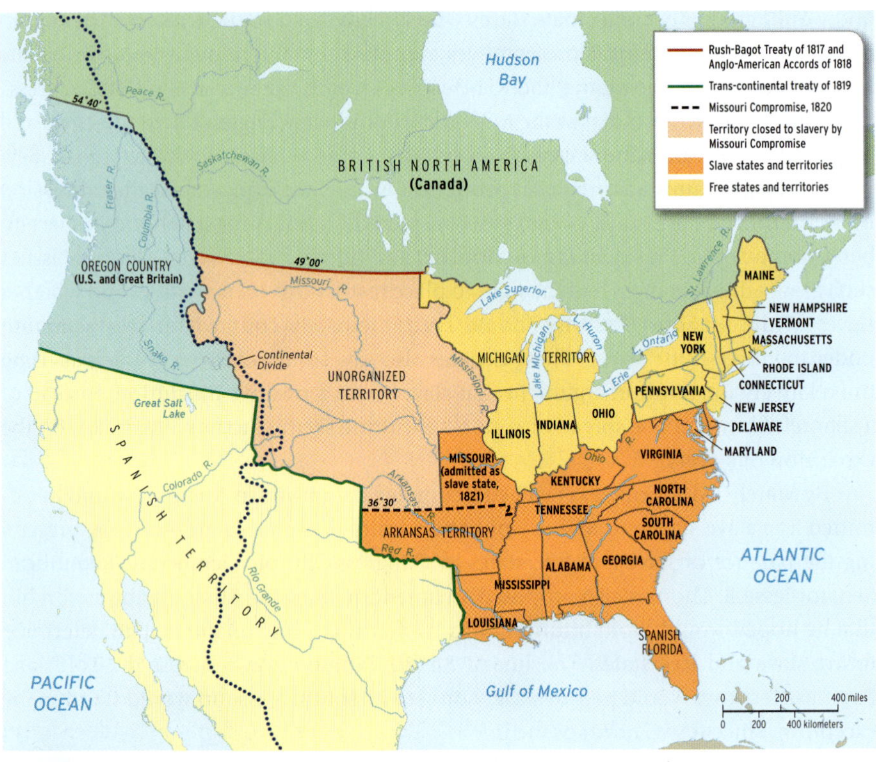


▲ **Map 9.2**

**U.S. Expansion and Slavery, 1820** The expansion of U.S. territorial borders held great consequences for the development of the institution of slavery and for conflicts over slavery.

The Northwest Ordinance of 1787 had outlawed slavery in the Northwest Territory, but that prohibition did not mean the northern territories were hospitable to African Americans. Concerned that slaves might escape to freedom in the territories or to Canada, Congress passed the first federal Fugitive Slave Act in 1793. The act empowered local government officials to help masters recover runaways and imposed a fine on anyone who helped a "fugitive from justice." Some slave owners who migrated to Indiana and Illinois smuggled slaves with them, and many towns and states had laws governing where and how free African Americans could live and work. In 1813, Illinois forbade free African Americans to settle there, and voters narrowly defeated a proposal to legalize slavery in Illinois in 1824.

Some free African Americans reacted against this kind of animosity by expressing an interest in migrating out of the United States altogether. In 1815, the Quaker sea captain Paul Cuffee, who was of African and Indian heritage, settled a shipload of free African Americans in the African British colony of Sierra Leone. In 1816 Presbyterian minister Robert Finley founded the **American Colonization Society** (ACS), which counted among its supporters Kentucky congressman Henry Clay, President James Monroe, and other mildly antislavery whites who did not think the races could continue to coexist in North America. In 1821 the ACS transported its first free African American settlers to Liberia, the west African colony that the ACS would govern into the 1830s.

The colonization movement, as it was known, received most of its support from whites who hoped for the opportunity to gradually phase out the institution of slavery by transporting black people to Africa. Many free African Americans rejected the racism expressed by the ACS, even if they were interested in migration themselves. The ACS convinced only 22 of the 10,000 free blacks in Philadelphia to embark for Africa in its first two years of effort. In 1824, some prominent free African Americans in New York and Philadelphia, including minister **Richard Allen** and sailmaker James Forten, founded the Haytian Emigration Society of Coloured People to help African Americans settle in Haiti, whose president Jean-Pierre Boyer had agreed to pay for their passage as part of his bid for national recognition by the United States. Forten was a great supporter of the black republic in Haiti, although he utterly rejected the white vision of African colonization.

## Spanish Expansion in California

The United States was not the only country expanding on the North American continent between 1789 and 1824. The Spanish empire (independent Mexico after 1822) also pushed its boundaries outward during that period. Although the Spanish had traded with Indians in California since the 1500s, they did not establish colonies there until the 1760s. During the 1780s and 1790s Spanish officials took steps to expand the colonized area in California to create a greater buffer between the silver mines in Mexico and Russian and British settlements in Oregon that were moving south.

The main vehicle for Spanish colonial expansion in California was the mission system, which extended government control over territory through a mixture of religious and military means. Franciscan friars, supported by Spanish soldiers, would establish a mission church, baptize nearby Indians, and employ them—sometimes by force—in farming and other trades. Between 1769 and 1821, friars baptized more than 70,000 Indians at the 20 missions that spread quickly across the territory of Alta California. Many Indian people, like the Ipai, resisted being colonized, but their defenses were weakened by the population collapse brought on by the introduction of European diseases. Other Indians, like some of the Chumash, embraced baptism but retained a syncretic view of the world that maintained their native beliefs alongside Roman Catholicism. Sometimes Christian Indians later rejected baptism, and the Chumash eventually rebelled against the Spanish in 1824.

Severe drought in the 1790s caused many Indians to seek refuge in the missions, where Spanish friars provided food in exchange for labor and conversion. Hispanic settlers called *Californios,* many of them mixed-race Mexicans and descendents of earlier Spanish soldiers and southern Indians, claimed land, and their livestock degraded native land use. Spanish soldiers compelled Indian laborers to build the system of presidio forts that further consolidated control over California territory.

The mission of San Juan de Bautista was founded in 1797 by Fr. Fermín de Lasuén, the successor to Junípero Serra, the Franciscan friar who spearheaded the spread of the Spanish mission system northward in California. This illustration pictures the church building at the mission that was begun in 1803.

**STUDY QUESTIONS FOR SHIFTING BORDERS**

1. **How did Spanish expansion in California compare to efforts of the United States to expand westward between 1789 and 1824?**
2. **In what ways and for what reasons did the westward expansion of the United States revive and exacerbate conflicts over slavery?**

# SOCIAL AND CULTURAL SHIFTS

The movement of goods, people, and ideas across and beyond North America at the beginning of the 19th century affected the creation of an "American" culture within the United States. Americans sought ways to define their places in the social order, even as society itself constantly shifted. Indians, white women, African Americans, and evangelicals all assumed new roles as culture and society changed.

## Indian Acculturation

At the turn of the 19th century, native women and men adopted a variety of strategies ranging from acculturation to native cultural revival to deal with change and demographic pressure. Indian groups who lived within the United States continued to adapt after more than a hundred years of intensive contact with Europeans and Americans—even as California Indians and some Plains peoples were facing such contacts for the first time. During the same years in which **Tecumseh** and Tenskwatawa led movements for cultural revival and military resistance among the Shawnee and their allies (see Chapter 8), some Indian people who lived further south used a different strategy—of acculturation and accommodation. Some groups within the Cherokee, Choctaw, Chickasaw, and Creek accepted U.S. Indian policies that encouraged them to "civilize" by adopting European-style agriculture, clothing, and culture. The Creek fought a civil war during the War of 1812 partly because of internal disagreements over assimilation, but the pro-acculturation forces triumphed with the backing of Andrew Jackson and U.S. military power.

The Cherokee pursued survival by ceding land in exchange for education and the promise of good relations with the United States. American government agents and missionaries lived within Cherokee society and were accepted by many. Although they never adopted private land ownership, the Cherokee did adapt to other American customs: they changed their gender roles to match American family structure, some owned slaves, and they centralized their government under a National Council structure in 1808 that took many matters away from the control of the traditional matrilineal clans. The council also extended citizenship to the biracial children of Cherokee men and white women (who could not belong to a clan), and mixed-race Cherokee became prominent leaders in the next decade. **Sequoyah** standardized the Cherokee alphabet, which made printing possible, and more than 25 percent of Cherokee people could read by the 1820s—a high figure that gained international attention.

Cherokee leaders disagreed about the degree to which acculturation would solve their problems, and some agreed to move their families to Arkansas territory to gain favor with the United States. Tensions continued to rise after the War of 1812, and white population growth near the Cherokee in Tennessee, Alabama, and Georgia meant that the debate over survival and acculturation was far from over.

## Gender in Early Republican Society

White women also experienced quick changes in their social roles. In colonial society it would have been far more difficult for a single woman like Anne Royall to travel alone so extensively. Following on the heels of the revolutionary ideology of republican motherhood, women were expected to play a role in creating a better republican society through their ability to raise educated children to be good citizens. Women also claimed the ability to augment male political virtue by leading benevolent and refined social activities.

White women's educational opportunities expanded dramatically during the early republic, in part as a reaction to the theories of British feminist **Mary Wollstonecraft**, who was read widely in the United States. Women's rights advocate **Judith Sargent Murray** wrote that "women have a talent" and "should be taught to depend on their own efforts." New schools and academies for girls were founded in every region, and girls increasingly participated in the public education that was offered most widely in the North. After 1789, women also began to find career opportunities as teachers, and many of the most important girls' academies were founded by women such as **Emma Willard** and Julia Tevis. Most girls were not offered the same education as boys—for example, classical languages were largely off limits. But more serious academic subjects like math and history joined girls' education in needlework and dancing. Educators differed on whether girls should be educated for their own intellectual fulfillment or more to serve the interests of family and society, but in either case greater education meant progress as female literacy rates soared.

This sampler was sewn by Catharine Ann Speel in Philadelphia when she was 12 or 13 years old, in 1805. Girls often sewed samplers like this to practice stitches and to show off needlework skill, which they learned from family members and at schools. Speel's sampler is typical in showing a house, the alphabet, animals, and a man, and it includes a typical moral poem. Speel identifies herself as her mother's daughter on the sampler, emphasizing female lineage.

Advances in women's legal status proved to be more modest, as state **coverture** laws continued to view married women as legally subsumed under their husbands' control. In the 1790s, it became easier for women to obtain divorces. Women petitioned both state and federal legislatures, they participated in political rituals such as Fourth of July celebrations and French Revolutionary festivals, and some wrote for newspapers and magazines. Single women and widows, who could own property, ran businesses such as the Brandywine Ironworks, the successful boilerplate manufactory controlled by Pennsylvania Quaker **Rebecca Lukens**. The vast majority of poorer women and all black women led less public lives, and changing gender roles affected their daily lives more slowly.

## Literature and Popular Culture

Women formed one of the quickest-growing audiences in the United States for the dramatic increase in books, magazines, newspapers, and other kinds of print culture, which simultaneously connected the United States to Europe and helped its inhabitants to establish distinct identities. Historians estimate that by 1790 more than 90 percent of the white population in the United States could read—a figure some estimate to be twice as large as in Britain. A much smaller percentage of African Americans were literate, since many slaves were prohibited from learning. As the postal service expanded in the early years of the republic, subscription newspapers and magazines made up the majority of mail. By 1822, the United States had more newspaper readers than any other country, and hundreds of papers were printed in small towns in every state and territory.

Until after 1825, when improvements in printing occurred, most books in the United States remained expensive and were imported from Britain. But publishers such as Philadelphia's Matthew Carey showed interest in producing a truly "American" literature even before then. Many books relied on the American Revolution for plot, and authors like Mason Locke Weems sought to inspire their readers with biographies such as his *Life of Washington* (1800). **Hugh Henry Brackenridge**'s *Modern Chivalry*

(1804) satirized the social climbing of Americans on the move. **Susannah Rowson**'s best seller *Charlotte Temple* (1791) appealed to legions of middle-class female readers by transporting the English seduction novel to the United States—it emphasized the fragility of women's virtue in highly sentimentalized language. Following the precedent of Rowson and Charles Brockdon Brown, author of the gothic novel *Wieland*, more writers—including Washington Irving and James Fenimore Cooper—began to earn their living by publishing. The transatlantic book culture also nourished American Christianity, as the American Bible Society (1816) and the American Tract Society (1823) grew out of English efforts to spread religious publications.

This photograph from the early 20th century shows the grave at Trinity Church, New York, constructed around 1804 for the fictional character Charlotte Temple. The fictional character created by Susannah Rowson was such a popular figure of tragic romance that after this grave was installed visitors flocked to leave flowers, pieces of hair, and love letters as tributes to her. Alexander Hamilton is buried nearby.

By the time Susannah Rowson died in 1824, young middle- and upper-class white women who avidly read *Charlotte Temple* and other novels had turned her into the first U.S. literary celebrity. They bought, passed around, and discussed her book, and some even made pilgrimages to a gravestone for the character Charlotte Temple in New York's Trinity church. By consuming novels like *Charlotte Temple*, women showed their power to influence American culture, even as religious and literary critics warned that novel reading was a dangerously immoral activity.

## African American Culture: Slaves and Free People

Even though the institution of slavery denied slaves control of their own lives, African American men and women strengthened black culture between 1789 and 1824. Black culture varied by region and among slave and free populations. The end of the legal slave trade in 1808 meant that blacks could establish their own fully native-born culture, be it still influenced by many different regional African traditions in religion, food, clothing, funeral and burial traditions, and other areas of life. Black culture and white culture continued to be intertwined, since many slaves lived with their masters on small farms.

For slaves, nurturing cultural traditions helped them to survive the violent reality of day-to-day life, especially on larger plantations. Josiah Henson remembered how he and his fellow slaves balanced misery with the pleasure of family life during his youth in the 1790s: "Along with memories of miry cabins, frosted feet, weary toil under the blazing sun, curses and blows, there flock in others, of jolly Christmas times . . . midnight visits to apple orchards, broiling stray chickens, and first-rate tricks to dodge work." Despite the wide variation in slave life caused by working conditions, the density of the black population, and even the personality of individual slave masters, all black people tried to maintain pieces of their own identities despite the institution that controlled them.

The free African American population experienced huge growth in the new republic, especially in the northern states that had abolished or phased out slavery since the end of the American Revolution. The free black population in the United States grew from around 60,000 in 1790 to approximately 235,000 by 1820. Both northern and southern free African Americans tended to live in cities. In Boston, New York, Philadelphia, Richmond, Charleston, and New Orleans distinct free African American cultures emerged. Many African American social and cultural groups worked to end slavery.

African Americans in cities, who were often excluded from white institutions, set about establishing their own mutual aid societies, black fraternal lodges, schools, and churches. Most urban black men and women were poor laborers, but a rising class of well-to-do shop owners, hairdressers, doctors, and ministers formed political and social organizations, especially in Philadelphia and Boston. Two former slaves, Richard Allen and **Absalom Jones**, founded the first independent black Protestant church, the Bethel Church, in Philadelphia in 1792, and similar congregations sprang up across the North. In 1816, the independent black churches banded together to form the African Methodist Episcopal denomination. Efforts to found AME churches in the South were blocked after the thwarted 1822 slave revolt plot attributed to Denmark Vesey. Vesey, who was a fervent Christian, was convicted of planning a violent rebellion in South Carolina, whose state legislature promptly forbade separate black churches from being founded. Wherever black churches could thrive, however, they nurtured African American cultural aspirations and efforts toward freedom.

## Roots of the Second Great Awakening

Many African Americans belonged to Methodist, Baptist, and other Protestant churches that had dramatically increased their membership by the 1790s. The new denominations born in the 18th-century Great Awakening began to experience a new surge of growth by the turn of the century.

The rise of church membership was not the only reflection of renewed religious energy. A new wave of revivalism took hold across the United States at the turn of the century, and many different kinds of people were swept up in it. Popular preachers held outdoor camp meetings that attracted a mixed audience of whites and blacks, unchurched and church members. Nineteenth-century camp meeting revivals provided

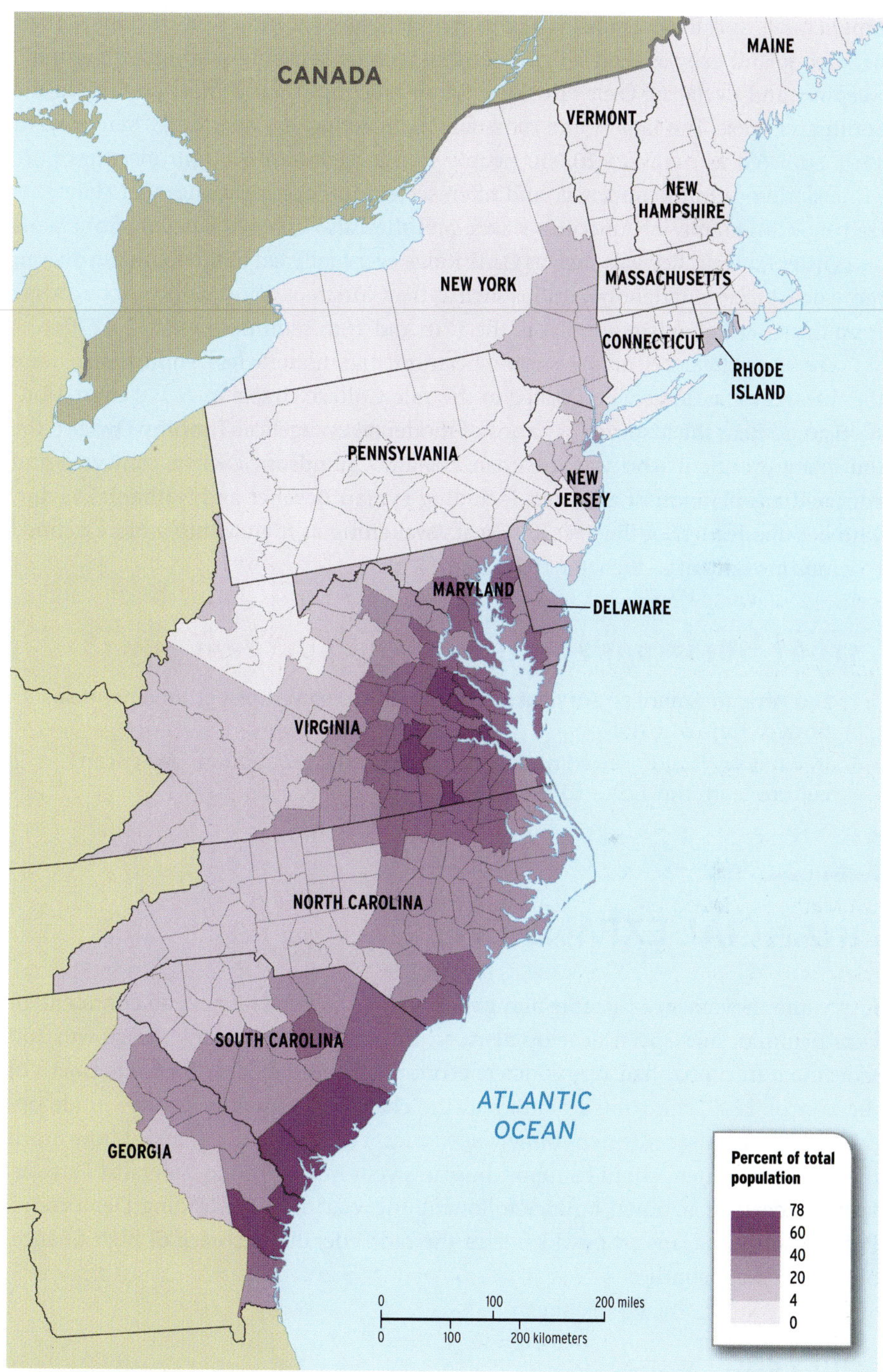


**▲ Map 9.3**

**African Americans as a Total Percentage of Population, 1790** What is significant about the geographic location of densely populated African American communities?

experiential, social occasions when people gathered to hear sermons, meet their neighbors, and express their religious enthusiasm by speaking in tongues, shouting, weeping, and declaring their salvation. Camp meetings proved most popular in the South and West. The largest and most famous meeting at Cane Ridge, Kentucky, in 1801 attracted as many as 20,000 people to the backwoods. Camp meetings bore some similarity to the informal, and often secret, outdoor gatherings that characterized the Christianity of American slaves, and they also adapted customs from Scots and Ulster revivals. Revivals such as Cane Ridge eventually led to the founding of even more new Protestant denominations such as the Church of Christ, which strayed away from the strict Calvinism popular in the 17th and 18th centuries.

On the other end of the social spectrum, but nonetheless enthusiastic, were the throngs of students who flocked to the Yale College chapel in New Haven, Connecticut, to hear the inspiring sermons of moderate evangelical **Timothy Dwight**, the university president who was Jonathan Edwards' grandson. Dwight converted and educated a generation of ministers including **Lyman Beecher** and **Nathaniel Taylor**, who became leaders of the **Second Great Awakening** as it grew into a more defined religious movement in the later 1820s and 1830s.

**STUDY QUESTIONS FOR SOCIAL AND CULTURAL SHIFTS**

1. **Did African American survival strategies differ from those of Indians? If so, how? If not, why not?**
2. **In what ways did printed materials influence the creation of "American" culture from the 1790s to the 1820s?**

# FINANCIAL EXPANSION

Just as the movement of people and goods across the North American continent affected cultural and social developments in the early 19th century, the growth and movement of capital had very concrete economic consequences. In the aftermath of the War of 1812, the United States had the chance to capitalize on new trade opportunities and the settlement of new territories. Debates persisted about how much the U.S. government should support business ventures. With the Federalist Party effectively dead in national politics following the War of 1812, leading Democratic-Republican politicians adopted some of the old Federalist embrace of high finance, but not without conflict.

## Banks and Panics

President James Madison had been convinced by the War of 1812 that the United States must do more to encourage domestic manufacturing. During and after the war, Madison proposed to build roads and canals, to enact tariffs on foreign products, and to reauthorize the charter of the **Bank of the United States** (BUS). Madison had bitterly opposed the BUS on constitutional grounds when Alexander Hamilton proposed it in the 1791, but he believed that the "expediency and almost necessity" of wartime finance meant that the United States now needed a federal bank. Even Thomas Jefferson himself embraced Madison's vision by 1816 when he wrote that "We must now place the manufacturer by the side of the agriculturalist."

The BUS consisted of a partnership between federal government and private investors, and their intertwined interests became difficult to separate at the end of the War of 1812. Financial speculators, including John Jacob Astor and his fellow merchant **Stephen Girard**, bought up bonds and other guaranteed notes, and as their investments fluctuated so did their commitment to central banking. In January 1815, President Madison vetoed Congress' proposed recharter of the BUS, because the bill gave too much private advantage to merchants like Astor and Girard. True to his roots as a strict interpreter of the U.S. Constitution, Madison also vetoed the 1816 "Bonus Bill" that would have funded transportation from public land sales, even though he supported internal improvements, because the Constitution did not expressly grant Congress authority to pass such legislation.

Madison still hoped for a central bank, but Congress was contending over a variety of financial issues. Each of the more than 200 private and state banks issued its own bank notes, a practice that drove up inflation. Madison's supporters in Congress, including South Carolinian **John C. Calhoun** and Speaker of the House Henry Clay, proposed a charter for a Second Bank of the United States. The new federal bank, to be based in Philadelphia, would stabilize U.S. currency and would exert stronger control over its private investors. President Madison approved the new charter of the Second Bank of the United States in April 1816. In the same month a 25 percent tariff on foreign wool cloth, cotton, and iron went into effect. Congress also passed legislation authorizing a National Road and other internal improvements advocated by Madison and Henry Clay.

In the spring of 1817, James Monroe, the newly elected president, embarked on a tour of the northern states to reach out to disgruntled Federalists, but before he

The Second Bank of the United States building in Philadelphia was designed in the Greek revival style by William Strickland and constructed between 1818 and 1824. Between its incorporation in 1816 and the bank war with the Jackson administration that caused it to fold in 1836, the Second Bank of the United States was the most important financial institution in the country.

could depart, Monroe had to deal with more controversy over the Second Bank of the United States. The House of Representatives had investigated the bank's books and uncovered what one member called "a system of fraud, stock-jobbing, and speculation" that enriched the bank's private directors and threatened public finance. The directors of the Baltimore branch of the Bank of the United States alone had embezzled over $1.5 million, an astronomical sum at the time. The public lost confidence in the bank, but a bill to revoke its charter failed in Congress in February 1819.

At the same time, a severe depression halted business expansion. Since the end of the War of 1812, U.S. exports had increased by over 100 percent and agricultural prices had soared. But by the end of 1818, rampant speculation in cotton and land, a shortage of gold and silver to back up U.S. currency, and the recovery of the British economy spelled trouble. The plummet of cotton prices in Europe and the United States demonstrated how that product had tightened the links in the transatlantic economy. In 1819, banks and businesses backed by inflated currency began to fail in droves, and the Second Bank of the United States reacted too slowly to prevent a collapse of the economy. When the bank did react, it made matters worse by suspending payments in hard currency. The effects were traumatic. Personal bankruptcies soared, land prices plummeted, and the financial crisis even temporarily slowed down the tide of settlers who were willing to uproot and seek new farmland on the frontier.

## Corporations and the Supreme Court

Less than two weeks after the Second Bank of the United States survived its fresh challenge in the House of Representatives in 1819, the Supreme Court entered the political debate over federal economic power and issued one of its most important decisions

Samuel F. B. Morse painted this portrait of President James Monroe in 1819. Monroe's presidency was marked by the strong influence of cabinet ministers, especially Secretary of State John Quincy Adams, and by nationalist policies that encouraged territorial expansion. The Monroe Doctrine that bore his name warned European countries not to intervene in the affairs of the Western Hemisphere.

ever. The court unanimously decided in the case of *McCulloch v. Maryland* that central banking was constitutional. Furthermore, Chief Justice John Marshall's opinion supported the idea that the federal government represented the people of one, unified United States. According to Marshall, even though the Constitution did not explicitly grant Congress the right to charter national banks, it implied that Congress could do so, since it could exercise powers given by the people "for their benefit." The decision struck down a hefty tax that Maryland had imposed on the Baltimore branch of the Bank of the United States and declared that federal laws must supersede state action. In the future, the decision would hold great power even beyond the issue of banking, since it declared that Congress could use broad powers implied by the Constitution so long as Congress avoided anything expressly forbidden in that document.

John Marshall, an old Federalist whose market ideas matched the new economic climate, led the Supreme Court to deliver several other opinions that buoyed businessmen who were interested in federal investment and financial expansion. In 1819, the court decided in *Dartmouth College v. Woodward* that the state of New Hampshire could not alter the Dartmouth College charter because Dartmouth was a private corporation, whose property the state should not violate. The decision encouraged the development of business corporations, which provided a great advantage to entrepreneurs by limiting their personal liability for business failures. In 1824, the court ruled in a case concerning steamboat monopolies, *Gibbons v. Ogden*, that the Commerce Clause of the Constitution granted the federal government the sole right to regulate interstate commerce. Marshall and the Supreme Court helped to fuel business development for decades to come.

### STUDY QUESTIONS FOR FINANCIAL EXPANSION

1. **In what ways did the three branches of the federal government each affect the national economy during the 1810s?**
2. **In what ways did the Panic of 1819 reveal the strengths and weaknesses of U.S. economic development?**

## POLITICS AND HEMISPHERIC CHANGE

Although financial crisis slowed settlement for a time after 1819, a new wave of political and military engagements would soon again spark frontier movements. In the aftermath of the War of 1812, the United States showed a new confidence in foreign policy. The United States claimed to have no imperial ambitions, but aggressive military action by General Andrew Jackson and assertive diplomacy from Secretary of State **John Quincy Adams** added territory and enhanced the international stature of the nation. The United States linked itself firmly to the rest of the Western Hemisphere when it took an interest in revolutions in Latin America. But how could the United States solidify its new position without igniting more political trouble with European nations?

GLOBAL PASSAGES

## Texas Filibustering

Some Americans were unhappy with the Transcontinental Treaty, especially with the clause that agreed to forgo U.S. claims on Texas and to set the Sabine River as the western boundary of the Louisiana Purchase. In June 1819, a group of businessmen including John Sibley and John G. Burnett organized a military expedition out of Louisiana to capture Nacogdoches, Texas. They hired James Long, a veteran of the Battle of New Orleans, to lead their force. After capturing Nacogdoches Long was made president of their self-declared Republic of Texas. Long attempted to enlist the support of **Jean Laffite**, the pirate who had aided Andrew Jackson at New Orleans and whose privateers now controlled Galveston Island. Laffite betrayed Long to the Spanish government. When the Spanish sent troops, the United States refused to support Long's military actions, and his small force fled back to Louisiana to regroup.

Long then formed an alliance with Mexican rebel José Felíx Trespalacios, who was in Louisiana trying to drum up support for the republican insurgency against Spain's colonial government in Mexico. Long hoped that he would be able to link his military efforts to the cause of Mexicans who were seeking to overthrow Spanish colonial rule. Late in 1819, Long and Trespalacios led a new invasion onto the Bolivar Peninsula in Galveston Bay, where they faced off against Laffite's forces. Long and Trespalacios languished for over a year, plagued by lack of funds and by disloyalty

## First Seminole War

Since acquiring Louisiana in 1803, U.S. officials had tried various measures to gain Spain's territory in Florida. In 1818, conflict with the Seminole Indians gave them new opportunity to act. Although it is not clear whether Secretary of War John C. Calhoun and Secretary of State John Quincy Adams intended to endorse belligerent action, they nonetheless capitalized on aggressive tactics employed by General Andrew Jackson to gain control of Florida. The Seminole, a mixed group of native peoples and runaway slaves, encouraged runaways from the United States to seek refuge in their territory in Spanish East Florida. The Seminole also harbored Creek who had fled south and west after Andrew Jackson crushed the Red Sticks rebellion in 1814. The United States refused to return Creek lands after the War of 1812, in spite of agreeing to do so in the Treaty of Ghent. In November 1817, U.S. general Edmund Gains burned the Creek village of Fowltown, Georgia, an action that caused reprisals from Florida Creek and Seminole against American settlers across the border. Calhoun sent Jackson to pacify the situation.

among their men, who lacked supplies and pay. When news reached Galveston in September 1821 that republican forces had taken control of Mexico City and had won Mexican independence, Trespalacios sailed for the capital, where he pledged his support to republican leader Augustín de Iturbide. Long left Galveston for La Bahia, but he was arrested and sent to Mexico City, where his lack of support for Iturbide probably cost him his life. He was shot by a sentry and killed.

Although Long had failed at his filibustering (defined as private military action by U.S. citizens seeking to take over Latin American territory), his actions paved the way for the colonization of Texas by other U.S. citizens. José Trespalacios was appointed the first Mexican territorial governor of Texas. In 1822, he arrived in the Texas capital of San Antonio, where he granted land to Stephen Austin, an American who established the first private colony in Texas and laid the foundations for U.S. involvement in the province. Jane Long, James Long's widow, received a pension from the Mexican government and became a pioneer settler in Austin's colony. Trespalacios was replaced as governor of Texas in 1823 after Iturbide fell from power. Stephen Austin and other American *empresarios* who ran private colonies in Texas cooperated with the Mexican government for the time being, but by the 1830s their actions would lead to more warfare and dissention.

- Compare James Long's filibustering to Andrew Jackson's takeover of Florida in the First Seminole War.
- How do you think Thomas Jefferson's vision of the West influenced filibustering?

In March 1818, Jackson arrived on the border with a force of Tennessee volunteers, regular army soldiers, and Creek allies hostile to the Red Sticks. He then proceeded to invade Spanish territory. Jackson had told President Monroe in January that he wanted to seize "the whole of East Florida," and when he received no reply from Monroe he took it as license to act freely. On April 6 Jackson captured the Spanish fort at St. Mark's, and he then attacked the Seminole villages on the Suwannee River. In addition to burning property while fighting Indians and African Americans in these actions, Jackson also arrested and executed two British citizens whom he accused of helping the Seminole. On May 28, Jackson occupied the Spanish capitol of Pensacola, expelled governor **José Mascot**, appointed a U.S. territorial governor, and declared that Spain would have to give up Florida if it could not control the Seminole.

Jackson's actions caused an uproar in Washington, DC. Although most of Monroe's cabinet believed that Jackson had exceeded his orders, Secretary of State John Quincy Adams acted to restrain the reaction against Jackson. Adams, who had entered treaty negotiations with Spanish diplomat **Luis de Onís**, used the Seminole war as leverage and stressed that Spain had to demonstrate mastery of the Seminole in order to be trusted. In November 1818, after Onís pulled out of talks, Adams returned control of Pensacola and St. Marks to the Spanish, but controversy over Jackson's actions continued. In January 1819, in his annual message to Congress, President Monroe disavowed intentions to take over Spanish Territory. Congress immediately began to investigate and to debate whether Jackson's actions had been correct. Henry Clay delivered a blistering speech denouncing Jackson, but resolutions to censure Jackson were roundly defeated. Mississippi representative George Poindexter declared that Jackson had "fulfilled the measure of his country's glory," and many Americans seemed to agree as they thronged to praise him on a February triumphal tour around the eastern seaboard.

## Transcontinental (Adams-Onís) Treaty

President Monroe relied heavily on Secretary of State John Quincy Adams to guide him through many different policy decisions. Adams carefully balanced rivalries with other cabinet ministers including Treasury Secretary William H. Crawford and Vice President Daniel D. Tompkins. Adams put his stamp on a whole new era of U.S. foreign policy, and he did much to consolidate the status of the United States in the world. Upon taking office Adams immediately improved U.S. relations with Great Britain. He oversaw the Rush-Bagot Agreement in 1817, in which the British agreed to demilitarize the Great Lakes. In the midst of the diplomatic controversy over the Seminole War, Adams and U.S. Minister to Great Britain **Richard Rush** also cemented the Convention of 1818, in which the British agreed to set the border between the United States and Canada at the 49th parallel. After Adams sent a warship to the Oregon coast, the British also agreed to return Astoria to the United States and to recognize some U.S. territorial rights in Oregon.

Shocked by the lack of response from Great Britain to U.S. aggression in Florida and facing growing pressure from the independence movements in Latin America, Spanish officials decided to cut their losses and cede Florida when Luis de Onís returned to his negotiations with Adams in late 1818. Now confident that he could gain Florida, Adams made an even bolder proposal to acquire new territory from the Spanish, who still resisted U.S. claims on the southwestern border of the Louisiana Purchase territory. Adams proposed that Spain cede territory all the way to the Pacific Ocean to the north of California at the 42nd parallel. This was the first U.S. government bid to extend its territory across the entire continent of North America, a move that Adams wrote in his diary would form "a great epoch in our history." In exchange for Spanish recognition of U.S. rights in Oregon, Adams consented to forgo all claim to Texas. Adams and Onís agreed to these terms in the Transcontinental Treaty in February 1819.

## The United States and Latin American Revolutions

The U.S. Senate ratified the Adams-Onís Treaty just two days after Adams presented it. But Madrid held up final agreement until 1821, in large part because of arguments over U.S. response to the revolutions that by 1810 had spread across most of Latin America. The United States had proclaimed neutrality in Spain's wars with its colonies in September 1815, but many U.S. traders and private citizens sought to aid Latin American rebels. In August 1817, Washington diplomats remained neutral.

Spain demanded that the United States not aid the Latin American rebels, but public opinion was in the rebels' favor. The successes of Simón Bolívar against Spanish forces in Colombia, Ecuador, and Venezuela between 1819 and 1821, Augustín de

▲ **Map 9.4**

**Latin America and the Caribbean, c. 1830** This map shows the dates that various Latin American and Caribbean countries attained their colonial independence.

Iturbide's securing of Mexican independence in 1821, and San Martín's independence victory in Peru in 1821 helped to convince the Monroe administration to alter its course and propose recognition of the Latin American independence movements in March 1822. By 1826, Congress had agreed to recognize the Republic of Greater Colombia, Mexico, Chile, Argentina, Brazil, the Provinces of Central America, and Peru. Only the black republic of Haiti would have to wait until 1862 for U.S. acceptance.

## The Monroe Doctrine

The U.S. recognition of Latin American independence did not end its wrangling with Spain, and in 1822 other European powers also indicated that they might intervene in the region. By April 1823, Spain retained only Cuba and Puerto Rico as colonies. Although John Quincy Adams agreed to let Spain maintain control there, he warned that the United States would not approve if Spain let any other European power intercede and the United States might be prepared to invade Cuba if Spain disagreed. Adams also took a hard line in British trade negotiations and objected to a Russian claim on American territory in Oregon. British foreign minister **George Canning** opposed European intervention in Latin America, but American officials worried that he would be ignored by other Alliance powers. Canning told U.S. diplomat Richard Rush that he would be willing to issue a joint British-American statement warning Europeans against Latin-American intervention. Secretary of State John Quincy Adams was

### TIMELINE 1789–1823

**1789**

**March** Pennsylvania lifts its ban on theater

**1790**

**May** The first U.S. copyright law takes effect, although it is largely ineffective

**1791**

**March** Vermont becomes the 14th state

**1792**

**May** Robert Gray claims the Columbia River and part of the Oregon Territory for the United States

**June** Kentucky admitted to the union as a state

**1793**

**October** Eli Whitney refines his cotton gin design

**1794**

Susannah Rowson's novel *Charlotte Temple* is published

**May** Eli Whitney receives the patent for his cotton gin

**June** Richard Allen founds the Bethel Church in Philadelphia

**1796**

**June** Tennessee becomes the 16th state

**1798**

Charles Brockdon Brown publishes his novel *Wieland*

**1800**

Mason Locke Weems publishes his biography of George Washington

**1801**

**August** Cane Ridge Revival in Bourbon County, KY

**1803**

**March** Ohio becomes the 17th state in the union

**August** The Lewis and Clark expedition is commissioned

**1804**

**May** The Corps of Discovery sets out on the Lewis and Clark expedition

**November** Lewis and Clark take up winter quarters with the Mandan Indians

**1805**

Hugh Henry Brackenridge publishes *Modern Chivalry*

**April** The Lewis and Clark expedition reaches the mouth of the Yellowstone River

**August** Zebulon Pike explores for the source of the Mississippi River

**November** Lewis and Clark reach the Pacific Ocean

**1806**

**July** Lewis and Clark split the Corps of Discovery into two parties

**July** Zebulon Pike sets out to explore the southwestern Louisiana Territory

**September** The Lewis and Clark expedition ends in St. Louis

**1808**

**April** John Jacob Astor incorporates the American Fur Company

**November** The Osage cede lands in Missouri and Arkansas to the United States in a treaty signed at Ft. Clark, KS

**1810**

The Campbellite Church of Christ splits from the Presbyterian Church

**June** John Jacob Astor founds the Pacific Fur Company

**October** President Madison annexes part of West Florida to Louisiana

**1811**

**January** Congress authorizes President

suspicious of Canning's motives, however, and he decided the United States should respond alone.

Adams took a bold approach and decided to warn Europe in no uncertain terms. Adams drafted Monroe's seventh annual message to Congress, and in it he enunciated what would become known as the **Monroe Doctrine**. In the December 1823 address Monroe declared that the United States shared common interest with other states in the Western Hemisphere and that the political system in Europe was "essentially different" from that of the democratic republics in North and South America. Monroe maintained that the United States would not interfere in European politics or with existing European colonies in the Western Hemisphere, but neither should Europe insert itself any further in the West. Europe could not be allowed to extend its power or monarchical political system in North or South America without, in Monroe's words, "endangering our peace and happiness." European powers should not seek future colonies in the Western Hemisphere and should not seek to re-conquer independent states.

In later decades and centuries, the Monroe Doctrine would be used as a justification of U.S. intervention in Latin American countries, but for the time being it was mostly a bold statement of independence from European influence. Since 1789, the United States had more than tripled the area of its territory, and its growing population was settling larger areas every year. But the United States did not yet have the military power to entirely enforce its grand vision.

Madison to acquire East Florida

**1812**

**April** Louisiana becomes the 18th state in the union

**June** The Missouri Territory is organized

**1814**

Emma Willard opens her first school in Middlebury, VT

**1815**

**September** United States declares neutrality in Latin American wars of independence

**1816**

Indiana admitted to the union as a state

**April** Congress passes 25% trade tariff

**December** James Monroe elected President

**1817**

**March** John Quincy Adams becomes Secretary of State

**April** Rush-Bagot agreement improves relations between United States and Britain

**1818**

**February** Bernardo O'Higgins and José de San Martín declare independence in Chile

**April** Gen. Andrew Jackson takes control of West Florida in the First Seminole War

**December** Illinois admitted to the union

**1819**

**January** Cotton prices drop, touching off the Panic of 1819

**February** Adams-Onís Treaty signed

**February** Motions of censure against Andrew Jackson fail in Congress

**1820**

**March** Missouri Compromise—Missouri and Maine become U.S. states

**December** President Monroe is reelected

**1821**

Adams-Onís Treaty ratified

**February** Mexico declares independence

**July** José de San Martín declares the independence of Peru

**September** Mexico cements its independence from Spain

**1822**

**March** President Monroe suggests that the United States should recognized Latin American countries

**1823**

**December** Monroe Doctrine articulated in Monroe's annual message to Congress

## STUDY QUESTIONS FOR POLITICS AND HEMISPHERIC CHANGE

1. **In what ways did the Monroe Doctrine indicate that the United States aspired to a new status in the world?**
2. **John Quincy Adams has been called one of the most talented Secretaries of State the United States has ever had. Why?**

## Summary

- Between 1789 and 1824 the United States, Spain, Great Britain, and Russia expanded on the North American continent through exploration, settlement, and trade.
- Different Indian peoples responded to pressures on their lives through various combinations of warfare, trade, diplomacy, and cultural assimilation.
- The physical expansion of the United States and the expansion of cotton farming led to conflicts over slavery.
- A new "American" culture reflected the changing social roles of women, African Americans, Christians, and others.
- The United States was increasingly connected to the rest of the world through trade even as new foreign policy following the War of 1812 defined a more assertive position for the country.

## Key Terms and People

**Adams, John Quincy** *349*
**Allen, Richard** *339*
**American Colonization Society (ACS)** *338*
**Astor, John Jacob** *331*
**Bank of the United States (BUS)** *347*
**Beecher, Lyman** *346*
**Brackenridge, Hugh Henry** *342*
**Calhoun, John C.** *347*
**Canning, George** *354*
**Clark, William** *329*
**Clay, Henry** *336*
**coverture** *342*
**Dwight, Timothy** *346*
**Girard, Stephen** *347*
**Jones, Absalom** *344*
**Laffite, Jean** *350*
**Lewis, Meriwether** *328*
**Lukens, Rebecca** *342*
**Mascot, José** *351*
**Monroe Doctrine** *355*
**Monroe, James** *337*
**Murray, Judith Sargent** *341*
**Onís, Luis de** *351*
**Pike, Zebulon** *330*
**Rowson, Susannah** *343*
**Rush, Richard** *352*
**Sacagawea** *329*
**Second Great Awakening** *346*
**Sequoyah** *341*
**Tallmadge, James, Jr.** *336*
**Taylor, Nathaniel** *346*
**Tecumseh** *340*
**Wilkinson, James** *330*
**Willard, Emma** *341*
**Wollstonecraft, Mary** *341*
**yeomen** *335*

## Reviewing Chapter 9

1. Both government policies and individual initiative were crucial to the expansion of the United States. Which was more important, and why?
2. How did the movement of people around North America influence political events between 1789 and 1824?
3. What were some of the most important ways that attitudes towards nature and natural resources shaped actions of U.S. citizens between 1789 and 1824?

## Further Reading

Chasteen, John Charles. *Americanos: Latin America's Struggle for Independence.* NewYork: Oxford University Press, 2008. This book traces Latin American wars for independence starting in 1808 and examines how various Latin American colonies became independent nations. Chasteen shows the interplay between the United States and many Latin American revolutionary nations.

Forbes, Robert Pierce. *The Missouri Compromise and Its Aftermath: Slavery and the Meaning of America.* Chapel Hill: University of North Carolina Press, 2007. Forbes analyzes the complex political history of American expansionism that led to the delicate Missouri Compromise and traces the consequences of the Compromise for U.S. politics and society.

Hackel, Stephen. *Children of Coyote, Missionaries of Saint Francis: Indian-Spanish Relations in Colonial California, 1769–1850.* Chapel Hill: University of North Carolina Press, 2005. In this book, Hackel examines how California Indians coped with and resisted Spanish religious and military colonial control, even as their populations were decimated by disease. The presents a particularly in-depth case study of the Mission of San Carlos Borromeo.

Howe, Daniel Walker. *What Hath God Wrought: The Transformation of America, 1815–1848.* New York: Oxford University Press, 2007. Howe's sweeping overview of U.S. history from 1815–848 integrates excellent discussion of territorial expansion, slavery, religious revival, and the development of American literature. This narrative account is also a gripping read.

Nash, Gary B. *Forging Freedom: The Formation of Philadelphia's Black Community, 1720–1840.* Cambridge: Harvard University Press, 1988. Nash's account of the free black community in Philadelphia shows how ties of kinship, economic activity, and religion provided the means to create the urban center of free black society in the United States. Nash shows how many African Americans succeeded, despite racism and growing segregation.

# Visual Review

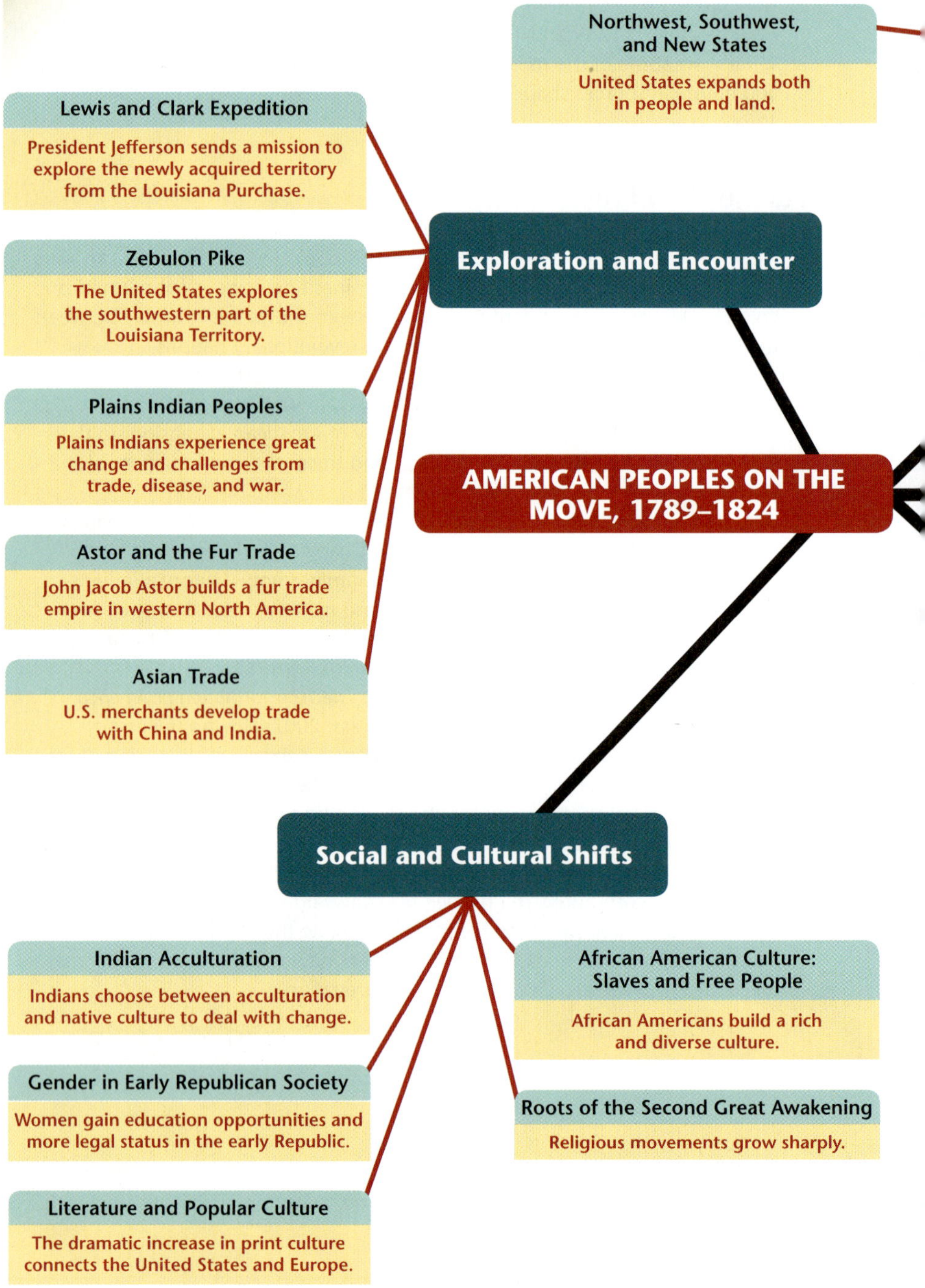

**AMERICAN PEOPLES ON THE MOVE, 1789–1824**

## Exploration and Encounter

**Jeffersonian Agrarianism**
An ideology that valued land and farming fuels activity in the United States.

**Northwest, Southwest, and New States**
United States expands both in people and land.

**Lewis and Clark Expedition**
President Jefferson sends a mission to explore the newly acquired territory from the Louisiana Purchase.

**Zebulon Pike**
The United States explores the southwestern part of the Louisiana Territory.

**Plains Indian Peoples**
Plains Indians experience great change and challenges from trade, disease, and war.

**Astor and the Fur Trade**
John Jacob Astor builds a fur trade empire in western North America.

**Asian Trade**
U.S. merchants develop trade with China and India.

## Social and Cultural Shifts

**Indian Acculturation**
Indians choose between acculturation and native culture to deal with change.

**Gender in Early Republican Society**
Women gain education opportunities and more legal status in the early Republic.

**Literature and Popular Culture**
The dramatic increase in print culture connects the United States and Europe.

**African American Culture: Slaves and Free People**
African Americans build a rich and diverse culture.

**Roots of the Second Great Awakening**
Religious movements grow sharply.

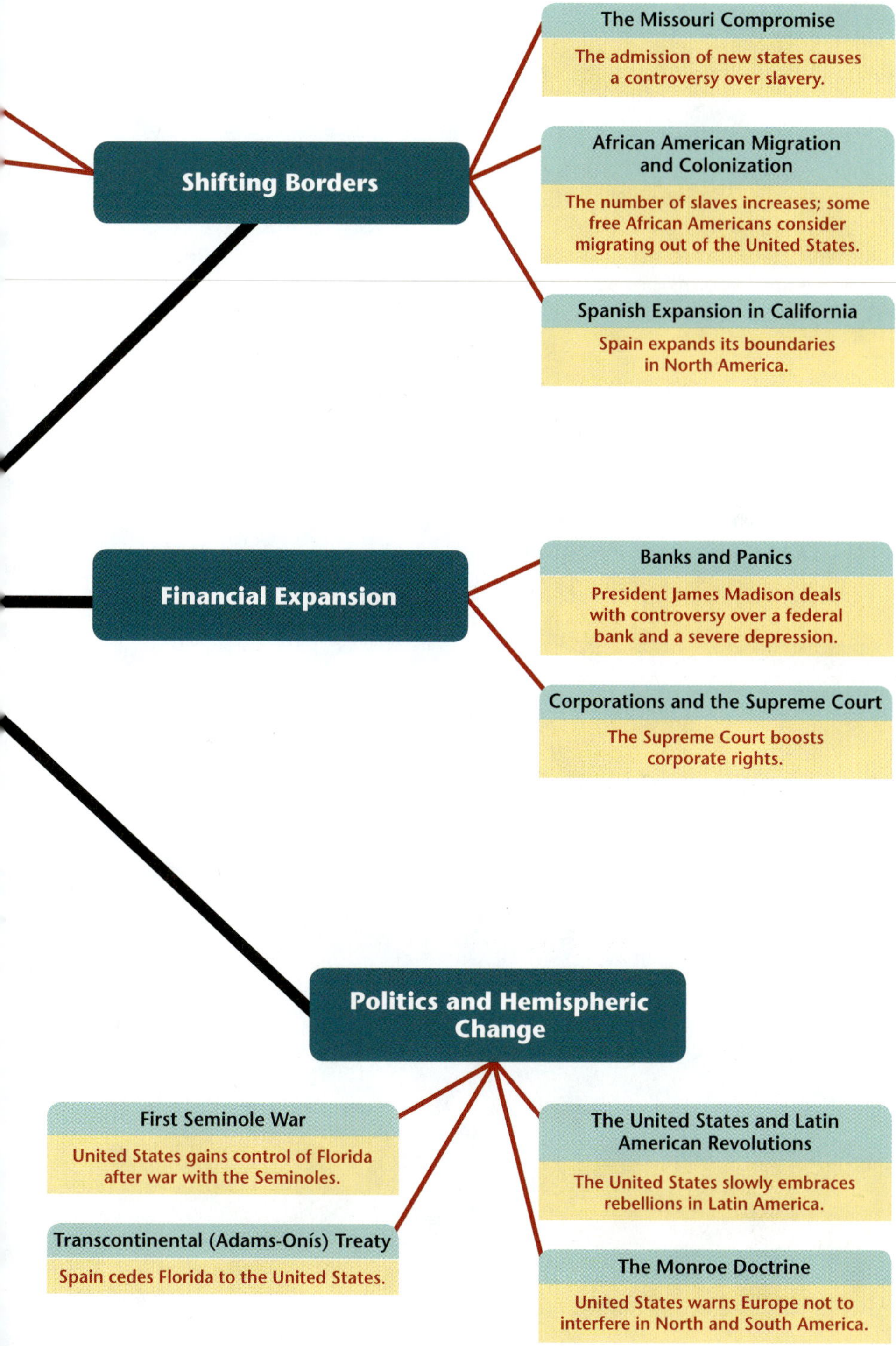

**Shifting Borders**

**The Missouri Compromise**

The admission of new states causes a controversy over slavery.

**African American Migration and Colonization**

The number of slaves increases; some free African Americans consider migrating out of the United States.

**Spanish Expansion in California**

Spain expands its boundaries in North America.

**Financial Expansion**

**Banks and Panics**

President James Madison deals with controversy over a federal bank and a severe depression.

**Corporations and the Supreme Court**

The Supreme Court boosts corporate rights.

**Politics and Hemispheric Change**

**First Seminole War**

United States gains control of Florida after war with the Seminoles.

**Transcontinental (Adams-Onís) Treaty**

Spain cedes Florida to the United States.

**The United States and Latin American Revolutions**

The United States slowly embraces rebellions in Latin America.

**The Monroe Doctrine**

United States warns Europe not to interfere in North and South America.

# 10 Market Revolutions and the Rise of Democracy

## 1789–1832

On July 4, 1830, the residents of Portland, Maine, found themselves bitterly divided by politics. Instead of holding one celebration of Independence Day, Democrats who supported Andrew Jackson held their own separate event, as they no longer wished to celebrate alongside Jackson's opponents, who controlled local government and festivities. The two factions were in the process of splitting into two parties—the Democrats and the Whigs. Both sides used Fourth of July parades, ritual toasting, celebrations, and newspapers not only to celebrate the nation's birthday but also to blast their opponents.

After the rival parades directly passed one another in the center of town, each side adjourned to separate locations, where partygoers could enjoy the company of those who agreed with them. The Jacksonian Democrats met at Mr. Attwood's boarding house, where elaborate decorations, including a live bald eagle and two miniature fully rigged commercial sailing ships, displayed Democratic principles. The anti-Jacksonians repaired to the City Hall, which was also "handsomely decorated" for their celebration.

The ritual toasts—long an Independence Day tradition—revealed the bitter partisan divide between Portlanders. The Jacksonians cast President Jackson as the "youngest political son of the late Thomas Jefferson," "the sincere and untiring friend of the *simple* mechanic," and a supporter "of the rights of the People, and worthy of their suffrages." Several toasters wished for Democratic electoral success in the Fall elections, and Ebenezer

Portrait of Andrew Jackson by Ralph Eleaser Whiteside Earl

**CHAPTER OUTLINE**



*continued on page 365*

# America in the World

Mexico blocked American colonization in Texas (1830).

The Santa Fe Trail expanded trade markets westward (1821).

 U.S. event that influenced the world

 International event that influenced the United States

 Event with multinational influence

 Conflict

Textile mills gave birth to the American Industrial Revolution (1790).
The Erie Canal made New York state the center of economic growth in the United States (1825).

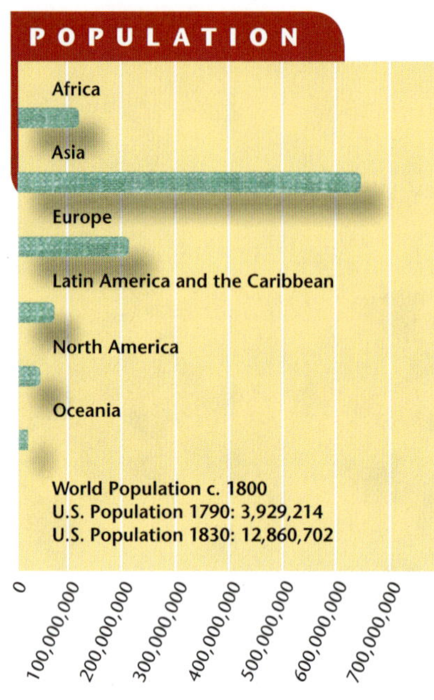


Webster hailed the Democrats' electoral opponents in an aggressive tone: "We will toast them . . . and baste them with democratic butter." Meanwhile, back at City Hall, the anti-Jacksonians labeled their opponents "political skunks and other vermin."

Portland's role in the transatlantic economy helped drive political disagreements. Maine grew rapidly in the decade between its admission to the Union in 1820 and 1830, and its expanding population benefited from thriving agriculture, fishing, lumber, and shipbuilding industries. Maine served as an entry port for cotton, feeding the new textile mills throughout New England. Advertisements in the local newspapers announced regular commercial and passenger ship traffic between Portland, Boston, and European cities including Belfast and Frankfort. The Cumberland and Oxford canal opened in 1830 to connect the interior of southern Maine to the port of Portland.

Andrew Jackson's supporters in Portland made a clear distinction between their support of this state effort, financed by the locally chartered Canal Bank, and what they considered to be the unconstitutional "**American System**" of Henry Clay that promoted the use of federal government funds for the same kinds of projects. The Jacksonian Democrats in Maine drew most of their support from poor fishermen, working men, and small merchants, while the anti-Jacksonian Whigs attracted wealthier business supporters.

The partisanship displayed in Portland, Maine, characterized the growing splits in national and local politics taking place all over the United States. Disagreements over how government should best manage the burgeoning capitalist and commercial enterprise in the developing nation would change the character of U.S. politics as the country entered the worldwide Industrial Revolution.

## THE MARKET SYSTEM

Americans had grown increasingly used to buying and selling goods since the mid-1700s. The pace and scale of these economic exchanges accelerated, however, and between 1789 and 1832 a fuller market economy took shape in the United States. In a market economy market forces influence the production, distribution, and consumption of goods. Before 1789, most rural Americans lived on interdependent family farms, although many, like southern tobacco planters, raised staple crops and participated in international trade. At the turn of the 19th century, more and more farmers began to produce surplus goods that they could sell locally, regionally, or internationally for cash. Although the vast majority of Americans remained in rural areas, a greater percentage of Americans were moving into towns and cities, where manufacturing took place. The greater supply of foreign and domestic manufactured goods that fueled the market system allowed farm families to specialize, since they could purchase goods instead of having to produce or trade locally for everything they needed. The market system intensified economic competition, changed business and labor patterns, and had a profound effect on the lives of everyone in the United States. Technological change, government interaction with the economy, and international exchanges all intensified the development of market capitalism.

CHAPTER OUTLINE

*continued from page 361*



## Internal and External Markets

The U.S. market economy emerged from the connection of local, regional, national, and international networks of exchange—all of which grew between 1789 and 1832. By 1800 everyday economic activities were more and more influenced by market prices and wider economic forces. In a free-market economy open competition and the exchange of products, credit, and cash balance the optimum production and price of goods. As new kinds of transportation and machinery became available by 1820, many farmers made decisions about what to grow, when to grow it, and how to process it based on market forces.

As Americans had more opportunities to sell their goods farther away, the connections between domestic markets and international markets grew in importance for both agricultural and manufactured products. After the turn of the 19th century, for example, cotton planters in Georgia and Alabama shipped their products to New England textile mills that manufactured and sold cloth across the United States and into the South and West.

European manufacturing could also affect prices and supplies, and international trade played an important role in the market process. The towns and cities inside the United States that grew most rapidly were those, like Providence, New York, St. Louis, and Philadelphia, that had links both to internal networks of agricultural trade and to external ports and waterways that could facilitate international exchange.

Examining one particular product, such as butter, can show how the market transformation worked. Butter went from a product that families produced for themselves to the stuff of international commerce. Dairying and butter making were practiced widely by farm women in the Mid-Atlantic states at the end of the 18th century, and by 1790 surplus butter was already being traded between farms and sold in Philadelphia. After the War of 1812, more and more women specialized in butter making and started to produce large quantities for sale as a commodity. The stable price for butter, between 17 and 25 cents per pound between the 1790s and 1830s, meant that women could provide income from butter when other farm products fluctuated. Martha Ogle Forman, a Maryland dairywoman, wrote in her diary in 1824, "We now make more butter than we know what to do with." In fact, she did know what to do with the surplus butter: she sold it for profit.

Women like Forman could spend more time making butter because they were able to purchase manufactured cloth instead of spinning and weaving at home. As supplies of store-bought cloth accelerated into the 1830s, so did the production of butter. Farms also adopted new milking methods and new breeds of cows that gave more milk. Butter could be preserved with salt for over a year, and Mid-Atlantic butter was increasingly sold in central markets in Philadelphia, Providence, Annapolis, Charleston, Boston, and other port cities. And the international market also grew. Between 1802 and 1835 Americans exported 67 million pounds of dairy products overseas to Europe, the Caribbean, and China.

The same kind of story could be repeated for scores of other commodities—for example: cheese, grain, whiskey, pork, and lumber. Homemade and farm goods spread through local, regional, national, and international markets. The market economy

Butter churning, a traditional part of women's work in the dairy producing Mid-Atlantic states, became an increasingly market-oriented economic activity in the early 19th century. Women could sell surplus butter for cash they could use to buy other household products. Eventually, butter became an international trade commodity.

grew through a million single decisions about what to buy, what to produce, and how to sell it.

## Technology: Domestic Invention and Global Appropriation

The invention and adoption of new technologies also fueled market activity. In the Patent Act of 1790 Congress granted inventors a 14-year monopoly on successfully patented machinery and processes, and patents provided an economic incentive for invention. The federal government went from issuing three patents in 1790 to 573 in 1831. The new interest in manufacturing during the War of 1812, when foreign trade was severely restricted, especially spurred domestic invention.

Americans invented new technologies to improve both agriculture and manufacturing. By 1792, Delaware inventor **Oliver Evans** licensed his designs for continuous-processing flour mills and grain elevators to more than 100 mills. In 1819, Jethro Wood patented an iron plow constructed from interchangeable parts. After revolutionizing the production of cotton with his mechanized cotton mill in 1793, **Eli Whitney** turned his ingenuity to manufacturing muskets with interchangeable parts. In 1831 Illinois inventor **Cyrus McCormick** built his first mechanical reaper, a machine that would revolutionize harvesting in the decades to come.

Americans also appropriated some new technologies from abroad—especially from Great Britain. By the early 1780s British textile mills used mechanized looms and carding machines, but textile workers were discouraged from emigrating out of the country and could be fined if they gave up trade secrets. American agents in New York, Maryland, Pennsylvania, and Massachusetts tried to pay English mechanics to build machinery for them, and they openly advertised in newspapers for men willing to divulge the secrets of British inventor **Richard Arkwright**. Trying to stop the smuggling of British textile machinery into the United States, British consul Phineas Bond, Jr., even inspected cargo in the port of Philadelphia. **Samuel Slater**, a former British textile worker, emigrated to the United States in 1789 and parlayed his knowledge of both machinery and labor management practices into the first successful mechanized mill in the United States.

## Water and Steam Power

Steam power was just part of a revolution in the commercial use of water power. Although water power had been harnessed for centuries at saw mills, leather tanneries, and grist mills, in the 1790s water power began to be applied to manufacturing in greater magnitude. The power created by waterfalls turned water wheels that could be connected by gears and belts to power machinery. Because of favorable geographical conditions, by the early 19th century, Americans were global leaders in harnessing water power for manufacturing. Across the North and Northwest, water power contributed to the growth of textile mills that used machinery to card, spin, and weave cotton and woolen cloth. After the turn of the century, water powered cotton gins, sugar mills, and rice mills in the South. Waterwheels drove furnaces and forges essential to ironworks. By 1830, there were an estimated 50,000 water mills in the United States, and the first industrial towns and cities all grew near bodies of water. Location near a water source was so important to all these industries that competition for land near waterways was fierce.

Harnessing steam power from heated water was probably the most important technological innovation in the early market economy. Steam power, although weaker and slower to develop, allowed greater mobility than pure water power because machinery did not have to be near a waterway. British inventor **James Watt** perfected the first modern steam engine in 1769, although it took several decades of constant innovation by engineers to make steam power more efficient. In the first decade of the 19th century, Oliver Evans, the successful American flour mill inventor, patented a high-pressure steam engine that would be used in the first railroad locomotive and in other industrial applications.

Steamboats were probably the first significant American contribution to international technology. Steam-powered transportation had the ability to increase the speed of trade and transportation dramatically. Pennsylvanian **John Fitch** first used steam to power a boat in August 1787. After several decades of scrambling by various inventors to produce a commercially viable steamboat, **Robert Fulton** combined ingenuity with principles he observed on a trip to Europe and perfected a usable high-powered boat engine. Fulton worked with investor and politician **Robert Livingston** to obtain

Robert Fulton's ship "*Clermont*" was the first commercially viable steamboat in the world. Fulton and Robert Livingston received a monopoly on New York Hudson River steamboat travel, even before it was technologically viable. They launched the *Clermont* in 1807.

a monopoly on steamboat traffic in New York waters, and in August 1807 he launched the *North River Steamboat*—also known as the *Clermont*—the world's first fully successful commercial steamboat.

Steamboats quickly spread throughout America's inland waterways, and by 1812 steamboats plied waters in the transappalachian West. French engineer Jean Baptiste Marestier observed in 1819 that "America now possesses several hundred [commercial steamboats] and the people of the New World are already reaping immense benefits." He worried about American "superiority over other nations" in steamboat travel. That same year the *Savannah*, the first American ship with auxiliary steam power, crossed the Atlantic Ocean. By 1830, hundreds of steamboats, traveling nearly twice as fast as in the 1810s, traded goods up and down the coasts and on the Mississippi River.

## Transportation and Communication

Improvements in transportation—including steamboats, roads, canals, and early railroads—played a crucial role in the spread of the market economy throughout the United States in the early decades of the 19th century. Both federal and state governments invested heavily to speed up and lower the cost of moving goods around the country. Despite political controversy over use of too much federal power, federal government expenditures on transportation improvements went from less than $100,000 in 1789 to over $1.5 million in 1832. In 1804, **Albert Gallatin**, Thomas Jefferson's Treasury Secretary, initially proposed the first comprehensive plan for internal improvements.

Henry Clay—who served as a U.S. senator, Speaker of the House of Representatives, and Secretary of State between 1809 and 1832—later became the leading advocate of publicly funded transportation. Subsidies for roads and canals, in particular, became one of the cornerstones of his "American System"—a group of laws intended to spur domestic economic development that also included **tariffs** and currency regulation. Clay's plans for public improvements, however, ran afoul of several presidents who opposed the overuse of federal power. In 1817, James Madison vetoed the "Bonus Bill" that would have used Bank of the United States funds to pay for roads and canals because he judged it to be an unconstitutional use of federal power.

Road building increased exponentially in these decades and proved a key to increased market activity. In the 1790s, turnpikes—roads tailor-made for wagons bearing goods—were constructed up and down the eastern seaboard; by the 1820s they carried hundreds of thousands of tons of freight per year. Many roads, including turnpikes, were built by private companies, encouraged by state subsidies and charters. Congress also took action and authorized the Cumberland Road from Cumberland, Maryland, to Ohio in 1806. Efforts to revive funding for a National Road after the War of 1812 were blocked by arguments that road building could not serve a truly "national" interest. In 1822, Congress authorized repairs to the Cumberland Road and extended it to Vandalia, Illinois, but President Monroe, calling the bill unconstitutional, vetoed it.

Following the War of 1812, several states supplemented road-building projects with early efforts at canal building. Canals promised to expand steamboats and to

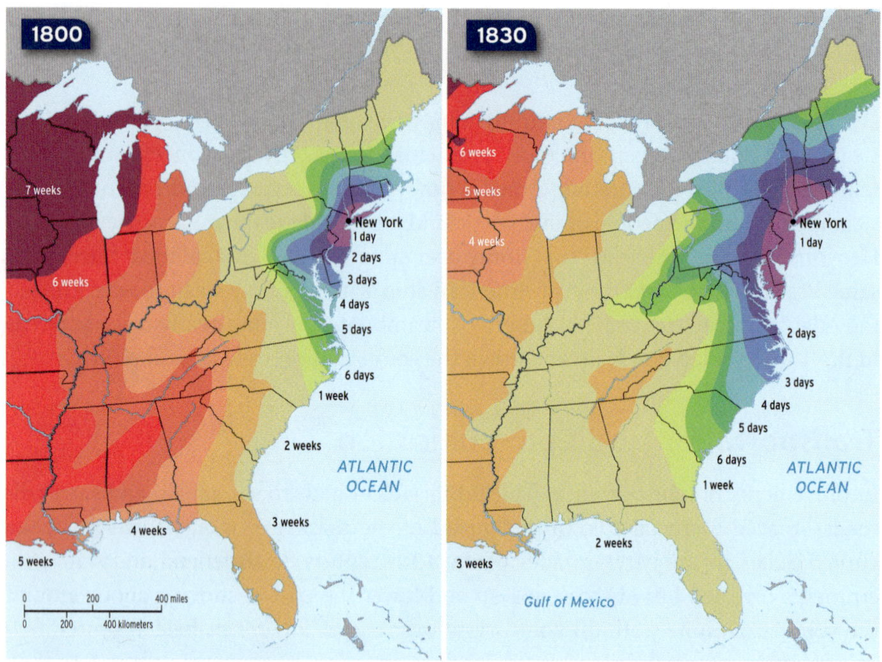


▲ **Map 10.1**

**Transportation Times Inside the United States, 1800–1830** This map shows how long it took to travel from New York City to other points in the United States. Transportation improvements and technological developments dramatically improved travel time between 1800 and 1830.

widen market activity, since they mainly aimed to connect inland waters to major avenues of river and oceanic trade.

Early railroads also promised to further economic development. In 1830, the Baltimore and Ohio Company founded the first railroad in the United States and opened 13 miles of passenger service between the Baltimore port and Sandyhook, Maryland. Between 1830 and 1833, a rail line between Charleston and Hamburg, South Carolina, used steam-powered locomotives to transport hundreds of passengers along the world's longest run of track. These relatively small beginnings would inspire an entire era of growth in industry and transportation.

Transportation advances also improved communication between towns, states, and regions. Congress created the U.S. Postal System in 1789, and by the 1820s it delivered mail along nearly 2,500 postal routes. Increased business activity led to even faster growth: 5,000 post offices opened across the United States between 1819 and 1832. The mail provided an important means for both private and public communication. A letter could cost as much as 25 cents to mail, but newspapers could be sent for only one and a half cents. The mails also carried political pamphlets, and advances in papermaking meant that they could be printed more cheaply. Although more expensive to send, business documents also traveled through the mail and made market connections across great distances possible.

**STUDY QUESTIONS FOR THE MARKET SYSTEM**

1. **In what ways were the market changes in the U.S. economy between 1789 and 1832 revolutionary?**
2. **What role did transportation play in U.S. economic development in this period?**

# MARKETS AND SOCIAL RELATIONSHIPS

In addition to changes in manufacturing, technology, and transportation, the transition to a capitalist market economy in the United States also changed the ways that people related to one another in families, workplaces, and neighborhoods. As with any huge change in an economic system, individuals felt the effects unevenly and experienced them in ways that defy simple description. Journeymen or agricultural wage laborers, who might have once counted on advancing to shop or farm ownership, now often found themselves working permanently for wages. Patterns of labor on farms and in households changed the relationships between husbands and wives, children, and hired help. Slaves, who both provided labor and were defined as commodities in slaveholding areas, also saw themselves subject to market forces.

## Manufacturing and the Factory System

The factory system of production radically changed the ways that workers related to business owners and to one another. The factory system referred to the centralization of manufacturing under the ownership of one person or a corporation. Instead of the manufacture of goods in homes or in small family-owned workshops, the factory system brought together many unrelated workers under one roof. Instead of working for master craftsmen in a hierarchical system, factory workers labored for wages in defined jobs—usually concentrating on one aspect of production. In its purest form the factory system did not have to include the widespread use of machines; it was more about ownership and the organization of labor. But as U.S. factories developed, they also began to become mechanized.

British textile manufacturing firms instituted the factory system in the 1770s, and as Americans turned their attention to domestic production by the 1790s, they became interested in this system. The transition from home work to factory work took place slowly at first, but several early New England industries, including textile mills, shoemaking, and clock making, began to centralize production as they also adopted mechanization.

In 1790, British immigrant Samuel Slater and wealthy American merchant **Moses Brown** founded the first mechanized cotton mill in the United States in Pawtucket, Rhode Island. By 1793, Slater and Brown had expanded into an even larger factory on the Blackstone River, where they housed 1,500 water-powered spindles under one roof. The women wageworkers at Slater's mills used spinning skills they had developed at home, and they now applied them in an industrial setting. The operations also employed children as spinners and men as mechanics. Slater and his associates, spreading out through New England in the 1790s and early 1800s, founded scores of additional mechanized mill operations. By 1810, 31 mechanized mills were operating in the United States, most in Rhode Island or near Philadelphia. As mills spread they also began to use more machines and to draw more workers away from home production.

The Boston Associates, a corporation formed by wealthy men including **Samuel Cabot Lowell** and **Nathaniel Appleton**, raised the stakes in 1814 when they founded their mill operation in Waltham, Massachusetts. The Boston Associates centralized all aspects of cloth production under one roof. In an effort to manufacture truly mass-produced cloth and to capture market share, the Waltham mill owners introduced a labor system that was different from the British model adopted by Slater. They recruited young farm women, who provided the bulk of their mill work and lived in

Samuel Slater founded the first successful mechanized spinning mill in North America in Pawtucket, Rhode Island, in 1790. Water-powered mills, such as Slater's, soon spread across southern New England, changing employment patterns in the region and fueling the industrial revolution.

This engraving of the work floor of a cotton mill shows the power looms at work weaving cloth. Note the gendered division of labor: women operate the looms, while the sole visible man is there to repair one of the leather straps that used water power to run the looms. Working on a factory floor like this in the 1830s was a huge change in atmosphere from home textile production.

company-controlled boarding houses at the mill. The boarding houses enforced strict rules of conduct both on and off the factory floor. Most of these young "Mill Girls" viewed wage work as temporary, until they could marry and return to farming. The mills paid relatively high wages, but the work was difficult—with one woman in charge of 128 fast-moving spindles or two power looms. The Boston Associates mills were so profitable that they soon established large company towns at Lowell, Chicopee, and Lawrence, Massachusetts, and Manchester, New Hampshire. By the mid-1830s, when the "Mill Girls" began to be replaced by a more permanent class of immigrant workers, the boardinghouses became less important. But the mills continued to influence the character of life in New England into the 20th century.

Whether in a mill town or in a town like Lynn, Massachusetts, where hundreds of families manufactured shoes, workers saw their lives changed by the advent of the factory system. Working conditions were generally better than they were in British textile cities like Manchester and Barmen, where poverty, malnutrition, and disease were rampant. Even for people accustomed to hard work, however, labor in mechanized factories posed challenges. As mill worker Lucy Davis explained it, "The work was much harder than I expected and quite new to me." Factory work was often unsafe, and by the 1830s working conditions deteriorated as work sped up. It is no coincidence that the first widespread strikes and forms of labor resistance accompanied the rise of the factory system. Instead of being defined primarily by family relationships, workers began to see themselves in terms of their labor.

## Slavery and Markets

The burgeoning capitalist market economy also held deep consequences for slaves, who did not own their own labor and who were regarded as market commodities to be bought, sold, and traded. Slavery had for centuries played a vital role in the transatlantic market economy, especially for products like sugar and cotton, and slaves provided the labor for many of the raw materials for factories in the United States and in Great Britain. As cotton agriculture intensified between 1789 and 1832, slaves played an increasing role in the market economy, although many historians argue that the southern economy itself resisted a full integration into capitalism. As commodities, slaves were bought and traded in large open-air slave markets in most southern cities. One master wrote in Louisiana in 1818 that "Negroes will yield a much larger income than any Bank dividends."

This market logic helped to intensify the racism that increasingly defined all African American lives. Newspapers across the country advertised slaves as products for sale alongside agricultural produce, manufactured items, luxury goods, and livestock. After the expansion of the cotton economy in Alabama, Mississippi, and Louisiana, the internal slave trade followed the demand for cotton, and in the 1820s 155,000 slaves were sold into those areas from other states. Some estimates indicate that the domestic slave trade comprised as much as 15 percent of the Southern economy. Each

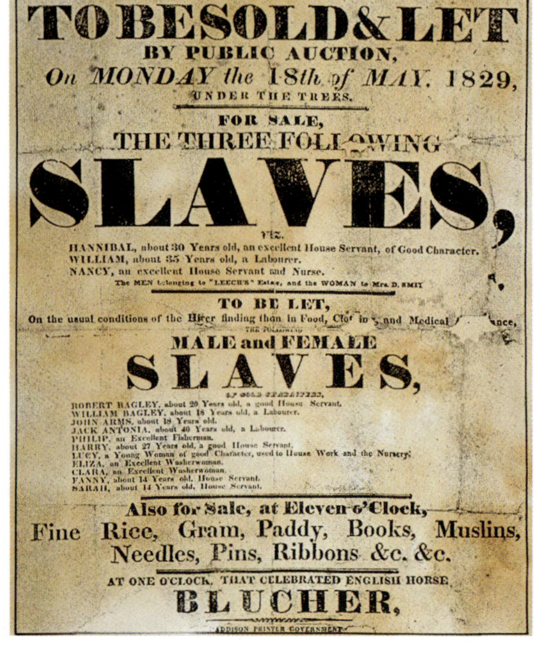


This advertisement for a runaway slave was typical of ads that ran throughout the South up until the 1860s. Slaves were viewed as valuable property, although the ads also recognized their humanity in the ways they were described by physical traits, skills, and personality. Runaway slave ads also provide historians with some clues about how slaves might have liberated themselves.

slave sale, of course, represented the rupture of a family and the misery of countless individuals who lived in the slave system.

## Class and Consumerism

Whereas slaves were characterized by race, free workers came to be defined as members of a working class. The relationship of workers to capital helped to create the economic power structures that divided people by social class. Social class also contributed to the feelings of affinity and connection that people in different strata of society developed with one another in opposition to those of lower or higher rank.

Class took shape in both work and social life. Americans in the early republic bought and sold goods, belonged to organizations, and engaged in other activities that displayed and strengthened their ties to other members of their social class. As the breakdown of the artisan system relegated more Americans to ranks of permanent wage earners, many workers felt an increasing identification with fellow

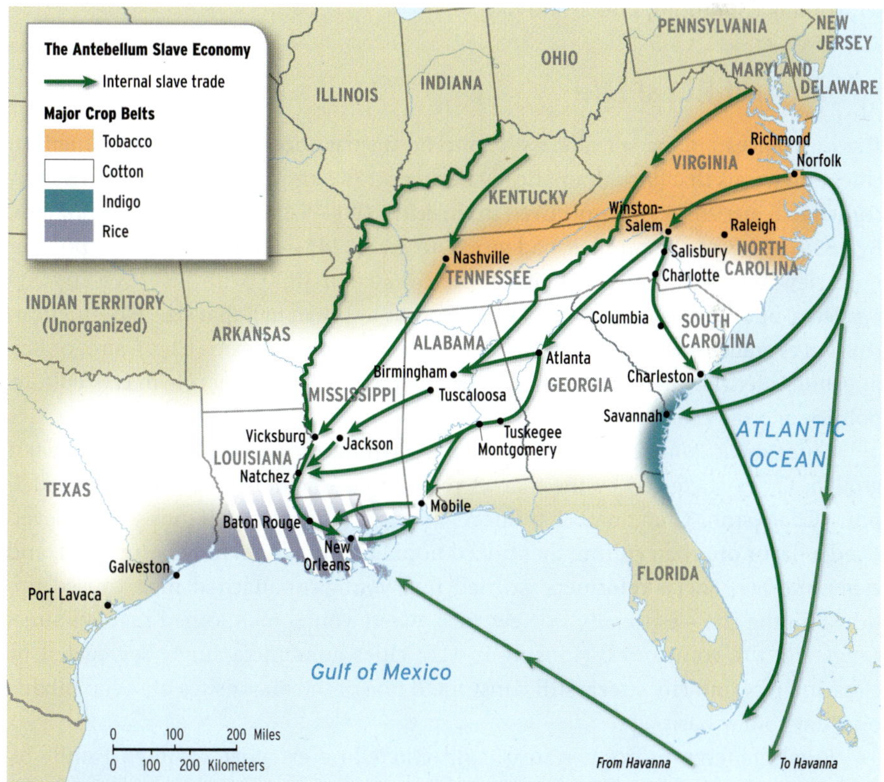


**Map 10.2**

**The Antebellum Slave Economy** This map depicts the internal slave trade that continued after Congress outlawed the international trade in 1808 and also depicts some illegal trade that continued with Cuba. The map also notes the location of staple crops that relied on slave labor.

workers across different trades and industries. Although the United States had a more equal income distribution than Europe, the divide between rich and poor grew significantly.

Wealthy planters, professionals, western landowners, and industrialists all displayed their earnings in the consumption of luxury goods and housing. Emerging middle-class Americans—such as tradesmen, clerks, and housewives—also had access to a growing array of consumer goods such as clothing, furniture, and imported house wares that reinforced their sense of refinement. Middling Americans tended to live in modest-sized houses but to decorate them more elaborately than poorer workers could. If the factory did not provide housing, many factory workers rented rooms in boarding houses, where they might lodge with relatives or other workers.

One sign of working-class identification came when workers began to band together to strike against their employers. After journeyman shoemakers organized one of the first labor protests in American history in 1806, strikes became more common. Boardinghouse life at the Lowell textile mills bred a sense of "sisterhood" among the workers there that reinforced the women's decision to strike in the late 1820s for better working conditions, hours, and pay.

## Urban and Rural Life

The differences among social classes were on display most clearly in the American cities and towns that grew dramatically between 1789 and 1832. The U.S. Census recorded that just 201,655 people lived in cities in 1790—5.1 percent of the population. By 1830, however, the number had grown to 1,127,247—8.8 percent of the population. New York was the largest city in the country in 1830, with just over 200,000 residents, but the next largest city, Baltimore, was less than half that size. No American city was as grand or well developed as London, Amsterdam, Mexico City, Cairo, or Beijing, but American cities were growing fast and assuming a greater role in U.S. culture, politics, and the economy.

Cities most connected to markets and manufacturing experienced the fastest growth. Cities energized by the market revolution—including New York, Philadelphia, Charleston, Cincinnati, Baltimore, New Orleans, and St. Louis—each developed a flavor of urban culture that mixed popular entertainment, vice, religion, and economic life. Social reformers worried that young, unattached men caused upheaval in the city—especially in New York, where young men joined raucous street gangs and fire companies. Housing in U.S. cities grew increasingly segregated by class and race, but city streets still constituted one of the major sites of social mixing on a day-to-day basis.

Rural life, even in frontier areas, still centered on extended families. Family remained the dominant social and economic unit in the experience of the vast majority of Americans. In the first half of the 19th century, economic growth relied on rural agricultural production in both Europe and the United States, and a high rate of rural mobility enhanced economic opportunity. The growth of larger towns also energized rural areas. The trading post and steamboat stop of Madison, Indiana, for example, grew from a few hundred residents in 1812 to well over a thousand by 1830. Towns like Madison housed the mills, markets, and shops that fueled the growth of both rural and urban capitalism.

**STUDY QUESTIONS FOR MARKETS AND SOCIAL RELATIONSHIPS**

1. **Why did the shift to wage work change the relationship between workers and bosses?**
2. **Did the market economy affected urban and rural areas differently?**

# DEMOCRACY AND THE PUBLIC SPHERE

Alongside the rise in the market economy, by the 1820s U.S. political life grew more democratic than ever before. Democratization spread political power to new groups, especially to poor white men who had never held much direct power in American public life. The consolidation of political power in the hands of white men that had begun in the 1790s and that excluded women, African Americans, and Indians picked up speed. The spread of communications and expanded opportunities for participation in political rituals like Fourth of July parades—especially in growing cities—also meant that a wider group of men and women had a chance to influence public life, even if they had little direct power. The ability to debate, celebrate, and influence political life in this expanded "public sphere" developed in the United States just as voting also gained importance. Politicians had to place new emphasis on persuading the public to support them.

## Voting and Politics

The U.S. Constitution had guaranteed a republican government, but it had not specified anything about who would vote to determine representatives in that republic. After 1800, voting took on added importance in U.S. life, and participation in politics became one of the hallmarks of American democracy. At the turn of the 19th century, American leaders still expected deference from common men and women, and politicians could be criticized for campaigning too vigorously on their own behalf.

Once the Federalist party, associated with social elites, died out after the War of 1812, the expansion of white male suffrage took off. No new state admitted to the union after 1815 required property for white men to vote. Even though Congress in the 1780s had set high property-holding requirements for voting in western territories, after the turn of the century Congress removed most impediments to white male voting. A revised Massachusetts state constitution ratified in 1820 removed a religious test and property requirements for white men to vote, and New York followed suit in 1821. By 1824, virtually all white men in the United States were eligible to vote, although several states, notably South Carolina and Virginia, resisted removing property requirements until decades later.

Black men saw their voting rights constrict in the same era. The 1821 New York constitution, which expanded white male suffrage, retained property requirements for black men to vote. Every state admitted to the union after 1819, with the exception of Maine, disenfranchised black men altogether. By 1830, the Jacksonian Democrats, the chief proponents of universal white male suffrage, lost the support of propertied African American men who could vote in northern states.

Even though race proscribed voting rights, by 1828 vastly more American men possessed voting rights than in other countries worldwide. Even France and many countries in Latin America—which had undergone revolutions similar to that in the United States—did not spread the franchise as widely. Great Britain reserved voting for men who held large quantities of property, and even many middle-class white men could not cast ballots there. The U.S. focus on suffrage as a fundamental right and an important factor in politics also energized voter turnout, which soared to 57 percent in the 1828 presidential election. Voting now also more directly influenced presidential selection than it did previously. In 1800 only two states chose their members of the electoral college by popular vote, but by 1832 only South Carolina did not.

## Election of 1824

The emphasis on white men's voting rights changed the character of the 1824 presidential election, as the old Democratic-Republican party came apart—the victim of its own success. State conventions nominated presidential candidates—all of whom were Democrats, but many of whom differed in political outlook. By the fall of 1824, the four leading candidates were Treasury Secretary **William Crawford**, Secretary of State John Quincy Adams, Speaker of the House Henry Clay, and war hero Andrew Jackson. Crawford and Jackson, from Georgia and Tennessee, respectively, enjoyed strong southern support, while Kentuckian Henry Clay drew support from the West. Massachusetts' John Quincy Adams locked up New England. Jackson had long clashed with both Adams and Crawford, but he was an even stronger nemesis of Clay's—especially since Clay had criticized Jackson's actions in the Seminole War. Crawford, who had the support of **Martin Van Buren** and his highly organized faction of New York "Bucktail" Democrats, emerged as the early front-runner in the race, but a stroke left his health impaired and hurt his chances.

Andrew Jackson received 42 percent of the popular vote, which was recorded for the first time, as opposed to 33 percent for Adams and 13 percent for both Clay and Crawford. But when the electoral college met, no candidate emerged with the clear majority prescribed by the Constitution: Jackson got 99 electoral votes, Adams got 84, Crawford earned 42, and Clay received 37. The Twelfth Amendment to the Constitution (1804) stipulated that the House of Representatives would decide the election from among the top three candidates—and as Crawford's health deteriorated, the race boiled down to Jackson and Adams.

Henry Clay, a longtime congressman, was Speaker of the House during the contested presidential election of 1824. Clay's support in the House helped John Quincy Adams win the election, and his rival Andrew Jackson claimed the two men had struck a "corrupt bargain" after Adams appointed Clay as secretary of state in 1825.

Each state delegation in the House received one vote, and Henry Clay—as Speaker of the House—exercised great influence over the election he had just lost. In January, Clay met with Adams. When Congress met in February, Clay supported Adams, who was then elected president, even though Andrew Jackson had won more popular and more electoral college votes. Jacksonians accused Clay and Adams of striking a "corrupt bargain" to elect Adams. The election splintered the Democratic-Republican party and set the stage for a dramatic comeback by Jackson in 1828.

## John Quincy Adams

John Quincy Adams, who had been a powerful and successful Secretary of State under President Monroe, served one largely unsuccessful term as president. In his inaugural address he announced that "the will of the people" should be the guide "of all legitimate government upon earth," but throughout his term he fell prey to the very "collisions of party spirit" that he pledged to avoid. Adams appropriated federal funds for road and canal-building projects, but he had less success when promoting the program of high trade tariffs of Clay's "American System." The vote of Vice President **John C. Calhoun** defeated an 1827 bill to raise the trade tax on woolen cloth. Calhoun renounced his previous support of Clay and Adams when he decided trade taxes would hurt his native South Carolina. Calhoun's further outspoken critique of a broad 1828 trade tax, dubbed "The Tariff of Abominations," helped to solidify his and Jackson's opposition to the "National Republicans" as the

Adams-Clay wing of the Democratic party had become known. Adams even lost the upper hand in foreign policy. He was roundly criticized for his willingness to participate in a Panama conference on North and South American solidarity proposed by Simón Bolívar in 1826.

## Andrew Jackson, "The People," and the Election of 1828

Andrew Jackson spent most of John Quincy Adams's term renewing his own campaign for the election of 1828, and Adams's own sitting vice president, John C. Calhoun, became Jackson's running mate. Losing the 1824 election, despite receiving the majority of popular votes, convinced Jackson that democratic suffrage was vital to the health of the republic. In the 1828 campaign he took his appeal directly to the people. Martin Van Buren, the savvy New York politician who pioneered modern political electioneering, orchestrated a campaign to attract votes promoting Jackson as a war hero and dubbing him "old Hickory"—a strong leader who wouldn't break under pressure. Jackson won the election by a landslide; he got 56 percent of the popular vote and 68 percent of the electoral vote.

Jackson's ascendency benefitted from the tensions in society created by the market revolution. Although the internal improvements championed by Clay and Adams fueled capitalist growth, they also inspired fears that government worked to benefit a limited class of elites. Jackson was a wealthy plantation owner by the time he was elected president, but he cultivated the image of a backwoods commoner and expressed an absolute commitment to democratic equality, at least among white men. Jackson did not endorse any of the labor-oriented working-men's (or "Workey") third parties that sprang up in the 1820s and early 1830s, but he did oppose the use of government power to advance the interests of the moneyed few. Much of Jackson's democratic appeal was based on his personal presence, and when he threw open the White House to "the people" for his inauguration in March 1829, hundreds flooded in to greet him. In his inaugural address Jackson thanked the "free people" for choosing him as president and promised them "accountability" as he undertook the "task of reform" of American government.

## Jackson and the Veto

Jackson had ample opportunity to put his beliefs in reform, limited government, and direct democracy into action during his first term as president. Many of Jackson's efforts centered around putting men loyal to him in power and alienating those who opposed him. By the middle of his first term, Jackson had gathered around him a "kitchen cabinet" of informal advisors from outside his cabinet composed of loyal politicians, including Secretary of State Martin Van Buren, Attorney General **Roger B. Taney**, and Senators **Thomas Hart Benton** and **James K. Polk**. Jackson positioned himself as the protector of "the people," who would wield his presidential veto as a way to prevent Congress from authorizing actions that would not benefit the majority.

As part of this reform program, Jackson challenged the American System both as it had been enacted during Adams's presidency and as it continued to be championed by Henry Clay and other political rivals. In Jackson's first annual message to Congress in December 1828 he declared that "Every member of the Union . . . will be benefited by the improvement of inland navigation and the construction of highways in the several states," but he also warned that such projects should be funded by the states since federal action may not be "warranted by the Constitution." In the spring of 1830, Congress voted to invest $150,000 in a turnpike company that sought to improve 64 miles of road across Kentucky from Lexington to Maysville. Arguing that he could not allow federal expenditure on a road built within one state, Jackson vetoed the "**Maysville Road" Bill**. He subsequently vetoed other road-building projects. The Maysville Road and other vetoes hastened the division of national politics into pro- and anti-Jacksonian camps.

Jackson took an even harder line against the Second Bank of the United States (BUS), the financial source for much of the investment in the American System. Jackson had long been suspicious of centralized banking—indeed, of most banking—and he viewed the BUS as a "hydra of corruption" that manipulated the paper currency market, benefited elites, and suppressed the financial hopes of common Americans who would benefit from a greater reliance on gold and silver currency. Many national politicians, even some of Jackson's staunchest supporters, were deeply involved with the BUS, but this connection just increased the president's fear that the BUS might have "power to control the Government" and that it benefitted "a few Monied Capitalists." The bank legitimately raised the credit of the U.S. government and the stability of the U.S. economy, but Jackson styled it as a political enemy.

Although the congressional charter of the BUS did not expire until 1836, the Bank's president, **Nicholas Biddle**, applied for renewal in January 1832, and Congress passed a new charter in June of that year. President Jackson quickly vetoed the charter and sent a message to Congress declaring that the BUS was unconstitutional. Biddle fought back by opposing Jackson's reelection that fall, but after he assumed his second term. Jackson installed his staunch supporter Roger B. Taney as Treasury Secretary. Taney removed federal deposits from the BUS and chose to do federal banking with smaller state banks instead. Biddle continued to fight by contracting credit, but the bank was never rechartered, and it died after 1836. Jackson's strength in "the Bank War" effectively killed centralized federal banking in the United States until the 20th century.

## STUDY QUESTIONS FOR DEMOCRACY AND THE PUBLIC SPHERE

1. **What factors contributed to the expansion of white male suffrage by the 1820s?**
2. **In what ways and by what means did Andrew Jackson harness anxieties over the market economy to his political advantage?**

# ECONOMIC OPPORTUNITY AND TERRITORIAL EXPANSION

The culture of economic growth pushed some U.S. citizens to expand further into western territories during the era of the market revolution. One western settler remembered that when she first came to St. Louis in 1817, "it was a small place, the population not exceeding fifteen hundred, and four brick buildings," but after 1820 "emigrants began to pour in from all parts . . . bringing with them wealth and enterprise." As U.S. citizens populated western territories in the Louisiana Purchase and beyond, they constantly looked for new resources and new trade opportunities. Some, pushing beyond U.S. boundaries, even sought to establish colonies in foreign territory or to conquer Indian territory.

## Texas Colonization

**Moses Austin** was typical of many Americans who saw booms and busts during the market revolution, and he moved west looking for greater economic opportunity. In 1798, Austin established the first American settlement in Missouri at Potosi, where he built up a substantial fortune in lead mining and smelting. After losing much of his fortune when the Bank of St. Louis, which he cofounded, failed during the Panic of 1819, Austin decided to seek a new fortune in Spanish territory. By looking for opportunity in Texas—a northern province of Mexico—Austin pushed his business horizons further than most entrepreneurs. Moses, and his son **Stephen Austin**, would become the most important founders of private colonies in Texas—run by American citizens with the permission of Mexican authorities.

Moses Austin died shortly after securing permission to found a settlement in Texas from Spain's royal governor in San Antonio in December 1820. Stephen Austin took up the plan to settle 300 families along the Brazos River. However, he was forced to travel to Mexico City to seek fresh permission to establish his colony after the newly independent Mexican government refused to honor the Austins' Spanish land grant. Austin successfully negotiated new land grants under the Imperial Colonization Law of 1823 and began to parcel out the settlements along the Brazos, Colorado, and Bernard rivers in Texas.

Over the next several years Austin received additional grants, and he was the most successful of the *empresarios*, colonization agents who headed private colonies, whom the Mexican government had granted permission to start Texas settlements. He attracted over 1,200 families to his lands, and many of them established profitable ranches and farms. Austin and the other *empresarios* remained largely independent throughout the late 1820s, as they appointed their own civil authorities and conducted raids against Krankawa and Tonkawa Indians.

Although Mexican authorities frowned on it, Austin allowed settlers to bring slaves into Texas as long as they were officially classified as indentured servants. When the Mexican government outlawed slavery in Texas in 1830, Austin garnered an exception for his own colonists. Slaves comprised 10 to 15 percent of the Texas population by 1835. Most of the 10,000 Anglo-American settlers in Texas held onto their Protestant religion despite mandatory pledges to become Catholic. Many prominent Tejanos who lived near the Anglo colonies engaged in ranching and trade with the colonists, even though Anglos outnumbered them by 1830. After 1831, when new Mexican governments began to raise taxes and to exert stronger control over Texas, tensions between Mexican officials and Anglo and Tejano settlers quickly rose.

## Santa Fe Trail

Texas was not the only contact point between the United States and Mexico that touched the international market economy. Between the 1790s and 1830s, the Santa Fe Trail facilitated the growth of New Mexico as a major outpost of international trade. By 1810, New Mexico emerged as an important trade site in northern New Spain. Following Mexican independence in 1821, Americans entered the New Mexico trade when **William Becknell** led a group of traders from Missouri across Plains Indian trails to Santa Fe. With little investment Becknell's group realized a 2,000 percent profit by selling cotton cloth, iron hardware, and other manufactured goods to Indian and Spanish inhabitants. In 1822 Becknell began to lead wagon trains between Missouri and New Mexico.

The Santa Fe Trail quickly became a lucrative trade route between the United States and Mexico. By 1825, the U.S. government surveyed the Santa Fe Trail and secured treaties with the Kansas and Osage people allowing commercial traffic across their lands. Indians disagreed about the validity of treaties allowing U.S. trade across their lands, and American traders complained that some Osage were still "lurking about the main pass way—seeking whom they may rob or murder." In 1829 President Jackson authorized U.S. infantry troops to escort shipments of U.S. goods. Despite Indian conflicts and high Mexican trade tariffs, both Mexican and U.S. traders regularly earned 40–100 percent profits in the Santa Fe trade.

## The Black Hawk War

In the Old Northwest the competition between Indians and Americans for resources was even fiercer, and instead of establishing trade, the United States moved to push Indians off their land. Between 1800 and 1820, American settlers streamed into Illinois, which became a state in 1818. The white population grew from nearly zero to over 55,000. In northwestern Illinois the Sac and Fox Indians retained land where they farmed and mined lead, despite a probably invalid 1804 treaty in which some representatives agreed that their tribes would move west of the Mississippi River. In the decades following the War of 1812, they were pushed across the river into the Iowa

▲ **Map 10.3**

**Texas and the Santa Fe Trail, c. 1830** In the 1820s, greater numbers of Americans were drawn to the Southwest to trade along the Santa Fe Trail or to settle in the Mexican colonies of Texas. The Santa Fe Trail linked up major international trade networks.

Territory, as the federal government issued leases to lead miners, who then invaded Sac and Fox land in northwestern Illinois. The ouster of the Sac and Fox fit the desire of U.S. citizens to seize economic resources in the northwest and also fit Andrew Jackson's plans to remove all recalcitrant Indian peoples west of the Mississippi.

In May 1832, the Sac leader **Black Hawk**, who had fought with Tecumseh's Pan-Indian forces against the United States in the War of 1812, returned to Illinois with hundreds of Sac, Fox, and Kickapoo people. Black Hawk had clashed with **Keokuk** and other Sac and Fox leaders who favored accommodation to U.S. terms. The governor of Illinois, John Reynolds, called out the militia to drive Black Hawk's people out of the state. When Black Hawk tried to surrender, the militia fired on him, but Indian warriors fought them off. Secretary of War **Lewis Cass** ordered federal troops to reinforce the Illinois militia and some Sioux allies, and the combined force, including future national leaders **Zachary Taylor**, **Jefferson Davis**, and **Abraham Lincoln**, pursued Black Hawk into Wisconsin territory. An August battle at the Bad Axe River ended with most of Black Hawk's band (including women and children) being shot, despite the display of a white surrender flag. Black Hawk himself sought refuge with

This painting depicts the 1832 Battle of Bad Axe River, where Sac and Fox followers of Black Hawk were brutally defeated, ending the Black Hawk War. Black Hawk, a Sac leader who had fought with Tecumseh's Pan-Indian forces in the War of 1812, led a movement to reclaim land in Illinois in 1832, but the defeat and his subsequent capture ended the movement.

the Winnebago Indians, who subsequently turned him over to American authorities. The treaties that ended the short Black Hawk War ceded additional Sac, Fox, and Winnebago land to the United States.

**STUDY QUESTIONS FOR ECONOMIC OPPORTUNITY AND TERRITORIAL EXPANSION**

1. **What factors drove Anglo colonization of Texas?**
2. **How was the market economy different in the West than in the Northeast and the Southeast?**

# EXPANDING MARKETS

In the 1820s and 1830s, market activity in the United States expanded even more rapidly than it had in the preceding decades, and the United States played an increasing role in the transoceanic world economy. While not yet on par with major world economic powers, the United States began to undergo its own version of the Industrial Revolution that was transforming western Europe. By 1830, the world of markets influenced the everyday lives of more and more Americans.

## The Legal Structures of Capitalism

In the 1810s and early 1820s, the U.S. Supreme Court delivered several rulings that encouraged federal involvement in commerce and the rise of the business corporation—one of the major financial tools of capitalist development. John Marshall, a proponent of economic activity, continued to guide decisions that encouraged

GLOBAL PASSAGES

# Whaling

Although Americans had hunted whales starting in the 17th century, following the American Revolution, commercial whaling grew in scale. By the 1790s, U.S. vessels were engaged in widespread operations that took them all over the world in search of whales, which could be broken down into a variety of trade commodities: oil for lamps, bone stays for corsets and other clothing, and ivory. Between 1794 and 1803, U.S. whale ships harvested between 3,000 and 12,000 thousand tons of whales per year—but that total plummeted during the trade embargoes leading up to the War of 1812.

After the war, the industry began another huge expansion, with American ships traveling record distances around the world in search of whales. After 1818, American whalers shifted from mainly fishing off the coast of Peru, New Zealand, and Chile to taking advantage of newly discovered concentrations of sperm whales in the central Pacific Ocean, off the coast of Japan, and in the Indian Ocean. British whalers dominated the North Atlantic, but American ships were a significant presence in these other waters, where ice was less of an impediment to profitable fishing. By 1830, American whaling ships went to sea for as long as five years at a time and often sailed halfway around the world.

The American whaling industry was based on Nantucket Island, Massachusetts, until the early 1820s, when New Bedford, Massachusetts, became the dominant whaling town. New Bedford's deeper port accommodated larger ships, and its connection to inland markets helped speed the trade of whale products. Before 1825, most crew members on American ships were American citizens, but after that date more sailors from the areas where whaling occurred began to appear on ship crew lists. Herman Melville, the author of the famous whaling novel *Moby Dick*, demonstrated how these sailors could frighten 19th-century Americans when he wrote that "in New Bedford, actual cannibals stand chatting at street corners; savages outright . . . it makes a stranger stare." By 1835, 35 different U.S. port cities launched whaling ships.

Whaling captains, whose wives often ran family trade businesses in port cities, often became wealthy from the products of whaling. Average sailors, who performed difficult work breaking down and processing whales while they were still at sea, received wages commensurate to those of most textile workers, although skilled craftsmen might do well on an especially successful voyage.

Whaling provided raw materials for scores of trade products and introduced Americans to important parts of the world—including Japan and Hawaii. Whaling

This engraving shows whalers trying to take a whale in the Arctic Ocean and dramatizes the danger, a common theme in visual depictions of whaling. Several small boating parties set out from the main whaling ship to harpoon the whale, but one boat is overturned, plunging the sailors into the icy water. The boat that has been upended flies the American flag.

and its transoceanic reach also influenced American culture, as writers like Herman Melville and popular-culture depictions of sailors made a mark on the public mind. Whales and their by-products became one of the most important engines of capitalist development—by the middle of the 19th century whaling was the fifth-largest industry in the United States.

- Why do you think American culture was so fascinated with whaling if it was just another capitalist industry?
- Compare and contrast how whaling and butter making contributed to the growth of the market economy.

capitalist development during the last years of his long tenure as Chief Justice. Between 1825 and 1835, however, Marshall's Supreme Court came under withering attacks by Jacksonian politicians, who accused it of "judicial tyranny," claiming that the court encouraged the same kind of the elitist economic power as the Second Bank of the United States. Jackson was able to appoint three associate justices, who took an active role as Chief Justice Marshall became increasingly infirm in his old age. Although on the defensive, Marshall managed to promote the federal control of commerce, which he had advocated in 1824 in *Gibbons v. Ogden*. Marshall also wrote the opinion in *Craig v. Missouri* (1834), which invalidated a law that had allowed Missouri to issue its own paper money.

When John Marshall died in 1835, Andrew Jackson seized the opportunity to put the Supreme Court firmly in the hands of his Democratic supporters. Jackson appointed his Maryland ally, Roger B. Taney, as Chief Justice in 1836. Although Taney supported economic development, he favored less federal intervention than Marshall had. Ruling in the 1837 case of *Charles River Bridge v. Warren Bridge*, Taney had the chance to make his legal mark early in his first term as Chief Justice. The state of Massachusetts had chartered the Charles River Bridge in 1785, and its owners made spectacular profits from tolls they charged to cross from Boston into Charlestown. When a rival company constructed a new bridge just 260 feet away in 1828, the Charles River Bridge Company, citing a violation of their 45-year state charter, sued. Writing for the majority, Chief Justice Taney ruled that the Charles River Bridge charter had not guaranteed exclusive rights and stated that courts should not be overly involved in matters of economic development better left to state legislatures. Taney's rival on the court, Justice Joseph Story, wrote a blistering dissent charging that the majority allowed the interference with sacred corporate rights. But Taney had deftly supported economic modernization, while also preserving a narrow interpretation of federal power that pleased Democrats and helped to alienate the newly forming Whig party.

## The Inland Empire

One of the best indications of the increasing scale of the market economy and the willingness of state governments to encourage it was the successful completion of the Erie Canal. The canal, which greatly expanded inland commercial traffic by connecting Lake Erie to the Hudson River, which flows to the Atlantic, had first been considered in the late 18th century, but the New York legislature did not authorize the survey for the massive engineering project until 1808. When the federal government refused to participate, New York State funded the entire project. **DeWitt Clinton**, the New York governor and former mayor of New York City, ceremonially broke ground for the project in 1817. Detractors, who doubted the value of the project, dubbed the canal "Clinton's Big Ditch." At the opening of the Erie Canal in 1825 Clinton poured a ceremonial cask of Lake Erie water into the Atlantic Ocean and declared, "May the God of Heavens and the Earth smile . . . and render it subservient to the best interests of the human race."

The Erie Canal was the world's largest canal at the time, and it contained several impressive feats of engineering—largely constructed by Irish immigrant laborers. The 363-mile long, four-foot-deep canal contained a series of aqueducts and locks that allowed traffic to flow smoothly over ravines and rivers, and it could carry boats each loaded with 50 tons of freight pulled by horses or mules walking alongside the canal. The canal also carried steamboats and passenger traffic. Each of the cities along the canal—Buffalo, Rochester, Syracuse, Utica, and Albany—experienced exponential growth and quickly became a commercial center. Moreover, the canal ensured that New York City would continue to grow as the major U.S. Atlantic trading port. The Erie Canal quickly became a symbol of American economic prosperity and ingenuity. Over the next half century, the Erie Canal, and other canals like it, would help to expand U.S. commerce and helped unite easterners and westerners.

## The Industrial Revolution

Americans declared the Erie Canal to be the greatest in the world because they were increasingly interested in their place in the world economy. Any accomplishment that exceeded those of Europe seemed to be a special point of pride. As the Industrial Revolution in England rapidly expanded textile-producing towns, scores of agricultural workers moved from farm labor into factory work, and for the first time ever England became a net importer of food products—many of them grown in the United States. In 1830 American workers enjoyed 40 percent higher wages than their counterparts in England. The global labor market seemed to favor colonies and former colonies, with American and Canadian factory workers earning higher wages than many comparable workers in Europe.

As part of the early Industrial Revolution, Americans especially excelled at textile production, since it combined their agricultural system, talent for mechanization, and the rapid adoption of new technologies. In 1831 the United States contained almost 700 textile firms that operated 1.2 million cotton spindles and 33,500 mechanized looms. Before 1830 France and England both consumed large quantities of American cotton, which fed European industrialization. Although working conditions in the United States were generally more comfortable than in England, the high level of child labor and the deteriorating conditions in some mills meant that greater labor woes would soon follow.

The Industrial Revolution in England helped to transform world markets and increase the importance of wage labor and technology—and as the United States began an Industrial Revolution of its own, it contributed to the first global transformation to capitalism. Southerners grew cotton that fed mills in the northern United States and Britain, and—although they held onto a slave system that many historians have characterized as "pre-capitalist"—they participated in systems of international credit, trade, and exchange. One historian has characterized Americans as playing a crucial role in the "pan-hemispheric plantation complex." Agriculture, fueled by market activity, continued to expand in all regions of the United States. Overall, U.S. exports grew from $20 million in 1790 to $82 million in 1832.

The rise of democratic participation in politics by white men in the United States helped to divide political responses to the acceleration of the U.S. market economy. Even as the United States grew more democratic than ever before and was more democratic than most other nations, market forces intensified slavery, and many Americans were left out of democratic politics. Jacksonian Democrats, who walked a fine line between encouraging innovation and economic development as they supported limited federal government while touting the rights of the common man, faced a particularly challenging set of political choices as the economy continued to grow after 1830.

## STUDY QUESTIONS FOR EXPANDING MARKETS

1. **Where and for what reasons did Jacksonian Democrats and their opponents agree and disagree about "internal improvements?**
2. **How were changes in the U.S. economy related to changes in U.S. politics between 1815 and 1832?**

## TIMELINE 1789–1832

**1789**

Samuel Slater emigrates to the United States from England

**September** Congress creates the U.S. Postal Service

**1790**

Samuel Slater and Moses Brown found the first mechanized cotton mill in the United States

**April** Congress establishes the U.S. Patent Office and grants inventors a 14-year monopoly on their inventions

**1791**

Alexander Hamilton sends his report on encouraging domestic manufacturing to Congress

**1800**

**January** Eli Whitney demonstrates interchangeable parts by assembling a musket from pieces selected from a pile by President Thomas Jefferson

**1804**

Treasury Secretary Albert Gallatin proposes a comprehensive plan of national canals and roads

**July 27** The 12th Amendment to the Constitution is ratified

**1807**

**August** Robert Fulton begins commercial steamboat service on the Hudson River

**1810**

Oliver Evans installs the first steam-powered flour mill in Pittsburgh

**1814**

The Boston Associates incorporate their mill business in Waltham, MA

**1817**

**July 4** Construction on the Erie Canal begins

**1819**

**May** The vessel *Savannah* uses backup steam power to cross the Atlantic

**1821**

William Becknell opens trade from Missouri to New Mexico on the Santa Fe Trail

**1824**

**March 2** The U.S. Supreme court decides the case of *Gibbons v. Ogden*

**December 1** When the electoral college reveals its votes, no presidential candidate receives a clear majority

## Summary

- Between 1789 and 1832, the United States underwent what some historians call a "market revolution," and a capitalist economy took shape.
- Economic changes altered social relationships among workers, slaves, business owners, and many other Americans.
- By the 1820s, U.S. politics were becoming increasing democratic by opening up suffrage and political participation to almost all white men.
- U.S. citizens had economic interest in Western territories—which led to open trade, colonization of Texas, and warfare with several Indian groups.
- By the 1820s and 1830s, the United States was part of a new system of world markets, especially influenced by the early industrial revolution in Western Europe.

**1825**

**February 25** The U.S. House of Representatives elect John Quincy Adams President

**March 7** President Adams appoints Henry Clay as Secretary of State, part of what their enemies dub "the corrupt bargain"

**June** Britain cuts off U.S. trade to its colonies in the West Indies

**October 26** The Erie Canal is completed and opened with great ceremony

**1828**

**May** Congress passes a trade tax, dubbed the "Tariff of Abominations" by opponents

**December** Andrew Jackson is elected President

South Carolina legislature protests the "Tariff of Abominations"

**1829**

**September** Mexico outlaws slavery in Texas, but exempts Stephen Austin's colony

**1830**

The Baltimore & Ohio Railroad becomes the first U.S. railroad to carry passengers and freight

Mexico forbids further colonization of Texas by American citizens

**1831**

Cyrus McCormick builds the first mechanical reaper, making crops much easier to harvest

**1832**

**January** Second Bank of the United States president Nicholas Biddle applies for a recharter of the bank and begins "The Bank War" with President Jackson

Black Hawk leads a group of Sac and Fox Indians from Iowa Territory back into their vacated lands in Illinois, touching off the Black Hawk War

**August** Black Hawk's Indians are destroyed in a battle on the Bad Axe River

**December** Andrew Jackson reelected president

## Key Terms and People

**American System** *364*
**Appleton, Nathaniel** *372*
**Arkwright, Richard** *367*
**Austin, Moses** *382*
**Austin, Stephen** *382*
**Becknell, William** *383*
**Benton, Thomas Hart** *380*
**Biddle, Nicholas** *381*
**Black Hawk** *384*
**Brown, Moses** *372*
**Calhoun, John C.** *379*
**Cass, Lewis** *384*
**Clinton, DeWitt** *388*
**Crawford, William** *378*
**Davis, Jefferson** *384*
**Evans, Oliver** *367*
**Fitch, John** *368*
**Fulton, Robert** *368*
**Gallatin, Albert** *369*
**Keokuk** *384*
**Lincoln, Abraham** *384*
**Livingston, Robert** *368*
**Lowell, Samuel Cabot** *372*
**Maysville Road Bill** *381*
**McCormick, Cyrus** *367*
**Polk, James K.** *380*
**Slater, Samuel** *367*
**Taney, Roger B.** *380*
**tariff** *369*
**Taylor, Zachary** *384*
**Van Buren, Martin** *378*
**Watt, James** *368*
**Whitney, Eli** *367*

## Reviewing Chapter 10

1. How did the market changes in the United States after 1789 continue economic developments that had begun during the colonial period?
2. How did the transformation to a market economy increase tensions between equality and inequality in U.S. society?
3. What were the most important global influences on the U.S. economy?

## Further Reading

Bernstein, Peter L. *Wedding the Waters: The Erie Canal and the Making of a Great Nation*. New York: W.W. Norton, 2005. This book offers an engaging narrative of the construction and success of the Erie Canal and argues that it was one of the most important achievements of the century, not only technically, but because it helped to unite the East and West and to tie the United States to European trade.

Dolin, Eric Jay. *Leviathan: The History of Whaling in America*. New York: W.W. Norton, 2007. This book charts over three hundred years of the history of American whaling. In addition to presenting gripping tales of whaling voyages, Dolin shows how whaling led to New England's economic growth and helped to connect the United States to the rest of the world through an extensive trade network.

Deyle, Steven. *Carry Me Back: The Domestic Slave Trade in American Life*. New York: Oxford University Press, 2005. This book is an economic history of the domestic slave trade that developed after Congress outlawed the international slave trade in 1808. It shows how buying and selling slaves became an integral part of the U.S. domestic economy and involved thousands of individual slave owners in transactions that split up black families.

Jensen, Joan. *Loosening the Bonds: Mid-Atlantic Farm Women, 1750–1850*. New Haven: Yale University Press, 1986. This is the classic account of how Mid-Atlantic farm women contributed to the growth of the U.S. market economy, especially through their dairying and butter-making activities.

Wilentz, Sean. *The Rise of American Democracy: Jefferson to Lincoln*. New York: W.W. Norton, 2005. Wilentz traces the rise of democracy in the United States in this narrative that covers the 1790s to the 1860s. Wilentz devotes special attention to Andrew Jackson and the development of democratic politics and ideology in the 1820s and 1830s.

# Visual Review

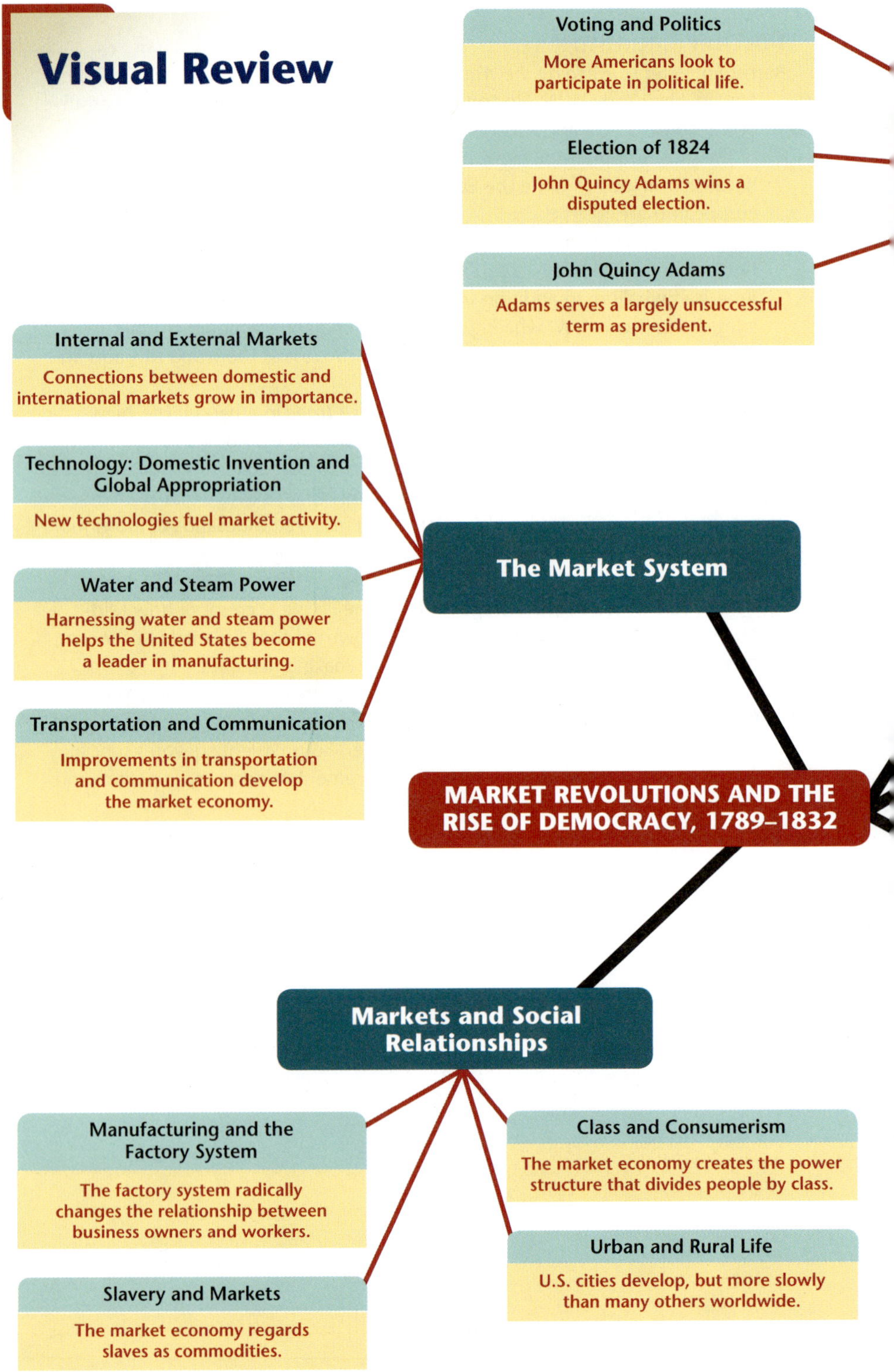

**Voting and Politics**
More Americans look to participate in political life.

**Election of 1824**
John Quincy Adams wins a disputed election.

**John Quincy Adams**
Adams serves a largely unsuccessful term as president.

**Internal and External Markets**
Connections between domestic and international markets grow in importance.

**Technology: Domestic Invention and Global Appropriation**
New technologies fuel market activity.

**Water and Steam Power**
Harnessing water and steam power helps the United States become a leader in manufacturing.

**Transportation and Communication**
Improvements in transportation and communication develop the market economy.

## The Market System

## MARKET REVOLUTIONS AND THE RISE OF DEMOCRACY, 1789–1832

## Markets and Social Relationships

**Manufacturing and the Factory System**
The factory system radically changes the relationship between business owners and workers.

**Slavery and Markets**
The market economy regards slaves as commodities.

**Class and Consumerism**
The market economy creates the power structure that divides people by class.

**Urban and Rural Life**
U.S. cities develop, but more slowly than many others worldwide.

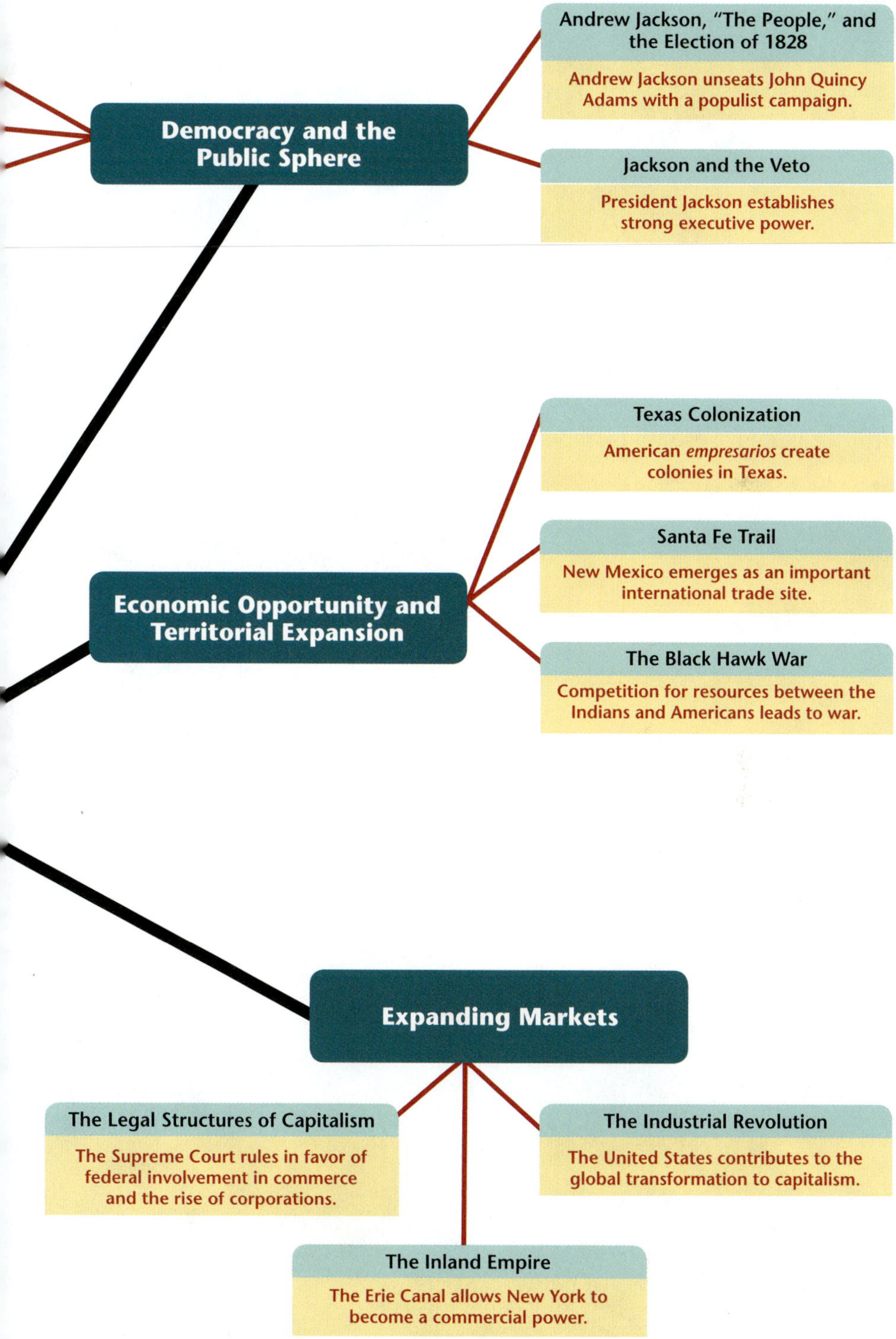

**Democracy and the Public Sphere**

**Andrew Jackson, "The People," and the Election of 1828**

Andrew Jackson unseats John Quincy Adams with a populist campaign.

**Jackson and the Veto**

President Jackson establishes strong executive power.

**Economic Opportunity and Territorial Expansion**

**Texas Colonization**

American *empresarios* create colonies in Texas.

**Santa Fe Trail**

New Mexico emerges as an important international trade site.

**The Black Hawk War**

Competition for resources between the Indians and Americans leads to war.

**Expanding Markets**

**The Legal Structures of Capitalism**

The Supreme Court rules in favor of federal involvement in commerce and the rise of corporations.

**The Inland Empire**

The Erie Canal allows New York to become a commercial power.

**The Industrial Revolution**

The United States contributes to the global transformation to capitalism.

# 11 New Boundaries, New Roles

## 1820–1856

CHAPTER OUTLINE



In early 1836, reports surfaced in the United States that a mixed band of American and Mexican separatists had been killed down to the last man in the defense of an old mission compound in San Antonio, Texas, called the **Alamo**. Led by the Anglo **Sam Houston** and the Hispanic **Lorenzo de Zavala**, the Texas independence movement brought together a diverse group united by their opposition to receiving orders from remote Mexico City. Former Mississippi governor John A. Quitman led some of the many Americans who supported the independence movement. Quitman crossed the Sabine River into Mexico with 17 men and the confidence that he fought for freedom. "If I must die early, let me die with these brave fellows and for such a cause," he proclaimed. Quitman and his band joined Houston's army and helped Texas declare its independence from Mexico. U.S. president Andrew Jackson, serving out the last of his tumultuous eight years, did not interfere with Quitman or the other Americans who crossed the border to fight against Mexico, even though their actions clearly violated American neutrality laws.

Less than a year after Quitman helped separate Texas from Mexico, a different American invasion generated a much different presidential response. In the wake of "Patriot Uprisings" in Upper and Lower Canada (today's Ontario and

*Emigrants Crossing the Plains* by Albert Bierstadt, 1867

# America in the World

The siege of the Alamo inspired Texas to declare independence from Mexico (1836).

The Second Seminole War decimated the Seminole nation (1835–1842).

The Cherokee ratified a tribal constitution modeled on the U.S. Constitution (1827).

 U.S. event that influenced the world

 International event that influenced the United States

 Event with multinational influence

 Conflict

The Neutrality Act aimed at preventing private entanglement in foreign wars (1818).
The Indian Removal Act forced the relocation of Native Americans to western states (1830).

Quebec), Canadian rebels retreated across the U.S. border into northern cities such as Rochester, Buffalo, and Detroit. During 1837, thousands of Americans joined these Canadian separatists fighting the British, just as Americans had joined Texans fighting the Mexicans. In December 1837, the U.S.-born Rennselaer Van Rennselaer led a small group of men across the Niagara river to establish a beachhead for the return of a well-known Canadian rebel, but Jackson's successor as president, Martin Van Buren, dealt aggressively with this group of American adventurers. Van Buren issued a proclamation denouncing the actions, alerted customs agents and U.S. marshals along the border, and eventually sent General Winfield Scott to manage relations in the region. Despite the heavy military presence, Canadian Patriots and their American supporters coordinated attacks along the border throughout the year. Pressed by armies on both sides, the men went underground in early 1838 but sporadic attacks occurred into 1841.

Neither the Texas nor the Canadian episodes received official government support, but Jackson's hands-off approach offered implicit support for the former. Mexico had only recently freed itself from Spanish control and many Americans viewed it as a weak neighbor, ripe for American conquest. Texas independence angered the Mexicans and America's harboring of Canadian rebels angered the British. In both situations, America negotiated solutions that demonstrated its rising status as a continental power, but also one that remained loose at the seams.

## AN EXPANDING NATION

The three decades of peace following the War of 1812 gave Americans an opportunity to consolidate the territory that had been won permanently from the British. But even as settlers pushed west and traders sailed around the world, American control of the land within the boundaries of the original colonies remained incomplete, underscored by the extensive Cherokee and Creek landholdings in Georgia. Two substantial obstacles blocked American expansion west of the Mississippi River: Mexican control of most of today's Southwest and the presence of substantial numbers of Native Americans. On the west side of the river, the United States claimed only a few military forts strung out across a vast expanse of plains and mountain territory controlled by a variety of Indian communities. Intermingled with the western Indians lived tens of thousands of Spanish-speaking residents, most born while Spain still ruled the region. Anglo settlers who headed west into this landscape embodied the dynamism of the era. At the same time, many other Americans moved against their will. The sale of slaves from eastern states to the emerging cotton belt and the removal of Indians from the southeast to Oklahoma involved more people and implicated the United States in one of the historical paradoxes faced by other large nations. A growing population and a robust economy encouraged the United States to expand but that expansion created new problems. Military difficulties arose as the settlers and explorers encountered people with existing claims to the land; political problems developed as leaders wrestled with whether the United States should follow the pattern of previous empires; and cultural conflicts grew as the country sought to incorporate people of widely different backgrounds into an already diverse nation.

## Andrew Jackson and the Trail of Tears

Strong native communities stood opposed to the United States in the east as well. In the southeast alone, the Cherokee, Choctaw, Chickasaw, Seminole, and Creek counted 75,000 members compared to 330,000 white people and 230,000 black people in the region in 1820. The state and federal governments worked sometimes in cooperation and other times at odds with each other to push Indians farther to the west. Andrew Jackson came to the presidency strongly opposed to the presence of Indians in territory that could be profitably settled by whites and strongly opposed to the practice of the federal government negotiating with Indians as equals. As early as 1817, Jackson had described "treaties with the Indians as an absurdity." Although he professed that resettlement should be voluntary, Jackson's aggressive nationalism had a long history of conflict with Indians, "Spanish dons," and others standing in the way of U.S. expansion. Jackson sought "to reclaim them [Indians] from their wandering habits and make them a happy, prosperous people," and as president he used the executive power to force this policy on Indians across the country. Most Anglo-Americans supported his policies.

Jackson's most public battle with Indians resulted from the expulsion of the Cherokee people from Georgia. The Cherokees, the largest native community in the Southeast, had adapted to American customs more than neighboring tribes. But as new Anglo settlers generated conflicts, states and the federal government steadily increased pressure on Indians to sell their lands. The government of Georgia, where most Cherokee landholdings lay, harassed the tribe. After gold was discovered on Cherokee-controlled land in 1829, white miners flooded into the region. With their numbers nearing 10,000 they had the clout to convince state leaders to seek the complete expulsion of the tribe.

Following Jackson's lead, Congress passed the **Indian Removal Act of 1830**, which nullified 50 years' worth of treaties between the United States and many tribes. The law committed the federal government to creating an Indian Territory west of the Mississippi, in present-day Oklahoma, and to moving Indians by force into this new region. The state of Georgia also sought expulsion, but the Cherokee, well-educated and protective of their treaty rights, vigorously resisted. Cherokee leaders sought legal protection against Georgia laws that asserted authority over the tribe. In a series of seminal cases, the Supreme Court, led by Chief Justice **John Marshall**, declared the Cherokee, like all recognized Indian tribes, "domestic dependent nations." In the 1832 *Worcester v. Georgia* decision, the court ruled against Georgia's claim that it held authority over the tribe, but the state ignored the ruling. Andrew Jackson, who supported state efforts to expel the Cherokee, famously remarked after reading Marshall's decision, "let him enforce it." Without recourse to the army, which could have protected Indian lands from settler encroachment, Marshall could not.

Under Georgia's protection, white settlers continued to move into Cherokee territory in the early 1830s. Still seeking a peaceful conclusion, in 1835 the federal government negotiated a new treaty with a minority group of Cherokee. This new agreement exchanged all Cherokee claims to land in the east for claims in Indian Territory and a cash settlement. When U.S. forces arrived in early 1838 few Cherokee had prepared

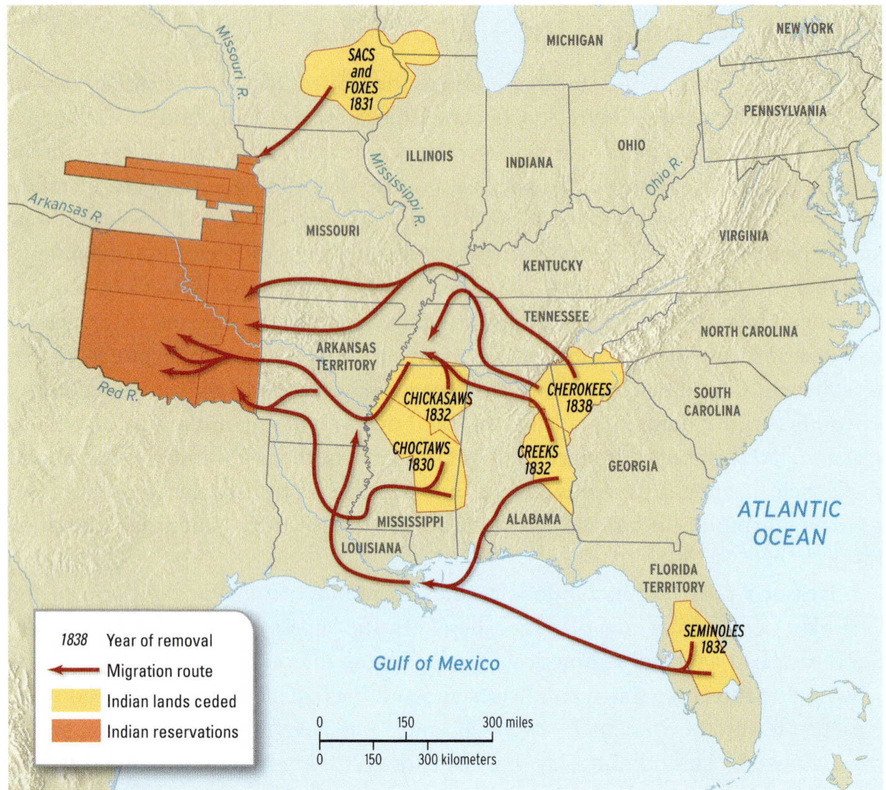


**Map 11.1**

**Indian Removals, 1830s** This map shows the routes along which Indians were driven by the U.S. army during the forced relocations of the 1830s. Jackson's policies moved the last large Indian communities living east of the Mississippi River into the frontier regions of the Oklahoma Territory.

for the trip, and soldiers rounded up and confined people over the summer. Contaminated water, inadequate food, and disease killed many of those restricted in stockades, and many more perished on the 800-mile journey west. Estimates of fatalities connected with the "**Trail of Tears**," as Indians referred to the forced march, range from 4,000 to 8,000. The blatant abrogation of property rights backed by clear title to the land worried many white citizens, even those generally opposed to Indians. **Davy Crockett**, the legendary frontiersman, lost his congressional seat for opposing Jackson's policy. The violence and trauma of the forced march to the new western lands created more political enemies for Jackson and a shameful legacy for the American government.

While Jackson and white Georgians were expelling the Cherokee from the northern reaches of the state, the Second Seminole War raged in the south. In a dramatically different approach than the legal maneuvering of the Cherokee, Seminole fighters

The forced removal of Indians by the U.S. government created a demographic and historical catastrophe for Indian communities. The Cherokee removal, represented here in a modern painting, began in the winter and imposed physical hardships as it alienated Indian people from their ancestral homelands.

used their knowledge of the land and ecology to stymie American forces for years. Most of the fighting in the second conflict occurred within the Okefenokee Swamp and its hinterlands, a shifting maze of wet and dry ground that disoriented all but the most experienced soldiers. Led by Osceola, a skilled commander, the Seminole developed a pattern of attacking and retreating that frustrated and debilitated American troops, who also suffered disease and discomfort in the swamps. Despite the high cost to U.S. forces, the Army persevered and by 1842, a staggering 90 percent of the Seminole community had been killed. The remaining 600 were permanently expelled into the wild region of southern Florida.

## Re-Peopling the West

In the late 18th and early 19th century, settlers moved out of the Northeastern region—with a population density of 31 people per square mile—into the Midwestern territories (which held only eight people per square mile) and farther west to the Great Plains. The result was an emigration stream that paralleled the expulsion of Cherokee and other Indians to the south, with the important difference that Anglo settlers moved voluntarily. Would-be westerners first had to reach the Missouri River. From there, they had to travel 2,000 miles to reach the Pacific shore. Between one-quarter and one-half of a million migrants made the trip between 1843 and 1870. Because wagons and the oxen that pulled them required a fairly easy grade and regular access to water, travelers could use only a few routes. Fur traders had pioneered these routes, which California and Oregon promoters began advertising in the mid-1830s.

With the successful journey of a large wagon train of over 100 people, emigration began in earnest after 1842. If the trip was not quite the "pleasure excursion" that the

▲ **Map 11.2**

**Major Overland Trails** Western emigrants followed well-established routes across the continent. Starting at the Missouri River, the paths converged in the narrow passes through the Rocky Mountains and then diverged to head toward northern or southern towns on the Pacific Coast.

*Daily Missouri Republican* claimed, it was at least possible. Most groups traveled about 15 miles per day, leaving Missouri in early May, crossing through the South Pass in early July at 8,000 feet and only then reaching the hardest part of the trip. The mountains and the wide western rivers made the journey both dangerous and physically demanding. If they survived disease, thirst, and bad weather, the settlers might make it to California or Oregon by October.

The fantastical advertisements crafted by western boosters rarely conveyed the challenges of living in the West. In 1830, the boundaries of the United States extended far west of the Mississippi River, but the federal government exercised little influence over the region beyond the great "national highway." Mexico nominally controlled most of today's U.S. West, although they paid little attention to the region because of problems in areas farther south. Instead, native peoples actually dominated the region west of the Mississippi. Indians had long warred with and occasionally allied with the Spanish, but except for those southwestern tribes who had to contend with a persistent Spanish presence, the Plains Indians viewed each other as their most important threats. But the American settlers, who started arriving in the 1830s and then increasingly after 1841, posed a threat. Unlike the Spanish or French, these new inhabitants did not come to trade; they built farms and forts and intended to stay. Americans sometimes recognized differences within the larger native population and even established friendly relations, but generally, settlers' attitudes displayed their ignorance and fear.

In the deeper Southwest, many American settlers regarded the Mexican and Indian residents, whom they rarely distinguished, with a mix of loathing and disgust. At best, settlers treated them as obstacles to the expansion of American power in the region. An 1846 issue of the *Illinois State Register* described Mexicans in the region as "reptiles in the path of progressive democracy . . . they must either crawl or be crushed." The combination of biology and politics in the paper's explanation reflected contemporary American thinking that certain races might die out because they were "unfit" for the modern world. Few Americans demonstrated much sympathy for Indians or Mexicans displaced by settler encroachment. Ethnographers and scientists like Harvard's **Louis Agassiz** added scientific weight to the biological explanation by using skull-size measurements—usually "proven" with comprised and faulty data—to generate an intellectual hierarchy of the races. Agassiz's methods were hardly scientific: his data were faulty, and he failed to rigorously test and separate evidence from hypothesis.

Spanish-speaking residents proved another obstacle to U.S. expansion. Mexican independence in 1821 barely affected the northern provinces of New Mexico and California. Living on Mexico's northern edge, far from the administrative center in Mexico City, these settlers maintained their largely pastoral and agricultural economy and Catholic beliefs. In 1834, Mexico had moved to reduce the power of the Catholic Church over the country by secularizing the mission lands, but this allowed elite landholders in many places to acquire still more property and social control. In some cases, especially the California territory, the ranchero elite allied themselves with Anglo settlers, but in others they maintained autonomy. In other cases, the villages created out of mission lands ensured local control and mutual dependency among the

Hispanic residents, who retained control over land and resources into the 1870s despite Americans' efforts.

## Latin American Filibustering and the Texas Independence Movement

As legal settlers ventured into U.S. holdings across the Mississippi, adventurers like John A. Quitman and Rennselaer Van Rennselaer pushed south and west into the Spanish borderlands or north into Canada. Americans launched some of these expeditions while living outside the United States, but other groups organized within the United States proper and then invaded foreign soil. After the Louisiana Purchase in 1803, Americans began pushing into Spanish West Florida, which then extended from Pensacola across the gulf coast into modern-day Louisiana. In 1810, a group of Anglo settlers pushed into the western edge of this territory and claimed it as an independent republic; Congress soon annexed the area into Louisiana. Despite military reprisals and vigorous diplomatic protests by the Spanish, the American government implicitly sanctioned the practice by incorporating the new settlements into the United States whenever possible. Between 1800 and 1860, U.S. citizens launched at least 19 separate expeditions into Spanish colonies or Latin American republics. Americans described these actions and the people who took them as filibusters, from the Spanish *filibustero* and before that, the Dutch term for "freebooter."

Filibusters clearly violated the U.S. Neutrality Act of 1818, which outlawed private warfare. Yet because so many people supported the cause of American expansion, Americans often regarded filibusters as heroes despite their frequent executions as spies and insurrectionaries in the countries they invaded. After tapering off in the 1840s, a new wave of filibusters pushed deep into Central America in the 1850s. John Quitman, who had led a charge into Texas to support independence and again into Mexico in 1846 organized an expedition to liberate Cuba from Spanish rule in 1855. Quitman backed out but the organization's sponsor replaced him with Henry Maury—a southern lawyer and sea captain—who quickly found eager supporters. **William Walker**, who invaded Mexico once and Nicaragua three times, replaced Quitman and Maury and became famous across America as the most successful and infamous filibuster of the age. The following poem ran in southern newspapers at the time:

> Success to Maury and his men
> They'll safely cross the water
> Three cheers for Southern enterprise
> Hurrah for General Walker

Walker succeeded briefly in Nicaragua, occupying the post of "president" for several months in 1856, only to be expelled and later executed in Honduras. As the poem indicates, Southerners led most of the efforts in the 1850s, intending to add new slaveholding territory to the Union. As a result, filibustering in this decade became embroiled in the larger sectional conflicts over slavery.

Filibusters raised a set of questions related to American expansion and power, although few at the time considered the issue in such systematic detail. Who acted for the United States? Did privately organized ventures represent the interests of the nation? Would American expansion happen violently or peacefully? To what extent would the residents of a place be consulted before American acquisition? Did this style of expansion constitute imperialism? American leaders offered vague and shifting answers to these questions. As filibustering demonstrated, private ventures could sometimes serve as an advance guard for national expansion. Force and persuasion operated simultaneously as Americans expanded their borders.

Some historians argue that Texas should be counted as the grandest filibuster victory, because so many Americans poured over the border in 1835–1836 to fight on behalf of the independence movement. But the roots of the Lone Star Republic were more complex. By 1835, two distinct groups in Texas, Tejanos (or Spanish-speaking Texans) and Texians (English-speaking Texans), both criticized Mexican misrule in its northernmost colony. Texians, including Davy Crockett, who had come south to recover his reputation after his electoral defeat, began the movement for Texas's independence, but many Tejanos supported it as well. By early 1836, Crockett and a small group of English- and Spanish-speaking rebels retreated into an old Spanish mission in San Antonio called the Alamo. After a pitched battle lasting nearly two weeks, the Spanish forces, led by president and general **Antonio López de Santa Anna**, broke into the compound and killed all the Alamo defenders.

Despite this setback, independence forces, rallying to the famous cry "Remember the Alamo," defeated the main Spanish army and captured Santa Anna in fighting along the San Jacinto River a few months later. The victors issued a Texas Declaration of Independence signed by prominent Texians like Sam Houston, a former Tennessee congressman, who became president of the new republic, and prominent Tejanos, like Lorenzo de Zavala, who served as vice president. The success of the Texas independence movement built on widespread discontent among settlers over the failures of Spanish administration. Its most immediate changes reflected a desire to mimic its neighbor to the north. Mexico had abolished slavery in 1829, but Texas reinstated it and prohibited free blacks from residing in the new nation. The presence of a new slaveholding nation to the south worried those Northerners eager to stop the spread of slavery within the Union. Even with the exclusion of black men and women, Texas contained a diverse population. Spanish- and English-speaking communities contested for power over the next decade and, after the republic became part of the United States, Protestant Americans worried about the inclusion of so many new Catholics into the country.

## Pacific Explorations

One of the hallmarks of the global ascendancy of western Europeans after 1500 was their use of the sea for warfare and trade. The Portuguese, who perfected a ship that could travel against the wind, used this new technology to begin exploring the West African coast in the mid-1400s. Spanish, English, French, and Dutch explorers soon followed, establishing direct trading links with African and then Asian peoples whose wares had only been accessible via the long overland routes across the Sahara or along the Silk Road, connecting China and the Middle East. Military expeditions often followed or accompanied the traders though Europeans could rarely do more than provide protection to the traders who remained behind. The second wave of European exploration consisted of naturalists and ethnographers, who took notes and gathered specimens on voyages across the oceans. The drafting of maps, the exhibition of plants and animals (and sometimes, of people), and the use of new ingredients in food and beverages offered evidence of European command of the globe. Americans emulated European powers by making similar expeditions.

In 1838, the U.S. Navy launched the South Seas Exploring Expedition. Lieutenant **Charles Wilkes**, a young but domineering sailor, commanded a six-ship flotilla that traveled 87,000 miles over four years of sailing. Like European expeditions of earlier centuries, the American mission carried a bevy of scholars—including naturalists, botanists, artists, and a linguistics expert—to gather information about parts of the world still quite foreign to most Americans. Wilkes sailed around South America, across the Pacific to Australia, south through the Antarctic Sea, east to Hawaii, up the American Pacific Coast, then west through the Philippines, around the Cape of Good Hope to New York. Harkening back to the exploits of British captain **James Cook**,

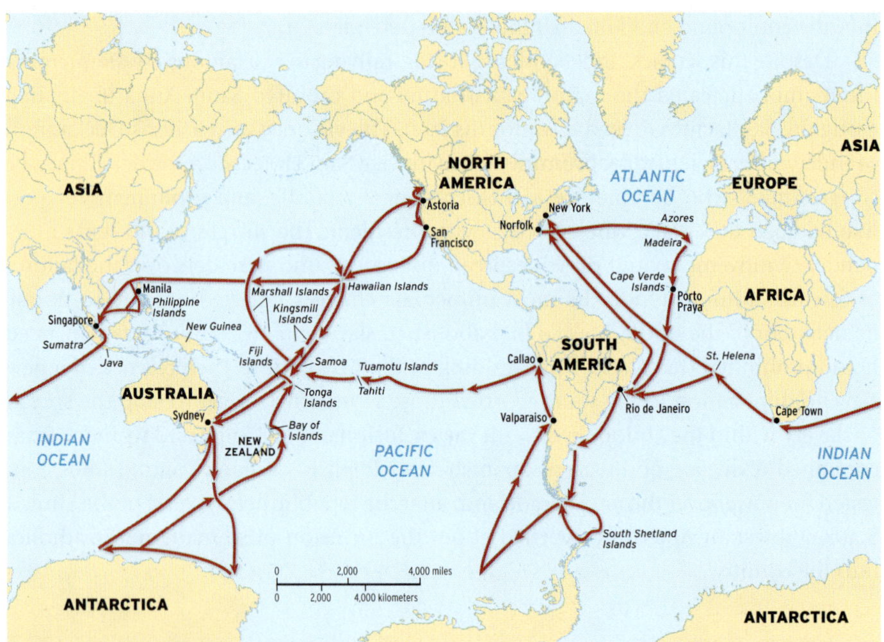


▲ **Map 11.3**

**Path of the United States Exploring Expedition, 1838–1842** Navy lieutenant Charles Wilkes led the first American circumnavigation of the globe. His flotilla included scientists who sought to map and identify places and products of interest to American traders and politicians.

who explored the Pacific Ocean in the late 18th century, Wilkes's naturalists collected samples everywhere the ship stopped. The 60,000 plant and bird specimens collected by scientists during the Wilkes Expedition formed the basis for the Smithsonian Institution when Congress created it a few years later.

Wilkes himself led the effort to memorialize the expedition, writing the 5-volume narrative of the journey and editing the 20-volume scientific reports. Reflecting the growing curiosity among Americans about the rest of the world, the reports detailed both the expedition's travels and also the history of the countries and people encountered along the way. Endorsing the common "civilizational" view, Wilkes described different countries at different levels of development depending on how closely they mirrored European attitudes and institutions. Wilkes's full circumnavigation of the globe also put the United States in a small group of modern nations whose explorers could claim to have traveled around the whole world. For Americans the journey signaled their membership in the exclusive community of nations whose reach extended around the world. It also marked out for American businessmen and traders those places of potential interest for future investment and trade. A midshipman on Wilkes's expedition ominously anticipated the future course of interactions between Americans and those people they encountered in the Pacific: "I could not help thinking, how much better it would be to let them [the indigenes] go their own way, but No, No! We must have all the world like us, if we can."

### STUDY QUESTIONS FOR AN EXPANDING NATION

1. **Compare the various forms of expansion undertaken by Americans in the 1830s and 1840s. What are the similarities and differences among them?**
2. **What justifications did Americans offer for the dislocation of native and other long-settled peoples in areas within or adjacent to U.S. borders?**

## THE NEW CHALLENGE OF LABOR

Supporters of U.S. expansion drew a sharp distinction between the United States and Europe because of the absence of a formal class system in the United States and the presence of "free land." Ignoring the presence of Indians, Mexicans, and others who controlled much of the hemisphere, such boosters believed that new territory would provide space for future settlers and prevent the consolidation of land that sustained Europe's aristocracies. They worried particularly about the social effects of the increasing economic transformations that threatened to create a working class dependent on the whims of factory owners. Nearly every American visitor to Europe's industrializing cities observed the problem. In 1845, American poet **William Cullen Bryan** described the poor in Edinburgh, Scotland as "a throng of sickly-looking, dirty people . . . [a] wretched and squalid class" that according to his guide comprised more than half the city's population. The Jeffersonian ideal of a republic of free, self-sufficient farmers became even more compelling as Americans watched the changes wracking western Europe. There, industrialization produced an increasingly disaffected class of workers, and the influx of new workers and rapid technological and institutional changes in the United States in the 1830s and 1840s threatened to generate the same problems. Despite the vigorous efforts of filibusters and others, land acquisition alone did not solve the problem. The emerging industrial economy demanded workers who sold their labor as a commodity. For these men and women, the prospect of land ownership and self-sufficiency stayed forever out of reach. But laboring people in the United States, like those abroad, adopted new forms of politics and economic practice as a way to sustain the egalitarian promise of the country.

## White Workers, Unions, and Class Consciousness

Building on an old European tradition, American artisans—such as bookbinders, wheelwrights, or cobblers—owned their own tools, supervised themselves (and often a team of apprentices), and enjoyed lives of respectability and modest comfort. The burgeoning use of steam power and mechanical reproduction in the early 1800s allowed factory owners to underprice and outproduce artisans. This process took several decades, but by 1830, the outlines of a new national economy had emerged. American consumers might have benefited from cheaper and more uniform goods, but skilled workers suffered. The rise of unskilled labor as a major category of work was the most visible symbol of this shift. Between 1820 and 1860, the number of factory workers in the United States increased nearly sevenfold, from 350,000 to 2 million. This transformation impacted the nation well beyond the economy, shaping politics, social relationships, and the very nature of American cities.

This period saw the rise of machine production; wherever possible, industrialists began substituting machines for the older system of handwork that had dominated production for centuries. In economic terms, artisans became wage laborers. In the process, they began selling their work to employers as they would any another good that could be bought and sold on the market. When workers struck bargains with honest employers who observed the rules of their contracts, the process of selling one's labor could appear normal and even beneficial. Some laborers maneuvered their way up the income ladder in this period, working, saving, and seizing opportunities when possible, but many more spent their lives as unskilled workers at jobs that did little more than keep them and their families barely alive. When employers did not respect contracts or used the glut of laborers as leverage to exploit the longest workday for the lowest salary, workers suffered terrible deprivation. In New York City, for instance, real wages among the city's major trades declined through the 1830s and 1840s, leaving workers' families earning only half of the $600 per year needed to support a family of four at the time. This decline hit unskilled workers hardest, who typically earned only 60 percent of a skilled workers' wages.

The first decades of the 19th century encompassed such a tangle of growth and decay, of success and failure, it resists easy summary. But most Americans at the time clearly saw the rise of a distinct American working class. The change had visible

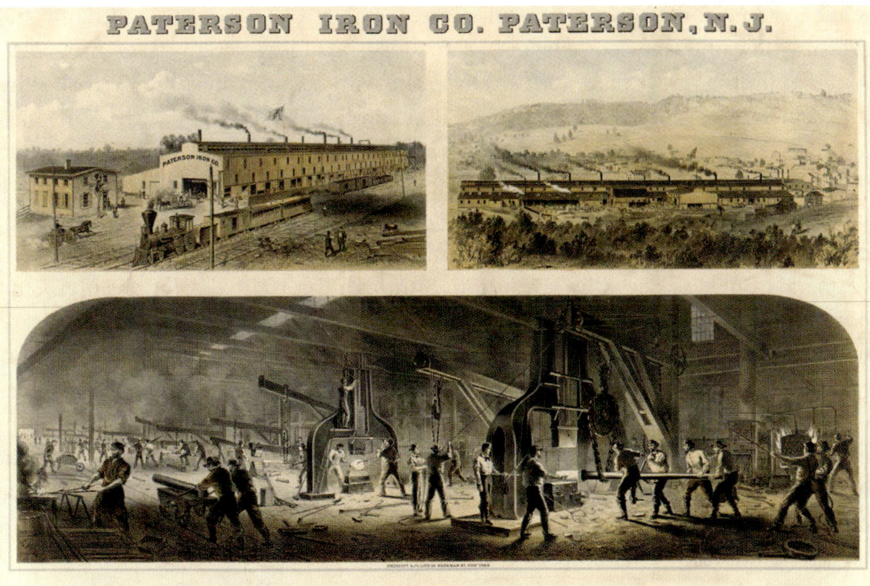


The factories of the mid-19th century operated on a vastly larger scale than anything previously seen in early America. Industrial workers adjusted to laboring alongside a large and diverse array of individuals, but racial, ethnic, and gender differences inhibited worker organization.

consequences in the northeastern cities with the greatest industrial growth. New York, Philadelphia, and Boston all developed neighborhoods defined by class. As production moved out of the master's home or a home-based workshop, workers had less contact with the owner and his family and more contact with others in their same economic position. They lived in boarding houses and spent their leisure time with other working men in their own venues: bars, boxing arenas, and minstrel halls. In the mid-1830s labor organizing reached a high point in many northeastern cities, particularly among the skilled trades. New York artisans engaged in at least 35 strikes. The General Trades Union (GTU), an umbrella organization created in 1833, coordinated some of these but others—by locksmiths, tailors, carpenters, sheet-iron workers, and machinists—were initiated by craft workers seeking better pay and working conditions.

Protests over working conditions and wages pushed owners and workers further apart in the 1830s. Skilled workers had long used strikes as measures of last resort. In the 1790s, Philadelphia shoemakers, dockworkers, and others struck. In 1824, female textile workers in New England struck against factory owners. Over the next two decades, male and female workers initiated more strikes, but usually with little effect, partly because the trade unions organizing among urban residents segregated themselves by gender, race, ethnicity, and craft. The ever-increasing pool of new workers provided a ready supply of strikebreakers for owners. In addition, the depression of 1837 made matters worse for workers. Union membership rolls dropped significantly and pressure on workers to accept owners' demands—including lower wages—increased.

During the 1830s and 1840s, European workers and their intellectual allies urged increasingly radical solutions to their problems. Most famously, Karl Marx and Frederick Engels issued the *Manifesto of the Communist Party*, which predicted the **abolition** of private property and the rise of the industrial working class to a position of political dominance. The *Manifesto*, published in 1848, expressed in print what Americans saw in the streets of Paris, Berlin, Vienna, and Budapest that year as Europe was seized by revolution. Although the 1848 Revolutions drew support from a wide range of reformers and sought political changes that Americans had already adopted (such as universal white male suffrage), most U.S. observers saw only violence and destruction. The June days, when French government forces violently suppressed a mixed force of workers and National Guard troops, epitomized the danger. One French conservative described the June days as not "a political struggle . . . but a class conflict, a sort of 'servile war,'" and this specter haunted American business and political leaders the way the legacy of the Haitian Revolution haunted American slaveholders.

American workers, for their part, more closely followed the actions and the writings of English, German, and French reformers than revolutionaries. European writers and activists toured American cities in the 1830s, encouraging the formation of class-based political parties. These activists held other surprising ideas as well. **Frances Wright**, a Scotswoman, emerged as one of the most famous labor leaders of the day. Wright advocated free thought and women's rights, offering a vigorous critique of American inequality to thousands of rapt New Yorkers during her 1829 tour of the city. Her performance, one of the first public addresses on politics by a woman in the United States, scandalized and energized audiences in equal measure. Wright, like fellow activists **Robert Dale Owen** and **George Henry Evans**, called on American workers to use their voting power to alleviate the worst effects of industrialization. Born in England, Evans came to the United States in 1820 and published his own papers, first the "Workingman's Advocate" and later "The Man." His papers, and the intellectual and organizational efforts of Wright, Owen, and others, inspired independent "Workingmen's Parties" in several northeastern cities, but these parties achieved little change at the level of government policy.

## Foreign-Born Workers

Some of the people who found their working lives unbearable in their home countries made their way to the United States. Between 1820 and 1860, just over five million immigrants entered the country, with nearly 95 percent coming from northwestern Europe. Although immigrants never comprised more than 2 percent of the total population in any given year, their cumulative impact grew considerably during this period. By the Civil War, the foreign-born comprised 13.2 percent of the population. And despite the relative homogeneity of their region of origin, compared to immigration later in the century, they possessed diverse, often urban, backgrounds. German migrants tended to come from rural backgrounds and made the exodus with a strong faith in democracy and opportunity. Irish immigrants, mostly Catholic during the same period, left Europe under the pressure of famine and dislocation. They possessed little optimism. Irish immigrants composed at least a third of all those newcomers to American shores between 1820 and 1860. Many were driven by desperation produced by the "Great Hunger," as the Irish called the famine that plagued their country between 1845 and 1849. But many others came because Protestant English domination of the island's Catholic inhabitants ensured little chance for economic success. Although many immigrants found greater opportunities in the new world, American Protestants displayed strong prejudice against the Irish as well. An 1830 newspaper advertisement for domestic help in New York revealed the routine discrimination faced by many Irish immigrants: "Wanted. A Cook or Chambermaid . . . must be American, Scotch, Swiss or African—no Irish." Irish immigrants tended to settle in the northeast, and they typically came without the skills to help them succeed. As a result, the Irish took on mostly unskilled positions—in public works like road building, in nascent factories, and in homes—and formed a substantial part of the poorest class by midcentury. Women comprised a majority of Irish immigrants at this time, which was unique for immigration patterns in the 19th century, and the lower wages paid for women's work further weakened their ability to earn enough to support themselves after the difficult and costly

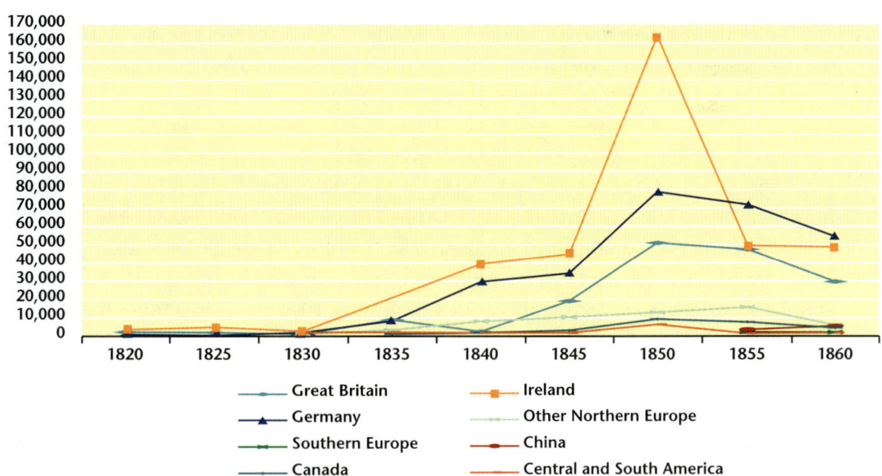


▲ **Figure 11.1**

**Immigrants, by country or region, 1820–1860** Northwestern Europe sent the most immigrants to the United States in the 19th century, especially during the Famine Years in Ireland. By midcentury, however, an increasingly diverse array of immigrants found their way to the United States.

GLOBAL PASSAGES

## Middlemen Abroad

Europe was not the only destination for interested travelers, and not all travelers toured for pleasure. A growing cadre of American merchants, missionaries, and officials began to circulate in the Pacific in the wake of Charles Wilkes's South Seas Expedition. These men joined a stream of European businessmen eager to trade for Chinese goods. Despite the linguistic and cultural differences within this group, they shared a common orientation as members of the commercial middle class—entrepreneurs from industrializing nations that sought opportunities to buy and sell in the massive and lucrative Chinese market. A marked feature of these new western traders was their willingness to break the law to achieve high returns. One trader noted about his company's new ship that he hoped it would "make us some money . . . How, I dont care, so it is made." Because the Chinese had little interest in American goods, one of the few ways to accomplish this was through the illegal trade in opium. British merchants pioneered this practice, smuggling the drug from India or Turkey into China against the wishes of Chinese officials. American traders, like Warren Delano (Franklin Delano Roosevelt's grandfather) entered the opium trade alongside them. The British, like the Americans, strongly discouraged the use of opium in their own countries, but showed no reluctance to sell it to Asians, and both nations profited handsomely from the early global drug trade.

One of those new businessmen who enriched himself through the opium trade was Augustine Heard, born in 1795 to a prominent trading family in Ipswich, Massachusetts. By the time he was 45, Heard had made a dozen voyages to Indian and Chinese ports and many others in the Atlantic and Mediterranean. One of Heard's partners in China, George Dixwell, also drew on a distinguished New England lineage and counted doctors, businessmen, and teachers among his relatives. Dixwell's aunt cautioned him against the greed that characterized so many New England men who traveled to the Pacific. "I pray you not be over anxious about lucre," she warned him, "do not have an Eldorado [a reference to a mythical city of gold sought by Spanish explorers] the object of your pursuit . . . it is unphilosophical, it is unchristian." No doubt Dixwell's aunt would have condemned the opium trade

transatlantic journey. The influx of Irish workers allowed managers to push wages down. This economic pressure and the immigrants' Catholic faith stimulated anti-Irish riots led by native workers in the 1830s and, in the 1850s, the virulently anti-immigrant nativist movement.

German immigrants composed another 25 percent of the total immigrant flow between 1830 and 1860, but unlike the Irish, Germans emigrated in larger family in even stronger terms but the profits proved too attractive. Heard's firm, which became one of the largest American trading enterprises in 19th-century China gained a sure footing through trading opium in the 1840s. The results in China were devastating as addicts multiplied and drug-related crime destabilized the government.

Heard's company formed valuable relationships with opium producers and sellers in India. Kessressung Khooscalchund, a major Bombay trading firm, proved to be an important ally as the Americans contended with varieties in the quality of the drug, storage fees, competition among shippers, and Chinese anger over the drug's impact on its citizens. John Heard, Augustine's nephew, played an active role in soliciting Indian contacts and increasing the firm's commission profits. At the conclusion of a meeting with Kavaldass Luxmichund, an Indian manager for the Kessressung firm, Heard reported that Luxmichund "dipped his thumb into a dish of paint and gave me a mark on the forehead between the eyes, where . . . Hindoos wear the mark of their cast, so that I suppose I may now consider myself a baptized Hindoo . . . He threw a heavy cashmere shawl over my shoulders, and put a diamond ring on my finger—true Oriental liberality and magnificence." This deep immersion in Asian cultures marked these rising businessmen as members of a cosmopolitan class. Their families bore the marks of their success as well. On his way home, John wondered what to do with Luxmichund's gifts because his mother and aunt already owned Indian cashmere shawls. Heard diversified his company's activities, supplying and selling tea, silk, and other Chinese goods to American companies. Most importantly, the firm established itself as commission merchants, acquiring information about the volume, quality, and price of Chinese goods and selling this information to American buyers. The shrewd diversification of Augustine Heard and Co., their willingness to engage in the drug market, and their appreciation for the global structure of modern capitalism produced real profit for its investors and an expanded sense of American commercial accomplishments for those who read about the firm in American papers.

- How does the importance of the early global drug trade challenge the traditional notion of market exchanges as benevolent or mutually beneficial?
- How would the cultural exchanges (such as the one described previously by John Heard) have shaped his or his family's perceptions of Indians?

groups. One study of German immigration in the 18th and early 19th centuries revealed a ratio of 1.6 women and dependent children per adult man as opposed to 0.25 women and dependent children per adult man for English immigrants. The men who came tended to have labor skills that ensured they would not remain in unskilled positions for long, and this put them in starker competition with native-born Americans. The German women who emigrated tended to work within their homes or their own communities. Like the Germans, Scandinavian immigrants tended to move in family units, but they pushed even farther west, seeking out open land in the Midwest and Great Plains. Farming became the mainstay for these communities for the next several generations. In these sparsely settled areas in the mid-19th century, immigrants could recreate and maintain their home culture in ways that their families back in Europe could not. America demanded national loyalty from the newcomers but little in the way of cultural assimilation. With each ethnic group free to practice its own traditions, the United States contained an increasingly diverse population as the 19th century progressed.

## The New Middle Class

Even as the new immigrants struggled to secure day labor and unskilled jobs, better established Americans seized opportunities to move up the income ladder. A new middle class emerged in the 1830s and 1840s, partly as a result of the rapid urban growth occurring across the nation. Members of this community participated mostly in "nonmanual labor." They lacked the wealth to live without working, but they did not perform the physical labor on which most Americans depended. What we now call "white collar" work emerged at this time. As industrial and other businesses grew larger and more complex, office workers, including clerks and accountants typically attired in cleaner "white" clothes than their working-class peers, were needed to manage the companies' information.

New York City led the nation in new retail districts and Broadway epitomized the allure and diversity of products and services that such areas promised the burgeoning consumer class.

At 312,000 residents, New York City was the largest and wealthiest urban place in the United States in 1840, but the changes that occurred there reappeared in other cities over the next several decades. Cities provided the space for and stimulated the rise of a middle class. The anonymous nature of cities forced residents to identify and interact with one another as members of larger social or ethnic communities before they interacted as individuals. American cities, especially northeastern ones, also generated a diversity of living conditions, from the squalid shacks of New York's Bowery to the opulent mansions along Fifth Avenue. Commercial establishments revealed the changes as well. New York, Philadelphia, and Boston soon teemed with retail establishments selling a bewildering array of domestic- and foreign-produced goods. Mass-produced clothing sold best, followed by food, magazines, and books, all components of the increasingly commercialized, increasingly nationalized economy that defined the United States. The shops themselves, often several stories tall and outfitted with the latest light fixtures, paintings, and carpets, presented a new world of purchasing within which the burgeoning middle class could distinguish itself from those who bought their supplies in the small, single-room, family-run stores more common earlier in the century.

Few people used the term "middle class" in the United States before the 1830s, though its equivalents in foreign tongues would have been familiar to most western Europeans. Americans did not consciously imitate Europeans in the creation of a middle class, but they openly copied their cousins on matters of fashion and taste. American

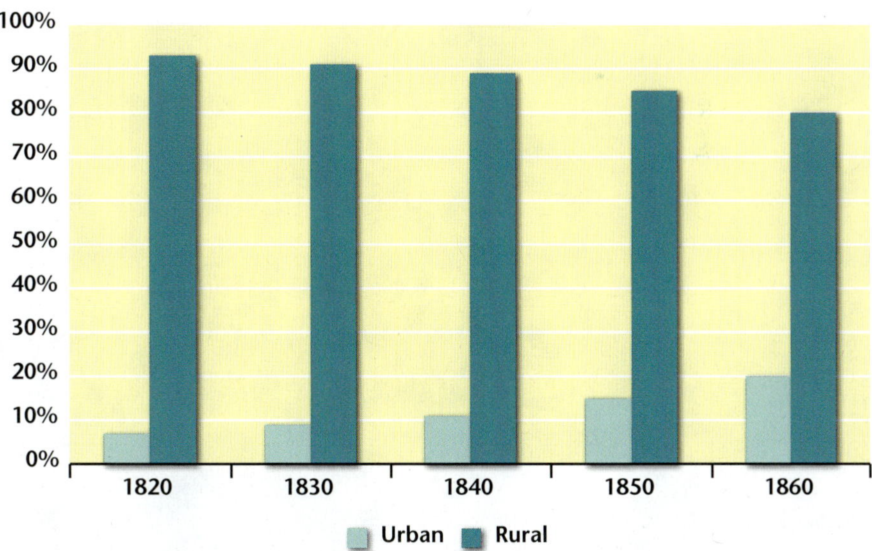


▲ **Figure 11.2**

**Urbanization, 1820–1860** Despite the increasing pace of urbanization in the United States, both North and South remained overwhelming rural and agricultural at the time of the Civil War. Note: Urban areas were defined by the census as incorporated places of 2,500 or more residents.

elites and the rising middle class looked to Europe on questions of style in art, music, dress, and literature. Magazines from London and Paris circulated across the Atlantic, allowing Americans to associate themselves with the latest European trends. For the sons of American elites (and much more rarely, daughters), no education was complete without a "Grand Tour," an extended journey of travel and education in European cities. The necessity of anchoring themselves to the traditions of Europe revealed the anxieties that beset the middle classes in the period of transition and change in 1830s and 1840s America. At home, these concerns manifested themselves in the injunctions in advice manuals and books to avoid "confidence men and painted women"—the male and female scoundrels who exploited the anonymity and openness of the new urban places to cheat honest people out of their money and their reputations.

## The Expansion of Slavery and Slaves as Workers

In contrast to the growing prominence and success of free labor in the North, white Southerners made increasingly effective use of slave labor. As Britain and France increased their appetite for the cotton to produce the textiles that they traded with empires around the globe, American investors saw new opportunities in the fertile lands of central Georgia, Alabama, and Mississippi. This region grew rapidly in the 1830s and 1840s, financed by the promise of high returns from cotton. But for African

The layout of homes changed to accommodate the purchasing power of the rising middle class. "Parlors" started to appear—private but comfortable rooms in which families could display the furniture, carpets, and chandeliers that signaled their status.

Americans, the cotton gin and the new southwestern settlements promised only more generations of bondage. The high demand for labor in the region encouraged slave owners along the Atlantic seaboard to sell some of their slaves into an expanding internal slave trade. The route from Virginia and the Carolinas west and south became a Second Middle Passage, marked by the violence and hardship of forced marches and deprivation. In the 1810s, 120,000 slaves marched over the Alleghany Mountains and down the river valleys of the Deep South; by the 1830s, the number had increased to 300,000. Those who remained had to refashion their families, shorn of parents, siblings, or children, under the threat of being sold "down the river."

Many of the planters moving into the new Southwest were the sons of established slaveholders on the eastern seaboard. These young men typically moved ahead of their families. Indian adversaries often slowed down travel and settlement, but after the mid-1830s, when the federal and state governments drove eastern Indians to the west, planters gained access to the rich soils of the region. Slaves on the new cotton plantations worked under unusually brutal conditions. The young masters, eager to pay off debts incurred in travel and to prove themselves independent men, drove slaves through long hours of clearing land and planting crops. Without their families and the network of social institutions that occasionally checked such behavior, southwestern masters subjected enslaved women to more sexual exploitation and enslaved men to harsher punishments than in the East. Despite the higher mortality rates that accompanied relocation and life in the region, profits remained high and so more planters flooded the area into the 1850s.

Slave owners' use of the task system, which flourished in regions dominated by staple-crop production (mostly cotton, sugar, and rice), large landholdings, and, often, absentee landowners, provided the sole bright spot for slaves on the new cotton plantations of the Deep South. In the Upper South, most owners organized enslaved laborers as a "gang"—usually a squad of three or four men and women—and set them to work for a specified period of time (typically sunup to sundown) with an overseer or driver ensuring that workers stayed busy throughout the day. Under the "task" system, by contrast, owners organized work around specific assignments. A group of workers might still function as a unit, but rather than simply laboring all day, they would be assigned a discrete unit of work to complete—so many acres of land to weed or so many pounds of cotton to pick. By allowing workers to use whatever time remained in the day after completing the task for their personal use, the task system thus built a small measure of incentive into slavery. Owners found the system advantageous for several reasons: slaves had an incentive to work more efficiently; because slaves typically used extra time gathering or producing supplementary food for their families, owners could reduce the rations they provided; and because most slaves spent extra time with their families, it decreased the likelihood that parents would run away. Even with these mercenary advantages for the owner, most enslaved people preferred the task system because it gave them at least some autonomy. Within the narrow space they could carve out, slaves built stronger families and a more resilient and sustaining culture.

Another feature of the slave system provided a similar mix of dangers and opportunities for slaves: the growing rental market. As southern cities and industries developed, the old tradition of wealthy slaveholders "loaning out" their enslaved laborers to poorer neighbors for short periods of time (harvest was the most common) evolved into a more formal system. In some cases, urban residents rented them and in others cases corporations dominated the markets, usually because they needed labor but did not want to invest the capital to buy slaves outright. Rented-out slaves sometimes lived with their temporary owners, in homes or barracks in the case of companies, but in many cases they found their own housing. Owners deducted some portion of a slave's total rental value to be applied to food and housing and gave this to the enslaved person who remained responsible for arranging for his or her own upkeep. This system benefited slaves by giving them a measure of daily autonomy from their owners although it also separated family members. It created new problems for city leaders responsible for policing slave behavior in place of absent masters. White workingmen also resented the competition from enslaved laborers.

### STUDY QUESTIONS FOR THE NEW CHALLENGE OF LABOR

1. **What were the effects of the increasing urbanization and industrialization in 1830s and 1840s America?**
2. **How did the rise of "free labor" and slavery both stabilize and unsettle the United States in this period?**

# MEN AND WOMEN IN ANTEBELLUM AMERICA

The economic changes confronting Americans in the antebellum era (the decades before the Civil War) produced and were shaped by changes in the size and very nature of families and gender relations. Drawing on a burgeoning market in parenting advice literature, parents began rethinking how to raise and relate to their children. Rather than viewing households as little kingdoms, with a spouse, children, and any other dependents recognizing the natural authority of the father as they would the king, parents began emphasizing the affectionate bonds that sustained families. Love and the open expression of emotion received much more attention in the early 19th century than they had in previous generations. Despite this new emphasis, the lines between men's and women's proper roles within both society and the family began to sharpen. Greater respect between spouses and the mutual obligations of all members of the "domestic" family did not necessarily lead to more liberal values with regard to women's place in the public world.

## Gender and Economic Change

Nearly all women in the United States suffered under similar restrictions with regard to their public rights: women could not vote or hold office, could not sue or establish contracts, were barred from positions of leadership in their churches, and were rarely allowed access to higher education or divorce, even from abusive husbands. The law of **coverture** ensured that when a woman married, her property and any wages she might earn became her husband's. These legal constraints clashed with an increasing sense of women as unique individuals who deserved the same moral respect as men. In many cases, legislatures maintained restrictions on women's rights from colonial practices, but as the nation developed and especially as the American economy created new opportunities and new situations, states articulated the differences between men and women in law. Differences emerged most noticeably in the North, where the expanding economy drew upper- and middle-class men away from household based production—principally farming—into paid employment at separate and dedicated work sites. Since the early colonial period, the household had been the basic social and economic unit, the site of both production and reproduction. As the new national and industrial economy took shape, paid work moved outside of the home. For the mostly urban upper classes, this meant that men left the home and women stayed inside it. Alexis de Tocqueville, the famous French visitor to the United States, observed of gender relations in the 1830s that "the inexorable opinion of the public carefully circumscribes [her] within the narrow circle of domestic interests and duties and forbids her to step beyond it."

Those families who experienced this transformation in work increasingly viewed the world outside the household as the "public" space and the domestic space of the home as "private." The men in these households, in particular, believed that women had substantial autonomy within the domestic world but should have little presence in the public one. Several factors converged to create this trend. The factories and offices that increasingly employed men outside of the home refused to hire women. Women had traditionally held greater authority in regard to childrearing and the daily household tasks. Finally, Americans regarded the public world of business and government as morally suspect if not corrupt. The market, they believed, functioned as a kind of free-for-all in which participants might engage in any noncriminal behavior in the pursuit of profit. Politics, they believed, operated according to similar principles. In this world, women's perceived strengths—a highly developed moral sense and strong sympathies for others—became liabilities. As a result, men sought to exclude women from the public world for their own protection and because they would have been ineffective in the face of male aggression and ruthlessness.

The middle-class women who staffed most of the nation's leading reform organizations rejected the intellectual assumptions that divided the genders. The leading female activists in the crusades for temperance, abolition, and women's rights drew scorn for their aggression rather than gentle treatment because of their natural sensitivity. Female volunteers performed much of the work done by a wide range of reform associations in the decades up to and through the Civil War. The **Grimké sisters**, Sarah and Angelina, ranked among the best-known abolitionists of the period and a trio of women—**Susan B. Anthony**, **Lucretia Mott**, and **Elizabeth Cady Stanton**—led the fight for women's rights. Despite this, most men believed that women belonged in the home and not in the office, factory, or store. The separation of space by gender did little to advance the modern notions of gender equality, but women could and

The new emphasis on domestic intimacy demanded new representations in family portraiture. The richness of the fabrics in this family portrait, the profusion of consumer items—tailored clothing, books, furniture, and furnishings—and the harmony with nature embodied by the open windows and doors all sought to demonstrate the virtue of this new model of family organization and presentation.

did use the special protections owed to them under the ideology of separate spheres to educate themselves and to organize the broader movement for full equality. "We are a band of sisters—we must have sympathy for each other's woes," wrote one female activist.

Many Americans knew that the divisions of social and economic labor along gender lines varied within the nation. Class position determined, to a large degree, the extent to which men and women could rigidly separate their duties. Poor families needed the income of their female members and could not afford to remove them from paid work. Slavery, with its identical demands on the labor of black men and women, clearly violated the new norms, as did the many rural white households where production and reproduction remained rooted in the same physical place. Indians, who still controlled most of the western half of the continent, maintained their own gendered divisions of labor. Most importantly, women usually controlled the agriculture within native communities. Because early white observers routinely ignored women's work they often overlooked the importance of farming to Indian economies and inaccurately criticized them for relying too heavily on hunting.

## Ladies, Women, and Working Girls

At the same time that state legislatures and churches restricted women's options, women themselves seized new opportunities in the whirl of changes brought on by the market revolution. Some women, of course, pursued paid work out of necessity because their families required the active contributions of all members in order to survive. In New England, thousands of young women entered schoolhouses as teachers and many more took employment in the textile mills dotting the region. The mills in Lowell, Massachusetts, in particular, gained renown for their large labor force of young women, who ranged between the ages of 15 and 35. The **Lowell Mill Girls**, as observers called them regardless of age, worked in one of the first large-scale, steam-powered industries in the United States—and one of the most fully globalized. They wove cotton, grown by slaves working on plantations in the southern United States, and shipped the finished products to consumers all across America and around the world. Less well known at the time were the female mill workers of the South. In Georgia, white women comprised a majority of the state's factory workers. In Macon, Columbus, Augusta, and the state capital of Milledgeville, textile factories employed thousands of young, mostly single women.

This cover of a literary journal produced by Lowell Mill workers revealed the awkward position occupied by female workers, poised between the domestic worlds of home and the mercenary world of factories.

Even in those places without the mechanized mills of Lowell or Augusta, women performed a wide variety of paid work. Most rural women already performed physically demanding and time consuming household work, and many also engaged in small-scale domestic production. They sold most of the goods produced in town or city markets—from candles and clothing to butter, eggs, and small farm animals. For many of these women, the money they generated was the only cash income a farm family might possess.

Cities presented other working opportunities that women sometimes sought and sometimes were reduced to accepting. As American cities developed in the 1830s and 1840s, more city dwellers with money to spare paid for services that they would have done for themselves in a previous era or a more rural setting. Women filled most of the roles as cooks, cleaners, launderers, seamstresses, and all-purpose domestic help. More ominously, poor women sometimes resorted to prostitution.

Enslaved women occupied the most ambiguous position within the prevailing visions of women's proper roles. Because of their enslavement, such women performed a range of tasks ordinarily undertaken by men. Female slaves in the field worked the same jobs as male slaves. Corporations sometimes owned or rented slave women, just like their male counterparts. In 1810, Virginia's Oxford Iron Works counted nearly one-third of its enslaved workforce as female, some of them cooking and cleaning for the male workers, but others performing regular foundry tasks alongside men. Slave women also contended with a high degree of sexual vulnerability that few free women ever experienced. Despite legal, religious, and social prohibitions, slave owners maintained sexual relationships with enslaved women. The increasing prevalence of **mulatto**, or mixed-race, people in the United States census offered physical proof of many of these relationships. Slave mothers educated their adolescent daughters in strategies to protect themselves from this omnipresent danger.

The wide variety of conditions within which American women lived and worked in the 1830s and 1840s ensured a diversity of attitudes about women and their place in American life, and these differences were clearly visible in the language of the time. Among white Southerners, the designation "lady" signaled membership in an exclusive club. Ladies were typically well educated, from wealthy families, and always white. "Women," in all regions, indicated a broader community and could include poor women and immigrants. As the Lowell experience demonstrated, working women often fit awkwardly into the prescribed social roles for the time—and thus found themselves labeled "girls." Those women who ignored or violated the rigid boundaries of acceptable

Enslaved women worked alongside men performing long hours of fieldwork on tobacco, cotton, and rice plantations. The lack of gender distinctions in slave labor encouraged many whites to view black women as less feminine than their white counterparts.

behavior, particularly with regard to sexual and racial norms, earned even more damning labels. No longer women, they were simply "low and degraded" or "ruined." Those who criticized women for working outside the home ignored the financial difficulties that many families were experiencing. It was one thing to stay at home with a comfortable middle-class income, but for women with low incomes and children to feed, earning a salary was a necessity.

## Masculinity on the Trail, in the Cities, and on the Farm

Despite men's dominance in American society in the 1830s and 1840s, notions of manhood changed as unpredictably as those of womanhood. Differences in region and ethnicity produced the sharpest distinctions among different expressions of masculinity. In the Northeast, with its concentration of urban areas and highly specialized economies, men found opportunities and incentives to build marriages and families on the basis of affection rather than the older model of hierarchy and authority. Although this transition promised more frequent demonstrations of love among spouses, it also required men to abandon long-held notions of what constituted manly behavior. In earlier decades, affronts to a man's honor demanded an immediate physical, usually violent, response. As new norms of manhood took shape in the increasingly crowded and anonymous northern cities, men placed a premium on self-control, a virtue that diminished conflict while allowing men to retain their honor. Another change was the open expression of emotion, particularly positive emotions, like love, which took root especially among younger men and reformers. Male abolitionists, for instance, wrote and spoke with each other in extraordinarily intimate and emotional terms. A letter from **Charles Sumner**, the Massachusetts senator elected on a strict antislavery platform, to his friend, the poet **Henry Wadsworth Longfellow**, remarked of their correspondence: "Yr letters seem warm as a lover's heart. I can almost feel the heat when I break the seal."

New attitudes toward manhood took root more slowly in the South, where older and more traditional forms of masculine expression retained favor. The conflict surrounding statehood in the new territory of Florida, only brought within the Union in 1819, revealed the importance of expressions of masculinity to political and social authority. As residents built the case for statehood, two political factions coalesced around competing leaders. Men within the territory aligned themselves with one group or the other and zealously guarded the honor and positions of their peers. When men found themselves in conflict, they had to sort through a complex hierarchy of verbal and physical responses before taking action. The southern code of honor, heightened among white men because of the presence of slaves, demanded retaliation for any sleight to one's own or one's group's public image or reputation. Floridians gouged eyes, bit off earlobes, and assaulted each other in ways calculated to produce shame by creating a public symbol of one's inferiority. The popular forms of ritualized violence among Southerners bonded white men in a shared ethos even as it alienated them from Northerners pursuing nonviolent expressions of masculinity.

At the same time, the growing importance of evangelical Christian values, which stressed charity, humility, and compassion, rather than revenge, competed with the system of honor, especially in the South. The shift in emphasis from the hyper-public nature of honor, in which men most valued the way their peers viewed them, to Christianity, in which an individual's most important relationship was with God, represented a profound shift in southern culture. As the *Religious Herald* boldly announced in 1837, "A public profession of Christianity is an avowal of our separation from the world, as regards it maxims, pursuits, and pleasures." This transformation happened slowly through the 1830s. As evangelical churches gained influence, the values they represented began to alter the tenor of southern culture. Northern religious reformers sought similar opportunities to direct the energy and morality of American men. The increasing popularity of bare-knuckle fighting, a sport imported from England complete with foreign fighters, drew scorn from those who emphasized restraint and nonviolence. According to one commentator, boxing was "nothing but brutality, ferociousness, and cowardness . . ." which tended to "debase the mind, deaden the feelings and extinguish every spark of benevolence." Despite such critiques, a wide swath of men from different classes watched, gambled on, and thrilled to matches that could last 50 rounds or two hours of fighting. The popularity of such spectacles revealed the tensions in American culture in the antebellum era—benevolence and sympathy existed alongside violence and aggression.

## Men and Women in the Southwest

The differentiation of male and female roles that began to occur in American society of the 1830s and 1840s emerged more fully in the eastern parts of the country than the west. Through the 1850s and beyond, among families who moved west of the Mississippi River, the household continued to be the center of economic activity, as it was in the South. Men and women in these regions generally spent their days alongside one another. Women were still responsible for domestic work and child rearing and they also usually participated in the agricultural or pastoral work that sustained most western families as well. The shared responsibilities in these households appeared as soon as they started on the trek west. The demands of the journey required that men and women, if they did not share the same labor, shared the same outlook on the experience. Men typically retained responsibility for the animals, for transportation, and for protection of the family; while women took primary care of feeding, clothing, and doctoring the family if necessary. But the hardships of the journey ensured that men's and women's duties and needs often overlapped.

The key difference between East and West in terms of gender was the lopsided male–female ratios in many parts of the Anglo West. The Hispanic West and those areas that received wagon trains included roughly equal numbers of men and women, but the mining towns, the newly formed ranches, and many of the large farms were overwhelmingly male. As a result the region possessed fewer of the social institutions—churches, schools, and civic groups—that moderated the actions of young men and, consequently, a higher degree of violence and disruptive behavior than the east.

Because the Spanish controlled the southwestern reaches of central North America until 1821 and Mexico controlled this region after its independence, the social atmosphere differed markedly from the eastern United States. Elites married exclusively within their own community throughout the Spanish colonial period, producing a discrete population that viewed itself as superior to both local Indians and American settlers to the region. Peasants and the poorer classes intermarried more often, as did Anglo settlers and Hispanics in the 1840s and 1850s. In the formerly Spanish Southwest, more modern formulations of marriage based on love and mutual consent had been gaining popularity. Thanks to efforts initiated by Spain's Bourbon rulers in the late 18th century to reduce the power of the Catholic Church, civil authorities held greater sway in sanctioning marriages and younger generations resisted their parents' efforts to use marriage as a form of alliance building. Women played a central role in most of the labor of the villages of northern New Mexico and southern Colorado; reflecting this importance, daughters often inherited land alongside sons.

The gender values carried into the region by Anglo settlers challenged those of the local residents, whether of Spanish, Indian, or mixed descent. Because settlers only gradually established their presence, their values stood alongside rather than instantly replacing the older systems in the region. Anglo-Americans worked particularly hard to displace the practice of trading unfree women among different Indian communities in the region. During the 18th and early 19th centuries, in both Spanish and Indian communities, females who had been captured through war or slavery were used to link communities and pay off debts. Anglo settlers criticized the practice as barbaric, a western echo of the charge brought by abolitionists that southern slaveholders deliberately "bred" female slaves so they could sell their children or fetch the higher prices that fertile women slaves commanded.

### STUDY QUESTIONS FOR MEN AND WOMEN IN ANTEBELLUM AMERICA

1. **How did men's and women's lives differ in the mid-19th century?**
2. **How did race, region, and class influence changes in masculinity and femininity in the period?**

## FREEDOM FOR SOME

The dynamism that characterized gender relations in this period could be seen in the political system as well, where politics developed in two different directions simultaneously. On the one hand, Americans broke away from European traditions by liberalizing democracy to include all white men. On the other, Americans increased their commitment to slavery, which created a society based on bonded labor that western Europe had left behind with the end of feudalism in the 1500s. In southern states, these two trends buttressed one another while in the North they began to generate concern about what kind of country America would become. The tension between liberty and slavery fueled several decades of conflict about the structure and the nature of American democracy. Did individual freedom include the right to enslave other people? Did the nation have the authority to prohibit slavery? Rather than confront these polarizing issues directly, politicians at the state and national level focused on questions about apportionment, voting qualifications, and the regional balance of power in the country. The changes they made expanded access to electoral politics and retained an awkward sectional peace, but skeptics wondered whether even the robust American political system could contain the transformations coursing through the country in the 1830s and 1840s.

## The Nature of Democracy in the Atlantic World

Americans drew inspiration from a wide variety of sources. The independence movements in Latin America—when various republics broke away from Spain's control between 1810 and 1825—fascinated and encouraged Americans in their own expansion of democracy. Americans found European democratic efforts equally compelling. **Louis Kossuth**, the journalist and political leader in Hungary, attained renown as a freedom fighter throughout the Americas. After his expulsion from Hungary in 1848 by the embattled Hapsburgs (the ruling family of the Austrian Empire), Kossuth toured the United States to great acclaim, receiving a 100-gun salute when his ship reached New Jersey and invitations to the White House and Congress.

The liberalization of politics in the United States dovetailed with the market liberalization that occurred at the same time. Despite the conservatism of most Jacksonian Democrats, a faction within the party—known as Young Democrats—began advocating the virtues of markets and global trade. Young Democrats applauded the British decision in 1846 to repeal its "**Corn Laws**," high tariffs on imported foodstuffs designed to protect Britain's agricultural sector. Pro–free-trade Americans hoped that the British move would spur the repeal of similar duties around the world and open foreign markets to American products. The same Young Democrats who applauded Wilkes's Pacific explorations and preached free trade celebrated and supported democratic movements all across the European continent. **John O. Sullivan**'s *Democratic Review*, the unofficial organ of the movement, chronicled the fortunes of Italian, German, and Central European rebels, who themselves looked backward to the American rebels of 1776, against the old aristocracy of Europe.

Whether Americans took inspiration from Spanish- or Hungarian-speaking Democrats, they heard the same message: authority should reside in the common people. The great accomplishment of the American Revolution had been to locate the government's sovereignty not in the divine right of a king but collectively, in the people. "The people," in this sense, referred to participants in the political order. In Jacksonian America, this still meant native-born white men. The influx of Catholic immigrants, the increasing numbers of free blacks in the North, and the efforts by women to attain the vote challenged assumptions about who could participate in the political process, but white men protected their interests effectively until the Civil War. For several decades after the Revolution, reformers trying to liberalize the political system focused on eliminating property requirements for voting and office holding and creating more elective, as opposed to appointive, offices while at the same time obstructing efforts by women and racial minorities to gain access to the political system.

When the United States adopted the Constitution, it created a larger republic than any other in the world. European experiments with republics had been significantly smaller in terms of geography and population, they had been substantially more homogenous in ethnic and racial composition, and they had usually developed amongst a people bound together by language, religion, history, and culture. Northern Italian city-states like Venice and Genoa, as well as the Netherlands, and England had all experimented at different times over the preceding centuries with republican institutions. The United States, in contrast, contained descendants of people from the four different continents bordering the Atlantic Ocean, speaking a multitude of languages, practicing a variety of religious faiths or none at all, and pursuing a variety of strategies for increasing their wealth. European political thinkers assumed that factions would tear apart all but the smallest and most cohesive republics. During the 1830s, Americans returned to issues raised by James Madison and other founders regarding the proper structure of democratic government and hoped to prove European skepticism wrong.

## The Second Party System

The practical results of political changes in the United States in the 1830s and 1840s shocked many Europeans, particularly elite Britons who distrusted the wisdom of granting voting rights to, or enfranchising, all white men. While European politicians and thinkers watched, many gleefully anticipating the imminent collapse of the American republic, Americans pushed ahead. In many states, reformers eliminated two requirements for voting and office holding that had kept the poor out of the political system: property restrictions had required that officeholders and voters own real estate, and poll taxes ensured that only men with disposable income could vote. Gender, race, age, and residency remained in place as key criteria for voting and office holding. Most of the millions of immigrants to the country could naturalize themselves as citizens and assume full participation in the political system within a few years of arrival. From our modern perspective, a democracy in which only white males could vote (universal white male suffrage) seems a shallow democracy. But for people at the time, who recalled the legacy of European governance that gave little power to common people, the change as momentous. The addition of transforming previously appointed positions into elected ones, including most local offices such as tax assessor, sheriff, and local judges, produced the most democratic system in the western world.

Another factor that broadened people's access to government was the rise of the second party system. Andrew Jackson's bold leadership over two terms in the White House generated a host of opposition. Reformers criticized the callousness of his Indian removal, commercial interests condemned his destruction of the bank, and state rights proponents had their own concerns about this slaveholding son of the South who put down South Carolina's attempt to "nullify" the federal tariff.

Jackson's enemies coalesced in the **Whig Party**, which took its name from the British opposition party. At first, they had little in common except their hatred of

Caleb Bingham's famous painting captured the social nature of voting in the first half of the 19th century. Men voted publicly, which created the possibility of coercion, intimidation, and fraud, but also reinforced the collaborative process of democracy.

"King Andrew the First" as opponents labeled him. During the 1830s, the Whig Party organized around a set of issues that enabled them to build a national coalition; they captured the presidency in 1840 and again in 1848. Whereas the Democrats encouraged the mass immigration of the 1830s and 1840s and welcomed many of these voters into the party, Whig supporters tended to distrust the largely Catholic and working class migrants. Coming largely from the ranks of native-born Protestants, Whigs espoused a vigorous nationalism, supported government investments in infrastructure to stimulate business, and, in some parts of the North, endorsed moderate antislavery politics. In contrast, the Democratic Party preferred state funding and control of development projects, which set them against the federal road, bridge, and river improvements that Whigs promised would energize the American economy. Sociocultural issues, such as closing all government services on the Christian Sabbath and advocacy of temperance, also energized Whig voters.

## Democracy in the South

To the surprise of many observers, southern states actually liberalized their rules regarding access to the vote and higher office earlier than many northern ones. The southern slaveholders who filled most statehouses rarely initiated change, although the most farsighted among them saw that incorporating nonslaveholding whites into the political order on a more equal footing could ensure the security of the system. By allowing nonslaveholders to have more power in the political system, slaveholders hoped the new voters would be less likely to challenge that system.

The democracy that evolved in the presence of slavery assumed the mastery and autonomy of white men. Although the system would find its fullest expression in the Confederate States of America (formed by the seceding southern states in 1861), the unique characteristics of a democracy based on race emerged several decades before the Civil War. In the nation as a whole, politics knitted the country together, connecting men and women across regions, classes, ethnicities, and religions. But because of the overwhelming endorsement of slavery within the South, neither party could risk being associated with any challenge to it. On this issue, the southern wings of the two parties competed to outdo each other in protecting the South's peculiar institution. This weakness in the party system proved to be central to the political collapse that produced secession and war. In addition, both northern and southern whites showed their preference for white rule. By 1840, free blacks could vote only in Maine, New Hampshire, Vermont, and Massachusetts. New York and Pennsylvania had recently repealed earlier grants of voting rights to black men.

O. S., VOL. XXII. APRIL, 1857. 3d S., VOL. II, NO. IV

DE BOW'S REVIEW, INDUSTRIAL RESOURCES, ETC.

EDITED BY J. D. B. DE BOW.

TABLE OF CONTENTS.



OFFICE OF REVIEW, 448 E STREET, NEAR POST OFFICE, WASHINGTON D. C.; NEW ORLEANS, 54 CAMP STREET; TRUBNER & CO., LONDON.

Remittances or payments may be made to either office. Those by letter will b more convenient to the Editor at Washington.

Although South Carolina lost the nullification debate, its actions inflamed a sense of injured pride across the South. A decade later, James D. B. DeBow launched his eponymous magazine, *DeBow's Review*, as a platform for advancing the southern economic and political agenda.

The power of slavery to warp democracy appeared most ominously in South Carolina in 1832. Over the course of that year, politicians in the Palmetto State initiated a conflict with the federal government over the tariff. Beginning during the War of 1812, New Englanders had promoted a tariff—a federal tax on imported (usually finished) goods—as a way to stimulate domestic manufacturing and curb the importing of European products. If European goods became more expensive, tariff supporters argued, Americans would buy fewer of them and more goods made at home. New England manufacturers naturally favored the tariff. Southerners, with little industrial development of their own, complained that the tariff helped the Northeast at the expense of their region. They felt forced to buy either expensive northern-made goods, which seemed to bolster the clout of a region many Southerners regarded as a rival, or pay the tariff-elevated prices for European merchandise. When George McDuffie, an upcountry South Carolina representative rose to speak about the issue, "his frame came alive with outrage. He shrieked. He kicked. He thumped. He spat. He seemed a revivalist in a death struggle with Satan." In 1828, President Adams supported a high tariff—known as the "tariff of abominations" by its enemies—that passed with strong northern support. Southerners in and out of Congress complained vociferously about the legislation, which doubled the tax on many imported goods.

When Jackson came to the White House many Southerners assumed he would push repeal of the tariff. But Jackson's home state of Tennessee benefited from a tariff on hemp imports and despite his state rights philosophy, Jackson moved slowly against the law. Congress reduced the 1828 tariff in 1832, though it proved too late for the increasingly radical South Carolinians. South Carolina politicians saw only potential gain from denouncing the tariff in stronger and stronger language. By late 1832, John Calhoun—once Jackson's vice president and possible successor—had thrown himself fully against the tariff. He penned an "exposition" against the policy that condemned it as unconstitutional and destructive of the liberty that the Union was founded to protect. Building on Calhoun's theory, the South Carolina legislature passed an act "nullifying" the federal law and refusing to collect the tariff at its ports. President Jackson issued the most famous denunciation of the doctrine of nullification: "I consider, then, the power to annul a law of the United States, assumed by

## TIMELINE 1818–1856

**1818**

**March** U.S. Congress passes Neutrality Act, designed to suppress private warfare waged by Americans

**1821**

Mexico secures independence from Spain

**1827**

**July** Cherokee Indians ratify a tribal constitution modeled on the U.S. Constitution

**1829**

Frances Wright delivers the first public address to a mixed-gender audience by a woman in U.S. history

**August** Discovery of gold on Cherokee land in Georgia

**1830**

**May 26** Congress passes the Indian Removal Act

**1831**

Alexis de Tocqueville arrives in the United States for a two-year study of the country, resulting in the publication (in 1835) of *Democracy in America*

**1832**

**March 3** U.S. Supreme Court issues decision in *Worcester v. Georgia* holding that Congress, not the states, had sole authority to regulate relations with Indian tribes

**November 24** South Carolina legislature passes an "Ordinance of Nullification" intending to nullify the federal tariff

**1833**

**March 2** U.S. Congress passes the "Force Act" giving President Jackson the power to suppress South Carolina's refusal to collect the federal tariff

**1835**

**December** Second Seminole War begins in southern Georgia/northern Florida

**1836**

**March 6** Mexican forces led by General Santa Anna defeat and kill a combined force of Texian and Tejano rebels inside the Alamo

**April 21** Mexican President and General Santa Anna defeated in fighting along San Jacinto River; Texas independence declared

**May 25** U.S. House of Representatives instates the "gag rule" prohibiting introduction or discussion of petitions calling for abolition

**1837**

**December 13** Rensselaer Van Rensselaer leads

one State, incompatible with the existence of the Union, contradicted expressly by the letter of the Constitution, unauthorized by its spirit, inconsistent with every principle on which It was founded, and destructive of the great object for which it was formed." Congress passed a Force Act and Jackson appeared ready to lead U.S. troops into the South when a compromise was reached. Congress reduced the tariff further, and South Carolina repealed its nullification ordinance. The nation had come dangerously close to secession and war.

## Conflicts over Slavery

Southern partisans lost the battle over nullification but this did not diminish their willingness to defend slavery. Because southern politicians controlled most of the top committee chairmanships and other leadership positions within Congress, they blocked discussion of slavery at the national as well as the state level by imposing the "**gag rule**." With abolitionists' opposition to slavery growing more forceful each year, southern representatives protested against the new petition from Maine and insisted that Congress "reject" it, an unprecedented request. **James Henry Hammond** of South Carolina, who made the original motion that produced what critics would call the gag rule, asserted that "he could not sit there and see the rights of the Southern people assaulted day after day, by the ignorant fanatics from whom these memorials proceeded." Hammond found support among his southern colleagues, many northern allies, and especially party leaders eager to see such a divisive issue removed from debate. For the next nine years, the U.S. Congress refused to consider or even print the memorials and petitions of citizens on the subject of abolition.

Partly owing to the dedicated efforts of former president **John Quincy Adams**, then representing Massachusetts in the House of Representatives, the House rescinded

American filibusters into Canada

**1838**

**January** General Winfield Scott sent to Canadian border to suppress violence

**May 17** General Winfield Scott arrives in Georgia and begins confining Cherokee people prior to their forced march to Indian Territory

**August 18** Wilkes Expedition sets sail from Hampton Roads, Virginia

**1839**

Mississippi passes first "Married Women's Property Act," granting married women independent rights to property brought into a marriage

**1842**

**June 10** Wilkes Expedition returns

**May 16** First successful large-scale wagon train departs Missouri for the Pacific Coast

**August 14** Second Seminole War ends; 90 percent of the Seminole killed during the conflict

**1844**

**December 3** U.S. Congress repeals the "gag rule"

**1845**

The Irish Famine begins

**1848**

**July 20** "Declaration of Sentiments" passed at Seneca Falls, NY, by prominent women's rights advocates calling for equality between men and women

Democratic Revolutions in Italy, Hungary, Germany, and France

**1851**

**December** Hungarian democracy activist Louis Kossuth tours the United States

**1856**

William Walker briefly holds office as "president" of Nicaragua before being executed the rule in 1844. In the meantime, however, the rule underscored the power of pro-slavery southern congressmen to control the institution and transformed the fight over abolition into a fight over free speech as well. Southern power, wielded arrogantly by men like Hammond, probably did more to stimulate antislavery sympathies among white Northerners than the work of dozens of dedicated abolitionists.

Hammond understood that an open debate over slavery could possibly move the nation to abolish it. Only a tiny minority of Northerners counted themselves as abolitionists in the years before the Civil War, and even most abolitionists wanted only gradual and peaceful emancipation. The power of persuasion, however, could move millions, and given the North's advantage in population, Southerners needed to win—not just stifle—the debate over slavery. Reacting to abolitionist pressure, Southerners developed a robust defense of slavery, marshaling history, religion, morality, and economics to demonstrate why Americans had to protect and even extend the system of racial slavery then dominant in the South.

The pro-slavery defense, as it has been called by historians, built on the idea of racial supremacy espoused by prominent scientists of the day, such as Harvard's Agassiz and the southern physician **Josiah Nott**. Both men articulated scientific explanations of white racial superiority based on an imputed link between skull size and intellectual ability. Slavery's defenders joined this modern argument to older endorsements of slavery, reaching back to the ancient Greeks and Romans and to the Bible. Many Protestant Christians at the time interpreted the biblical story of Ham as evidence that God had made black people to be the servants of white people. Pro-slavery theorists also built elaborate economic defenses of the institution, pointing to the remarkable wealth produced in southern states through the use of slave labor. James Henry Hammond explained the political defense of slavery in another famous Congressional speech that alienated as many Northerners as his earlier fight for the gag rule had. According to Hammond, every society required workers who performed the brute labor on which all else rested. He referred to this class as the "**mudsill**"and flatly stated that members of such a class, owing to their constant low-wage labor, could not develop the intellectual capacities to contribute productively to the political life of their society. Hammond condemned Northerners for forcing white men into this role while he lauded the South for using slaves in this capacity. According to Hammond, racial slavery enabled white men to educate themselves so that they could participate as fully free men in the political and social life of their region.

What could be called the "civilizational" aspect of the pro-slavery argument claimed that slaves could either be held in bondage in America or Africa. And, because America was a Christian nation and Africa was not, slavery in the United States must be better for the slaves. Over time, the argument went, slaves would adopt Christianity, ensuring eternal salvation for their souls. As Southerners knew, two awkward facts contradicted this part of the argument: after 1808, international law prohibited the importation of African slaves into the country, so all future slaves were native to the United States. Second, while Catholic Spain and Portugal made extensive efforts to convert its slaves to Christianity, Protestant England and later America made no similar effort. Before 1800, very few slaves had adopted Christianity. This failure became one of the chief criticisms of northern opponents of slavery and eventually prompted a slavery reform movement within the South.

## STUDY QUESTION FOR FREEDOM FOR SOME

1. **Did the changes in American politics in the 1830s and 1840s serve a more liberal or a more conservative social order?**

## Summary

- The 1830s and 1840s were a key phase in the expansion of the nation. Challenging Spain and Britain for dominance in North America, settlers flooded the landscape west of the Mississippi and dramatically changed the demography and the economy of the region.
- The economic growth spurred by new technology, especially the steam engine, helped drive the rise of a new middle class and of a more clearly defined and self-aware working class, mainly located in the cities.
- The new workplaces, distinguished from older household-based production, were almost entirely all-male places. This change helped generate the growing separation of men's and women's experiences in early America.
- In the South, the West, and among the variety of non-Anglo ethnic communities, men and women worked out different relationships with one another and different expectations of the future.
- Political elites imposed widespread progressive reforms, creating more democratic political systems across the country. Nevertheless, political power remained securely in the hands of wealthy white men.
- Partly because of the progressive reforms, outsiders of all sorts found ways to influence the political system. These groups, including Native Americans, women, new immigrants, and African Americans, also began using the language of American politics, especially the idea of an egalitarian democracy, to improve their own positions.

## Key Terms and People

**abolition** *412*
**Adams, John Quincy** *433*
**Agassiz, Louis** *405*
**Alamo** *397*
**Anthony, Susan B.** *421*
**Bryan, William Cullen** *409*
**Cook, James** *408*
**Corn Laws** *428*
**coverture** *421*
**Crockett, Davy** *402*
**Evans, George Henry** *412*
**gag rule** *433*
**Grimké sisters** *421*
**Hammond, James Henry** *433*
**Houston, Sam** *397*
**Indian Removal Act of 1830** *401*
**Kossuth, Louis** *428*
**Longfellow, Henry Wadsworth** *425*
**Lowell Mill Girls** *423*
**Marshall, John** *401*
**Mott, Lucretia** *421*
**mudsill** *434*
**mulatto** *424*
**Nott, Josiah** *434*
**Owen, Robert Dale** *412*
**Santa Anna, Antonio López de** *407*
**Stanton, Elizabeth Cady** *421*
**Sullivan, John O.** *428*
**Sumner, Charles** *425*
**Trail of Tears** *402*
**Walker, William** *406*
**Whig Party** *429*
**Wilkes, Charles** *408*
**Wright, Frances** *412*
**Zavala, Lorenzo de** *397*

## Reviewing Chapter 11

1. The most important boundary that changed in this period was the one between men and women. Do you agree with this statement? Why or why not?

## Further Reading

Aron, Stephen. *How the West Was Lost: The Transformation of Kentucky from Daniel Boone to Henry Clay*. Baltimore, MD: Johns Hopkins University Press, 1996. An insightful study of land and development politics during the first half of the 19th century.

Berlin, Ira. *Generations of Captivity: A History of African-American Slaves*. Cambridge, MA: Belknap Press, 2003. The best and most concise history of slavery in North America from the early 17th century through emancipation.

Guttierez, Ramon A. *When Jesus Came, the Corn Mothers Went Away: Marriage, Sexuality, and Power in New Mexico, 1500–1846*. Stanford, CA: Stanford University Press, 1991. An analysis of the effects of Spanish invasion and settlement on gender roles and relations in the Southwest.

May, Robert E. *Manifest Destiny's Underworld: Filibustering in Antebellum America*. Chapel Hill: University of North Carolina Press, 2002. An engaging survey of the practice of filibustering in 19th-century America.

Stansell, Christine. *City of Women: Sex and Class in New York, 1789–1860*. Urbana: University of Illinois Press, 1987. An analysis of the changes in family, work, and gender patterns in industrializing America.

Wilentz, Sean. *Chants Democratic: New York City and the Rise of the American Working Class, 1788–1850*. New York: Oxford University Press, 1984. The seminal study of a pivotal moment in the development of a working class in the United States.

# Visual Review

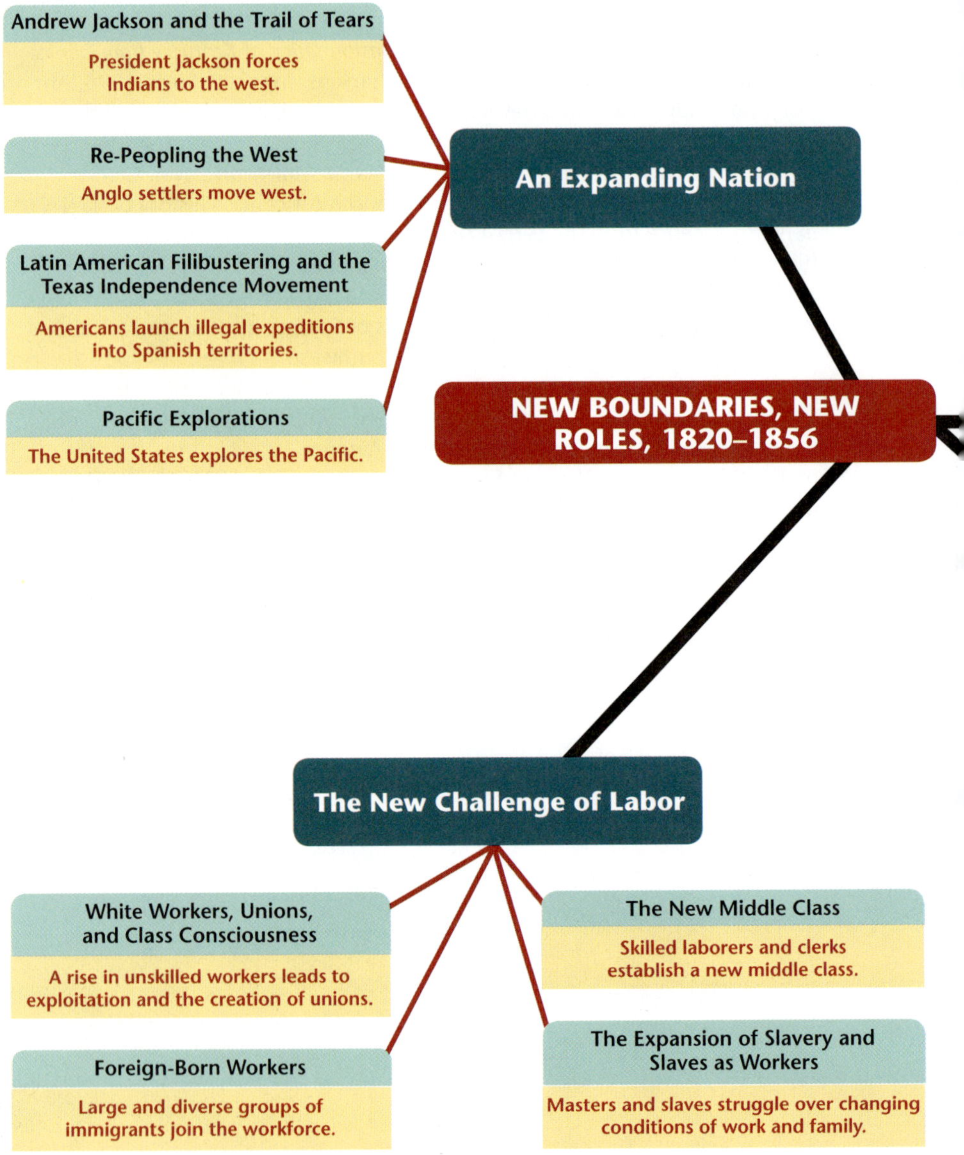

**NEW BOUNDARIES, NEW ROLES, 1820–1856**

## An Expanding Nation

**Andrew Jackson and the Trail of Tears**
President Jackson forces Indians to the west.

**Re-Peopling the West**
Anglo settlers move west.

**Latin American Filibustering and the Texas Independence Movement**
Americans launch illegal expeditions into Spanish territories.

**Pacific Explorations**
The United States explores the Pacific.

## The New Challenge of Labor

**White Workers, Unions, and Class Consciousness**
A rise in unskilled workers leads to exploitation and the creation of unions.

**Foreign-Born Workers**
Large and diverse groups of immigrants join the workforce.

**The New Middle Class**
Skilled laborers and clerks establish a new middle class.

**The Expansion of Slavery and Slaves as Workers**
Masters and slaves struggle over changing conditions of work and family.

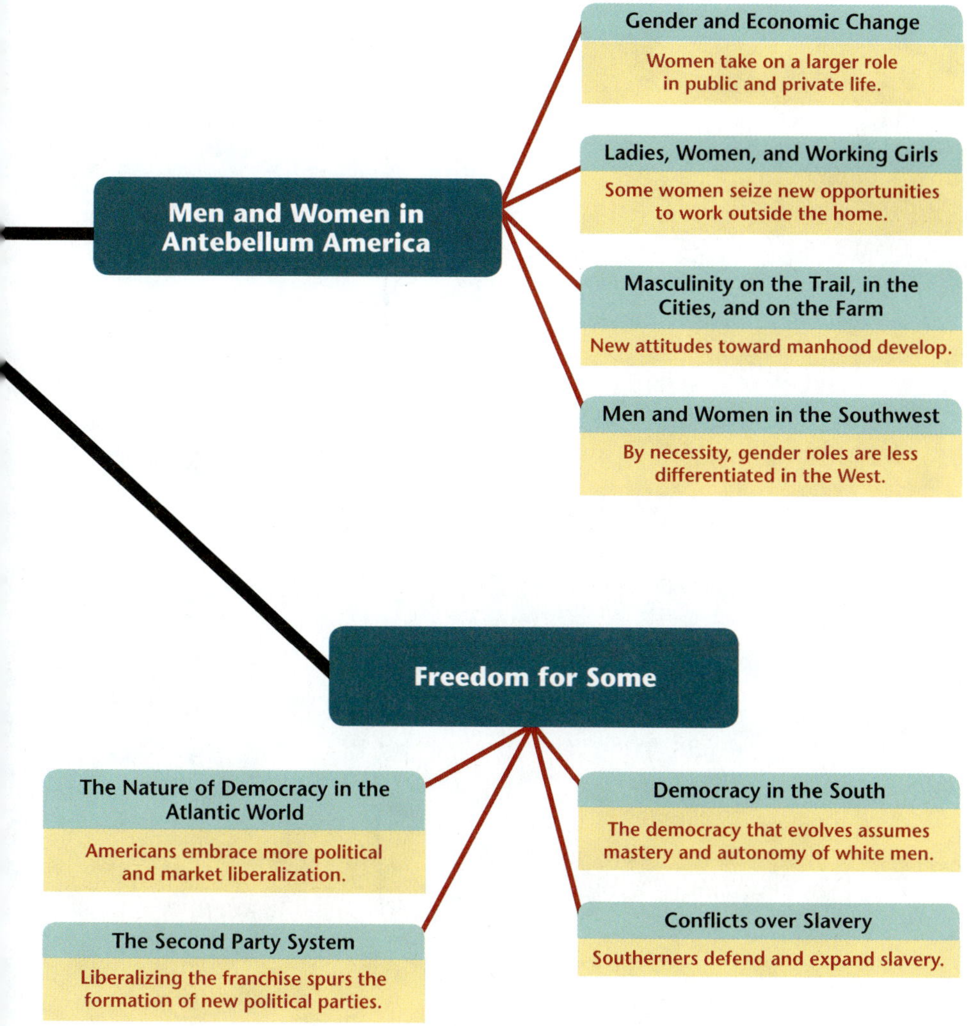

## Men and Women in Antebellum America

**Gender and Economic Change**
Women take on a larger role in public and private life.

**Ladies, Women, and Working Girls**
Some women seize new opportunities to work outside the home.

**Masculinity on the Trail, in the Cities, and on the Farm**
New attitudes toward manhood develop.

**Men and Women in the Southwest**
By necessity, gender roles are less differentiated in the West.

## Freedom for Some

**The Nature of Democracy in the Atlantic World**
Americans embrace more political and market liberalization.

**The Second Party System**
Liberalizing the franchise spurs the formation of new political parties.

**Democracy in the South**
The democracy that evolves assumes mastery and autonomy of white men.

**Conflicts over Slavery**
Southerners defend and expand slavery.

# 12 Religion and Reform

## 1820–1850

Tossing violently in a storm, a ship was driven ever closer to the shore of Fire Island, New York, on July 19, 1850. Out of the country for four years, Margaret Fuller was returning to the United States on that ship, with an Italian husband, a baby boy, and a new name, the Marchesa d'Ossoli. By the 1830s Fuller had become one of the best-known writers and thinkers in the United States. From 1846 to 1850 she worked, mostly in Italy, as one of America's first war correspondents, as she reported on the civil wars and nationalist movements wracking that country. A friend of Ralph Waldo Emerson and **Henry David Thoreau**, Fuller had edited the Transcendentalist magazine the *Dial*, offering insights into U.S. and European philosophy, literature, and art. She also wrote *Woman in the Nineteenth Century*, in which she argued for the full equality of men and women.

In 1844 Horace Greeley hired her as a full time critic for the *New York Tribune*. From that post she read and wrote widely. Like many Americans of the time she pursued a more Christian society. Her exposés took readers into the alms house, the asylum, and the prison, demanding reform and improvement. In addition to her religious faith Fuller drew inspiration from classical and contemporary history and politics. She closely followed the nationalist movements in Germany, Italy, Poland, and Hungary, and Fuller chronicled these movements during her stay in Europe. Although she did not find "the genuine democracy to which the rights of all men are holy," her writings broadened Americans' horizons.

◄

Nat Turner, American slave leader, with his confederates in conference. Steel engraving, 1863, after Felix O.C. Darley.

### CHAPTER OUTLINE

The first economic recession of the free banking era decimated the cotton industry (1837).

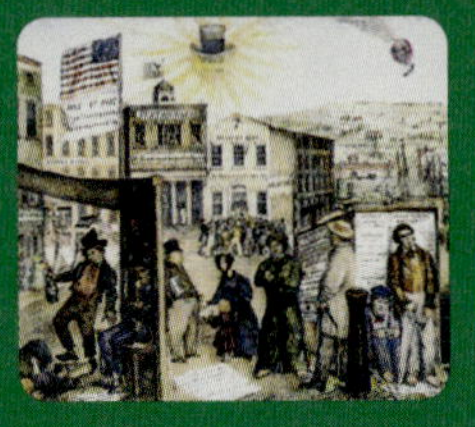

The Seneca Falls Convention produced the "Declaration of Sentiments," a cornerstone of the growing women's rights movement (1848).

U.S. event that influenced the world

International event that influenced the United States

Event with multinational influence

Conflict

Political upheaval across Europe led to American-influenced democratic revolutions (1848).
Britain ended slavery in the West Indies (1833).
WE ARE MEN AND BRETHREN
EMANCIPATION
Liberia was founded as a colony for freed American slaves (1820).

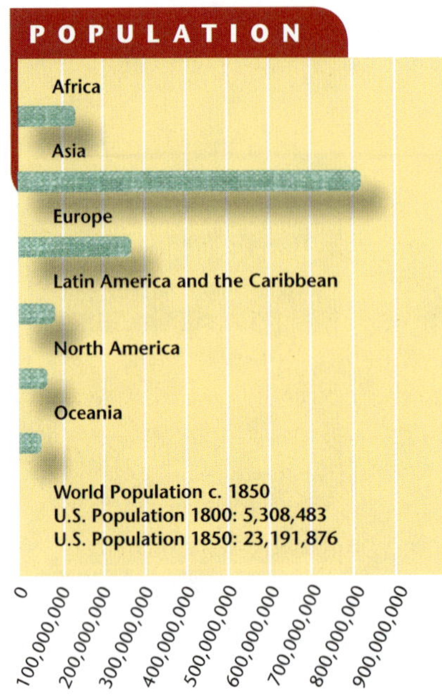


Tragically, in that July storm, Fuller's ship ran aground, and she and her husband and child drowned. The inscription on Fuller's tombstone encapsulated the reach of her vision: "By birth a child of New England; By adoption a citizen of Rome; By genius belonging to the world." Fuller served as a model, both intellectually and personally, for the first generation of women's rights activists. Susan B. Anthony said that Fuller "possessed more influence on the thought of American women than any woman previous to her time." Inspired by the global effort to achieve equality for women, Margaret Fuller embodied the possibilities and contradictions of the era of reform that defined the 1830s and 1840s. Although she was as deeply educated and as intellectually capable as any man, her family expected her to manage the household and attend to traditionally feminine duties. She demanded full equality, yet she reveled in the sensitivity of a "woman's heart" in her writings.

As Fuller's life demonstrated, Americans absorbed, transformed, and broadcast ideas that circulated around the globe in the 1830s and 1840s. Both Transcendentalists and evangelical Protestants created the transatlantic exchange networks. New theologies, new worship practices, and new reform movements spurred by these beliefs flowed back and forth across the Atlantic alongside the classical exchanges of philosophy and literature. Regardless of the source the era proved to be one of the most tumultuous thanks to dynamic exchange of ideas among Americans and their neighbors around the world.

## THE SECOND GREAT AWAKENING

In the early decades of the 19th century, a transatlantic revival movement spread from Britain to North America. This **Second Great Awakening**—following the similar religious dynamism of the 1730s—connected evangelical Christians on both sides of the Atlantic who exchanged ideas and strategies that inspired a broad set of social, cultural, and intellectual changes. Participants sought salvation and rebirth inside re-energized churches. The religious ferment of the 1820s and 1830s drew as much on the massive economic and social changes occurring in America as on theology. The increasingly rapid industrialization and urbanization of the country, the rise of a truly national commercial economy, and the surging middle class all spurred both celebration and anxiety. These changes also compelled Americans to rethink their world. Earlier generations of American engaged in mostly temporary and localized protest and reform. The evangelical reforms of the 1820s, 1830s, and 1840s, in contrast, drew on broad national support and lasted for decades. The issues they raised—the relationship between religious faith and politics, the responsibility of Christians to improve and uplift their society, and the tension between modernity and tradition—continue to engage us today.

## Spreading the Word

In September 1830 **Charles Grandison Finney**, a young man trained in the law but fired with religious zeal, arrived in Rochester, New York. After his moment of conversion Finney rebuffed a legal client by saying, "I have a retainer from the Lord Jesus Christ to plead his cause, I cannot plead yours." Finney intended to unsettle the complacent and energize the believers. He succeeded magnificently. Preaching every day and three times on Sunday, meeting privately with individuals, and organizing prayer groups, Finney lit the spiritual fire that would consume western New York over the next several years. He spoke directly to people—men and women, rich and poor alike—in their own language. Without a formal pulpit, Finney addressed his listeners as equals. He beseeched them to accept the salvation that he had experienced.

As Finney explained, accepting one's sinfulness only began the work of reformed Christians: he exhorted the converted to live every day in accordance with the gospel. Here lay the socially transformative power of the Second Great Awakening. Ministers like Finney encouraged Americans to reform their society, to bring it more clearly into line with God's plan. Despite diverse interpretations of what that world should look like and an uneven embrace of evangelicalism, revivals encouraged massive social action all across the country. Finney's religious experiences personified the journey that many converts took. He matured within the Presbyterian Church and studied law before turning to the ministry. Once engaged in the study of religion, Finney gravitated to the emotionalism of Baptist preaching and conversion. Convinced that the passive reception of scripture and predestination that he had learned as a boy had failed him, Finney implored his listeners to put the lessons of the gospel into practice in their lives. In the 1820s and 1830s, Finney and other revivalist ministers brought this message to listeners across the United States and overseas.

The "Burned Over" district of upstate New York earned its nickname because the scale and pace of conversions to the new evangelical faith suggested the wildfires that periodically devoured the countryside. Some converts had belonged to more established sects and others came from the ranks of unchurched Americans. The area west of the Adirondack Mountains and north of the Erie Canal supported a vibrant agricultural economy, which industrialized in step with the revivals. Finney, and other itinerant ministers, who moved from community to community setting up congregations, borrowed from the Methodist practice of camp meetings, outdoor religious events, to develop a new style of open and accessible religion. They hoped to emulate the success of the massive Cane Ridge Revival of 1801, which generated thousands of converts in Kentucky. Whereas their more conservative peers had eschewed public demonstrations of religion, evangelicals stressed the necessity of public revivals as a method of establishing and sustaining faith. This endorsement of public action and of the common sense of average people over the learned wisdom of trained ministers reinforced the accelerating democratization of American politics in the 1830s and 1840s.

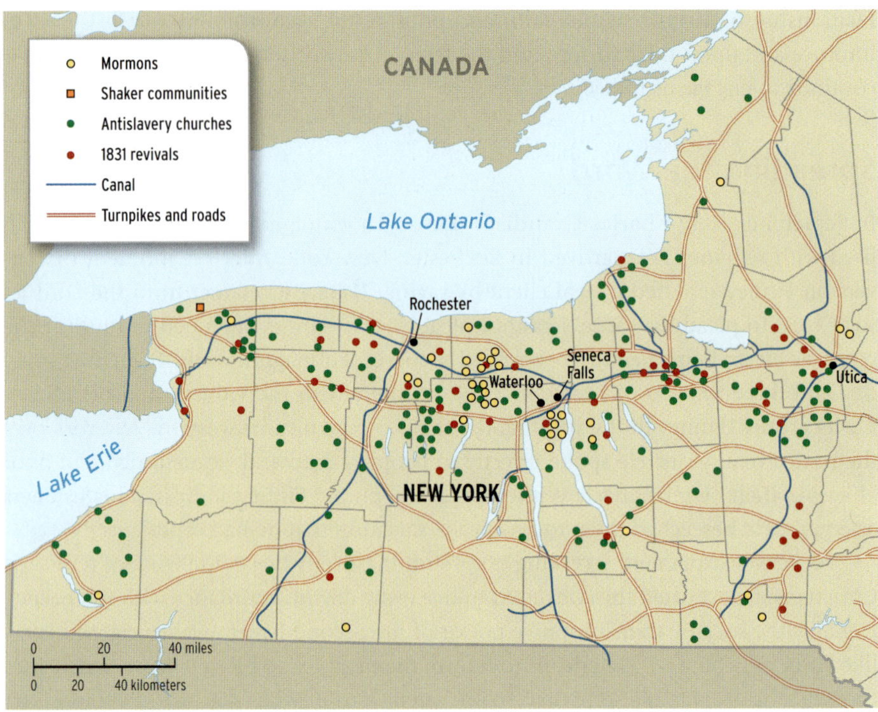


▲ **Map 12.1**

**New York State, 1830s** The new transportation networks of turnpikes, canals, and railroads carried itinerant ministers as well as produce around the nation. The result was that the Second Great Awakening flourished in well-connected market towns and urban areas as well as more remote rural areas.

## Building a Christian Nation

Between 1820 and 1860 Americans built 40,000 new churches, compared to the 10,000 they built in the 40 years before 1820. Although Protestant sects had dominated the religious life of the British colonies, a majority of citizens did not actively participate in organized religion. At the end of the revival period probably one-third of all Americans attended church regularly. The evangelical movement spread from New York throughout New England, through Ohio, and through Kentucky into the South. Because of their resistance to the emotionalism of revivals neither the Episcopalians, the American version of the Church of England, nor the Presbyterians benefited much from the movement. Instead, Methodists and the Baptists established themselves as leading American denominations as a result of the Second Great Awakening. The two faiths shared a close affinity with regard to doctrine, but the Baptists created a radically decentralized hierarchy that empowered local ministers and individual churches. In 1831, the year after Finney began his work in Rochester, evangelicals reported over 600 revivals in New York State alone, with most organized by the Methodists and Baptists but with some drawing followers from the more well-established sects.

The circulation of itinerant ministers further decentralized religion after the Revolution. Traveling preachers, often young, single men, adjusted to the physical rigors of long travel on horseback, rough accommodations, and long stretches away from home and family. The youth of most itinerants ensured they held less wealth and were less invested in established ways of thinking. These characteristics meant that they might challenge the authority of propertied elites, especially when they did not belong to a specific community and did not suffer the social repercussions of criticizing those in power. Once a critical mass of conversions had occurred, people often organized themselves into a formal church. This process might take months or it could take years. Beginning in fields, barns, and parlors, new congregations moved into actual churches as soon as they could raise the revenue to buy property.

Mimicking the institutional traditions of the more established sects, evangelicals established colleges at which ministers could be trained. A raft of small colleges built across the Midwest served both denominational and public needs. Charles Grandison Finney assumed the presidency of Oberlin College in 1833, one of the earliest and most influential of these institutions, established by evangelical Presbyterians. Oberlin received support from an influx of students from Lane Theological Institute, another midwestern evangelical institution whose administration had suppressed student activism against slavery. Southern evangelicals built as well; they founded Wake Forest,

EXHORTATION AND PREACHING AT THE CAMP MEETING AT EASTHAM.

▲ Outdoor revivals served as one of the chief conduits of the new evangelical faiths. Their informality and the mixed audiences—men and women, blacks and whites, slave and free, rich and poor—contributed to the democratic feeling of the movement.

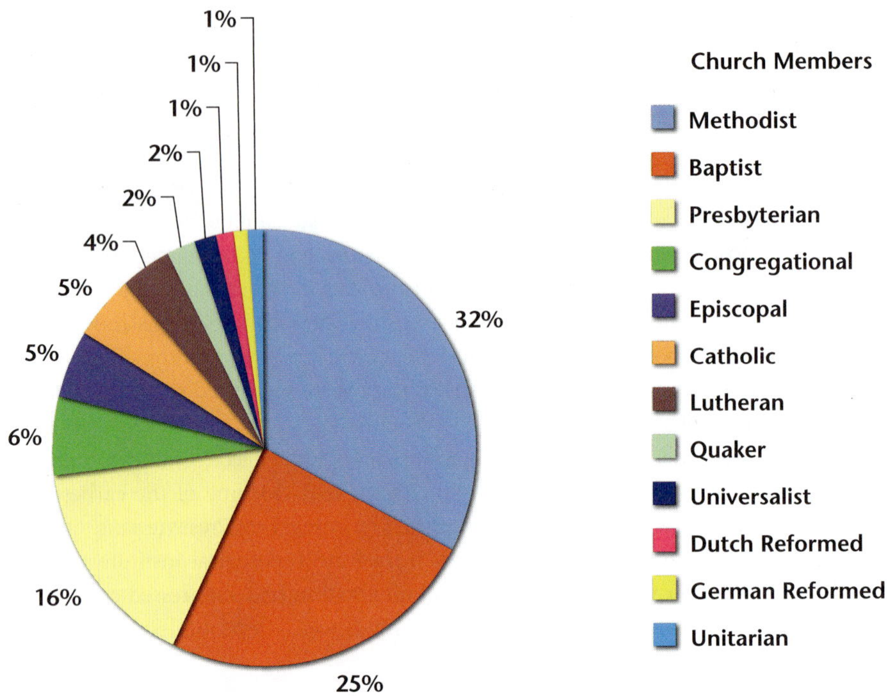


▲ **Figure 12.1**

**Church membership, 1850** The results of the Second Great Awakening were clearly visible by 1850, when Baptists and Methodists both counted millions of members, well ahead of other denominations. Note: Numbers are based on aggregate accommodations in churches as counted by the 1850 Census.

Richmond, Furman, Davidson, and Emory in the late 1830s and early 1840s. All told, evangelical reformers built 28 new denominational schools between 1820 and 1850.

The Second Great Awakening spurred religious growth well beyond the established Protestant sects. The Catholic Church, a presence since the early colonial period, grew on the strength of the immigrant population, to whom they ministered. Local, independent churches also sprang up across the nation. **Ann Lee**, a former English Quaker who had moved to the United States, organized followers around a rigid doctrine of gender equality and millennial prophecy. Believers regarded Lee as a second incarnation of Christ and adopted her celibate lifestyle in pursuit of a "heaven on earth." Known as the Shakers for a ritual dance they performed, their asceticism and devotion to high-quality agricultural production and craftwork left a folk art legacy that lived on long beyond Lee.

The most successful of these new sects were the **Mormons**, founded by **Joseph Smith** in the same upstate New York district in which Finney preached. Smith composed *The Book of Mormon* after receiving what he regarded as divine visions. Preaching a conservative theology of patriarchal authority, Smith drew thousands of followers. But the sect generated fear and anger among other Americans. The Mormons' defiant efforts to build a separate society, their advocacy of plural marriage, and their willingness to live under a theocratic hierarchy largely outside the regular democratic process spurred mainline Protestant Christians to regard them as a threat. Persecutions followed them as they moved from New York to Ohio and then to Missouri and Illinois. A confrontation in Illinois in 1844 left Smith dead and convinced **Brigham Young**, the new leader of the main community, that he must lead his people to a refuge. They chose as their destination the area around the Great Salt Lake, in today's Utah, then in largely ungoverned territory still belonging to Mexico. Young guided his community—more than 16,000 strong—over the mountains and out of the United States.

## Interpreting the Message

Many of the changes advanced by Finney and other revival ministers angered and scared orthodox religious leaders. Traditionalists opposed measures that democratized the churches, especially the use of vernacular language, immediate church membership after conversion, and mixed-sex audiences where both men and women prayed publicly. Without denying that God held the power to save souls, Finney demanded that people use their free will to reject sin and pursue a more Christian life. Many of the new evangelicals also endorsed millennialism, a belief system organized around an imminent apocalypse, which made salvation all the more urgent.

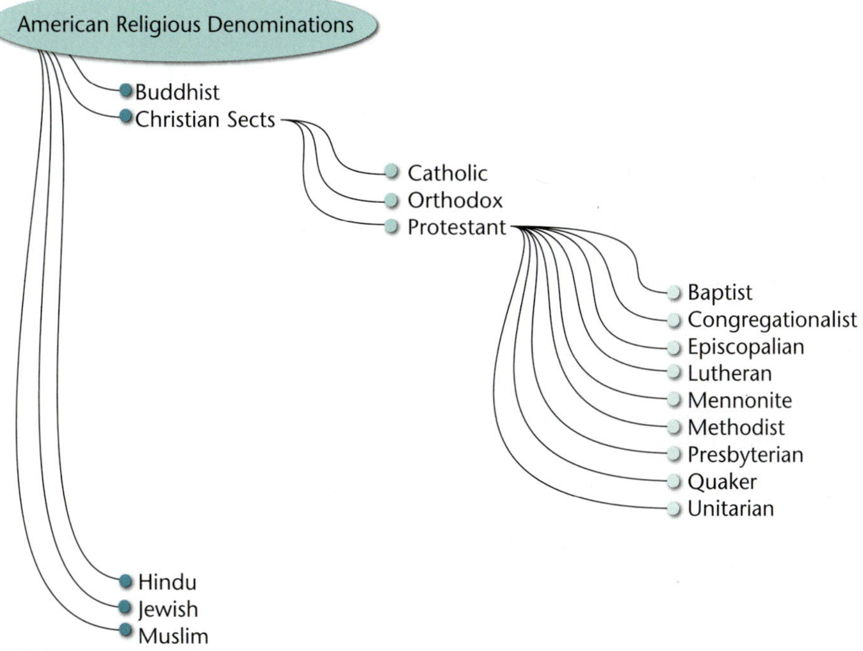


▲ **Figure 12.2**

**Subdivisions in American religious denominations** The First Amendment's prohibition on state supported churches and a great tolerance of religious diversity ensured that many sects flourished in the United States. Throughout the 19th century, immigrants brought new faiths to the United States that took root alongside the established denominations.

The religious diversity of the old Middle Colonies (New York and Pennsylvania) ensured that evangelicals' calls, even those that elevated the power of individuals at the expense of institutions, resonated within an already pluralistic atmosphere. In northern states generally, the call to act in a more Christian way evolved into an injunction to improve society. The Second Great Awakening targeted sin, both in the actions of individuals and in the effects these actions had on society. The pursuit of a Christian society propelled a host of reform movements including temperance; women's rights; prison, hospital, and asylum reform; better working conditions; and, most significantly, antislavery activism.

Religious reformers took advantage of two unique aspects of America's political system. In Britain the tight connection between social position and political power ensured that reform efforts proceeded through Parliament. The U.S. system, by contrast, was more decentralized and the result was that in early 19th-century America reformers more often went around government rather than went through it. Reform movements benefited from several changes in American law and society. Most importantly, the rapid growth of corporations and a variety of legal opinions establishing the autonomy of private institutions created a public sector and gave reformers the legal right and civic space within which to organize themselves.

At the same time the pursuit of perfection created tensions within American life about the role of religious institutions in democracy. Evangelical reform prompted people to ask doctrinal questions about the forces that could or should mediate the relationship between the individual and God and questions about the proper role for religious faith in politics and public policy. One abolitionist responded to fears of "mixing up" politics and religion with the call to "mix them, and mix them, and mix them, and keep mixing, until they cease to be mixed, and politics became religion and religion, politics." Other reformers and many outside the evangelical revival worried about the tension between encouraging Protestant Christian values and ensuring liberty at the same time.

### STUDY QUESTIONS FOR THE SECOND GREAT AWAKENING

1. **What strategies did evangelical ministers use to attract converts?**
2. **Why did so many people turn to evangelical Christianity in the 1830s and 1840s?**

## NORTHERN REFORM

The most prominent and disruptive reforms concerned abolition of slavery, women's rights, and temperance. These three movements challenged America's political, economic, and social structure. Supporting them required individuals to abandon deeply held beliefs about themselves, the natural world, society, and proper relations among human beings. Because reform movements represented such a broad and fundamental challenge to American life, they drew on a wide variety of inspirations. In most cases the Second Great Awakening and religious fervor energized reformers who created organizations within churches and drew explicitly on Christian doctrine to advocate particular changes. They often received funding from denominational institutions. But other reformers found their calling through secular channels, often by observing the plight of families broken by alcoholism, the slave trade, or domestic violence. Although reform movements appeared all across the country, northern communities demonstrated greater sympathy for them. The rapid changes that characterized this era in the North provided reformers with more projects and weakened the natural opposition to reform that developed among entrenched elites.

Each of the major reform movements contained its own specific contradictions. Many antislavery activists, for example, worried about the negative effects of slavery on democracy without much regard for slaves as people. Some women's rights advocates used prevailing biological teachings about women's greater sensitivity to argue for their greater voice in public policy, while their opponents used those same "facts" to argue for the exclusion of women from the public sphere. In certain cases, tensions between religious and secular reformers created friction, but generally they worked effectively together. The leadership of women in social reform movements created the greatest challenge. Women's active public role in reshaping American society in the 1830s, 1840s, and 1850s produced a backlash—such that even some friends of women's rights classified women's public protests as "out of place"—that curtailed many social movements, most noticeably the pursuit of equality between the sexes.

## The Temperance Crusade

Most female reformers, and some men too, began their work with a focus on individual moral reform, especially prohibition of alcohol. In 1826, evangelical ministers formed the **American Temperance Society** (ATS), which initiated an enormously successful campaign. It was the first major reform effort to grow out of the revivals and it drew support from ministers of all denominations. The movement did not end the consumption of alcohol in America, but it did help convince millions of people to rethink their relationship to drinking. In 1825, the average American 15 years of age or older consumed seven gallons of alcohol per year, or the equivalent of 110 eight-ounce glasses. By 1850 the per capita consumption rate had fallen to less than two gallons per year. Evangelical clergy argued that alcohol represented a serious threat to the moral order and condemned the social effects of alcohol, mostly on the men who lost jobs, fell away from the church, and abused or abandoned their families. Lyman Beecher, probably the best known preacher in the country, regarded intemperance as "the sin of our land . . . that river of fire, which is rolling through the land, destroying the vital air, and extending an atmosphere of death" that would "defeat the hopes of the world."

Beecher led the founding of the ATS, which called for a total prohibition of alcohol. Evangelicals succeeded in shifting public thinking about drinking by using statistics showing the deleterious effects of alcohol. By connecting moral reform to scientific analysis and data, reformers broadened the appeal and the argument for their proposals. They needed strong arguments because their appeals demanded a high degree of sacrifice. They insisted that good Christians refrain from all alcoholic beverages, including those used in communion rites, and they even denied church membership to those who drank. These demands helped evangelicals to differentiate themselves clearly from Catholics, most of whom used wine in communion rites and came from cultures where alcohol played an important social role. As a result, temperance rarely had the support of immigrant communities or the Democratic Party, which welcomed immigrants. Other Americans resented the campaign because they perceived it as an attack on individualism and basic freedom.

The desire to purify the body produced a variety of health reform movements. The first sustained call for vegetarianism in the United States emerged at this time. **Sylvester Graham**, a pioneer in the field, devised an entire health system emphasizing the moderate intake of stimulants—including tea, coffee, and alcohol—as well as sex, which he advised should be restricted to once a month. His vegetarian diet relied on bread made from Graham flour, which included bran in baking flour; the flour remains in use today in the United States in the crackers named after him. Other reformers focused on the body itself: phrenologists predicted intelligence, careers, and relationship patterns by interpreting the shape and contouring of people's skulls. Popular in Germany, Scotland, and other European nations, phrenology was predicated on the belief that the size of different sections of the skulls corresponded to the size of respective sections of the brain, which, in turn, determined the mental attributes that defined people.

## The Rising Power of American Abolition

The campaign against slavery grew from humble origins within minority religious communities in England and America. In the 1850s legislative debates over slavery—especially the 1850 Fugitive Slave Act and the 1854 Kansas-Nebraska Act—pushed many white Northerners into the antislavery camp, but in the 1830s and 1840s supporters came mostly from within the evangelical world. Quakers and Methodists both maintained historical opposition to the institution. **John Wesley**, Methodism's English founder, hated slavery and the early American Methodists Thomas Coke and **Francis Asbury** carried on the fight in the late 18th century when they organized the Methodist Episcopal Church of America. Slavery directly contradicted the egalitarian ethos of much Quaker teaching; although Philadelphia merchants heavily invested in the institution in the 18th century, Pennsylvania hosted the first antislavery organization in the world. **Granville Sharp**, the early English abolitionist, corresponded with Philadelphia Quakers when he built the British movement. Even in the South early evangelicals of all denominations often condemned chattel bondage as they pushed their congregants to pursue lives more closely aligned with Jesus's message of universal brotherhood. The key change within the movement came in the early 1830s as antislavery activists transformed into abolitionists began calling for an immediate end to slavery.

The transition from conservative, gradualist reform to the call for immediate abolition can be seen in the shift of power from the Pennsylvania Abolition Society (PAS), created in 1775 on Quaker principles of pacifism and antislavery, to the New England Antislavery Society (NEASS). The PAS, founded in the inspiring moment of the American Revolution, had pursued a largely legalistic course seeking individual emancipations of slaves within the state and gradual restrictions on slavery through state law. The PAS reflected a conservative faith in elite action. Black people could not join the organization and lawyers for the PAS made appeals strictly on the basis of reason. By the 1830s antislavery activists created a more vigorous and public campaign against the institution. Free African Americans in the North strongly opposed gradual emancipation, and their campaign educated and energized many white activists. In Massachusetts white activists joined their black peers to create a new model of abolition society. Drawing on the expanding democracy in the United States activists abandoned the older legalistic strategies and appealed directly to the people, often with stirringly emotional appeals. An 1831 edition of the *Abolitionist* included the following poem intended to shame white Northerners into action:

> White Lady, happy, Proud, and Free, Lend awhile, thine ear to me;
> Let the Negro Mother's Wail Turn Thy cheek yet more pale.

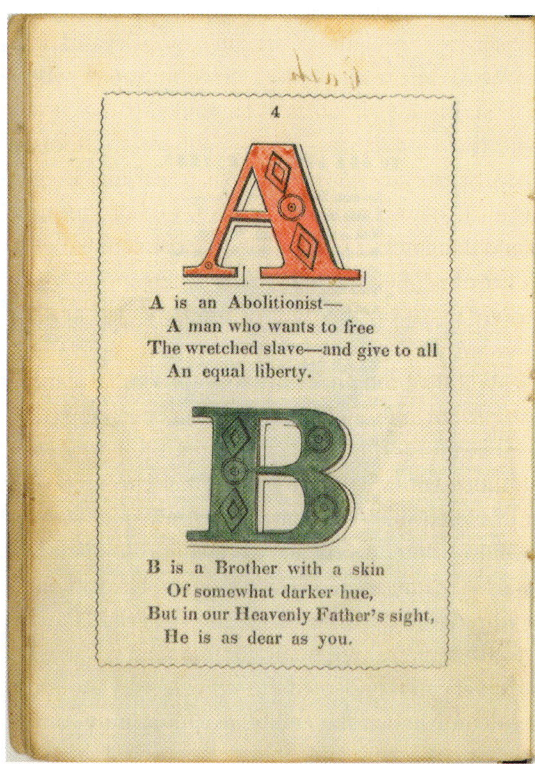
4

A is an Abolitionist—
A man who wants to free
The wretched slave—and give to all
An equal liberty.

B is a Brother with a skin
Of somewhat darker hue,
But in our Heavenly Father's sight,
He is as dear as you.

Much to the horror of white Southerners, abolitionists printed grammar and spelling textbooks, such as this one, to carry their messages to young people.

Appeals such as these, and the membership of the New England Anti-Slavery Society, nearly a quarter of whose members were black, signaled publicly that abolitionists had shifted both the nature of their critique of slavery and the method by which they explained that critique to the world. "Slavery is a crime," **William Lloyd Garrison** thundered, and "anything which serves as a substitute for the immediate and absolute emancipation of slavery is delusive, cruel, and dangerous." The NEASS became the model for the national **American Anti-Slavery Society** (AASS), organized by Garrison in 1833 with immediate abolition as its core message. The AASS organized local chapters, sent speakers who traveled the country preaching against the evils of slavery, published narratives of slave life, and eventually appealed directly to Congress for national action on the subject. Garrison, in particular, pursued immediate emancipation with a unique vigor and effectiveness through his newspaper *The Liberator*. By 1837 the AASS counted more than 1,000 chapters with 100,000 members, though abolitionists probably never comprised more than 5 percent of the northern population. Between 1833 and 1838, Britain ended slavery in its Caribbean colonies, emancipating 800,000 people. Garrison and others drew courage from the British, and later French, decision to abandon slavery, and they hoped that American leaders would soon follow course.

Garrison's stridency divided the abolition and reform communities as well as the country more broadly. His methods and his message, especially his pursuit of full racial equality for black Americans, frightened even some fellow antislavery activists. **Theodore Dwight Weld**, a convert to Garrisonian immediatism, initiated a series of discussions about slavery at Lane Theological Seminary in Cincinnati, Ohio, just across the river from Kentucky slavery. Emulating Garrison's racial egalitarianism, Weld and his students took up work in the city's black neighborhoods, where according to Weld, "if I ate in the City it was at *their* tables. If I attended parties it was *theirs—weddings—Funerals—theirs—Religious—meetings—theirs*—Sabbath schools—Bible classes—theirs." After the AASS began advocating immediate abolition, even other antislavery activists turned against them. Catherine Beecher, one of the most prominent reformers in the nation and daughter of Lyman Beecher, condemned abolitionists as "neither peaceful nor Christian." Beecher, like many others in American society, saw immediate abolition as an attack on the right of property, perhaps the central ideological component of New World capitalism.

In fact, radical abolitionists more typically brought down a reign of social isolation, expulsion, and violence on themselves. Sarah and Angelina Grimké had been forced to relocate from South Carolina to Pennsylvania as they made their opposition to slavery publicly known and opponents of abolition continually interrupted their meetings with force. The most notorious incident of violence, though hardly the only one, was the murder of **Elijah Lovejoy**, an abolitionist printer, who had relocated to Illinois in the mid-1830s. Despite warnings and attacks on his shop Lovejoy continued his work until a mob killed him. Despite the commitment to pacifism that most evangelicals maintained, Lovejoy's death and other acts like it radicalized many abolitionists.

Garrison, Weld, and the Grimké sisters all represented the white face of abolition. Well known and well financed, they demonstrated the ability of 19th-century Americans to see beyond racial differences. But enslaved people themselves proved the most effective opponents of slavery, none more so than **Frederick Douglass**, the most famous

*Douglass' Monthly* was one of several papers that Douglass edited in his lifetime. All were widely read and all devoted themselves to the destruction of slavery and the advancement of racial equality.

and most rhetorically skillful of his generation. Born Frederick Bailey on a Maryland plantation, Douglass learned to read and in 1838, at the age of 20, he escaped and ultimately made his way to Rochester, New York, where he threw himself into the work of abolition. Articulate in print and speech with a commanding physical presence, Douglass traveled the country to lecture to abolition societies. In Rochester he started his own paper, which circulated across the North. Douglass's narratives of his life sold tens of thousands of copies in the United States and abroad, and like other slave narratives at the time it introduced readers firsthand to the horrors of slavery.

Black activists targeted the scheme, popular among whites around the country, that slaves should be freed and then deported from the country. This was the platform of the **American Colonization Society** (ACS), which since its founding in 1817 continued to attract national leaders to its ranks. During the 1830s and 1840s the ACS counted among its members the most influential politicians of both regions and parties, including **Daniel Webster**, **Henry Clay**, and **Stephen Douglas**. Colonization generated intense opposition from black Americans. **James McCune Smith**, a New York City physician with an interracial practice, led the campaign against the plan. Black opposition to colonization in the 1820s helped drive Garrison and other white abolitionists to support immediate abolition.

## Women's Rights

Like the abolitionists and evangelical reformers more generally, advocates of women's rights drew inspiration and legitimacy by connecting their movement with predecessors in Europe. **Lydia Maria Child**, one of the most influential U.S. women's rights reformers, wrote biographies of an Englishwoman and two French women who provided models of active, virtuous womanhood. American women drew special inspiration from British author **Mary Wollstonecraft**'s *A Vindication of the Rights of Woman* (1792). Wollstonecraft's manifesto rejected the notion of natural differences between men and women and called for full gender equality. Women's efforts to challenge their second-tier status represented as profound a change as abolition. As one historian has noted, "to question sexual hierarchy and distinct spheres of gender was to question a pillar of traditional Christian society more basic and pervasive than the Sabbath."

The confidence to challenge that basic "pillar" came from women's success in other reform fields. According to a Boston minister in 1836, "it is to female influence and exertion that many of our best schemes of charity are due." Women played a crucial role in the abolition movement, perhaps the essential one. Many female reformers toiled first in the abolition movement and then in the 1830s moved into women's rights. Beyond the reform movement women began playing a more public role in formal politics. Whigs capitalized on their connections with moderate reforms such as temperance and protection of the Sabbath to make explicit appeals for women's support. Although women could not vote, party leaders believed that wives influenced their husband's votes and that more public support would only help the party. In the 1844 and 1848 presidential campaigns both Whigs and Democrats incorporated women into rallies and other events. The closest study of this process reveals no essentially female politics; rather, women's beliefs appeared, like men's, to be most directly affected by their region and their class position. Southern women, for instance, supported slavery and helped steer both parties toward a stricter line against emancipation.

This statue, located today in the rotunda of the U.S. Capitol, immortalizes three leaders of the fight for women's rights in the United States—Elizabeth Cady Stanton, Susan B. Anthony, and Lucretia Mott—and conveys the as-yet unfinished nature of the struggle.

Women themselves did not agree on reform. A famous debate between Catherine Beecher, part of a large and influential northern family, and Angelina Grimké clarified the challenges facing female reformers. In 1837 Beecher published her *Essay on Slavery and Abolitionism, with Reference to the Duty of American Females,* directed at Grimké' s abolition work. In it she declared that "petitions to congress, in reference to the official duties of legislators, seem, IN ALL CASES, to fall entirely without the sphere of female duty." Grimké responded to Beecher by articulating a strict egalitarian creed: "Whatever it is morally right for man to do . . . it is morally right for women to do." Grimké boldly proclaimed that "I believe it is women's right to have a voice in all the laws and regulations by which she is to be *governed,* whether in Church or State." Beyond participation, she asserted women's right to rule as well, "just as much right to sit upon the throne of England, or in the Presidential chair of the United States." Even though a woman had just assumed the English throne—Queen Victoria was crowned in 1837—the active role played by the Grimkés, and other women, generated increasing criticism in the late 1830s and eventually produced deep splits in the reform movement.

Frustrated by the conservative reaction of otherwise reform-minded men, a group of women in western New York organized a convention in 1848 to consider women's rights. The convention's "Declaration of Sentiments," modeled after the Declaration of Independence, listed the infringements on women's rights and called for change, including the right to vote. Elizabeth Cady Stanton, one of the convention organizers and one of the most important leaders of the 19th-century women's movement, drafted the declaration. Stanton accepted the need to sacrifice women's exceptionalism to further the causes she advocated, writing in 1842 that "I am in favour of political action, & the organization of a third party as the most efficient way of calling forth & directing action." Stanton declared that only Frederick Douglass, 1 of 32 men and the only person of color to attend the Seneca Falls Conference, could really understand what it meant to be disenfranchised. Douglass advocated strongly for women's full rights—his newspaper's masthead boldly declared "All Rights for All!"

Because many white and upper- or middle-class American women believed their responsibility was to raise moral children and preserve the domestic space, they regarded female public activism on politically contentious topics as inappropriate. But for other women the belief that females possessed a stronger innate moral sense compelled them to participate in the antislavery movement. They believed that women's greater respect for moral behavior obligated them to address slavery, the chief sin in the nation, even if the act of doing so, which required organizing, fundraising, and petitioning, brought them into fuller participation in the public world of men. The female reformers of this period encountered contradictions that have challenged American women to this day. Embracing women's distinctiveness could both empower and isolate—women used their special position to make real reforms and helped blunt the worst side effects of early industrialization. However, by endorsing women's difference they also ensured that women remain separated from men, especially as more formal politics overtook reform efforts after the Civil War.

GLOBAL PASSAGES

## Atlantic Evangelical Networks

Following his success in the United States in the 1830s, Charles Grandison Finney traveled and preached in Britain, where his *Lectures on Revivals of Religion* had sold 80,000 copies. His fellow American minister, James Caughey, claimed 20,000 conversions during his first visit. Both gained notoriety among members of the dissenting sects in Britain. All through the colonial period a reciprocal flow of culture and ideas moved back and forth between the home country and British colonies abroad. The role of British ministers in the United States and the journeys of American evangelicals through Britain in the 1830s and 1840s demonstrated that this Atlantic exchange continued to flourish after independence.

One of the most popular itinerant Methodists in the United States came from Ireland in 1819. John Newland Maffit, a theatrical and charismatic preacher, traveled continuously throughout America for nearly two decades, gaining fame as the man who brought President-elect **William Henry Harrison** to conversion in 1840. Partly because of the deep underlying cultural similarities and because of sufficient distance from the Revolution and the War of 1812, American evangelicals felt comfortable identifying themselves closely with the goals and means of their coreligionists in Britain. "England and America must love each other," declared a Methodist leader, because "they are the nations by whom God will work." The United States represented an important destination for British clergy seeking a location for missionary work. The size of the young republic, the relatively scarcity of its religious

## Making a Moral Society

A wide range of citizens participated in evangelical reforms, but the active support of a handful of wealthy elites ensured that the movement operated on a national, even global, basis. New York businessmen Arthur and Lewis Tappan occupied the pinnacle of this community. Arthur imported silk, and at its peak his business grossed a million dollars per year. He made huge donations to reform organizations from 1825 to1837, when the combination of a devastating fire and the national recession bankrupted him. During that period he contributed more to evangelical causes than anyone else in the nation, as he helped found, fund, or manage the American Tract Society, the American Education Society, the American Bible Society, and the Home Missionary Society, among others. His brother Lewis showed equal enthusiasm to bring a new Christian ethos to business and used his financial success to bankroll new spiritual enterprises.

Although there is no doubt that the Tappans cherished their faith—both gave enormous sums of money, time, and energy to propagate a variety of reforms—it is institutions, and the ample land all drew evangelicals to the New World. These ministers brought with them an intimate knowledge of revivals and an enthusiasm that made them popular visitors in America.

Unlike the established churches in the United States, which had been significantly weakened and in some places replaced by the Revolution, the Anglican Church remained an entrenched part of British life in the 1830s. Anglicans regarded the Methodists and Baptists who led most of the American revivals as "dissenting" sects. British Calvinists, Congregationalists, and others also emulated American practices. Despite concern about its theatrical elements the revival became a key feature of English and especially Welsh religious life. In 1839–1840, some 20,000 new members joined Independent Welsh churches as a result of the influence of Finney's revival model. Scottish Presbyterians likewise applied New World traditions to good effect. The circulation of British and American evangelicals within the Atlantic basin demonstrated the existence of a remarkably broad community of faith. Catholic missionaries had long celebrated the global reach of their church, with missionaries in every corner of the globe. But the evangelical Protestant networks that stretched across the Atlantic in the 1830s and 1840s revealed a uniquely Anglo-American connection and demonstrated how the larger social changes sought by evangelical reformers rested on global movements and ideas.

- In what ways did Britons and Americans share their faiths?
- How does the transatlantic appeal of evangelicalism reshape the traditional narrative that emphasizes America's unique experience with religious freedom?

also clear that the reforms they advocated made good business sense as well. Temperance offers the clearest example of how reforms often met the needs of both the new business elite and the evangelicals. As employers adopted new technologies, including clocks and steam-driven machinery, they expected workers to increase their own efficiency. Both owners and reformers targeted the old tradition of morning beer breaks, which artisans had retained from European cultures. U.S. prohibition also ensured that workingmen did not arrive late or incapacitated because of late nights at the bar. Job seekers at the Rochester Woolen Mills, in upstate New York, were told that they "must be of moral and temperate habits." Because workers increasingly resided on their own, away from the residences of factory owners, increased church attendance and religious programs gave owners a way to monitor employees after hours. The location of reform churches in upstate New York revealed the complex relationship between reform and the market. Many of the leading reform churches clustered along the Erie Canal and the emerging railroad lines, which provided better channels of communication, promoted urban growth, and attracted businessmen who appreciated the new religiosity that ensured more reliable workers.

**STUDY QUESTIONS FOR NORTHERN REFORM**

1. **What explains the militancy of abolitionists after 1831?**
2. **On what grounds did American women argue for greater freedom?**
3. **How did the various reform movements intersect with one another?**

# SOUTHERN REFORM

Southern evangelicals faced a far greater challenge than their northern coreligionists. Because slaveholders demanded absolute obedience from their slaves, they built a deeply conservative society. Any challenge to hierarchy and tradition threatened to undermine the foundation of that society. Despite this hurdle southern evangelical reformers confronted what they perceived as problems in southern society. Most evangelicals strongly supported temperance and denounced the personal violence that characterized the system of southern honor. A handful of brave reformers spoke out against slavery, but opponents often drove them from the region. Southern antislavery reformers were replaced by a new breed of thinkers who advocated for a more Christian slavery. Regardless of the measures they advocated, southern reformers proceeded more cautiously than their northern brethren. And, although southern reformers often corresponded or met with their northern or European peers, the emerging political culture of sectionalism curtailed cooperation across the regional divide.

## Sin, Salvation, and Honor

The dominant value system in the white South prior to the Second Great Awakening emphasized an ethos of honor inherited from ancient models. With little incentive to scrutinize their society many white Southerners clung to this secular value system in the face of mounting tensions within their society. The evangelical movement in the South of the 1820s and 1830s expressly challenged prevailing values. Evangelicals sought to replace the standing system in which a person's wealth and status determined one's worth with a system in which one's piety and moral purity determined rank. Attracting followers proved difficult if people had something to lose, as revealed by the response of a Kentucky sheriff who treated his local Methodist preacher well but who refused to commit to the church because "his worldly prospects were good, and he would not give up all for Christ." Southern evangelicals advocated many of the same reforms as their northerner counterparts. Hundreds of southern communities established local temperance societies, for example. Like Northerners, Southerners feared the effect of alcohol on families and society, but most of all, as one evangelical noted, because it was "one grand hindrance of the success of the gospel." Evangelicals supported Bible and tract societies, Sunday schools, home and foreign missions, and efforts to help prisoners and the disabled.

Southern women played a key role in the evangelical movement and reform, but they rarely extended their work into the broader public women's rights movement found in the North. Southern women tended to focus their efforts on the individual rather than societal level, they organized locally but not nationally, and increasingly by the 1840s they sought reforms that promoted the stability of the slaveholding South. For example, in Petersburg, Virginia, a mill town south of Richmond, evangelical women organized Sunday schools, an Education Society, a Young Ladies' Missionary Society, a Married Ladies' Missionary Society, a Tract Distribution Society, and a Ladies' Benevolent Society. In addition to real benefits for the community, local and private systems allowed community elites to retain control over aid recipients. To receive aid those in need had to pass the scrutiny of the "ladies." The insistence of southern evangelicals to pursue reform while respecting the hierarchy of the conservative South reveals how religious revivals and the development of a distinct southern political identity developed simultaneous throughout the 1830s, 1840s, and 1850s.

## Pro-Slavery Reform

The antislavery attitude of early evangelicals in the late 18th and early 19th centuries inhibited the larger reform movement in the South. Early evangelicals sometimes criticized slaveholding, but more often they sought ways to accommodate their religious faith with their racial beliefs. Over time, articulating a pro-slavery Christianity provided one way to claim both piety and respectability. The central evangelical reform project in the South became the **Mission to the Slaves**. Evangelical slaveholders came to regard the act of ministering to slaves as the purest expression of their faith.

Modeling their work on that of West Indian planters who pursued a similar movement in the 1810s, the Mission to the Slaves aimed to spur masters to improve the physical treatment of slaves with the threat of church or social sanctions for those who failed to do so. In addition, the mission advocated for laws to protect slaves from cruel treatment. Under southern law, slaves could not legally marry—although they formed de facto marriages—and evangelicals regarded this as a gross violation of the proper relationship between adult men and women who bore and raised children together. Female evangelicals also advocated protection of female slaves from sexual exploitation. The other main reform of the Mission to the Slaves fulfilled a basic Protestant obligation—ensuring that every person could read the Gospel for himself or herself. Because of the circulation of abolitionist propaganda in the mails and the power of literacy, southern states made it a crime to teach slaves to read. Evangelical reformers built Sunday schools and worked with individual masters to persuade them that limited literacy posed no threat.

As slaveholders increasingly found a home within evangelical churches, they articulated a more individualized and more paternalistic social order. They aimed especially to control those African Americans who converted to Christianity in large numbers for the first time and drew strength from their new faith. Southern evangelicals, by then firmly supporting the morality of slavery, used the occurrence of several major slave rebellions in the 1820s and 1830s to argue for the necessity of conversion. To pacify slaveholders' concerns that evangelical reforms would undermine control of their slaves, evangelicals emphasized that converted slaves would be more obedient. According to Basil Manly, "the dissemination of moral truth will always be found at once the cheapest & most effective support of law & order, the most certain check of incendiarism & turbulence."

Just as the secular pro-slavery theorists turned toward classical history and modern science to defend slavery, evangelical slaveholders reframed their slaveholding in a global perspective. Most white Southerners assumed that because American slaves had been sold out of Africa, those who remained in Africa would still be slaves, but the slaves of non-Christians. Combined with the myths and distortions of African life common among 19th-century Americans, evangelicals argued that leaving slaves in Africa only ensured that they would spend eternity in torment. At least as the slaves of Christians—who had an obligation to expose their slaves to the Gospel—African Americans would be assured eternal life.

## Nat Turner and Afro-Christianity

Similarities between West African practices and Christianity, including an emphasis on water as a conduit of spirituality, helped draw new worshippers to the faith; rivers, sacred places in African religions, became baptismal pools. The importance of burial practices and the belief that death brought a "homecoming," as well as a three-part hierarchy of gods that resembled the Christian trinity, made Christianity intelligible to West Africans. Muslim slaves brought to America in the colonial era by the French, Spanish, and the British provided another bridge between faiths. Malinke slaves in Spanish St. Augustine and Sengambians and northern Nigerians in Louisiana left ample evidence that they arrived in the New World already practicing Islam. The close kinship between

The more informal and emotionally expressive religious practices adopted by African Americans alienated some white Christians but gave black Christians a distinctive and rich spiritual practice.

the two faiths and the blended nature of Islam in West Africa ensured that New World Muslims could be expected to understand and perhaps absorb aspects of Christianity without much difficulty.

At least a quarter of all southern blacks participated in churches by the end of the 1850s and most of these would have been biracial churches. Although blacks sat in segregated pews, they received egalitarian treatment in many respects. Records reveal that mixed-race churches held blacks to the same moral standards as whites and disciplined them for the same reasons—drunkenness, lying, adultery, and other failures of evangelical belief. But these same churches never overtly challenged white assumptions of racial superiority. Following the Civil War blacks across the South split from the biracial churches and built their own institutions. This move may suggest dissatisfaction with the churches as they existed before the war but also reveals the existence of a spiritual community. Certainly the body of Afro-Christian hymns and spirituals that emerged at this period shows a community asserting its solidarity and searching for ways to resist the dehumanization of slavery.

O brothers, don't get weary
O brothers, don't get weary
O brothers, don't get weary
We're waiting for the Lord
We'll land on Canaan's shore
We'll land on Canaan's shore,
When we land on Canaan's shore,
We'll meet forever more.

Effort by slaveholders to control Christianity and African American belief generally failed. By the 1850s southern evangelical churches, particularly the Baptists and Methodists, had become major institutions in black American life. Instead of obedience Afro-Christian theology stressed the equality of all people before God, the necessity of discipline for a people held in bondage, and the promise of eventual deliverance. In their creative use of Christianity black evangelicals echoed the efforts of enslaved peoples in French and Portuguese colonies, particularly Haiti and Brazil, where a syncretistic Afro-Catholicism sustained generations of slaves in opposition to French, Portuguese, and later Brazilian slaveholders.

In the United States, evangelical religion's role in spurring resistance to slavery burst into public view with **Nat Turner**'s rebellion in Southampton County, Virginia. Turner's skills and literacy earned him the respect of local whites who allowed him to preach to their slaves. In 1831 Turner built a network of loyal men and launched a bloody uprising that killed nearly 60 whites and sent the state into a panic. Although the militia dispersed the rebels and eventually apprehended and executed Turner, the widespread and disciplined organization among slaves on diverse plantations brought home to whites the deepest fears they had harbored since the Haitian Revolution at the end of the 18th century. To fearful whites he seemed to portend the violence to come if they did not improve their treatment of slaves.

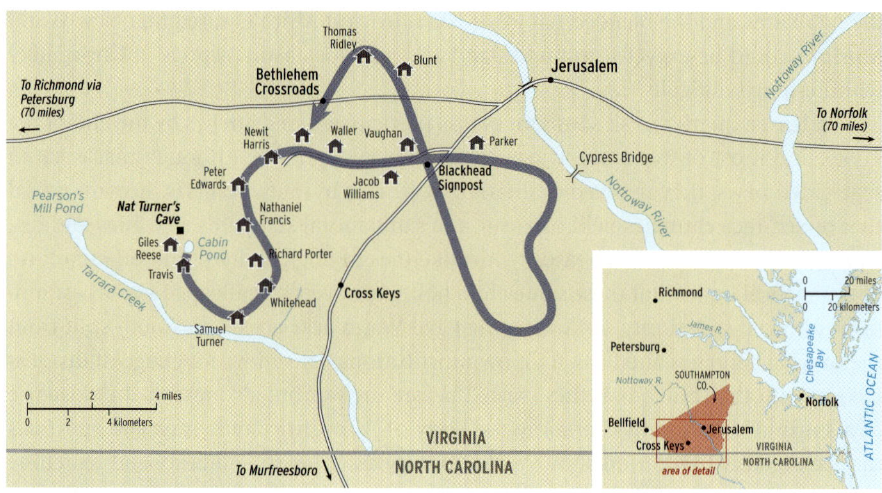


▲ **Map 12.2**

**Nat Turner's Route in Southampton County, Virginia, 1831** Nat Turner and his band moved from house to house in an attempt to contain news of their rebellion. The violence of their actions marked a trail in blood through Southampton County and seared itself into the mind of the white South.

Denmark Vesey preceded Turner but had less success. According to the charges against him, Vesey organized a multiethnic band of slaves and free blacks in Charleston in 1822 and planned a revolt. Captured before the plan could be sprung, investigators discovered religious leadership throughout the plot, including Morris Brown, an African Methodist Episcopal pastor. Vesey himself worked as a lay leader in the AME church and used scripture to draw supporters. According to one deposition against him, "his general conversation was about religion which he would apply to slavery, as for instance, he would speak of the creation of the world, in which he would say all men had equal rights, blacks as well as whites." **"Gullah" Jack Pritchard** surfaced as a leader in the Vesey conspiracy along with another AME member who also maintained a reputation in Charleston as a conjurer. One commonality among all the leaders of slave rebellions in the 1820s and 1830s was their use of religion to radicalize their communities and their positions of religious leadership to mobilize those communities.

## Southern Antislavery Reformers

Nat Turner's Rebellion occurred the same year that the abolitionist William Lloyd Garrison began publishing the *Liberator*, a confluence that most white Southerners did not regard as coincidental. Fearing additional slave rebellions, white Southerners quashed all criticism of slavery after 1831. James Henry Hammond's "gag rule" prevented congressional discussion of abolition from 1836 to 1844 and federal Postmasters before and after these dates prevented the circulation of abolitionist material in the southern mails. Sarah and Angelina Grimké, born into a wealthy Charleston slaveholding family, earned fame as the most prominent southern antislavery reformers. After a visit north and exposure to Quakers, Sarah embraced their faith, especially their opposition to slavery. Converting her sister, they challenged the very foundation of South Carolina society in their calls for emancipation. Isolated and silenced at home, they fled their family and their region, settling in Philadelphia, the leading Quaker city in the United States. After hearing Garrison speak, Angelina pushed beyond the staid boundaries of the Quaker world and entered antislavery work with a reformist zeal. Her *An Appeal to the Christian Women of the South* (1836) demanded emancipation on the grounds of Christianity and argued that the millennium would come only after slavery had been destroyed.

**David Walker**, another exile from the South, proved even more dangerous than the Grimké sisters. Born to an enslaved father and free black mother in North Carolina, Walker remained in the South until the mid-1820s, when he moved to Boston and immersed himself in the abolition movement. After writing briefly for a variety of journals Walker penned and published *An Appeal to the Coloured Citizens of the World*. Electrifying in its language and vigorous in its argument, the document created a firestorm of criticism in both the North and the South; even many abolitionists found its frank call for resistance too vigorous. Walker, flatly denying the legitimacy of slavery, asserted the universal rights of all people to freedom. He called on the "candid and unprejudiced of the world, to search the pages of history diligently, and see if [any group of people] ever treated a set of human beings, as the white Christians of America do us, the blacks, or Africans."

Walker drafted a brief global history of slavery, running from biblical and classical examples to the role played by European colonizers of the New World who created plantation slavery. Walker's "appeal" sought an international audience. He compared the plight of African Americans to other subjugated peoples—Native Americans, the Greeks, the Irish, and the Jews. The range of his learning—from ancient Egypt to the modern Spanish empire—and his use of these examples to make his argument reflected that black Americans could and did educate themselves to a degree that would have surprised most whites at the time.

In Boston, Walker worked within the larger maritime community. Since the early days of European exploration of the oceans black men had worked as sailors, and they remained, in the 1830s and 1840s, among the most worldly and most important members of the African diasporic community in the Americas. Keen to rebut charges that blacks were incompetent to rule themselves, Walker argued that "the inhuman system of *slavery*, is the *source* from which most of our miseries proceed." Like most antislavery evangelicals Walker condemned the hypocrisy of Christians holding fellow Christians in bondage. Again and again he warned "white Christians" against their continuing sanction of this most diabolical of evils. He closed with the ominous warning that "Americans may be as vigilant as they please, but they cannot be vigilant enough for the Lord, neither can they hide themselves, where he will not find and bring them out." Walker himself was not vigilant enough, despite death threats against him; less than a year after publishing the *Appeal* he was found dead outside his office in Boston.

**STUDY QUESTIONS FOR SOUTHERN REFORM**

1. **In what ways did southern reform resemble northern efforts? How were they different?**
2. **How did black Southerners conceptualize and experience evangelical Christianity?**

# CHALLENGES TO THE SPIRIT OF THE AGE

In many respects, the era from the late 1820s to the early 1850s can be defined as much by the role of religion as by economic change, geographic growth, and political development. The growth of evangelical Protestantism preoccupied the lives of many Americans through this period, produced social reforms that changed the lives of millions, and helped propel the sectional divisions that produced the Civil War and emancipation. At the same time, however, the rise of an increasingly secular culture, expressed through novels, newspapers, and the work of mass political parties matched the spiritual movements of the day. Some of this cultural work faced east, engaged with European questions expressed in largely British and continental idioms. In other cases authors self-consciously rejected older models and sought to build a uniquely American culture. Much of it was condemned by religious figures because of what they regarded as vulgar content or expression. Most frustrating for the traditionalists was the persistent popularity and wide reach of these new forms of media and communication. Americans were building their first truly national culture.

## Emerson, Thoreau, and the American Soul

Ralph Waldo Emerson began his professional life as a Unitarian minister but left the ministry in the midst of the tumult in the early 1830s. He wrote essays and criticism over the next several decades, patronized younger authors such as Henry David Thoreau and Margaret Fuller, and pushed for broad changes in American life. Unlike most of the evangelicals Emerson sought to reform the American mind. He celebrated a vigorous individualism, articulated most fully in his famous essay "Self-Reliance," in which he encouraged readers to reject tradition. "A foolish consistency is the hobgoblin of little minds, adored by statesmen and philosophers and divines," he wrote famously. Emerson's advice provided reassurance for the new classes that seized opportunities created by industrialization.

Henry David Thoreau attempted to live this philosophy when he retreated to a cabin outside Concord, Massachusetts, for two years. Unfortunately he failed as a farmer and survived through the largesse of friends who stopped by with gifts of food. Although Thoreau could not remove himself entirely from the modernizing world he so distrusted, his volume chronicling the experience, *Walden*, pushed readers to think critically about the costs of the rampant materialism that sustained the dynamic economic growth of the era. *Walden* also represented a challenge to traditional Anglo-American ideas about land use. Thoreau did not seek to maximize the land and encouraged a respectful appreciation for man's dependence on the natural world.

Thoreau and Emerson became associated with the philosophy of transcendentalism, an American variant of European Romanticism. Turning away from the rationalism of the Enlightenment, transcendentalists desired to know the world through emotion and intuition. Although it was often expressed in obscure prose, this philosophy, like Emerson's writing in general, proved compatible with trends toward democratization in American society. Transcendentalists put little value on formal education and degrees. Instead, experience and intimate contact with the natural world earned their praise. As Thoreau's experience indicates, their philosophy called for action rather than talk. Both writers supported abolition and other social reforms, but neither appreciated the staid evangelical tone of the movement. Emerson denounced the

WALDEN;

OR,

LIFE IN THE WOODS.

BY HENRY D. THOREAU,

AUTHOR OF "A WEEK ON THE CONCORD AND MERRIMACK RIVERS."

I do not propose to write an ode to dejection, but to brag as lustily as chanticleer in the morning, standing on his roost, if only to wake my neighbors up. — Page 92.

BOSTON:

TICKNOR AND FIELDS.

M DCCC LIV.

Thoreau's cabin and the image of man's relation to wildness articulated by *Walden* served for many readers as a counterbalance to the industrializing and urbanizing trends of the early 19th century.

hypocrisy that blinded would-be reformers from the full implications of their morality, demanding that "goodness must have some edge to it."

## The First Mass Culture

Steam power and industrialization, in addition to improving the efficiency of American manufacturing, lowered the price of leisure and recreation items. Printers began producing newspapers in greater volume at lower cost. In the early 1830s thousands of "penny presses" sprouted in every city and many small towns throughout the country. These newspapers distinguished themselves from their predecessors because, rather than relying on subsidies from political parties, they sought a mass readership. To accomplish this goal, reporters began writing "stories," largely human interest tales about murders, robberies, and rapes. **James Gordon Bennett**, the editor of the *New York Herald*, the most successful of the new breed of newspaper, realized that the average readers "were more ready to seek six columns of the details of a brutal murder, or the testimony of a divorce case, or the trial of a divine for improprieties of conduct, than the same amount of words poured forth by the genius of the noblest author of the times." Serialized fiction also began to appear, largely stories of romance and duplicity aimed at female readers.

Alongside the theater, which continued to offer performances of Shakespeare and other European classics, arose a much rowdier and uniquely American form of popular entertainment, minstrelsy. Minstrel shows began in northern cities, where white

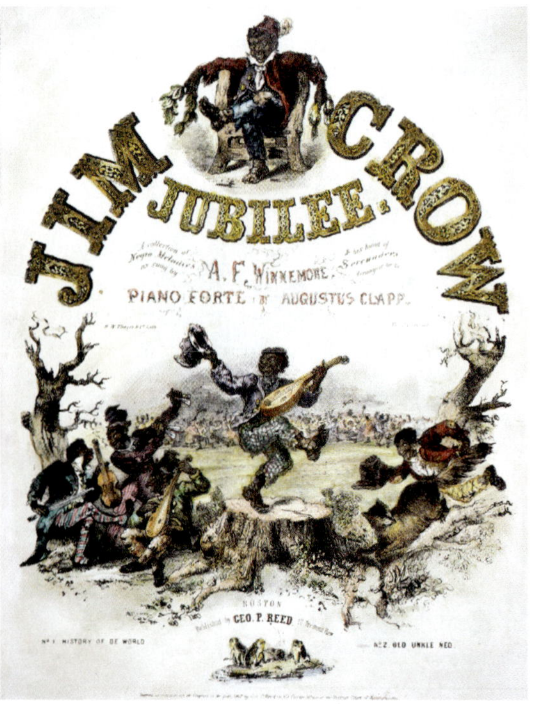


The degrading caricatures enacted in minstrel shows drew large white audiences and imprinted on many Northerners erroneous but lasting images of black life.

male performers blackened their faces and imitated what they imagined to be black behavior. The shows became enormously popular in New York, Boston, and other major cities, with a repertoire of songs and stock characters. **Stephen Foster**, America's first major songwriter, gained his fame penning minstrel tunes such as "Camptown Races" and "Oh! Susanna," though Foster later wrote songs that celebrated more complex black characters. Minstrel shows succeeded partly because of the way they transgressed boundaries, with whites imitating, celebrating, and lampooning blacks all at once. The all-male audiences and the vigorous physicality of the performances transformed the theaters into showcases for masculine expression. **Walt Whitman**, the bard of the common man, regularly patronized the Bowery Theater, one of New York City's most famous minstrel venues. He described the crowd there as "a vast sea of upturned faces and red flannel shirt, extending its roaring and turbid waves close up to the foot-lights on either side, clipping in the orchestra and dashing furiously against the boxes."

## The American Renaissance

The emergence of a group of American writers around midcentury—Emerson and Thoreau in essays, **Nathaniel Hawthorne** and **Herman Melville** in fiction, and **Edgar Allen Poe**, Walt Whitman, and **Emily Dickinson** in poetry—signaled for many Americans the maturation of their culture. In their settings, their language, and their themes, these authors made the United States a part of world literature. At the same time, however, they engaged in a dialogue with their peers across the Atlantic. They read and wrote with one eye on the European authors in whose traditions they worked—and European authors reciprocated the feeling. British novelist Anthony Trollope referred to Hawthorne as "a brother novelist very much greater than myself."

Hawthorne and Melville, in particular, wrote literature that reflected universal themes. Hawthorne went back in time, rather than far afield, to craft his most memorable work. In his *The Scarlet Letter* he used New England's witchcraft trials of late 17th century to explore contemporary morality. Melville first gained notoriety for a series of novels, *Typee, Omoo,* and *Redjacket,* drawn from his adventures as a young sailor in the Pacific Ocean. The novels blended travelogue and ethnography and provided detailed analyses of the lives of island inhabitants. Melville's most ambitious novel, *Moby Dick,* addressed universal questions of power, revenge, and madness. Nonetheless, Melville's work offers insights into mid-19th-century America. The ship that carries the whaling party in *Moby Dick,* the *Pequod,* carried a remarkably diverse crew, with Indian, African, and South Seas harpooners, white men and black, all bound together by their shared domicile and profession. Melville's imaginary ship mirrored the real-life diversity of America and the difficulty of reconciling so many competing interests and contradictory philosophies in one nation.

Melville's capacious imagination and welcome fictional embrace of diverse ethnic and racial types reflected a broad-mindedness common among this generation of writers. A number of writers, including Whitman, Dickinson, and Poe, took inspiration from what they called Oriental tales, which they read as a "symbol of the unfettered

Walt Whitman's poetry celebrated the physical and emotional energy unleashed by American growth in the 1840s and 1850s.

imagination." In many of his poems Poe adopted the form and message of Asian literature—especially in his use of visionaries and visionary moments—including borrowing from the Koran and Islamic practices. At the same time this trio of writers pioneered a distinct American poetry. Whitman advanced this project the furthest. His use of free verse, without either rhyme or meter, his frank sexuality, and his vigorous endorsement of the rough and authentic America distinguished his work. Rather than draw classical parallels or craft aspirational literature, Whitman celebrated the prosaic democracy of America, as in his most famous poem, "Song of Myself," where he writes:

I am of old and young, of the foolish as much as the wise,
Regardless of others, even regardful of others,
Maternal as well as paternal, a child as well as a man,
Sutff'd with the stuff that is coarse and stuff'd with the stuff that is fine,
One of the Nation of many nations, the smallest the same and the largest the same,

. . .

A learner with the simplest, a teacher of the thoughtfullest,
A novice beginning yet experient of myriads of seasons,
Of every hue and caste am I, of every rank and religion,
A farmer, mechanic, artist, gentlemen, sailor, quaker,
Prisoner, fancy-man, rowdy, lawyer, physician, priest.

Emily Dickinson, born in 1830, remained virtually unknown throughout her life. She remained in her parent's home in Amherst, Massachusetts, which she rarely left. She published only a handful of anonymous poems during her lifetime, but the posthumous discovery of her work has inspired fellow writers for the last century and a half. Moving beyond Whitman's experimentation with free verse, Dickinson unshackled every constraint, reimagining meter, rhyme, capitalization, grammar, and punctuation. Her work demonstrated new capacities in language that poets continue to explore. Dickinson professed her understanding of poetry in physical terms, ones that Whitman and Thoreau would well have understood: "If I read a book and it makes my whole body so cold no fire ever can warm me, I know *that* is poetry."

## Politics as Gospel

The vitality and diversity of American culture in the 1830s and 1840s could be seen in the political system as well. Senators, congressmen, and presidents recognized the power and importance of the reform movements initiated by evangelicals, but they could not control it. The new issues of the 1830s and 1840s, especially the transformation of artisans into workers and the rapid commercialization of the national economy, spurred the rise of working men's parties in northeastern cities, but these lasted only a few years and rarely influenced policy. As slavery began to assume greater national significance, antislavery reformers organized political parties under different names—the Liberty Party in 1840 and 1844 and the Free Soil Party in 1848—that likewise failed to take root. These failures, however, should not obscure the extent to which the nation's political culture reflected the larger dynamism and unpredictability of the era. The promise and the possibilities represented by these short-lived political parties and by the broader rise and fall of the Whig Party encouraged Americans to take politics seriously.

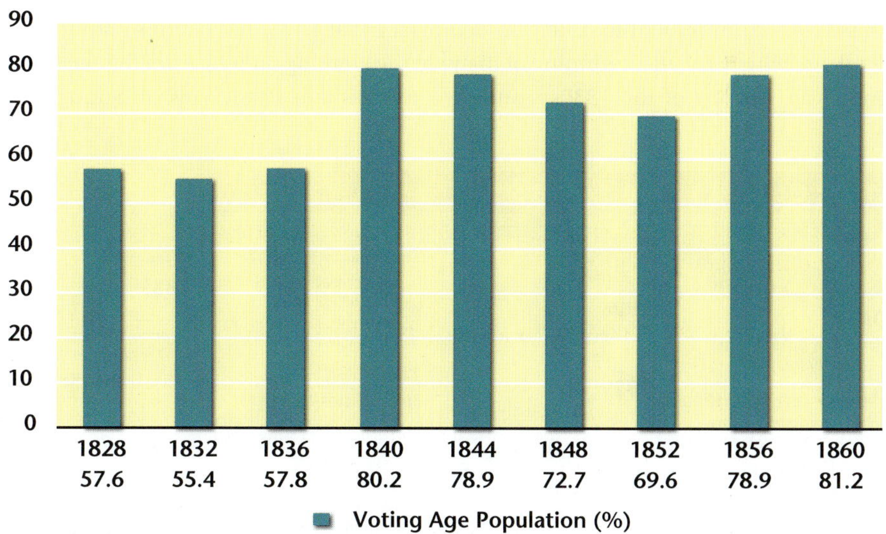


**Figure 12.3**

**Voter turnout at presidential elections, 1828–1860** As states made more men eligible to vote both Democrats and Whigs mobilized supporters in huge numbers. The political controversies of the 1850s further ensured that voting rates remained very high.

The Whig Party emerged as the main opposition to Democratic dominance. The Whigs coalesced around their shared antipathy for **Andrew Jackson**—they took their name from the English political party that opposed absolutist kings. By 1840—the first year the Whigs won the White House—the party had emerged with both a guiding ideology and an official organization. Whigs feared that Jackson had dangerously empowered the executive branch at the expense of the representative parts of government. Thus, the Richmond *Whig* defined their supporters as those who "prefer liberty to tyranny—who support privilege against prerogative—the rights and immunities of the people . . . against the predominance of the Crown or Executive power." Clay led the party during its two decades in existence, and his "American system" drew the support of Whig businessmen who wanted the federal and state governments to sponsor the construction of the infrastructure—roads, bridges, canals, and railroads—on which private enterprise could build American markets and cities.

The Whig Party also drew in reformers—from humanitarian groups protesting the treatment of Indians to some of the antislavery forces spread around the country. Whigs attracted primarily Protestant voters, often denouncing Catholic immigrants as "dupes" of the Democrats. They drew strength primarily in the North and the Upper South—Virginia, Kentucky, Tennessee, and North Carolina all saw strong Whig Parties. Citizens' enthusiasm for the Democrats, the Whigs, and the smaller third parties made the 1830s, 1840s, and much of the 1850s a period of political dynamism and flux. Men and women invested significant amounts of energy in organizing new parties and advocating new policies. "The spirit of the age," observed the English visitor **Fanny Wright**, was "to be a little fanatical."

The willingness of people to spend time, money, and energy on politics demonstrates a commitment to American democracy that few other nations manifested. England, which saw the beginning of many of the working men's parties that inspired American workers of the 1830s, continued to maintain restrictions on voting and

## TIMELINE 1801–1855

**1801**
Cane Ridge, Kentucky, evangelical revival held

**1817**
American Colonization Society founded

**1820**
Liberia is founded as a colony for freed American slaves

**1822**
Denmark Vesey arrested for organizing a slave conspiracy in Charleston, SC

**1825**
Charles Grandison Finney leads his first revival

Robert Dale Owen founds Utopian colony in New Harmony, IN

**1826**
The American Temperance Society founded

**1829**
David Walker publishes *An Appeal to the Coloured Citizens of the World*

Angelina Grimké joins her sister Sarah in Philadelphia where they became leading women's rights and antislavery activists

**1831**
William Lloyd Garrison founds *The Liberator*, America's leading abolitionist newspaper

Nat Tuner leads the deadliest slave rebellion in U.S. history in Southampton County, VA

**1833**
Britain passes West India Emancipation Act, ending slavery in the British West Indies

Massachusetts is the last state to disestablish its support of an official church

Charles Grandison Finney assumes the presidency of Oberlin College

The American Anti-Slavery Society is organized under Garrisonian principles

**1835**
Alexis de Tocqueville publishes Vol. 1 of *Democracy in America*

James Gordon Bennett begins publishing the *New York Herald*

**1837**
Abolitionist printer Elijah Lovejoy is murdered in Alton, IL, by an anti-abolitionist mob

Catherine Beecher and Angelina Grimké debate nature of women

Severe recession strikes the United States

office holding that excluded a significant number of even white men from the polls. To international observers Americans invested more of themselves in their public world. Many visitors from abroad saw this practice as unfortunate, as a degradation of republican government, which depended on men of virtue—not the common people. One of the most trenchant observers, the Frenchman Alexis de Tocqueville, expressed some skepticism about democratic forms of government. But de Tocqueville also drew inspiration from Americans' enthusiasm for politics and for their public world. He believed that Americans' willingness to create associations and parties would help restore the organic bonds that had once tied together the Old World's societies before the rise of capitalism and democracy. Whereas conservatives feared that the "tyranny of the majority" would overrule reason and liberty in open democracies, de Tocqueville predicted associations of "a thousand different types" would forestall the "tyranny of parties or the arbitrary rule of a prince."

When de Tocqueville observed that Americans were insatiable "joiners," he testified to the emergence of a new civic space in the United States. European countries had official spheres and private spheres and—increasingly after the 16th century—marketplaces, but little room for organized public actions. The reform movements that flourished in America in the 1830s and 1840s did so because a strong evangelical impulse sustained them—many people understood their reform work as saving their own souls as well as those they helped—and because of changes in American law. Some of these latter changes—especially the rise of general incorporation laws as a part of the expansion of capitalism during Andrew Jackson's administration—created the opportunity for reformers to organize themselves in ways that would have been impossible in previous years. Social reformers also benefited from the larger process of political democratization underway at the same time, which drew new participants into politics and empowered individual citizens to believe that they could solve problems in American life. However, this optimism waned somewhat in the 1850s as

**1838**

Frederick Douglass escapes slavery

**1840**

Liberty Party nominates James G. Birney for president on an antislavery platform

**1844**

Mormon founder Joseph Smith is killed in Illinois; Brigham Young leads Mormons to Utah

Liberty Party again nominates James G. Birney for president on an antislavery platform

**1845**

Frederick Douglass published first edition of his *Narrative of the Life of Frederick Douglass*

**1846**

Lewis Tappan helps found the American Missionary Association, which joins antislavery churches in the eastern and western United States

**1848**

Nationalist movements occur in Italy, Germany, France, and Hungary

Lucretia Mott and Elizabeth Cady Stanton lead the Seneca Falls Convention, which produces the "Declaration of Sentiments" calling for women's rights

Free Soil Party nominates Martin Van Buren for president on platform opposing the expansion of slavery in western territories

**1850**

Nathanial Hawthorne publishes *The Scarlet Letter*

Margaret Fuller dies on her return to New York

**1851**

Herman Melville publishes *Moby Dick*

**1854**

Henry David Thoreau publishes *Walden*

**1855**

Walt Whitman publishes the first edition of *Leaves of Grass* reformers found that some problems resisted easy solution, especially slavery and the continuing growth of poverty among urban residents.

### STUDY QUESTIONS FOR CHALLENGES TO THE SPIRIT OF THE AGE

1. **How did Transcendentalism relate to the evangelical reform efforts that defined the era?**
2. **Did the literature of Hawthorne, Melville, Whitman, and Dickinson create a more insular or more open America?**

## Summary

- Evangelical Christians on both sides of the Atlantic exchanged ideas and strategies during the Second Great Awakening and inspired a broad set of social, cultural, and intellectual changes in all parts of America.
- Northern women initiated reform efforts—including temperance, women's rights, and abolition—that targeted the same broad range of social ills as did their British counterparts.
- In the South slaveholders harnessed the power of the Protestant churches to articulate a more individualized and more paternalistic social order, especially as a way to control those African Americans who converted to Christianity in large numbers for the first time and drew strength from their new faith.
- These spiritual movements were matched by the rise of an increasingly secular culture, expressed through novels, newspapers, and the work of mass political parties.

## Key Terms and People

**American Anti-Slavery Society (AASS)** 454
**American Colonization Society (ACS)** 455
**American Temperance Society (ATS)** 451
**Asbury, Francis** *452*
**Bennett, James Gordon** *468*
**Child, Lydia Maria** *455*
**Clay, Henry** *455*
**Dickinson, Emily** *469*
**Douglas, Stephen** *455*
**Douglass, Frederick** *454*
**Finney, Charles Grandison** *445*
**Foster, Stephen** *469*
**Garrison, William Lloyd** *454*
**Graham, Sylvester** *452*
**Harrison, William Henry** *458*
**Hawthorne, Nathaniel** *469*
**Jackson, Andrew** *472*
**Lee, Ann** *448*
**Lovejoy, Elijah** *454*
**Melville, Herman** *469*
**Mission to the Slaves** *461*
**Mormons** *448*
**Poe, Edgar Allen** *469*
**Pritchard, "Gullah" Jack** *464*
**Second Great Awakening** *444*
**Sharp, Granville** *452*
**Smith, James McCune** *455*

## Reviewing Chapter 12

1. How were political democratization and religious awakening related during the antebellum era?
2. What distinguishes the evangelicalism of the 1830s and 1840s from the practice of Christianity in earlier periods?

## Further Reading

Carwardine, Richard. *Transatlantic Revivalism: Popular Evangelicalism in Britain and America, 1790–1865*. Westport, CT: Greenwood Press, 1978. This book traces the intellectual and personal links that bound people together across the Atlantic.

Ginzberg, Lori D. *Women and the Work of Benevolence: Morality, Politics, and Class in the Nineteenth-Century United States*. New Haven, CT: Yale University Press, 1990. An analysis of how women's reform work both challenged and reinforced gender conventions in 19th-century America.

Heyrman, Christine Leigh. *Southern Cross: The Beginnings of the Bible Belt*. New York: Knopf, 1997. A study of the origins and maturation of evangelical denominations in the southern United States through the Second Great Awakening.

Howe, Daniel Walker. *What Hath God Wrought: The Transformation of America, 1815–1848*. New York: Oxford University Press, 2007. A comprehensive history that reveals the intimate relationship between the emergence of new technologies, new ideologies, and new structures of politics in early 19th-century America.

Newman, Richard S. *The Transformation of American Abolitionism: Fighting Slavery in the Early Republic*. Chapel Hill: University of North Carolina Press, 2002. A clear analysis of the shift in strategy and goals from first generation abolition in the 18th century to the more radical 19th-century activists.

Ryan, Mary. *Civic Wars: Democracy and Public Life in the American City during the Nineteenth Century*. Berkeley: University of California Press, 1997. A thoughtful study that chronicles how the development of American cities challenged public and political life.

# Visual Review

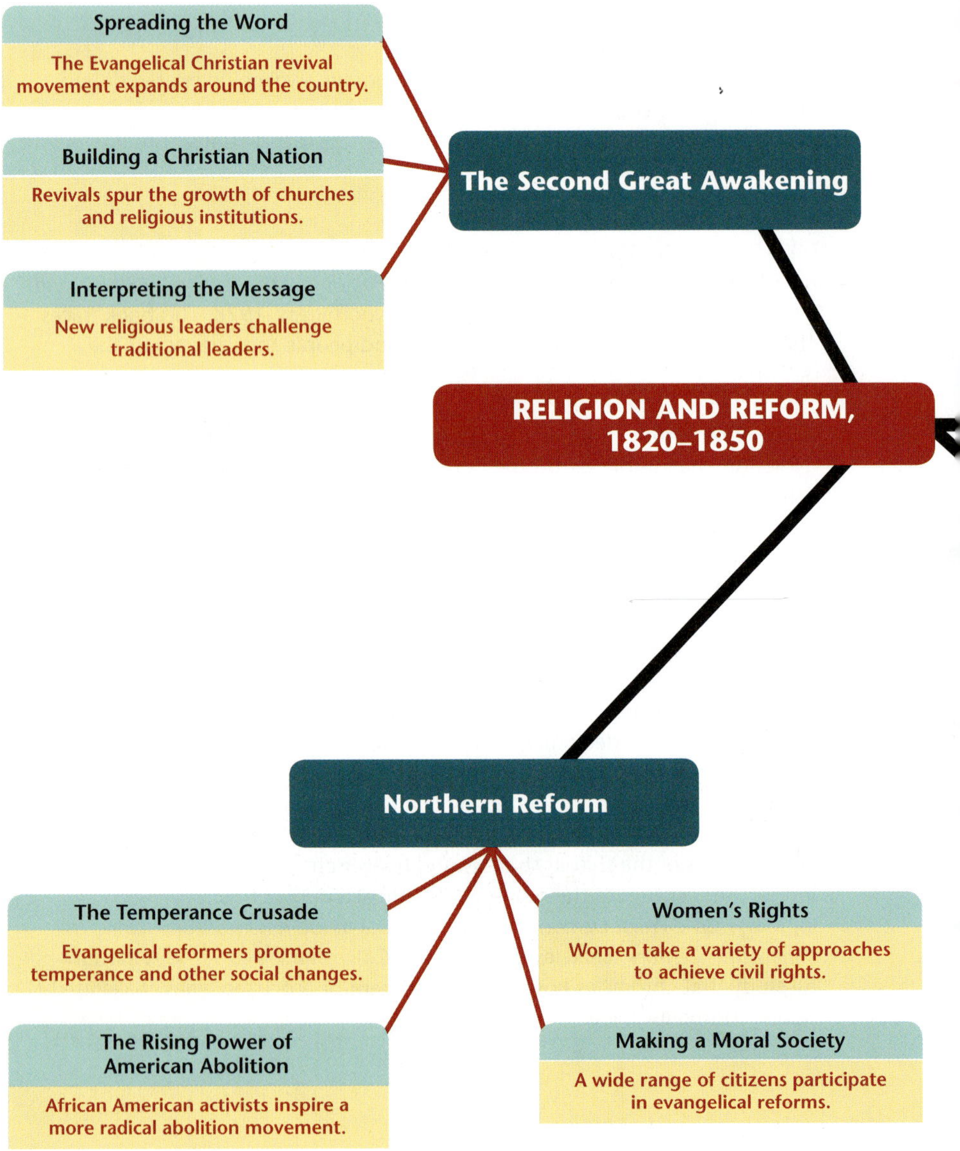

## RELIGION AND REFORM, 1820–1850

### The Second Great Awakening

**Spreading the Word**

The Evangelical Christian revival movement expands around the country.

**Building a Christian Nation**

Revivals spur the growth of churches and religious institutions.

**Interpreting the Message**

New religious leaders challenge traditional leaders.

### Northern Reform

**The Temperance Crusade**

Evangelical reformers promote temperance and other social changes.

**The Rising Power of American Abolition**

African American activists inspire a more radical abolition movement.

**Women's Rights**

Women take a variety of approaches to achieve civil rights.

**Making a Moral Society**

A wide range of citizens participate in evangelical reforms.

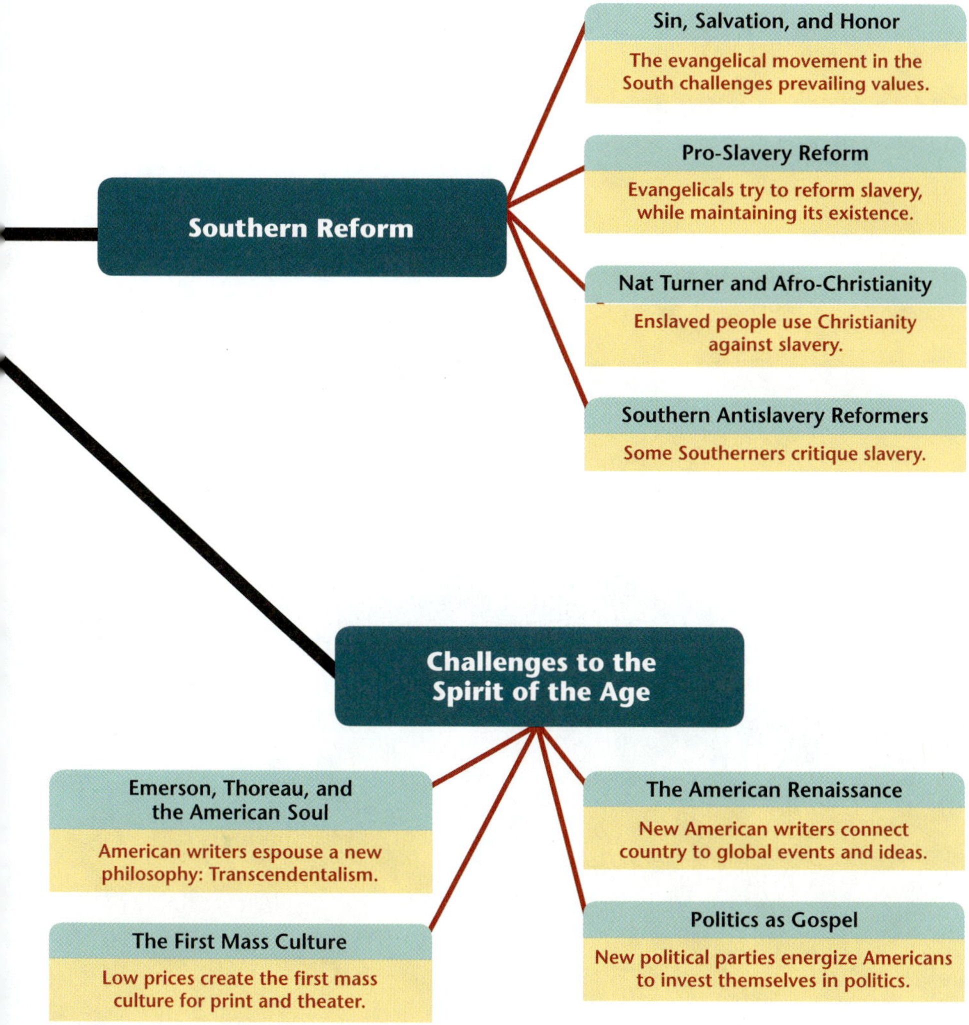

## Southern Reform

**Sin, Salvation, and Honor**
The evangelical movement in the South challenges prevailing values.

**Pro-Slavery Reform**
Evangelicals try to reform slavery, while maintaining its existence.

**Nat Turner and Afro-Christianity**
Enslaved people use Christianity against slavery.

**Southern Antislavery Reformers**
Some Southerners critique slavery.

## Challenges to the Spirit of the Age

**Emerson, Thoreau, and the American Soul**
American writers espouse a new philosophy: Transcendentalism.

**The First Mass Culture**
Low prices create the first mass culture for print and theater.

**The American Renaissance**
New American writers connect country to global events and ideas.

**Politics as Gospel**
New political parties energize Americans to invest themselves in politics.

# 13 A House Dividing

## 1844–1860

In November 1852 U.S. Commodore Matthew C. Perry left Norfolk, Virginia, with a fleet of "Black Ships"—the new steam-powered warships of the United States. He sailed for the closed society of Japan, which Americans saw as a potential trading partner, as a colonial target, and as a port and refueling base for whaling ships. Only the Chinese, the Koreans, and the Dutch had limited access to Japan, but Britain—which had defeated China in the First Opium War of 1839–1842—opened Western trade to the Pacific Rim and encouraged the United States to try its own brand of gunboat diplomacy.

Perry drew on decades of experience protecting U.S. commercial interests and suppressing piracy and illegal slave trading around the globe. For the Japan mission the U.S. government instructed Perry to be "courteous and conciliatory, but at the same time, firm and decided." The Japanese should be impressed with "a just sense of the power and greatness" of the Americans. After several months of negotiation, backed by threats that the steam-driven warships would shell the city of Tokyo, Perry secured a meeting with a high-ranking official. Coming ashore in early 1854, nearly 5,000 Japanese greeted the Americans. With the Treaty of Kanagawa, the Japanese acceded to U.S. demands that American whaling ships in distress in the region be provided with provisions.

◄ *Storming of Chapultepec—Pillow's Attack* by Carl Nebel

Once the Americans had come ashore, cultural and gift exchanges complemented the official business.

**CHAPTER OUTLINE**

# America in the World

Congress passed the Texas Annexation Act, expanding the U.S. territory into Texas (1845).

The Treaty of Guadalupe called for the United States to annex southwest territories from Mexico (1846–1848).

The Compromise of 1850 and Fugitive Slave Act allowed slave owners to retrieve runaway slaves from the North (1850).

 U.S. event that influenced the world

 International event that influenced the United States

 Event with multinational influence

Conflict

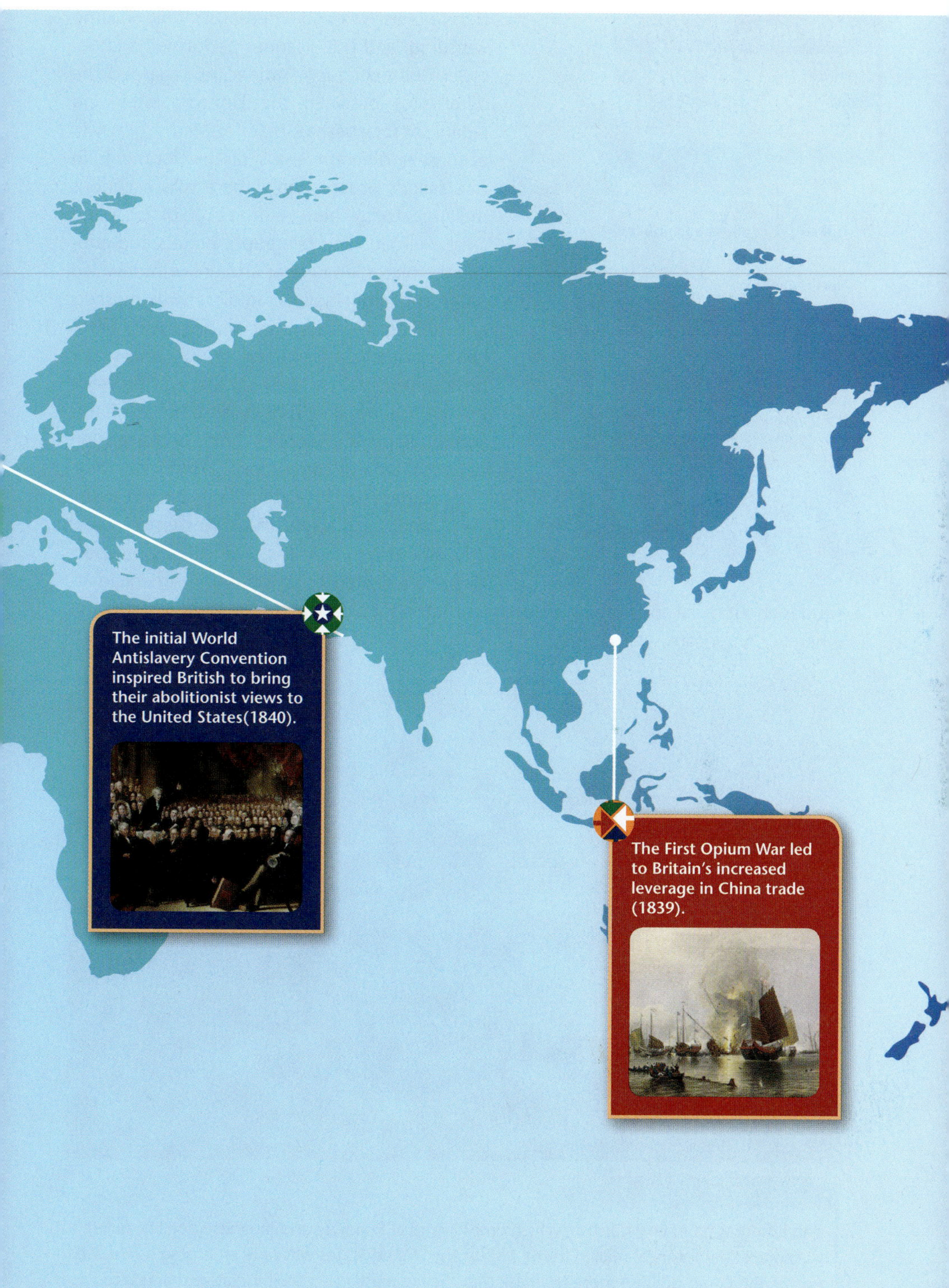
The initial World Antislavery Convention inspired British to bring their abolitionist views to the United States(1840).
The First Opium War led to Britain's increased leverage in China trade (1839).

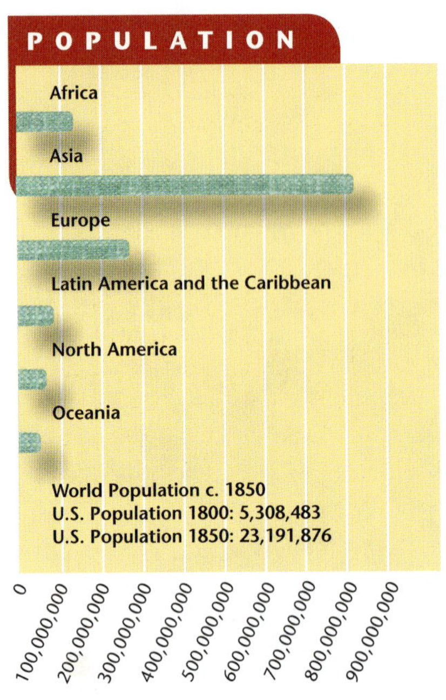


U.S. soldiers watched a demonstration of sumo wrestling, and U.S. Marines performed a close-order drill exhibition. Americans regarded the differences between the United States and Japanese societies as manifestations of civilizations at different levels of development. In one sailor's observation, "there was a curious mélange today here, a function of east and west, railroads and telegraph, boxers and educated athletes, epaulettes and uniforms, shaved pates and night-gowns, soldiers with muskets and drilling in close array, soldiers with petticoats, sandals . . . all these things, and many others, exhibiting the difference between our civilization and usages and those of this secluded, pagan people." The condescension in this statement came mostly from ignorance. The Japanese had insulated themselves from the West, and, as a result, most Westerners knew little about Japanese life. The sailor's perspective also reflected common Anglo-American attitudes about racial and cultural differences that shaped debates in the United States and wherever Americans went abroad.

▲ This lithograph of Perry's arrival, which emphasized U.S. power and Japanese docility, failed to capture the historical reality. In the 1850s, the United States was only emerging as a naval power and could do little more than ask that the Japanese open their lucrative markets to U.S. imports.

After he returned to the United States, Perry sought to quell criticism that he had not returned with a trade agreement. He assured his critics commercial exchange with both Japan and China would come, either through diplomacy or force. "The duty of protecting our vast and rapidly growing commerce will make it not only a measure of wisdom, but of positive necessity," to promote U.S. interests in the Pacific. Perry described the ascension of America to world power as inevitable and frankly admitted the likelihood of colonial acquisitions. "In the developments of the future, the destinies of our nation must assume conspicuous attitudes: we cannot expect to be free from the ambitious longings for increased power, which are the natural concomitants of national success." Although few politicians spoke this openly about American interventions overseas, Perry's vision of American power reflected the essence of what both Democrats and Whigs heralded in their campaigns and from the floors of Congress. Even as the United States shifted from throwing off its own history as a freed colony to become a colonizer itself, Perry excited Americans' interest in Asia as a trading partner and potential sphere of influence.

## THE EXPANSION OF AMERICA

Just a few years before Perry's trip, U.S. victory in the Mexican War brought the territory between the Louisiana Purchase line and the Pacific Ocean under U.S. control. At the same time European immigrants, continuing to arrive in high numbers, generated ethnic and political conflicts. Expansion intensified the conflict between Americans over whether new states should be organized with or without slavery. Political disputes over slavery in the territories generated increasing sectional animosities. During the mid-1850s Northerners fashioned a new political coalition based around opposition to the expansion of slavery, a conservative approach to immigration and naturalization, and federal support for economic development. Concerned about the effect of a sectional party in U.S. politics, Southerners reacted angrily and raised the possibility of leaving the Union.

In 1852, however, Perry's journey rose above politics. Democrats and Whigs, Northerners and Southerners all supported the mission and celebrated his accomplishment. It was one of the few genuinely bipartisan events during an era in which partisan divisions hardened considerably. The first Whig president, **William Henry Harrison**, elected in 1840, died after a month in office. The conservative Virginian **John Tyler**, a former Democrat, replaced him and quickly alienated the Whigs. In actuality, Tyler governed without a party from 1841–1845. The 1844 presidential election offered Democrats an opportunity to retake the White House and Whigs a chance to put a true party leader in office. The Whigs ran **Henry Clay** and the Democrats **James K. Polk**. In addition to their predictable differences over economic development, immigration, and slavery, expansion became one of the key issues of the campaign. In particular, the Democrats advocated the annexation, or territorial incorporation, of Texas. Polk won the election and entered office six days after the United States annexed Texas.

## The American Invasion and Conquest of Mexico

The open belligerence of the Polk administration inspired the war party inside Mexico, which took Texas annexation as an affront to the nation's honor. Throughout the period from 1836 to 1847 Mexican officials had contended with rebellions in a host of states. These weakened the Mexican national government at the moment that it entered into war with a more unified and militarily proficient foe. Even as the United States ostensibly pursued diplomatic negotiations in late 1845 and early 1846, Polk created the pretext for war by ordering troops into territory south of the Texas border along the Nueces River. When Mexican forces predictably attacked U.S. troops, Polk asserted that "American blood has been shed on American soil" and galvanized the country to support war. Most citizens eagerly endorsed the war. Proclaiming "Ho, for the Halls of Montezuma," volunteers flocked to the service.

The United States launched a three-pronged invasion of Mexico. As General **Zachary Taylor** and Colonel A. W. Doniphan invaded Mexico's northern territories, **Stephen Kearny** led an expedition across New Mexico and into California. The

**▲ Map 13.1**

**Mexican War** The United States launched a three-pronged invasion of Mexico—with Stephen Kearny going into New Mexico, Zachary Taylor securing the southern border of Texas, and Winfield Scott leading the main army on its successful attack on Mexico City. The war added half a million square miles to the United States, more than a third of its prewar territory.

Americans possessed a significant technological advantage with moveable artillery, which they used to devastating effect against Mexican forces. But with no sign of Mexican capitulation, in May 1847, General **Winfield Scott**, the highest ranking officer in the United States, landed at Veracruz and marched westward toward the capital. After several clashes with the Mexican Army, Scott reached the outskirts of Mexico City in August.

As Scott's men advanced through the country, many read a recently published history of Cortés's conquest of Mexico. William Prescott's epic account served as a kind of travel guide—some soldiers read the Spanish version to learn the language. Americans saw in their campaign a historic parallel to the first great clash of civilizations in Mexico. Navy lieutenant **Raphael Semmes** read the book and observed that "every step of our progress was fraught with the associations of three hundred years . . . Time, with his scythe and hourglass, had brought another and a newer race . . . Nothing could exceed the beauty of this spectacle." Some Mexicans too, drew the same analogy, as one politician commented that "the soldiers are telling terrible tales that bring to mind the Conquest."

Even though U.S. soldiers prided themselves on liberating the country from the thrall of centuries of Catholic and Spanish tyranny, many chroniclers reflected the longstanding attitudes that had shaped western settlement for decades. Characterizations of Mexican soldiers as "degraded," "hideous," and possessing minds "rather animal than intellectual" flowed back home in letters and newspaper reports. For most of these soldiers victory in the war demonstrated the superiority of Anglo institutions and provided an opportunity for Mexicans to reform their fractious nation. In describing the conflict one soldier wrote that "the American eagle seemed to spread his broad pinions and westward bar the principles of Republican government." Nevertheless, the U.S. invasion did little to stabilize the nation. Mexico continued to roil with racial, class, and regional conflicts, and after U.S. victory these rebellions flared into the open.

The war retained its popularity in the United States partly because American forces defeated Mexican forces in every major engagement in the 16-month conflict. Nonetheless, many Whigs and their supporters opposed the war and expansion because they feared it would lead America into the imperial mode that had ruined so many European nations. Whig politicians, like Illinois representative **Abraham Lincoln**, who maintained their opposition to the war, paid a high political price. Lincoln, a freshman congressman in 1847, hoped that by requiring the Polk administration to identify the precise location of the war's start in the "Spot Resolutions," the war's false origins would be exposed. But enthusiasm from battlefield victories overwhelmed debates over the war's initial legitimacy, and Lincoln lost his reelection to the House to a Democrat. Despite the tactical success that U.S. forces enjoyed during the war, the conflict turned out to be the bloodiest in U.S. history when measured on a per capita basis. The death rate for U.S. servicemen—110 out of every 1,000—remains the highest for any American war. More than 10 times as many U.S. soldiers died of disease during the war as died in combat, with 10,970 deaths from illness and 1,548 in battle. Northern victory in the war concluded a 20-year history of Mexican-U.S. relations marked by conflict, mistrust, and violence.

## The Geography and Ecology of the New American West

Once the war officially began, President Polk explained his goals: "I declared my purpose to be to acquire for the United States, California, New Mexico, and perhaps some of the Northern Provinces of Mexico." Mr. Polk's War, as critics called it, proved spectacularly successful in this regard. The Treaty of Guadalupe Hidalgo, which ended the war, ceded Texas north of the Rio Grande, California, and New Mexico to the United States for $15 million. It brought 500,000 square miles, nearly 55 percent of prewar Mexico, into U.S. possession, and expanded the continental United States by over 40 percent. Americans coveted California because of its resources and because its coast provided access to the Pacific Ocean and Asian markets. As in Texas in the 1830s, U.S. settlers had been moving into California since the early 1840s. Like the early Texas colonists these residents pledged nominal allegiance to Mexico but desired independence and annexation to the United States. In 1846 Lieutenant **John Frémont** reached northern California on a mapping expedition for the U.S. Topographical Engineers. One month after Frémont supported a settler uprising that declared the "Bear Flag Republic" independent of Mexico, the U.S. Navy arrived off the coast of San Francisco. Although fighting in southern California stretched later into the year, it involved small numbers and relatively few casualties. In January 1847 the Californios, Spanish-speaking Californians, capitulated to the U.S. Navy.

Farther up the coast Americans were already consolidating new territorial gains. Starting in the late 18th century British, Spanish, and Russian adventurers had clashed over the right to trade with the Indians along the coast of today's Oregon and Washington. U.S. traders joined the fray in the early 19th century, and by the 1820s Spain and Russia abandoned the region. Long after the American Revolution the United States and Britain struggled for supremacy in the region. When Polk ran for the presidency in 1844, his campaign slogan promised "Fifty-Four Forty or Fight!"—a reference to the northernmost boundary, measured in latitude, for U.S. claims in the Oregon Territory. This claim would have extended U.S. jurisdiction halfway into today's British Columbia. Cynics saw in the call Polk's attempt to balance the acquisition of Texas with more free land to the north. His decision to settle well south of that line exacerbated sectional tensions.

With the exception of the extreme Pacific Northwest and sections along the eastern front of the Rocky Mountain range, the western regions annexed to the United States in the 1840s possessed a markedly different climate and topography than that of the eastern United States. The most important marker of this difference was the drop in rainfall for those regions located west of the 100th Meridian. Regions across the Great Plains and over the Rocky Mountains received, on average, only 10 inches of rainfall per year. Early travelers reported on the aridity, giving rise to the label "Great American Desert." Lured by travel pamphlets promising fertile lands and their own experience in the East, settlers moving west brought expectations of profitable farming, but the dry western ecology forced them to modify their plans.

The 1859 discovery of gold in Colorado initiated the settlement of mid-America, which included ranching, freight hauling, and support services for the burgeoning towns in eastern Colorado and western Kansas. The consolidation of the broad middle of North America under U.S. control alleviated security concerns that had troubled Americans since the early 19th century, when a host of European powers remained ensconced on the continent. Even if they did not know what to do with the land and even if, as some Americans feared, organizing the new territories would precipitate political conflicts, most celebrated the accomplishment. Most citizens probably agreed with President Polk when he announced in his 1848 state of the Union: "we are the most favored people on the face of the earth."

## Conestogas, Comanches, and Californios

In that same speech Polk revealed yet more evidence for America's most "favored" status: the discovery of gold in California. Previous finds in Colorado, Alabama, and Georgia had drawn thousands of miners, but California's discovery overshadowed them all. Tens of thousands of men abandoned jobs and families and hurried west. As one East Coast clerk noted, "the thirst for California gold appears to be unabated and young men are enticed away from their business haunts, and daily occupations, for the sake of acquiring the filthy lucre." In 1849 80,000 men came to California, where, as Mark Twain observed, they "fairly reveled in gold, whiskey, fights, and fandangos." Immigrants were overwhelmingly male, from a wide variety of ethnic and racial backgrounds. The mining adventures that drew men from all over the world to California also drew global financial backing. Investors in New York, Philadelphia, London, and Berlin underwrote the hard labor provided by men from all over North America and from many European nations. Unlike the monetary capital, which mingled indiscriminately, laborers in western mines segregated themselves by ethnicity and race. Irish workers in Idaho, Italians in Arizona, and Greeks in Utah defended parochial boundaries from those laborers they perceived as different, especially Chinese and Indian miners.

Anglo migrants to the west regarded Catholic superstition and sin, combined with "cowardly, ignorant, lazy" habits inherited from the Spanish, as the main impediment to fruitful use and development of the region. "If the one half be true that is told of the abomination of the priesthood," one American wrote of the Franciscans, "that order there must be a perfect embodiment of every wicked attribute that darkens the character of corrupt human nature." Anglo settlers believed every outrageous tale of Catholic corruption and depravity. By displacing the native Mexican elite and developing California, Anglos could make money, purify the "American" character, and fulfill their Christian duty to bring their world into harmony with God's plan.

Not every American came with a sense of scorn. A long tradition of open trading brought early American travelers together with Mexicans, French, British, and Native peoples. The earliest permanent settlers usually trapped and hunted, intermarried with locals, and spoke both Spanish and English. For these men, and for later emigrants, California represented an escape from the pressures of the East, from dirty cities, tired land, and debts. Because of its location at the western edge of North America and because it promised access to a fantastic new world in the Pacific, Americans embodied

Gold captured the imagination of Americans east and west. Although the popular image of a "gold seeker" was a young, single, white man, the allure of the precious metal drew men and women from all around the globe.

California with their dreams. Even Henry David Thoreau, the poet of the eastern woods, felt that "my needle always settles between west and southwest. The future lies that way to me."

Controlling the new territory proved nearly as great a challenge as acquiring it. The Conestoga wagons that had already begun carrying Anglo settlers across the Great Plains began heading south in greater numbers, but doing so brought them into the orbit of two powerful Indian nations—the Apache and the Comanche—that generations of Spanish and then Mexican settlers had tried and failed to pacify. In 1850 the Apache community probably numbered only 5,000, but their attacks on settler communities had inspired the Mexican government to offer bounties for Apache scalps, men, women, and children. The Comanche represented an even more serious threat. More numerous and better organized than the Apache, they had lived along the northwestern edges of Texas and in the New Mexico Territory since the early 18th century. The Comanche dominated the region well into the second half of the 19th century.

The Comanche controlled parts of northern Mexico, known as Comanchería, through their ability to reinvent themselves as the Spanish began to push north. Seizing new weapons and tools—especially horses—they wedded these technologies to existing practices such as raiding and slave taking, which served to create extended networks of kin and dependency across the Southwest. The result was a native power that existed independently though in connection to the Europeans and later Americans. Unknown to the Americans who came to rule the area after the Mexican War, and probably to the Comanche themselves, Comanche society was entering a period of internal conflict and decline that weakened them substantially and paved the way for U.S. forces to displace them. The most serious threat to their community was biological rather than political: the collapse of the bison population. Decades of overhunting and a decade-long drought beginning in the mid-1840s destroyed the main source of food, a key commodity, and an essential part of the Comanche spiritual world. In 1852, weakened by starvation, Comanche chiefs appealed to a U.S. Indian agent for "a country we can call our own, where we might bury our people in quiet." The Comanche people did not all die—and, while some conceded to U.S. policies that placed Indians on reservations, others resisted and defended their autonomy into the 1870s.

Despite the threats posed by the Comanche and others, the prospect of gold drew immigrants to California. Creating a chaotic mix of languages, cultures, and values, Anglo settlers, European travelers, and Asian migrants all poured into California in 1849. Chinese and Irish migrants ranked at the top of the foreign-born contingent, followed by Germans, English, Welsh, Scottish, French, Chileans, Brazilians, Mexicans, and Canadians. Of these 70,000 new residents probably 15 percent were from Central or South America, and they all labored alongside 6,000–7,000 Miwok Indians. All these new Californians also lived alongside 75,000 Mexican Americans who remained in California after the Mexican War.

Two diverse immigrant streams reveal the global reach of gold and the divergent experiences of immigrants once they landed in America. Chinese, especially Cantonese, migrants came in pursuit of "**Gum Shan**"or "Gold Mountain," as the Cantonese referred to California. The Chinese came largely as contract laborers, usually relegated to the service industries that supported mines, and later worked in railroads and construction work. Like the thousands of African American men who came west, Chinese immigrants were segregated in their housing and were offered low-wage jobs with little chance for upward mobility. These men were especially prized by American miners as cooks and cleaners, because without them the dramatically unbalanced sex ratios of the gold rush required that men do work that traditionally fell to women. After placer mining had exhausted the surface gold, prospectors turned to hard rock mines—where large rock or quartz deposits had to be carefully excavated and the material brought to the surface before it could be crushed and chemically processed to extract the gold. The specialized knowledge required to operate hard rock mines drew men from Cornwall, England, who knew how to dig deep mines and set explosive charges safely. By 1870 Cornish miners comprised a majority of the miners in Grass Valley, one of the most lucrative parts of the California gold fields. Because of their English background these men blended easily into the new Anglo culture of the state in ways that were denied to Chinese workers.

Despite being neither "North" nor "South," California could not escape the sectional controversies that roiled the country throughout the 1850s. Some southern migrants to the state brought their slaves. Others waited until they received assurances that their property would be safe. That day never came, as both California residents and the U.S. Congress voted to approve California's statehood as "free soil." Even as Southerners denounced the establishment of free soil in California, they maintained the fight for slavery in the West. Democrats dominated the state, but the party split into pro-slavery and antislavery factions. As in Kansas, where the conflict over the expansion precipitated bloodshed, the factions in California came to blows. In late 1859 one of California's U.S. senators—**David Broderick**—was killed in a duel with **David Terry**, the chief justice of the state's supreme court. Broderick had assented to the duel but his

GLOBAL PASSAGES

## Global Gold

The first thing Edward Hargraves would have noticed were the smells. The pungent aroma of five-spice powder and the fermented complexity of soy sauce competing with roasting chilies and smoky corn carried along with the heady aroma of beef stewed with vegetables. Then, the breeze would have carried a cacophony of voices, accents, and languages: Mandarin, Portuguese, perhaps a smattering of Gaelic. Entering a gold mining camp in 1849 would have disoriented even someone with as global a background as Harvgraves. Born and educated in England, he moved to Australia when he was 16. In 1833 Hargraves embarked as a crew member on a ship that became infested with fever. Rescued in the Torres Straits between today's Queensland, Australia, and Papua New Guinea, he recovered in England and then returned to Australia. After a decade and a half of unpromising work in Australia, Hargraves seized on the opportunity presented by the discovery of gold in California. As one man described San Francisco in 1849, "the very air [is] pregnant with the magnetism of bold, spirited, unwearied action." That magnetism lured Hargraves, as well as the Chinese, Brazilian, and Irish prospectors whose diverse cuisines and speech would have greeted him as he entered the California fields.

The Australian *Sydney Herald* had broken news of the rush in December 1848, just as many East Coast Americans heard the news from President Polk, and Hargraves

supporters attributed his death to his opposition to the extension of slavery. The violent conflict between pro-slavery and antislavery expansion forces in California revealed how deeply the sectional conflict had impressed itself into the fabric of the nation.

### STUDY QUESTIONS FOR THE EXPANSION OF AMERICA

1. **What were the challenges facing U.S. control of the new western territory?**
2. **Why did the United States enter war with Mexico and how did the results transform the nation?**

## CONTESTED CITIZENSHIP

Even as the United States extended its power across the West and over the Pacific, citizens disputed with one another over who could be an American. The influx of an increasingly diverse stream of immigrants into the country made this discussion even more fraught. Native-born Americans, especially Protestant ones, reacted to the set sail from Australia for California. Arriving in mid-1849, Hargraves learned the craft of excavating but found little gold. The fields had already become crowded and competitive. Some men abandoned prospecting and made money provisioning the men who were toiling for gold. Levi Strauss was one of these. A 24-year-old German immigrant, Strauss intended to open a dry goods business but responded to the necessity of miners for durable pants. Using a French fabric, denim, Strauss designed a rugged but comfortable pair that became the foundation of his company, and the origin of blue jeans in America.

Hargraves, however, intent on seeking out the terrain that reminded him of the California gold fields, returned to Australia in 1851. At home he found success, finding gold on a tributary of the Macquarie River. Hargraves demonstrated the circular nature of information, skills, and capital in the increasingly global economy of the 1850s. The links between Australia and the United States also underscored the growing importance of the Pacific. The interconnectedness of these economies revealed itself as California gold spread around the world—miners dug out more gold in the first decade of California production than had appeared on world markets in the previous 150 years, reversing the global deflation that had marked the previous three decades.

- Why did the California gold rush inspire foreign immigration?
- What did the gold rush reveal about the nature of global information and economies in the mid-19th century?

growing diversity by trying to narrowly define citizenship and the rights that came with it. The political and cultural conflicts spurred by these changes wrought a massive transformation on the American electorate and partisan alignments. The failure of American politics as a result of these crises eventually helped bring the nation to war in 1861. The first phase of this process saw the collapse of the Whig Party in the face of a challenge from the nativist **Know-Nothing Party**.

## The Patterns of Migration

After the conclusion of the Mexican War immigrants flooded the Pacific Coast both from the eastern United States and from around the globe. Chinese laborers comprised the largest group of Asian immigrants into America at this time. Between 1840 and1920 two and a half million people left China for Hawaii, the United States, Canada, Australia, New Zealand, Southeast Asia, South America, and Africa. Although domestic disturbances and economic hardship compelled these moves, the vast majority of migrants to North America chose their destination. After the Gold Rush, news of fortunes circulated widely. One resident in China reported on the effect of the news: "Letters from Chinese in San Francisco and further in the country have been circulated . . . the accounts of the successful adventurers who have returned would, had the inhabitants possessed the means of paying their own way across, have gone far to depopulate considerable towns."

The Chinese immigrants who came to the United States in the 1840s and 1850s joined a larger immigrant stream from China to disparate locations around the globe. Before reaching the California shore one young man from South China worked aboard a British ship, a French whaler, and a Russian Man-of-War. During this same period he worked in Honolulu, Japan, and along the Chinese-Russian border. Despite the worldliness that some Chinese immigrants brought to the United States, the California legal system established in 1849 created a rigid binary system of classifying its residents. Laws grouped Chinese, African Americans, and Indians together as "nonwhite" and denied them access to the vote, the state court system, and the schools.

In contrast to California, the New Mexico territory remained as fluid as it had been under Mexican control, largely because the United States imposed little military control. Instead, the Indian communities—Comanche, Apache, Navajo, Cheyenne, and Kiowa—continued to practice older forms of war making, diplomacy, and trade. Even as these borderland areas displayed continuity in terms of Indian traditions and authority, the rapid decline of buffalo herds on the southern Plains, the continued

Immigrants entered the United States through coastal port cities. Many remained in the region where they landed, but others followed transportation corridors into the heart of the country, often tracing the routes laid down by earlier immigrants from their home countries.

spread of diseases like smallpox, and expansion of the Anglo commercial economy increased U.S. authority in the region. American officials worried about the raiding and slave taking among southwest Indians, a practice Anglos compared to the racial slavery of the Deep South.

Although California and the West drew migrants from Mexico and the Pacific, the countries around the Atlantic basin remained the main source of immigrants bound for the United States in this period. As in earlier decades, German states and Ireland continued to send the most immigrants, though the numbers of central and southern Europeans increased. The rate of immigration rose with each passing year, but the destination of most immigrants remained consistent: the North. The ports of Boston, Philadelphia, and New York attracted a majority of the nation's shipping traffic, both for human cargo and for goods. The combination of free labor policies and a booming economy drew most immigrants to the North. Cities such as Pittsburgh, Cleveland, Detroit, Cincinnati, and Chicago saw their populations explode, based partly on the strength of the new arrivals. These second-tier cities grew at remarkable rates—Chicago increased from 5,000 residents in 1840 to 109,000 in 1860—and achieved a size that the leading coastal ports had required centuries to reach.

But not all of the immigrants went west or north. Some immigrants went south, to such ports as Baltimore, Richmond, Charleston, Mobile, New Orleans, and Galveston. Immigrants who entered southern ports were more likely to remain in those cities or the surrounding area. Irish migrants established large expatriate communities in many of the southern Atlantic seaboard cities. These newcomers joined native Southerners, both black and white, who helped make the urban parts of the South the most dynamic places in the region. Despite their eagerness to accumulate new technology, however, few white Southerners wanted to replicate the massive urban centers of the Northeast. They anticipated that the anonymity and size of large cities would weaken the ability of masters to control their slaves. Many also resisted the rise of a large community of working class whites, who someday might see little reason to support slavery. In addition, southern elites continued to profit handsomely from staple crop agriculture. Because Southerners invested most of their capital in land and slaves, they had little left for the bond-driven commercial development that predominated in other parts of the country.

## Immigrants in America

Among southern ports, New Orleans was unique for its size, its cultural diversity, and its centrality to dynamic new trade patterns. Occupied by the French and Spanish before entry into the United States through the Louisiana Purchase, the polyglot population consisted of the descendants of various European ethnic groups, an equally wide array of African ethnicities, and a large population of people of mixed descent that Louisianans referred to generally as "**Creole**." After the expulsion of French settlers from the Canadian province of Acadia during the Seven Years' War, many relocated to France's colony in southern Louisiana. Here they came to be called "Cajuns" in a corruption of the name of the area from which they came.

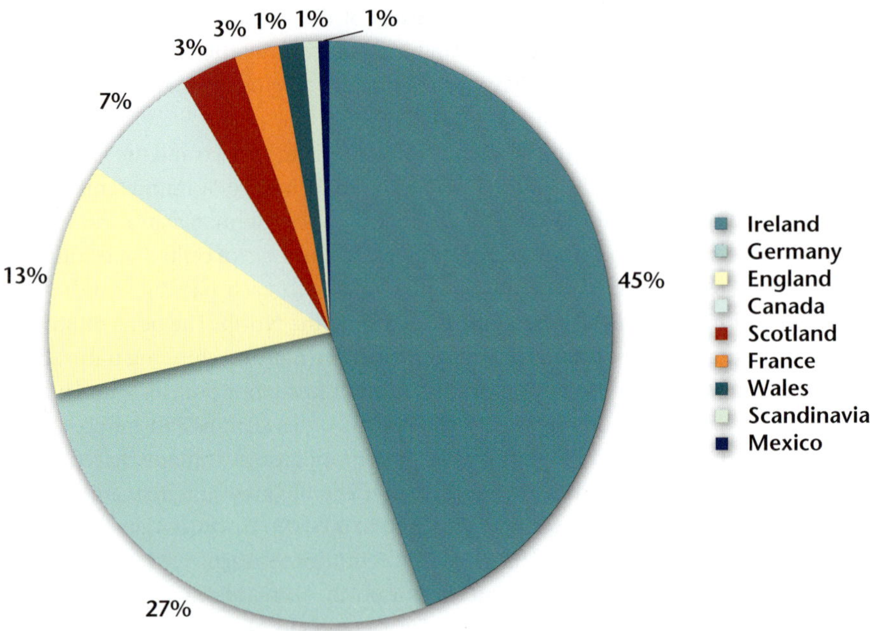


▲ Figure 13.1

**Foreign-born population subdivided by nationality, 1850** The high numbers of Irish immigrants, many of whom were Catholic, entangled public discussions of immigration policy with questions of religion. Note: Table includes only 10 largest emigrant countries, which collectively accounted for 96% of all immigrants.

The visible presence of the Roman Catholic faith produced much of the difference between the people of New Orleans. The French and Spanish built cathedrals and other public symbols of Catholicism in the city, and most Anglo-Americans continued to regard the faith as both foreign and hostile to democratic life. The entry of millions of new Catholics into the country over the 1840s and 1850s only increased fears about their presence in the country. Although most Protestant Americans remained oblivious, the U.S. Catholic community contained several different branches. A substantial body of English Catholics and French Catholics had migrated south from Canada and established themselves during the colonial era. The influx of Irish Catholics alarmed many native-born Catholics who feared that the Irish rejection of Anglo practices and values would further alienate all Catholics within U.S. society.

The political conflicts between old Protestants and new Catholic immigrants in the eastern states propelled much of the public policy toward immigration, but western territories possessed their own share of ethnic conflict. The movement of Chinese workers into the West after the Mexican War generated opposition from native-born workers. Many of the charges leveled at Chinese and other Asian immigrants were similar to the ones used against African Americans. According to the *San Francisco*

*Chronicle*, "When the [Chinese worker arrives here he is as rigidly under the control of the contractor who brought him as ever an African slave was under his master in South Carolina or Louisiana." In 1851 **Hinton Helper**, a leading critic of slavery, told Californians that "I should not wonder at all, if the copper of the Pacific yet becomes as great a subject of discord and dissension as the ebony of the Atlantic." Like his recommendations for freeing the South from slavery—which in his view involved removing African Americans along with slavery—Helper thought Asian immigrants had no role to play in settling the West.

## Race, Ethnicity, and the Invention of Americanism

The quick conclusion that Hinton Helper reached regarding the challenge of ethnic and racial diversity revealed one of the most pernicious aspects of mid-19th-century U.S. culture. Helper's advice—that black people should be removed from the South and Asian people removed from the West—drew on older traditions, like those maintained by the American Colonization Society, and the newer science of race, which was predicated largely on unreliable skull size measurements. Increasingly, white people in America expressed a harsher and more absolute conception of race and racial difference. Most white members of the Revolutionary generation believed implicitly in the intellectual, physical, and moral superiority of white people over darker-skinned people, but they rarely articulated this idea in their writings. What distinguished the antebellum generation was the centrality of racial thinking. The more diverse America became, the more its white residents emphasized racism as a central aspect of their worldview.

The lasting legacy of racist thought on American life has obscured the virulent ethnocentrism that also emerged in the 1840s and 1850s in response to the influx of new immigrants. The conflict pitted native Protestants on one side and immigrant Catholics on the other. By that time most states had endorsed universal white manhood suffrage; thus, following a short period of residence, new immigrants could participate in the political system. The high numbers of urban immigrants, especially in northeastern cities, raised concerns that these men would corrupt the political system. As one wealthy New York merchant worried, "these Irishmen, strangers among us, without a feeling of patriotism or affection in common with American citizens, decide the elections in the City of New York. They make Presidents and Governors, and they send men to represent us in the councils of the nation." The men who expressed such sentiments supported an increasingly aggressive response to what they perceived as a Catholic disruption of American civic life. A weekly New York journal of the 1830s, the *American Protestant Vindicator and Defender of Civil and Religious Liberty against the Inroads of Papacy*, expressed its agenda in its title.

Public schools became one of the key battlegrounds in the fight over religion and public life. The strong Protestant bias of "nondenominational" schools in Ireland left many Irish Catholics who emigrated in the 1840s and 1850s with a profound distrust of nonparochial schools. In 1843 one American Catholic organization warned parents to guard their heritage: "you must, therefore, use all diligence that your child be instructed at an early age in the saving truths of religion, and be preserved from the contagion of error." Accordingly, Catholics requested that public schools respect Catholic beliefs or simply divert public funds to parochial schools. When a Philadelphia bishop criticized the use of the Protestant King James Bible, it incited anti-Catholic riots that left 40 people dead and 60 injured. Although some states did divert funds to Catholic schools, Protestant Americans grew deeply suspicious and often violent over what they perceived as the deliberate refusal of Catholics to assimilate.

## The Know-Nothing Movement

New York, long the center of Irish immigrant life in the United States, experienced the most severe and most well-organized nativist movement. Beginning in the mid-1840s different political organizations calling themselves some variant of the American Party formed. They shared general goals: to restrict office holding to Native Americans; to retain the Bible in schools; and to extend the naturalization process from 5 to 21 years. Although these groups had little electoral success, they established the basis for the network of secret fraternal associations known collectively as the Know Nothings that emerged in the 1850s as well as the public and political wing of this movement that flourished at the same time. Nativists feared that the mainstream political parties would not sanction their policies for fear of alienating the immigrant vote. If asked about the organization, members answered that they "knew nothing." The openly public nature of the movement by the early 1850s demonstrated that either nativists had outgrown their fears or public sentiment was shifting toward their policies.

The Know-Nothing Party benefited from the collapse of the Whigs. Conflicts over allowing slavery into lands gained in the Mexican War weakened the Whig Party substantially. In some cases northern Whigs supported restrictions on slavery, but this stance mostly had the effect of driving their southern peers out of the party. The election of 1852 saw Whig losses at the presidential, congressional, gubernatorial, and state legislative levels. New York *Tribune* editor Horace Greeley angrily concluded that the party had been "not merely discomfited but annihilated." In the fall of 1856 the resounding failure of the Know-Nothing **Millard Fillmore** demonstrated the complete collapse of the party. The Republican nominee John Frémont won 114 electoral votes to Fillmore's 8. Pennsylvania Democrat **James Buchanan** won 174 votes, partly by pledging not to interfere with slavery.

Nativists benefited from this crisis by creating an alternative party that antislavery Northerners could support; as a result they drew away Whig voters in droves. Their strength became clearer after passage of the **Kansas-Nebraska Act** in 1854, which repealed the Missouri Compromise. The bill's new policy of "**popular sovereignty**," which was intended to allow settlers in a territory to decide the status of slavery, initiated a strenuous debate about the future of slavery in the western territories. Politicians immediately saw the impact of the bill. Edward Everett, governor of Massachusetts, complained that what he called the Know-Nothing "mischief" "has been needlessly brought about by the introduction of the Kanzas [sic] & Nebraska bill." The Know-Nothing Party flourished and then disappeared, absorbed by the Republican Party. The brief existence of the party and the fact that it was mostly confined to the North suggests that its appeal was temporary and limited. But the movement tapped into long-standing fears, and nativism did not end with the collapse of the official movement. At the party's height, in the election of 1854, eight governors, more than 100 Congressmen, thousands of local officials, and nearly a million citizens proclaimed themselves Know Nothings.

By advocating anti-immigrant, antislavery, and pro-temperance policies, Know Nothings tapped into the vital issues among a sizeable portion of the northern electorate. The most coherent parts of their platform celebrated Protestantism as naturally American and condemned Catholicism as impossible to reconcile with basic American values. "We are not now contending against foreigners, but against the principles of Roman Catholicism and its devotees," a Cleveland newspaper announced. Because the party relied on the strength of secret fraternal organizations, it remained substantially decentralized and state organizations pursued their own initiatives. In some states, Know Nothings succeeded in restricting public funds for parochial schools, disbanding immigrant militias, imposing literacy tests for voting, and reforming church property ownership rules.

The Know-Nothing Party collapsed on the same issue that had proved the key to their initial success: antislavery. During their 1855 national meeting, Know Nothings urged their followers to accept the Kansas-Nebraska Act allowing settlers in a territory to decide the status of slavery. Incensed by this, many Northerners bolted for the Republican Party, which had made opposition to the expansion of slavery a central plank in their ideology. The Republicans adopted some of the milder aspects of the Know-Nothing critique of immigrant voting corruption but they repudiated the movement's ugly anti-Catholicism. As concerns over slavery grew in 1855 and 1856, northern voters turned to the Republican Party in increasing numbers. From a political perspective one Know-Nothing party leader's diagnosis was accurate: "the cursed question of '*slavery*' is at the bottom of all our troubles."

### STUDY QUESTIONS FOR CONTESTED CITIZENSHIP

1. **How did the entry of new immigrants into the United States in the 1840s and 1850s alter American life?**
2. **What were the political responses by native-born Americans to this movement?**
3. **Why did the Know Nothings fail to make themselves a permanent party?**

## SLAVERY AND ANTEBELLUM LIFE

The persistent efforts of enslaved people to escape bondage, to alter the conditions of their slavery, and to assert their own humanity destabilized the system and forced slaveholders to constantly adjust. The increasing defensiveness of slaveholders in the 1840s and 1850s stemmed as much from this internal pressure as from the external pressure applied by abolitionists. The basis of mid-19th-century slavery remained the physical domination that whites could and did exercise over slaves, the monopoly on weapons and state power, and the social network of support for slavery that manifested itself in slave patrols and a legal system that oppressed black people at the expense of whites. At the same time slaves and masters struggled over the psychological, cultural, and social conditions of bondage. The complexity of these relationships, their continuous evolution over time, and the profoundly uneven distribution of power within the system of antebellum slavery taxes the empathetic sensibilities of modern readers, but the importance of understanding the perspectives of the different participants in the system demands that we make the effort.

## The Paradox of Slavery and Modernity

The persistence of slavery into the 1850s surprised many Americans. Members of the Revolutionary generation expected that slavery would disappear over time. Most philosophical thought in late $18^{th}$- and 19th-century Western Europe favored freedom and condemned slavery as inefficient and inhumane. But the United States proved a curious exception within the larger Western world. Even as states expanded democratic practices among white men, slavery gained greater strength. Defenders of the institution offered increasingly elaborate intellectual and religious justifications. Slavery in North America proved to be a remarkably adaptable economic strategy. Because southern cities did not receive the same surge of foreign immigrants as northern ones, the growth of urban slavery proved vital to southern cities.

Enslaved workers, often hired by companies from their rural masters, labored alongside white men in a host of occupations in antebellum cities. The tobacco factories of the Upper South used this system extensively. By 1860 hired slaves constituted fully one-half of the tobacco workers in Virginia. Richmond's Tredegar Iron Works, the largest industrial facility in the South, with over 1,000 employees, employed hundreds of enslaved men and women. Masters regarded slave hiring as advantageous because they could sign a contract, receive guaranteed compensation, and dispense with the day-to-day management of slaves. Many of the urban slaves, especially those hired in the 1850s, lived in rented rooms or boarding houses. Masters required them to deduct rent and food expenses from their wages, but enterprising slaves could work overtime or scrimp on necessities and actually set aside money for themselves. Urban slavery produced other complications as well. With masters absent, enslaved people supervised themselves after working hours. If they congregated in noisy bars and gambling saloons as white workers did, who would oversee them? If they committed crimes, who would be held responsible? Savannah, Charleston, Mobile, and New Orleans all experienced similar complications with managing this new type of slavery.

Urban slavery also generated class tensions within the white community and threatened its stability at a time when sectional politics demanded solidarity. In the 1850s Tredegar's white workers, for instance, went on strike repeatedly over the use of enslaved workers in the factory. Joseph Anderson, the plant's owner, responded

SCENE ON THE LEVEE, AT NEW ORLEANS.

The dynamism of the southern economy thrived on slave labor, applied to all sorts of farm, urban, and industrial work. Slavery's supporters understood this and fashioned an intellectual defense of the practice to sustain their lifestyle.

aggressively, but most white elites treaded carefully. A handful of southern advocates of free labor framed a critique of slavery that cut to the heart of slaveholders' assumption of their natural rule over the white and black South. Hinton Helper, a North Carolinian, issued the most famous attack on slavery from within the South in his book *The Impending Crisis* (1857). Helper called on nonslaveholding whites to overthrow the planter class, destroy slavery, and exile black people from the country. "The lords of the lash are not only absolute masters of the blacks . . . they are also the oracles and arbiters of all nonslaveholding whites, whose freedom is merely nominal, and whose unparalleled illiteracy and degradation is purposely and fiendishly perpetuated," Helper wrote.

Helper and the white strikers at Tredegar raised the central dilemma of protecting white labor inside a slave society. In the North, free labor theorists and politicians argued that white laborers could never be fairly treated in a slave society, whereas in the South defenders of slavery sought a middle ground. Their precarious position rejected the natural equality of rights that lay at the heart of the American polity and advanced a hierarchical model in its place. South Carolina Senator and former Vice President **John C. Calhoun**, the most prominent defender, framed the argument clearly: "all men are not created equal. According to the Bible, only two—a man and a woman—ever were—and of those one was pronounced subordinate to the other. All others have come into the world by being born, and in no sense . . . either free or equal."

## The West Indies, Brazil, and the Future of Slavery

Slaveholders knew from recent history that a false step could collapse the edifice of their power. By 1838 the British government had abolished slavery in its empire, most importantly on the sugar islands of the West Indies. Their proximity to the United States, the common language and cultural background, and the political parallels to the situation facing American planters ensured that Southerners would study the example. What they saw alarmed them. Although British emancipation granted compensation to owners, gave no land to ex-slaves, required a transition period of bonded labor by former slaves, and did not inspire the racial war that many whites had predicted, U.S. slaveholders regarded it as a radical and dramatically unsuccessful act. Their evidence for the failure of emancipation rested on the decline in West Indian sugar production, which plummeted after the end of the apprenticeship period. Abolitionists, by contrast, hailed the "mighty experiment" as a success. Less concerned with staple crop production, they celebrated the rise of free labor and the self-sufficiency that many ex-slaves pursued.

If the West Indies gave white Southerners doubts about the long-term security of slavery, looking farther south buoyed their hopes. Brazilian planters, independent of Portuguese rule since 1822, remained as committed to slavery as did their U.S. peers. Brazil persisted as one of the last holdouts violating the ban on the Atlantic Slave trade; between 1835 and 1855 alone, over half a million Africans were smuggled into Brazil, many of them on ships captained by Americans. The active role of U.S. nationals in the trade drew scorn even from conservatives like Supreme Court Justice **Joseph Story**. A Northerner and a vigorous nationalist, Story wrote the 1842 ***Prigg v. Pennsylvania*** decision, which established federal protection for Southerners seeking to reclaim fugitive slaves who escaped to the North. He could not, however, countenance participation in the illegal trade from Africa. "American citizens are steeped up to their very mouths (I scarcely use too bold a figure) in this stream of iniquity," Story wrote in 1852. From shipbuilding to sailing to the commerce itself, Americans played a key role in the importation of Africans into Brazil long after the trade had been closed. The fervent dedication to slavery displayed by Brazilians encouraged John C. Calhoun to remark that "between her [Brazil] and us there is a strict identity of interest on almost all subjects, without conflict, or even competition." Reflecting American concerns about British antislavery work, which included patrolling the waters off the African and Brazilian coasts with the intention of returning illegally captured Africans, Calhoun supported "our mutual interest in resisting [London's] interference with the relation in either country."

## Inside the Quarter

By 1860 four million black people were held in bondage in the American South. Viewed in financial terms, they represented the single largest investment of any kind in the United States, with a total aggregate value of roughly three billion dollars. During the 1830s, 1840s, and 1850s, slaveholding concentrated even as the slave population expanded; that is, fewer white people owned more and more black people. By 1860, 25 percent of southern households owned slaves and, of these, only 10 percent owned more than 12 individuals. But the majority of slaveholders owned only one or a few slaves. In these situations, slaves worked alongside family members, slept under the same roof, and remained in close contact with white people throughout their lives. Slaves on plantations lived in their own "quarter," a collection of small cabins usually apportioned one to a family. Within this space enslaved people fashioned families, communities, and their culture. Links—of love, friendship, trade, or rivalry—connected slaves from one plantation to another. Despite the best efforts of whites, news and rumor always traveled faster from quarter to quarter than from big house to big house.

Slaveholders alternated between the stark choices laid out by one master who professed "the surest and best method of managing negroes, is to love them" and another who advised that "we have to rely more and more on the power of fear." Some adopted both these routines. Bennet Barrow, a notoriously harsh Louisiana master, ordered periodic whippings of all his slaves but also gave frequent holidays and brought Christmas presents back to his slaves from New Orleans. Owners had a strong economic incentive to keep slaves healthy and satisfied enough with their material conditions that they did not see flight or revenge as a better option. It did not require a humanitarian slaveholder to see that better treatment could return more profits in the long run.

Without denying the violence and brutality that underlay American slavery, the evidence also reveals that enslaved people used every opportunity to seek small measures of freedom within the system. These actions did not signal acceptance of slavery nor were they incompatible with the more public and physical acts of resistance that marked so much of the relationship between masters and slaves in the antebellum South. But these measures gave enslaved African Americans the ability to carve out space for spouses, for children, sometimes for literacy or advanced skills, and most importantly, for themselves. Each small victory required enormous sacrifice and discipline to achieve, but the body of evidence that scholars have recovered from all aspects of slaves' lives demonstrates the vitality and richness of that life even within bondage.

Owners never spent more than the bare minimum to house slaves, but despite their rough surroundings, enslaved men and women built strong and loving families and protective communities whenever they could.

The families and communities created by enslaved people reveals the ways in which they created alternate value systems. Because enslaved people could not legally marry, some slaveholders regarded slave marriages as unions of convenience that they could sunder with a sale while others flattered themselves that slave marriages proved that they offered good lives to their bondmen. Evidence from enslaved people themselves reveals that families occupied the center and the whole of most slaves' lives. Because of the importance of family, the sale of enslaved people represented the greatest tragedy they could face. Sales may have disrupted one-third to one-half of enslaved families nationwide. Sales revealed the truly mercenary quality of American slavery. One of the largest and most dynamic such markets was located in New Orleans, where slaves arrived by ship, rail, and on foot, before being sold and parceled out to the brutal sugar plantations in the region. The high walls of the slave market, built according to city code to keep the transactions out of sight, concealed the raw fact of people as property that underlay the uniquely commercial nature of slavery in the New World.

## The Creation of African America

The tremendous diversity of African backgrounds inherited by enslaved people in America complicated and enriched the efforts of African Americans to identify themselves as one people. By the early 19th century, free African Americans felt secure enough to claim Africa as a proud ancestral homeland, a practice that went back at least to the African Methodist Episcopal (AME) Church, founded in Philadelphia in the 1790s. To assert a positive affiliation with Africa, as increasing numbers of free blacks did in the early 19th century, represented a fundamental challenge to the racist attitudes held by most white Americans. **Martin Delaney**, a free black man from Virginia, who moved to Pennsylvania and later worked with Frederick Douglass, built on earlier efforts to connect black Americans with Africa in historical, emotional, and physical terms. Before the Civil War, Delaney advocated the necessity of a separate black nation in Africa composed of émigrés from the United States, where they could show their superiority in "the true principles of morals, correctness of thought, religion, and law or civil government."

Positive images of Africa played a central role in the music and folklore of the enslaved people. By the mid-19th century black Americans had blended these images and ideas with European and Native American traditions to create a uniquely African American culture. Slave spirituals and songs revealed this syncretism and gave enslaved people an opportunity to say what they were really feeling.

> Hail! all hail! ye Afric clan,
> Hail! ye oppressed, ye Afric band,
> Who toil and sweat in slavery bound
> And when your health and strength are gone
> Are left to hunger and to mourn,
> Let independence be your aim,
> Ever mindful what 'tis worth.
> Pledge your bodies for the prize,
> Pile them even to the skies!

Alongside the folk traditions that have formed a basis for much of the investigation into the lives of American slaves grew a burgeoning Afro-Christianity. Careful studies have documented varying rates of African American participation in the different Protestant denominations, which suggest that enslaved people may have been able to chose the denomination to which they belonged. Before Nat Turner's Rebellion in 1831 black ministers had played a key role in the leadership of enslaved evangelicals; however, following that event, southern communities policed such activities much more closely. Even without their own ministers, Afro Christians continued to join churches and profess their faith.

The Afro-Christian faith differed in important ways from what white evangelicals believed. The nature of African American religion in the post-Civil War period offers some insights into the beliefs of enslaved people before the war. Whereas proslavery evangelicals focused on submission to God and to masters, Afro Christians celebrated the day of jubilee, of deliverance from evil, and of the salvation that awaited those who believed. As one slave noted, "the idea of a revolution in the condition of whites and blacks, is the corner-stone of the religion of the latter." The prophetic tradition offered enslaved Christians an explanation of their world that recognized suffering but promised redemption. **David Walker**, author of the incendiary pamphlet *Appeal to the Coloured People of the World* (1829), took solace from God's omnipotence by quoting the Book of Common Prayer:

> The wicked swell'd with lawless pride,
> Have made the poor their prey;
> O, let them fall by those designs
> Which they for others lay

**STUDY QUESTIONS FOR SLAVERY AND ANTEBELLUM LIFE**

1. **In what ways did enslaved men and women challenge the system of slavery?**
2. **How did they create families and lives even while still enslaved?**
3. **How did slaveholders respond to this challenge?**

## THE RISE OF THE REPUBLICANS

The dispute over slavery that consumed Northerners and Southerners in the 1850s rarely recognized the humanity or the suffering of enslaved people that emerged so clearly from their music, stories, and actions. White Northerners opposed slavery—and principally the expansion of slavery in the western territories—because it corrupted and weakened the American political and economic system. Abolitionists appreciated the true horror of slavery—mostly as a result of the role played by black people in the movement after 1830—but they remained a tiny minority of Northerners. Unlike the social and cultural issues that gave rise to the Know-Nothing Party, this dispute

**Table 13.1 Political parties, 1830–1860** The mid-19th century was one of the most vibrant and fluid periods in American politics. Different groups formed and dissolved a variety of partisan organizations before the emergence of the Republican Party in the 1850s.

| **Majority Party** |
| --- |
| Democrats (1800–): supported state rights, slavery, and immigration |
| **Primary Opposition Parties** |
| Whigs (1830–1850s): supported federal investment in infrastructure and social reforms stemming from Second Great Awakening |
| American Know Nothing (early to mid-1850s): supported strong nativist platform |
| Republican (mid-1850s–): supported antislavery policies in western territories and federal investment in development |
| **Issue-Specific Parties** |
| Workingmen's (1830s): locally organized parties supporting workers' rights |
| Liberty Party (1840s): abolition party |
| Free Soil Party (1848 to early 1850s): opposed expansion of slavery into western territories |
| Anti-Masons (1828 to mid-1830s): opposed Freemasonry |
| Southern Rights (1850s): supported southern interests, especially protection of slavery |
| Union (early 1850s): southern offshoot of the Whig Party |
| Constitutional Union (1860): conservative compromise party dedicated to preserving the Union |

mapped itself along sectional lines and so held the potential to fracture the nation. Northerners emerged from the political turmoil of the second half of the 1850s with a new Republican Party, which brought stability to northern politics, but whose sectional posture ultimately inspired white Southerners to abandon the Union.

## Free Soil and Free Labor

Disputes over the expansion of slavery into the western territories stretched back to the Confederation Congress, which adopted the Northwest Ordinance banning slavery in the Upper Midwest region. Because the legal restrictions applied only to existing territory and because slavery continued to be profitable, the expansion of U.S. territory forced this problem on each succeeding generation. The 1820 Missouri Compromise settled the conflict that arose regarding the incorporation of the Louisiana Purchase lands by establishing a boundary between slave and free territory along Missouri's southern border. The acquisitions after the Mexican War precipitated a new round of conflict when Pennsylvania Democrat David Wilmot proposed that slavery be excluded from any new territory gained during the war. Congress voted repeatedly on the Wilmot Proviso but never passed it. Each vote exacerbated and highlighted sectional rather than partisan differences. As the *Boston Whig* explained of the Wilmot Proviso, "As if by magic, it brought to a head the great question which is about to divide the American people."

Although northern enthusiasm for "free soil"—territories organized without slavery—had a long history, political mobilization on this topic failed to unsettle the traditional parties, as the short-lived Liberty and Free Soil Parties demonstrated. The men who organized the Republican Party in the early 1850s possessed the foresight to wed free soil to the emerging philosophy of free labor. Building on midcentury discussions that capitalism and labor were taking place all across the Atlantic world, free labor theorists sought to incorporate propertyless men into the electorate without jeopardizing the stability of law and government. European nations had long restricted voting because they believed that propertyless men embittered by their failures might call for land redistribution if given the right to vote. The vast majority of unskilled (and even many skilled) workers in the United States owned no property. But, rather than being defined negatively by the land they did not own, free-labor theorists defined them by what they possessed—their labor to sell. This view ensured that workers accepted certain responsibilities when they signed a contract—such as assuming liability for personal harm or death in hazardous jobs—but also that employers had to respect contracts as well and could not arbitrarily fire or lower the wages of an employee without risking legal retribution. With this change laboring men entered the governmental system in a responsible manner; they now had an investment in the legal and political status quo. Free labor relied on continuous upward mobility. Men who entered the workforce laboring for others would save their money, succeed to independence, and employ younger men, and the virtuous cycle would repeat to enrich families and society. This Republican ideology juxtaposed the virtue and efficiency of the North's autonomous workers with the immorality and inefficiency of the South's slave economy.

Whig, and later, Republican, economic policies promoted the expansion of a commercial economy into the new regions of the West. Before companies, creditors, and cash could reach the region, however, the West needed laws and governments. Only with the area securely organized, including the all-important court system to resolve the inevitable conflicts over land deals, would investors commit resources. Because Northerners and Southerners clashed over whether the territory should be organized as free or slave land, territorial organization remained stalled. As a result, one of the most important legislative initiatives of the era—the **Transcontinental Railroad**—only passed Congress during the Civil War when the exit of southern Democrats from Congress gave Republicans the votes to organize the territories and pass the bill. Conflict over slavery's expansion effectively deadlocked Congress on major legislation for over a decade.

## The Politics of Slave Catching

Outside Congress problems manifested themselves along the border between slavery and freedom, where slaveholders complained about the lack of cooperation they received from northern state and local governments when their slaves escaped. The southern boundaries of Ohio and Pennsylvania emerged as the key battlegrounds. The 1842 Supreme Court case of *Prigg v. Pennsylvania* opened the subject on the national stage. Edward Prigg, acting for a Maryland slaveholder, entered Pennsylvania to reclaim a woman and her children who had escaped from bondage five years earlier. Prigg carried them off and Pennsylvania officials convicted him of kidnapping. A proslavery, southern majority on the Supreme Court used the case to create a national defense of slavery. The opinion, stating that no state law could "in any way qualify, regulate, control, or restrain" actions taken by slaveholders to reclaim their property, established a broad right of recapture. Accordingly, the Court set Prigg free and voided the Pennsylvania statute under which he was arrested.

Even more ominously, the sectional disputes over slave and free territory manifested themselves in religious institutions, which worried moderates everywhere. After a decade of controversy over whether Christianity sanctioned slaveholding, the Baptist and Methodist Churches divided over the issue of slavery in 1845. The subject had created controversy at national religious conventions for years, with antislavery forces from northern churches sponsoring resolutions to inhibit the ability of ministers to own or churches to use slave labor. At the same time southern ministers crafted the biblical defense of slavery. For Northerners this amounted to an unwarranted interference in politics and a gross misinterpretation of Christ's message of brotherly love. Southerners regarded the separation as cleansing.

The tangled problems of slavery, territories, and economic expansion reached a critical point in 1850. With the discovery of gold in California and the resulting flood of people to the region, Congress had been under pressure to admit the territory to statehood. Deadlocked over the question of whether California would be free or slave, Congress extended its session into the summer of 1850, and a mood of apprehension and fear gripped the capitol. The final legislation—known as the **Compromise of 1850**—admitted California as a free state, organized the remainder of the New Mexico Territory, banned the slave trade in the District of Columbia, empowered the Treasury to assume Texas's debts from its independence struggle, and gave the South a much stronger federal Fugitive Slave Law. This last provision proved to be the most controversial. It nationalized the process of slave capture and return by requiring federal judges to appoint "commissioners" to overhear cases of accused fugitives and by requiring the active complicity of state officers. Northerners, who assumed that most "slave catchers" simply kidnapped free blacks from the North, were appalled by the legislation, which assumed the guilt of the charged party, refused to allow blacks to testify, obviated the standard rules for evidence that would have been present in a court of law, and provided financial incentives for commissioners to find fugitives guilty ($10 as opposed to $5 for those found innocent).

All across the North individuals protested passage of the legislation, which they believed made them complicit in slavery: "A filthy law," "an outrage to humanity," proclaimed northern papers. Anyone who obeyed it ought to be "marked and treated as a moral leper," wrote one, while another advised those who did to "repent before God and ask His forgiveness." Bostonians made the most vigorous response, with abolitionists protesting and blocking the removal of accused fugitives through legal and illegal means. The 1854 rendition of the Virginia fugitive **Anthony Burns**, which precipitated an attack on federal marshals that left one dead, required President Pierce to mobilize the U.S. Marines in order to escort Burns from the city, as tens of thousands of Bostonians went out into the streets to protest. Burns, marched to the wharf past buildings hung with black bunting to symbolize the shame of the act, was the last fugitive slave returned from Boston.

In the context of the fight over the return of fugitive slaves, Harriet Beecher Stowe published *Uncle Tom's Cabin*, which quickly became the most popular novel of the 19th century. It sought to characterize the central crime of slavery as the destruction of slave families through sale and violence. Stowe, the daughter, sister, and wife of prominent northern ministers, drew enthusiasm for abolition from her involvement with the evangelical movement. Stowe's frank depiction of the hypocrisy, the sexual exploitation of enslaved women, and the cruelty inherent in the system aroused violent opposition in the South, where book burnings and mass protests greeted the novel. Spurred by Stowe's novel, which was read around the world, a half-million women in England, Ireland, and Scotland sent a petition calling for emancipation to the U.S. Congress.

The reality of federal protection for slave catchers rather than fugitive slaves, dramatized so effectively by Stowe, inspired several northern state legislatures to pass Personal Liberty laws designed to inhibit the operation of the **Fugitive Slave Act**. Despite the irony of their position, Southerners denounced these statutes as unconstitutional nullifications of federal law. When the federal government opposed slavery, Southerners increasingly used the language of state rights to criticize the actions, but when the federal government supported slavery, most white Southerners stood firmly behind its protection.

## The Politics of Expansion

The sundering of religious ties, the widening cultural differences, and the continuing political conflicts revealed internal tensions that contrasted sharply with the international optimism that the United States projected. As Commodore Perry launched his expedition to Japan, the author James Fenimore Cooper noted that Americans had "a longing to see distant lands" to determine the "differences which exist between the stranger and ourselves." Those global aspirations grew from a rapidly expanding economy and the new continental reach of the country itself even as some Americans worried that expansion could initiate an internal collapse like those that had beset previous empires.

If that collapse came, it would be on the plains of Kansas. After the admission of Missouri, Iowa, and Minnesota, territories farther to the west proved more difficult to organize. The controversies of the 1850s revolved around Kansas and Nebraska. As disputes over slavery heated up, pro-slavery settlers from Missouri pushed to make Kansas a test. They entered the Kansas territory with slaves or in support of slaveholding as a way to dominate the territorial government so that when it presented Congress with a plan for admission the state constitution would include slavery. Equally

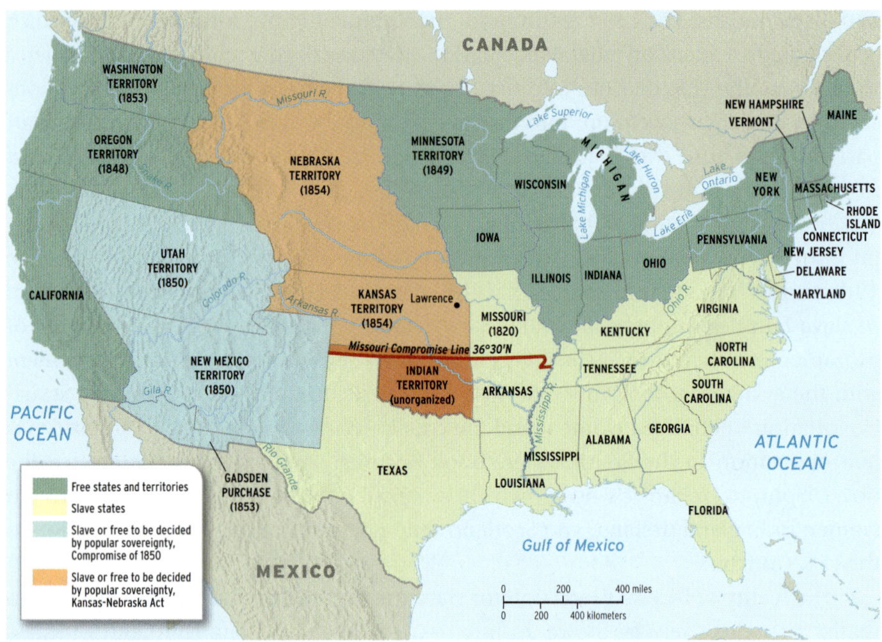


**Map 13.2**

**Territorial Organization, 1840s–1850s** After the Mexican War, Americans fought, first rhetorically and then physically, over whether the new territory should be opened to slavery. The 1854 Kansas-Nebraska Act, intended to settle the controversy, only stoked more anger among Northerners who condemned its repeal of the Missouri Compromise line.

motivated to "win" Kansas, free-state settlers mobilized in the East and headed to the territory to combat the pro-slavery "ruffians." Organized by entities such as the New England Emigrant Aid society, free-state settlers understood themselves as the advance guard in a growing war over slavery within the United States. Armed with "Beecher's Bibles," local slang for the Springfield rifles carried by emigrants and named for abolitionist minister Lyman Ward Beecher, antislavery and pro-slavery forces knew this would not be a war of words.

**Stephen Douglas**, the northern leader of the Democratic Party and champion of the Transcontinental Railroad, sought to pacify the Kansas conflict by organizing the territory under the banner of what he called "popular sovereignty." This would have left the decision for or against slavery up to the people present in a territory when it voted for organization. To allow popular sovereignty, Douglas had to engineer the removal of the Missouri Compromise, which, with its prohibition on slavery in territory north of 36°30′, prohibited a slaveholding Kansas. This policy change came in the Kansas-Nebraska Act. Despite fearing that the bill would "raise a hell of a storm" in the North, Douglas hoped it would resolve sectional conflict. Southerners appreciated the legislation, but the northern response—overwhelming in its dissatisfaction—went a long way toward ruining Douglas's political prospects toward higher office. Tens of thousands of Northerners protested the act's removal of a 30-year-old policy that had, they argued, successfully obviated the more violent sectional disagreements that were sure to appear without it. The most well-publicized critique, "The Appeal of the Independent Democrats," arraigned "this bill as a gross violation of a sacred pledge; as a criminal betrayal of precious rights; as part and parcel of an atrocious plot to exclude from a vast unoccupied region immigrants from the Old World and free laborers from our own States, and convert it into a dreary region of despotism, inhabited by masters and slaves." The bill undermined support among Northerners for the Democratic Party and inspired the formation of the Republicans. Concerned about what he regarded as an unwarranted acquiescence to pro-slavery forces, Abraham Lincoln reentered politics in 1854. The repeal of the Missouri Compromise was "wrong in its direct effect, letting slavery into Kansas and Nebraska—and wrong in its prospective principle, allowing it to spread to every other part of the wide world," Lincoln said.

Rather than stemming the bloodshed, the Kansas-Nebraska Act seemed to encourage it. Newspapers carried weekly reports about bloody attacks and reprisals between free and slave state settlers. **John Brown**, an evangelical abolitionist from the East, perpetrated one of the most infamous such episodes, when he and his sons attacked a family of pro-slavery settlers along Pottawatomie Creek, hacking them to death with broad swords. Possibly influenced by groups of revolutionary activists from Europe with whom he collaborated, Brown had abandoned the pacifism and

SACKING OF LAWRENCE.

▲

As the status of slavery in the territories consumed the attention of politicians and citizens in the East, pro-slavery and antislavery factions engaged in personal and communal violence on the ground in Kansas. For Northerners, the infamous attack on the free-state capital of Lawrence represented slavery's chaotic and violent influence on American life.

moderate approach of his eastern counterparts. This group included two Britons energized by the Chartist movement, a Polish revolutionary, a Bavarian, and a Vienna-born Jew who fought under Hungary's Kossuth. After the failures of 1848 to produce liberal states, European radicals may well have seen America as a more hospitable climate. Brown's actions reflected a similar frustration with slow pace of change. He and his sons escaped punishment for the massacre, but his infamy preceded him as he headed back east. The violence reached a head with the "Sack of Lawrence" in 1856, when a pro-slavery posse entered the city, destroyed two printing presses, and burned down the Free State Hotel.

In response to the attack on Lawrence, Massachusetts Republican **Charles Sumner**, the first abolitionist senator, took to the Senate floor for a two-day speech titled "The Crime Against Kansas." Because the speech mocked one of South Carolina's senators, Democratic Congressman Preston Brooks, the senator's cousin, attacked Sumner in the Senate and beat him into unconsciousness. For Northerners Sumner was a martyr to the unchecked violence and incapacity for rational actions that typified the slaveholding South. Was it any surprise, said Northerners, that men who grow up beating their slaves should turn their whip on those with whom they disagree? Brooks resigned his seat after a modest censure by the House, and his constituents immediately reelected him. Sumner earned the drubbing he received, Southerners said, and to replace the lost cane thousands of them sent Brooks new ones, with inscriptions such as "Bully for Brooks!"

## The Politics of Sectionalism

The rise of the Republican Party challenged the Democratic supremacy that had reigned since Andrew Jackson's day. Because of the population disparity between the sections, the North possessed more electoral votes and more seats in the House of Representatives. To stay viable at the national level northern Democrats had to retain their bisectional coalition, and to accomplish this they had to respect the wishes of their southern colleagues. Stephen Douglas observed this rule when he pushed for the repeal of the Missouri Compromise. But doing too much endangered the standing of northern Democrats with their constituents. Those who sacrificed all to retain the support of southern slaveholders were called "doughfaces." President **Franklin Pierce**, who had signed the Kansas-Nebraska Act and then supported an aggressively pro-slavery constitution when the territory petitioned for confirmation as a state, was a doughface. So was James Buchanan, a Pennsylvania Democrat elected president in 1856, and the last Democratic president until Grover Cleveland in 1885. Despite the public scorn for men like Buchanan, the Democratic Party remained one of the last truly national institutions in the late 1850s. Gone were the churches, the voluntary associations, the businessmen's alliances, and the Whig Party. The presidential election of 1860 would put the Democrats to the test as well.

The thorny problem of the status of slaves and of the territories emerged again publicly with the Supreme Court's ***Dred Scott* decision** in 1857. Widely regarded as one of the worst decisions of the High Court, it was yet another attempt to settle the pressing questions of the day that instead intensified them. Scott had been enslaved to an army surgeon who spent years posted to the Illinois and Wisconsin territory when those areas were under the Northwest Ordinance. Scott's lawyers claimed that he had been illegally held as a slave in free territory. Justice **Roger B. Taney**, a Maryland slaveholder who had already freed his slaves but held a deep contempt for black people, wrote the majority opinion. Taney ruled that Scott lacked the standing to bring the case and consequently dismissed it. His opinion also included the infamous line that the black man "had no rights which the white man was bound to respect." In direct contravention of the case law on the subject, Taney ruled that black people could not be citizens. On the question of where slaveholders could take their property in safety, Taney issued a broad federal protection of slavery. Taney ruled that the Missouri Compromise, although already defunct, had been unconstitutional because Congress could not legislate on slavery in the territories.

This sweeping denunciation of a right that Northerners had presumed existed for the past 70 years shocked and outraged them. Republicans made the decision a key rhetorical weapon in their arsenal, evidence of a grand conspiracy among slaveholders and their allies in Washington to foist a fully nationalized protection of slavery on northern states. What Northerners knew was that from the Mexican War through the disputes over organizing Kansas and returning fugitive slaves, the South seemed able to manipulate the federal government to buttress its interests while the North stood by haplessly. The *Dred Scott* decision fulfilled Southerners' highest hopes for protecting slavery in the territories, though in doing so through federal rather than state power it undercut southern arguments that state rights provided the surest foundation for slavery.

Dred Scott's lawsuit made him perhaps the most famous enslaved person in the United States. The decision inflamed sectional tensions still more rather than extinguishing them as Chief Justice Roger Taney had hoped.

Abraham Lincoln reflected moderate northern antislavery opinion on the decision, which he condemned strongly as wrong in legal, political, and moral terms, but pledged to obey while it stood. Other Americans were not so willing to acquiesce. John Brown, of Kansas fame, came east after the Pottawatomie massacre and planned a more direct response to the problem of slavery. Brown, along with his sons and a handful of black and white supporters, attacked the U.S. arsenal at **Harpers Ferry**, Virginia, in late 1859. Funded secretly by six prominent abolitionists, Brown had organized and drilled his men in a small southern Pennsylvania town not far from Harpers Ferry. During preparation Brown approached Frederick Douglass for support. Douglass, denouncing the plan and pleading with Brown to put off the attack, argued that it was sure to fail and in the process alienate moderate Northerners while encouraging the pro-slavery forces in the South. Brown ignored Douglass, whose concern proved well founded. The plan to seize the town and the arsenal misfired from the start. The first victim was a free black man, a night watchman for the Baltimore & Ohio Railroad. News of the attack reached Washington, DC, and a squadron of U.S. Marines, led by Colonel **Robert E. Lee**, arrived in Harpers Ferry the next morning. Lee's forces penned Brown's men in a barn and killed several and captured the rest, including Brown. Brown was charged with attempting to incite a slave insurrection, and as expected was found guilty and executed. Virginia Governor **Henry Wise** expressed the will of the white South when he wrote that "we cannot suffer such insults without suffering worse than the death of citizens—without suffering dishonor, the death of a state."

Brown retained his composure in jail and on the scaffold. His famous pronouncement at his trial recognized that he could do more as a martyr than as a man: "Now,

## TIMELINE 1829–1860

**1829**

David Walker publishes *An Appeal to the Coloured Citizens of the World*

**1833**

Britain passes West India Emancipation Act, ending slavery in the British West Indies

**1839**

Britain begins First Opium War in China (ends 1842)

**1840**

William Henry Harrison elected first Whig President but dies after a month in office and succeeded by John Tyler

First World Antislavery Convention held

**1842**

*Prigg v. Pennsylvania* establishes national authority for reclaiming fugitive slaves

**1844**

Methodist Episcopal Church, South formed in dispute over slavery

Anti-Catholic riots in Philadelphia

**February 26** U.S. Congress passes Texas Annexation Act

**1845**

**December 29** United States formally annexes Texas

Baptists divide over slavery

**1846**

**April** United States declares war on Mexico

**June 14** "Bear Flag" Revolt initiates collapse of Mexican authority in California

**August 8** Pennsylvania Democrat David Wilmot proposes amendment to Mexican War Appropriations Bill outlawing slavery in lands acquired from the war

**1847**

**March** General Winfield Scott lands at Veracruz, Mexico, defeats Mexican forces, and begins march toward Mexico City

**September** U.S. Army captures Mexico City

**1848**

**February** Treaty of Guadalupe Hidalgo ends the Mexican War and cedes 500,000 square miles of Mexican territory to the United States

**July** Last U.S. troops leave Mexico

**November** Whig Zachary Taylor elected president

**December** Gold discovered near Sutter's Mill in California

**1850**

Compromise of 1850 passes, which includes provisions admitting California as a free state; opening New Mexico territory to organization under popular sovereignty; banning the slave trade in Washington, DC; and creating a strong federal Fugitive Slave Act if it is deemed necessary that I should forfeit my life for the furtherance of the ends of justice, and mingle my blood further with the blood of my children and with the blood of millions in this slave country whose rights are disregarded by wicked, cruel, and unjust enactments, I submit; so let it be done!"

The public reaction in each section to John Brown's raid, like reactions to the caning of Charles Sumner three years before, reflected the yawning chasm between the people of the North and South. For Southerners Brown was the predictable conclusion of the increasingly radical rhetoric of abolitionists bent on exterminating the southern people. "Every village bell which tolled its solemn note at the execution of Brown proclaims to the South the approbation of that village of insurrection and servile war," wrote one prominent Southerner. Radicals in the North celebrated and lionized Brown—Henry David Thoreau eulogized him, saying "some eighteen hundred years ago Christ was crucified; this morning, perchance, Captain Brown was hung. These are the two ends of a chain which is not without its links. He is not Old Brown any longer; he is an angel of light."

Most Northerners were less effusive. Democrats and conservatives denounced him in no uncertain terms, and Republicans like Lincoln condemned Brown's method while trying to respect his motive. Any sympathy, no matter how mild, proved too much for Southerners. The fire-eaters of the South used Brown's raid, ineffectual as it was, to spur Southerners on to support secession. Brown's plan and timing may have failed at Harpers Ferry, but in the context of his day he could scarcely have chosen a better time. A perfect storm of politics and sectionalism had gathered force throughout the 1850s, before Brown's raid concluded the decade and sent Americans into the most contentious and important presidential election in U.S. history.

**1852**

Harriet Beecher Stowe publishes *Uncle Tom's Cabin* giving expression to northern antislavery sentiment

Election of Democratic Franklin Pierce to the presidency

**1853**

Commodore Perry arrives in Tokyo Bay, Japan

**1854**

Kansas-Nebraska Act passed abolishing the Missouri Compromise Line of 1820

Rendition of fugitive slave Anthony Burns from Boston inflames northern opposition to Fugitive Slave Act

First Republican Party convention held in Jackson, MI

**1855**

American Party formally organized linking various nativist parties across the country

**1856**

**May 18–19** Charles Sumner delivers "Crime Against Kansas" speech in U.S. Senate

**May 22** Preston Brooks beats Charles Sumner in Senate chamber

Pro-slavery guerrillas from Missouri lead "Sack of Lawrence" in Kansas Territory

**November** Democrat James Buchanan elected president

Whig party collapses in most states

**1857**

*Dred Scott* denies citizenship to African Americans

Hinton Helper publishes *The Impending Crisis,* denouncing slavery's effect on the political and economic freedom of poor white men in the South

**1859**

Gold discovered near Pike's Peak in Colorado

**December** John Brown leads failed slave insurrection at Harpers Ferry, VA

**1860**

Black population in the United States reaches four million

### STUDY QUESTIONS FOR THE RISE OF THE REPUBLICANS

1. **Why did Northerners and Southerners fight over Kansas and in what ways did such violence reshape national politics?**
2. **How did the dispute over slavery (in all parts of the country) escalate in the 1850s?**

## Summary

- American expansionists pushed the nation into conflict with Mexico and in the process dramatically changed the ethnic profile of the nation, as they drew within its borders Spanish-speaking residents of California and the Far West.
- Combined with the continuing influx of Irish and German immigrants, this demographic transformation scared Anglo-Americans into a repressive movement, known as nativism, designed to guarantee political control by Protestant elites.
- The acquisition of new territory inspired an escalating battle in Congress among pro-slavery and antislavery forces and mirrored the tensions within the South itself.
- As slaves fought against the system from within, and pro-slavery and pro-free-soil citizens fought each other in Kansas, Republicans coalesced around a policy opposing the expansion of slavery.

## Key Terms and People

## Reviewing Chapter 13

1. How did the movement of people into and around the United States affect political developments of the period?
2. What was the relationship between slavery and the sectional politics of the 1850s?

## Further Reading

Davis, David Brion. *Inhuman Bondage: The Rise and Fall of Slavery in the New World.* New York: Oxford University Press, 2006. A global history of the commercial slavery that dominated the Western Hemisphere during the 17th, 18th, and 19th centuries.

Foner, Eric. *Free Soil, Free Labor, Free Men: The Ideology of the Republican Party Before the Civil War,* 2d ed. New York: Oxford University Press, 1995. The clearest analysis of the various forces that shaped the early Republican Party.

Holt, Michael. *The Political Crisis of the 1850s.* New York: Norton, 1978. A concise history of the partisan collapse that prefigured the sectional crisis.

Johnson, Walter. *Soul By Soul: Life Inside the Antebellum Slave Market.* Cambridge, MA: Harvard University Press, 1999. An insightful cultural and economic analysis of the operation of slave markets.

Rugemer, Edward Bartlett. *The Problem of Emancipation: The Caribbean Roots of the American Civil War.* Baton Rouge: Louisiana State University, 2008. A hemispheric history of the relationship between British emancipation and secession and war.

West, Elliott. *The Contested Plains: Indians, Goldseekers, and the Rush to Colorado.* Lawrence, KS: University Press of Kansas, 1998. A fascinating history of the 1859 Colorado gold rush and the competing forces over development and settlement in the middle of the continent.

# Visual Review

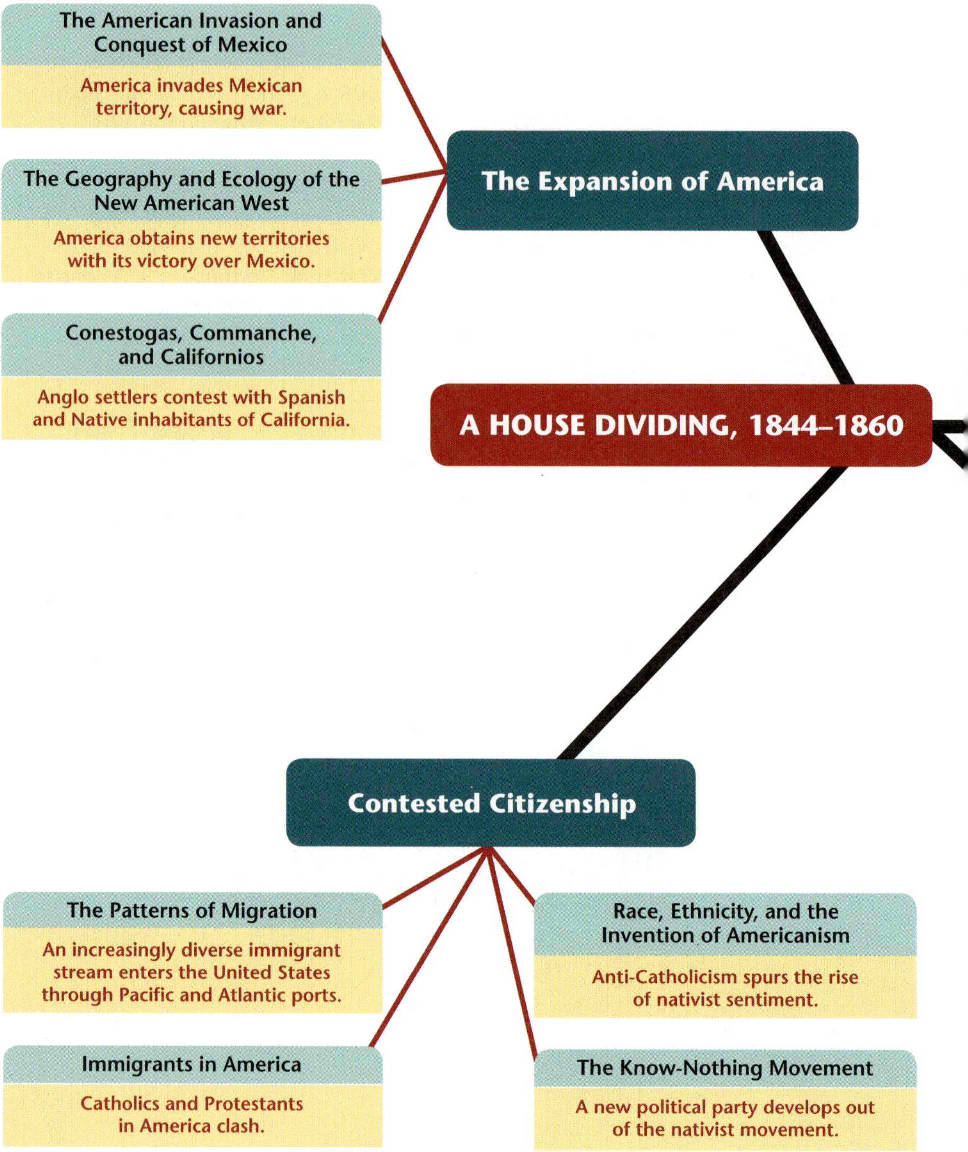

## A HOUSE DIVIDING, 1844–1860

### The Expansion of America

**The American Invasion and Conquest of Mexico**
America invades Mexican territory, causing war.

**The Geography and Ecology of the New American West**
America obtains new territories with its victory over Mexico.

**Conestogas, Commanche, and Californios**
Anglo settlers contest with Spanish and Native inhabitants of California.

### Contested Citizenship

**The Patterns of Migration**
An increasingly diverse immigrant stream enters the United States through Pacific and Atlantic ports.

**Immigrants in America**
Catholics and Protestants in America clash.

**Race, Ethnicity, and the Invention of Americanism**
Anti-Catholicism spurs the rise of nativist sentiment.

**The Know-Nothing Movement**
A new political party develops out of the nativist movement.

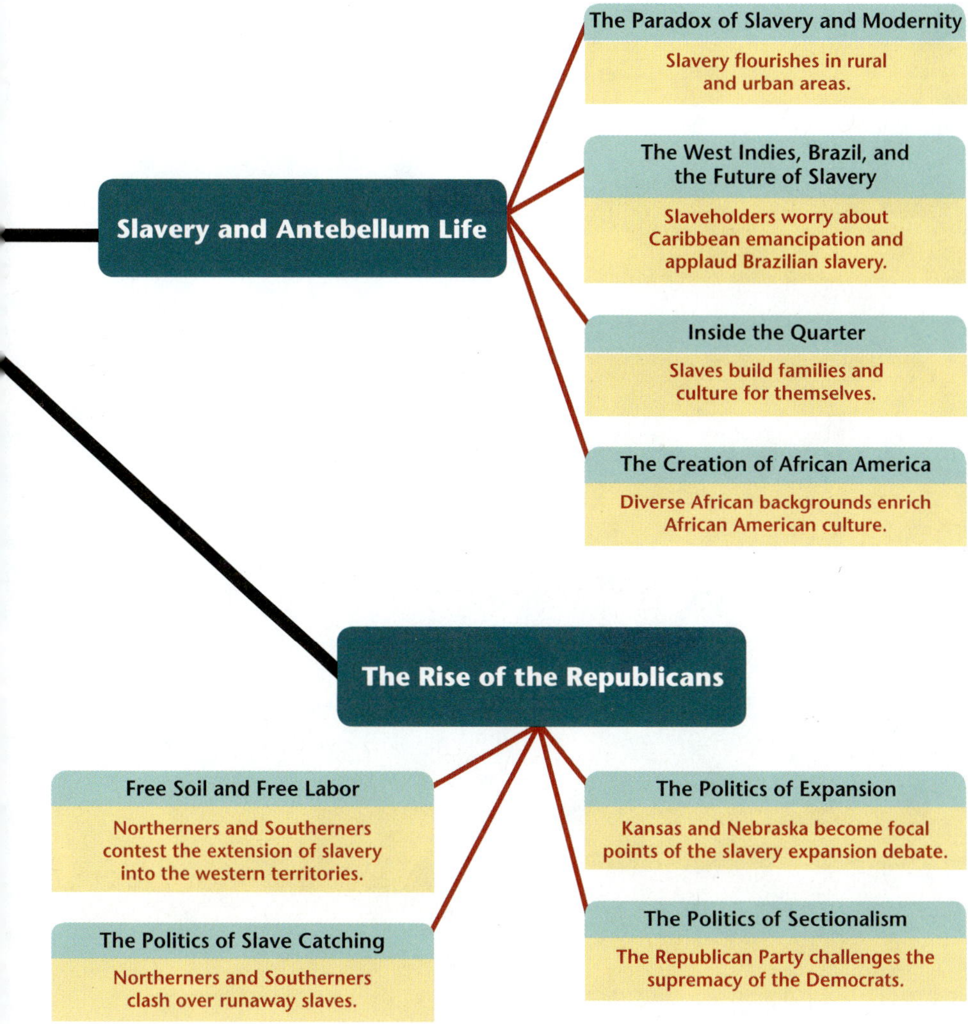

## Slavery and Antebellum Life

**The Paradox of Slavery and Modernity**
Slavery flourishes in rural and urban areas.

**The West Indies, Brazil, and the Future of Slavery**
Slaveholders worry about Caribbean emancipation and applaud Brazilian slavery.

**Inside the Quarter**
Slaves build families and culture for themselves.

**The Creation of African America**
Diverse African backgrounds enrich African American culture.

## The Rise of the Republicans

**Free Soil and Free Labor**
Northerners and Southerners contest the extension of slavery into the western territories.

**The Politics of Slave Catching**
Northerners and Southerners clash over runaway slaves.

**The Politics of Expansion**
Kansas and Nebraska become focal points of the slavery expansion debate.

**The Politics of Sectionalism**
The Republican Party challenges the supremacy of the Democrats.

# 14 The Civil War

## 1860–1865

In early 1865 the top labor reform activists in Europe wrote to Abraham Lincoln to express their support. The International Workingmen's Association, which included representatives from France, Poland, Switzerland, Italy, Denmark, Germany, and England, applauded Lincoln's effort to destroy the "oligarchy" of slaveholders that dominated American politics. "The workingmen of Europe," they proclaimed, "felt instinctively that the star-spangled banner carried the destiny of their class." Lincoln, who had proclaimed the Union "the last, best hope of earth," would have agreed; by liberating slaves from their masters and the South from slavery, the North enlarged the meaning of freedom for all people.

The letter writers participated in a global debate about the meaning of democracy, a fluid concept in the 1850s and 1860s. Great Britain, ruled by a king within a constitutional democracy, steadily liberalized important features of its political system. German reformers pressed for more autonomous parliaments to operate without monarchs. Hungarian and Polish activists challenged the power of kings and nobles. The United States maintained the most fully developed democracy and so served as an inspiration to radicals and a warning to conservatives across the globe.

British reformers, more than anyone, studied the American experience. In 1832 the British parliament passed the first Reform Act, granting the vote to upper-middle-class men. Support for expanding suffrage continued to grow and in 1867 the conservative Tories expanded the franchise to most men, though they retained a property requirement (finally

◄ Jefferson Davis and Cabinet with General Lee in the council chamber in Richmond, c. 1866

**CHAPTER OUTLINE**



*continued on page 523*

# America in the World

President Lincoln and Congress outlawed slavery in the United States, although Confederate States resisted (1862).

Final Emancipation Proclamation signed, freeing all slaves in Confederate territory (1863).

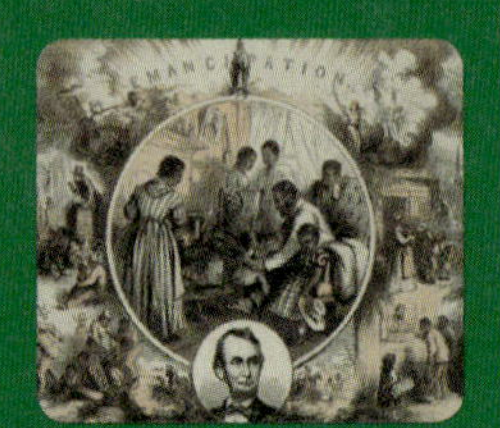

U.S. event that influenced the world

International event that influenced the United States

Event with multinational influence

Conflict

Thirteenth Amendment ratified, abolishing slavery in the United States (1865).

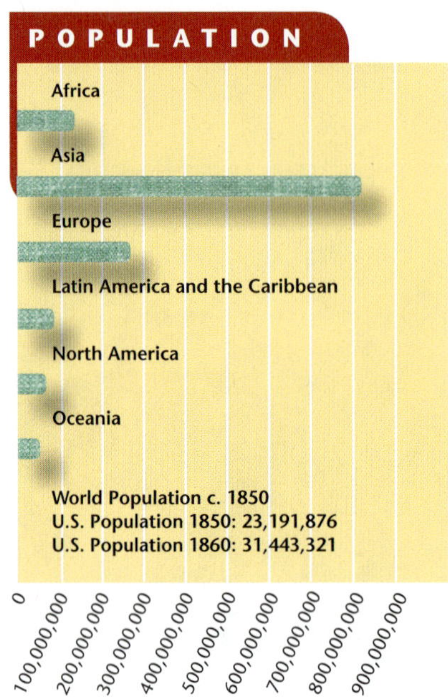


lifted in 1884). Britons drew contrasting lessons about the meaning of the U.S. Civil War. Aristocrats saw the proof they needed to oppose the liberalization of British society. Universal manhood suffrage, in their view, had led to the dissolution of the United States and revealed the inability of most men to handle the responsibility of voting. Reformers, on the other hand, took solace from the fact that the Union eventually persevered and, in the process, abolished slavery. For them the survival of American democracy gave legitimacy to the institution worldwide. German reformers likewise cheered on the republic, hopeful that it could help them resuscitate the changes initiated in the 1848 revolutions.

The members of the International Workingmen's Association saw in Lincoln's efforts a continuation of what they had begun in their own countries in the 1830s and 1840s. Latin American reformers like **Simón Bolívar** likewise would have recognized something familiar occurring north of the border. The national independence movements from Spain coincided with efforts to broaden access to land and political power within their countries. But as all these well-intentioned men could testify, the scale of change they envisioned provoked resistance from the entrenched elite in every country. In the United States, as in Europe and Latin America, the clash of these forces produced bloodshed and destruction.

## SECESSION, 1860–1861

In 1860 widespread violence still lay in the future and adversaries sparred through politics alone. From the perspective of white Southerners, the rapid growth of the northern states, built on immigration from northwestern Europe and increasingly extensive economic ties around the globe, threatened the balance of power within the United States. Fearful about the future of slavery under a Republican administration, a majority of slaveholding states seceded from the Union. Few anticipated anything more than a short war, if that. Many Southerners assumed that their central place as cotton-supplier to French and British textile manufacturers would bring recognition of their new nation before any real war began. For their part Northerners interpreted secession as a repudiation of self-government, a threat to both America and the future of democracy around the world. Northerners went to war in 1861 to reunify the nation. Determined southern resistance compelled increasingly severe measures from the North. A war for union evolved into a war for emancipation with a twisted legacy of violence, anger, hope, and joy.

## The Secession of the Lower South

**CHAPTER OUTLINE**

*continued from page 519*



The battle began with the election of 1860. The Democrats convened their party in Charleston, South Carolina, home to the most rabid pro-secession wing of the party. The convention deadlocked when the northern wing, led by Stephen Douglas, refused to adopt a slave code to ensure federal protection for slavery in the western territories. Fire-eaters, advocates of immediate secession, from Deep South states abandoned the meeting rather than accept defeat on this measure. Northern Democrats reconvened in Baltimore several weeks later and nominated Douglas, while southern Democrats nominated Senator **John Breckinridge** of Kentucky. Republicans likewise entered their convention in Chicago divided over who should lead the party. Most regarded party leaders **William Henry Seward** and **Samuel Chase** as too radical on the question of slavery. Local favorite **Abraham Lincoln** won the nomination partly because of his strong national showing in the 1858 senatorial campaign against Stephen Douglas and partly because he did not have a long track record. Lincoln had long made his personal opposition to slavery clear, but as a strict constitutionalist he also recognized that neither Congress nor the president had authority over slavery where it already existed. One more party organized itself out of the remnants of the southern Whigs and nominated Kentuckian **John Bell**. Calling themselves the Constitutional Union Party, they advocated little beyond a moderate appeal to "Union" in their campaign platform. The four-way contest thus presented voters with the most complex ballot since the election of 1824.

The campaign mirrored the deep sectional divisions in the country. Lincoln appeared only before northern audiences and many southern registrars refused to even print his name on ballots. Breckinridge campaigned in the South and Bell toured mostly the middle of the country. Douglas was the only candidate who campaigned nationally, reprimanding both southern and northern extremists whom he believed threatened the Union. Breckinridge never advocated secession, though he was clearly the candidate most sympathetic to the cause of southern rights. Lincoln's strategy was to attract the support of the Lower North—Illinois, Indiana, Ohio, and Pennsylvania in particular—and combine it with Republican New England. Because Lincoln had never belonged to the Know-Nothing Party, he remained attractive to immigrant voters who would have rejected nativist Republicans. Although Lincoln was not an abolitionist, his firm opposition to the expansion of slavery into the western territories alarmed those Southerners who regarded slavery's expansion as essential to its survival and angered those Southerners who regarded limits to slavery's expansion an affront to the region's honor as well as a violation of constitutionally protected

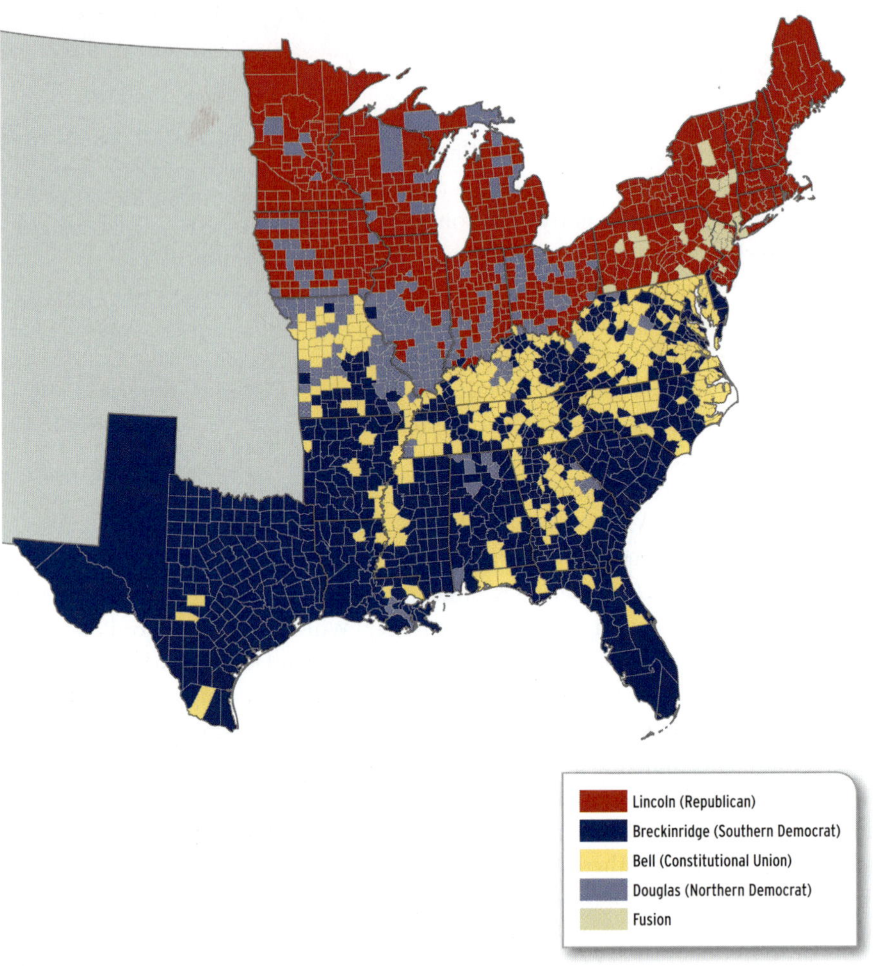


▲ **Map 14.1**

**1860 Presidential Election, by County** The four-way contest exacerbated sectional discontent. Abraham Lincoln won the northern states and enough electoral votes to secure the office, while John Breckinridge won the South, and John Bell and Stephen Douglas shared states in the country's middle.

property rights. Although he captured only 40 percent of the popular vote, Lincoln won the November 6 election by securing a majority in the electoral college.

South Carolina responded first to Lincoln's election. On December 20, 1860, the state "dissolved" its relationship to the Union. The "Declaration of Causes" issued by the convention began with a stark explanation of slavery's centrality to secession: "our position is thoroughly identified with the institution of slavery—the greatest material interest of the world." Although Lincoln had not yet assumed office and had explicitly condemned the actions of John Brown and other radical abolitionists, his Republican affiliation convinced them that the institution was doomed. Fellow fire-eaters in Mississippi would soon state the case in equally stark language: "There was no choice left us but submission to the mandates of abolition, or a dissolution of the Union, whose principles had been subverted to work out our ruin." The next step was for South Carolina to persuade other slaveholding states to leave the Union as well. Alabama, and over the next six weeks Florida, Georgia, Mississippi, Louisiana, and Texas, followed suit, though none demonstrated as much unity as South Carolina. In each of these states substantial minorities opposed immediate secession. Despite this conflict, prosecession forces in Texas and other southern states won the day and led their states out of the Union. On February 4, 1861, representatives of the seven Deep South states assembled in Montgomery, Alabama, and created the Confederate States of America.

## Fort Sumter and the Secession of the Upper South

During the long interim between the election and Lincoln's inauguration in March 1861, President **James Buchanan** did little to address the crisis. Buchanan believed that secession was unconstitutional but that he was powerless to intervene. Buchanan's "hands-off" policy gave seceding states the false impression that the U.S. government would do nothing to impede their exit. Lincoln waited out the lame-duck period at his home in Springfield, Illinois, where he reiterated his oft-stated position that the president had no power over slavery in the states where it already existed but that Congress could regulate or ban slavery in the territories.

Lincoln's inauguration on March 4, 1861, was a solemn affair; it occurred under the cloud of uncertainty about the Union's future that he had pledged to preserve. In his inaugural speech, Lincoln appealed to Southerners to remain loyal—"we are not enemies, but friends"—and to respect the shared history ("the mystic chords of memory") that bound them to the United States. Lincoln's supporters regarded the speech as moderate and conciliatory, whereas opponents considered his declaration that the Union would "hold, occupy, and possess the property and places belonging to the government" a threat to their peace and security. Both Lincoln and Mississippian **Jefferson Davis**, who resigned from Congress and accepted the presidency of the Confederacy, moved cautiously. Both faced similar challenges, and for both the momentum of events initiated by others pushed them along. Northerners demanded that Lincoln restore control over federal property—principally coastal forts and armories in the South—while Southerners pushed Davis to assert Confederate control over the same places.

Even as both sides considered the possibility of war, Upper South representatives continued to embrace negotiation. Pro-secession forces knew they represented a minority view in the region, so they inflamed fears of Lincoln. Pro-Union forces sought conciliatory agreements from Lincoln and Congress that would reassure Southerners that slavery would be protected. Congress passed and two states ratified a new amendment that would have guaranteed slavery in the states where it existed. But with most southern representatives resigned from Congress, these compromise measures were too little too late. To entice their slaveholding brethren in the Upper South to join them, several Deep South states sent commissioners to the region to argue for the necessity of a unified slaveholding South. The Alabama Commissioner, Stephen Hale, told Kentuckians that Northerners "had been waging an unrelenting and fanatical war" against slavery since the 1830s. Under a Lincoln administration whites would "be degraded to a position of equality with free negroes . . . or else there will be an eternal war of races, desolating the land with blood, and utterly wasting and destroying all the resources of the country." Hale's conclusion was clear: "Disunion is inevitable."

The crisis peaked at Fort Sumter, an unfinished earthen fort located in Charleston Harbor. The U.S. commander at the fort, a Kentuckian named Robert Anderson, notified Washington that he could not last without provisions. Lincoln sent an unarmed ship to restock the food supplies for the small garrison. On April 12, 1861, before the ship reached the harbor, Confederate batteries on neighboring islands opened fire on Fort Sumter. This artillery duel initiated war. The veteran British journalist **William Howard Russell**, arriving in Charleston on April 17, observed that "the streets of Charleston present some such aspect of those of Paris in the last revolution." Just as the French Revolution had global implications, so too did the Civil War, and Europeans watched the conflict carefully. European reformers had already witnessed the power of civil wars to derail nascent democracy movements in 1848 and strongly supported the North, especially once it turned decisively against slavery. British elites and commercial interests, however, felt a kinship with the proud southern planters and saw economic advantage in a divided North America.

RICHMOND
SECESSION EGG
"Whew! That Old Hen, Jeff Davis, has been trying to hatch a Rotten Egg."

This cartoon reveals northern scorn for secession and the easy assumption among Northerners that curtailing the process would be quick and painless.

## Mobilization for War

In the wake of the battle at Fort Sumter Lincoln called up the militia, requesting 75,000 men enlisted for 90 days to help restore obedience to the law of the United States. This action, combined with the drama of the showdown in Charleston Harbor, forced Upper South states to choose sides. Upper South politicians who had resisted secession regarded Lincoln's decision to mobilize an army as an act of betrayal after the months of quiet negotiation that had filled the late winter and early spring. Four more slave states—Virginia, North Carolina, Tennessee, and Arkansas—left the Union for the Confederacy while four others (Missouri, Kentucky, Maryland, and Delaware) remained loyal. A wave of martial enthusiasm swept both the North and the South. **George Templeton Strong** detailed changes in New York City: "The Northern backbone is much stiffened already. Many who stood up for 'Southern rights' and complained of wrongs done the South now say that, since the South has fired the first gun, they are ready to go to all lengths in supporting the government." At county courthouses, town squares, and city centers, hundreds of thousands of men volunteered for the Union and Confederate armies. The mobilization process demonstrated that the Civil War would be a truly popular conflict, fought by two democracies with the consent of a majority of their citizens. Women in both sections eagerly supported mobilization. Each side contained dissidents, including Unionists in the

The local nature of enlistment and mobilization in the Civil War generated enthusiasm among soldiers and civilians alike. Both groups anticipated a short, relatively bloodless affair.

South who volunteered to serve in U.S. units or actively aided northern troops as they came south. But the war proved to be one of the first truly popular wars, in which the people themselves initiated and sustained the fighting.

In retrospect the North's military advantages seem so significant that southern enthusiasm looks arrogant or rash. At the time, however, most Southerners and many Northerners identified differences more important than manpower and supplies. On paper the North was much better equipped to fight. It possessed a 5:2 advantage in terms of eligible soldiers, over twice as many draft animals, and a vastly greater industrial capacity. Most importantly the North had a more modernized, commercialized, and dynamic economic system. Southerners invested their money in land and slaves, and neither could easily be sold to pay for the war. But the South held both geographic and psychological advantages. The land mass of the Confederacy was three-quarters of a million square miles—larger than the size of continental Europe—with a 3,000 mile coastline; thus, it seemed too large to be fully conquered by Union forces. Southerners also fought a defensive war—they knew the terrain and took pride and strength in the fact that they were defending their homes against invasion.

The U.S. Army contained only 15,000 men in 1860, and nearly one-third of the officers and enlisted men resigned to join the Confederacy. The navy had only three functional vessels in U.S. waters ready for duty. As a result, northern advantages, especially its larger population and greater economic resources, would matter only in a long war. Both sides anticipated a brief struggle—perhaps lasting no longer than the fall of 1861. Washington was unprepared for the influx of men who arrived in the late spring—tens of thousands more than Lincoln's initial call—and without proper facilities they slept in the Patent Office, the hallways of the capitol building, and any other federal facility that had space. The Confederacy established a training camp outside Richmond to accommodate the influx of troops from around the South.

Even more pressing for the North than space to house soldiers was a vision of the war's purpose. Frederick Douglass and other abolitionists saw the war as an opportunity to destroy slavery. In the May 1861 issue of *Douglass' Monthly* Douglass began his campaign to forge the link between Union and emancipation. Douglass wrote, "Fire must be met with water, darkness with light, and war for the destruction of liberty must be met with war for the destruction of slavery. *The simple way then, to put an end to the savage and desolating war now waged by the slaveholders, is to strike down slavery itself,* the primal cause of the war." Democrats and conservative Republicans condemned bloodshed and the destruction (or confiscation) of property from other Americans. Lincoln seemed personally aligned with the broad middle of the country. A passionate defender of the Union, he insisted that the first and only goal for the North was the restoration of the rule of law and the obedience of southern state governments to national law. White Southerners had a shorter explanation for their behavior—they were defending their autonomy, their independence, as free people. They openly acknowledged that their freedom depended on the preservation of racial slavery. The vice president of the Confederacy, **Alexander Stephens**, famously proclaimed black slavery "the cornerstone" of the new republic.

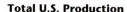

**Total U.S. Population and Military Service**

100%
90
80
70
60
50
40
30
20
10
0

Total population
Free male population, age18–60 years
Freeman, age 18–60 years, in military service 1864

Union States
Confederate States

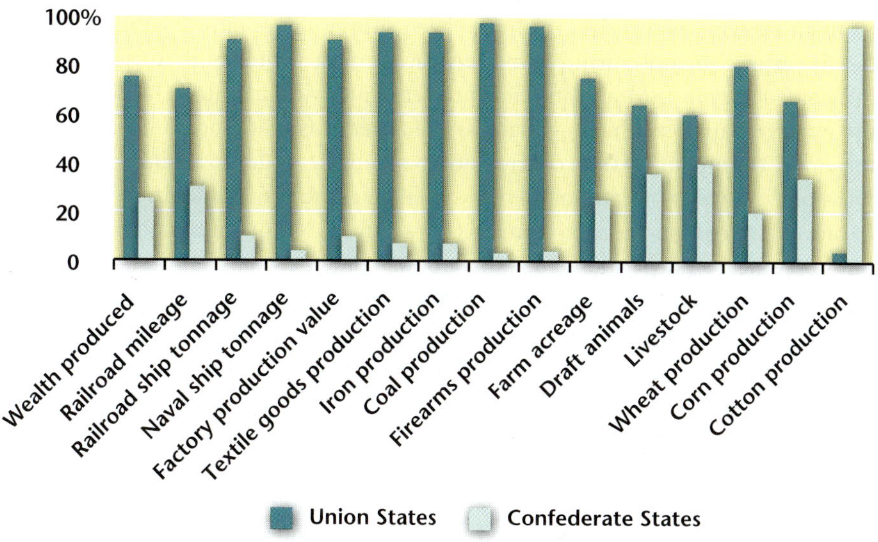


▲ **Figure 14.1**

**Resource comparison, USA and CSA** The North possessed significant advantages in industrial and agricultural resource production (except cotton), but this only became a factor over time. Confederates entered the conflict aware of their material deficiencies but confident that the war would not last long enough for them to greatly matter.

## From the Ballot to the Bullet

An outside observer coming to the United States in 1860 might have had a hard time understanding the source of differences between North and South. Both derived their values from the same historical and religious foundations—western Europe and Protestant Christianity. Both conceived of themselves as democratic and capitalistic. They spoke the same language, shared foodways, fashion, literature, and a developing popular culture of theater, music, and stage entertainment. Both used the American Revolution to justify their way of life. How could two people so similar conceptualize themselves as so different and fight such a catastrophic war? Most people at the time identified slavery as the key difference between the two sections. Despite the absence of the institution in the North, white citizens held racial views similar to those of their southern peers. Nonetheless, the presence, durability, and dynamism of slavery in the American South produced, over time, sharply different understandings of freedom, citizenship, and the natural rights accorded to all human beings. Northerners had grown especially alarmed by what they saw as the corrupting influence of slavery on American life and institutions. Lincoln saw his challenge as proving that in democracies there could be "no appeal from the ballot to the bullet."

The challenge for the North was to compel the South back into the Union without alienating it any further. Lincoln believed in the loyalty of the majority of white Southerners who, he thought, had only been swayed temporarily by the rhetoric of the fire-eaters. His optimism proved misplaced; most white Southerners supported the Confederacy in 1861 and still did at the end of the war in 1865. The North began the war by treating southern civilians as the Americans that Lincoln always insisted they were. Union armies were ordered not to confiscate or destroy southern property. This policy aimed to placate Southerners and their conservative allies in the North and to prove that reunion posed no threat. Radicals in the North lambasted the policy as the "rosewater" strategy and argued that no war could be won by sprinkling perfume on one's opponent. General-in-Chief **Winfield Scott**, a hero of the War of 1812 and the Mexican War, proposed a more vigorous strategy to encircle the Confederacy along the rivers and coastlines and slowly constrict their ability to wage war.

Just as public demand for action drove Jefferson Davis to attack Fort Sumter, by midsummer northern public opinion drove Lincoln to attack the Confederate forces assembled near the railroad junction of Manassas, Virginia, about 20 miles southwest of Washington, DC. The battle attracted curious onlookers hoping to see the rebels sent running and convinced, that this would be a bloodless war. The battle of Bull Run, named by the North for the creek that flowed through the area, turned out to be far bloodier than anyone on either side had imagined. Although Union forces pushed Confederates back through the morning's fighting, a pause at midday allowed southern troops to regroup and counterattack. The untrained Union soldiers broke and abandoned the field, scattering the tourists in a hasty retreat back to Washington. By the end of the day Confederate forces had lost close to 2,000 men and Union forces close to 3,000. Although the Confederate victory embarrassed the North, it inspired greater mobilization and a stronger training regimen through the fall and winter of 1861. Confident that it represented their true superiority, Confederates basked in the victory.

**STUDY QUESTIONS FOR SECESSION, 1860–1861**

1. **Why did the Civil War start in 1861?**
2. **Which played a greater role in the coming of the war: reason or emotion?**

# WAR IN EARNEST, 1862–1863

In many respects 1862 proved to be the most important year of the Civil War. Because the war extended in time, it imposed increasing burdens on the populations of both sections. All of these costs—physical, ideological, and psychological—became clear during 1862, yet both sides fought on. As the bloodshed increased, soldiers and civilians on both sides longed for peace. As they moved further away from peace, however, they increasingly came to view the other side as a mortal enemy. This prospect worried Abraham Lincoln, who understood the devastating nature of civil wars—the more energetically his commanders pursued Confederate defeat the harder it became to achieve his goal of rebuilding the Union.

## The North Advances

Although Northerners, Southerners, and European observers focused on fighting in the East, the war's center of gravity in early 1862 was in the West. There, Lincoln found a commander who won and the beginnings of a strategy that would eventually bring victory to the Union. The general was **Ulysses S. Grant**, a 40-year-old former army officer whose prewar failures in a variety of businesses did little to predict his success in the war. Grant first achieved fame by conquering Forts Henry and Donelson, located in Tennessee on the Tennessee and the Cumberland rivers, respectively. Rivers were the one geographic weakness faced by the Confederacy—all the major ones flowed into or through the South and were used as avenues of invasion by Union forces. The capture of the two forts gave federal forces access to all of Tennessee, as they took 14,000 Confederate prisoners and provided a much-needed hero for northern newspapers.

By early April 1862 Grant's soldiers had marched to the southern boundary of Tennessee, where they clashed with Confederate forces in a cataclysmic battle around Shiloh Church. Although the battle was a stalemate—with Confederate forces winning the first day and Union forces the next—northern soldiers retained their position on the battlefield while Confederates retreated into northern Mississippi. The scale of the battle garnered the most attention, with nearly 24,000 total casualties over the two days of fighting. General Grant grimly noted that "I saw an open field . . . so covered with dead that it would have been possible to walk across the clearing, in any direction, stepping on dead bodies, without a foot touching the ground." The horrific

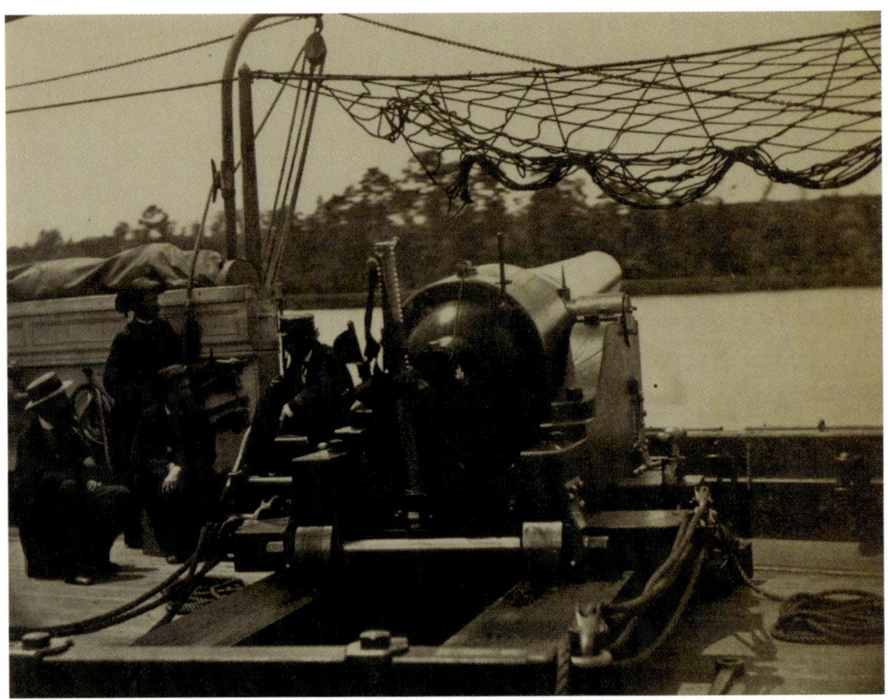

Grant effectively coordinated his movement into Tennessee with naval commanders. The North's rapidly expanding "brown water navy" allowed the Union to bring heavy guns into range of forts along the Mississippi and Tennessee Rivers.

nature of Civil War battles resulted from the new rifled musket, which increased the accuracy and the killing range of weapons, and more powerful and accurate artillery. Officers on both sides failed to adjust the tactics they used in battle despite these new technologies. Trained in grand frontal and flanking (side) attacks, both armies continued to launch assaults against entrenched opponents despite the considerable advantage that the new weapons gave to the defensive side. With a few rare exceptions, attacking armies always suffered higher casualties than defenders and rarely emerged from battles victorious.

As regular forces engaged in more deadly conflict, civilians experienced the terror and chaos of guerrilla conflict. In several parts of the Confederacy, civilians loyal to the United States harassed and attacked Confederate forces; in other places Confederate civilians targeted Union forces. Eastern Tennessee proved a hotbed of Unionism throughout the war. Although central and western Tennesseans had supported secession and sent tens of thousands of men to fight for the Confederacy, residents of the mountainous region of east Tennessee remained loyal to the United States. Through much of 1861 and 1862 Unionist east Tennesseans violently resisted Confederate control. In mid-1862 a Confederate captain in the region explained to his wife that "the people here they are nearly all Lincolnites or Toryes it is dangerous to go eny distance from camp." The Richmond government responded to the violence with increasingly harsh policies intended to pacify the region.

In central Virginia, central Tennessee, and much of Kentucky the roles were reversed. In these areas, pro-Confederate civilians spied on, sabotaged, and attacked Union soldiers as they advanced into the region. Pro-Confederate women, many with fathers or husbands in military service, often assisted guerrillas with food and information. U.S. soldiers grew increasingly wary of southern white women and by war's end regarded their defiance as a major reason why the war lasted as long as it did. Increasingly vigorous methods to curtail guerilla actions adopted by both national governments failed to solve the problem.

The worst violence occurred in those places with the lightest presence of regular troops. Western Virginia, western North Carolina, and nearly all of Missouri were exposed to continuous guerrilla conflict. In these areas, noncombatants—including men, women, and children—enacted violence according to old grudges, political resentments, and economic opportunity. The Civil War's guerilla conflict often had little to do with the war itself and instead offered people the chance to enact revenge on neighbors for old conflicts. The famous Hatfield-McCoy feud, which lasted into the 20th century, had its origins partly in wartime conflicts in the mountains of Tennessee and Virginia. Civilians recognized early on that armies ensured their safety and as a result increasing numbers of people fled to occupied towns over the course of the war. Cities like Nashville, Little Rock, and Memphis saw their populations double or triple during the war as a result of the influx of refugees seeking security.

## Stalemate in the East

As Union forces moved decisively into Confederate strongholds in the West, they remained stalemated in the East. After the battle of Bull Run, Lincoln appointed General **George B. McClellan** the new commander of the Army of the Potomac. McClellan spent the winter reorganizing, outfitting, and training his men. When the spring weather improved enough to initiate a campaign, McClellan ferried his soldiers down the Chesapeake Bay to Fort Monroe—a Union outpost on the tip of the peninsula between Virginia's York and James Rivers. McClellan then squandered his advantage by proceeding with agonizing slowness up the Peninsula toward the Confederate capital of Richmond. From Washington, President Lincoln urged McClellan forward and paced the halls of the telegraph office set up across the street from the White House waiting for news. Unlike Jefferson Davis, Lincoln entered the war with no real knowledge of warfare or the military, but, reading tactical and strategy manuals late into the night, he learned rapidly on the job. For his part McClellan took nearly two months to cover the 60 miles against a much smaller Confederate force. On May 31, after a climactic battle within earshot of Richmond, McClellan pulled his forces back to a base on the York River and gave the Confederates a chance to regroup.

This pause coincided with the elevation of General **Robert E. Lee** to command of Confederate forces in Virginia. Whereas Lee's predecessors had been prone to retreat and delay, Lee favored the offense. His approach to war generated enormously high casualties for Confederate forces but because he produced victories. Confederate civilians favored him above all other commanders. For many Lee embodied the spirit of the Confederate nation. Although Lee never became a political figure on the order of Napoleon, his stature proved important in convincing the public to continue fighting. In late June, Lee succeeded in pushing McClellan's troops back to the James River. The campaign, known as the Seven Days, immortalized Lee for saving Richmond and for defeating a much larger Union force. For the North the Peninsula campaign was a costly and humiliating defeat.

Another seminal feature of the Peninsula Campaign was how Union forces eroded slavery as they moved toward Richmond. The official policy of the United States still protected slavery, and Democratic generals like McClellan enforced this policy with special vigor. But the army's disruption of civilian life inevitably weakened the system. With most white men in military service, communities could not muster slave patrols and use the state to catch runaways and stop slave conspiracies. As the Union army lumbered up the Peninsula, enslaved people seized opportunities to flee. White women left in charge of homes and plantations assumed a new burden in managing adult male slaves in their agricultural duties, something few had done before the war. The erosion of slavery had actually begun in the war's opening moments, when three male slaves fled to the security of Fortress Monroe in May 1861. Union general **Benjamin Butler**, refusing to return them to their owners, held them as "contraband of war." Although Butler's order continued to recognize enslaved people as property, it gave supporters of abolition an important tool in the war against slavery. So far in the conflict, however, Lincoln insisted the war was about union, not the end of slavery. He hoped to retain the support of the slaveholding border states—Missouri, Kentucky, Maryland, and Delaware—even at the expense of alienating abolitionists in the North.

If Confederates drew dire lessons from the ancillary effects of the Peninsula campaign, they received great sustenance from the success of their armies in the Shenandoah Valley, on the other side of the state. In Spring 1862 a new hero joined Lee in the pantheon of Confederate history—Thomas Jonathan **"Stonewall" Jackson—** widely praised for his effective leadership and aggressive approach to warfare. In the Valley, Jackson outmaneuvered several Union armies. In a sequence of battles lasting through May, Jackson eluded larger Union forces and prevented them from reinforcing McClellan on the Peninsula. When Jackson was killed by friendly fire in mid-1863, he became the Confederacy's best known martyr and part of the emerging culture of patriotic sacrifice that defined the new nation.

The Union worked to build a culture of national unity as well. Seeking to turn the ethnic diversity of the region into a strength, military recruiters encouraged communities to send regiments with specific ethnic identities into the northern armies. Irish and German groups led the way in 1861, as they enlisted in the "Irish Rifles" (39th New York Infantry), the "Fighting Irish" (69th New York State Militia), and "Die Neuner" (9th Ohio Infantry). Many of the men who enlisted in these units had been born abroad and military service offered one way to establish their claim to full

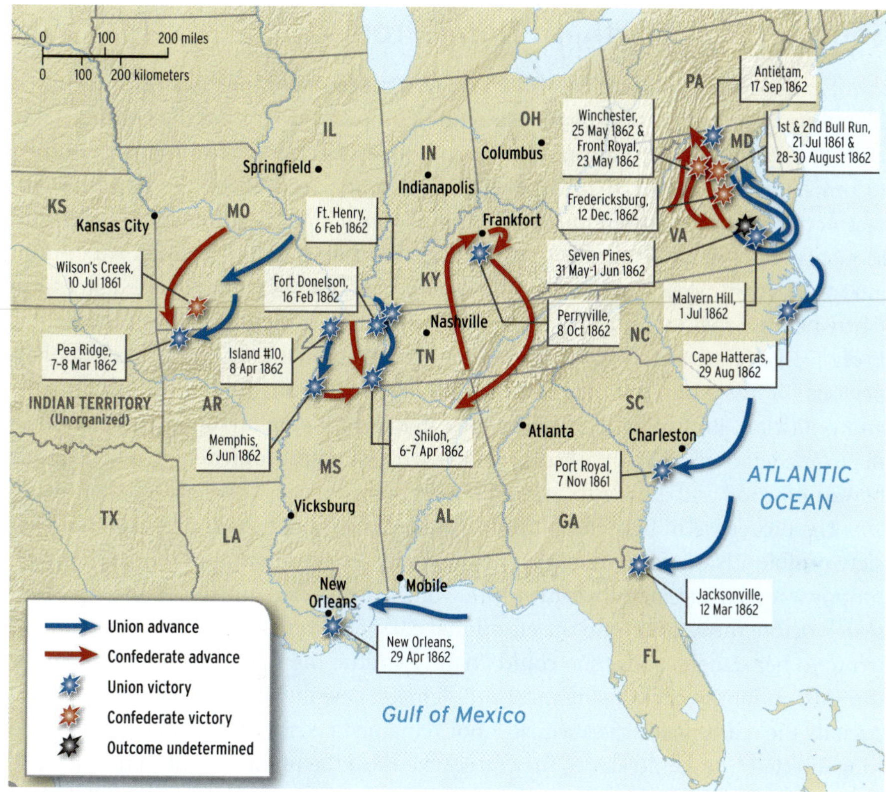


▲ **Map 14.2**

**Major Battles and Campaigns, 1861–1862** Early in the war, Confederate forces established a de facto boundary along the Rapidan-Rappahannock River corridor in Virginia that they maintained through 1862. In the West, the Union experienced more military success, principally along the major rivers leading into the southern interior.

citizenship in the United States. Others felt an obligation to defend their new home and the honor of their old ones. As an Irish-American sergeant explained to his relatives in Ireland, "when we are fighting for America we are fighting in the interest of Irland [sic] striking a double blow cutting with a two edged sword For while we strike in defence of the rights of Irishmen here we are striking a blow at Irland's enemy and oppressor England." But the unpredictable nature of the war and the suspicion with which many native-born Americans viewed foreigners, especially Catholics, upset that hope. German troops serving in the Union Army of the Potomac's 11th Corps were poorly officered and earned a black name after being involved in several widely reported battlefield defeats. Germans across the country felt the sting of nativist scorn, and in 1865 many identified more closely as German than American. The Irish experience likewise turned sour when conservative Irish soldiers and politicians refused to support a war for emancipation.

## Southern and Northern Home Fronts

European national revolutions of the late 1840s demonstrated the tension between liberal social reformers seeking to restructure European society and the unpredictable nature of war. In many countries revolutions failed and conservative regimes returned to power through violence. In the U.S. Civil War, to some extent, the opposite process occurred. The chaos and unpredictability of war created unintended social consequences that white Southerners who initiated secession did not foresee. Paramount among these was class conflict: some poor and middle-class whites rejected secession partly because they saw it as a policy designed to protect the interests of the wealthy. Every Confederate state witnessed this tension. One of the most articulate spokespersons for this group was Tennessee's **William G. "Parson" Brownlow**. A journalist and politician, Brownlow made clear the extent and the nature of his opposition to the Confederacy in 1861: "We can never live in a Southern Confederacy, and be made hewers of wood and drawers of water for a set of aristocrats."

The process of military mobilization altered the gender dynamic of southern society profoundly, if unintentionally. Because southern communities sent such a high proportion of white men to fight, white women had to assume duties that few possessed before the war. Beyond the emotional costs for women left alone—one mother wrote to her daughter that she could "hardly endure the sadness of the change, the diminished family circle"—the most problematic new duty was managing slaves, especially the adult male slaves whose labor remained essential. Although women had long directed household slaves, they rarely exercised the physical control necessary to keep order on farms. In Macon and Augusta, Georgia, they staffed textile mills, while in Richmond, they worked in munitions factories, and a sizeable number served as clerks in various Confederate Departments. Rural women took over virtually all the tasks that were necessary on farms, including making decisions about which crops to raise, how to grow them, and when to sell. By 1863, Michael Raysor, a Floridian serving in Mississippi, finally admitted to his wife that she had bested him as a farmer. "You said that you thought we would have near a hundred head of hogs to fatten this fall. This is doing well, aint it. I think you are a better farmer than I am you have done exceedingly well since I left." With the conclusion of the war men reclaimed the roles that they had traditionally filled before the war, but women rarely forgot the importance of their self-reliance.

The main push for social change in the North came not in the area of class or gender equality but in racial justice. Abolitionists, long derided as outcasts and denied access to political power, seized opportunities to press their agenda. From the beginning of the conflict Frederick Douglass worked to frame the conflict as a war of liberty versus slavery. Even as they succeeded in turning the U.S. government away from its cozy relationship with slavery, abolitionists had little luck improving the attitudes of white Northerners toward black people. Discrimination remained commonplace across the North, and whites manifested a much greater passion for punishing slaveholders than they did for helping slaves. The conflict over slavery broke roughly along partisan lines. The Republican Party had already established its opposition to the institution and the Democratic Party had long harbored slavery's staunchest defenders. The result was that each party, using the issue to press for partisan advantage, complicated an already bloody political landscape.

As the war dragged on, the Democratic Party split into two wings: a pro-war faction that supported the Union while distancing itself from the Lincoln administration, and an increasingly shrill antiwar wing known as the "Copperheads." Even as Democrats functioned as a loyal opposition, they condemned and lampooned Lincoln in the harshest possible language, asserting that Lincoln was "willing to destroy his country, his party, himself, if he can destroy his opponents." The party gained support from this approach in the congressional elections of 1862, when Democrats reclaimed 28 seats. The northern war effort was badly stalled in late 1862, and this delay played as important a role in Democratic victories. Republican electoral fortunes rose and fell with the successes and failures of the Union army.

Despite popular sympathy for the president personally, many elites in the country, including prominent Republicans, regarded Lincoln as an uncouth backwoodsman not fit for higher office. Lincoln enjoyed the coarse popular humor of the day—he often read aloud from his favorite humorists while waiting in the telegraph office for battle reports—but his stories revealed a keen mind. Lincoln's use of language—both grand and commonplace—proved one of the North's greatest assets during the conflict. Unlike Jefferson Davis, who had little interest in or ability to communicate with his constituents, Lincoln framed the key issues of the war in powerful phrasings, often using accessible metaphors and analogies. Democrats responded with fear mongering and openly racist rhetoric. They condemned emancipation and Lincoln for adopting it. "The only true policy for the American government," a Democrat wrote, was "the Constitution as it is, the Union as it was, and the Negroes where they are." This tactic that reached a crescendo in the 1864 presidential election, when Democrats argued that Lincoln's policies promoted blacks at the expense of whites and that he even supported interracial sexual relations.

The political landscape of the South was less partisan but no less complex or destructive. One of the Confederate government's first acts was to ban political parties. In the utopian vision of the Confederacy's founders, parties created social conflict where none existed; therefore, by abolishing parties, they could eliminate an important source of friction. This approach ignored the very real divisions—by class, region, religion, and ethnicity—that already existed within southern communities, and it did little to quell social conflict. Instead of organizing a policy-based critique of Jefferson Davis and other leading officeholders, dissenting politicians targeted their venom directly at Davis.

## The Struggle for European Support

From the outset of the war both Lincoln and Davis, courting international support for their side, engaged in diplomacy in Europe—primarily with Europe's two great powers, Great Britain and France. Although Confederate emissaries traveled east, they had little luck, especially in Russia, which maintained a steadfast dedication to the North.

France leaned toward the Confederacy but refused to act without Britain, so the two sides primarily struggled to capture British support. Whereas the British aristocracy sympathized with the Confederacy, based on a cultural and intellectual familiarity, the laboring classes seem to have supported the Union because of the Republican Party's devotion to the workingman and its opposition to slavery.

The first major international crisis in the Civil War revolved around the seizure of a British ship, the *Trent*, by the U.S. Navy in the Caribbean in late 1861. The U.S. commander, **Charles Wilkes**, arrested two Confederate commissioners sailing to London and France. The complexities of admiralty law during war clouded the legality of Wilkes's actions, but Britain—responding defiantly—came close to declaring war on the United States. Lincoln quietly sought a peaceful resolution, and Britain backed down when the commissioners were released. The peaceful solution dashed Confederate hopes for a permanent break between the Union and Britain.

The North's diplomatic effort benefited from the increasingly close economic ties forged with Britain over the previous decade. Confederates, pinning their hopes on King Cotton diplomacy, initiated an embargo on cotton sales to Britain and France in May 1861, as they believed that economic pressure would force them to recognize the Confederacy. When the British journalist William Howard Russell traveled through the South in 1861, he found great faith in this strategy. A South Carolinian assured him, "we know John Bull very well. He will make a great fuss about non-interference at first, but when he begins to want cotton he'll come off his perch." Confederate leaders failed to appreciate two important facts. Britain and France both held substantial stockpiles of cotton, which postponed the embargo's impact for well over a year, and for Britain the volume and substance of northern trade—especially food—was just as important as the southern trade in cotton. Confederates also failed to recognize the values of English textile workers, who derived their livelihood from southern cotton but supported the Union cause through the war.

Nonetheless, influential members of the British Cabinet viewed the U.S. conflict as a net gain for Europe and division of the country as inevitable given southern military prowess and the course of the war in 1861 and 1862. Momentum to recognize the Confederacy as a fully independent nation in the eyes of the world peaked in 1862. **William Gladstone**, the liberal statesman and later prime minister, asserted that "there is no doubt that Jefferson Davis and other leaders of the South have made an Army; they are making, it appears, a Navy; and they have made—what is more than either—they have made a Nation." Gladstone and others nearly succeeded in convincing Prime Minister Palmerston to recognize the Confederacy when Union forces rebuffed Robert E. Lee's September 1862 invasion of Maryland at Antietam. After this defeat, and especially after Lincoln issued the preliminary **Emancipation Proclamation** in its wake, Britain never again came close to recognizing the Confederacy.

Emancipation proved to be one of the most useful tools in Lincoln's diplomatic arsenal. Britain and France emancipated the slaves held in their overseas colonies in the 1830s and 1840s. Britain took the lead in policing the Atlantic Slave Trade. British naval ships patrolled the waters off the western coast of Africa and seized illegal slaving ships sailing to Brazil and Cuba after the international ban on the slave trade took effect. Once Lincoln set U.S. policy firmly against slavery there was little chance of Britain endorsing the Confederacy. In line with his increasingly progressive shift on emancipation, Lincoln initiated diplomatic recognition of Haiti in 1862, a first for the United States since the black republic established its independence from France in 1804. Emancipation also put the United States in synchrony with other global movements toward liberty. In 1861, Tsar Alexander II signed the "Emancipation Manifesto," freeing Russia's serfs. Like Lincoln's emancipation of slaves, Russia's change reflected an emerging liberal consensus around the supremacy of individual freedom and of freedom as a precondition for modern economic growth.

### STUDY QUESTIONS FOR WAR IN EARNEST, 1862–1863

1. **How was the war changing in 1862 in ways that people did not anticipate in 1861?**
2. **Who was winning the war in 1862?**

# A NEW BIRTH OF FREEDOM

The centrality of emancipation as a global concern appears obvious in retrospect, but the most revolutionary change of the war came gradually and against the wishes of both northern and southern leaders. Although Lincoln had clearly expressed his personal antipathy toward slavery, as president he initially believed he had little constitutional authority to affect the institution. The action of enslaved people who seized opportunities to escape forced the North to endorse emancipation and destroyed the world's largest and most influential slave society.

## Slaves Take Flight

Over the course of the war, at least 500,000 slaves fled to the safety of Union lines. Running away was an especially risky decision before the United States had officially committed itself to emancipation. After Butler issued his contraband order, the United States maintained a contradictory policy. At the top, Lincoln denied any interest in emancipation, largely to ensure the continued loyalty of the Border states. In a famous exchange with New York newspaper editor **Horace Greeley** in August 1862, Lincoln proclaimed "If there be those who would not save the Union, unless they could at the same time save slavery, I do not agree with them. If there be those who would not save the Union unless they could at the same time destroy slavery, I do not agree with them. My paramount object in this struggle is to save the Union, and is not either to save or to destroy slavery."

Politically conservative generals followed Lincoln's lead and returned slaves to masters who came to Union camps to reclaim runaways. A handful of liberal generals adopted more aggressive policies and usually refused to return escapees. Abolitionists

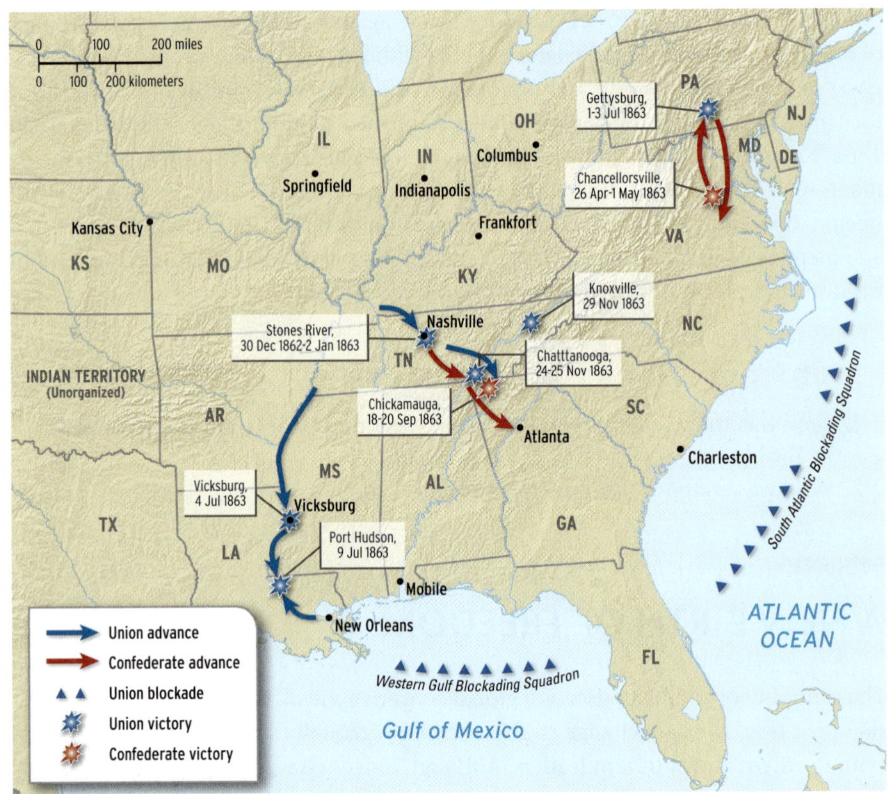


**Map 14.3**

**Major Battles and Campaigns, 1863** As in 1862, Union forces had little success against Confederates in the East in 1863, although the repulse of Robert E. Lee's army at Gettysburg inspired jubilation. In the West, Union successes were striking. They reclaimed all of Tennessee, took full control of the Mississippi River, and pressed into the northern tier of Deep South states.

celebrated two events in particular. In August 1861, General **John Frémont**, the 1856 Republican presidential candidate, ordered all property of all rebels in Missouri subject to confiscation. Recognizing the damage this action would do to Unionist sympathy in the slaveholding Border states, Lincoln immediately revoked the order. In May 1862, General **David Hunter**, commander of the occupied territories of low country South Carolina, Georgia, and Florida, issued an order freeing all the slaves in his department. Again to the great dismay of abolitionists, Lincoln rescinded the order.

Despite the government's resistance, enslaved people continued to flee. Like northern abolitionists, they recognized that the war grew out of a conflict over slavery. By actively supporting the Union they could both achieve their own freedom and establish a claim to American citizenship. As one ex-slave explained to his former master after the war, "as to my freedom, which you say I can have, there is nothing to be gained on that score, as I got my free papers in 1864 from the Provost-Marshal-General of the

Department of Nashville." To facilitate the continued movement of Union armies into the South, those who fled to Union lines lived in supervised facilities know as contraband camps. Falling between civilian and military control, the camps were usually unsanitary and overcrowded. The military also exploited contrabands—often in support services for nearby soldiers' camps—and generally treated them only marginally better than they had been as slaves.

If contraband camps represented the worst of the Union's response to emancipation, the actions of many Union soldiers in the field represented the best. Only a small minority of soldiers came into the army as abolitionists, but over the course of the war a great number changed their attitudes toward the practice. Exposure to slaves themselves, which few Northerners had experienced before the war, inspired sympathy for their suffering and anger at the abuse they received from masters. In the best circumstances northern soldiers used their power to rescue enslaved people and alleviate the suffering of those who had run away. Sergeant E.C. Hubbard of Illinois entered the war angry that white men were killing one another "all for a detestable black man" but, as he explained to his brother, after seeing how slavery worked in practice, he was "*forced* to change my opinion." In early 1864 he wrote home to his staunchly Democratic family that "*Slavery is gone*. Peace propositions to Richmond won't save it . . . The war could never be ended without [slavery's] destruction." African Americans knew this certainty intuitively and they made vigorous efforts to join the army so they could participate. At the war's start the U.S. Army excluded black men from service. However, by 1862 black units had been organized in Louisiana and along the South Carolina, Georgia, and Florida Sea Islands. These early regiments were incorporated into the U.S. Army when official black enlistment began in 1863.

## From Confiscation to Emancipation

On the issue of emancipation, soldiers were often ahead of both their families at home and politicians across the North. While soldiers grappled with the lived reality of slavery, most Northerners continued to discuss it in the abstract, as only a piece of the larger political conflict. In 1861 Congress codified Butler's contraband order with the First Confiscation Act, which provided the army with the authority to retain runaway slaves when their labor was being used directly for the Confederate war effort. They expanded this policy in 1862 by declaring free any slave belonging to a rebel owner living in those areas controlled by the Union army, parts of Tennessee, Virginia, Louisiana, and Mississippi. As the war extended into 1862, northern war planners recognized that by relying on slave labor to produce food supplies and other essentials, the Confederacy could mobilize an enormously high percentage of its military-age men; in most counties the enlistment rate was well above 60 percent, nearly double that of northern counties. By attacking slavery directly the Union weakened the South's ability to fight.

Lincoln came to this conclusion well before he announced it publicly. After watching the hapless retreat of McClellan's army from the gates of Richmond in mid-1862 and the subsequent march of Lee's Confederates through Virginia and into Maryland in the fall of 1862, Lincoln endorsed the use of emancipation as a war policy. Although he risked alienating border state conservatives, Lincoln had given them ample time to see how the war destroyed the institution regardless of policy, and he knew the advantages that would accrue in foreign policy and Confederate manpower.

In August 1862 Lee's Army crashed through a Union force under General John Pope on the fields of Manassas, Virginia, the exact site where they had fought almost a year earlier. The outcome was eerily similar. Despite Pope's loudly proclaimed intention to rid Virginia of Lee, the retreat of his army to Washington allowed Lee to march freely into the North in early September. Lincoln reinstated McClellan as commander of the Army of the Potomac and sent him north to stop Lee. On September 18, the armies clashed outside the small town of Sharpsburg along the banks of Antietam Creek. The battle proved to be bloodiest single day of the war, with nearly 23,000 casualties between the two sides. Despite a nearly 2:1 advantage in numbers, McClellan failed to break Lee's army and the Confederates retreated safely back across the Potomac River. Although far from the clear-cut victory he had hoped for, Lincoln issued the Emancipation Proclamation on September 22.

Jefferson Davis regarded the measure as intended to encourage slaves to murder their masters and condemned the authors of emancipation as "those who have attempted the most execrable measure recorded in the history of guilty man." Lincoln offered a more noble interpretation when he commemorated a national cemetery at Gettysburg. The war heralded a "new birth of freedom," Lincoln said, not just by preserving the Union but by expanding the meaning of freedom to include black Americans as well. For black Americans the day of jubilee arrived when the proclamation took effect on January 1, 1863. Henry Tuner, a free black minister in Washington,

Photographer Matthew Brady captured the devastation of the Battle of Antietam when he arrived two days after the fighting. The exhibition of his photos, "The Dead of Antietam," traveled to northern cities where horrified civilians saw photographic representations of war's costs.

Thomas Eastman's painting captured the risk and drama of the flight undertaken by over 500,000 enslaved people who sought their freedom in the moments of change produced by the war.

DC, recalled the celebration that evening: "Great processions of colored and white men marched to and fro and passed in front of the White House and congratulated President Lincoln on his proclamation. The president came to the window and made responsive bows, and thousands told him, if he would come out of that palace, they would hug him to death . . . It was indeed a time of times, and a half time, nothing like it will ever be seen again in this life."

## Government Centralization in Wartime

Emancipation emerged as what one historian has called the "crown jewel" in the Union's hard war policy, which targeted the ability of Confederates to fight by destroying infrastructure, transportation networks, and food supplies for the army. In addition to being a moral act, emancipation allowed the North to seize a vital war resource from the Confederacy. Over the course of the war the Union gradually increased the pressure it applied to the Confederacy. Emancipation denied Confederates the one resource they had to retain without which they could not hope to win or even prolong the war even as it generated intense criticism in the North because it altered the balance of power between the federal government and the states. Slavery had always been a "domestic institution," that is, one controlled by state law. Emancipation in the

North happened through the mechanism of state constitutional changes, mostly in the decade after the Revolution. By abolishing slavery through executive order—even in the midst of war—Lincoln reshaped the nature of American federalism. U.S. emancipation also stood out as unique among other slaveholding nations, which generally adopted gradual and compensated strategies to end slavery.

Confederate leaders claimed that they had seceded from the Union to protect state rights. In one of the many ironies of the Civil War the first challenge to state rights came not in the North but from those same Confederate leaders. In early 1862 imminent expiration of the term of service of most Confederate soldiers confronted Jefferson Davis with a massive problem. Most soldiers had enlisted in mid-1861 for one year; thus, their service would end at the start of the next campaign season. With reenlistments stalled Davis deployed both a carrot and a heavy stick. The government offered furloughs and bounties for men who reenlisted, and for those who refused Davis signed into law a national draft. American authorities had never resorted to a draft before, and southern soldiers were galled by the policy, especially because the law automatically reenlisted men currently in uniform for an additional three years. Many soldiers believed that exemptions to the law—for certain categories of industrial workers, for state government employees, and for the clergy—amounted to class privilege. Letters of complaint filled newspapers and desertion reached a war-time high. Confederate leaders gradually adopted progressive policies to address concern about unequal sacrifice. Although dissent remained a persistent problem within the Confederacy, civilians and soldiers alike accepted the draft and other policies as necessary

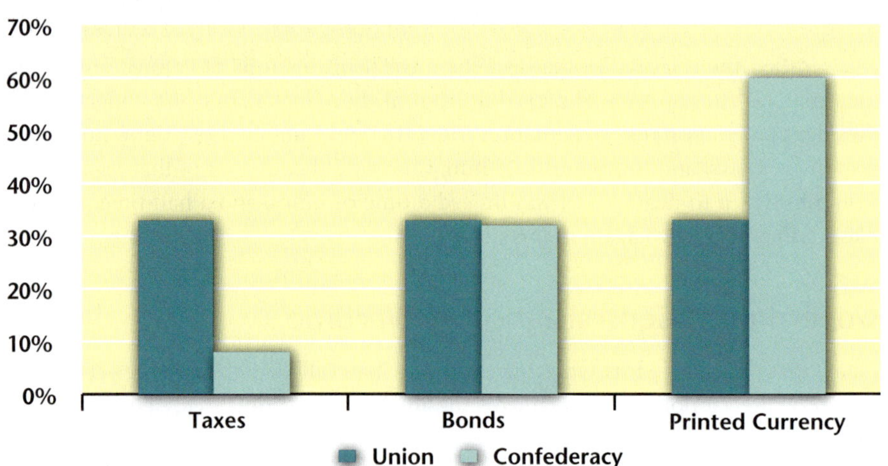


**Figure 14.2**

**War financing, 1861–1865** The Union maintained a balanced assortment of funding devices throughout the war. Because most Southerners invested their wealth in land and slaves, they had less capital to shift into war production. Instead, the Confederacy relied more heavily on printed currency, which depreciated rapidly and contributed to a very high inflation rate.

measures to help win their independence. The Union also adopted a draft, and it spurred similar resentment and anger among northern men.

Still, it was the Confederacy that led the way in centralizing measures during wartime. In 1863 the Confederacy adopted two new policies—impressment and a tax-in-kind—that gave significant power to Richmond at the expense of the states. Impressment allowed army quartermasters to seize necessary supplies in exchange for Confederate script. With no gold reserves Confederate economic policy relied on printed money, rather than on metallic coin, and bonds. The new currency devalued so quickly that most civilians regarded impressment as little more than theft. The Confederacy also relied on new taxes. Because these failed to generate the necessary revenue, the Richmond government created a tax-in-kind, which levied 10 percent of all major foodstuffs. Southern civilians complained bitterly about the tax-in-kind and dodged it whenever they could, but the resources gained by the Confederacy were redistributed to needy families, often the widows of soldiers, in an attempt to equalize the suffering on the Confederate home front. The North imposed its own taxes and its more dynamic commercial economy produced more revenue. Over the course of the war the North generated one-third of its revenues from taxes, one-third from currency, and one-third from bond sales.

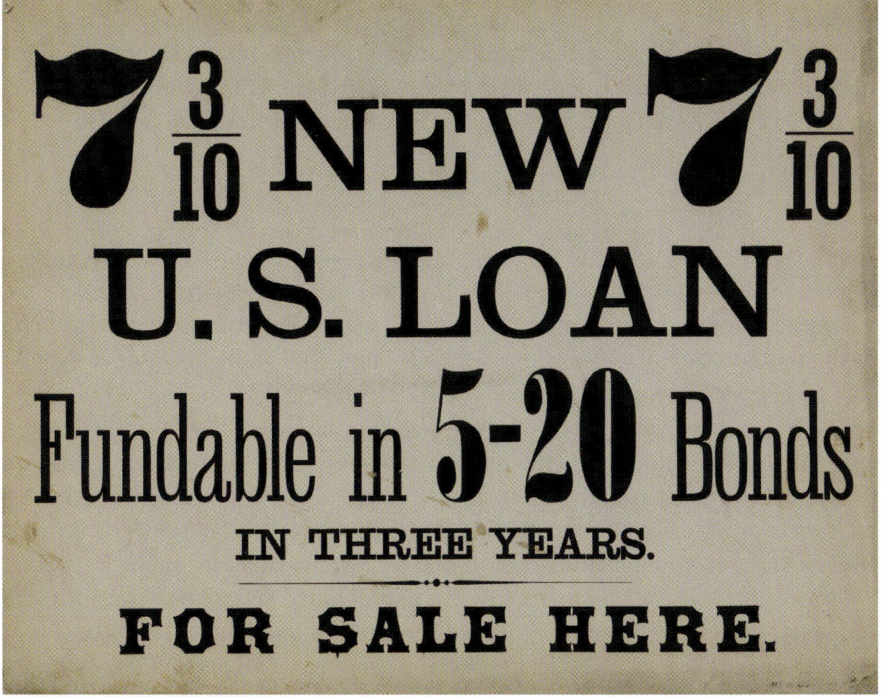


The Union's war bond campaign tied Americans to the war effort both patriotically and economically through the promise of interest on the notes that citizens bought.

**STUDY QUESTIONS FOR A NEW BIRTH OF FREEDOM**

1. **Why did the North endorse emancipation in 1862?**
2. **What role did African Americans play in shaping that change?**

# THE HARD WAR, 1863–1864

The North's economic vitality played a substantial role in helping it win the war. The southern economy, though enormously profitable in the antebellum era, was not well suited to financing a capital-intensive modern war. But money and resources alone did not win the war for the North. Military success eluded them partly because northern commanders like McClellan were reluctant to engage with the full weight of the region's strength. But that stance changed in late 1863, when Lincoln promoted Ulysses S. Grant, the victor in many western theater battles, to general-in-chief of all Union forces and transferred him to Washington, where he could consult with the president and direct the Army of the Potomac against Lee. Grant's approach, implemented by his lieutenants **William T. Sherman** and **Philip Sheridan**, exploited the North's manpower advantage and took aim directly at the Confederacy's ability to wage war. Grant, however, did not advocate unrestrained warfare. Despite popular memories of the burning Georgia by Sherman, U.S. troops did not target civilians and focused their destruction on public resources and facilities that sustained Confederate troops.

## Invasion and Occupation

Southerners received an early example of the North's hard war policy during the battle of Fredericksburg, Virginia, in December 1862. After the battle of Antietam, Lee moved his troops east and **Ambrose Burnside**, who replaced McClellan in October 1862, followed. Northern troops moved swiftly and reached the town of Fredericksburg, a major tobacco port. Burnside needed to cross the Rappahannock River to establish a position in town, but Confederate sharpshooters posted in buildings on the south bank fired on northern engineers trying to build pontoon bridges. Union General Edwin V. Sumner advised the town's mayor that since Confederate troops assaulted Union soldiers "under cover of the houses of your city" and since "your mills and manufactories are furnishing provisions and the material for clothing for armed bodies in rebellion against the Government of the United States," he demanded "the surrender of the city . . . at or before 5 o'clock this afternoon." Should the mayor refuse, Sumner allowed 16 hours for the removal of "women and children, the sick and wounded and aged, &c., which period having expired, I shall proceed to shell the town." The mayor evacuated the town and the Union besieged it. After the Confederates pulled back to a high ridge south of town, Union soldiers entered and, in their frustration, opened private residences and destroyed furniture and household materials. Confederates portrayed the looting as predictable Yankee vandalism and venerated the suffering of the Fredericksburg refugees, mostly women and children, who fled south. Although Union policy never sanctioned the wanton destruction of private property, the tenacity of Confederate resistance forced a shift in Union policy toward more destructiveness.

Military leaders formulated new strategies as Union armies advanced slowly through the southern countryside. The Union seized New Orleans and other coastal spots in late 1861 and early 1862, victories that allowed Union troops to move into Louisiana and the Carolinas. In Tennessee and Virginia the contest between Union and Confederate troops consumed scarce resources and left little for civilians. Southern women were often left to confront Union troops. In some cases they acquiesced, but in many others they maintained a defiance that landed some in jail. The U.S. Provost-Marshal in Kentucky jailed female Confederate sympathizers who refused to stop aiding pro-Southern guerilla forces in the state. In New Orleans, Confederate women famously disrespected Union soldiers until General Benjamin Butler threatened to arrest those who did so as "women of the town plying their avocation." By treating these women who now acted in public as "public women," Butler used southern class and gender values as a weapon and established a quieter occupation. Despite its manpower advantage the Union did not have the resources to hold all the territory they seized from Confederates permanently. Instead, they created garrisons in major towns that controlled, to the best of their ability, the regions around them. The result was a three-tiered system, with garrison towns at the center providing the highest degree of security and normal economic and social life. Beyond these were "frontier" regions, where armies provided a looser degree of control. Most dangerous of all were the "no-man's land" regions, places that neither army held but that they frequently raided. Social and economic life in these areas—central Virginia, Tennessee, and Louisiana and northern Alabama and Mississippi—barely resembled life in the prewar period.

At the same time Northerner officers strove to keep their method of fighting in synchrony with northern war aims. By 1860 most West Point graduates were familiar with Prussian military strategist Carl von Clausewitz who had penned the definitive text for understanding the purpose and scope of war. His maxim—that "war was politics by other means"—impressed on the leaders of both sides the importance of keeping war goals firmly in mind. Lee understood this aim and shaped his campaign with garnered information from northern newspapers about northern morale. Likewise, Grant and Sherman understood that the purpose of the war was not killing Southerners but reestablishing the authority of the national government in the shortest possible time.

## Black Soldiers, Black Flags

The laws of war helped regulate the violence regular troops committed in battle and on the march. It did little to stem guerilla violence and it did little to control the violence meted out to the new Union soldiers in 1863 and 1864: the **U.S. Colored Troops** (USCT). After the Emancipation Proclamation took effect on January 1, 1863, the

Union began enrolling and organizing units of black soldiers. Some were free black men from the North—Frederick Douglass's sons enlisted early—but many others were former slaves. Enlistment generated controversy in the North, most infamously as one of the causes of the New York City Draft Riots, five days of brutal violence waged by New York's white workingmen against the city's black residents. The riot started at draft offices but quickly turned into an attack on Republican institutions and leaders across the city and the black New Yorkers. Over 50 deaths, many of them brutal lynchings, shocked the nation and required the services of regular U.S. troops to suppress.

The proving grounds came in mid-1863 on the South Carolina coast and along the Mississippi River. At Fort Wagner, in Charleston Harbor, and at Port Hudson, north of Baton Rouge, black units participated valiantly in bloody attacks on Confederate positions. Northern newspapers reported both battles as evidence that black soldiers could perform as well as white troops. Although discrimination within the army remained—virtually no black men served above the level of sergeant and black soldiers were paid less than white ones—prejudice against black troops gradually subsided in the North. By war's end over 180,000 black men had donned the Union blue and their participation late in the war proved a crucial source of manpower. For black soldiers and their families, military service was also a path to citizenship. As Frederick Douglass made clear, "once let the black man get upon his person the brass letters US, let him get an eagle on his button, and a musket on his shoulder, and bullets in his pocket, and there is no power on earth or under the earth which can deny that he has earned the right of citizenship in the United States." Black veterans throughout the hemisphere used military service to claim citizenship, beginning with Revolutionary War veterans in the 18th century and extending to places like Colombia in the 19th and Cuba in the early 20th centuries.

For Confederates, however, black soldiers represented the worst threat that could be imagined. For decades, white Southerners had lived in fear of slave rebellions.

Although black sailors did not receive full equality they often earned fairer treatment than their land-bound peers. Since the colonial era, trading and military ships had contained racially and ethnically diverse crews, and U.S. naval warships carried on this tradition with black and white seamen working alongside one another throughout the war.

Despite precautions enslaved people had taken up arms against slaveholders from the earliest days of the colonial era. Abraham Lincoln, understanding the potency of the black soldier, remarked that "the bare sight of fifty thousand armed and drilled black soldiers on the banks of the Mississippi would end the rebellion at once." Confederates initially responded by classifying black soldiers as slaves in a state of insurrection. State law prescribed death for this action and for the white officers who commanded them. Confederates also threatened to sell as slaves black soldiers captured in the South. The public nature of this debate put U.S. soldiers and their officers on notice and President Lincoln threatened retaliation against Confederate soldiers if any northern ones were killed indiscriminately. At Fort Pillow, Tennessee, on the banks of the Mississippi, Confederates under the command of cavalry general **Nathan Bedford Forrest** killed 300 members of the garrison, many of them black troops murdered after they had surrendered. The U.S. House of Representatives formally investigated what came to be known as the Fort Pillow Massacre. Although that event received the most notoriety, similar atrocities occurred in Virginia, Arkansas, Florida, North Carolina, and elsewhere, demonstrating the toxic potential for civil conflicts that crossed racial as well as regional lines.

## The Campaigns of Grant and Sherman

Even without the complicating factor of racial difference, by 1863 the fighting had grown in scale and in violence. The most important battles of the year concluded on the same day—July 4, 1863. At Gettysburg, Pennsylvania, Union forces defeated Robert E. Lee's Confederates in a three-day battle that produced nearly 50,000 casualties. It marked the first clear defeat of Lee by a Union general, which produced jubilation in the North and confusion in the South. The more strategically significant victory came at Vicksburg, Mississippi, the last major Confederate position on the Mississippi River. Grant had tried to take the city for six months and his inability to do so drove some Northerners to question his competence. When the city finally fell, Grant captured a 40,000-man army and the Union won full control of the river. "The father of waters flows unvexed to the sea," Lincoln remarked. The Union had cut the Confederacy in half. Control of water, whether the rivers or the Confederate coastline through the blockade imposed by the Union navy, proved essential to the North's eventual victory. Lincoln's vigorous Secretary of the Navy **Gideon Welles** oversaw the dramatic expansion of the Navy's fleet; by 1865 the blockading squadron consisted of 471 ships.

In late 1863 Grant and his lieutenants, pushing back Confederate forces at Chattanooga, Tennessee, effectively reduced the western Confederacy to the Deep South states of Mississippi and Alabama. After Lincoln called Grant east, he made Sherman commander in the region and gave him instructions to take Atlanta, the second most important Confederate city after Richmond. After several months of hard fighting the Confederate Army abandoned the city to Sherman and moved north. Sherman reorganized his forces, destroyed the industrial base of the city, and left late in the fall. Sherman instructed his army to live off the land, taking what they needed. His Army, divided into four columns, marched to Savannah with little opposition.

GLOBAL PASSAGES

## Learning from the War

Starting in the 18th century, European military practice began to emphasize a professional staff instead of the traditional patronage system, with officers appointed to curry favor with wealthy or well-connected elites. The change encouraged officers to educate themselves in military science and the best way of doing that was through personal observation. Through the Napoleonic Era many of these men attached themselves to foreign armies as retainers, but their primary purpose was to learn from and evaluate new technologies and tactics. The U.S. Civil War drew a host of foreign visitors to observe and learn from the conflict. Throughout the war British observers circulated through the armies of both sides. The Frenchman Prince de Joinville traveled with McClellan during the Peninsula Campaign and later wrote up an assessment of the tactical blunders committed by the Union staff. Separately, two representatives of the French Artillery Corps—François de Chanal and Pierre Guzman—traveled around the North, inspecting hospitals, munitions factories, and forts. Their goal was to assess the new technologies being developed by Union engineers and scientists. Several Prussians also visited, including the cavalry commander Heros von Borcke, who joined J. E. B. Stuart's command for much of the war and used his insights to shape German cavalry tactics in the 1870s. For all these men the U.S. Civil War promised new insights into communication, tactics, weapons, defensive fortifications, and training.

The Prussian General Staff sent Captain **Justus Scheibert** to observe the conflict, and he compiled his evaluation in a series of articles and books. The practice of warfare changed rapidly as a result of industrialization and the increasing professionalization of the military in Europe. The U.S. Civil War thus offered observers an especially important point from which to assess the directions that combat was

Soldiers inflicted serious damage to Georgia's infrastructure, liberated thousands of slaves, and terrified the populace as rumors of an army of locusts preceded them. Most of the personal violence and property destruction in the state came at the hand of "Bummers"—deserters from both armies—who followed Sherman's troops and took advantage of the chaotic conditions left behind. Sherman reached Savannah in late December—he presented the city "as a Christmas gift" to Lincoln—and then turned north into the Carolinas.

As historians have probed beneath the mythology of Sherman's March, they have discovered significant damage but not the ruthless campaign of extermination so often portrayed in popular memory. Like Philip Sheridan in the Shenandoah Valley late in 1864, Sherman targeted resources, not people. A great deal of food was likely to take in coming years. Scheibert's main assignment was to evaluate artillery and fortifications. The technological breakthroughs on both sides of the Atlantic in artillery rendered the traditional European masonry fort infeasible, although Scheibert was surprised at the durability of earthen forts such as Fort Sumter, in Charleston Harbor. Later, Scheibert recognized the value of building on the advances made by Americans during the war, as he noted that "we Europeans have excelled because of what the Americans did."

Rifled muskets and rifled artillery attracted special interest as well. A British field officer who had traveled 3,000 miles across the North to evaluate gun foundries, factories, and the front lines predicted that before "this struggle closes there will be so great a development and improvement in all kinds of arms, both for military and naval warfare, that the world will act wisely in leaving itself open to profit by American ingenuity." Nearly all of the European observers, however, shared a scorn for the amateur nature of American armies, the "armed mobs from which nothing could be learned" according to a comment supposedly made by **Helmuth von Moltke**, the famed Chief of the Prussian General Staff. Ardant du Picq, a French military theorist, condemned the "lack of discipline and organization" in both armies that had made the war longer and bloodier than necessary. Nonetheless, European writers could hardly fail to appreciate the sustained power that armies on both sides exhibited over the course of the conflict. Only a nonspecialist, the German novelist Karl Bleibtreu, grasped the success of the American approach. He regarded the armies on both sides as having obtained "the highest grade of martial perfection" and anticipated that European nations would eventually adopt more democratic methods of staffing their armies.

- Why did Europeans observe the Civil War?
- What lessons did they take from it?

destroyed—much, as Sherman said, "simple waste and destruction"—but he did so to weaken Confederate armies, not starve civilians. Sherman's campaign and its legacy raise the issue of whether the Civil War was a "total war." Like most other Civil War commanders Sherman respected the distinction between civilian noncombatants, who could not be deliberately harmed, and lawful combatants, whom he could target with lethal force. New technologies, especially the powerful new artillery and the reliance of regional economies on existing railroad lines, blurred that distinction as the destruction waged by Sherman's troops affected everyone in its path.

From the perspective of Confederate civilians, the war must surely have seemed total. Emma LeConte, a college student living in Columbia, South Carolina, witnessed firsthand Sherman's invasion of that city. Although Confederates set the fires that consumed much of Columbia, LeConte laid the blame squarely on Sherman. "There is not a house, I believe, in Columbia that has not been pillaged," she wrote, and "those that the flames spared were entered by brutal soldiery and everything wantonly destroyed. The streets were filled with terrified women and children who were offered every insult and indignity short of personal outrage—they were allowed to save nothing but what clothes they wore, and there is now great suffering for food." She concluded, "It would be impossible to describe or even to conceive of the pandemonium and horror."

Rather than the compressed horror of Sherman's march, residents of central Virginia experienced the steady grind of military occupation and battles. After Gettysburg the armies of both sides returned to the state and, although there were no grand battles, their mere presence imposed hardship. At its largest the Army of the Potomac was equivalent in size to the biggest city in the Confederacy and it required enormous resources to supply it—600 tons per day. In early 1864, when Grant assumed command, his aim was the defeat of Lee's army. Rather than following McClellan's 1862 water route, the Army of the Potomac headed directly to Richmond, and the spring campaign was the bloodiest yet. In six weeks of fighting, Grant lost over 55,000 soldiers and Lee over 30,000, the equivalent of fighting a battle of Bull Run every day for that month and a half. Grant trapped Lee's army outside Petersburg, a railroad town that served as the conduit for all supplies entering Richmond. The two armies entrenched along ever-lengthening lines stretched between the two cities, a preview of the trench warfare that distinguished World War I.

**STUDY QUESTIONS FOR THE HARD WAR, 1863–1864**

1. **Why did the level of violence and destruction increase in 1863 and 1864?**
2. **What role did race play in this process?**

# VICTORY AND DEFEAT, 1865

By late 1864 even staunch Confederates recognized that they were losing the war. Still, the Davis government refused to concede to the two essential terms that Lincoln demanded—reunion and emancipation. As a result, the war stretched into the spring of 1865, with increasing hardship for Confederate civilians facing scarcity imposed by the war and the blockade.

## American Nationalism, Southern Nationalism

Lee knew that Grant would eventually break his lines in front of Petersburg and that when he did the Confederate capital would fall and the war would end. Lee's main hope in the fall of 1864 was that Lincoln would be defeated by the Democratic candidate, former Union general George McClellan, who had been nominated on a platform committed to ending the war immediately. As late as August, Lincoln himself assumed he would lose, so unpopular was his administration and the course of the war effort, which once again had bogged down. But Sherman's victory in Atlanta, Sheridan's in the Shenandoah Valley, and the capture of Mobile Bay in early August reversed his fortunes and Lincoln was reelected. In his Second Inaugural Address, a speech comparable in power and eloquence to the Gettysburg Address, Lincoln set out a beneficent vision for postwar America—"with malice toward none and charity toward all"—but also offered a sobering assessment of responsibility for the war and American slavery. He argued that both the North and the South bore blame for the war's enormous human cost—over 620,000 dead. He did not claim to know God's will but believed the nation's punishment—in which "every drop of blood drawn with the lash shall be paid with one drawn by the sword"—revealed God's displeasure for the wrongs done to generations of enslaved Africans and African Americans.

In late March, as Sherman's men tramped mostly unscathed through North Carolina, Lee realized that he would have to abandon Petersburg and Richmond. His

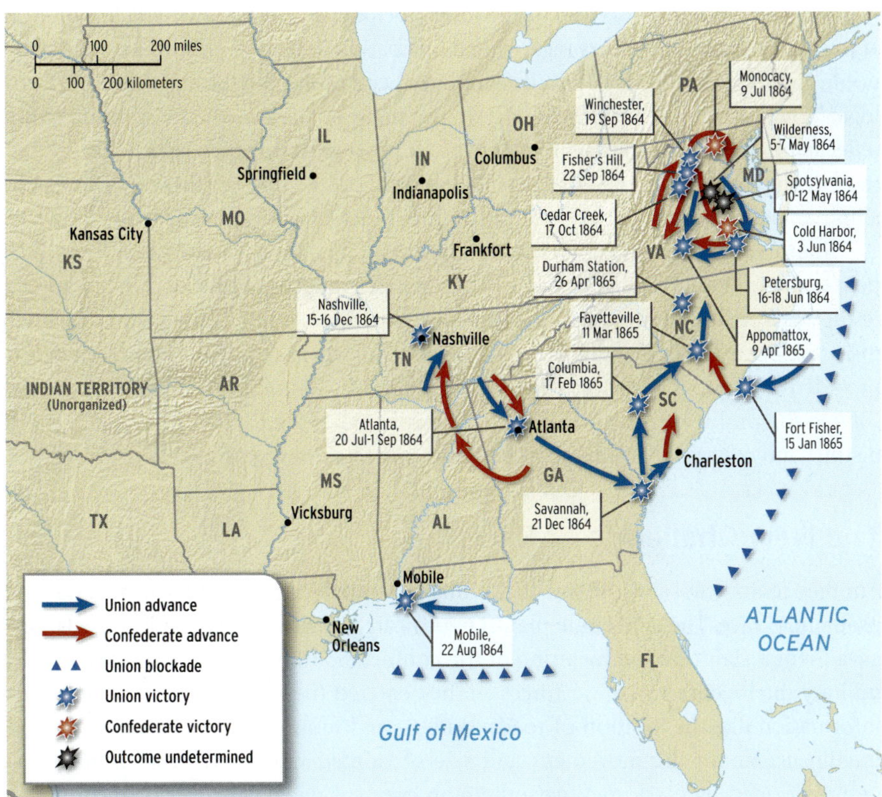


▲ Map 14.4

**Major Battles and Campaigns, 1864–1865** William Sherman's capture of Atlanta and his ensuing march to the coast demonstrated the ability of Union forces to move through the center of the Confederacy. His army eventually moved north to join Ulysses S. Grant to trap the two remaining Confederate armies.

men's rations had dwindled to virtually nothing, soldiers had deserted, leaving for home in the face of imminent defeat, and Grant nearly surrounded his army. Lee hoped to move west, resupply his troops, and connect with the small Confederate force in North Carolina, but Union cavalry cut off his retreat. On April 9, 1865, Lee surrendered at the small crossroads town of Appomattox Courthouse. Joseph Johnston's army surrendered to Sherman on April 26 at Durham Station, North Carolina, although most people, both Northerners and Southerners, saw Lee's surrender as the end of the war. As cannons tolled across the North, citizens took stock of their victory.

For most white Americans the reestablishment of the Union was the war's principal accomplishment. Some people today may regard that outcome as trivial, given the seeming inevitability of the current geographic configuration of the United States. But it was hardly inevitable at the time. As Lincoln had warned at the start of the war, if Southerners successfully left the Union, the process would replicate itself and self-government would disappear. Union victory, not a legal opinion or constitutional amendment established the incompatibility of secession and democracy in the United States.

Most Northerners also took pride in emancipation, even if few had supported it at the war's start. Northerners regarded emancipation as further ennobling an already noble victory. **John Wesley Powell**, who later became the first head of the U.S. Geologic Survey, fought in an Illinois unit during the war. His sweeping vision of victory reflected the thinking of many northerners; "It was a great thing to destroy slavery, but the integrity of the Union was of no less importance." Victory confirmed the sense of a unique destiny that most 19th-century white Americans regarded as theirs alone.

South of the Mason-Dixon Line, Southerners now shared with most of the world's people the experience of having been invaded, occupied, and defeated in a war. The result was a profound rupture in the historical experience of the United States. Despite the Confederacy's internal divisions the sacrifices of war and the humiliation of defeat provided a common basis for white southern identity in the postwar era. Rather than solving the problem of sectionalism, in many respects the Civil War created a more distinct and coherent "South" than had ever existed earlier in American history.

## The New Challenge of Race

Another central cause of the war that remained unresolved at its conclusion was the problem of race. The active role played by African Americans on behalf of the Union gave them a claim on the meaning of the conflict. Southern blacks provided crucial military intelligence to Union forces as they entered the region, ranging from basic information like the location of roads, bridges, and mountain gaps to more detailed intelligence about the movement and size of Confederate forces. The military service performed by black men gave them an even stronger claim to citizenship. In a letter to the Democratic Congressman Roscoe Conkling, Lincoln explained the impact of blacks' willingness to fight. After the war, he wrote, "there will be some black men who can remember that, with silent tongue, and clenched teeth, and steady eye, and well-poised bayonet, they have helped mankind on to this great consummation; while, I fear, there will be some white ones, unable to forget that, with malignant heart, and deceitful speech, they strove to hinder it." In many ways Lincoln's attitudes toward emancipation and black Americans reflected the average white Northerner. He came reluctantly to emancipation and he never adopted a modern conception of full racial equality, but he stood resolutely behind emancipation once it was Union policy, and by the war's end he advocated limited political rights for black men.

## Environmental and Economic Scars of War

As the war rearranged human relations, it also forced a reevaluation of the relationship between people and the environment. Since before the Revolution Americans had envisioned themselves as developing and enhancing nature. The environmental costs of industrialization and urbanization were already visible in the mid-19th century, and although some citizens felt the costs were too high, the majority of Americans believed that they had a productive and responsible relationship to the land. For four years Federals and Confederates did little but destroy and consume. Sherman's marches through Georgia and the Carolinas left significant environmental devastation. In this region a conservative estimate puts his destruction at 18,600 mules and horses, 13,300 head of cattle, 19 million pounds of fodder, 22 million pounds of grain and corn, and another 7 million pounds of foodstuffs. As one historian has explained, "In taking away their tools, animals, slaves, and produce, Sherman's forces interrupted—or completely rearranged—Southerners' fundamental relationship with nature."

Although Sherman's troops did not salt the earth, their destruction of industrial resources did considerable damage to the landscape. Armies on both sides had torn up railroads and bridges as a way to slow down the advance of the enemy, but both sides also developed engineer corps to rebuild that infrastructure. Sherman found a more permanent solution, which entailed creating huge fires from creosote-soaked

The war's physical impact on the South marked the region as distinctive. Although the detritus of conflict was soon removed or repaired, the psychological impact and memories of the conflict lasted for generations.

railroad ties, heating the rails until pliable, and using animals and men to twist them into knots or around trees. This practice—known variously as "Sherman neckties" or "Davis gimlets"—required returning the rails to a forge where they could be re-rolled, something that Confederates could not do during the war. After the war Georgians and South Carolinians, in particular, were confronted with a deeply scarred and damaged land. They also confronted a deeply depressed regional economy. The infrastructural and environmental damage, the destruction of fencing, the inability to tend farmland during the war, the loss of capital as a result of emancipation, and the disorganization of the labor market ensured a slow road to recovery in the South.

In the North the experience was nearly the opposite. Although the North experienced substantial inflation, the war stimulated a boom in many northern industries. Meat production, oil extraction, and all manner of military supplies, from clothing and tents to weapons and ships, saw rapid technological growth. The war hastened the use of mechanization and standardization in production, especially with regard to shoes and clothes, which had to be supplied to the army in huge volumes and standard sizes. The meat-packing plants of Chicago devised a "disassembly" line along which beef and hog carcasses were taken apart so that the constituent parts could be packaged—usually canned—and sold to the army.

## The Last Best Hope of Man?

Like sectionalism and race, the third of the great causes of the Civil War—the dispute over the proper balance of federal and state authority—was not solved by the war. To be sure, the war established the supremacy of the Union and of the federal government. Congressional Republicans, with Lincoln's support, carved out new areas of

### TIMELINE 1861–1865

**1861**

**December 1860 to February 1861** Secession of Lower South (TX, LA, MS, AL, FL, GA, SC)

**April 12** Confederates open fire on Fort Sumter in Charleston Harbor

**April 15** Lincoln calls up 75,000 militia; precipitates secession of Upper South (VA, NC, AR, TN)

**May 24** Benjamin Butler, Union commander at Fortress Monroe on the York Peninsula, declares 3 slaves who made their way into his camp "contraband" and refuses to return them to their owners

**July 21** Confederates win Battle of Bull Run (VA) and drive Union Army back to Washington, DC

**August 6** U.S. Congress passes the First Confiscation Act which provides the U.S. Army with the authority to confiscate slaves whose owners employ them in direct support of the Confederate military

**1862**

**February 6–16** Union forces capture Forts Henry and Donelson (TN), giving the North control of the Tennessee and Cumberland Rivers

**April 6–7** Union wins Battle of Shiloh (TN) forcing Confederates back to Corinth, MS

**April 16** President Lincoln signs legislation abolishing slavery in DC, with compensation for the owners

**June 19** U.S. Congress outlaws slavery in U.S. territories

**July 17** U.S. Congress passes the 2nd Confiscation Act that declares free the slaves of any rebel in those areas of the Confederacy controlled by the Union army and giving Lincoln the authority to use contrabands as soldiers

**June 26 to July 2** Lee repulses McClellan's advance on Richmond during Seven Days' Battles (VA)

**August 29–30** Confederates win Battle of Second Bull (VA) and drive Union forces back toward Washington, DC

**September 17** McClellan claims victory in the Battle of Antietam (MD) after forcing retreat of Lee's army back across the Potomac

**September 22** Lincoln issues Preliminary Emancipation Proclamation

**October 7** Battle of Perryville (KY) forces Braxton Bragg to abandon Confederate invasion of Kentucky

**December 11–13** Confederates win Battle of Fredericksburg (VA)

federal power, though these were all initiatives that Republicans had supported before the war but passed only because of the lack of Democratic opposition. On the larger question of ideology the war did little to resolve the historical tensions between states and the central government. Northern Democrats maintained a steady criticism of the Lincoln administration for the measures it adopted, especially those that altered the traditional balance of American federalism.

Americans celebrated the preservation of democracy not just for the United States but for all the world. The vision articulated by the North, intended to inspire, worried foreign friends and enemies alike. The *New York Herald* cheered the liberating potential of northern armies at the war's end. "Their [northern soldiers'] souls and those of their slain comrades will be marching on. On—till the thrones shake and crumble at the sound of their coming, and are crushed beneath their steady tramp. On—till the people everywhere rise and demand their liberties with invincible voices. On—till no despot tyrannizes over his fellow men, and no aristocracy lords it over the down-trodden masses. On—till every nation is a republic, and every man a freeman. On—till the soldiers of Grant, Sherman and Sheridan have saved the world as they have saved the Union. On, and on, and on!" Close to home the Civil War hastened the consolidation of a unified Canada concerned about America's emboldened and expansionist spirit, and it alerted the globe to a new world power.

At the same time the war demonstrated that political movements inspired by a strong sense of nationalism could sustain liberal politics. In western Europe, in the years after 1848, nationalist movements often aligned themselves with conservative or reactionary politics, most famously in Germany. Lincoln's frequent exhortations for Americans to identify themselves with the nation—the "mystic chords of memory"—and his rhetorical efforts to place equality and justice at the center of American

with heavy Union casualties

**1863**

**January 1** Lincoln signs Final Emancipation Proclamation, freeing all slaves held in Confederate controlled territory

**May 1** Confederates win Battle of Chancellorsville (VA)

**July 1–4** Union wins Battle of Gettysburg (PA)

**July 4** Union captures Vicksburg, MS, and gains control of the Mississippi River

**September 19** Confederates win Battle of Chickamauga (TN) forcing Union troops back into Chattanooga

**November 23–25** Union wins Battle of Chattanooga (TN) forcing Confederates back into Georgia

**1864**

**May 5–6** Battle of Spotsylvania (VA)

**May 10–11** Battle of the Wilderness (VA)

**June 1–3** Confederates win Battle of Cold Harbor (VA) but Union forces push south toward Petersburg

**Mid-June** Siege of Petersburg, VA, begins

**September 5** Fall of Atlanta, GA

**November 12** Sherman's forces leave Atlanta for Savannah

**Late September–October** Union wins decisive victories in Battles of Winchester, Fisher's Hill, and Cedar Creek, VA, giving Federals control of the lower Shenandoah Valley

**November–December** Union wins decisive victories in Battles of Franklin and Nashville, completing Union control of the western theater

**December 20** Sherman occupies Savannah, GA

**1865**

**February 14** Fall of Columbia, SC

**March 13** Confederate Congress passes legislation providing for the enlistment of black men into Confederate military units

**April 4** Petersburg and Richmond evacuated

**April 9** Lee surrenders to Grant at Appomattox Courthouse, VA

**April 22** Joseph Johnston surrenders to William T. Sherman at Durham Station, NC

**December 18** 13th Amendment ratified, abolishing slavery in the United States national identity (a "new birth of freedom") tied American nationalism to a liberalizing political agenda that sundered the government's long embrace of slavery and advocated development policies designed to support the homesteader as well as the speculator. Observers outside the United States affirmed Lincoln's sense of the liberal progress as a consequence of the war and saw how the Union's triumph could help them in their own reforms. The British statesman John Morley drew the connection: "The triumph of the North . . . was the force that made English liberalism powerful enough to enfranchise the workmen, depose official Christianity in Ireland, and deal the first blow at the landlords."

### STUDY QUESTIONS FOR VICTORY AND DEFEAT, 1865

1. **How did Americans (of all sorts) understand the meaning of the Civil War when it ended?**
2. **How does the history of the Civil War portrayed here compare to popular and/or family stories about the war?**

## Summary

- The rapid growth of the northern states, built on immigration from northwestern Europe and increasingly extensive economic ties with that part of the globe, threatened the balance of power within the United States.
- Conflicts over the future of slavery in the West propelled a majority of slaveholding states to secede, a decision buttressed by Southerners' assumption that their central place as cotton supplier to the burgeoning French and British empires would bring recognition of their new nation before any real war began.
- The North interpreted secession as a repudiation of the essence of self-government, a threat to both America and the future of democracy around the world.
- The most revolutionary change of the war came as enslaved peoples seized opportunities to escape, forced the North to endorse emancipation, and destroyed the world's largest and most influential slave society.
- The war spurred the development of new military technologies and new rules about the relationship between soldiers and noncombatants in wartime that circulated within the Western world, raised concerns about America's emboldened and expansionist spirit, and alerted the globe to a new world power.
- Like similar nationalist struggles in Europe at the same time, the U.S. Civil War strengthened the central government but also created new problems of sectionalism and race, as an embittered white South sought to subjugate and control the three and a half million African Americans freed during the war.

## Key Terms and People

**Bell, John** *523*
**Bolívar, Simón** *522*
**Breckinridge, John** *523*
**Brownlow, William G. "Parson"** *536*
**Buchanan, James** *525*
**Burnside, Ambrose** *546*
**Butler, Benjamin** *534*
**Chase, Samuel** *523*
**Davis, Jefferson** *525*
**Emancipation Proclamation** *538*
**Forrest, Nathan Bedford** *549*
**Frémont, John** *540*
**Gladstone, William** *538*
**Grant, Ulysses S.** *531*
**Greeley, Horace** *539*
**Hunter, David** *540*
**Jackson, "Stonewall"** *534*
**Lee, Robert E.** *533*
**Lincoln, Abraham** *523*
**McClellan, George B.** *533*
**Moltke, Helmuth von** *551*
**Powell, John Wesley** *554*
**Russell, William Howard** *526*
**Scheibert, Justus** *550*
**Scott, Winfield** *530*
**Seward, William Henry** *523*
**Sheridan, Philip** *546*
**Sherman, William T.** *546*
**Stephens, Alexander** *528*
**Strong, George Templeton** *527*
**U.S. Colored Troops (USCT)** *547*
**Welles, Gideon** *549*
**Wilkes, Charles** *538*

## Reviewing Chapter 14

1. Why did the North win the Civil War?
2. How does the U.S. Civil War compare to other civil conflicts in the 19th and 20th centuries?

## Further Reading

Ash, Stephen V. *When the Yankees Came: Conflict and Chaos in the Occupied South.* Chapel Hill: University of North Carolina Press, 1995. The clearest analysis of the nature and experience of occupation for both Southern civilians and Northern soldiers.

Gallagher, Gary W. *The Confederate War.* Cambridge: Harvard University Press, 1997. A probing book that argues for the durability and resiliency of Confederate nationalism.

Grimsley, Mark. *The Hard Hand of War: Union Military Policy Toward Southern Civilians, 1861–1865.* Cambridge: Cambridge University Press, 1995. The most compelling explanation of the shift in Union policy toward a more destructive conflict.

McCurry, Stephanie. *Confederate Reckoning: Power and Politics in the Civil War South* Cambridge: Harvard University Press, 2010. A vigorous reinterpretation of the Confederate political experience, focusing on the challenges presented by white women and enslaved people.

Rable, George C. *The Confederate Republic: A Revolution Against Politics.* Chapel Hill: University of North Carolina Press, 1994. The best analysis of the political tension between nationalists and libertarians in the Confederacy.

Whites, LeeAnn. *The Civil War as a Crisis in Gender: Augusta, Georgia, 1860-1890.* Athens: University of Georgia Press, 1995. An insightful study of the dynamic relationship between gender conventions and war in the South.

# Visual Review

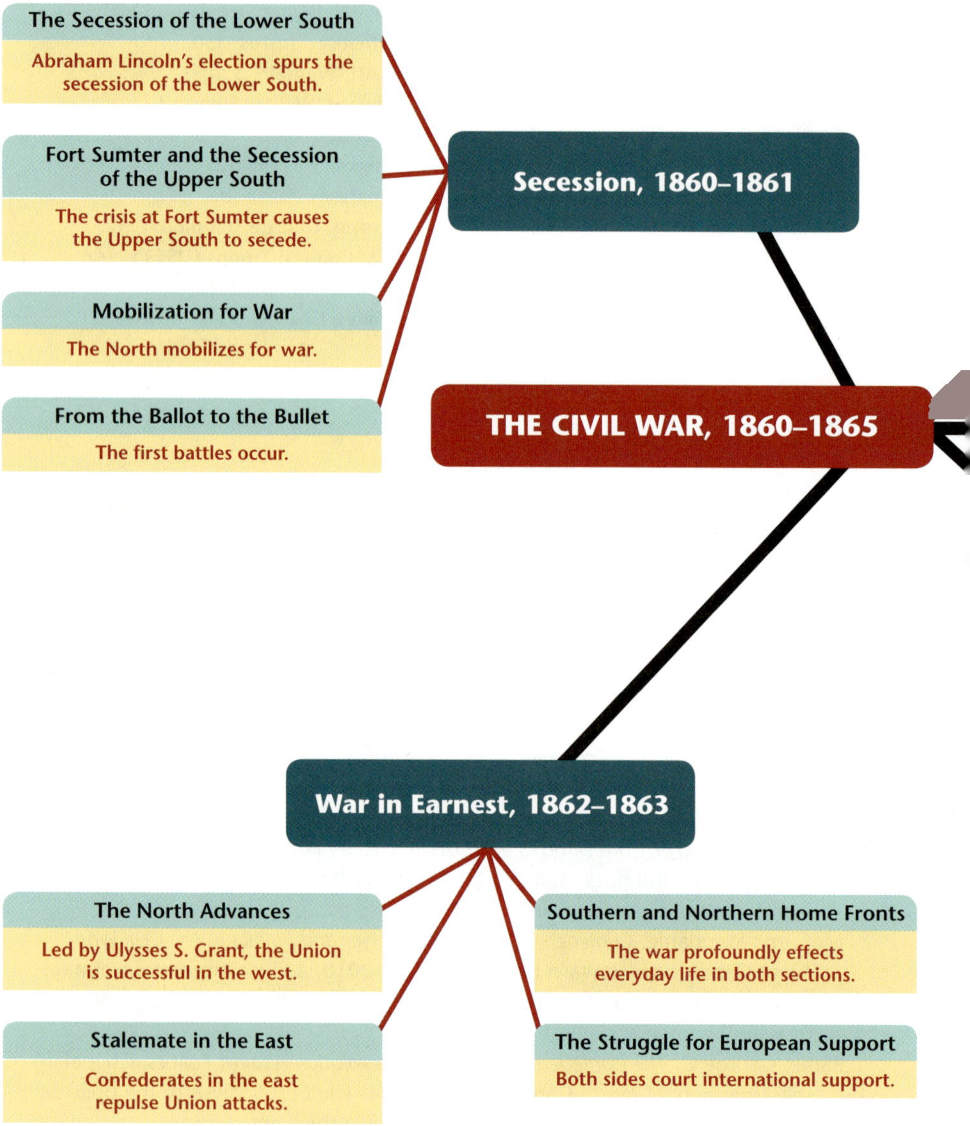

## THE CIVIL WAR, 1860–1865

### Secession, 1860–1861

**The Secession of the Lower South**
Abraham Lincoln's election spurs the secession of the Lower South.

**Fort Sumter and the Secession of the Upper South**
The crisis at Fort Sumter causes the Upper South to secede.

**Mobilization for War**
The North mobilizes for war.

**From the Ballot to the Bullet**
The first battles occur.

### War in Earnest, 1862–1863

**The North Advances**
Led by Ulysses S. Grant, the Union is successful in the west.

**Stalemate in the East**
Confederates in the east repulse Union attacks.

**Southern and Northern Home Fronts**
The war profoundly effects everyday life in both sections.

**The Struggle for European Support**
Both sides court international support.

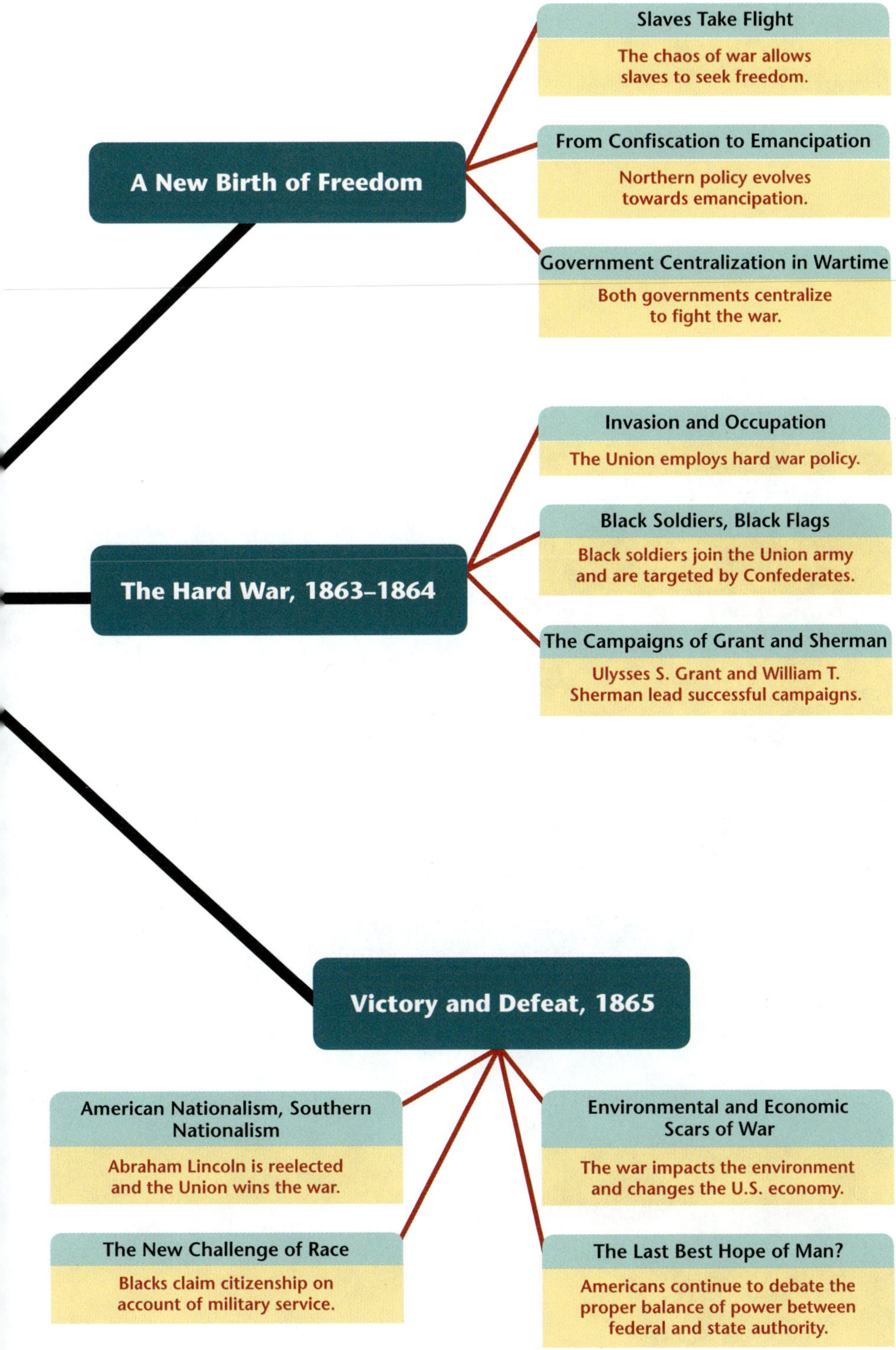

## A New Birth of Freedom

**Slaves Take Flight**
The chaos of war allows slaves to seek freedom.

**From Confiscation to Emancipation**
Northern policy evolves towards emancipation.

**Government Centralization in Wartime**
Both governments centralize to fight the war.

## The Hard War, 1863–1864

**Invasion and Occupation**
The Union employs hard war policy.

**Black Soldiers, Black Flags**
Black soldiers join the Union army and are targeted by Confederates.

**The Campaigns of Grant and Sherman**
Ulysses S. Grant and William T. Sherman lead successful campaigns.

## Victory and Defeat, 1865

**American Nationalism, Southern Nationalism**
Abraham Lincoln is reelected and the Union wins the war.

**The New Challenge of Race**
Blacks claim citizenship on account of military service.

**Environmental and Economic Scars of War**
The war impacts the environment and changes the U.S. economy.

**The Last Best Hope of Man?**
Americans continue to debate the proper balance of power between federal and state authority.

# 15 Reconstructing America

## 1865–1877

Cato, Patience, Peggy, Jane, Porter, and Stepney were among many enslaved black Southerners who lived on plantations in Liberty County, Georgia. In early 1865, they watched as the first wave of "Bummers," or deserters from Sherman's Union army, came through the county. The Union deserters raided plantation houses and slave cabins alike, taking everything edible (and much that was not) and shooting animals they could not carry away. One Confederate described the raiders as "lost in the world of eternal woe. Their throats were open sepulchers, their mouths filled with cursing and bitterness and lies." Despite the hardship that ensued, enslaved people living in the region did nothing to obstruct the Union Army. Cato and Stepney, who both worked as drivers organizing and managing slave labor under the eye of a white overseer, effectively supported the Union by their inaction. Their stature in the community surely influenced others. They behaved, in the bitter but accurate words of a local slaveholder, as though they "now believe themselves perfectly free." In Liberty County, and throughout the rural South, whites and blacks shared a world based in the hierarchy of slavery and racial dominance, and organized around the production schedules of staple crops. As Cato and the others observed the Yankee conquest of Georgia they saw the dawning of a new era and began to work out what freedom meant. A wide range of choices, opportunities, and perils awaited black Southerners across the region.

Cato and his wife Jane, who lived on a nearby plantation, bided their time through the collapse of the Confederacy. Cato's long experience working the land and managing workers

◄ *Driving the Last Spike* by Thomas Hill, 1881

**CHAPTER OUTLINE**



*continued on page 567*

# America in the World

The Colfax Massacre showed that racially motivated violence remained a serious issue during Reconstruction (1873).

The Force Act was passed to crack down on Ku Klux Klan actions to keep Blacks from voting (1865–1871).

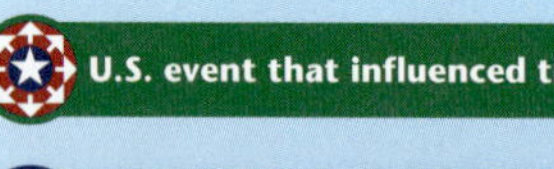


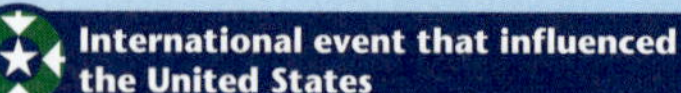

Event with multinational influence

Conflict

The Fourteenth Amendment established citizenship rights and due process (1867).
Although rarely enforced, the Civil Rights Act was intended to eliminate segregation by race in public spaces (1875).
The Fifteenth Amendment prohibited voting discrimination based on race or servitude (1870).

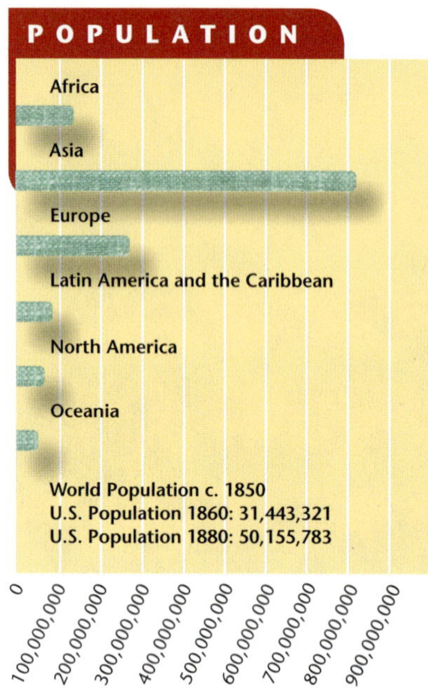


led him to reject the authority of a new overseer hired in late summer 1865. Cato's former owner denounced him as "a most insolent, indolent, and dishonest man." In response, Cato and his wife exercised their freedom in most fundamental sense—they left Liberty County altogether, moving to nearby Savannah. No longer able to control her former slaves, Cato's ex-owner lashed out by asserting that black people would not last: "with their emancipation must come their extermination."

Despite the rising anger among whites, many freedmen and freedwomen remained in Liberty and set about making contracts for their work. Porter and Patience stayed in the area and, in spite of the fluctuating labor and pay agreements with area planters, managed to buy their own farm outright. Patience's brother Stepney resided on Arcadia, a coastal plantation that supported two lucrative crops: rice and sea island cotton. He began to manage much of the former plantation land at Arcadia and helped coordinate the rental and purchase of land by freed people. The close family networks established among the Gullah people, as the black Southerners in this region were known, undoubtedly aided many in their transition to freedom.

Unfortunately, few freed people experienced the success they did. Peggy, who had lived on the same plantation as Cato, moved to Savannah but contracted smallpox and died. Some freed people began to labor for wages on the plantations that they had once farmed as slaves, but this rarely brought them the financial independence they desired. Others rented land or farmed on shares, splitting the proceeds from the yearly crop with the landlord. This latter sharecropper system, adopted widely across the South, trapped tenant farmers in cycles of debt and prevented the southern agricultural sector from diversifying as the world cotton market collapsed. In Liberty County, as elsewhere in the South, the reintegration of the southern economy into the larger global market reflected the efforts Southerners and Northerners made to reconstruct the nation. But Southerners' failure to build a sustainable and humane economy or a just social and political system in the postwar South reinforced the larger failure of the nation in Reconstruction.

## THE YEAR OF JUBILEE, 1865

The dramatic changes underway in the South and the nation produced surprising outcomes. At the end of the Civil War, white Southerners were defeated and resentful, while black Southerners celebrated Jubilee, their deliverance from bondage. Northerners likewise celebrated, because they had preserved the Union and extinguished slavery in the United States. But great questions remained: what role would recently freed slaves play in American life? What rights would they possess? What obligations did the federal government have to ensure a meaningful freedom? For Washington, the first order of business was reestablishing loyal governments in the South and bringing the region back into a normal relationship with the nation. No precedents guided this process and grand constitutional questions about the nature of the Union and the meaning of republican government acquired immediate political weight. Republicans and Democrats, Northerners and Southerners, and blacks and whites, divided over the answers to these questions. The wartime task of reunion gave way to the postwar task of reconstruction, which entailed the reorganization of the southern political system and the rebuilding of shattered public and private institutions.

CHAPTER OUTLINE

*continued from page 563*



## African American Families

Of the nearly four million enslaved people in the South before the Civil War, approximately 500,000 fled to freedom during the war and the rest claimed their freedom at the war's conclusion. The most important task confronting freed people was reestablishing families broken by slavery. White Southerners wanted to restore what they considered normal labor relations, but most black Southerners' desire to locate displaced family members outweighed even the desire for a steady wage. According

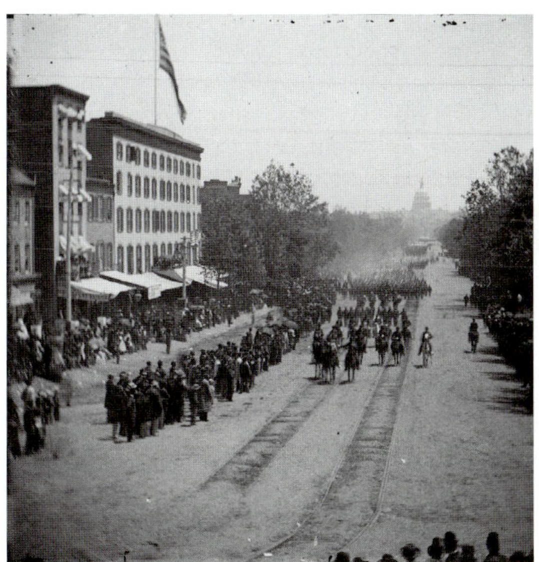

After four long years, Northerners celebrated Union victory in the Civil War and the end of slavery. But the war's conclusion only began the struggle to define what freedom would mean in practice.

to many enslaved people, the central crime of slavery was the destruction of black families. Through the late spring and summer of 1865, as white southern soldiers headed home in defeat, black Southerners took to the road, following letters, reports, and rumors to track the exodus of children, parents, siblings, and loved ones as a result of slave sales. This movement added to the uncertainty of the postwar period and alarmed whites who expected blacks to stay and continue the work they had done before emancipation.

The next question that confronted freed people was what work they would do. Across the South, black Southerners faced several choices: wage labor, renting land to farm themselves, sharecropping, or some combination of the three. But the question of where that work happened often took precedence. "If I stay here, I'll never know I'm free," explained one freedwoman as she left the plantation on which she had labored as a slave. Many thousands made the same choice, leaving behind farms and plantations on which they had been raised in favor of a new, if uncertain, life somewhere else. Often, they moved to cities, most overcrowded from the influx of refugees during the war. Memphis and Nashville both grew by more than a third between 1860 and 1870, while Atlanta's population more than doubled.

In rural areas, labor contracts and work were the most pressing priorities. Very few enslaved people owned any real estate before the war, which required them to work for wages. The main challenge was working out fair and enforceable contracts

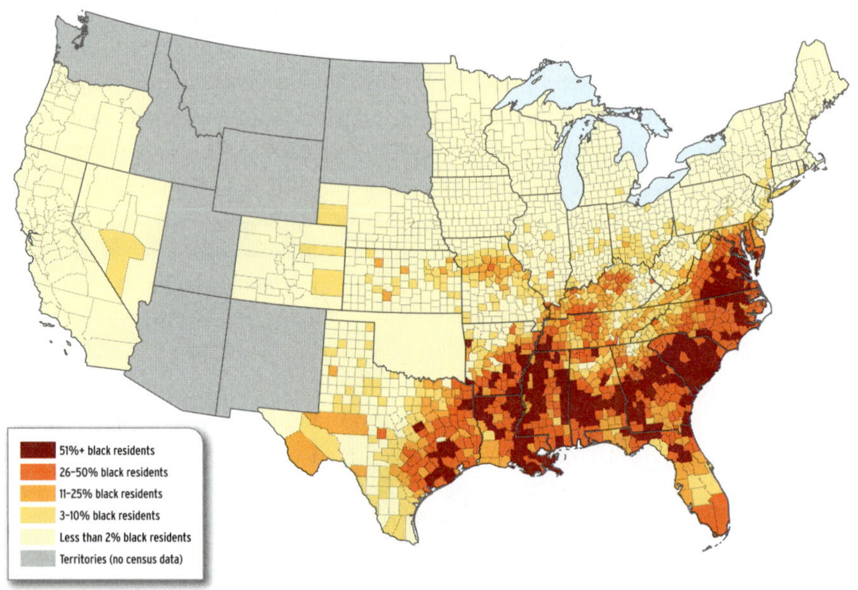


▲ **Map 15.1**

**Black Population of the United States, 1880** Despite the opportunities for movement created by emancipation, few former slaves had the resources to make a full relocation out of the region. As a result, black Americans continued to live predominately in the South until the second and third decades of the 20th century.

with former masters or other whites. The Bureau of Refugees, Freedmen, and Abandoned Land (usually called the **Freedmen's Bureau**), established within the Army in early 1865, helped adjudicate labor disputes in the summer and fall of 1865. Led by former Union general **Oliver Otis Howard**, the Bureau also distributed food rations to blacks and whites during the hard winter that followed and initiated the building of schools, hospitals, and other communal institutions. Despite this important work, elite Southerners resented the intrusion of the federal government and joined with northern Democrats to denounce the Bureau as an unnecessary federal imposition on states' rights. Because slaves had labored without incentive, whites did not expect them to understand paid work. In fact, most African Americans adjusted quickly, even when they could not rely on landowners to fairly fulfill the terms of labor contracts. One man, who had relocated to Ohio at the war's end, responded to a request from his former master to return to Tennessee, by asking "you to send us our wages for the time we served you." "Here I draw my wages every Saturday night," wrote Jourdan Anderson, "but in Tennessee there was never any pay day for the negroes any more than for the horses and the cows."

## Southern Whites and the Problem of Defeat

The spring and summer of 1865 exhilarated and bewildered Americans throughout the country. The most shocking event was the assassination of **Abraham Lincoln**. After celebrating the official surrender of Lee's Army of Northern Virginia on April 12, 1865, Lincoln attended a play on the evening of the 14th, Good Friday. **John Wilkes Booth**, a member of America's most famous acting family, organized a conspiracy to kill Lincoln and several cabinet members. Booth shot Lincoln in his box at Ford's Theater while a conspirator stabbed Secretary of State **William Seward** in his home. Lincoln, unconscious but still alive, was taken to a house across the street from the theater, where doctors tried to save him. Cabinet members, generals, and other officials visited the room where he lay before Lincoln died just after dawn. Secretary of War **Edwin Stanton** summarized the grim morning and its effect on America's memory of Lincoln: "now he belongs to the ages." Booth escaped into Maryland before being killed by U.S. troops. Grief and anger flooded across the North, with many citizens blaming the conspiracy on **Jefferson Davis**, who fled south after evacuating Richmond in early April. Despite the controversies he stoked as president, Lincoln earned the deep appreciation of Northerners by steering the country through the crisis of disunion. Walt Whitman, who had seen Lincoln on his melancholy early morning walks around Washington, spoke for many when he lamented:

> O the bleeding drops of red,
> Where on the deck my Captain lies,
> Fallen cold and dead.

Some Southerners, **Robert E. Lee** among them, recognized Lincoln's turn toward generosity late in the war and regarded his murder as damaging to their interest.

Others, however, could not help but exalt this final turn of events. "Hurrah! Old Abe Lincoln has been assassinated!" a South Carolina woman wrote in her diary. "Our hated enemy has met the just reward of his life." Northerners could not comprehend such an attitude. For them, the restoration of the Union brought relief and confirmation of God's favor over their society. Even as Southerners struggled to reconcile their religious understanding of defeat—many believed it was another test offered by God for his chosen people—they resisted the political consequences of Union victory. A number of high-ranking Confederate military officers fled to South America, fearful of punishment they might receive from the Union government. **Edward Porter Alexander**, Lee's chief of artillery, laid his plans on the retreat to Appomattox: "I had made up my mind that if ever a white flag was raised I would take to the bushes. And, somehow, I would manage to get out of the country & go to Brazil. Brazil was just going to war with Paraguay & I could doubtless get a place in their artillery. . . ." Several thousand white Southerners relocated to Brazil, where they created an expatriate community in one of the last two major slave societies remaining in the western hemisphere. More than 10,000 Confederates exiled themselves after the war. This exodus carried men, and sometimes their families, around the world. Many ended up serving as military advisors to foreign governments, including Britain, France, Germany, and several employed by the Khedive of Egypt.

Even as white Southerners lamented the war's outcome, they sought the easiest path toward readmission to the Union in hopes of restoring some measure of normality in the South and because it might allow them to retain authority over the freed people. So, despite their vigorous pursuit of independence and their wartime insistence that the Confederacy was a separate nation, many Southerners assumed that they could quickly and easily resume their old position within the United States. Northern Democrats largely agreed. They had long believed that Southerners could not leave the Union and so restoration of rights, especially property rights for southern whites, would be a simple matter of affirming their future loyalty. Republicans resisted these easy terms but fought amongst themselves about the proper way to rebuild the nation's political system.

White Southerners also grappled with restoring order in their communities and explaining defeat to themselves. This proved particularly challenging for southern men. In the prewar era, white men had claimed authority by promising to protect and care for members of southern society they viewed as inferior to them, including women, children, and black people. Confederate defeat revealed the failure of **paternalism**. Southern women, in particular, had been forced to assume new burdens and responsibilities during the war. On Virginia plantations the economic consequences of defeat and emancipation forced men and women to share tasks and roles that were distinct before the war. By the 1870s, local agricultural organizations were encouraging men and women to cooperate in running their households and their farms. The **Farmers' Alliance**, a national version of these local bodies, maintained this policy. In their journal, distributed to hundreds of thousands of farming households across the country, the Alliance advised that "It is not too much to say that there is no other occupation in which men and women are engaged, whose work and cares and responsibilities fall with such nearly equal weight on the husband and wife, as do those of farming." The ethic of mutuality that developed in some rural communities around the South came more from necessity than ideology, but it still challenged one of the core aspects of prewar gender relations. In other places, the effects of the war compelled some women to reaffirm the hierarchy rather than press forward with changes. To do this, white women relinquished their wartime responsibilities and advocated traditional gender relationships. As one editorial in a Georgia newspaper noted, "a married man falling into misfortunes is more apt to retrieve his situation in the world than a single one, chiefly because . . . although abroad may be darkness and humiliation, yet there is still a little world of love at home of which he is monarch."

## Emancipation in Comparative Perspective

Americans followed neither an inevitable nor an entirely distinct path after emancipation. Both Jamaica and South Africa experienced similarly sudden and disruptive emancipation moments in the mid-19th century. Although both places functioned as British colonies when they freed their slaves, in all three societies, whites followed emancipation by vigorously pursuing racial supremacy. This pursuit took different forms. In Jamaica, white elites used the emerging scientific consensus behind racial hierarchy to abdicate local control to London. As a consequence, white property holders on the island were protected at the expense of black workers. In South Africa, local whites achieved greater autonomy from the colonial office, and although they allowed black voting, whites retained economic and social power. Unlike Jamaica, which had a society sharply divided between a small number of white elites and a high number of landless blacks, South Africa possessed a sizeable rural white population. Like its southern counterpart in the United States, rural whites joined with elites to resist emancipation and, when resistance proved futile, work to establish white supremacy.

A pivotal moment in Jamaican emancipation came 30 years after the start of the process. In the fall of 1865, as Americans were struggling to devise the rules and goals of their own post-emancipation Reconstruction, word spread through the hemisphere of a rebellion of black farm workers in Jamaica. The **Morant Bay Rebellion** stemmed from inequities in post-emancipation Jamaica. The black laboring class continued to be denied access to land or political power, a consequence of policies designed by white leaders that restricted blacks to working as agricultural laborers. The rebellion consumed the eastern half of the island and left hundreds of black laborers dead and hundreds more beaten by state militia forces. American newspapers tracked the event and filtered it through the perspectives of the ongoing struggle over the role of the freedmen in American life. A southern paper described "terrible massacres of the whites" by bands of deranged blacks. In contrast, American abolitionists used the event as an object lesson in why full equality and political rights were necessary for all Southerners. According to Senator **Charles Sumner**, the freedmen of the South "were not unlike the freedmen of San Domingo or Jamaica . . . and have the same sense of wrong."

The United States avoided a Morant Bay Rebellion, though it did not grant freed people the degree of freedom Sumner recommended. A key distinction between the three experiments in Reconstruction proved to be the nature of political change in each society. In Jamaica, a mulatto elite, composed mostly of the descendents of slave-holders and their slaves, entered into the political system, but they mostly sided with the white elite. When legislators granted blacks the right to vote in South Africa, they also enacted a property restriction that ensured white domination. In contrast, black southern men received the vote without restriction. This helped make American Reconstruction the most radical of those slave societies that experienced emancipation in the 19th century.

**STUDY QUESTIONS FOR THE YEAR OF JUBILEE, 1865**

1. **How did white and black Southerners respond to the end of the Civil War?**
2. **What did each group want for the postwar world?**

# SHAPING RECONSTRUCTION, 1865–1868

In 1865, a small group of Republican congressmen and senators had high hopes for a vigorous Reconstruction plan. Some were former abolitionists, and others had emerged during the war as advocates for a transformed South. These men—and a substantially more diverse body of black and white male and female reformers who urged them on—foresaw not just the expansion of free labor but a redistribution of southern wealth and an egalitarian political order that included black male suffrage. Between 1865 and 1866, this group—known as the "radical Republicans"—went from the margins to the center of the political debate, and they did so largely because Northerners perceived President Andrew Johnson as currying favor with an unrepentant South. The fight that erupted between Johnson and his own party in Congress opened strange new rifts in American politics and propelled Republicans toward a surprising and dramatic shift in Reconstruction. In a series of clashes with Johnson, Congressional Republicans adopted increasingly radical measures meant to secure the fruits of Union victory in the war and protect the rights of the freed people. The different phases of Reconstruction that followed illuminate the unpredictability of events after the war and the importance of partisan and sectional alignments in American politics.

## Andrew Johnson's Reconstruction

As the uncertainty of spring gave way to summer, southern whites confidently assumed they would be allowed to continue with "self-reconstruction." Under this theory, white Southerners reaffirmed their loyalty to the United States through existing political systems. With Congress out of session, Andrew Johnson, the Tennessee Unionist who had become president after Lincoln's assassination, set the terms. Despite radicals' hopes that Johnson would impose strict conditions on the reentry of southern states, he set the bar low. Southerners needed to repudiate secession and state debts incurred during the war and confirm emancipation by ratifying the **Thirteenth Amendment**, which outlawed slavery in the United States. Johnson also extended amnesty to most of the high-ranking military and civilian officials of the Confederacy. Before the war, Johnson was a bitter enemy of the plantation elite, championing the cause of the white artisans and nonslaveholding farmers of East Tennessee. But in his efforts to keep pace with the shifting political alignments of the postwar era, Johnson became a staunch defender of white supremacy and recast himself as the defender of embattled white elites.

In fall 1865, southern states held new state elections. In the Upper South, a significant number of former Whigs and Unionists won, but voters in the Lower South largely reelected Democratic Party elites who led the region during the war. **Alexander Stephens**, the former vice president of the Confederacy, was elected U.S. senator from Georgia. Most Northerners, and even some Democrats, reacted with shock and anger. Did the South really imagine it could send the very men who had led a bloody rebellion against the United States to serve in Congress? Andrew Johnson, while frustrated that the election of openly disloyal men would prejudice the North against the region, accepted the results as a product of the democratic process. Radical Republicans grew increasingly uneasy with Johnson's leniency.

Forced to accept emancipation, reconstituted state governments across the region adopted a series of laws known collectively as the "**black codes**"in the fall of 1865, which proscribed both the extent and the limits of freedom for black residents in the region. The rights granted to freed people included the right to marry, to own property, and to participate in the judicial process, through suing and being sued and giving testimony in court cases, but the legislators paid much more attention to restrictions on black freedom. The most nefarious of these were the "apprenticeship" laws, which gave county courts the authority to take children away from parents if those parents were not capable of providing for them. Black Southerners and many Northerners perceived this as a blatant attempt to reimpose slavery. The codes also focused not just on ex-slaves but on "all freedpeople, free negroes, and mulattoes," effectively creating a new legal designation in southern law that singled out black people where previously status (free or slave) had been the key distinction among residents.

For Northerners, the second half of 1865 proved nearly as disorienting as the first half. Just as they experienced the elation of victory and anguish over Lincoln's assassination, Northerners moved from supporting Johnson's initial measures to reconstruct the South quickly to anger at Johnson's capitulation to Southern arrogance. Carl Schurz, a prominent Civil War general and radical Republican, had been sent on a tour of the South by Johnson in late 1865 to assess the situation, but his findings undercut support for Johnson's policies. White Southerners did not think of themselves as Americans and did not trust black Southerners to work in a new free labor economy. Schurz concluded that "it is not only the political machinery of the States and their constitutional relations to the general government, but the whole organism of southern society that must be reconstructed, or rather constructed anew, so as to bring it into harmony with the rest of American society." As Congress reconvened in December 1865, its members weighed the merits and methods of reconstructing the

South. After much debate, Congress slowed down the process of Reconstruction by refusing to seat the delegations recently elected from southern states.

## The Fight over Reconstruction

The desire to punish the South for its refusal to accept the verdict of war manifested itself in the first session of the 39th Congress. These were the men elected in fall 1864, at the moment of the Union's triumph at Atlanta, Mobile Bay, and the Shenandoah Valley. They came into office on Lincoln's coattails, and they were overwhelmingly Republican. They held more than a 2-to-1 advantage in the House of Representatives and a 3-to-1 advantage in the Senate. Further, as Johnson alienated himself from moderate Republicans the balance of power in the party shifted toward the radicals. So it was with relative ease that Republicans overcame Democratic objections and refused to seat the delegations sent to Washington by the former Confederate states. Doing so amounted to a public challenge to Johnson's leadership and signaled a clear desire to slow down Reconstruction. Although Republicans would never have a free hand from their constituents, who worried about Reconstruction's costs and duration, a majority of Northerners and many southern unionists wanted to reevaluate the purpose and direction of Reconstruction policy in late 1865 and early 1866.

Republican congressmen worried about the economic state of the former Confederacy. Union and Confederate forces alike had destroyed huge swathes of the southern landscape, tearing down fence rails for firewood and tearing up railroads to weaken the Confederates' ability to fight. Most economically damaging of all was emancipation, which represented a capital loss of at least $3 billion for white Southerners. By one estimate, slave property comprised 60 percent of the wealth of the Deep South cotton states. The results on the Civil War in per capita terms were striking: the average total wealth of all southern farm operators dropped from $22,819 in 1860 to $3,168 a decade later. Freed people thus entered the labor market during a period of severe contraction, with most farmers possessing little cash with which to pay workers.

Because of the immediate necessity for freed people to sign a contract of some sort and begin earning money, they were in a poor position to negotiate with landowners. Agents of the Freedmen's Bureau served as the only check on exploitative labor agreements. In southwest Georgia, the bureau received a complaint from **Felix Massey**, a former slave who stated that "Sidney Burden had ambushed him along a country road, attempted to gouge out his eyes, and then fired a pistol his way 'contrary to the laws of the United States.'" Freedmen's Bureau agents settled labor disputes when they arose, but the Bureau never fielded more than 900 agents in the whole South, which rarely amounted to more than one per county. Despite the importance of their work, Johnson and Congressional Democrats denounced the Freedmen's Bureau as an unwarranted extension of federal power. White Southerners were much less subtle in their critique. **Josiah Nott**, an Alabamian and prominent prewar doctor, fumed against the reorganization of Mobile's public space to accommodate African Americans. "See how the damd Military, the nigger troops, the Freemen's Bureau spit upon us and rub it in." Republicans remained committed to a limited government, and many were concerned about the constitutional issues raised by the Bureau, but most regarded the work as too important to abandon. In 1866, Congress approved a one-year renewal of the Bureau. Johnson vetoed the bill and, in a sign of growing Republican solidarity, Congress overrode his veto.

Partisan politics played a large role in shaping the nature of Reconstruction. The Republican Party was only a decade old and had yet to establish any presence in the southern United States, which it needed if it was to remain a viable entity. Republicans sought to build a coalition of "loyal" voters—drawing on former Unionists in the South and African Americans if they were enfranchised, along with their core base in the North. A key component of their rhetoric in the period focused on the "Bloody Shirt," a patriotic appeal to reward Republicans for steering the country through the Civil War. They condemned Democrats as traitors who abetted the Confederacy. Republicans benefited from the rise of the veteran as an American icon during this period. In previous wars, veterans had been honored, but only after the Civil War was military service promoted as the purest expression of civic pride. Veterans themselves played a key role in promulgating this idea.

Fresh from his defeat over the renewal of the Freedmen's Bureau, Johnson picked another fight with Congress, this time over the 1866 Civil Rights Act. The first instance of federal law designed expressly to protect the rights of citizens, rather than prohibiting the actions of government, the bill was authored by moderate Republican **Lyman Trumball** of Illinois and was intended as a middle ground between radicals who wanted strong intervention in southern states to ensure racial equality and conservatives who feared the centralizing nature of such action. The bill established a common national citizenship for all people born in the United States and promised the "full and equal benefit of all laws and proceedings for the security of person and property." Although as one northern senator noted, "this species of legislation is absolutely revolutionary," because the bill did not spell out the rights that citizens enjoyed, it concealed continuing differences among Republicans. Johnson refused to accept even this moderate measure and he vetoed the bill. Johnson's explanation, as with his earlier veto of the Freedmen's Bureau, conveyed his refusal to accept the "centralization" of power initiated by the bill. Johnson also made white supremacy an important part of his veto, arguing that by granting black Americans equal access to the law, it denied rights to whites. To Johnson's horror, the bill seemed to grant "a perfect equality of the white and colored races . . . to be fixed by Federal law in every State of the Union." Congress again overrode Johnson and enacted the legislation. Johnson's opposition to these two central measures and his intemperate veto messages isolated him politically and pushed the sizeable body of moderate Republicans closer to the radicals.

## The Civil War Amendments and American Citizenship

After the Civil Rights bill passed, Republicans began debating a broader protection of individual rights. As they discussed what would become the **Fourteenth Amendment**, Republicans again quarreled among themselves about the propriety of creating federal safeguards for individual rights. And again, moderates won the day, this time crafting a broad guarantee of national citizenship and equality before the law, but offering no specific protection of freed people's political rights. The second section of the amendment punished states that denied the vote to black men by reducing their representation in Congress. Under the prewar constitution, enslaved people counted as three-fifths of a free person for the purposes of apportionment; under the Fourteenth Amendment, if not enfranchised, they would effectively count as zero-fifths. This feature might compel southern states to enfranchise black men, but it put little pressure on Northern states to do the same because ignoring their small black populations did not substantially reduce northern representation in Congress. The amendment also repudiated the debt accumulated by the Confederate and Southern state governments, leaving the millions of dollars issued during the war in bonds and currency worthless.

In post-emancipation Jamaica, the British had pursued a similarly bold plan for full civil equality, although it imposed through the policies of the colonial secretary, Lord Glenelg, rather than through a constitution. In 1837, Glenelg explained that the "great cardinal principle of the law for the abolition of slavery is, that the apprenticeship of the emancipated slaves is to be immediately succeeded by personal freedom, in the full and unlimited sense of the term in which it is used in reference to the other subjects of the British Crown." Glenelg's policies held for a decade, but by the late 1840s, the government imposed restrictions on the right to vote and eventually suspended Jamaican self-government entirely. In Jamaica and the United States, the central governments issued broad grants of civil equality to recently freed slaves only to back away from these to give landholders more control over their labor force and to prevent black people from entering the political system.

During the debate over the Fourteenth Amendment, the moderate Republican senator from Maine **William Pitt Fessenden** inserted two words into the first section. His change, adopted without a vote, granted citizenship to "naturalized" residents alongside African Americans. This change extended America's protection of its foreign-born citizens around the globe. It proved particularly important for Irish Americans who had emigrated to the United States but who continued to participate in the effort to free Ireland from British rule. By declaring all naturalized residents of the United States citizens, the Fourteenth Amendment brought under the protection of the constitution immigrants who had persevered through the 1850s when nativist sentiment drove the creation of laws that denied them the vote or otherwise singled them out as second-class citizens. For the Fenians, U.S. citizenship also provided a crucial level of protection against arbitrary British imprisonment or conscription. Even as the amendment expanded rights for some, it contracted rights for others. For the first time, constitutional language restricted voting specifically to "males." Article I of the constitution refers only to "people" in sections on voting, but the Fourteenth Amendment set the minimum requirements as "male inhabitants" at least 21 years of age.

The issue of black voting lurked just beneath the surface of the disputes among Southerners, Johnson, and Congressional Republicans. Radicals and even some moderates had long believed in the wisdom and justice of the measure. In 1864, as loyal representatives of Louisiana considered a new state constitution, Abraham Lincoln had suggested voting privileges for the men of color, "especially the intelligent and former soldiers." A partisan imperative was at work as well. Republicans knew that the end of slavery also meant the end of the three-fifths principle in the constitution, where five enslaved people were counted as three free people for the purposes of enumeration. The result of emancipation would be a substantial gain for the South in terms of representation in the House of Representatives and the Electoral College. Enfranchising black men would give Republicans the means to defend themselves and also ensure that the party could build a base of support in the South. Participants in the struggle to adapt political and civil frameworks in a post-emancipation world understood their effort in a global context. Henry Turner, a leading black minister, equated emancipation and the postwar amendments with "the almost instantaneous liberation of the Russian serfs, and their immediate investiture with citizens' immunities."

Shortly after passage of the Fourteenth Amendment, Republicans began work on the **Fifteenth Amendment**. Ratified in 1870, the amendment issued a blanket prohibition against denying the right to vote on the basis of race. The amendment's failure to enfranchise women incensed women's suffrage advocates who had been working since the 1830s to win women the right to vote. Leading suffrage activists, like **Susan B. Anthony** and Elizabeth Cady Stanton, had essentially paused their work on this project during the war to help further emancipation. Congress's failure to consider women's suffrage created deep bitterness and led to tensions within the movement along racial lines. Elizabeth Cady Stanton railed, "think of Patrick and Sambo and Hans and Ung Tung who do not know the difference between a Monarchy and a Republic, who never read the Declaration of Independence . . . making laws for Lydia Maria Child, Lucretia Mott, or Fanny Kemble." Stanton's angry comparison of immigrants with the leaders of the women's rights movement underscored the personal nature of the issue.

The fighting between the radicals and the president had long-term significance. It empowered Congress to act decisively when the president would not. Georges Clemenceau, the future prime minister of France, came to the United States in 1865 as a journalist. He followed Washington politics carefully and succinctly summarized the status of affairs in September 1867: "The war between the President and Congress goes on, complicated from time to time by some unexpected turn. Contrary to all that has happened, is happening, and will happen in certain countries, the legislative power here has the upper hand." Clemenceau, an ardent liberal who had come to the United States to study the course of democracy after the war, approved. "Congress may, when it pleases, take the President by the ear and lead him down from his high seat, and he can do nothing about it except to struggle and shout . . . At each session they add a shackle to his bonds, tighten the bit in a different place, file a claw or tooth, and then when he is well bound up, fastened, and caught in an inextricable net of laws and decrees, more or less contradicting each other, they tie him to the stake of the Constitution and take a good look at him."

## Congressional Reconstruction

**Thaddeus Stevens**, a Pennsylvania Republican, played a key role in the conflict with Johnson and the creation of federal protections for individual rights. Stevens helped lead the radical Republicans in Congress and served as perhaps the ablest and most dedicated white proponent of meaningful freedom for African Americans. Like other radicals, Stevens regarded the southern states as having actually left the Union. He believed that southern states could now be subjected to specific terms before they were granted reentry into the Union. For Stevens, the most important change—one compelled by humanity and justice as well as political necessity—was to diminish the clout of the white elites in southern life and elevate the freed people. Stevens believed that this could only be accomplished if the government broke up the great landholdings of the prewar era and distributed the land to former slaves, but President Johnson killed a brief experiment with resettlement undertaken by General **William T. Sherman** in early 1865. Despite Stevens' urging, Republicans could not bring themselves to advocate the redistribution of property.

For Stevens, the Southern reaction to the Fourteenth Amendment proved the necessity of radically reordering southern politics. After quick passage by Congress, white Southerners overwhelmingly rejected the measure. The boldness of the Southern refusal to consider the Fourteenth Amendment and the increasingly violent racial politics of the region—whites killed dozens of African Americans in Memphis and New Orleans during riots in the summer of 1866—pushed Congress to seize control of Reconstruction completely. In March 1867, Congress passed the first of a series of Reconstruction Acts. Dramatic in their scope, the legislation consolidated the 10

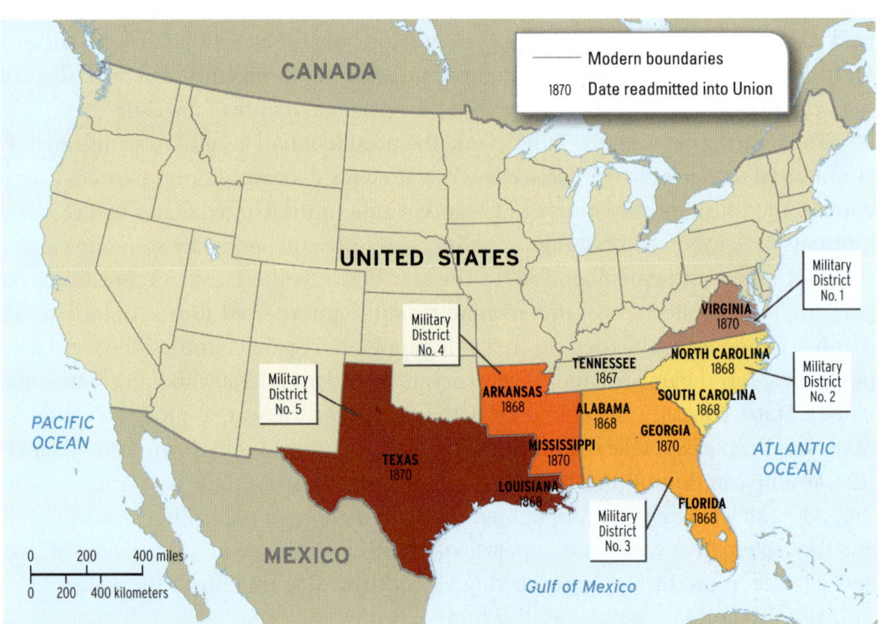


**Map 15.2**

**Military Districts Established by the Reconstruction Acts, 1867** One of the most radical pieces of legislation passed by the Reconstruction Congresses, these acts divided the South into five districts commanded by a military governor (usually a former Union army general). States had to revise their own constitutions to provide for universal manhood suffrage and ratify the Fourteenth Amendment before being returned to state status.

remaining ex-Confederate states into five military districts with former Union generals acting as military governors. Additionally, to return to the Union, states had to ratify the Fourteenth Amendment and revise their constitutions to provide for black male voting.

The legislative changes of 1867 signaled the decisive shift of power within Washington to Capitol Hill. Angry Republicans hamstrung Johnson with laws of bewilderingly intricacy in the hopes of creating a pretext for impeaching him. The "Tenure of Office" act, for example, restricted the president's ability to remove appointees that required Senate approval for their positions. After clashing with Congress over the constitutionality of this law in mid-1867, the House of Representatives impeached Johnson. The first U.S. president to ever be impeached, Johnson remained in office because the Senate failed to convict him by one vote. However, politically he was powerless. By the end of the year, Republicans turned with relief to selecting Johnson's successor, choosing the enormously popular Union general **Ulysses S. Grant**. Grant won election easily in 1868, running on a platform of sectional reconciliation under the slogan "Let Us Have Peace."

The first charge to the military governors now administering the southern states was to hold elections to select delegates for state constitutional conventions. Black

The impeachment of Andrew Johnson and his subsequent trial in the Senate (pictured here) established the clear dominance of Congress over the process and politics of Reconstruction.

men participated in the election and helped produce a strong Republican victory, including the election of a majority of black delegates in South Carolina and Louisiana. In other southern states, black delegates comprised only a small percent of the delegates, but even that small number invalidated the entire process for most white Southerners. The victories in the South confirmed that the Republican Party would stay competitive in the region as long as they could maintain the full support of the African American community.

**STUDY QUESTIONS FOR SHAPING RECONSTRUCTION, 1865–1868**

1. **Why did Republicans endorse a more radical Reconstruction policy than Andrew Johnson?**
2. **How did the changes made by Congress reshape the relationship between state and federal power?**

# RECONSTRUCTION IN THE SOUTH, 1866–1876

Even as congress and the president fashioned and refashioned Reconstruction in Washington, black and white Southerners shaped the postwar world on the ground. They disputed the terms of work, housing, property, politics, and social relationships. For black Southerners, the first order of business was to create autonomous lives. True emancipation required not just free individuals but communities dedicated to uplifting and supporting its members. Politically, Reconstruction entailed creating Republican governments that would implement the policies articulated by Congress. Politics monopolized the public's attention but the success of Reconstruction, and the ability of African Americans to make their freedom real, hinged on rebuilding the southern economy.

## African American Life in the Postwar South

The efforts that black Southerners made to reconstitute their families in the wake of emancipation laid the foundation for their postwar communities. The neighborhoods that defined the life of enslaved men and women in the plantation districts became the basis for new free communities. Churches occupied the heart of these new communities. In some cases, they were new congregations; in others, they were biracial parishes from before the war that split into separate white and black churches after the war. By 1866, 62 percent of black Methodists had left their prewar churches. But more people came to the independent black churches after the war, and those who did joined a community that played a key role in reconstructing the South.

Another key change came with the Freedmen's Bureau and their drive to build schools. Before the Civil War, no southern state maintained a public education system. Northerners viewed education as essential to both political and economic progress. Many Northerners believed that secession resulted from an undereducated white population. African Americans, in particular, viewed education as essential. Beginning in contraband camps during the war, freed people sought out **literacy**. Denied to them as slaves, literacy and higher education promised a life beyond the fields and satisfied many people's desire to read the Bible themselves. People of all ages lined up at churches and schools, where instruction was available throughout the day and usually well into the evening. Despite complaints from white Southerners about the cost, public education proved one of the lasting accomplishments of Reconstruction-era governments.

The eagerness with which black Americans embraced their new lives as full citizens of the United States manifested itself in public celebrations of Emancipation Day and the Fourth of July. The first of these events began during the war itself, in Union-occupied territory on the Sea Islands of South Carolina, where Union general **Thomas Wentworth Higginson** listened to a crowd of freed people spontaneously burst into the national anthem when the flag was raised. "I never saw anything so electric; it made all other words cheap . . . it seemed the choked voice of a race at last unloosed." Such celebrations formed the bedrock of an emerging black culture. The most enduring of these events, "Juneteenth," began in Texas as a commemoration of the war's end and evolved into a celebration of African American freedom that continues to be marked today.

The parades and festivals that accompanied these events provided an opportunity for community leaders—teachers, ministers, and politicians—to speak on themes both historical and contemporary. The messages they broadcast varied by place,

The act of voting signaled a bedrock equality between white and black men that few on either side could have imagined at the beginning of the Civil War in 1861.

gender, class position, and political ideology. Some emphasized cooperation with whites while others preached self-help. **Martin Delaney**, the highest-ranking black officer during the Civil War, told a South Carolina audience in 1865, "I tell you slavery is over, and shall never return again. We have now 200,000 of our men well drilled in arms and used to War fare and I tell you it is with you and them that slavery shall not come back again, if you are determined it will not return again." Some spoke through the language of religion and salvation, while others used the secular language of rights and law. Regardless of their differences, all of the speakers emphasized that black people would remain a permanent and progressive force for change and democracy within America. Rather than distancing themselves from the past, southern African Americans proudly remembered the perseverance of their ancestors through generations of slavery.

The festivals through which black Americans celebrated emancipation and Union victory also provided an opportunity for political organization. The Union League emerged as the most important institutional support for black politics. Started during the war as an adjunct to the Republican Party in the North, Union Leagues became social and political centers in many of the North's largest cities. After the war, the Leagues transformed into a grass-roots movement that helped black Southerners organize themselves politically. Albion Tourgee, a northern lawyer who lived in North Carolina during Reconstruction, wrote a famous novel, *A Fool's Errand*, that chronicled his experiences with Reconstruction. He described the Union Leagues as intended to "[cultivate] . . . an unbounded devotion for the flag in the hearts of the embryonic citizens, and [keep] alive the fire of patriotism in the hearts of the old Union element." The "fool" who comes south in the novel failed to appreciate the depth of hostility manifested by white Southerners against both their black neighbors and Northerners who came south. Inculcating love of the old flag was bad enough, but throughout the southern states, Republicans organized local Union Leagues that helped educate and mobilize voters.

Even though the Civil War ended the split in the U.S. economy between free and slave labor, it did not equalize wages between the two sections or between the races. The South replaced slavery with a low-wage free labor system and within that, African Americans consistently received lower pay for equivalent work done by white workers. The majority of black Southerners remained agricultural workers, but very few worked their own land. Instead, Southerners expanded a little-used prewar practice called sharecropping, in which landless workers signed contracts to take up residence and farm plots of land, often on property belonging to former slaveholders. In exchange for leasing land, property owners claimed 50 percent or more of the profits at harvest time. When sharecropping first came into use it met the needs of property owners who needed labor to farm the land but had no money with which to pay wages and workers who wanted more autonomy. **Sharecroppers** set their own schedules and supervised themselves in the field, but crucially it was usually landowners who chose the crop.

All across the Deep South and much of Arkansas, Tennessee, and North Carolina, that choice was cotton. Merchants, among the few actors in the postwar southern economic system with access to credit, insisted on receiving cotton. The changes in the

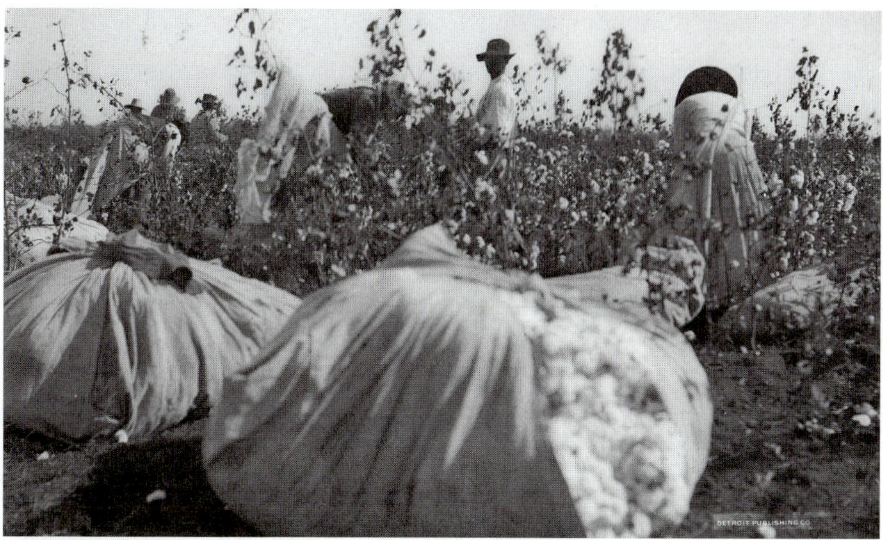


The political opportunities African Americans experienced during Reconstruction were not matched by economic opportunities. Across much of the Deep South, the only work available to black men and women continued to be agricultural labor in cotton fields.

global cotton market, however, produced price fluctuations and great uncertainty for growers. Adding to the structural problems, white landowners exploited their laborers and merchants squeezed them on prices for goods and supplies. Egypt and India entered the global cotton market during the Civil War, adding competition and uncertainty for U.S. producers. As a result, sharecropping quickly trapped farmers in cycles of debt. The results ensured overuse and poor treatment of southern lands, a stunted regional economy, and little progress for African American farmers. As Georges Clemenceau, who toured the country in the late 1860s, observed, "The real misfortune of the negro race is in owning no land of its own. There cannot be real emancipation for men who do not possess at least a small portion of the soil."

## Republican Governments in the Postwar South

The Republican state governments established after the round of constitutional conventions in 1867–1868 were fragile and awkward alliances between groups with widely divergent interests. Black Southerners represented by far the largest component of the party. They wanted to receive a genuinely fair opportunity to perform work, buy land, gain an education, and live autonomous lives. White northern Republicans, labeled "carpetbaggers" by conservatives because they assumed Northerners were only coming South to make quick money, focused on economic development. As the national party shifted to support black voting, its southern wing did so as well, though this was never a priority for the leaders who represented the region in Congress and

GLOBAL PASSAGES

## Reconstruction Abroad

As Clemenceau's presence demonstrated, emancipation was of interest to people around the globe. Before the Civil War, American abolitionists focused on the Caribbean, where the Haitian Revolution and British abolition formed two different alternatives to ponder as they sought to destroy slavery. Despite their opposition to the practice of slaveholding, only a few black radicals advocated anything like the Haitian Revolution. The vast majority of antislavery activists sought to emulate British emancipation, a legalistic event that left property and lives intact. As more time elapsed from their transition to free labor, American slaveholders also had more material with which to evaluate the effects of emancipation. According to one observer in 1860, "In St. Domingo, the French have been destroyed by the blacks; in Jamaica, the English are being fully absorbed by them." American slaveholders initiated secession and civil war to avoid the fate of either of these Caribbean neighbors.

For decades before the Civil War, hemispheric emancipation experiments had been discussed, written about, and pondered, but the shock and force of U.S. emancipation spread through the region with remarkable speed. Alongside the United States, in 1860 only Brazil and Cuba remained major slave powers in the western hemisphere. During the war, the absence of the South from the global cotton market proved a boon to Brazilian growers even as it weakened the Brazilian coffee industry, which relied on sales to the United States. In Brazil, this dynamic produced strong incentives for coffee growers to scale back slave purchases at the same time that southern Brazilian cotton growers increased them. This worried Brazilians who already knew, from the U.S. experience, that a regionally bifurcated slave economy could produce disaster. As one Brazilian senator noted in 1862, "was it not the case, that when some years ago in the United States the Northern states abolished

state houses. Native white Southerners proved the most troublesome part of the coalition. They had to brave the scorn of fellow whites when they joined the party. Usually prewar Whigs or wartime Unionists, white Southerners rarely came to the party with any interest in black voting or civil rights. Democrats eagerly exploited the conflicting interests in the Republican Party.

In those states with well-established free black communities before the Civil War, black voters demonstrated a greater diversity of political opinion. Charleston, Savannah, and New Orleans all included independent, educated, and prosperous communities of free people of color, many of whom carried into the postwar world conservative values on economics and community leadership. The split within black communities can be seen clearly in the case of Mobile, Alabama. After the Union navy captured the slavery, and it remained in the Southern States, the industrial interests of the Southern States became entirely opposed to those of the Northern States? Was it not after the creation and growth of this diversity of interests that the explosion took place which has not yet terminated?"

The surprising end of the U.S. Civil War, with full, immediate, and uncompensated emancipation, worried Brazilian slaveholders much more than the problem of regional balance. Brazil, independent of Portugal since 1822, aspired to join the first rank of new world nations. Many of its leading politicians soon realized that doing so against the tide of global opinion that ranked slavery as a relic of the barbarous past would prove difficult if not impossible. The leading British diplomat in Brazil noted that after 1865, he detected "a rapidly growing feeling among the leading men of the necessity of the abolition of slavery." By 1871, Brazil had adopted a law freeing the children of enslaved mothers, the first step on a path to full abolition that concluded in 1888. In Cuba, which remained under the control of the Spanish empire, similar fears about the future of slavery manifested themselves as soon as the war concluded. In 1865, a conservative Spanish politician concluded, "the war in the United States is finished, and being finished, slavery on the whole American continent can be taken as finished." Like the Brazilians, the Spanish in Cuba implemented a much slower and more cautious emancipation policy. In the latter case, violent independence movements intersected with emancipation to complicate the situation still more. But Brazilians and Cubans saw clearly in 1865 that slavery's end in the United States shifted global opinion against the practice and left them intellectually and politically isolated. The interconnectedness of the American economies that had done so much to enrich Brazil and Cuba in the first two-thirds of the century proved a central part of their undoing in the last third.

- How did Americans respond to British and French emancipation in the Caribbean?
- How did U.S. emancipation affect other slave regimes in the hemisphere?

port city in August 1864, enslaved people flooded into it seeking freedom. After the initial flush of enthusiasm in the late 1860s, a deep division opened within the black community. On one hand, well-educated, middle-class blacks pursued a moderate politics focused mostly on economic recovery and the protection of property. To achieve these goals, they advocated cooperation with white Southerners who would work with the Republicans. A larger group, mostly freed people, pushed more aggressively for the protection of civil rights and education and they did so without white allies. Over the next several years, these groups competed to court black voters and even attracted the interest of white Southerners who saw a chance to dilute Republican strength.

In many places, white conservatives had initially boycotted elections that resulted from the constitutional conventions of 1867–1868. Hoping to undermine the

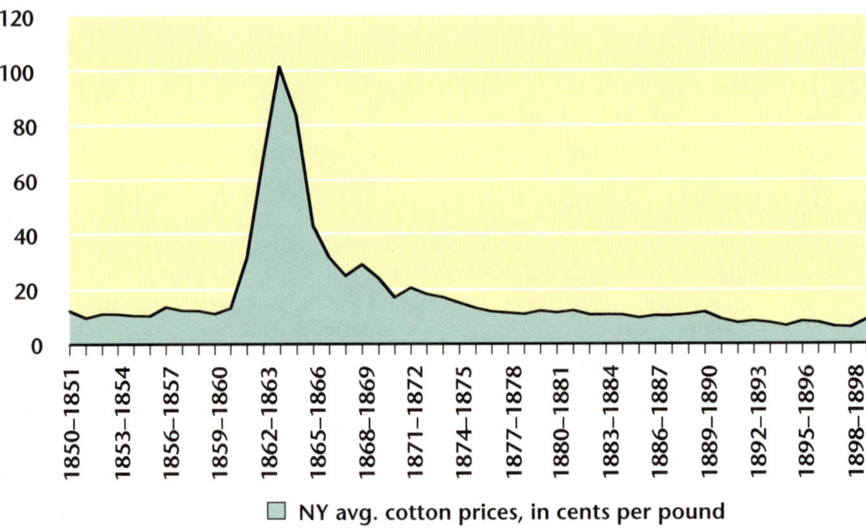


▲ **Figure 15.1**

**U.S. cotton prices, 1850–1900** The stable and lucrative cotton market changed significantly because of the Civil War. Responding to the Confederate embargo on cotton sales, England and France turned to new suppliers in Asia and the Middle East, which drove prices down for the remainder of the century.

legitimacy of these new governments, they succeeded only in hastening Republican dominance. In other states, some conservatives made alliances with Republicans to create coalition governments. But the 1872 national elections, in which Ulysses S. Grant was reelected despite substantial opposition within his own party, revealed a weakness that Democrats longed to exploit. Beginning in 1873, white conservatives returned to the political system and used charges of corruption and profligacy to defeat the Republicans. Both charges contained some merit—Republican legislators in the South, like those of both parties in state governments all across the country, were susceptible to the bribes and favors of the rich and well connected. The wide scale of corruption within Grant's administration had even threatened his reelection. Also, the policies that Republicans implemented—especially public education—required new taxes. Before the war, slaveholders and large property owners shouldered most of the tax burden, but with no slave property to tax, postwar state governments imposed property taxes on a much broader range of people. Even though the children of white property owners benefited from public education, they condemned the taxes required to pay for them. Democrats capitalized on these legitimate policy disputes and campaigned vigorously on the platform of white supremacy to retake state governments.

## Cotton, Merchants, and the Lien

In 1865, the southern United States was part of a region, extending south through Central America and the Caribbean and into northeastern Brazil, where plantation agriculture predominated. In the United States, cotton predominated; in the Caribbean,

Despite the numerous obstacles to cotton production, southern river and ocean ports looked much as they had before the Civil War, with bales of cotton stacked and ready for transport, only now into an increasingly competitive global market.

sugar; and in Brazil, coffee. This style of agriculture required huge plots of land, a large labor force, and high volumes of capital and credit. The plantation system changed but did not disappear after the Civil War. The major change entailed the use of tenant labor or sharecropping in place of the gang labor used under slavery, but land continued to be owned in large allotments and management functioned as it had before the war. Even though many sharecroppers worked with some autonomy, landowners determined crop choices, fertilizer use, and harvest dates.

Even with the scattered residential pattern typical of the postwar era and the substantial effort made by sharecroppers to claim ownership of the crop, landowning planters continued to dominate southern agriculture. They did so partly through the effective control of the **crop lien**, which represented farm workers' claim to ownership of the crops they raised. In Georgia, North Carolina, and Tennessee, the state supreme courts all ruled that the portion of crops given to a sharecropper constituted a wage. This removed from the sharecroppers any legal claim over the crops that they planted, raised, and harvested.

One of the few groups of workers to exercise some control over labor conditions and wages were sugar workers. Sugar's value had spurred Europeans' initial effort to import large numbers of Africans to the New World. Sugar growing and especially the process of harvesting earned an infamous reputation as the most deadly agricultural work in the Americas. It also required significant skill. Because the sugar cane had to be harvested at exactly the right moment and quickly processed, those workers with knowledge of the crop possessed more leverage to negotiate better terms with their employers. In the decade after emancipation, sugar workers—mostly in Louisiana's southern parishes—used politics and collective action to halt wage cuts and pursued the right to produce garden plots. Even after the Democrats regained power in the states, black sugar workers stayed their ground. Several large strikes in the early 1880s, some with white and black workers cooperating, laid the ground for the broader organization of workers under the **Knights of Labor** at the end of the decade. In the other major sugar-producing country in the hemisphere—Cuba—the post-emancipation story evolved differently. By the 1880s, when Cuba's emancipation took full effect, sugar work was not done exclusively by people of African descent. Black Cubans, mixed-race Cubans, and more recent Spanish immigrants all labored together, and their solidarity as workers undercut the use of racism that had been so effective in Louisiana. The comparatively stronger and more diverse community of Cuban sugar workers revealed another route that emancipation could take in the Americas.

Because sharecropping allowed white property owners to make their money from land, and related merchant work, they had no incentive to pursue industrial development. Between 1860 and 1880, the number of manufacturing establishments in the South increased from 30,000 to 50,000 and from 1880 to 1900 they grew from 50,000 to nearly 120,000, although this was still significantly lower than the northern total from 1860. The failure to build factories in the Reconstruction-era South was not for lack of trying. The Republicans who assumed power in southern states in the late 1860s and 1870s set economic development as their number one goal. The most important vital element of this plan was the railroad. Northern Republicans especially had a mystical faith in the railroad's ability to spur development of all sorts. As a Tennessee Republican asserted, "A free and living Republic [will] spring up in the track of the railroad as inevitably, as surely as grass and flowers follow in the spring." Unfortunately, southern states and southern investors could not meet the capital demands of new railroad construction. Northern and foreign investors found more lucrative and less risky places to put their money and despite significant public attention, few new lines were built. Further, frequent charges of corruption surrounding railroads weakened Republicans at the polls. Other Republican policies did more to earn the support of their constituents, most importantly Republican efforts to give sharecroppers and tenant farmers control over crop liens.

### STUDY QUESTIONS FOR RECONSTRUCTION IN THE SOUTH, 1866–1876

1. **What was the experience of Reconstruction like for freed people in the South?**
2. **How did they protect their interests? How did whites seek to subvert those interests?**

## THE END OF RECONSTRUCTION, 1877

For most of the 100 years following the end of Reconstruction, historians described the period as its contemporary white critics did—as the unconscionable elevation of blacks to positions of power from which they deprived whites of their rights and bankrupted southern states. Sympathetic to southern whites and grounded in openly racist assumptions about the moral and intellectual inferiority of black people, these historians promoted a factually inaccurate and deeply compromised view of the era as one that attempted too much and failed. Thanks to a fundamentally different attitude about the meaning of race and a generation of research, historians today hold a nearly opposite view. They regard Congressional Reconstruction as well intentioned and appropriate to the situation. In their view, Reconstruction failed because the federal government did not persevere against southern white resistance. The demise of Reconstruction—defined as the end of Republican governments in the region—came because of forces both internal and external to the South. The changes in how historians have accounted for that end and the meanings they have attached to it reveal how long it took America to outgrow the racial and political values of the era.

## The Ku Klux Klan and Reconstruction Violence

The bitterest and most violent opponents of Reconstruction, and black freedom more generally, emerged at the very start of the era. In late 1865, a small group of men gathered in Pulaski, Tennessee, and organized the **Ku Klux Klan**. Membership in the group spread by word of mouth across the state and soon through the region. Within a year, Klan members made denying African Americans any legitimate role in the public

The Ku Klux Klan, a terrorist group bent on reestablishing white supremacy after the end of slavery, came to dominate many regions of the South. They pursued black leaders of all stripes—politicians, ministers, businessmen, and teachers—and their white allies with brutal violence.

sphere their principle goal. As a white newspaper enthusiastically reported about the Memphis chapter in 1868, "it is rapidly organizing wherever the insolent negro, the malignant white traitor to his race and the infamous squatter are plotting to make the South utterly unfit for the residence of the decent white man. It will arrest the progress of that secret negro conspiracy which has for its object the establishment of negro domination." They also targeted white Republicans—especially native white Southerners who cooperated with the party—for their efforts to build an interracial democracy in the South. Klan members whipped, beat, burnt, and killed all manner of community leaders through the South. They targeted ministers, teachers, political leaders, and successful businessmen or farmers. The high point of Klan-related violence came in response to the Reconstruction Acts and to the prominent role played by Africans Americans in the reorganization of southern life between 1868 and 1871.

Klan violence grew so public and so extreme that Congress finally took action. In 1870–1871, Republicans passed a series of laws, collectively known as the Force Acts, designed to impede the operation of the Ku Klux Klan. They did this by punishing as a federal crime any attempt to obstruct a person in the practice of a designated civil right. One of the Klan's most effective weapons was intimidation of black voters. The Enforcement Acts targeted this practice directly by designating as conspiracies any attempts to coerce black men at the polls or deny them access to the vote. Congress created the Department of Justice and tasked it with bringing cases against those men who used violence to enforce white supremacy. On a few occasions, President Grant sent the army itself into southern districts to disrupt and capture Klan cells. Finally, during 1871, Congress held hearings at which the testimony of both victims and alleged members of the Klan told their stories to a national audience. Although the Justice Department was underfunded and less energetic in their prosecutions than southern Republicans wished, they initiated thousands of prosecutions and secured hundreds of convictions across the South, driving the Klan underground.

Even with their success against the Klan, Northerners did not eradicate violence in southern life. Klan members became, in effect, an arm of the Democratic Party. In Louisiana, the Knights of the White Camellia and the White League superseded the Klan. Mississippi saw the creation of "rifle clubs." Regardless of the terminology, after 1871, southern whites reorganized their attack on Republican governments in the states. Louisiana saw a particularly bitter struggle. White conservatives in the state opposed the election of **Henry Warmoth**, a northern lawyer and Civil War officer who operated mostly as a party of one, appointing men loyal to him alone and throwing the state into chaos. He was succeeded by **William Kellogg**, a radical Republican even more noxious to Louisiana Democrats.

All across Louisiana in 1873, conservatives began organizing themselves and turning legally elected Republican officeholders out of office. Sometimes, they simply intimidated the local sheriffs, judges, and tax assessors who comprised the body of local government in the state. Others times, they committed violence against officeholders or the families. The most notorious episode involved an attack on the northern parish town of Colfax. Residents of the town learned of the plan in advance, and perhaps 200 black men from the area converged on the courthouse on the morning

THE LOUISIANA MURDERS—GATHERING THE DEAD AND WOUNDED.—[See Page 396.]

The Colfax Massacre embodied the ultimately successful strategy used in Louisiana, Mississippi, and South Carolina to drive the last Republicans from the region. The failure of local, state, and federal authorities to find any justice for the victims stands as one of the worst tragedies of Reconstruction.

of Easter Sunday, 1873. Armed with a variety of weapons, they came to protect the men they had elected. A white militia composed of several hundred men organized in neighboring Montgomery rode into town and drove the defenders back into the courthouse, which they set afire. The attackers shot men as they escaped and captured more, executing 37 that evening. By nightfall, they had killed around 150 defenders in the worst racial massacre in U.S. history. The lesson to Republicans around the state was clear—white Democrats would stop at nothing to purge them from office. Whites in other southern states observed the success of Louisiana conservatives, and many adopted the same strategy.

## Northern Weariness and Northern Conservatism

Governor Kellogg's metropolitan police force helped keep order in New Orleans, but without the support of the federal government, he could do little to protect fellow Republicans in outlying parishes. In a few isolated instances, President Grant sent U.S. troops back into the South to help quell disorder. Interventions like these exposed

Grant to the charge that his administration had failed to secure the peace he promised in 1868. It opened Republicans to criticism from fiscal conservatives about the continuing expense of Reconstruction and, more cynically, to those who felt that black Southerners needed to defend themselves from whites or suffer the consequences. The violence in Mississippi in 1875 drove the governor, a young white Northerner named Adelbert Ames, to request federal troops. Grant had responded positively in 1874, sending a small contingent of troops to Vicksburg. The situation deteriorated even more the following year. Ames's telegram to the White House explained the dire situation: "I am in great danger of losing my life. Not only that, all the leading Republicans, who have not run away, in danger . . . The [White] league here have adopted a new policy, which is to kill the leaders and spare the colored people, unless they 'rise'." This time Grant worried more about weakening Republicans at the polls in the North than with defending Republicans in the South. "The whole public are tired out with these annual autumnal outbreaks in the South . . . [and] are ready now to condemn any interference on the part of the Government," he told his attorney general. Grant, who had conquered Vicksburg, Mississippi, for the Union in 1863, sent no troops this time.

Federal courts likewise reflected northern impatience with the duration and expense of Reconstruction in their increasing reluctance to support black or Republican plaintiffs. The most important of these cases revolved around the defendants arrested for leading the Colfax Massacre. Unable to secure justice in local courts, federal prosecutors sought a conviction on charges of violating the civil rights of the murdered officeholders. In *Cruikshank v. U.S.*, the Supreme Court ruled that the Fourteenth Amendment only protected citizens against official state actions not private violence. Because the massacre's ringleader, William Cruikshank, operated without state sanction, the amendment offered no protection. Cruikshank went free, and in the process the court dramatically narrowed the scope of protection offered by the Fourteenth Amendment. The *Cruikshank* case was decided in 1876, the same year that a new Republican won the presidency. Rutherford B. Hayes secured the office after the contested election of 1876, when Republicans and Democrats clashed over the returns from Louisiana, Florida, and South Carolina. Both sides agreed to count the presidential ballots for Hayes, but gave Democrats control at the state level. This ended the last three Republican state governments in the South and initiated an era of Democratic dominance that lasted for most of the next century. Shortly after his inauguration, Hayes recalled the last few thousand U.S. troops out of the South, officially ending the period of Reconstruction.

Northerners' fatigue with Reconstruction also resulted from their preoccupation with the rapid changes happening in their own region. The wave of city building in the 1840s and 1850s that had developed during the technological boom of that era (telegraph, canals, and railroads) increased after the war. Immigrants continued to pour into northern cities, where their rapid incorporation changed the political contours of the region. Legislation passed by the dynamic wartime Congress also began to bear fruit. The most important of these was the **Homestead Act**, which allowed families to claim 160 acres of land if they improved it over five years of residence. The bill opened the western United States to white settlement. Accompanying settlers in the

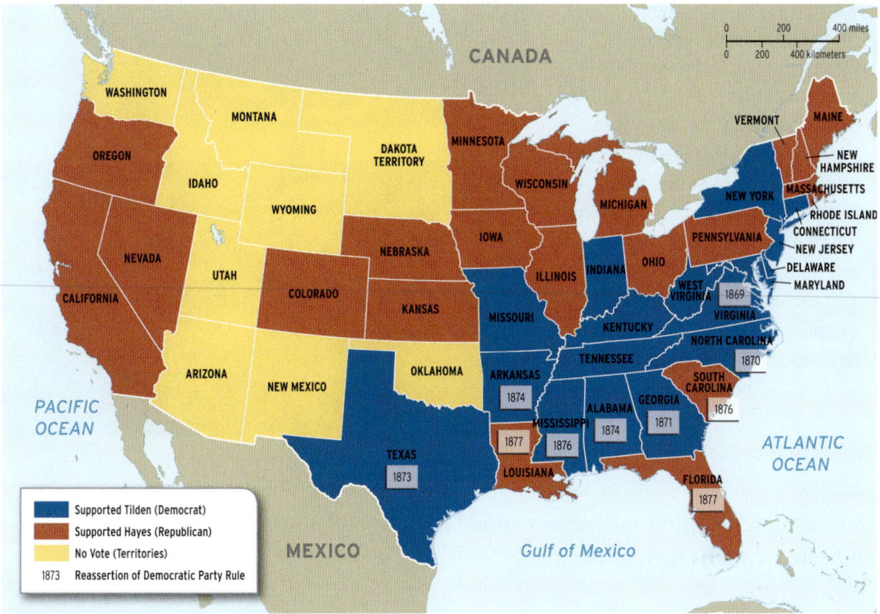


**▲ Map 15.3**

**1876 Presidential Election, by State** Although the Republican presidential candidate, Rutherford B. Hayes, was credited with the electoral votes of Louisiana, South Carolina, and Florida, these states all elected Democratic governors and legislatures. This ended the presence of statewide Republican rule in the South and marked the end of political Reconstruction.

movement west was the nation's first Transcontinental Railroad, which had also been authorized by the 37th Congress. Congressmen, land developers, and businessmen regarded the railroad line, which reduced travel time between the Atlantic and Pacific coasts from months to days, as the nation's most important economic development measure.

As the Union Pacific laid track, Indian communities of the West resisted. During the Civil War, the U.S. Army had largely ceded the region back to Indian control. Indians exploited the opportunity of a distracted United States and undermanned forts to reestablish their historic position. With the coming of peace in 1865, a newly expanded, trained, and disciplined U.S. Army moved west. The Sioux, in particular, had challenged U.S. authority during the war, culminating in a wide-scale uprising in Minnesota that was violently suppressed by the army. Military tribunals had originally sentenced 303 men to death for crimes against settlers during the Minnesota conflicts, but Lincoln commuted the death sentences for 264 prisoners and allowed the execution of 39 others. After the war, western Indians faced an emboldened army without the aid of a sympathetic executive. The shift away from Indian's hunting and low-impact farming practices to the more intensive style of American agriculture caused significant change throughout the Great Plains and the West and within a few decades

By settling the long-standing political conflicts over the future of slavery, the Civil War set in motion massive white migration into the western states and territories. This process brought white Americans into more intimate contact, both benign and malignant, with native peoples all across the western landscape.

spurred a preservation movement aimed at balancing the development of the region and conserving its natural beauty.

## Legacies of Reconstruction

Before **John Muir**, one of the most important environmental activists of the era, gained fame as a protector and champion of the American West, he toured the South during Reconstruction. Leaving his home in Indianapolis in early 1867, Muir walked south to Florida, observing flora, fauna, and the human wildlife along the way. In addition to wry observations about the "long-haired ex-guerillas" of the Tennessee and North Carolina mountains, Muir chronicled the attitudes of the white and black citizens with whom he interacted on his trip. In Georgia, he observed, "the traces of war

### TIMELINE 1865–1888

**1865**

**January 31** Congress proposes the 13th Amendment

**March 3** Congress establishes the Bureau of Refugees, Freedmen, and Abandoned Lands

**April 9** Robert E. Lee's Army surrenders to Ulysses S. Grant at Appomattox, VA

**April 14** Abraham Lincoln assassinated by John Wilkes Booth

**April 26** Joseph Johnston's Army surrenders to William T. Sherman at Durham, NC

**October** Morant Bay Rebellion in Jamaica

**December 6** Ratification of the 13th Amendment abolishes slavery in the United States

Southern state legislatures pass "Black Codes"

Ku Klux Klan organized in Pulaski, TN

**1866**

**February 19** President Andrew Johnson vetoes the Freedmen's Bureau reauthorization bill

**March 27** President Andrew Johnson vetoes the 1866 Civil Rights Act

**May 1** Memphis race riot

**June 13** Congress proposes the 14th Amendment

**July 16** Congress overrides Johnson's veto of the Freedmen's Bureau Act and the Civil Rights Act

**July 30** New Orleans race riot

**1867**

**March** Congress passes Reconstruction Acts

Southern state constitutional conventions begin across the South with mixed race delegates

**1868**

**February 24** House of Representatives votes to impeach Andrew Johnson

**April 9** Senate votes not to convict Andrew Johnson

**June 9** Ratification of 14th Amendment establishes citizenship rights and due process for citizens

**November 3** Republican Ulysses S. Grant elected president

**1869**

**February 26** Congress proposes the 15th Amendment

are not only apparent on the broken fields, burnt fences, mills, and woods ruthlessly slaughtered, but also on the countenances of the people. A few years after a forest has been burned, another generation of bright and happy trees arises . . . So with the people of this war-field. Happy, unscarred, and unclouded youth is growing up around the aged, half-consumed, and fallen parents." The sadness that Muir observed in 1867 had changed to anger a decade later. Southern whites ended Reconstruction embittered against African Americans for the efforts they had made to claim civil rights, contemptuous of the federal government for assistance—however meager—they had given that effort, and deeply suspicious of the open, bipartisan politics that flourished briefly in the 1870s. All three of these attitudes weakened the South over time and encouraged whites to regard the most important political and social goal for their communities as the violent protection of white supremacy.

The unwillingness of federal authorities to enforce the civil rights laws and especially the Fourteenth and Fifteenth Amendments left southern African Americans isolated, but blacks were never solely victims. From the earliest days of North American slavery, they had resisted the institution, and their actions during and after Reconstruction reveal a similar refusal to be defined by white actions. In early 1866, a group of "colored citizens" in Florida complained to then Secretary of War Grant that "the Civil authoritys here are taking from the Colord People all the fire arms that they find in their Persesion, including Dubble barrel Shot Guns, Pistols of any kind." Without the means of self-defense they would be reliant on the government for their protection. Years before, Frederick Douglass had observed of black Americans, "It is enough to say, that if a knowledge of the use of arms is desirable in any people, it is desirable in us." As the Florida men who petitioned Ulysses Grant made clear, it remained desirable, sadly, imperative, after the war as well. Perhaps anticipating the day when Northerners would abandon the effort, they closed by noting that "if Congress Do not Stand Squarely up for us, and Make Laws that Will Protect us, over the heads of the States,

**1870**

**February 3** Ratification of the 15th Amendment prohibits discrimination in voting on the basis of race or previous condition of servitude

**May 31** U.S. Congress passes "Force Act" giving it the power to crack down on the Ku Klux Klan (followed by complementary legislation later in 1870 and 1871)

**1871**

Brazil passes gradual emancipation law

Congress holds Ku Klux Klan Hearings to assess and publicize violence against freed people and their white allies in the South

**1872**

**November 29** Republican Ulysses S. Grant reelected president

**1873**

**April 13** Colfax Massacre in northern Louisiana kills approximately 150 people

**1874**

**November** Democrats gain control of U.S. House of Representatives

**1875**

**March 1** Congress passes 1875 Civil Rights Act

**1876**

**March 27** Supreme Court issues *U.S. v. Cruikshank* verdict, which restricted meaning of 14th Amendment to protection against actions taken by state actors

**1877**

**March 4** Rutherford B. Hayes inaugurated president; recalls last U.S. troops from the South

Democrats seize control of last three southern states (Florida, South Carolina, and Florida) still governed by Republicans

**1879**

Albion Tourgee publishes *A Fool's Errand*

**1886**

Cuba abolishes slavery

**1888**

Brazil abolishes slavery

We are Nothing More than Searfs." Congress did not stand up "squarely," but southern African Americans forged ahead on their own. They pursued an egalitarian politics through the Republican Party, and many protected and used that vote until the end of the century. They also built communities, churches, schools, and businesses. These institutions and the networks of support and self-improvement that developed among them sustained black Southerners until another struggle against Southern violence produced America's Second Reconstruction—the Civil Rights Movement of the 1950s and 1960s—and the nation finally stood square.

### STUDY QUESTIONS FOR THE END OF RECONSTRUCTION, 1877

1. **Why did Reconstruction end in 1877?**
2. **What explains the northern willingness to abandon the policies they initiated in 1867?**

## Summary

- In common with Brazil and Cuba, the two other major slave societies in the hemisphere, the American South struggled to reorganize its labor and landholding systems in the wake of emancipation.
- Unlike in those two nations, in America, blacks gained the vote and helped build new systems of public education over the opposition of southern whites and their allies in Washington.
- Southerners desperately needed money to rebuild and modernize the region's infrastructure, but stripped of capital by war and relying primarily on agricultural enterprises, Southerners had little success attracting American or European funds.
- Conservative southern whites used both voting and violence, the latter formalized in the Ku Klux Klan and white militias, to defeat the Republican governments that represented such a sharp break with the region's past and end Reconstruction.
- Northerners, eager to develop the West and extend American influence within the Caribbean and across the oceans and weary of the expense and trouble of the South, consented to a return to Democratic rule, but the community building and education already enacted by African Americans created the networks that sustained them through the years of Jim Crow.

## Key Terms and People

**Alexander, Edward Porter** *570*
**Anthony, Susan B.** *577*
**black codes** *537*
**Booth, John Wilkes** *569*
**crop lien** *587*
**Davis, Jefferson** *569*
**Delaney, Martin** *582*
**Farmers' Alliance** *570*

**Fessenden, William Pitt** *576*
**Fifteenth Amendment** *577*
**Fourteenth Amendment** *575*
**Freedmen's Bureau** *569*
**Grant, Ulysses S.** *579*
**Higginson, Thomas Wentworth** *581*
**Homestead Act** *592*
**Howard, Oliver Otis** *569*
**Kellogg, William** *590*
**Knights of Labor** *588*
**Ku Klux Klan** *589*
**Lee, Robert E.** *569*
**Lincoln, Abraham** *569*
**literacy** *581*
**Massey, Felix** *574*
**Morant Bay Rebellion** *571*
**Muir, John** *594*
**Nott, Josiah** *574*
**paternalism** *570*
**Seward, William** *569*
**sharecroppers** *582*
**Sherman, William T.** *578*
**Stanton, Edwin** *569*
**Stephens, Alexander** *573*
**Stevens, Thaddeus** *577*
**Sumner, Charles** *571*
**Thirteenth Amendment** *573*
**Trumball, Lyman** *575*
**Warmoth, Henry** *590*

## Reviewing Chapter 15

1. How did the United States experience of emancipation and nation building compare to other countries in the mid-19th century?
2. Was the Civil War and Reconstruction a "watershed" in American life? Explain what changed and what remained consistent.

## Further Reading

Blight, David W. *Race and Reunion: The Civil War in American Memory*. Cambridge: Belknap Press, 2001. The fullest account of changes in the memory of the Civil War, especially the willingness of white Northerners to marginalize the history of slavery and emancipation in the conflict.

Foner, Eric. *Reconstruction: America's Unfinished Revolution, 1863–1877*. New York: Harper and Row, 1988. A comprehensive history of Reconstruction with particular attention to labor and emancipation in the South.

Litwack, Leon F. *Been in the Storm So Long: The Aftermath of Slavery*. New York: Vintage, 1980. A vivid chronicle of the experience of emancipation for black Southerners.

Perman, Michel. *The Road to Redemption: Southern Politics, 1869–1879*. Chapel Hill: University of North Carolina Press, 1984. The clearest analysis of the national- and state-level politics that produced the end of Reconstruction.

Ransom, Roger L. and Richard Sutch. *One Kind of Freedom: The Economic Consequences of Emancipation*. Cambridge, UK: Cambridge University Press, 1977. A comprehensive economic analysis of the effects of the Civil War on the South.

Silber, Nina. *The Romance of Reunion: Northerners and the South, 1865–1900*. Chapel Hill: University of North Carolina Press, 1993. An elegant study that emphasizes the cultural dimensions of the northern shift toward reconciliation after the Civil War.

# Visual Review

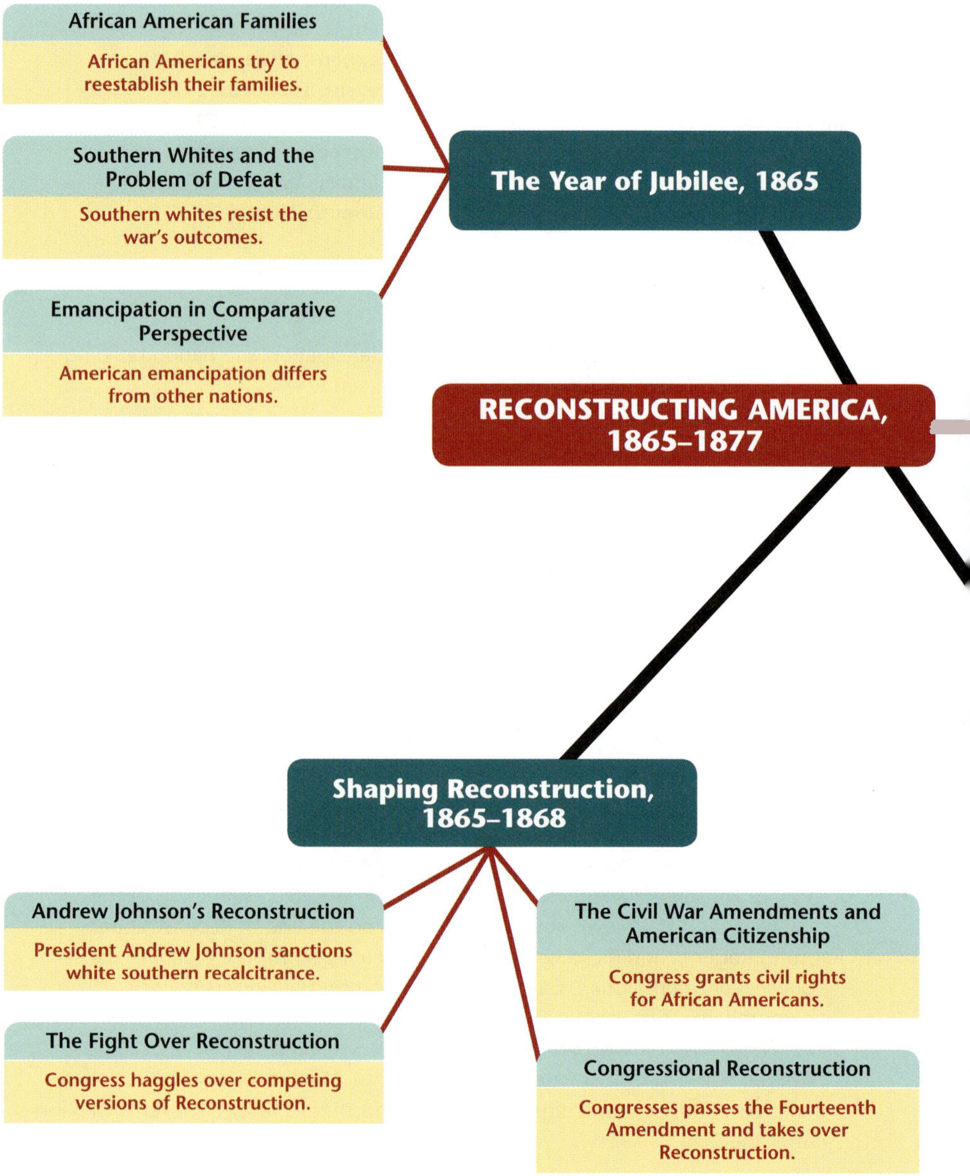

## RECONSTRUCTING AMERICA, 1865–1877

### The Year of Jubilee, 1865

**African American Families**

African Americans try to reestablish their families.

**Southern Whites and the Problem of Defeat**

Southern whites resist the war's outcomes.

**Emancipation in Comparative Perspective**

American emancipation differs from other nations.

### Shaping Reconstruction, 1865–1868

**Andrew Johnson's Reconstruction**

President Andrew Johnson sanctions white southern recalcitrance.

**The Fight Over Reconstruction**

Congress haggles over competing versions of Reconstruction.

**The Civil War Amendments and American Citizenship**

Congress grants civil rights for African Americans.

**Congressional Reconstruction**

Congresses passes the Fourteenth Amendment and takes over Reconstruction.

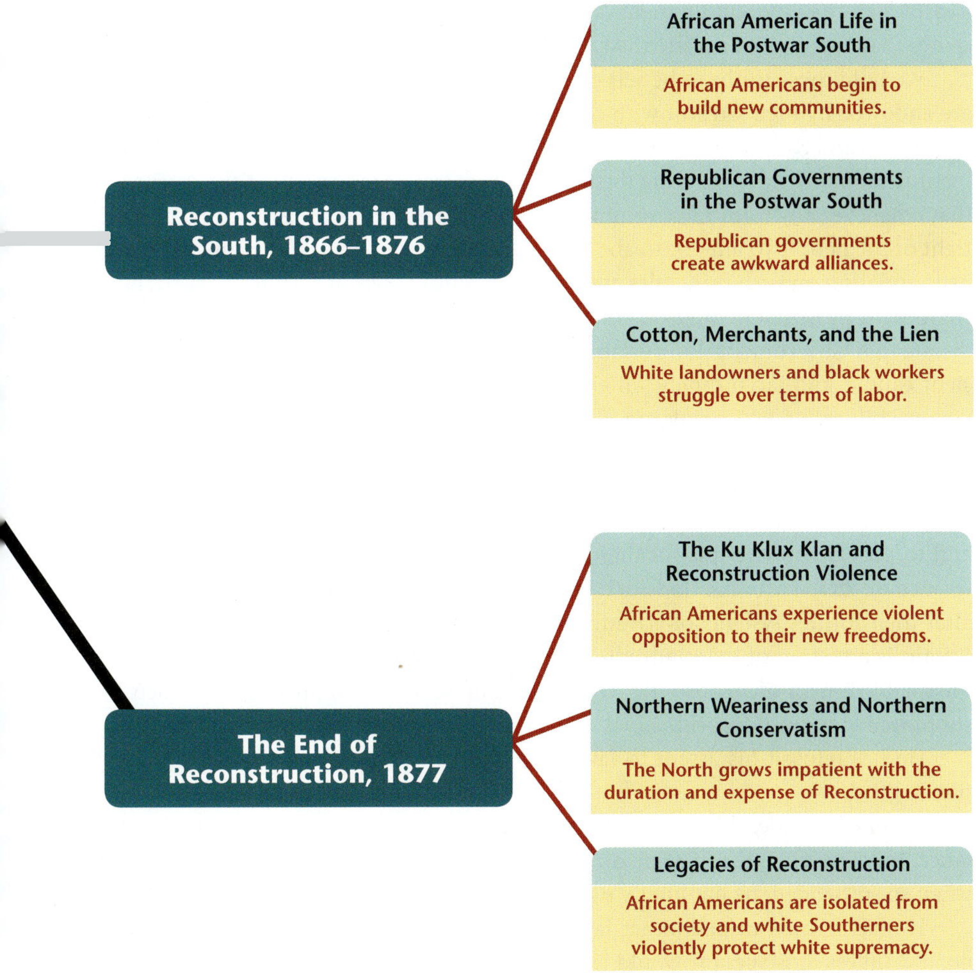

**Reconstruction in the South, 1866–1876**

**African American Life in the Postwar South**
African Americans begin to build new communities.

**Republican Governments in the Postwar South**
Republican governments create awkward alliances.

**Cotton, Merchants, and the Lien**
White landowners and black workers struggle over terms of labor.

**The End of Reconstruction, 1877**

**The Ku Klux Klan and Reconstruction Violence**
African Americans experience violent opposition to their new freedoms.

**Northern Weariness and Northern Conservatism**
The North grows impatient with the duration and expense of Reconstruction.

**Legacies of Reconstruction**
African Americans are isolated from society and white Southerners violently protect white supremacy.

# Appendix A

## HISTORICAL DOCUMENTS

### The Declaration of Independence

When in the course of human events, it becomes necessary for one people to dissolve the political bands which have connected them with another, and to assume, among the powers of the earth, the separate and equal station to which the Laws of Nature and of Nature's God entitle them, a decent respect to the opinions of mankind requires that they should declare the causes which impel them to the separation.

We hold these truths to be self-evident, that all men are created equal, that they are endowed by their Creator with certain unalienable Rights, that among these are life, liberty and the pursuit of happiness. That to secure these rights, governments are instituted among men, deriving their just powers from the consent of the governed; that whenever any form of government becomes destructive of these ends, it is the right of the people to alter or to abolish it, and to institute new Government, laying its foundation on such principles and organizing its powers in such form, as to them shall seem most likely to effect their safety and happiness. Prudence, indeed, will dictate that Governments long established should not be changed for light and transient causes; and, accordingly, all experience hath shown, that mankind are more disposed to suffer, while evils are sufferable, than to right themselves by abolishing the forms to which they are accustomed. But when a long train of abuses and usurpations, pursuing invariably the same object evinces a design to reduce them under absolute despotism, it is their right, it is their duty, to throw off such government, and to provide new guards for their future security. Such has been the patient sufferance of these colonies; and such is now the necessity which constrains them to alter their former systems of government. The history of the present King of Great Britain is a history of repeated injuries and usurpations, all having in direct object the establishment of an absolute tyranny over these States. To prove this, let facts be submitted to a candid world:

He has refused his assent to laws, the most wholesome and necessary for the public good.

He has forbidden his governors to pass laws of immediate and pressing importance, unless suspended in their operation till his assent should be obtained; and, when so suspended, he has utterly neglected to attend to them.

He has refused to pass other laws for the accommodation of large districts of people, unless those people would relinquish the right of representation in the legislature, a right inestimable to them and formidable to tyrants only.

He has called together legislative bodies at places unusual, uncomfortable, and distant from the depository of their public records, for the sole purpose of fatiguing them into compliance with his measures.

He has dissolved representative houses repeatedly, for opposing with manly firmness his invasions on the rights of the people.

He has refused for a long time, after such dissolutions, to cause others to be elected; whereby the legislative powers, incapable of annihilation, have returned to the People at large for their exercise; the State remaining in the mean time exposed to all the dangers of invasion from without, and convulsions within.

He has endeavored to prevent the population of these States; for that purpose obstructing the laws for naturalization of foreigners; refusing to pass others to encourage their migrations hither, and raising the conditions of new appropriations of lands.

He has obstructed the administration of justice, by refusing his assent to laws for establishing judiciary powers.

He has made judges dependent on his will alone, for the tenure of their offices, and the amount and payment of their salaries.

He has erected a multitude of new offices, and sent hither swarms of officers to harass our people, and eat out their substance.

He has kept among us, in times of peace, standing armies without the consent of our legislatures.

He has affected to render the Military independent of, and superior to, the civil power.

He has combined with others to subject us to a jurisdiction foreign to our constitution and unacknowledged by our laws; giving his assent to their acts of pretended legislation:

For quartering large bodies of armed troops among us;

For protecting them, by a mock trial, from punishment for any murders which they should commit on the inhabitants of these States;

For cutting off our trade with all parts of the world;

For imposing taxes on us without our Consent;

For depriving us, in many cases, of the benefits of Trial by Jury;

For transporting us beyond Seas to be tried for pretended offences;

For abolishing the free System of English Laws in a neighbouring Province, establishing therein an Arbitrary government, and enlarging its Boundaries so as to render it at once an example and fit instrument for introducing the same absolute rule into these colonies;

For taking away our charters, abolishing our most valuable laws, and altering fundamentally the forms of our governments;

For suspending our own legislatures, and declaring themselves invested with power to legislate for us in all cases whatsoever.

He has abdicated government here, by declaring us out of his protection and waging war against us.

He has plundered our seas, ravaged our coasts, burnt our towns, and destroyed the lives of our people.

He is at this time transporting large armies of foreign mercenaries to complete the works of death, desolation and tyranny, already begun with circumstances of cruelty and perfidy scarcely paralleled in the most barbarous ages, and totally unworthy the head of a civilized nation.

He has constrained our fellow citizens taken captive on the high seas to bear arms against their country, to become the executioners of their friends and brethren, or to fall themselves by their hands.

He has excited domestic insurrections amongst us, and has endeavored to bring on the inhabitants of our frontiers, the merciless Indian savages, whose known rule of warfare, is an undistinguished destruction of all ages, sexes and conditions.

In every stage of these oppressions we have petitioned for redress in the most humble terms; our repeated petitions have been answered only by repeated injury. A prince whose character is thus marked by every act which may define a tyrant, is unfit to be the ruler of a free people.

Nor have we been wanting in attentions to our British brethren. We have warned them from time to time of attempts by their legislature to extend an unwarrantable jurisdiction over us. We have reminded them of the circumstances of our emigration and settlement here. We have appealed to their native justice and magnanimity, and we have conjured them by the ties of our common kindred to disavow these usurpations, which, would inevitably interrupt our connections and correspondence. They, too, have been deaf to the voice of justice and of consanguinity. We must, therefore, acquiesce in the necessity, which denounces our separation, and hold them, as we hold the rest of mankind, enemies in war, in peace friends.

We, therefore, the representatives of the United States of America, in general Congress, assembled, appealing to the Supreme Judge of the world for the rectitude of our intentions, do, in the name, and by the authority of the good people of these colonies, solemnly publish and declare, that these united colonies are, and of right ought to be free and independent states; that they are absolved from all allegiance to the British Crown, and that all political connection between them and the state of Great Britain, is and ought to be totally dissolved; and that, as free and independent states, they have full power to levy war, conclude peace, contract alliances, establish commerce, and to do all other acts and things which independent states may of right do. And for the support of this declaration, with a firm reliance on the protection of Divine Providence, we mutually pledge to each other our lives, our fortunes and our sacred honor.

## The Constitution of the United States of America

**We the People** of the United States, in Order to form a more perfect Union, establish Justice, insure domestic Tranquility, provide for the common defence, promote the general Welfare, and secure the Blessings of Liberty to ourselves and our Posterity, do ordain and establish this Constitution for the United States of America.

### ARTICLE I

#### Section 1.

All legislative Powers herein granted shall be vested in a Congress of the United States, which shall consist of a Senate and House of Representatives.

### Section 2.

The House of Representatives shall be composed of Members chosen every second Year by the People of the several States, and the Electors in each State shall have the Qualifications requisite for Electors of the most numerous Branch of the State Legislature.

No Person shall be a Representative who shall not have attained to the Age of twenty five Years, and been seven Years a Citizen of the United States, and who shall not, when elected, be an Inhabitant of that State in which he shall be chosen.

Representatives and direct Taxes shall be apportioned among the several States which may be included within this Union, according to their respective Numbers, which shall be determined by adding to the whole Number of free Persons, including those bound to Service for a Term of Years, and excluding Indians not taxed, three fifths of all other Persons. The actual Enumeration shall be made within three Years after the first Meeting of the Congress of the United States, and within every subsequent Term of ten Years, in such Manner as they shall by Law direct. The Number of Representatives shall not exceed one for every thirty Thousand, but each State shall have at Least one Representative; and until such enumeration shall be made, the State of New Hampshire shall be entitled to choose three, Massachusetts eight, Rhode-Island and Providence Plantations one, Connecticut five, New York six, New Jersey four, Pennsylvania eight, Delaware one, Maryland six, Virginia ten, North Carolina five, South Carolina five, and Georgia three.

When vacancies happen in the Representation from any State, the Executive Authority thereof shall issue Writs of Election to fill such Vacancies.

The House of Representatives shall choose their Speaker and other Officers; and shall have the sole Power of Impeachment.

### Section 3.

The Senate of the United States shall be composed of two Senators from each State, chosen by the Legislature thereof for six Years; and each Senator shall have one Vote.

Immediately after they shall be assembled in Consequence of the first Election, they shall be divided as equally as may be into three Classes. The Seats of the Senators of the first Class shall be vacated at the Expiration of the second Year, of the second Class at the Expiration of the fourth Year, and of the third Class at the Expiration of the sixth Year, so that one third may be chosen every second Year; and if Vacancies happen by Resignation, or otherwise, during the Recess of the Legislature of any State, the Executive thereof may make temporary Appointments until the next Meeting of the Legislature, which shall then fill such Vacancies.

No Person shall be a Senator who shall not have attained to the Age of thirty Years, and been nine Years a Citizen of the United States, and who shall not, when elected, be an Inhabitant of that State for which he shall be chosen.

The Vice President of the United States shall be President of the Senate, but shall have no Vote, unless they be equally divided.

The Senate shall choose their other Officers, and also a President pro tempore, in the Absence of the Vice President, or when he shall exercise the Office of President of the United States.

The Senate shall have the sole Power to try all Impeachments. When sitting for that Purpose, they shall be on Oath or Affirmation. When the President of the United States is tried, the Chief Justice shall preside: And no Person shall be convicted without the Concurrence of two thirds of the Members present.

Judgment in Cases of Impeachment shall not extend further than to removal from Office, and disqualification to hold and enjoy any Office of honor, Trust or Profit under the United States: but the Party convicted shall nevertheless be liable and subject to Indictment, Trial, Judgment and Punishment, according to Law.

### Section 4.

The Times, Places and Manner of holding Elections for Senators and Representatives, shall be prescribed in each State by the Legislature thereof; but the Congress may at any time by Law make or alter such Regulations, except as to the Places of chusing Senators.

The Congress shall assemble at least once in every Year, and such Meeting shall be on the first Monday in December, unless they shall by Law appoint a different Day.

### Section 5.

Each House shall be the Judge of the Elections, Returns and Qualifications of its own Members, and a Majority of each shall constitute a Quorum to do Business; but a smaller Number may adjourn from day to day, and may be authorized to compel the Attendance of absent Members, in such Manner, and under such Penalties as each House may provide.

Each House may determine the Rules of its Proceedings, punish its Members for disorderly Behaviour, and, with the Concurrence of two thirds, expel a Member.

Each House shall keep a Journal of its Proceedings, and from time to time publish the same, excepting such Parts as may in their Judgment require Secrecy; and the Yeas and Nays of the Members of either House on any question shall, at the Desire of one fifth of those Present, be entered on the Journal.

Neither House, during the Session of Congress, shall, without the Consent of the other, adjourn for more than three days, nor to any other Place than that in which the two Houses shall be sitting.

### Section 6.

The Senators and Representatives shall receive a Compensation for their Services, to be ascertained by Law, and paid out of the Treasury of the United States. They shall in all Cases, except Treason, Felony and Breach of the Peace, be privileged from Arrest during their Attendance at the Session of their respective Houses, and in going to and returning from the same; and for any Speech or Debate in either House, they shall not be questioned in any other Place.

No Senator or Representative shall, during the Time for which he was elected, be appointed to any civil Office under the Authority of the United States, which shall have been created, or the Emoluments whereof shall have been increased during such time; and no Person holding any Office under the United States, shall be a Member of either House during his Continuance in Office.

## Section 7.

All Bills for raising Revenue shall originate in the House of Representatives; but the Senate may propose or concur with Amendments as on other Bills.

Every Bill which shall have passed the House of Representatives and the Senate, shall, before it become a Law, be presented to the President of the United States: If he approve he shall sign it, but if not he shall return it, with his Objections to that House in which it shall have originated, who shall enter the Objections at large on their Journal, and proceed to reconsider it. If after such Reconsideration two thirds of that House shall agree to pass the Bill, it shall be sent, together with the Objections, to the other House, by which it shall likewise be reconsidered, and if approved by two thirds of that House, it shall become a Law. But in all such Cases the Votes of both Houses shall be determined by yeas and Nays, and the Names of the Persons voting for and against the Bill shall be entered on the Journal of each House respectively. If any Bill shall not be returned by the President within ten Days (Sundays excepted) after it shall have been presented to him, the Same shall be a Law, in like Manner as if he had signed it, unless the Congress by their Adjournment prevent its Return, in which Case it shall not be a Law.

Every Order, Resolution, or Vote to which the Concurrence of the Senate and House of Representatives may be necessary (except on a question of Adjournment) shall be presented to the President of the United States; and before the Same shall take Effect, shall be approved by him, or being disapproved by him, shall be repassed by two thirds of the Senate and House of Representatives, according to the Rules and Limitations prescribed in the Case of a Bill.

## Section 8.

The Congress shall have Power

To lay and collect Taxes, Duties, Imposts and Excises, to pay the Debts and provide for the common Defence and general Welfare of the United States; but all Duties, Imposts and Excises shall be uniform throughout the United States;

To borrow Money on the credit of the United States;

To regulate Commerce with foreign Nations, and among the several States, and with the Indian Tribes;

To establish an uniform Rule of Naturalization, and uniform Laws on the subject of Bankruptcies throughout the United States;

To coin Money, regulate the Value thereof, and of foreign Coin, and fix the Standard of Weights and Measures;

To provide for the Punishment of counterfeiting the Securities and current Coin of the United States;

To establish Post Offices and post Roads;

To promote the Progress of Science and useful Arts, by securing for limited Times to Authors and Inventors the exclusive Right to their respective Writings and Discoveries;

To constitute Tribunals inferior to the supreme Court;

To define and punish Piracies and Felonies committed on the high Seas, and Offences against the Law of Nations;

To declare War, grant Letters of Marque and Reprisal, and make Rules concerning Captures on Land and Water;

To raise and support Armies, but no Appropriation of Money to that Use shall be for a longer Term than two Years;

To provide and maintain a Navy;

To make Rules for the Government and Regulation of the land and naval Forces;

To provide for calling forth the Militia to execute the Laws of the Union, suppress Insurrections and repel Invasions;

To provide for organizing, arming, and disciplining the Militia, and for governing such Part of them as may be employed in the Service of the United States, reserving to the States respectively, the Appointment of the Officers, and the Authority of training the Militia according to the discipline prescribed by Congress;

To exercise exclusive Legislation in all Cases whatsoever, over such District (not exceeding ten Miles square) as may, by Cession of particular States, and the Acceptance of Congress, become the Seat of the Government of the United States, and to exercise like Authority over all Places purchased by the Consent of the Legislature of the State in which the Same shall be, for the Erection of Forts, Magazines, Arsenals, dock-Yards, and other needful Buildings;—And

To make all Laws which shall be necessary and proper for carrying into Execution the foregoing Powers, and all other Powers vested by this Constitution in the Government of the United States, or in any Department or Officer thereof.

## Section 9.

The Migration or Importation of such Persons as any of the States now existing shall think proper to admit, shall not be prohibited by the Congress prior to the Year one thousand eight hundred and eight, but a Tax or duty may be imposed on such Importation, not exceeding ten dollars for each Person.

The Privilege of the Writ of Habeas Corpus shall not be suspended, unless when in Cases of Rebellion or Invasion the public Safety may require it.

No Bill of Attainder or ex post facto Law shall be passed.

No Capitation, or other direct, Tax shall be laid, unless in Proportion to the Census or enumeration herein before directed to be taken.

No Tax or Duty shall be laid on Articles exported from any State.

No Preference shall be given by any Regulation of Commerce or Revenue to the Ports of one State over those of another; nor shall Vessels bound to, or from, one State, be obliged to enter, clear, or pay Duties in another.

No Money shall be drawn from the Treasury, but in Consequence of Appropriations made by Law; and a regular Statement and Account of the Receipts and Expenditures of all public Money shall be published from time to time.

No Title of Nobility shall be granted by the United States: And no Person holding any Office of Profit or Trust under them, shall, without the Consent of the Congress, accept of any present, Emolument, Office, or Title, of any kind whatever, from any King, Prince, or foreign State.

### Section 10.

No State shall enter into any Treaty, Alliance, or Confederation; grant Letters of Marque and Reprisal; coin Money; emit Bills of Credit; make any Thing but gold and silver Coin a Tender in Payment of Debts; pass any Bill of Attainder, ex post facto Law, or Law impairing the Obligation of Contracts, or grant any Title of Nobility.

No State shall, without the Consent of the Congress, lay any Imposts or Duties on Imports or Exports, except what may be absolutely necessary for executing it's inspection Laws: and the net Produce of all Duties and Imposts, laid by any State on Imports or Exports, shall be for the Use of the Treasury of the United States; and all such Laws shall be subject to the Revision and Control of the Congress.

No State shall, without the Consent of Congress, lay any Duty of Tonnage, keep Troops, or Ships of War in time of Peace, enter into any Agreement or Compact with another State, or with a foreign Power, or engage in War, unless actually invaded, or in such imminent Danger as will not admit of delay.

## ARTICLE II

### Section 1.

The executive Power shall be vested in a President of the United States of America. He shall hold his Office during the Term of four Years, and, together with the Vice President, chosen for the same Term, be elected, as follows:

Each State shall appoint, in such Manner as the Legislature thereof may direct, a Number of Electors, equal to the whole Number of Senators and Representatives to which the State may be entitled in the Congress: but no Senator or Representative, or Person holding an Office of Trust or Profit under the United States, shall be appointed an Elector.

The Electors shall meet in their respective States, and vote by Ballot for two Persons, of whom one at least shall not be an Inhabitant of the same State with themselves. And they shall make a List of all the Persons voted for, and of the Number of Votes for each; which List they shall sign and certify, and transmit sealed to the Seat of the Government of the United States, directed to the President of the Senate. The President of the Senate shall, in the Presence of the Senate and House of Representatives, open all the Certificates, and the Votes shall then be counted. The Person having the greatest Number of Votes shall be the President, if such Number be a Majority of the whole Number of Electors appointed; and if there be more than one who have such Majority, and have an equal Number of Votes, then the House of Representatives shall immediately choose by Ballot one of them for President; and if no Person have a Majority, then from the five highest on the List the said House shall in like Manner choose the President. But in choosing the President, the Votes shall be taken by States, the Representation from each State having one Vote; A quorum for this purpose shall consist of a Member or Members from two thirds of the States, and a Majority of all the States shall be necessary to a Choice. In every Case, after the Choice of the President, the Person having the greatest Number of Votes of the Electors shall be the Vice President. But if there should remain two or more who have equal Votes, the Senate shall choose from them by Ballot the Vice President.

The Congress may determine the Time of choosing the Electors, and the Day on which they shall give their Votes; which Day shall be the same throughout the United States.

No Person except a natural born Citizen, or a Citizen of the United States, at the time of the Adoption of this Constitution, shall be eligible to the Office of President; neither shall any Person be eligible to that Office who shall not have attained to the Age of thirty five Years, and been fourteen Years a Resident within the United States.

In Case of the Removal of the President from Office, or of his Death, Resignation, or Inability to discharge the Powers and Duties of the said Office, the Same shall devolve on the Vice President, and the Congress may by Law provide for the Case of Removal, Death, Resignation or Inability, both of the President and Vice President, declaring what Officer shall then act as President, and such Officer shall act accordingly, until the Disability be removed, or a President shall be elected.

The President shall, at stated Times, receive for his Services, a Compensation, which shall neither be increased nor diminished during the Period for which he shall have been elected, and he shall not receive within that Period any other Emolument from the United States, or any of them.

Before he enter on the Execution of his Office, he shall take the following Oath or Affirmation:—"I do solemnly swear (or affirm) that I will faithfully execute the Office of President of the United States, and will to the best of my Ability, preserve, protect and defend the Constitution of the United States."

### Section 2.

The President shall be Commander in Chief of the Army and Navy of the United States, and of the Militia of the several States, when called into the actual Service of the United States; he may require the Opinion, in writing, of the principal Officer in each of the executive Departments, upon any Subject relating to the Duties of their respective Offices, and he shall have Power to grant Reprieves and Pardons for Offences against the United States, except in Cases of Impeachment.

He shall have Power, by and with the Advice and Consent of the Senate, to make Treaties, provided two thirds of the Senators present concur; and he shall nominate, and by and with the Advice and Consent of the Senate, shall appoint Ambassadors, other public Ministers and Consuls, Judges of the supreme Court, and all other Officers of the United States, whose Appointments are not herein otherwise provided for, and which shall be established by Law: but the Congress may by Law vest the Appointment of such inferior Officers, as they think proper, in the President alone, in the Courts of Law, or in the Heads of Departments.

The President shall have Power to fill up all Vacancies that may happen during the Recess of the Senate, by granting Commissions which shall expire at the End of their next Session.

### Section 3.

He shall from time to time give to the Congress Information of the State of the Union, and recommend to their Consideration such Measures as he shall judge necessary and expedient; he may, on extraordinary Occasions, convene both Houses, or either of them, and in Case of Disagreement between them, with Respect to the Time of Adjournment, he may adjourn them to such Time as he shall think proper; he shall receive Ambassadors and other public Ministers; he shall take Care that the Laws be faithfully executed, and shall Commission all the Officers of the United States.

### Section 4

The President, Vice President and all civil Officers of the United States, shall be removed from Office on Impeachment for, and Conviction of, Treason, Bribery, or other high Crimes and Misdemeanors.

## ARTICLE III

### Section 1.

The judicial Power of the United States shall be vested in one supreme Court, and in such inferior Courts as the Congress may from time to time ordain and establish. The Judges, both of the supreme and inferior Courts, shall hold their Offices during good Behaviour, and shall, at stated Times, receive for their Services a Compensation, which shall not be diminished during their Continuance in Office.

### Section 2.

The judicial Power shall extend to all Cases, in Law and Equity, arising under this Constitution, the Laws of the United States, and Treaties made, or which shall be made, under their Authority;—to all Cases affecting Ambassadors, other public Ministers and Consuls;—to all Cases of admiralty and maritime Jurisdiction;—to Controversies to which the United States shall be a Party;—to Controversies between two or more States;—between a State and Citizens of another State;—between Citizens of different States;—between Citizens of the same State claiming Lands under Grants of different States, and between a State, or the Citizens thereof, and foreign States, Citizens or Subjects.

In all Cases affecting Ambassadors, other public Ministers and Consuls, and those in which a State shall be Party, the supreme Court shall have original Jurisdiction. In all the other Cases before mentioned, the supreme Court shall have appellate Jurisdiction, both as to Law and Fact, with such Exceptions, and under such Regulations as the Congress shall make.

The Trial of all Crimes, except in Cases of Impeachment, shall be by Jury; and such Trial shall be held in the State where the said Crimes shall have been committed; but when not committed within any State, the Trial shall be at such Place or Places as the Congress may by Law have directed.

### Section 3.

Treason against the United States, shall consist only in levying War against them, or in adhering to their Enemies, giving them Aid and Comfort. No Person shall be convicted of Treason unless on the Testimony of two Witnesses to the same overt Act, or on Confession in open Court.

The Congress shall have Power to declare the Punishment of Treason, but no Attainder of Treason shall work Corruption of Blood, or Forfeiture except during the Life of the Person attainted.

## ARTICLE IV

### Section 1.

Full Faith and Credit shall be given in each State to the public Acts, Records, and judicial Proceedings of every other State. And the Congress may by general Laws prescribe the Manner in which such Acts, Records and Proceedings shall be proved, and the Effect thereof.

### Section 2.

The Citizens of each State shall be entitled to all Privileges and Immunities of Citizens in the several States.

A Person charged in any State with Treason, Felony, or other Crime, who shall flee from Justice, and be found in another State, shall on Demand of the executive Authority of the State from which he fled, be delivered up, to be removed to the State having Jurisdiction of the Crime.

No Person held to Service or Labour in one State, under the Laws thereof, escaping into another, shall, in Consequence of any Law or Regulation therein, be discharged from such Service or Labour, but shall be delivered up on Claim of the Party to whom such Service or Labour may be due.

### Section 3.

New States may be admitted by the Congress into this Union; but no new State shall be formed or erected within the Jurisdiction of any other State; nor any State be formed by the Junction of two or more States, or Parts of States, without the Consent of the Legislatures of the States concerned as well as of the Congress.

The Congress shall have Power to dispose of and make all needful Rules and Regulations respecting the Territory or other Property belonging to the United States; and nothing in this Constitution shall be so construed as to Prejudice any Claims of the United States, or of any particular State.

### Section 4.

The United States shall guarantee to every State in this Union a Republican Form of Government, and shall protect each of them against Invasion; and on Application of the Legislature, or of the Executive (when the Legislature cannot be convened), against domestic Violence.

## ARTICLE V

The Congress, whenever two thirds of both Houses shall deem it necessary, shall propose Amendments to this Constitution, or, on the Application of the Legislatures of two thirds of the several States, shall call a Convention for proposing Amendments, which, in either Case, shall be valid to all Intents and Purposes, as Part of this Constitution, when ratified by the Legislatures of three fourths of the several States, or by Conventions in three fourths thereof, as the one or the other Mode of Ratification may be proposed by the Congress; Provided that no Amendment which may be made prior to the Year One thousand eight hundred and eight shall in any Manner affect the first and fourth Clauses in the Ninth Section of the first Article; and that no State, without its Consent, shall be deprived of its equal Suffrage in the Senate.

## ARTICLE VI

All Debts contracted and Engagements entered into, before the Adoption of this Constitution, shall be as valid against the United States under this Constitution, as under the Confederation.

This Constitution, and the Laws of the United States which shall be made in Pursuance thereof; and all Treaties made, or which shall be made, under the Authority of the United States, shall be the supreme Law of the Land; and the Judges in every State shall be bound thereby, any Thing in the Constitution or Laws of any State to the Contrary notwithstanding.

The Senators and Representatives before mentioned, and the Members of the several State Legislatures, and all executive and judicial Officers, both of the United States and of the several States, shall be bound by Oath or Affirmation, to support this Constitution; but no religious Test shall ever be required as a Qualification to any Office or public Trust under the United States.

## ARTICLE VII

The Ratification of the Conventions of nine States, shall be sufficient for the Establishment of this Constitution between the States so ratifying the Same.

The Word, "the," being interlined between the seventh and eighth Lines of the first Page, the Word "Thirty" being partly written on an Erazure in the fifteenth Line of the first Page, The Words "is tried" being interlined between the thirty second and thirty third Lines of the first Page and the Word "the" being interlined between the forty third and forty fourth Lines of the second Page.

Attest William Jackson Secretary

Done in Convention by the Unanimous Consent of the States present the Seventeenth Day of September in the Year of our Lord one thousand seven hundred and Eighty seven and of the Independence of the United States of America the Twelfth In witness whereof We have hereunto subscribed our Names,

G°. Washington
*Presidt and deputy from Virginia*

**Delaware**
Geo: Read
Gunning Bedford jun
John Dickinson
Richard Bassett
Jaco: Broom

**Maryland**
James McHenry
Dan of St Thos. Jenifer
Danl. Carroll

**Virginia**
John Blair
James Madison Jr.

**North Carolina**
Wm. Blount
Richd. Dobbs Spaight
Hu Williamson

**South Carolina**
J. Rutledge
Charles Cotesworth Pinckney
Charles Pinckney
Pierce Butler

**Georgia**
William Few
Abr Baldwin

**New Hampshire**
John Langdon
Nicholas Gilman

**Massachusetts**
Nathaniel Gorham
Rufus King

**Connecticut**
Wm. Saml. Johnson
Roger Sherman

**New York**
Alexander Hamilton

**New Jersey**
Wil: Livingston
David Brearley
Wm. Paterson
Jona: Dayton

**Pennsylvania**
B Franklin
Thomas Mifflin
Robt. Morris
Geo. Clymer
Thos. FitzSimons
Jared Ingersoll
James Wilson
Gouv Morris

## Articles

In addition to, and Amendment of the Constitution of the United States of America, proposed by Congress, and ratified by the Legislatures of the several States, pursuant to the fifth Article of the original Constitution.

(The first ten amendments to the U.S. Constitution were ratified December 15, 1791, and form what is known as the "Bill of Rights.")

## AMENDMENT I

Congress shall make no law respecting an establishment of religion, or prohibiting the free exercise thereof; or abridging the freedom of speech, or of the press; or the right of the people peaceably to assemble, and to petition the Government for a redress of grievances.

## AMENDMENT II

A well regulated Militia, being necessary to the security of a free State, the right of the people to keep and bear Arms, shall not be infringed.

## AMENDMENT III

No Soldier shall, in time of peace be quartered in any house, without the consent of the Owner, nor in time of war, but in a manner to be prescribed by law.

## AMENDMENT IV

The right of the people to be secure in their persons, houses, papers, and effects, against unreasonable searches and seizures, shall not be violated, and no Warrants shall issue, but upon probable cause, supported by Oath or affirmation, and particularly describing the place to be searched, and the persons or things to be seized.

## AMENDMENT V

No person shall be held to answer for a capital, or otherwise infamous crime, unless on a presentment or indictment of a Grand Jury, except in cases arising in the land or naval forces, or in the Militia, when in actual service in time of War or public danger; nor shall any person be subject for the same offence to be twice put in jeopardy of life or limb; nor shall be compelled in any criminal case to be a witness against himself, nor be deprived of life, liberty, or property, without due process of law; nor shall private property be taken for public use, without just compensation.

## AMENDMENT VI

In all criminal prosecutions, the accused shall enjoy the right to a speedy and public trial, by an impartial jury of the State and district wherein the crime shall have been committed, which district shall have been previously ascertained by law, and to be informed of the nature and cause of the accusation; to be confronted with the witnesses against him; to have compulsory process for obtaining witnesses in his favor, and to have the Assistance of Counsel for his defence.

## AMENDMENT VII

In Suits at common law, where the value in controversy shall exceed twenty dollars, the right of trial by jury shall be preserved, and no fact tried by a jury, shall be otherwise re-examined in any Court of the United States, than according to the rules of the common law.

## AMENDMENT VIII

Excessive bail shall not be required, nor excessive fines imposed, nor cruel and unusual punishments inflicted.

## AMENDMENT IX

The enumeration in the Constitution, of certain rights, shall not be construed to deny or disparage others retained by the people.

## AMENDMENT X

The powers not delegated to the United States by the Constitution, nor prohibited by it to the States, are reserved to the States respectively, or to the people.

## AMENDMENT XI

Passed by Congress March 4, 1794. Ratified February 7, 1795.

**Note:** Article III, Section 2, of the Constitution was modified by Amendment XI.

The Judicial power of the United States shall not be construed to extend to any suit in law or equity, commenced or prosecuted against one of the United States by Citizens of another State, or by Citizens or Subjects of any Foreign State.

## AMENDMENT XII

Passed by Congress December 9, 1803. Ratified June 15, 1804.

**Note:** A portion of Article II, Section 1, of the Constitution was superceded by the Twelfth Amendment.

The Electors shall meet in their respective states and vote by ballot for President and Vice-President, one of whom, at least, shall not be an inhabitant of the same state with themselves; they shall name in their ballots the person voted for as President, and in distinct ballots the person voted for as Vice-President, and they shall make distinct lists of all persons voted for as President, and of all persons voted for as Vice-President, and of the number of votes for each, which lists they shall sign and certify, and transmit sealed to the seat of the government of the United States, directed to the President of the Senate;—the President of the Senate shall, in the presence of the Senate and House of Representatives, open all the certificates and the votes shall then be counted;—The person having the greatest number of votes for President, shall be the President, if such number be a majority of the whole number of Electors appointed; and if no person have such majority, then from the persons having the highest numbers not exceeding three on the list of those voted for as President, the House of Representatives shall choose immediately, by ballot, the President. But in choosing the President, the votes shall be taken by states, the representation from each state having one vote; a quorum for this purpose shall consist of a member or members from two-thirds of the states, and a majority of all the states shall be necessary to a choice. [And if the House of Representatives shall not choose a President whenever the right of choice shall devolve upon them, before the fourth day of March next following, then the Vice-President shall act as President, as in case of the death or other constitutional disability of the President.—]* The person having the greatest number of votes as Vice-President, shall be the Vice-President, if such number be a majority of the whole number of Electors appointed, and if no person have a majority, then from the two highest numbers on the list, the Senate shall choose the Vice-President; a quorum for the purpose shall consist of two-thirds of the whole number of Senators, and a majority of the whole number shall be necessary to a choice. But no person constitutionally ineligible to the office of President shall be eligible to that of Vice-President of the United States.

*Superceded by Section 3 of the Twentieth Amendment.

## AMENDMENT XIII

Passed by Congress January 31, 1865. Ratified December 6, 1865.

**Note:** A portion of Article IV, Section 2, of the Constitution was superceded by the Thirteenth Amendment.

### Section 1.

Neither slavery nor involuntary servitude, except as a punishment for crime whereof the party shall have been duly convicted, shall exist within the United States, or any place subject to their jurisdiction.

### Section 2.

Congress shall have power to enforce this article by appropriate legislation.

## AMENDMENT XIV

Passed by Congress June 13, 1866. Ratified July 9, 1868.

**Note:** Article I, Section 2, of the Constitution was modified by Section 2 of the Fourteenth Amendment.

### Section 1.

All persons born or naturalized in the United States, and subject to the jurisdiction thereof, are citizens of the United States and of the State wherein they reside. No State shall make or enforce any law which shall abridge the privileges or immunities of citizens of the United States; nor shall any State deprive any person of life, liberty, or property, without due process of law; nor deny to any person within its jurisdiction the equal protection of the laws.

### Section 2.

Representatives shall be apportioned among the several States according to their respective numbers, counting the whole number of persons in each State, excluding Indians not taxed. But when the right to vote at any election for the choice of electors for President and Vice-President of the United States, Representatives in Congress, the Executive and Judicial officers of a State, or the members of the Legislature thereof, is denied to any of the male inhabitants of such State, being twenty-one years of age,* and citizens of the United States, or in any way abridged, except for participation in rebellion, or other crime, the basis of representation therein shall be reduced in the proportion which the number of such male citizens shall bear to the whole number of male citizens twenty-one years of age in such State.

### Section 3.

No person shall be a Senator or Representative in Congress, or elector of President and Vice-President, or hold any office, civil or military, under the United States, or under any State, who, having previously taken an oath, as a member of Congress, or as an officer of the United States, or as a member of any State legislature, or as an executive or judicial officer of any State, to support the Constitution of the United States, shall have engaged in insurrection or rebellion against the same, or given aid or comfort to the enemies thereof. But Congress may by a vote of two-thirds of each House, remove such disability.

### Section 4.

The validity of the public debt of the United States, authorized by law, including debts incurred for payment of pensions and bounties for services in suppressing insurrection or rebellion, shall not be questioned. But neither the United States nor any State shall assume or pay any debt or obligation incurred in aid of insurrection or rebellion against the United States, or any claim for the loss or emancipation of any slave; but all such debts, obligations and claims shall be held illegal and void.

### Section 5.

The Congress shall have the power to enforce, by appropriate legislation, the provisions of this article.

*Changed by Section 1 of the Twenty-sixth Amendment.

## AMENDMENT XV

Passed by Congress February 26, 1869. Ratified February 3, 1870.

### Section 1.

The right of citizens of the United States to vote shall not be denied or abridged by the United States or by any State on account of race, color, or previous condition of servitude.

### Section 2.

The Congress shall have the power to enforce this article by appropriate legislation.

## AMENDMENT XVI

Passed by Congress July 2, 1909. Ratified February 3, 1913.

**Note:** Article I, Section 9, of the Constitution was modified by Amendment XVI.

The Congress shall have power to lay and collect taxes on incomes, from whatever source derived, without apportionment among the several States, and without regard to any census or enumeration.

## AMENDMENT XVII

Passed by Congress May 13, 1912. Ratified April 8, 1913.

**Note:** Article I, Section 3, of the Constitution was modified by the Seventeenth Amendment.

The Senate of the United States shall be composed of two Senators from each State, elected by the people thereof, for six years; and each Senator shall have one vote. The electors in each State shall have the qualifications requisite for electors of the most numerous branch of the State legislatures.

When vacancies happen in the representation of any State in the Senate, the executive authority of such State shall issue writs of election to fill such vacancies: *Provided,* That the legislature of any State may empower the executive thereof to make temporary appointments until the people fill the vacancies by election as the legislature may direct.

This amendment shall not be so construed as to affect the election or term of any Senator chosen before it becomes valid as part of the Constitution.

## AMENDMENT XVIII

Passed by Congress December 18, 1917. Ratified January 16, 1919. Repealed by Amendment XXI.

### Section 1.

After one year from the ratification of this article the manufacture, sale, or transportation of intoxicating liquors within, the importation thereof into, or the exportation thereof from the United States and all territory subject to the jurisdiction thereof for beverage purposes is hereby prohibited.

### Section 2.

The Congress and the several States shall have concurrent power to enforce this article by appropriate legislation.

### Section 3.
This article shall be inoperative unless it shall have been ratified as an amendment to the Constitution by the legislatures of the several States, as provided in the Constitution, within seven years from the date of the submission hereof to the States by the Congress.

## AMENDMENT XIX

Passed by Congress June 4, 1919. Ratified August 18, 1920.

The right of citizens of the United States to vote shall not be denied or abridged by the United States or by any State on account of sex.

Congress shall have power to enforce this article by appropriate legislation.

## AMENDMENT XX

Passed by Congress March 2, 1932. Ratified January 23, 1933.

**Note:** Article I, Section 4, of the Constitution was modified by Section 2 of this amendment. In addition, a portion of the Twelfth Amendment was superceded by Section 3.

### Section 1.
The terms of the President and the Vice President shall end at noon on the 20th day of January, and the terms of Senators and Representatives at noon on the 3d day of January, of the years in which such terms would have ended if this article had not been ratified; and the terms of their successors shall then begin.

### Section 2.
The Congress shall assemble at least once in every year, and such meeting shall begin at noon on the 3d day of January, unless they shall by law appoint a different day.

### Section 3.
If, at the time fixed for the beginning of the term of the President, the President elect shall have died, the Vice President elect shall become President. If a President shall not have been chosen before the time fixed for the beginning of his term, or if the President elect shall have failed to qualify, then the Vice President elect shall act as President until a President shall have qualified; and the Congress may by law provide for the case wherein neither a President elect nor a Vice President shall have qualified, declaring who shall then act as President, or the manner in which one who is to act shall be selected, and such person shall act accordingly until a President or Vice President shall have qualified.

### Section 4.
The Congress may by law provide for the case of the death of any of the persons from whom the House of Representatives may choose a President whenever the right of choice shall have devolved upon them, and for the case of the death of any of the

persons from whom the Senate may choose a Vice President whenever the right of choice shall have devolved upon them.

### Section 5.

Sections 1 and 2 shall take effect on the 15th day of October following the ratification of this article.

### Section 6.

This article shall be inoperative unless it shall have been ratified as an amendment to the Constitution by the legislatures of three-fourths of the several States within seven years from the date of its submission.

## AMENDMENT XXI

Passed by Congress February 20, 1933. Ratified December 5, 1933.

### Section 1.

The eighteenth article of amendment to the Constitution of the United States is hereby repealed.

### Section 2.

The transportation or importation into any State, Territory, or Possession of the United States for delivery or use therein of intoxicating liquors, in violation of the laws thereof, is hereby prohibited.

### Section 3.

This article shall be inoperative unless it shall have been ratified as an amendment to the Constitution by conventions in the several States, as provided in the Constitution, within seven years from the date of the submission hereof to the States by the Congress.

## AMENDMENT XXII

Passed by Congress March 21, 1947. Ratified February 27, 1951.

### Section 1.

No person shall be elected to the office of the President more than twice, and no person who has held the office of President, or acted as President, for more than two years of a term to which some other person was elected President shall be elected to the office of President more than once. But this Article shall not apply to any person holding the office of President when this Article was proposed by Congress, and shall not prevent any person who may be holding the office of President, or acting as President, during the term within which this Article becomes operative from holding the office of President or acting as President during the remainder of such term.

### Section 2.

This article shall be inoperative unless it shall have been ratified as an amendment to the Constitution by the legislatures of three-fourths of the several States within seven years from the date of its submission to the States by the Congress.

## AMENDMENT XXIII

Passed by Congress June 16, 1960. Ratified March 29, 1961.

### Section 1.

The District constituting the seat of Government of the United States shall appoint in such manner as Congress may direct:

A number of electors of President and Vice President equal to the whole number of Senators and Representatives in Congress to which the District would be entitled if it were a State, but in no event more than the least populous State; they shall be in addition to those appointed by the States, but they shall be considered, for the purposes of the election of President and Vice President, to be electors appointed by a State; and they shall meet in the District and perform such duties as provided by the twelfth article of amendment.

### Section 2.

The Congress shall have power to enforce this article by appropriate legislation.

## AMENDMENT XXIV

Passed by Congress August 27, 1962. Ratified January 23, 1964.

### Section 1.

The right of citizens of the United States to vote in any primary or other election for President or Vice President, for electors for President or Vice President, or for Senator or Representative in Congress, shall not be denied or abridged by the United States or any State by reason of failure to pay poll tax or other tax.

### Section 2.

The Congress shall have power to enforce this article by appropriate legislation.

## AMENDMENT XXV

Passed by Congress July 6, 1965. Ratified February 10, 1967.

**Note:** Article II, Section 1, of the Constitution was affected by the Twenty-fifth Amendment.

### Section 1.

In case of the removal of the President from office or of his death or resignation, the Vice President shall become President.

### Section 2.

Whenever there is a vacancy in the office of the Vice President, the President shall nominate a Vice President who shall take office upon confirmation by a majority vote of both Houses of Congress.

### Section 3.

Whenever the President transmits to the President pro tempore of the Senate and the Speaker of the House of Representatives his written declaration that he is unable to discharge the powers and duties of his office, and until he transmits to them a written declaration to the contrary, such powers and duties shall be discharged by the Vice President as Acting President.

### Section 4.

Whenever the Vice President and a majority of either the principal officers of the executive departments or of such other body as Congress may by law provide, transmit to the President pro tempore of the Senate and the Speaker of the House of Representatives their written declaration that the President is unable to discharge the powers and duties of his office, the Vice President shall immediately assume the powers and duties of the office as Acting President.

Thereafter, when the President transmits to the President pro tempore of the Senate and the Speaker of the House of Representatives his written declaration that no inability exists, he shall resume the powers and duties of his office unless the Vice President and a majority of either the principal officers of the executive department or of such other body as Congress may by law provide, transmit within four days to the President pro tempore of the Senate and the Speaker of the House of Representatives their written declaration that the President is unable to discharge the powers and duties of his office. Thereupon Congress shall decide the issue, assembling within forty-eight hours for that purpose if not in session. If the Congress, within twenty-one days after receipt of the latter written declaration, or, if Congress is not in session, within twenty-one days after Congress is required to assemble, determines by two-thirds vote of both Houses that the President is unable to discharge the powers and duties of his office, the Vice President shall continue to discharge the same as Acting President; otherwise, the President shall resume the powers and duties of his office.

## AMENDMENT XXVI

Passed by Congress March 23, 1971. Ratified July 1, 1971.

**Note:** Amendment XIV, Section 2, of the Constitution was modified by Section 1 of the Twenty-sixth Amendment.

### Section 1.

The right of citizens of the United States, who are eighteen years of age or older, to vote shall not be denied or abridged by the United States or by any State on account of age.

**Section 2.**
The Congress shall have power to enforce this article by appropriate legislation.

## AMENDMENT XXVII

Originally proposed Sept. 25, 1789. Ratified May 7, 1992.

No law, varying the compensation for the services of the Senators and Representatives, shall take effect, until an election of representatives shall have intervened.

## Lincoln's Gettysburg Address

Four score and seven years ago our fathers brought forth on this continent, a new nation, conceived in Liberty, and dedicated to the proposition that all men are created equal.

Now we are engaged in a great civil war, testing whether that nation, or any nation so conceived and so dedicated, can long endure. We are met on a great battle-field of that war. We have come to dedicate a portion of that field, as a final resting place for those who here gave their lives that that nation might live. It is altogether fitting and proper that we should do this.

But, in a larger sense, we can not dedicate—we can not consecrate—we can not hallow—this ground. The brave men, living and dead, who struggled here, have consecrated it, far above our poor power to add or detract. The world will little note, nor long remember what we say here, but it can never forget what they did here. It is for us the living, rather, to be dedicated here to the unfinished work which they who fought here have thus far so nobly advanced. It is rather for us to be here dedicated to the great task remaining before us—that from these honored dead we take increased devotion to that cause for which they gave the last full measure of devotion—that we here highly resolve that these dead shall not have died in vain—that this nation, under God, shall have a new birth of freedom—and that government of the people, by the people, for the people, shall not perish from the earth.

# Appendix B

## HISTORICAL FACTS AND DATA

### U.S. Presidents and Vice Presidents

| | PRESIDENT | VICE-PRESIDENT | POLITICAL PARTY | TERM |
|---|---|---|---|---|
| 1 | George Washington | John Adams | No Party Designation | 1789–1797 |
| 2 | John Adams | Thomas Jefferson | Federalist | 1797–1801 |
| 3 | Thomas Jefferson | Aaron Burr<br>George Clinton | Democratic-Republican | 1801–1809 |
| 4 | James Madison | George Clinton<br>Elbridge Gerry | Democratic-Republican | 1809–1817 |
| 5 | James Monroe | Daniel D Tompkins | Democratic-Republican | 1817–1825 |
| 6 | John Quincy Adams | John C Calhoun | Democratic-Republican | 1825–1829 |
| 7 | Andrew Jackson | John C Calhoun<br>Martin Van Buren | Democratic | 1829–1837 |
| 8 | Martin Van Buren | Richard M. Johnson | Democratic | 1837–1841 |
| 9 | William Henry Harrison | John Tyler | Whig | 1841 |
| 10 | John Tyler | None | Whig | 1841–1845 |
| 11 | James Knox Polk | George M Dallas | Democratic | 1845–1849 |
| 12 | Zachary Taylor | Millard Fillmore | Whig | 1849–1850 |
| 13 | Millard Fillmore | None | Whig | 1850–1853 |
| 14 | Franklin Pierce | William R King | Democratic | 1853–1857 |
| 15 | James Buchanan | John C Breckinridge | Democratic | 1857–1861 |
| 16 | Abraham Lincoln | Hannibel Hamlin<br>Andrew Johnson | Union | 1861–1865 |
| 17 | Andrew Johnson | None | Union | 1865–1869 |
| 18 | Ulysses Simpson Grant | Schuyler Colfax<br>Henry Wilson | Republican | 1869–1877 |
| 19 | Rutherford Birchard Hayes | William A Wheeler | Republican | 1877–1881 |
| 20 | James Abram Garfield | Chester Alan Arthur | Republican | 1881 |

*(continued)*

| | PRESIDENT | VICE-PRESIDENT | POLITICAL PARTY | TERM |
|---|---|---|---|---|
| 21 | Chester Alan Arthur | None | Republican | 1881–1885 |
| 22 | Stephen Grover Cleveland | Thomas Hendricks | Democratic | 1885–1889 |
| 23 | Benjamin Harrison | Levi P Morton | Republican | 1889–1893 |
| 24 | Chester Alan Arthur | Adlai E Stevenson | Democratic | 1893–1897 |
| 25 | William McKinley | Garret A. Hobart<br>Theodore Roosevelt | Republican | 1897–1901 |
| 26 | Theodore Roosevelt | Charles W Fairbanks | Republican | 1901–1909 |
| 27 | William Howard Taft | James S Sherman | Republican | 1909–1913 |
| 28 | Woodrow Wilson | Thomas R Marshall | Democratic | 1913–1921 |
| 29 | Warren Gamaliel Harding | Calvin Coolidge | Republican | 1921–1923 |
| 30 | Calvin Coolidge | Charles G Dawes | Republican | 1923–1929 |
| 31 | Herbert Clark Hoover | Charles Curtis | Republican | 1929–1933 |
| 32 | Franklin Delano Roosevelt | John Nance Garner<br>Henry A. Wallace<br>Harry S. Truman | Democratic | 1933–1945 |
| 33 | Harry S. Truman | Alben W Barkley | Democratic | 1945–1953 |
| 34 | Dwight David Eisenhower | Richard Milhous Nixon | Republican | 1953–1961 |
| 35 | John Fitzgerald Kennedy | Lyndon Baines Johnson | Democratic | 1961–1963 |
| 36 | Lyndon Baines Johnson | Hubert Horatio Humphrey | Democratic | 1963–1969 |
| 37 | Richard Milhous Nixon | Spiro T. Agnew<br>Gerald Rudolph Ford | Republican | 1969–1974 |
| 38 | Gerald Rudolph Ford | Nelson Rockefeller | Republican | 1974–1977 |
| 39 | James Earl Carter, Jr. | Walter Mondale | Democratic | 1977–1981 |
| 40 | Ronald Wilson Reagan | George Herbert Walker Bush | Republican | 1981–1989 |
| 41 | George Herbert Walker Bush | J. Danforth Quayle | Republican | 1989–1993 |
| 42 | William Jefferson Clinton | Albert Gore, Jr. | Democratic | 1993–2001 |
| 43 | George Walker Bush | Richard Cheney | Republican | 2001–2008 |
| 44 | Barack Hussein Obama | Joseph Biden | Democratic | 2008– |

## Admission of States into the Union

| | STATE | DATE OF ADMISSION |
|---|---|---|
| 1 | Delaware | December 7, 1787 |
| 2 | Pennsylvania | December 12, 1787 |
| 3 | New Jersey | December 18, 1787 |
| 4 | Georgia | January 2, 1788 |
| 5 | Connecticut | January 9, 1788 |
| 6 | Massachusetts | February 6, 1788 |
| 7 | Maryland | April 28, 1788 |
| 8 | South Carolina | May 23, 1788 |
| 9 | New Hampshire | June 21, 1788 |
| 10 | Virginia | June 25, 1788 |
| 11 | New York | July 26, 1788 |
| 12 | North Carolina | November 21, 1789 |
| 13 | Rhode Island | May 29, 1790 |
| 14 | Vermont | March 4, 1791 |
| 15 | Kentucky | June 1, 1792 |
| 16 | Tennessee | June 1, 1796 |
| 17 | Ohio | March 1, 1803 |
| 18 | Louisiana | April 30, 1812 |
| 19 | Indiana | December 11, 1816 |
| 20 | Mississippi | December 10, 1817 |
| 21 | Illinois | December 3, 1818 |
| 22 | Alabama | December 14, 1819 |
| 23 | Maine | March 15, 1820 |
| 24 | Missouri | August 10, 1821 |
| 25 | Arkansas | June 15, 1836 |

| | STATE | DATE OF ADMISSION |
|---|---|---|
| 27 | Florida | March 3, 1845 |
| 28 | Texas | December 29, 1845 |
| 29 | Iowa | December 28, 1846 |
| 30 | Wisconsin | May 29, 1848 |
| 31 | California | September 9, 1850 |
| 32 | Minnesota | May 11, 1858 |
| 33 | Oregon | February 14, 1859 |
| 34 | Kansas | January 29, 1861 |
| 35 | West Virginia | June 20, 1863 |
| 36 | Nevada | October 31, 1864 |
| 37 | Nebraska | March 1, 1867 |
| 38 | Colorado | August 1, 1876 |
| 39 | North Dakota | November 2, 1889 |
| 40 | South Dakota | November 2, 1889 |
| 41 | Montana | November 11, 1889 |
| 43 | Idaho | July 3, 1890 |
| 44 | Wyoming | July 10, 1890 |
| 45 | Utah | January 4, 1896 |
| 46 | Oklahoma | November 16, 1907 |
| 47 | New Mexico | January 6, 1912 |
| 48 | Arizona | February 14, 1912 |
| 49 | Alaska | January 3, 1959 |
| 50 | Hawaii | August 21, 1959 |

# Glossary

**Abolition** A pre-Civil War social movement devoted to the emancipation of slaves and their inclusion in American society as citizens with equal rights.

**Abu Ghraib** Iraqi correctional facility near Baghdad that was widely publicized in 2004 for abuses of Iraqi prisoners of war by the U.S. military and CIA operatives.

**Act of Supremacy (1534)** English parliamentary act that abolished papal authority over England, making King Henry VIII the head of the Church of England.

**Acts of Union (1707)** Parliamentary acts that created the United Kingdom by merging the kingdoms and parliaments of England and Scotland.

**Adamson Act (1916)** Congressional act that granted railroad workers an eight-hour workday and overtime pay.

**Agricultural Adjustment Administration (AAA, 1933)** U.S. government agency created by the Agricultural Adjustment Act to provide credit, loans, and other subsidies to farmers.

**Alamo** A mission outpost in San Antonio, Texas, that was defended down to the last man by American and Mexican separatists in the Texas War for Independence of 1836.

**Albany Congress (1754)** A conference of representatives of seven British North American colonies, held in Albany, New York, to consider strategies for diplomacy with the Indians and dissuade the Iroquois from becoming French allies.

**Alien and Sedition Acts (1798)** Four congressional acts that severely restricted immigration into the United States and gave the president power to deport anyone thought to be dangerous—even for spreading radical political ideas.

**Alliance for Progress (1961)** A multibillion-dollar aid program for Latin America aimed at establishing economic cooperation between the United States and South America.

**American Antislavery Society** An abolitionist society organized by William Lloyd Garrison in 1833 with immediate abolition as its core objective.

**American Colonization Society (ACS)** A society of antislavery whites, founded in 1817, that advocated the return of freed slaves to Africa.

**American Expeditionary Forces** American armed forces, commanded by General John J. Pershing, sent to Europe during World War I to fight alongside British and French allied units.

**American Federation of Labor** A collective of craft unions, founded in 1881, comprised of highly skilled, mostly white, carpenters, plumbers, and electricians. The organization largely ignored the plight of lower paid industrial workers, excluded minority laborers, and often supported Republican candidates.

**American Indian Movement** Formed in Minneapolis in 1968, an activist organization devoted to protecting Indian rights and to upholding established treaties, particularly over land, with federal, state, and local governments.

**American Philosophical Society** Scholarly organization founded in Philadelphia in 1743 to promote the dissemination of knowledge in the science and humanities.

**American Protective Association (APA)** An anti-Catholic nativist organization founded in 1887. The APA advocated strict immigration laws and spread conspiracy theories about Roman Catholics.

**American Railway Union (ARU)** Founded in 1893, the ARU was one of the first industrial unions in the United States and the largest labor union of its time. ARU was founded on the belief that railway workers would increase their power if they would organize one industry-wide union.

**American Recovery and Reinvestment Act (2009)** Congressional act allocating $787 billion in economic stimulus funds. The package combined government spending on infrastructure, unemployment benefits, and food stamps, with tax cuts.

**American System** Senator Henry Clay's proposal of 1824 intended to spur domestic economic development as well as tariffs and currency regulation.

**American Temperance Society** Organization established in 1826 to advocate abstinence from distilled beverages. The movement did not end the consumption of alcohol in America, but it did help convince millions of people to rethink their relationship with drinking.

**Americans with Disabilities Act (ADA)** Congressional act of 1990 that provided equal rights for people with disabilities.

**Anarchism** A term meaning without rulers or without government.

**Anti-Imperial League** American organization formed in 1898 by those who opposed American colonization of the Philippines.

**Articles of Capitulation (1664)** English policies regarding Dutch residents of New Amsterdam, which granted them religious liberty, freedom from military conscription, property rights, the ability to leave New York within 18 months, and free trade and freedom of movement within the English Empire.

**Articles of Confederation** The first written framework for a government of the United States, drafted by Congress and in effect from 1781 to 1788.

**Astrolabe** A navigation instrument used to pinpoint and predict the location of the stars, Sun, Moon, and planets for determining longitude and latitude while sailing at sea.

**Atlantic Charter (1941)** A joint policy statement issued by the United States and Great Britain that defined the goals and objectives of their alliance at the beginning of World War II. The charter called for disarming defeated aggressors and establishing a permanent system of general security.

**Atlantic slave trade** The enslaving, trade, and transport of African people to Europe and the Americas, begun by the Portuguese in the early 1440s.

**Atlantic world** Name given to the area of exploration bordering the Atlantic Ocean and including the five continents of North America, South America, Antarctica, Africa, and Europe.

**Baby boom** The temporary but noteworthy increase in birth rate in the United States, Great Britain, and Europe in the years immediately following World War II.

**Balance of powers** A model of governance in which authority is distributed to several different branches of government, providing checks and balances against one another. Also known as the separation of powers.

**Bank of the United States (BUS)** The first federal bank, founded in 1791, that operated until 1811 and provided for the issuance of a national currency and centralization of federal tax collection.

**Barbados slave code (1661)** English America's first slave code; it prescribed different treatment and contrasting levels of legal protection for enslaved Africans and white servants.

**Battle of the Bulge** The last major offensive by Axis powers in World War II, fought in Belgium in 1944.

**Bay of Pigs Invasion** Failed operation approved by President Kennedy to invade Cuba with a small CIA-led military force of political Cuban exiles with hopes of liberating the country and removing Fidel Castro from power.

**Bill of Rights** The first 10 amendments to the United States Constitution, ratified by the states in 1791.

**Black Codes (1865–1866)** Congressional acts that granted rights to former slaves. These included the right to marry, to own property, and to participate in the judicial process.

**Black Legend** Politically motivated, factually exploitative conviction that the Spaniards indiscriminately slaughtered Indians, tyrannized them, and imposed Catholicism on them during their 16th-century conquests in the Americas.

**Black Panther Party** A radical civil rights organization founded in Oakland in 1966 by Huey Newton and Bobby Seale. Members of Black Panthers advocated black self-determination and armed self-defense against police brutality.

**Black Tuesday (October 29, 1929)** The day that marked the start of the Great Depression, precipitated by a calamitous crash of the stock market.

**Board of Trade (1696)** An advisory council created by King William III of England that was charged to oversee colonial matters. The act testified to the colonies' growing significance to England's economy.

**Boston Massacre (1770)** An altercation between occupying British troops and a Boston mob, resulting in the death of five colonists. This was a significant incident in the buildup of tensions between Britain and the colonies in the years leading up to the American Revolution.

**Boston Tea Party (1773)** An act of defiance on the part of Boston colonists to protest the British Tea Act of 1773, a new tax on imported tea; 30 to 60 men disguised as Mohawk Indians stormed British tea ships and dumped 90,000 pounds of tea into Boston Harbor.

***Bracero* Program (1942)** Agreement between the governments of Mexico and the United States that granted annual entry to hundreds of thousands of seasonal agricultural workers. Control of the border was generally loosened and hundreds of thousands of other Mexicans were drawn north by growing opportunities in the greatly expanding U.S. economy.

**Bretton Woods agreements (1944)** Multinational agreements that established a system for international trade and monetary values to promote economic recovery following World War II.

***Brown v. Board of Education* of Topeka Kansas** U.S. Supreme Court decision that outlawed racial segregation in public schools.

**Bunker Hill, Battle of** The first significant battle of the American Revolution. It actually took place on Breed's Hill, where colonial forces claimed victory and demonstrated that they could resist larger British forces.

**Bush Doctrine** Foreign policy principles of President George W. Bush, the centerpiece of which was a policy wherein the United States had the right to engage in preemptive war to secure itself against terrorist groups and countries that harbored them.

***Bush v. Gore*** U.S. Supreme Court decision that determined the winner of the 2000 presidential race between Al Gore and George W. Bush.

**Calvinism** A Protestant religion that followed the teachings of theologian John Calvin that was practiced by European and American Puritans.

**Central Powers** Name given during World War II to the alliance of Germany, Austria-Hungary, and Ottoman Turkey.

**Charter of Freedoms and Exemptions (1640)** A Dutch West India Company policy that granted 200 acres to whoever brought five adults to New Netherland and promised prospective colonists religious freedom and local self-governance; these offers attracted English Puritans from Massachusetts to eastern Long Island.

**Chinese Exclusion Act (1882)** Congressional Act that barred the immigration of Chinese laborers. This law all but ended Chinese immigration and remained in effect until 1943.

**Church of England (Anglican Church)** English Christian church established by King Henry VIII after his break from papal authority in 1534.

**Civil Rights Act of 1964** Congressional act that prohibited discrimination in employment or the use of public places on the basis of race, sex, religion, or national origin.

**Code Noir (1685)** Slave code mandated by imperial France governing the rights and treatment of African slaves in their colonial territories from the French West Indies to Louisiana.

**Coercive Acts/Intolerable Acts (1774)** Four British parliamentary decrees enacted in response to unrest and protests in Boston. The acts reorganized the Massachusetts government and placed more authority in the hands of royal appointees. The acts also imposed royal control over local courts and authorized troops to be forcibly housed in private homes and buildings.

**Coinage Act of 1883** Congressional act that made gold the nation's monetary standard and halted the making of silver dollars.

**Cold War** Term given to the political, economic, and military tensions that existed between the United States and its allies and the Soviet Union between 1945 and the dissolution of the Soviet Union in 1989.

**Columbian exchange** The historic movement of people, plants, animals, culture, and pathogens between the Americas and the rest of the world that began during the time of Columbus.

**Common law** Law based on decisions previously made by judges and courts, as opposed to statutory, or written laws and statutes; the common law system was rooted in English legal practices.

**Commons** Lands open to all residents.

**Compromise of 1850** Congressional measures created to resolve a series of regional tensions in the United States. The measures admitted California as a free state, organized the remainder of the New Mexico Territory, banned the slave trade in the District of Columbia, empowered the Treasury to assume Texas's debts from its independence struggle with Mexico, and gave the South a much stronger federal Fugitive Slave Law.

**Congress of Industrial Organizations (CIO)** Umbrella group of labor unions, formed in 1935, to represent semiskilled workers in major industrial sectors. Unions within the Congress accepted black and other minority workers.

**Containment** Name given to the foundation of U.S. foreign policy during the Cold War. George F. Kennan argued that Soviet communism was "impervious to the logic of reason," inherently expansionist, and only controllable through "long-term, patient but firm and vigilant containment."

**Contract with America** A document conceived by Republican Congressman

Newt Gingrich in 1993 that promised to make Congress more accountable, balance the federal budget, reverse the tax increases passed in 1993, and reduce the capital gains tax.

**Conversion test** An exercise developed by Massachusetts Bay Puritans to test prospective church members for membership in their congregation; prospects had to testify to their relationship with God and offer proof that God had saved them.

**Counterculture** In the 1960s and early 1970s, the name given to the subculture of college-age young Americans who developed distinctively liberal beliefs and practices regarding sexuality, race, gender, politics, and culture; these values stood in contrast to those of the dominant culture of their parents.

**Covenant** As practiced by New England Puritans, an agreement with God that required them to translate their faith into actions that obeyed God's will as revealed in the Bible.

**Covenant Chain (1677)** An alliance between the Iroquois and English colonies from New England south to Maryland that joined their forces against the French.

**Coverture** A principle of British and American law wherein a married woman lost her legal identity as an individual and in which her economic resources would be controlled by her husband. This law prevented married women from owning property.

**Creoles** People born in the United States, particularly in Louisiana, who were direct descendants of French and Spanish colonial settlers.

**Crop lien system** A credit system widely used by Southern farmers from the 1860s to the 1920s. This was a way for farmers to get credit before the planting season by borrowing against the value for anticipated harvests.

**Cuban missile crisis** A tense standoff between the United States and Soviet Union in October 1962 when the United States discovered that the Soviets had begun installing nuclear missiles in Cuba. The incident was the most dramatic nuclear standoff of the Cold War.

**Dawes Act (1877)** Congressional act that divided two-thirds of Indian tribal lands to be sold off or confiscated. Many Indians who had lived on reservations became essentially landless.

**Declaration of Independence (1776)** American revolutionary document that declared that the United States was free and independent of the British Empire.

**Defense Advanced Research Projects Agency (DARPA)** U.S. defense agency that created the Internet, originally founded in 1958 to counter Soviet advances in space science.

**Defense of Marriage Act (1996)** Congressional act that decreed that no state would be compelled to recognize a same-sex marriage conducted in another state, nor would the federal government recognize the existence of such a marriage even if it were performed legally in a state.

**Desert Lands Act (1877)** Congressional act, applicable in 11 Western states, that allowed for homesteading on 640-acre parcels of arid land at 25 cents per acre and provided title within three years for a dollar an acre for settled, irrigated land.

**Détente** Term given to the U.S. relaxation of tension with the Soviets during the 1970s.

**Dominion of New England (1686–1689)** A union of English colonies imposed by the English monarchy; it comprised eight contiguous colonies, from New England to New Jersey, under one governor, Edmond Andros, who dissolved representative assemblies, jailed dissidents, and imposed taxes on lands already owned outright.

***Dred Scott v. Sandford* (1857)** U.S. Supreme Court ruling that slaves were not citizens of the United States and were therefore unable to sue in a federal court of law. As a consequence, the federal government had no authority to outlaw slavery in the territories, leaving that choice up to the states.

**Dust Bowl** Locations in the Great Plains, including Kansas, Colorado, Oklahoma, and Texas, afflicted by a severe drought that destroyed farmland during the 1930s, leading to the mass relocation of farm families.

**Dutch West India Company (DWIC)** Dutch trading company whose merchants were granted trade monopolies in parts of the New World, and whose activities included the acquisition of territories in the Hudson River Valley in New York.

**Edict of Nantes (1598)** Proclamation by King Henry IV of France granting rights to Huguenots (French Calvinist Protestants).

**Eighteenth Amendment (1919)** Constitutional amendment that barred the manufacture and sale of alcohol in the United States.

**Emancipation Proclamation (1863)** Proclamation by Abraham Lincoln that freed the slaves living in Confederate states.

**Emergency Banking Relief Act (1933)** Congressional act that followed the market crash of 1929; it reopened banks and restored bank solvency under Treasury Department supervision. The act also removed U.S. currency from the gold standard.

**Emergency Economic Stabilization Act (2008)** Congressional act that authorized the U.S. Treasury to budget up to $700 billion to bail out banks and other financial institutions affected by a crisis in subprime mortgage values.

**Emergency Immigration Act of 1921** Congressional act that created specific immigration limitations based on national origin. The act banned all immigration from Asia, but it allowed free immigration from the Western Hemisphere, as the Southwest depended on Mexican and Central American labor.

**Encomienda** System whereby the Spanish government granted land, villages, and indigenous people to its military leaders who conquered land in the Americas.

**Epic of Deganawidah** Iroquois legend that explained the establishment of the Great League of Peace between Indian nations.

**Equal Rights Amendment (ERA)** Proposed amendment to the U.S. Constitution that banned the denial or abridgment of rights on the basis of gender.

**Espionage Act (1917)** Congressional act passed on the eve of America's entrance into World War I that expanded the definition of treason and defined a variety of acts deemed to comprise espionage. The Act was enacted to fight sabotage, spying, or interference with the war effort.

**Executive Order 9981 (1948)** Order by President Truman that established equality in the armed services on the basis of race, color, religion, and national origin.

**Fair Deal** Domestic programs for social reform proposed by the Truman administration. The 21-point program called for an increase in the minimum wage, comprehensive housing legislation for returning veterans, full employment and expanded unemployment benefits, permanent federal farm subsidies, expanded public works projects, and expanded environmental conservation programs.

**Farmers' Alliance** An umbrella movement of agricultural organizations, founded in Texas in 1876, that encouraged men and women to cooperate in running their households and their farms. The Alliance provided the foundation for what would become the Populist Party.

**Federal Reserve Act (1913)** Congressional act implemented to create a central banking system that significantly strengthened the nation's monetary policy and provided regulation of banks.

**Federalism** A system of government that divides powers between a centralized national administration and state governments.

**Federalist Papers** A series of anonymously authored essays, published in newspapers, supporting ratification of the U.S. Constitution of 1787 by Madison, Hamilton, and Jay.

**Feitoria** Portuguese name for a fortified trading post, early examples of which were first established in Africa in the 15th century during the early years of the Atlantic slave trade.

**Fifteenth Amendment (1870)** Constitutional amendment that prohibited the denial of voting rights on the basis of race.

**Fireside Chats** Weekly radio addresses by President Franklin Roosevelt in which he explained his proposals, policies, and actions to the American people.

**First Continental Congress** Representatives of the colonies who met in Philadelphia for the first time in 1774 to articulate their positions and form policies against grievous British laws and regulations. The group charged committees in each colony to vigorously enforce boycotts; endorsed a declaration of rights and grievances on October 14, 1774; and then adjourned, hoping that the King would change the course of imperial policy.

**First hundred days** President Franklin Roosevelt's first days in office, during which he prevailed on Congress to pass 14 major pieces of legislation including bills to raise agricultural prices, put the unemployed to work, regulate the stock market, reform banking practices, and assist home owners and farmers in paying mortgages.

**Fourteenth Amendment (1868)** Constitutional amendment that guaranteed national citizenship and equality to former slaves, detailed changes related to the former Confederate states, but offered no specific protection of freed people's voting rights.

**Franciscans** A Roman Catholic religious order, active in establishing Spanish missions in Southwestern North America in the 18th and 19th centuries.

**Fugitive Slave Act (1850)** Congressional act that nationalized the process of slave capture and return by requiring federal judges to appoint "commissioners" to hear cases of accused fugitives and by requiring the active complicity of state officers.

**Fur trade** The trading of furs, primarily through the St. Lawrence River region, that served as the primary gateway for European goods into North America into the 1600s.

**Gag rule** Rule adopted by Congress in 1836 to block the discussion of slavery at the national as well as the state level. The rule was repealed in 1844.

**Gang system** One of two general types of division of labor of plantation slaves, the other being the task system. The gang system involved the work of coordinated groups, supervised by a driver, to maintain an even level of productivity during the work day.

**General Allotment Act (1887)** Congressional act that divided Indian reservation land into smaller parcels of property.

**Gentlemen's Agreement (1907)** Agreement reached by President Theodore Roosevelt and the Japanese government that stated that the United States would no longer exclude Japanese immigrants if the Japanese promised to voluntarily limit the number of its immigrants to the United States, primarily adult male laborers.

**Glass-Steagall Banking Act (1933)** Congressional act that established strict guidelines for banking operations and expanded the power of the Federal Reserve System. The act also founded the Federal Deposit Insurance Corporation. Some regulations associated with the original act were repealed in 1999, leading to mismanagement and scandals in the banking and finance industries, and the recession beginning around 2009.

**Globalization** A term that was popularized in the 1990s to refer to the knitting together of the world's economies through new information technology and the end of the artificial political barrier of the Cold War.

**Glorious Revolution (1688)** Uprising of the English Parliament against King James II that transformed the English system of government from an absolute monarchy to a constitutional monarchy and the rule of Parliament.

**Grand Settlement of 1701** A pair of treaties between the Iroquois and the French that stabilized relations between the two in the Great Lakes and Northeast parts of North America.

**Grandfather clause** Allowance created by southern state legislatures in the 1890s permitting any person who had voted before 1867, or had a father or grandfather who had voted, to be exempt from the literacy test or other restrictions. The unspoken aim of this law was to increase the number of eligible white male voters.

**Great Depression** America's worst economic downturn to date. Beginning at the end of 1929 and lasting for 10 years; the catastrophe spread to every corner of the country, wrecking lives and leaving people homeless, hungry, and desperate for work.

**Great Migration** The large scale movement of African Americans from the South to the North during and after World War I, where jobs were more plentiful.

**Great Recession** An international economic collapse of 2008, where credit markets around the world froze and banks stopped lending to one another. Businesses dependent on lending began to downsize and fail. The meltdown affected financial institutions and governments throughout the world.

**Great Society** President Lyndon Johnson's name for a series of social and economic reforms, begun in 1965, to end racial discrimination, expand educational opportunities, end hunger and poverty, and make health care available for all.

**Gulf of Tonkin Resolution** Congressional authorization requested by President Lyndon Johnson in 1964 that gave him the power to escalate military action in Vietnam without additional congressional approval.

**Half-freedom** Conditional freedom given to former African slaves and residents of New Amsterdam by the Dutch West India Company in 1644, allowing them to work for themselves and live where they wished, as long as they paid the DWIC and bound themselves and their children to serve the company.

**Half-way covenant** A plan by New England Puritans, whose church was losing members by the 1660s, to offer partial church membership to the children of parents who were not church members, thus bypassing established conversion practices.

**Harlem Renaissance** An African American cultural and arts movement of the 1920s centered in the Harlem neighborhood of New York City.

**Harpers Ferry Raid (1859)** Failed raid led by abolitionist John Brown on the U.S. arsenal in Harper's Ferry, Virginia. Brown's capture and execution led to greater regional tensions leading up to the Civil War.

**Helsinki Accords** A set of principles that accepted the post-1945 division of Europe into East–West spheres. The accords recognized the right of all Europeans to seek peaceful change, and the Soviets agreed in a general way to respect human rights in their sphere.

**Homestead Act (1862)** Congressional act that allowed families to claim 160 acres of land if they improved it over five years of residence. The act opened the Western United States to settlement.

**House of Burgesses** The first representative government assembly and ruling body established in the English settlements in America; founded by the Virginia Company in 1619, this assembly replaced martial law with English common law, setting in motion the development of the county court system.

**House Committee on Un-American Activities** Congressional committee formed in 1938 to search for communists and conspiracies within the United States including penetration into the labor movement and federal agencies. Although discredited during the 1950s for its investigations of entertainment and media figures, the committee was not abandoned until 1975.

**Huguenots** Name given to the French followers of Calvinism, a Protestant religion founded by theologian John Calvin.

**Huron Confederacy** A union of several tribes of Huron people, formed to established peaceful relations and trade.

**Immigration Restriction League** An anti-immigration organization founded in Boston in 1894 that promoted legislation to restrict the immigration of Southern and Eastern Europeans.

**Indentured servitude** An arrangement offered by various English enterprises to attract English people to the colonies, exchanging free passage by ship to America for up to seven years labor.

**Indian Removal Act (1830)** Federal law that nullified 50 years' worth of treaties between the United States and many tribes. The law resulted in the relocation of more than 45,000 Indians living east of the Mississippi to points further west, opening up lands for white settlers. The law committed the federal government to creating an Indian Territory west of the Mississippi.

**Indian Reorganization Act (1934)** Congressional act that slowed the division of reservation land into small plots, encouraged tribal self-government, and established Indian-run corporations to control communal land and resources.

**Industrious revolution** Preindustrialization period associated with 18th century British North America during which there was a diversification of labor, development of a market-oriented society, and a labor shift from services to marketable goods.

**iinitiative, referendum, recall** First proposed by Populists in the 1890s, the initiative and referendum, adopted originally in Oregon, made it possible for voters to place legislation directly before the electorate for a vote in general elections; the referendum allowed voters to repeal state legislation with which they disagreed; the recall gave voters the power to remove any public official who did not, in their view, act for the public good.

**Insular Cases (1901–1904)** A series of U.S. Supreme Court cases that would be applied to all of the new territories added to the United States in which it was ruled that American constitutional rights and liberties did not extend to all lands under U.S. control.

**Interstate and Defense Highways Act (1956)** The largest public works program in American history, approved by President Dwight Eisenhower, that facilitated the growth of suburban America and the businesses and industries that sustained them.

**Iroquois League** Also known as the Great League of Peace. A confederation formed c. 1400 and originally composed of five Iroquoian-speaking peoples of today's Upstate New York: the Seneca, Cayuga, Onondaga, Oneida, and Mohawk.

**Jamestown** The first permanent English settlement in America, founded in 1607 and located in what is today coastal Virginia.

**Jay's Treaty (1794)** Treaty with Britain granting the United States trade rights on the Mississippi, in the British East Indies, and removing remaining British forts on American territory.

**Jesuits (Society of Jesus)** A Catholic male religious order, founded in Spain in 1534, that was active in winning converts overseas.

**Jim Crow laws** State and local laws that originated in the South in the mid 1880s and legally separated people according to race. These laws spread to many public facilities and established a policy of racial segregation that favored white citizens.

**Johnson–O'Malley Act (1934)** Congressional act that provided federal aid to improve health care and education to Indian tribes.

**joint-stock company** An early form of shareholding company that was used by the British to finance development of the colonies.

**kachinas** In Pueblo culture, ancestral beings believed to bring rain and communal harmony.

**Kansas-Nebraska Act (1854)** Congressional act that repealed the Missouri Compromise. The bill's new policy of "popular sovereignty," intended to allow settlers in a territory to decide the status of slavery, initiated a strenuous debate about the future of slavery in the Western territories.

**Keating–Owen Child Labor Law (1916)** Law that banned interstate commerce in goods produced by child labor.

**Kellogg–Briand Pact (1928)** Also known as the "Pact of Paris," an agreement signed by 62 nations that agreed not to use war as an instrument of national policy. The pact was initiated by the United States and France.

**Kiva** An underground chamber used by Pueblo Indians for religious ceremonies.

**Knights of Labor** The first national labor union, founded in Baltimore, in 1869. The Knights aimed to organize all laboring people into one large, national union. The union offered membership regardless of race, gender, or national origin, excluding only "social parasites" such as lawyers, bankers, and liquor salesmen. African Americans and Mexican Americans belonged to the Knights and the organization's emphasis on equal rights for all workers and equal pay for equal work attracted many women as well.

**Know-Nothing Party** Antiforeign, anti-Catholic political organization established in 1854 and consisting of a network of secret fraternal associations, largely a nativist reaction against large-scale European immigration. The organization's name stemmed from its secrecy; if asked about the organization, members would essentially deny any knowledge of it, saying that they "knew nothing."

**Ku Klux Klan** An organization associated with the bitterest and most violent opponents of Reconstruction and black freedom. Formed in Pulaski, Tennessee, in late 1865, Klan members devoted themselves to denying African Americans any legitimate role in the public sphere, stressing the superiority of white, Protestant, Anglo-Saxon citizens.

**Laissez-faire economics** An economic doctrine that insisted that government should not interfere with businesses or the market. The term is from the French meaning, "leave it alone."

***Lawrence v. Texas* (2003)** U.S. Supreme Court decision that overturned most state antisodomy laws used to criminalize homosexual behavior.

**League of Nations** Organization proposed by President Woodrow Wilson in 1918, following World War I, the purpose of which was to guarantee the sovereignty of individual nations, large and small, and provide a forum for mediating disputes.

**Limited Test Ban Treaty (1963)** An agreement between the United States and the Soviet Union that ended above-ground atomic weapon testing but permitted continued testing underground.

**Linen Act of 1705** British parliamentary act that encouraged the export of Irish linen to North America. In turn, the act increased the demand in Northern Ireland for colonial flaxseed, the source of linen.

**Literacy Act (1917)** Clause of the U.S. Immigration Act of 1917 that barred the entry of any persons unable to read in their own language on the grounds that this lack demonstrated their ignorance.

***Lochner v. New York* (1905)** U.S. Supreme Court decision that struck down a New York Law limiting the hours that male bakers could work because, in the court's opinion, the state had no right to regulate their hours.

**Lowell Mill Girls** Female workers associated with the textile mills in Lowell, Massachusetts. The mills had a large labor force of young women, who ranged between the ages of 15 and 35 and worked in one of the first large-scale, steam-powered industries in the United States.

**Ludlow Massacre (1914)** An attack by local deputies and state militia on striking United Mine Workers in Ludlow, Colorado. At the request of mine owners, the militia attacked a camp of striking miners who had been evicted from company-owned housing. Drenching the miner's tents with kerosene and setting them on fire, they shot up the encampment with machine guns and killed 14 people, included 11 children. Soon labeled the Ludlow Massacre, the gruesome deaths of the victims sparked violent retaliation by the miners.

***Lusitania*** British passenger liner torpedoed by a German submarine in 1915 while sailing between New York and England. The attack killed 1,200 of the 2,000 passengers and crew, including 128 Americans.

**lynching** The murder of African American individuals by a mob, often by hanging, shooting, or burning. Lynchings were most prevalent in the southern United States between the 1880s and 1960s.

***Maine* (battleship)** A U.S. battleship that exploded on February 15, 1898, killing 260 American sailors. Americans blamed Spain for the explosion, drawing the United States closer to war with Spain, which was declared two months later.

**Malintzín** A native Nahua woman from the Gulf Coast of Mexico who figured importantly in the Spanish conquest of Mexico by acting as the translator and advisor to Hernán Cortés, leader of a Spanish expedition.

**Manhattan Project** Secret U.S. scientific and military program during World War II dedicated to the development of an atomic bomb. The project was led by J. Robert Oppenheimer and employed 150,000 people at a top secret location in New Mexico.

**Mann Act (1910)** Congressional act that outlawed the transport of women across state lines for "immoral purposes."

**Manumission** The freeing of slaves by their owners.

***Marbury v. Madison* (1803)** U.S. Supreme Court decision that firmly established the principle of "judicial review," the right of the U.S. Supreme Court to rule on the constitutionality of legislation and executive actions.

**March on Washington for Jobs and Freedom** Historic civil rights march on August 28, 1963, during which over 200,000 black and white demonstrators marched from the Washington Monument to the Lincoln Memorial where Martin Luther King, Jr., delivered his "I Have a Dream" speech.

**Marshall Plan (European Recovery Plan) (1948)** A massive foreign aid program approved following World War II, it called for aid packages to help Western Europe, including West Germany, and Japan rapidly rebuild their devastated economies, restore industries and trade, and rejoin the free world.

**Massachusetts Bay Company** A business enterprise founded by English Puritans and merchants in 1629 that founded the Massachusetts Bay Colony, resulting in a swell of English emigration to the colonies.

**Matrilineal** A society in which social identity is based on kinship and descendency from the mother.

**McCarran International Security Act (1950)** Congressional act requiring the registration of American Communist Party members; the act reinforced perceptions of immigrants as a source of radicalism during the Cold War and set the tone for a contentious debate about immigration in the coming decade.

**McCarthyism** A national communist witch hunt in post-World War II America led by Senator Joseph McCarthy.

**McKinley Tariff (1890)** Congressional act that ended the practice of allowing Hawaiian sugar to enter the United States duty free, ending Hawaii's favored status and threatening its sugar industry.

**McNary–Haughen Acts (1927–1928)** Congressional acts that required the government to support crop prices by buying basic farm commodities.

**Meat Inspection Act (1906)** Congressional act that required federal inspectors from the U.S. Department of Agriculture to inspect livestock in slaughterhouses and to guarantee sanitary standards.

**Medicaid** A health care plan that originated with President Lyndon Johnson's Great Society program in which the federal government provided states matching grants to pay for medical costs of poor people of all ages.

**Medicare** A health plan that originated with President Lyndon Johnson's

Great Society programs that provided universal hospital insurance for Americans over 65.

**Medicare Modernization Act (2003)** Congressional act that subsidized the cost of some, but not all, medication taken by seniors.

**Mercantilism** An economic philosophy of English and French governments founded on the belief that control of foreign trade—including the acquisition of raw materials from their colonies—was key to securing the kingdom that ruled them.

**Methodists** A Protestant evangelical sect, rooted in the 18th century Anglican revival movement, that accepted slaves and freed blacks and opposed government intervention in religion.

**Minute men** In Revolutionary War times, local militias in Massachusetts and Connecticut that went on alert in response to pending British military action.

***Miranda v. Arizona*** U.S. Supreme Court decision that expanded the Fifth Amendment's prohibition on self-incrimination.

**Mission to the slaves** The responsibility of evangelical slaveholders to provide religious teaching and ministering to their slaves.

**Mississippi Bubble** Name given the financial collapse in 1720 of the Company of the Indies, an investment scheme intended to finance the French colonization of Louisiana.

**Mississippian societies** Name given to Indian societies of the Mississippi Valley, formed around 700 CE and peaking between 1100 and 1300.

**Model Cities Program** Federal urban aid program created by President Lyndon Johnson to encourage physical and economic revitalization of the nation's poorest urban areas.

**Modernists** Religious leaders, influenced by the Social Gospel movement of the late 19th century, as well as Darwin's theory of evolution and archaeological discoveries, who believed Christianity should respond positively to new knowledge and social conditions.

**Monetarists** Proponents of a conservative economic movement that favored a change to tax and spending policies. Led by Milton Friedman, these economists insisted that prosperity and freedom required reduced government spending along with more stringent control of the money supply.

**Monopoly** A business enterprise that is the only supplier of a particular service or commodity.

**Monroe Doctrine (1823)** Policy introduced by President James Monroe who declared that the United States shared common interest with other states in the Western Hemisphere and that the political system in Europe was "essentially different" from that of the democratic republics in North and South America.

**Monroe–Pinckney Treaty (1806)** An agreement that established new trade relations between Great Britain and the United States.

**Montgomery Improvement Association** An organization of black clergy and community leaders, formed in 1955, and led by Martin Luther King, Jr., who refined a philosophy of nonviolent protest for boycotters.

**Moral Majority** A political lobbying group designed to mobilize evangelical Christian voters and "get them saved, baptized and registered" to vote.

**Morant Bay Rebellion (1865)** A revolt of black farm workers in Jamaica. It consumed the eastern half of the island and left hundreds of black laborers dead and hundreds more beaten by state militia forces.

**Moravians (United Brethren)** A Protestant religious sect, revived in Germany in 1727 and brought to Georgia in 1735, that sought to create closed, economically autonomous, sex-segregated communities in which Christian liturgical rituals and piety infused daily life.

**Mormons** A Protestant religious sect, founded by Joseph Smith, who preached a conservative theology of patriarchal authority.

**Mourning wars** Skirmishes associated with Eastern North American Indians to avenge the death of relatives by capturing or killing members of neighboring tribes.

**Muckraking** An early form of investigative journalism in America. Believing that exposing facts could rouse the American public to demand change, "muckraking" helped bring about major reforms in the late 19th and early 20th centuries.

**Mudsill theory** A sociological theory first proposed by South Carolina Senator James Henry Hammond in 1858 who stated that a division of upper and lower classes was the natural order of society, a view that was interpreted by many as a thinly veiled excuse for exploiting slavery.

**Mujahideen** Islamic-inspired Afghan and foreign guerrillas who fought the occupying Soviets in Afghanistan during the 1980s. They counted among their ranks Saudi fundamentalist Osama Bin Laden.

**Mulatto** Mixed race people in the United States.

***Muller v. Oregon* (1908)** U.S. Supreme Court decision that upheld an Oregon law limiting the work day of female laundry workers to 10 hours per day.

**My Lai massacre (1968)** Massacre by American troops of 504 unarmed Vietnamese villagers during the Vietnam War.

**National American Woman Suffrage Association** Organization of women founded in 1890 whose leaders sought a constitutional amendment to give women the right to vote.

**National Association for the Advancement of Colored People (NAACP)** Civil Rights organization founded in 1910 that was innovative in establishing legal action as a powerful basis in the fight for African American rights.

**National Municipal League** A national organization, founded in 1894, made up progressives from both parties committed to reforming government in U.S. cities.

**National Organization for Women** Founded in 1966, this organization advocated an end to laws that discriminated against women, opportunity to work at any job, and equal pay for equal work.

**National Origins Act (1924)** Congressional act that defined strict quotas regulating the flow and character of U.S. immigration.

**National Parks Act (1916)** Congressional act that created the National Park Service and aimed, in part, to preserve national park lands and "leave them unimpaired for the enjoyment of future generations."

**National Recovery Administration (NRA)** World War I programs that brought together industry leaders and labor groups to boost production. The NRA wrote "production codes" for each industry that encouraged cooperation among competing businesses to set stable prices and wages.

**National Security Act (1947)** This act consolidated the U.S. military command; a representative from each military branch would advise a newly created Secretary of Defense and the president through the Joint Chiefs of Staff Office.

**Nativism** Name given to a strong anti-immigration, anti-Catholic activist movement that flourished in America from the 1830s to the 1850s. The term "nativists" was giving to those who strongly opposed the influx of immigrants into American society.

**Navigation Act of 1696** One of a series of English regulations and taxes on colonial trade dating from 1650 to 1775.

**Neo-cons** "Neo-conservatives," a small but influential group of conservative Democrats who bolstered Republican ranks during the presidency of George W. Bush.

**New Deal** Name collectively given to President Franklin Roosevelt's programs to fight the Great Depression, first articulated during his 1932 presidential campaign. He pledged to use federal power to ensure a more equitable distribution of income and rebuild the economy from the bottom up.

**New Freedom** Phrase used by President Woodrow Wilson who attacked all "bigness," whether in government or business, and advocated small business and fair competition enforced by only minimal government interference.

**New Frontier** Name given to President John F. Kennedy's phrase for a collection of programs to expand economic and social opportunities in the United States.

**New Left** Counterculture protest movement of the 1960s whose young activists intentionally distanced themselves from the ideological infighting, Marxist leanings, and labor organizing of the Old Left of the 1930s and 1940s.

**New Look** President Dwight Eisenhower's military reorganization of 1954 that established the central philosophy of the doctrine of "massive retaliation" as more economically feasible than containment alone.

**New Nationalism** Name given to President Theodore Roosevelt's platform in 1912 that advocated expansive government activism and regulation for the public interest.

**New World Order** George H. W. Bush proclaimed the dawn of a New World Order in 1989, in which the United States, the world's preeminent superpower, would lead multinational coalitions to enforce its standards of international behavior.

**Nineteenth Amendment (1920)** Constitutional amendment granting women the right to vote.

**No Child Left Behind Act (NCLB)** Program proposed by President George W. Bush in 2001 to improve educational outcomes for poor and minority children. It renewed federal funding for several existing school programs and provided some additional money for reading and math instruction. In return, all states had to implement "standards based educational reform," a term that in practice meant standardized testing of students in reading and math.

**Non-Intercourse Act (1809)** Congressional act that reopened trade with countries other than Britain and France.

**North American Free Trade Agreement (NAFTA)** Trade agreement approved by Democrats and Republicans in 1993 during the administration of President Bill Clinton. This agreement lifted barriers to trade between the United States, Mexico, and Canada, and nearly all conventional economists believed that it would lift living standards in these countries.

**Olive Branch Petition (1775)** Petition sent by the Continental Congress to King George III of England seeking his intervention to avoid the Revolutionary War.

**Open Door Policy** Principles drafted in 1899 by Secretary of State John Hay requesting that European powers put an end to the further partitioning of China and open up areas of China claimed by each power to allow them to compete fairly for Chinese trade. These policies asked for unhindered access to markets where they could compete successfully against economic rivals.

**Orders in Council (1807)** British policies during the Napoleonic wars that required U.S. ships to stop in British ports for licensing and inspection before they could trade with France or French colonies.

**Organization of Petroleum Exporting Countries** The oil cartel formed in 1960 that supported Egypt and Syria.

**PAC**—see Political Action Committee

**Panama Canal** Opened in 1914, the canal, linking the Atlantic and Pacific Oceans, enhanced access to U.S. colonies in the Pacific as well as trade with Asia, but poisoned U.S. relations with Latin American countries because of the questionable way that the United States gained rights to build the canal.

**Parliament** Legislative body of the British government.

**Paternalism** In pre-Civil War America, the belief by white slave owners that it was their duty to protect and care for members of Southern society they viewed as inferior to them, including slaves and their families but also white women.

**Peace Policy** Organized by General Ely Samuel Parker, the Indian commissioners and leaders of various Christian denominations provided Indians with food and clothing in exchange for promises to abandon cultural traditions and to assimilate into American society.

**Pendleton Civil Service Act (1883)** Congressional act that established the modern Civil Service and initiated an examination for a classified list of federal jobs, including most government departments, custom house jobs, and post office positions.

**Pentagon Papers** Popular name given to a collection of classified government documents that were illegally made public in 1971. The documents outlined decision making by the U.S. Defense Department during the period from World War II to the Vietnam War.

**People's (Populist) Party** A third party, made up largely of rural people frustrated with the unresponsiveness of the Republican and Democratic parties to their pressing needs. The People's Party ran candidates for president in 1892 and 1896 on a platform demanding major reforms, including the government ownership of railroads, a graduated income tax, and the free coinage of silver.

**Pietism** A Protestant religious movement that linked North America, Britain, the Netherlands, and central Europe. Pietists promoted the personal piety of believers and the evangelization of all, including American Indians and enslaved Africans.

**Pinckney's Treaty (1795)** A treaty with Spain that fully opened Mississippi River trade to the United States, provided tax-free markets in New Orleans, settled Florida border issues, and guaranteed Spanish help against southwest Indians who moved to block U.S. settlers from expanding west.

**Plantation Act of 1740** British parliamentary act that allowed non-Catholic aliens who resided for at least seven years in British North America, received communion in a Protestant church, swore allegiance to George II, and paid two shillings, to become citizens.

**Platt Amendment (1901)** Amendment to the new Cuban constitution that gave the United States broad authority to intervene to preserve Cuban independence and required Cuba to sell or lease land for U.S. naval stations and coaling bases.

***Plessy v. Ferguson* (1896)** U.S. Supreme Court decision that upheld the legality of Jim Crow laws. This led to the establishment of the NAACP and vigorous legal battles to overturn such laws.

**Political Action Committees (PACs)** A private group dedicated to the election of a given political candidate or to influence a policy decision in government.

**Polygamy** A marriage custom of having more than one partner at the same time, such as a man with more than one wife.

**Popular sovereignty** A policy established in the mid-19th century that permitted settlers in newly established Western territories to decide on the policy of slavery for themselves.

***Prigg v. Pennsylvania* (1842)** U.S. Supreme Court decision that established federal protection to Southerners seeking to reclaim fugitive slaves who escaped to the North.

**Privateer** A government contracted but privately owned warship used to attack foreign ships and disrupt trade.

**Proclamation of 1763** An order issued by King George III of England that prohibited settlements west of the Appalachians.

**Protestantism** A Christian reform movement that arose in Europe during the 1500s and denied the authority of the Catholic Church.

**Pullman Strike** Led by Eugene V. Debs and the American Railway Union in 1894 in response to massive wage cuts at the Pullman Palace Car Company, the strike and boycott of trains pulling Pullman cars froze rail service in the Midwest and slowed it elsewhere until federal troops helped crush the strike.

**Pure Food and Drug Act (1906)** Congressional act that outlawed adulterated or mislabeled food and drugs and gave the federal government the right to seize illegal products and fine and jail those who manufactured and sold them.

**Puritans** Europeans who followed the Christian teachings of theologian John Calvin, defied the Catholic Church, and sought to place the governance of church affairs in the hands of local officials, ministers, and elders.

**Quitrent** A land tax or rent imposed on colonists by their European governing body.

**Reconquista** Expansion of western European Christian nations during the 1400s into Muslim settlements on the Iberian peninsula.

**Reconstruction Finance Corporation (1932)** Federal program of President Herbert Hoover to loan money to struggling banks, railroads, manufacturers, and mortgage companies during the Great Depression.

**Redemptioners** In the 18th century, indentured servants who paid for their passage across the Atlantic by selling their services when they landed.

**Rerum novarum** A papal encyclical from Pope Leo XIII, issued in 1891, condemning the exploitation of laborers and supporting state intervention to promote social justice.

**Revivalists** Leaders and advocates of various evangelical Protestant campaigns of the First Great Awakening (18th century). Revivalists sought to rekindle widespread religious enthusiasm in the American colonies.

***Roe v. Wade*** U.S. Supreme Court decision affirming a woman's right to terminate a pregnancy.

**Roosevelt Corollary** Articulated by President Theodore Roosevelt in 1904, this corollary to the Monroe Doctrine declared that the United States had the right to intervene in the affairs of Latin American nations to ensure order.

**Rough Riders** Colonel Theodore Roosevelt and his First Volunteer Cavalry

Regiment, known as "The Rough Riders," became national heroes for their daring exploits during the Spanish-American War (1898).

**Royal Orders for New Discoveries (1573)** Decree by King Philip II of Spain that missionaries should play the principal role in exploring, pacifying, and colonizing new territories and mandated that baptized Indians should live on missions, learn to speak Spanish, keep livestock, cultivate European crops, and use European tools to master European crafts.

**Russo-Japanese War** Rival imperial claims in Asia sparked this war between Russia and Japan in 1904. President Theodore Roosevelt brokered a peace treaty between the two countries in 1905, earning him the Nobel Peace Prize.

**Saint Augustine, Florida** First Spanish settlement in America, founded in 1565.

**Salutary neglect** Name given to the practice of colonists to defy or ignore British laws that they found onerous, often with the complicity of those charged to enforce them.

**Second Bill of Rights** List of "economic bill of rights," proposed by President Franklin D. Roosevelt in 1944, that guaranteed every citizen a job, a living wage, decent housing, adequate medical care, educational opportunity, and protection against unemployment in postwar America.

**Second Great Awakening** Religious revivalist movement of the early 19th century that echoed the Great Awakening of the 1730s. The movement linked evangelical Christians on both sides of the Atlantic to exchange ideas and strategies that inspired a broad set of social, cultural, and intellectual changes.

**Securities Act of 1933** Congressional act that required companies selling stock to the public to register with a federal agency and provide accurate information on what was being sold.

**Securities Exchange Act of 1934** Congressional act that created the Securities Exchange Commission to regulate stock markets and activities by brokers.

**Sedition Act (1918)** Amendments to the Espionage Act of 1917 that added a variety of offenses to the list of prohibited acts, including the use of "disloyal, profane, scurrilous, or abusive language about the form of government of the United States, or the Constitution of the United States."

**Separation of powers** Political concept as articulated by French Enlightenment philosopher the Baron de Montesquieu that each state establish a balance between executive, legislative, and judicial powers.

**Seven Years' War (1756–1763)** Also known as the French and Indian War, a conflict between Britain and France and their respective Indian allies in colonial America. This was largely a conflict between empires for territorial and economic control of the colonies and related trade routes.

**Seventeenth Amendment** Ratified in 1913, the Seventeenth Amendment to the U.S. Constitution mandated the direct election of U.S. senators.

**Sharecroppers** Farmers who rented land or farmed on shares, splitting the proceeds from the yearly crop with the landlord.

**Shays' Rebellion (1797)** An attempt by indebted Massachusetts farmers, led by Daniel Shays, to prevent the state government from seizing their property.

**Sherman Antitrust Act (1890)** Congressional act aimed at dismantling "combination in the form of trust" that restrained trade. It was the first American law to restrict business monopolies.

**Sixteenth Amendment (1913)** Constitutional amendment that authorized a federal income tax on both personal and corporate income.

**Smoot-Hawley Tariff** Passed in 1930 at the onset of the Great Depression, the tariff made it especially difficult for international manufacturers to sell their products in the United States, resulting in retaliatory tariffs that worsened the international economy.

**Social Darwinism** A theory, popularized by Herbert Spencer, which purported that Charles Darwin's theory of evolution could be applied to human society as well. This belief that society evolved and improved through survival of the fittest was supported by many business leaders of the 19th century as a rationalization for exploiting the working class.

**Social Gospel** A broad, multidimensional and international movement among liberal Protestant theologians in the late 19th and early 20th centuries that insisted that Christian principles needed to be applied to social problems.

**Social Security Act (1935)** Congressional act that established a government administered system funded primarily by contributions—payroll taxes—from workers and employers, not general tax revenues.

**Society for Promoting Christian Knowledge (SPCK)** English organization formed in 1699 to further the mission of Anglican reformers by publishing and disseminating Bibles and religious tracts to the colonies.

**Society for the Propagation of the Gospel in Foreign Parts (SPG)** Anglican reform organization founded in 1701 for the purpose of sending missionaries to North America and the West Indies.

**Society of Friends ("Quakers")** A Christian religious sect that broke from the Church of England and established itself in America during the 17th century.

**Sons of Liberty** Stamp Act protestors who spread awareness of colonial protests between colonies.

**Stagflation** A slowly growing economy with high rates of unemployment and inflation.

**Stamp Act (1765)** British parliamentary act that required many forms of printed materials and products be affixed with revenue stamps, or taxes, to the British.

**Tariff** A tax on imported goods.

**Task system** One of two general types of division of labor of plantation slaves, the other being the gang system. The task system assigned individuals with specific tasks. Rather than being part of a group that worked continuously to the day's end, the task system allowed individuals to end their work day when their task was done and thus granted them more autonomy.

**Teapot Dome Scandal** In 1924, investigations revealed that Secretary of the Interior Albert Fall, a member of President Harding's cabinet, took bribes in return for lucrative leases to drill for oil on government-owned land.

**Tennessee Valley Authority** Federal agency created in 1933 to construct a network of dams and hydroelectric projects to control floods, generate power, and promote growth in a chronically poor area of the South.

**Thirteenth Amendment (1865)** Constitutional amendment that outlawed slavery in the United States.

**Townshend Acts (1767)** British parliamentary acts that taxed commons goods in the colonies such as tea and other commodities. The acts represented Britain's resolve to control and regulate the colonies.

**Trail of Tears** Cherokee name for the United States' forced removal of their people from the Southeast to other lands. In early 1838, few Cherokee had prepared for the trip; contaminated water, inadequate food, and disease killed many of those restricted in stockades, and many more perished on the 800-mile journey west.

**Transcontinental Railroad** Completed in 1869, the first continuous train line connecting the Midwest to the West coast of America. It ran between Omaha, Nebraska, to Sacramento, California, and reduced travel time across the nation from weeks to days.

**Transportation Act (1718)** British parliamentary act that mandated the exile of convicted criminals to North America, mostly those who had committed property crimes such as theft.

**Treaty of Paris (1763)** The treaty ending the Seven Years' War. The terms of the treaty transformed eastern North America's political geography. France surrendered North America, swapping Canada for the return of Guadeloupe. France ceded Louisiana to Spain, and Spain traded Florida to the British to regain control of Havana. The British Empire claimed almost all of North America east of the Mississippi.

**Treaty of Tordesillas (1494)** Treaty signed by Spain and Portugal that divided newly discovered lands between them, specifically those in Africa (to Portugal) and those associated with Columbus (to Spain).

**Treaty of Versailles** The treaty that ended World War I and created independent Poland, Czechoslovakia, Yugoslavia, Hungary, Finland, and the Baltic states of Latvia, Lithuania, and Estonia.

**Triangle fire** In March 1911, a raging fire swept through the Triangle Waist Company in New York City, killing 146 workers, mostly young women, leading to a series of workplace reforms.

**U.S. Colored Troops** Black troops consisting of freed black men and former slaves, enlisted for the Union Army after the Emancipation Proclamation of January 1, 1863.

**United Colonies of New England (1643)** Union of the Massachusetts Bay, Plymouth, Connecticut, and New Haven colonies to bolster their mutual defenses and negotiations with Indians.

**United Fruit Company** A Boston-based company originally established for importing bananas to the United States from Latin America, it was known as "The Octopus" for its involvement and influence in the affairs of Honduras and Costa Rica.

**United Nations Organization** An organization open to all nations, established in 1945, for the purpose of maintaining world peace. It is headquartered in New York.

**Universal Negro Improvement Association** Civil rights organization led by black Nationalist leader Marcus Garvey; the association was active from 1916 to 1923.

**USA Patriot Act (2001)** Congressional act that expanded the Justice Department's powers to conduct surveillance on terrorist suspects at and home and abroad.

**Vice-admiralty courts** Colonial courts established by the English Board of Trade to enforce the Navigation Act of 1696.

**Virginia Company of London** English joint-stock company established in 1606 by a royal charter that gave it exclusive rights to colonize from New England south to Virginia.

**Voting Rights Act (1965)** Congressional act that outlawed literacy tests to vote and gave the Justice Department the power directly to register voters in districts where discrimination existed.

**Watergate** Washington office building in which White House operatives committed a series of illegal surveillance acts against political rivals from 1971 to 1973, resulting in a scandal that forced President Richard Nixon to resign in August 1974.

**Whig Party** American political party formed in 1834 that supported government investments in infrastructure to stimulate business, and, in some parts of the North, endorsed moderate antislavery politics.

**Whiskey Rebellion (1794)** Violent uprising in western Pennsylvania by farmers who refused to pay a federal tax on liquor.

***Williams v. Mississippi*** The U.S. Supreme Court ruled in 1898 that Mississippi's voting laws, put into effect in 1890 to disfranchise black voters, did not discriminate on the basis of race.

**Women's Christian Temperance Union (WCTU)** Formed in 1874, the nation's largest female reform organization of the 19th century, specifically dedicated to the banning of intoxicating beverages.

**Yellow journalism** Name given to sensationalist newspaper journalism of the late 19th century. This type of journalism provoked widespread public support for the Cuban rebels.

# Credits

## MAP, FIGURE, AND TABLE SOURCES

America in the World (Population) Source(s): United States Population Division; United Nations, Department of Economic and Social Affairs, Population Division (2011). *World Population Prospects: The 2010 Revision*; Massimo Livi Bacci, *A Concise History of World Population* (Wiley-Blackwell, 2001).

### Chapter 1

Map 1.1 Source(s): Helen Hornbeck Tanner, ed., *The Settling of North America: The Atlas of the Great Migrations into North America from the Ice Age to the Present* (New York: MacMillan, 1995), 29; Mark C. Carnes, ed., *Historical Atlas of the United States* (New York: Routledge, 2003), 20–21.

Map 1.2 Source(s): Michael Coe et al., *Atlas of Ancient North America* (New York: Facts on File, 1986), 44–45.

Map 1.3 Source(s): Mark Kishlansky et al., *Societies and Culture in World History* (New York: Harper Collins, 1995), 414; *The Oxford Atlas of Exploration*, 2nd edition (New York: Oxford University Press, 2008), 34; Patrick K. O'Brien, gen. ed., *The Oxford Atlas of World History*, concise ed. (New York: Oxford University Press, 2002), 116–17.

Map 1.4 Source(s): D. W. Meinig, *The Shaping of America: A Geographic Perspective on 500 Years of History: Volume 1: Atlantic America, 1492–1800* (New Haven and London: Yale University Press, 1986), 5; Alfred W. Crosby, *Ecological Imperialism: The Biological Expansion of Europe, 900–1900* (New York: Cambridge University Press, 1985), 110; Albert C. Jensen, *The Cod* (New York: Thomas Y. Crowell, 1972), 3; Patrick K. O'Brien, gen. ed., *The Oxford Atlas of World History*, concise ed. (New York: Oxford University Press, 2002), 116–17.

Map 1.6 Source(s): Peter Bakewell, *A History of Latin America*, 2nd edition (Malden, Mass.: Blackwell, 2004), xxii.

Map 1.7 Source(s): *The Oxford Atlas of Exploration*, 2nd edition (New York: Oxford University Press, 2008), 34, 124; Patrick K. O'Brien, gen. ed., *The Oxford Atlas of World History*, concise ed. (New York: Oxford University Press, 2002), 120.

### Chapter 2

Map 2.1 Source(s): *The Cambridge History of the Native Peoples of the Americas: Volume 1: North America: Part I*, ed. Bruce G. Trigger and Wilcomb E. Washburn (New York: Cambridge University Press, 1996), 345 and 346; *The Oxford Atlas of Exploration*, 2nd edition (New York: Oxford University Press, 2008), 124.

Map 2.2 Source(s): *The Cambridge History of the Native Peoples of the Americas: Volume 1: North America: Part I*, ed. Bruce G. Trigger and Wilcomb E. Washburn (New York:

Cambridge University Press, 1996), 341.

Map 2.3 Source(s): *The Cambridge History of the Native Peoples of the Americas: Volume 1: North America: Part I*, ed. Bruce G. Trigger and Wilcomb E. Washburn (New York: Cambridge University Press, 1996), 405; *The Settling of North America: the Atlas of the Great Migration into North America from the Ice Age to the Present*, ed. Helen Hornbeck Tanner (New York: MacMillan, 1995), 42; James Oakes et al., *Of the People: A History of the United States* (New York, Oxford: Oxford University Press, 2010), 77.

Map 2.4 Source(s): Jenny Hale Pulsipher, *Subjects unto the Same King: Indians, English, and the Contest for Authority in Colonial New England* (Philadelphia: University of Pennsylvania Press, 2005), 78.

## Chapter 3

Map 3.1 Source(s): *The Historical Atlas of Canada*, ed. R. Cole Harris (Toronto: University of Toronto Press, 1987), Volume 1, Plate 35.

Map 3.2 Source(s): David Eltis and David Richardson, *Atlas of the Transatlantic Slave Trade* (New Haven and London: Yale University Press, 2010), 18–19; Assessing the Slave Trade. 2009. *Voyages: The Trans-Atlantic Slave Trade Database.* http://www.slavevoyages.org (accessed November 29, 2011); Gregory O'Malley, "Beyond the Middle Passage: Slave Migration from the Caribbean to North America, 1619–1807," *The William and Mary Quarterly*, 3rd Series, 66 (January 2009), 141–42, 146, 160–61, 163.

Map 3.3 Source(s): Mark C. Carnes, ed., *Historical Atlas of the United States* (New York: Routledge, 2003), 48.

Map 3.4 Source(s): *The Cambridge History of the Native Peoples of the Americas: Volume 1: North America: Part I*, ed. Bruce G. Trigger and Wilcomb E. Washburn (New York: Cambridge University Press, 1996), 416, 426; Andrew K. Frank, ed., *The Routledge Historical Atlas of the American South* (New York and London: Routledge, 1999), 20.

Figure 3.1 Source(s): Assessing the Slave Trade. 2009. *Voyages: The Trans-Atlantic Slave Trade Database.* http://www.slavevoyages.org (accessed November 29, 2011).

Figure 3.2 Source(s): David Eltis, *The Rise of African Slavery in the Americas* (New York: Cambridge University Press, 2000), 9.

Figure 3.3 Source(s): David W. Galenson, *White Servitude in Colonial America: An Economic Analysis* (New York: Cambridge University Press, 1981), 83, 84.

Table 3.1 Source(s): Assessing the Slave Trade. 2009. *Voyages: The Trans-Atlantic Slave Trade Database.* http://www.slavevoyages.org (accessed November 29, 2011).

Table 3.2 Source(s): Richard Middleton, *Colonial America: A History*, 3rd edition (Oxford: Blackwell, 2002); Charles M. Andrews, *The Colonial Period of American History, Volume 4: England's Commercial and Colonial Policy* (New Haven: Yale University Press, 1938).

## Chapter 4

Map 4.1 Source(s): Carl Waldman, *Atlas of the North American Indian*, 3rd edition (New York: Facts on File, 2009), 79; Colin G. Calloway, *First Peoples: A Documentary Survey of American Indian History*, 3rd edition (Boston and New York: Bedford/St. Martin's, 2008), 295.

Map 4.2 Source(s): Paul Kelton, *Epidemics and Enslavement: Biological Catastrophe in the Native Southeast, 1492–1715* (Lincoln and London: University of Nebraska Press, 2007), 201.

Map 4.3 Source(s): David Eltis and David Richardson, *Atlas of the Transatlantic Slave Trade* (New Haven and London: Yale University Press, 2010), 18–19; Assessing the Slave Trade. 2009. *Voyages: The Trans-Atlantic Slave Trade Database.* http://www.slavevoyages.org (accessed November 29, 2011).

Map 4.4 Source(s): Mark C. Carnes, ed., *Historical Atlas of the United States* (New York: Routledge, 2003), 73.

Figure 4.1 Source(s): Assessing the Slave Trade. 2009. *Voyages: The Trans-Atlantic Slave Trade Database.* http://www.slavevoyages.org (accessed November 29, 2011).

Table 4.1 Source(s): Assessing the Slave Trade. 2009. *Voyages: The Trans-Atlantic Slave Trade Database.* http://www.slavevoyages.org (accessed November 29, 2011).

Table 4.2 Source(s): Assessing the Slave Trade. 2009. *Voyages: The Trans-Atlantic Slave Trade Database.* http://www.slavevoyages.org (accessed November 29, 2011).

Table 4.3 Source(s): Aaron S. Fogleman, "Migrations to the Thirteen British North American Colonies, 1700–1775: New Estimates," *Journal of Interdisciplinary History* 22 (1992), 691–709; Assessing the Slave Trade. 2009. *Voyages: The Trans-Atlantic Slave Trade Database.* http://www.slavevoyages.org (accessed November 29, 2011).

## Chapter 5

Map 5.1 Source(s): David Eltis and David Richardson, *Atlas of the Transatlantic Slave Trade* (New Haven and London: Yale University Press, 2010), 18–19; Assessing the Slave Trade. 2009. *Voyages: The Trans-Atlantic Slave Trade Database.* http://www.slavevoyages.org (accessed November 29, 2011).

Map 5.2 Source(s): Mark C. Carnes, ed., *Historical Atlas of the United States* (New York: Routledge, 2003), 59.

Map 5.3 Source(s): Mark C. Carnes, ed., *Historical Atlas of the United States* (New York: Routledge, 2003), 58; Andrew K. Frank, ed., *The Routledge Historical Atlas of the American South* (New York and London: Routledge, 1999), 20.

Map 5.4 Source(s): Robert H. Ferrell and Richard Natkiel, *Atlas of American History* (New York: Facts on File, 1987, 1993), 30; Mark C. Carnes, ed., *Historical Atlas of the United States* (New York: Routledge, 2003), 58.

Map 5.6 Source(s): Robert H. Ferrell and Richard Natkiel, *Atlas of American History* (New York: Facts on File, 1987, 1993), 16; *Historical Atlas of Canada*, ed. R. Cole Harris (Toronto: University of Toronto Press, 1987), Volume 1, Plate 30.

Map 5.7 Source(s): *Historical Atlas of Canada*, ed. R. Cole Harris (Toronto: University of Toronto Press, 1987), Volume 1, Plate 30.

Figure 5.1 Source(s): Assessing the Slave Trade. 2009. *Voyages: The Trans-Atlantic Slave Trade Database.* http://www.slavevoyages.org (accessed November 29, 2011).

Figure 5.2 Source(s): Jay Coughtry, *The Notorious Triangle: Rhode Island and the African Slave Trade, 1700–1807* (Philadelphia: Temple University Press, 1981), 34.

Figure 5.3 Source(s): Jacob Cooke, ed., *Encyclopedia of North American Colonies* (New York: Scribner's, 1993), 1, 470.

Table 5.1 Source(s): Assessing the Slave Trade. 2009. *Voyages: The Trans-Atlantic Slave Trade Database.* http://www.slavevoyages.org (accessed November 29, 2011).

Table 5.2 Source(s): Aaron S. Fogleman, "Migrations to the Thirteen British North American Colonies, 1700–1775: New Estimates," *Journal of Interdisciplinary History* 22 (1992), 691–709; Assessing the Slave Trade. 2009. *Voyages: The Trans-Atlantic Slave Trade Database.* http://www.slavevoyages.org (accessed November 29, 2011).

Table 5.3 Source(s): Richard Middleton, *Colonial America: A History*, 3rd edition (Oxford: Blackwell, 2002); Jack P. Greene, ed., *Settlements to Society: A Documentary History of Colonial America* (New York: W.W. Norton, 1975).

## Chapter 8

Figure 8.1 Source(s): Historical Statistics of the United States Millennial Edition Online, ed. Susan B. Carter, Scott Sigmund Gartner, Michael R. Haines, Alan L. Olmstead, Richard Sutch and Gavin Wright (Cambridge University Press, 2011). http://hsus.cambridge.org/HSUSWeb/ (accessed November 29, 2011).

## Chapter 10

Map 10.2 Source(s): Steven Dutch, University of Wisconsin–Green Bay; C.O. Paullin, *Atlas of the Historical Geography of the United States*, (Carnegie Institute, 1932, reproduced in facsimile by Greenwood Press, 1975).

## Chapter 11

Map 11.3 Source(s): Nathanial Philbrick, *Sea of Glory: America's Voyage of Discovery, the U.S. Exploring Expedition, 1838–1842* (New York: Viking, 2003).

Figure 11.1 Source(s): *Historical Statistics of the United States, 1789–1945*. Dept. of the Census, 1949. Series B 304–330 – Immigration – Immigrants by Country: 1820 to 1945.

Figure 11.2 Source(s): *Historical Statistics of the United States, 1789–1945*. Dept. of the Census, 1949. Series B 13–23: Population, Decennial Summary—Sex, Urban-Rural Residence, and Race: 1790 to 1940.

## Chapter 12

Map 12.1 Source(s): John H. Thompson, *Geography of New York State* (New York: Syracuse University Press, 1966).

Map 12.1 Source(s): Kenneth Greenberg, *The Confessions of Nat Turner* (Bedford/St. Martins, 1996).

Figure 12.1 Source(s): Eighth U.S. Census. Schedule 1.

Figure 12.3 Source(s): Lyn Ragsdale, *Vital Statistics on the Presidency* (Washington, D.C.: Congressional Quarterly Press, 1998), 132–38.

## Chapter 13

Figure 13.1 Source(s): Campbell J. Gibson and Emily Lennon, "Historical Census Statistics on the Foreign-Born Population of the United States: 1850–1990." Population Division, U.S. Bureau of the Census, Washington, D.C. 20233-8800 February 1999 POPULATION DIVISION WORKING PAPER NO. 29, Table 4. Region and Country or Area of Birth of the Foreign-Born Population.

## Chapter 14

Map 14.1 Source(s): Aaron Sheehan-Dean, *Concise Historical Atlas of the U.S. Civil War* (New York, Oxford: Oxford University Press, 2008).

Map 14.2 Source(s): Aaron Sheehan-Dean, *Concise Historical Atlas of the U.S. Civil War* (New York, Oxford: Oxford University Press, 2008).

Map 14.3 Source(s): Aaron Sheehan-Dean, *Concise Historical Atlas of the U.S. Civil War* (New York, Oxford: Oxford University Press, 2008).

Map 14.4 Source(s): Aaron Sheehan-Dean, *Concise Historical Atlas of the U.S. Civil War* (New York, Oxford: Oxford University Press, 2008).

Figure 14.2 Source(s): Douglas B. Ball, *Financial Failure and Confederate Defeat* (Urbana: University of Illinois Press, 1991); Randall, J.G. *The Civil War and Reconstruction*. Boston: D.C. Heath, 1937; Richard Cecil Todd, *Confederate Finance* (Athens: University of Georgia Press, 1954).

## Chapter 15

Map 15.1 Source(s): Aaron Sheehan-Dean, *Concise Historical Atlas of the U.S. Civil War* (New York, Oxford: Oxford University Press, 2008).

Map 15.2 Source(s): Aaron Sheehan-Dean, *Concise Historical Atlas of the U.S. Civil War* (New York, Oxford: Oxford University Press, 2008).

Map 15.2 Source(s): Aaron Sheehan-Dean, *Concise Historical Atlas of the U.S. Civil War* (New York, Oxford: Oxford University Press, 2008).

Figure 15.1 Source(s): James L. Watkins, *King Cotton: A Historical and Statistical Review, 1790–1908* (New York: James L. Wakins and Sons, 1908).

## Chapter 16

Map 16.1 Source(s): Steven Dutch, University of Wisconsin–Green Bay.

Map 16.2 Source(s): Samuel Truett, *Fugitive Landscapes: The Forgotten History of the U.S.-Mexico Borderlands* (New Haven, London: Yale University Press, 2006).

## Chapter 17

Map 17.2 Source(s): Mona Domosh, *American Commodities in an Age of Empire* (Routledge, 2006), 33.

Figure 17.1 Source(s): O.P. Austin, "The United States: Her Industries," *National Geographic* (August 1903): 313.

## Chapter 18

Map 18.1 Source(s): *London Times Atlas*.

Map 18.2 Source(s): *Historical Atlas of the United States*, Centennial Edition, ed. Wilbur E. Garrett (National Geographic, 1988).

Table 18.1 Sources(s): Eighth and Twelfth U.S. Censuses.

## Chapter 20

Map 20.1 Sources(s): Thomas Paterson et al., *American Foreign Relations* (D.C. Health, 1995), vol. 2, 55, 40.

Map 20.2 Source(s): Patrick K. O'Brien, gen. ed., *The Oxford Atlas of World History*, (New York: Oxford University Press, 1999, 2007), 270.

## Chapter 21

Table 21.1 Source(s): Michael Howard, *The First World War: A Very Short Introduction* (New York, Oxford: Oxford University Press, 2007), 122.

## Chapter 22

Map 22.1 Source(s): *Historical Atlas of the United States*, Centennial Edition, ed. Wilbur E. Garrett (National Geographic, 1988).

Map 22.2 Source(s): James A. Henretta, David Brody and Lynn Dumenil, *America's History*, Sixth Edition (New York: Bedford/St. Martin's, 2007).

## Chapter 23

Figure 23.1 Sources(s): United States Department of Commerce, *Historical Statistics of the United States* (1960), 70.

## Chapter 24

Table 24.1 Source(s): Hans Dollinger, *The Decline and Fall of Nazi Germany and Imperial Japan: A Pictorial History of the Final Days of World War II* (New York, NY: Bonanza Books, 1965, 1967), 422.

## Chapter 29

Figure 29.2 Source(s): U.S. Bureau of the Census, Current Population Reports, "Money Income in the United States: 2000."

## Chapter 30

Map 30.2 Source(s): Mark C. Carnes et al., *Mapping America's Past* (New York: Henry Holt and Co., 1996), 267; *Hammond Atlas of the Twentieth Century* (New York: Times Books, 1996), 166.

Figure 30.1 Source(s): $INDU (Dow Jones Industrial Average) INDX, May 1, 2009. Chart courtesy of StockCharts.com.

Figure 30.2 Source(s): Center for Immigration Studies, 1990 Immigration and Naturalization Service Yearbook.

## Chapter 31

Table 31.1 Source(s): U.S. Census Bureau, American Community Survey, 2009.

Figure 31.1 Sources(s): U.S. Census Bureau, American Community Survey, California Association of Realtors, Case-Shiller, National Bureau of Economic Research.

# PHOTO CREDITS

**Chapter 1** Page 2: *Monumenta Cartographia*, 1502 by © Royal Geographical Society, London, UK/ The Bridgeman Art Library; p. 4: (left) The Art Archive / National Anthropological Museum Mexico / Gianni Dagli Orti; (right) From *Brevis Narratio. . .* published by Theodore de Bry, 1591 / Service Historique de la Marine, Vincennes, France / Giraudon / The Bridgeman Art Library International; p. 5: (bottom) From The Discovery of America, 1878, Spanish School, (19th century) / Private Collection / Index / The Bridgeman Art Library International; (top) De Soto Discovering the Mississippi, 1541, Berninghaus, Oscar (1874–1952) / Private Collection / The Bridgeman Art Library International; (right) From *Newe Welt und Americanische Historien* by Johann Ludwig Gottfried, published by Mattaeus Merian, Frankfurt, 1631, Bry, Theodore de (1528–98) / Private Collection / The Stapleton Collection / The Bridgeman Art Library International; p. 8: Courtesy of The Bancroft Library, University of California, Berkeley; p. 10: Ira Block/ National Geographic/ Getty Images; p. 12: *Novae franciae accurata delineatio* 1657, Library and Archives Canada; p. 18: The Stapleton Collection / The Bridgeman Art Library; p. 21: © The Trustees of the British Museum; p. 24: Museo de America, Madrid, Spain / The Bridgeman Art Library; p. 27: Courtesy of Library and Archives Canada; p. 30: Courtesy of the Peabody Museum of Archaeology and Ethnology, Harvard University, 2004.24.29636; p. 33: ©The Trustees of the British Museum / Art Resource, NY.

**Chapter 2** Page 44: © The Trustees of the British Museum; p. 46: (top) The Signing of the Mayflower Compact, c.1900 (oil on canvas), Moran, Edward Percy (1862–1935) / Pilgrim Hall Museum, Plymouth, Massachusetts / The Bridgeman Art Library International; (bottom) The Granger Collection, NYC; p. 47: (all) The Granger Collection, NYC; p. 50: Private Collection / Archives Charmet / The Bridgeman Art Library; p. 51: ©Cindy Miller Hopkins / DanitaDelimont.com; p. 55: Lahontan, Louis Armand de Lom d'Arce, baron de. *New voyages to North-America: containing an account of the several nations* [. . .]. Vol. 2. London: H. Bomwicke et al., 1703. FC71 L313 1703. p. 59 [a]; p. 60: Indentured servant agreement between Richard Lowther and Edward Lyurd, 31st July 1627/ Virginia Historical Society, Richmond, Virginia, USA/ The Bridgeman Art Library; p. 63: Art Resource, NY; p. 67: Library and Archives Canada / C21404; p. 75: Machotick medal, observe (silver) by English School / Virginia Historical Society, Richmond, Virginia, USA/ The Bridgeman Art Library.

**Chapter 3** Page 84: Portrait of Elsie (Rutgers) Schuyler Vas, 1723. Albany Institute of History & Art, 1957.104; p. 86: (left) The Granger Collection, NYC; (right) American School, (19th century) / Private Collection / Peter Newark American Pictures / The Bridgeman Art Library International; p. 87: (bottom left) Title page of the Navigation Act of 1651 (print), American School, (17th century) / Private Collection / Peter Newark American Pictures / The Bridgeman Art Library International; (top right) National Maritime Museum, Greenwich, UK, Caird Collection; (bottom right) Private Collection / Peter Newark American Pictures / The Bridgeman Art Library International; p. 89: Center Historique des Archives Nationales, Paris, France / Giraudon / The Bridgeman Art Library; p. 92: © The Huntington Library, Art Collections & Botanical Gardens / The Bridgeman Art Library; p. 93: British Library, London, UK / © British Library Board. All Rights Reserved / The Bridgeman Art Library; p. 99: © The British Library Board; p. 104: Danita Delimont / Alamy; p. 114: Courtesy, National Museum of the American Indian, Smithsonian Institution [23/9269]; p. 120: New York State Archives.

**Chapter 4** Page 128: Library and Archives Canada, acc. no. 1977-35-4. Acquired with a special grant from the Canadian Government in 1977; p. 130: (bottom left) © Library and Archives Canada; (top right) © Historical Picture Archive/ CORBIS; p. 131: (left)

The Granger Collection, NYC; (right ) Library of Congress Geography and Map Division; (top) The Art Archive / Geographical Society Paris / Gianni Dagli Orti; p. 132: The Historic New Orleans Collection; p. 137: State Library of Louisiana; p. 146: © Trustees of the British Museum; p. 151: Courtesy Houghton Library, Harvard University EC7.A100.709s2; p. 156: The Granger Collection, NYC; p. 157: Portrait of an Unidentified Woman (oil on canvas), American School, (18th century) / © Collection of the New-York Historical Society, USA / The Bridgeman Art Library International; p. 164: The Granger Collection, NYC; p. 165: Mary Evans Picture Library.

**Chapter 5** Page 172: George Whitefield by John Wollaston oil on canvas, circa 1742 / © National Portrait Gallery, London; p. 174: (left) The Smugglers' Cave (litho), Pearse, Alfred (19th/20th Century) / Private Collection / Peter Newark Historical Pictures / The Bridgeman Art Library International; (right) Architect of the Capitol; p. 175: (left) ©Pictorial Press Ltd / Alamy; (center) The Emigrants (oil on canvas), Woltze, Berthold (1829–96) / Private Collection / © Odon Wagner Gallery, Toronto, Canada / The Bridgeman Art Library International; (top right) Copyright © North Wind / North Wind Picture Archives; p. 185: Document opposing the re-election of Benjamin Franklin to the Assembly, 1764 (print), Weiss, Lewis (1717–96) / New York Public Library, USA / The Bridgeman Art Library; p. 188: Courtesy of Texas Archeological Research Laboratory, University of Texas at Austin; p. 189: Courtesy Florida Museum of Natural History-Historical Archaeology Collections; p. 192: Courtesy American Antiquarian Society; p. 194: The Gansevoort Limner, Susanna Truax, Gift of Edgar William and Bernice Chrysler Garbisch. Image courtesy of the National Gallery of Art, Washington; p. 209: The Death of General Wolfe (1727–59), c.1771 (oil on panel) Benjamin West (1738–1820) / Private Collection / Phillips, Fine Art Auctioneers, New York, USA / The Bridgeman Art Library; p. 210: A View of the Plundering and Burning of the City of Grimross, 1758 by Thomas Davies (1737–1812), National Gallery of Canada (6270).

**Chapter 6** Page 218: Yale University Art Gallery / Art Resource, NY; p. 220: (top) The Battle of Lexington, April 19th 1775, from *Connecticut Historical Collections* by John Warner Barber, engraved by A. Doolittle, 1832 (coloured engraving), American School, (19th century) / Private Collection / The Bridgeman Art Library International; (bottom left) The Granger Collection, NYC; (bottom right) Private Collection / The Bridgeman Art Library; p. 221: (bottom left) Courtesy of United States National Archives and Records Administration; (bottom right) American School / Private Collection / Peter Newark Pictures / The Bridgeman Art Library; p. 223: George III, 1761–62 (oil on canvas), Ramsay, Allan (1713–84) / The Royal Collection © 2011 Her Majesty Queen Elizabeth II / The Bridgeman Art Library; p. 230: American School / Private Collection / Peter Newark Pictures / The Bridgeman Art Library; p. 231: Samuel Adams (colour litho) by John Singleton Copley (1738–1815) Private Collection/ Peter Newark American Pictures/ The Bridgeman Art Library; p. 235: Image copyright © The Metropolitan Museum of Art / Art Resource, NY; p. 238: The Granger Collection, NYC; p. 240: Private Collection / The Bridgeman Art Library; p. 244: Courtesy of the United States National Archives and Records Administration; p. 245: (top) © Christie's Images / The Bridgeman Art Library International; (bottom) Lebrecht 3/Lebrecht Music & Arts/Corbis.

**Chapter 7** Page 252: Image copyright © The Metropolitan Museum of Art / Art Resource, NY; p. 254: (bottom left) National Archives, Records of the Continental and Confederation Congresses and the Constitutional Convention; (bottom right) ©William Paarlberg; (top) U.S. Capitol paintings. Declaration of Independence, painting by John Trumbull in U.S. Capitol, Courtesy of Library of Congress; p. 255: (left) Bibliotheque des Arts Decoratifs, Paris, France / Archives Charmet / The Bridgeman Art Library International; (right) The Granger Collection, NYC; p. 256: Courtesy of Historical Society of Pennsylvania Collection / The Bridgeman Art Library; p. 263: The Granger Collection, NYC;

p. 267: Library of Congress Prints and Photographs Division; p. 272: Private Collection / Peter Newark American Pictures / The Bridgeman Art Library; p. 276: Art Resource, NY; p. 277: New York Public Library, USA/ The Bridgeman Art Library; p. 281: Mrs. James Warren (Mercy Otis) by John Singleton Copley, American 1738–1815. Photograph © Museum of Fine Arts, Boston.

**Chapter 8** Page 288: Schomburg Center for Research in Black Culture / New York Public Library; p. 290: (left) Courtesy of the artist, Rear Admiral John W. Schmidt, USN (Retired). Official U.S. Navy Photograph; (right) National Archives and Record Administration; p. 291: (top) Bibliotheque Nationale, Paris, France / Archives Charmet / The Bridgeman Art Library International; (bottom right) Courtesy Library and Archives Canada/C-115678; (bottom left) U.S. Naval Historical Center Photograph; p. 299: Gift of Mrs. Henry Nagle, 1894 / Philadelphia Museum of Art; p. 300: (left) ©Massachusetts Historical Society, Boston, MA, USA / The Bridgeman Art Library; (right) © Massachusetts Historical Society, Boston, MA, USA / The Bridgeman Art Library; p. 301: Dallas Museum of Art, The Faith P. and Charles L. Bybee Collection, anonymous gift; p. 302: Library of Congress; p. 307: Copyright © 2000–2011 The Metropolitan Museum of Art. All rights reserved. Source: Two dresses [French] (1983.6.1,07.146.5) | Heilbrunn Timeline of Art History | The Metropolitan Museum of Art; p. 316: Library of Congress; p. 319: Mid-Manhattan Library Picture Collection / New York Public Library.

**Chapter 9** Page 324: Image copyright © The Metropolitan Museum of Art / Art Resource, NY; p. 326: (top) The Granger Collection, NYC; (left) Library of Congress; (right) Copyright © North Wind / North Wind Picture Archives; 327 (top) Courtesy of Historical Society of Pennsylvania Collection / The Bridgeman Art Library; (bottom) The Granger Collection; p. 330: Library of Congress; p. 333: Library of Congress; p. 340: Library of Congress; p. 342: Whitman Sampler Collection, gift of Pet, Incorporated, 1969 / Philadelphia Museum of Art; p. 343: Schlesinger Library, Radcliffe Institute, Harvard University; p. 347: Historic American Buildings Survey / Library of Congress; p. 348: The White House Historical Association.

**Chapter 10** Page 360: Smithsonian American Art Museum, Washington, DC / Art Resource, NY; p. 362: (top) Artes e Historia México; (bottom) Copyright © North Wind / North Wind Picture Archives; p. 363: (both) The Granger Collection, NYC; p. 366: The Granger Collection, NYC; p. 368: Stephen A. Schwarzman Building / Manuscripts and Archives Division / New York Public Library; p. 372: Private Collection / Photo © Christie's Images / The Bridgeman Art Library; p. 373: Private Collection / Ken Welsh / The Bridgeman Art Library; p. 374: The Granger Collection, NYC; p. 379: © Philadelphia History Museum at the Atwater Kent, Courtesy of Historical Society of Pennsylvania Collection / Bridgeman Art Library; p. 385: Wisconsin Historical Society, image ID: 4522; p. 387: Dangers of the whale fishery, illustration from 'Penny Magazine', 1833 (engraving) by American School (19th century), New York Public Library, USA/ The Bridgeman Art Library.

**Chapter 11** Page 396: "Emigrants Crossing the Plains" 1867, Albert Bierstadt, artist. Permanent Art Collection, National Cowboy & Western Heritage Museum; p. 398: (top) Defending the Alamo, English School, (20th century) / Private Collection / © Look and Learn / The Bridgeman Art Library International; (center) The Granger Collection, NYC; (bottom) The Granger Collection, NYC; p. 399: (top) The Granger Collection, NYC; (bottom) "Morning Tears–winter, 1838–39." Copyright (c) John Guthrie, Guthrie Studios, www.guthriestudios.com p. 403: Morning Tears- winter, 1838–39. Copyright © John Guthrie, Guthrie Studios, www.guthriestudios.com; p. 411: The Granger Collection, NYC; p. 416: The Granger Collection, NYC; p. 418: © Stapleton Collection/Corbis; p. 422: © Francis G. Mayer/ CORBIS; p. 423: The Granger Collection, NYC; p. 424: The Granger Collection, NYC; p. 430: The County Election (oil on canvas), Bingham,

George Caleb (1811–79) / St. Louis Art Museum, Missouri, USA / The Bridgeman Art Library International; p. 431: De Bow's Review, April 1857.

**Chapter 12** Page 440: The Granger Collection, NYC; p. 442: (left) The Granger Collection, NYC; (right) Photograph courtesy of Oberlin College Archives; p. 443: (top right) bpk, Berlin / Knud Petersen / Art Resource, NY; (center) National Maritime Museum, Greenwich, UK, Michael Graham-Stewart Slavery Collection. Acquired with the assistance of the Heritage Lottery Fund; (bottom) Library of Congress; p. 447: The Granger Collection, NYC; p. 453: Courtesy of Mississippi Department of Archives and History; p. 455: The Granger Collection, NYC; p. 456: Library of Congress; p. 462: The Granger Collection, NYC; p. 467: © CORBIS; p. 468: The Granger Collection, NYC; p. 470: Library of Congress.

**Chapter 13** Page 478: Art Resource, NY; p. 480: (top) After the Battle of Monterrey, Mexican General Pedro de Ampudia surrenders the city to American General Zachary Taylor during the Mexican-American War of 1846–48 (colour litho), English School, (19th century) / Private Collection / Ken Welsh / The Bridgeman Art Library International; (bottom left) The Occupation of the Capital of Mexico by the American Army, 1846–48 (colour litho), American School, (19th century) / American Antiquarian Society, Worcester, Massachusetts, USA / The Bridgeman Art Library International; (bottom right) Library of Congress; p. 481: (right) National Maritime Museum, Greenwich, UK; (left) The Anti-Slavery Society Convention, 1840 by Benjamin Robert Haydon, 1841. Copyright © National Portrait Gallery, London 2011; p. 482: SSPL/Science Museum / Art Resource, NY; p. 488: Courtesy of UC Berkeley, Bancroft Library; p. 492: © Everett Collection / SuperStock; p. 499: The Granger Collection, NYC; p. 502: Copyright © North Wind / Nancy Carter\North Wind Picture Archives; p. 509: The Granger Collection, NYC; p. 511: The Granger Collection, NYC.

**Chapter 14** Page 518: The Granger Collection, NYC; p. 520: (both) Library of Congress; p. 521: Library of Congress; p. 526: Harper's Weekly, (1862) / Library of Congress; p. 527: Ohio Historical Society; p. 532: Andrew J. Russell, photographer / Library of Congress; p. 542: Gardner, Alexander, 1821–1882, photographer / Library of Congress; p. 543: A Ride for Liberty, or The Fugitive Slaves, c.1862 (oil on board) by Eastman Johnson (1824–1906) Brooklyn Museum of Art, New York, USA/ The Bridgeman Art Library; p. 545: The Historical Society of Pennsylvania; p. 548: Gibson, James F., b. 1828, photographer / Library of Congress; p. 555: Barnard, George N., 1819–1902, photographer / Library of Congress.

**Chapter 15** Page 562: The Granger Collection, NYC; p. 564: (left) © Bettmann / CORBIS; (right) Library of Congress; p. 565: (center) Library of Congress; (bottom) Beard, James Carter, 1837–1913 , artist / Library of Congress; (top) The Granger Collection, NYC; p. 567: Library of Congress; p. 579: Private Collection / Peter Newark American Pictures / The Bridgeman Art Library; p. 581: The Granger Collection, NYC; p. 583: Detroit Publishing Co. Photography Collection, no. 08148 / Library of Congress; p. 587: University of Washington Libraries, Special Collections Division, Captain S.E. Lancaster photograph collection. PH Coll 168; p. 589: © Bettmann / CORBIS; p. 591: The Granger Collection, NYC; p. 594: © Francis G. Mayer/CORBIS.

**Chapter 16** Page 600: Courtesy of The Forgotten Gateway Exhibit; p. 602: (top) South Castle Creek, a Temple of the Hills, Black Hills, South Dakota (oil on canvas), De Haven, Franklin (1856–1934) / Private Collection / Phillips, Fine Art Auctioneers, New York, USA / The Bridgeman Art Library International; (bottom) De Bow's Review, April 1857; p. 603: (left) Library of Congress; (right) James E. Hunt / McCracken Collection / Buffalo Bill Historical Center, Cody, Wyoming; P.69.1310c; p. 605: "The Heart of the Continent." Booster brochure of imagined West, Denver Public Library, Western History Collection / The Bridgeman Art Library; p. 614: James E. Hunt / McCracken Collection / Buffalo Bill Historical Center, Cody, Wyoming; P.69.1310c; p. 615: Courtesy of Nebraska State Historical

Society; p. 618: Courtesy of the Nevada Historical Society; p. 620: Atchison, Topeka, and Santa Fe Railway Company / Kansas Historical Society; p. 626: The Granger Collection, NYC; p. 628: Courtesy of the Burton Historical Collection, Detroit Public Library. ©1999; p. 634: The Grand Canyon of the Yellowstone, 1872 (oil on canvas), Moran, Thomas (1837–1926) / National Museum of American Art, Smithsonian Institute, USA / Lent by U.S. Dept. of the Interior, National Park Service / The Bridgeman Art Library.

**Chapter 17** Page 640: The Granger Collection, NYC; p. 642 (both) The Granger Collection, NYC; p. 643: (top) Library of Congress; (left) ©Illustrated London News Ltd/Mary Evans Picture Library; (right) Mary Evans Picture Library; p. 645: The Granger Collection, NYC; p. 650: © Bettmann/CORBIS; p. 656: The Granger Collection, NYC; p. 658: Early Office Museum Archives; p. 662: Library of Congress; p. 664: The Granger Collection, NYC; p. 666: © Bettmann / CORBIS; p. 673: The Granger Collection, NYC.

**Chapter 18** Page 680: Library of Congress; p. 682: (left) The Granger Collection, NYC; (right) Library of Congress; p. 683: (top) © Bettmann/CORBIS; (bottom left) Rue des Archives / The Granger Collection, NYC; (bottom right) The Granger Collection, NYC; p. 690: Rue des Archives / The Granger Collection, NYC; p. 692: The Granger Collection, NYC; p. 699: The Granger Collection, NYC; p. 703: Reproduced from an original postcard published by J. Valentine & Sons, New York; p. 704: Leopold Morse Goulston baseball collection in memory of Leo J. Bondy / New York Public Library; p. 706: Courtesy of Andrew Dolkart Collection; p. 709: © Moffett / Library of Congress; p. 710: The Granger Collection, NYC.

**Chapter 19** Page 722: The Granger Collection, NYC; p. 724: (left) Copyright © North Wind / North Wind Picture Archives; (right) View of one of the locks on the Panama canal (b/w photo), / Private Collection / Roger-Viollet, Paris / The Bridgeman Art Library International; p. 725: (top left) NHHC Collection; (bottom left) Detroit Publishing Company Photograph Collection / Library of Congress; (bottom right) Cover of Life magazine, Vol. 39, #1021 first published on May 22, 1902; p. 727: © CORBIS; p. 734: Rau Studios, Inc., Philadelphia / New York Public Library; p. 735: Courtesy Frederic Remington Art Museum, Ogdensburg, New York (Public Library Collection); p. 737: New York Public Library; p. 738: Fotosearch / Getty Images; p. 741: J.S. Pughe, *Harper's Weekly*, September 5, 1900; p. 743: Rau Studios, Inc., Philadelphia / New York Public Library; p. 748: Library of Congress.

**Chapter 20** Page 758: George Grantham Bain Collection / Library or Congress; p. 760: (left) The Granger Collection, NYC; (right) New York World-Telegram and the Sun Newspaper Photograph Collection (Library of Congress); p. 761: (right) Harris & Ewing Collection (Library of Congress); (top) New York Public Library; (bottom left) Library of Congress; p. 770: Library of Congress, LC-USZ62-31911; p. 771: New York Public Library; p. 772: Oscar B. Willis / New York Public Library; p. 778: The Granger Collection, NYC; p. 782: The Granger Collection, NYC; p. 783: Library of Congress; p. 789: War Department General and Special Staff / US National Archives and Records Administration (533769); p. 791: The Granger Collection, NYC.

**Chapter 21** Page 798: © Pictorial Press Ltd / Alamy; p. 800: (right) © Bettmann/ CORBIS; (left) Library of Congress; p. 801: (top) Rue des Archives / The Granger Collection, NYC; (bottom left) © Bettmann/CORBIS; (right) Mary Evans/Robert Hunt Collection; p. 802: New York Public Library; p. 807: Mary Evans/Robert Hunt Collection; p. 814: Library of Congress; p. 817: U.S. Signal Corps and Navy / Library of Congress; p. 820: Library of Congress; p. 824: U.S. Army Signal Corps / Library of Congress.

**Chapter 22** Page 840: The Jacob and Gwendolyn Lawrence Foundation / Art Resource, NY and © 2011 The Jacob and Gwendolyn Lawrence Foundation, Seattle/Artists Rights Society (ARS), New York; p. 842: (top) Lebrecht Photo Library; (center) The Granger Collection, NYC; (bottom) Del Rio Historical Photo Gallery / US Department of Homeland Security; p. 843: (top) Library of Congress; (bottom) Library of Congress; (center)

Scene of panic in Wall Street, New York, 24th October 1929 (b/w photo), American Photographer, (20th century) / Private Collection / Peter Newark American Pictures / The Bridgeman Art Library International; p. 844: Famous Players/Paramount / The Kobal Collection; p. 849: Mary Evans Picture Library; p. 850: The Granger Collection, NYC; p. 854: © David J. & Janice L. Frent Collection/Corbis; p. 855: Lebrecht Photo Library; p. 860: The Granger Collection, NYC; p. 863: © Bettmann/ CORBIS.

**Chapter 23** Page 878 © Associated Press; p. 880: ©Associated Press; p. 881: (left) Portrait of Hitler, 1933 (b/w photo), German Photographer (20th Century) / Private Collection / Peter Newark Military Pictures / The Bridgeman Art Library International; (right) Japanese tanks crossing a river in China, during the Second World War (b/w photo), German Photographer (20th Century) / © SZ Photo / The Bridgeman Art Library International; p. 886: ullstein bild / The Granger Collection, NYC; p. 891: Bureau of Reclamation, U.S. Dept of the Interior, 2006; p. 894: United Press International / New York World-Telegram & Sun Collection / Library of Congress; p. 896: Dorothea Lang / FSA/OWI Collection / Library of Congress; p. 908: © CORBIS.

**Chapter 24** Page 920: Library of Congress; p. 922: (top) Library of Congress; (bottom left) FSA/OWI Collection / Library of Congress; (bottom right) U.S. Signal Corps / Library of Congress; p. 923: (left) MCT / Landov; (right) Mary Evans / Sueddeutsche Zeitung Photo; p. 933: FSA/ OWI Collection / Library of Congress; p. 938: © Bettman/CORBIS; p. 941: © CORBIS; p. 947: Toni Frissell Collection / Library of Congress; p. 951: © National Archives/CORBIS; p. 954: Clem Albers / Farm Security Administration and Office of War Information Collection / Library of Congress; p. 960: U.S. Signal Corps / Library of Congress.

**Chapter 25** Page 966: H. Armstrong Roberts / ClassicStock.com; p. 968: (left) Central Intelligence Agency; (right) dpa /Landov; p. 969: (top) National Archives and Records Administration (NARA), 541959; (bottom left) Library of Congress; (bottom right) H. Armstrong Roberts / ClassicStock.com; p. 972: © Hulton-Deutsch Collection/ CORBIS; p. 975: *No Place to Hide* by David Bradley. Copyright © 1948 by David Bradley. Boston: Little, Brown & Company; p. 985: © Ann Ronan Picture Library / Heritage-Images / The Image Works; p. 986: What's Become of Rosie the Riveter? by FRIEDA S. MILLER, Director, Women's Bureau, United States Department of Labor *New York Times*, May 5, 1946. ProQuest Historical Newspapers The New York Times (1851–2003) pg. SM11; p. 987: © Bettmann/ CORBIS; p. 991: Courtesy of Bracero History Archive, item # 3020; p. 994: © Bettmann/ CORBIS; p. 998: New York World-Telegram and the Sun Newspaper Photograph Collection (Library of Congress).

**Chapter 26** Page 1004: Guy Gillette/Time & Life Pictures/ Getty Images; p. 1006: (top) © Bob Campbell/San Francisco Chronicle/Corbis; (center) © March of Dimes; (bottom) AP Photo; p. 1007: (top) © National Air and Space Museum; (bottom left) The G. Eric and Edith Matson Photograph Collection/ Library of Congress; (bottom right) © Bettmann/CORBIS; p. 1011: © Bettmann/CORBIS; p. 1012: From *Dark Sun: The Making of the Hydrogen Bomb* by Richard Rhodes. Simon & Schuster, 1995. Image reproduced by permission of Molecular Biophysics & Biochemistry Department, Yale University; p. 1017: CBS / Landov; p. 1023: Lin Shi Khan and Tony Perez, *Scottsboro, Alabama: A Story in Linoleum Cuts* (New York: New York University Press, 2001 [1935]; p. 1030: Domingos Alegres, Jaudi Dudi, No. 138, 18 de Noviembre de 1956, Sociedad Editora America, S.A.; p. 1031: © Bettmann/ CORBIS; p. 1034: The Granger Collection, NYC; p. 1036: ALLIED ARTISTS / The Kobal Collection.

**Chapter 27** Page 1050: © Flip Schulke/Corbis; p. 1052: (top) Courtesy of NASA; (center) Copyright © 2002 Robert Altman; (bottom) Library of Congress; p. 1053: (right) VONDERHEID/ dpa / Landov; (left) Library of Congress; p. 1054: Helen Nestor / Oakland Museum of California; p. 1056: Associated Press; p. 1073: The Granger Collection, NYC; p. 1074: Rue des Archives / The Granger Collection, NYC;

p. 1075: © Ted Streshinsky/ CORBIS; p. 1076: Courtesy of The Bancroft Library, University of California; p. 1078: © Bettmann/CORBIS; p. 1081: CBS / Landov.

**Chapter 28** Page 1088: Guido Alberto Rossi / GlowImages.com; p. 1090: (right) © Bettmann / CORBIS; (left) Dennis Brack / Landov; p. 1091: (both) © Bettmann/ CORBIS; p. 1092: AP Photo/ Nick Ut; p. 1093: AFP / Getty Images; p. 1101: © Bettmann/CORBIS; p. 1103: © Bettmann/CORBIS; p. 1108: Photo by Charles Ruppmann/NY Daily News Archive via Getty Images; p. 1114: United States Government Work (U.S. Foreign Policy History), Author unknown; p. 1119: Dennis Brack/Landov.

**Chapter 29** Page 1126: © mpworks / Alamy; p. 1128: (top) Carol Powers/ The Washington Times / Landov; (bottom) Corbis; p. 1129: (left) Bob Strong/ Reuters /Landov; (right) WH / MAI /Landov; p. 1137: Dirck Halstead / Time & Life Pictures/Getty Images; p. 1077: Jimmy Carter Presidential Library / MCT / Landov; p. 1139: © Bettmann/ CORBIS; p. 1140: Miami Herald/MCT /Landov; p. 1144: Charlotte Observer/ MCT /Landov; p. 1159: © Pascal Manoukian/Sygma/ CORBIS; p. 1160: Carol Powers/The Washington Times /Landov; p. 1162: WH / MAI /Landov.

**Chapter 30** Page 1168: H. ARMSTRONG ROBERTS / ClassicStock.com; p. 1170: (top) dpa /Landov; (bottom) NAFTA Secretariat; p. 1171: (top) From Lithuanian Wikipedia; (bottom left) Leighton Mark/UPI /Landov; (bottom right) © Jacques Pavlovsky /Sygma/Corbis; p. 1175: REUTERS/Rick Wilking /Landov; p. 1177: dpa /Landov; p. 1180: © Jacques Pavlovsky/Sygma/ CORBIS; p. 1187: © Bob Sacha/CORBIS; p. 1194: © Erik Freeland/CORBIS; p. 1199: REUTERS/Damir Sagolj /Landov; p. 1203: Bill Clark / UPI /Landov.

**Chapter 31** Page 1208: Chuck Kennedy/MCT / Landov; p. 1210: (left) Robert Galbraith/AFP/Getty Images; (right) © David Turnley/ CORBIS; p. 1211: (top) Goran Tomasevic/Reuters / Landov; (bottom left) U.S. Army Spc. Evan D. Marcy; (bottom right) REUTERS/ Hamid Mir /Landov; p. 1214: © David Turnley/CORBIS; p. 1218: U.S. Army Spc. Evan D. Marcy; p. 1219: AP Photo; p. 1222: AP Photo / Jim Mone; p. 1226: ROBERT GALBRAITH/AFP/Getty Images; p. 1229: Dennis Van Tine /Landov; p. 1230: REUTERS/Lucas Jackson / Landov; p. 1236: REUTERS/ Mark Avery /Landov.

# Index

WASHINGTON
Seattle
Olympia
Spokane
Portland
Columbia
OREGON
Salem
Eugene
Medford
IDAHO
Coeur d'Alene
Boise
Idaho Falls
Snake
MONTANA
Great Falls
Missoula
Helena
Billings
Missouri
Yellowstone
NORTH
SOUTH DA
Pierre
WYOMING
Casper
Laramie
Cheyenne
North Platte
NEBRAS
CALIFORNIA
Redding
Sacramento
San Francisco
San Jose
Monterey
Fresno
Los Angeles
San Diego
San Joaquin
NEVADA
Reno
Carson City
Ely
Las Vegas
UTAH
Great Salt Lake
Ogden
Salt Lake City
Cedar City
Colorado
COLORADO
Denver
Colorado Springs
Pueblo
Arkansas
ARIZONA
Flagstaff
Phoenix
Tuscon
NEW MEXICO
Santa Fe
Albuquerque
Las Cruces
El Paso
Rio Grande
TEXAS
Amarillo
Lubbock
Odessa
PACIFIC OCEAN
MEXICO
ARCTIC OCEAN
RUSSIA
ALASKA
Yukon
Fairbanks
Anchorage
Juneau
CANADA
Bering Sea
Gulf of Alaska
0 300 miles
0 300 kilometers
HAWAII
Honolulu
Hilo
PACIFIC OCEAN
0 150 miles
0 150 kilometers
0 100 200 miles
0 100 200 kilometers

CANADA
Lake Superior
Lake Michigan
Lake Huron
Lake Ontario
Lake Erie
St. Lawrence
MINNESOTA
Minneapolis
St. Paul
Mississippi
WISCONSIN
Green Bay
Madison
Milwaukee
MICHIGAN
Lansing
Flint
Detroit
MAINE
Bangor
Augusta
Portland
VERMONT
Montpelier
NEW HAMPSHIRE
Concord
MASSACHUSETTS
Boston
Providence
RHODE ISLAND
CONNECTICUT
Hartford
NEW YORK
Albany
Buffalo
Susquehanna
Hudson
New York
Erie
PENNSYLVANIA
Harrisburg
Pittsburgh
Philadelphia
Allegheny
NEW JERSEY
Trenton
DELAWARE
Dover
MARYLAND
Baltimore
Annapolis
Washington D.C.
Potomac
IOWA
Cedar Rapids
Des Moines
Chicago
ILLINOIS
Peoria
Springfield
Illinois
INDIANA
Fort Wayne
Indianapolis
Wabash
OHIO
Toledo
Cleveland
Columbus
Cincinnati
Ohio
WEST VIRGINIA
Charleston
VIRGINIA
Richmond
Norfolk
Roanoke
Kansas City
Jefferson City
St. Louis
MISSOURI
KENTUCKY
Louisville
Frankfort
TENNESSEE
Nashville
Knoxville
Memphis
Tennessee
NORTH CAROLINA
Raleigh
Charlotte
Asheville
Wilmington
Tulsa
Fort Smith
ARKANSAS
Little Rock
El Dorado
Red
SOUTH CAROLINA
Columbia
Charleston
Pee Dee
Savannah
GEORGIA
Atlanta
Augusta
Savannah
Valdosta
Chattahoochee
MISSISSIPPI
Tupelo
Jackson
Natchez
Mississippi
ALABAMA
Birmingham
Montgomery
Mobile
Alabama
LOUISIANA
Shreveport
Baton Rouge
New Orleans
Houston
Pensacola
Tallahassee
Jacksonville
FLORIDA
Orlando
Tampa
Miami
ATLANTIC OCEAN
Gulf of Mexico
BAHAMAS
PUERTO RICO
San Juan
Bayamón
Carolina
Ponce
0 30 miles
0 30 kilometers
Caribbean Sea

ARCTIC OCEAN
Beaufort Sea
Baffin Bay
Greenland (Denmark)
Greenland Sea
Davis Strait
ICELAND
Mackenzie
Peace
Hudson Bay
Gulf of Alaska
CANADA
Labrador Sea
IRELAND
Missouri
NORTH PACIFIC OCEAN
UNITED STATES
Mississippi
NORTH ATLANTIC OCEAN
PORTUGAL
SPAIN
MOROCCO
Gulf of Mexico
BAHAMAS
MEXICO
CUBA
HAITI
DOM. REP.
SAINT KITTS AND NEVIS
ANTIGUA AND BARBUDA
DOMINICA
SAINT LUCIA
SAINT VINCENT AND THE GRENADINES
BARBADOS
GRENADA
TRINIDAD AND TOBAGO
SURINAME
FRENCH GUIANA (France)
WESTERN SAHARA (Morocco)
MAURITANIA
CAPE VERDE
MALI
BELIZE
JAMAICA
Caribbean Sea
GUATEMALA
HONDURAS
EL SALVADOR
NICARAGUA
COSTA RICA
PANAMA
VENEZUELA
GUYANA
THE GAMBIA
SENEGAL
GUINEA-BISSAU
GUINEA
SIERRA LEONE
LIBERIA
COTE D'IVOIRE
GHANA
KIRIBATI
COLOMBIA
ECUADOR
Amazon
PERU
BRAZIL
BOLIVIA
PARAGUAY
Paraná
URUGUAY
SOUTH PACIFIC OCEAN
CHILE
ARGENTINA
Weddell Sea

ARCTIC OCEAN
Barents Sea
RUSSIA
FINLAND
ESTONIA
LATVIA
LITHUANIA
BELARUS
UKRAINE
MOLDOVA
ROMANIA
BULGARIA
GREECE
TURKEY
CYPRUS
SYRIA
LEBANON
ISRAEL
JORDAN
IRAQ
IRAN
KUWAIT
BAHRAIN
QATAR
U.A.E.
OMAN
SAUDI ARABIA
YEMEN
EGYPT
SUDAN
ERITREA
DJIBOUTI
ETHIOPIA
SOUTH SUDAN
SOMALIA
UGANDA
KENYA
RWANDA
BURUNDI
DEM. REP. OF THE CONGO
TANZANIA
ZAMBIA
MALAWI
MOZAMBIQUE
ZIMBABWE
BOTSWANA
SOUTH AFRICA
SWAZILAND
LESOTHO
MADAGASCAR
COMOROS
SEYCHELLES
MAURITIUS
GEORGIA
ARMENIA
AZERBAIJAN
KAZAKHSTAN
UZBEKISTAN
TURKMENISTAN
KYRGYZSTAN
TAJIKISTAN
AFGHANISTAN
PAKISTAN
INDIA
NEPAL
BHUTAN
BANGLADESH
SRI LANKA
MALDIVES
MONGOLIA
CHINA
NORTH KOREA
SOUTH KOREA
JAPAN
TAIWAN
MYANMAR
LAOS
THAILAND
VIETNAM
CAMBODIA
PHILIPPINES
BRUNEI
MALAYSIA
SINGAPORE
INDONESIA
TIMOR-LESTE
PAPUA NEW GUINEA
PALAU
FEDERATED STATES OF MICRONESIA
MARSHALL ISLANDS
NAURU
SOLOMON ISLANDS
VANUATU
FIJI
SAMOA
TONGA
AUSTRALIA
NEW ZEALAND
Sea of Okhotsk
Bering Sea
Sea of Japan
East China Sea
NORTH PACIFIC OCEAN
Philippine Sea
South China Sea
Bay of Bengal
Arabian Sea
Red Sea
INDIAN OCEAN
Mozambique Channel
Timor Sea
Coral Sea
SOUTH PACIFIC OCEAN
Tasman Sea
Great Australian Bight
Ob
Yenisey
Lena
Irtysh
Danube
Nile
Congo
Brahmaputra
Yangtze
Mekong
0 500 1,000 miles
0 500 1,000 kilometers
RCTICA